DOS: The Complete Reference,
Third Edition

DOS: The Complete Reference, Third Edition

Kris Jamsa

Osborne **McGraw-Hill**

Berkeley   New York   St. Louis   San Francisco
Auckland   Bogotá   Hamburg   London   Madrid
Mexico City   Milan   Montreal   New Delhi   Panama City
Paris   São Paulo   Singapore   Sydney
Tokyo   Toronto

Osborne **McGraw-Hill**
2600 Tenth Street
Berkeley, California 94710
U.S.A.

For information on translations or book distributors outside of the U.S.A., please write to Osborne **McGraw-Hill** at the above address.

DOS: The Complete Reference, Third Edition

67890 DOC 998765432

ISBN 0-07-881700-5

To Debbie,
Most people only dream at night,
with you my dreams last a lifetime...

Publisher —————————
Kenna S. Wood

Acquisitions Editor —————————
Allen L. Wyatt

Associate Editor —————————
Emily Rader

Project Editor —————————
Janis Paris

Copy Editor —————————
Paul Medoff

Technical Editor —————————
Phillip Schmauder

Proofing Coordinator —————————
Nancy McLaughlin Pechonis

Proofreaders —————————
Colleen Paretty
Valerie Haynes Perry
Gwendolyn Goss

Margaret Flynn
Ann Krueger Spivack

Indexers —————————
Lynn Brown
Richard Shrout

Computer Designers —————————
Peter F. Hancik
John Erick Christgau

Typesetters —————————
Jani Beckwith
Helena Charm
Marcela Hancik
Stefany Otis
Michelle Salinaro
Fred Lass

Illustrators —————————
Susie C. Kim
Peter F. Hancik

Cover Designers —————————
Bay Graphics Design, Inc.
Mason Fong

Contents at a Glance

1   Getting to Know Your Computer   1
2   Getting DOS Started   31
3   Issuing DOS Commands   43
4   Getting Started with DOS Files   61
5   Understanding Your Keyboard   81
6   Getting Around Your Disk   99
7   Preparing Disks for Use   111
8   Fundamental File Operations   131
9   DOS Wildcard Characters   147
10 Directories   163

11 Getting the Most from DOS Directories   185
12 Fundamental Copy Operations   207
13 Printing   217
14 Getting the Most from PRINT   231
15 Grouping Commands with Batch Files   245
16 Decision-Making Batch Files   265
17 Getting the Most from Batch Files   285
18 Automatic System Startup Commands
        with AUTOEXEC.BAT   303
19 The DOS Environment   315
20 The DOS Redirection Operators   329

21	The DOS Pipe	349
22	Protecting Your Files with BACKUP and RESTORE	365
23	Advanced File Manipulation	385
24	Customizing Your System with CONFIG.SYS	411
25	Using CHKDSK	435
26	DOS Pretender Commands	451
27	DOSKEY and DOS 5 Macros	465
28	DOS 5 Crisis Prevention	479
29	Using DEBUG	507
30	Another Look at Disks	537
31	Improving Your System Performance	553
32	Understanding DOS Memory Management	565
33	How DOS Actually Stores Files	597
34	ANSI.SYS	609
35	Advanced Disk Topics	627
36	Creating Simple Text Files with EDLIN	637
37	The DOS 5 Editor, EDIT	659
38	Support for International Users	675
39	Using the DOS 4 Shell	693
40	Advanced DOS 4 Shell Techniques	715
41	Using the DOS 5 Shell	725
42	Advanced DOS 5 Shell Techniques	755
43	DOS System Commands	767
44	Detecting and Correcting Disk Fragmentation	795
45	Disk Partitions and FDISK	807
46	The History of DOS	821
	Command Reference	827
A	Exit Status Values	1045
B	ASCII and Extended ASCII Character Sets	1049
C	DOS 4 and DOS 5 Shell Menu Maps	1053
D	International Keyboard Templates and Code Pages	1057

E Installing DOS Version 4   1071
F Upgrading to DOS 5   1081
G Common Error Messages   1087

   Index   1097

Contents

Acknowledgments xxi

Introduction xxiii

1

Getting to Know Your Computer 1

Looking at Your Computer's Hardware 1

Connecting the Pieces 2

How Disks Store Information 6

Floppy Disks in Detail 8

Looking at Disk Drives 13

Understanding Software 15

Understanding DOS 17

Hands On 19

Review 19

Answers 21

Advanced Concepts 23

2

Getting DOS Started 31

Before You Begin 31

Starting DOS from Floppy Disks 32

Turning On Your Computer 32

What DOS Will Display 33

Troubleshooting the DOS Startup 34

Hands On 36

Review 37

Answers 37

Advanced Concepts 38

Key Terms 41

3

Issuing DOS Commands 43

Executing Your First DOS Commands 43

Command-Line Parameters 50

External Versus Internal Commands 51

The "Bad command or file name" Message 52

Hands On 55

Review 57

Answers 57

Advanced Concepts 58

Key Terms 59

4

Getting Started with DOS Files 61

A Directory Is a List of Related Files 61

Using the DIR Command 62

Hands On 71

Review 73

Answers 73

Advanced Concepts 74

Key Terms 79

5

Understanding Your Keyboard   81

Keyboards Have Four Major
  Sections   81
Key Combinations   88
Hands On   90
Review   93
Answers   94
Advanced Concepts   94
Key Terms   97

6

Getting Around Your Disk   99

Changing the Default Drive   99
Accessing a Drive's Disk Without
  Changing Default Drives   100
The Abort, Retry, Fail? Prompt   102
Hands On   103
Advanced Concepts   106
Key Terms   108

7

Preparing Disks for Use   111

FORMAT Is an External Command   111
The Formatting Process   112
Not All Disk Sectors Are Capable
  of Storing Information   114
Preparing a Floppy Disk for Use   115
Formatting a Disk with Less Storage
  Capability than the Floppy Drive   117
Formatting Your Hard Disk   117
Hands On   118
Review   119
Answers   120
Advanced Concepts   121
Key Terms   128

8

Fundamental File Operations   131

TYPE Displays a File's Contents   131
COPY Duplicates a File's Contents   133
RENAME Changes a File's Name   137

DEL Deletes Files   138
Hands On   139
Review   142
Answers   142
Advanced Concepts   143
Key Terms   146

9

DOS Wildcard Characters   147

The * Wildcard   147
The ? Wildcard   155
Hands On   157
Review   159
Answers   160
Advanced Concepts   161
Key Terms   162

10

Directories   163

The Root Directory   163
The Current Directory   164
CHDIR Changes the Current
  Directory   165
MKDIR Creates Directories   168
RMDIR Removes Directories   173
Hands On   174
Review   177
Answers   178
Advanced Concepts   179
Key Terms   183

11

Getting the Most from DOS Directories   185

Displaying Your Directory Tree   185
Simplifying Execution of External
  Commands   189
Abbreviating Directory Names   194
FASTOPEN Improves System
  Performance   197
Hands On   200
Review   202
Answers   202
Advanced Concepts   203
Key Terms   205

12

Fundamental Copy Operations — 207

Copying Files from a Hard Disk to
  a Floppy Disk — 207
Copying from a Floppy Disk to a
  Hard Disk — 208
DISKCOPY Copies an Entire
  Disk's Contents — 209
Hands On — 213
Review — 213
Answers — 214
Advanced Concepts — 214
Key Terms — 215

13

Printing — 217

Using Your Printer — 217
Identifying Your Printer Type — 218
The Device Names PRN and AUX — 219
The Serial Port's Communication
  Settings — 220
Copying Files to Your Printer — 220
Printing the Screen — 221
Sending Information to Both
  Screen and Printer — 224
Telling Your Applications About
  Your Printer — 224
Hands On — 224
Review — 226
Answers — 227
Advanced Concepts — 227
Key Terms — 229

14

Getting the Most from PRINT — 231

Understanding PRINT — 231
Hands On — 236
Review — 238
Answers — 239
Advanced Concepts — 239
Key Terms — 244

15

Grouping Commands with Batch Files — 245

Creating Simple Batch Files — 245
Three Commonly Used Batch
  Commands — 251
Hands On — 254
Review — 258
Answers — 259
Advanced Concepts — 260
Using Extended ASCII Characters — 262
Key Terms — 263

16

Decision-Making Batch Files — 265

The IF Command — 266
IF EXIST Tests for Files — 266
Using IF to Compare Two
  Character Strings — 273
Passing Information to Your
  Batch Files — 273
Hands On — 278
Review — 280
Answers — 280
Advanced Concepts — 281
Key Terms — 284

17

Getting the Most from Batch Files — 285

Branching from One Location
  to Another Using GOTO — 285
Repeating a Command for a Set
  of Files — 288
Accessing More than Nine Batch
  Parameters — 290
Invoking One Batch File from
  Within Another — 293
Hands On — 295
Review — 298
Answers — 299
Advanced Concepts — 300
Key Terms — 302

18

Automatic System Startup Commands with AUTOEXEC.BAT   **303**

Common AUTOEXEC.BAT
Commands   304
A Sample AUTOEXEC.BAT   308
AUTOEXEC.BAT
and CONFIG.SYS   308
Change AUTOEXEC.BAT
with Caution   309
Hands On   310
Review   311
Answers   311
Advanced Concepts   312
Key Terms   313

19

The DOS Environment   **315**

The SET Command   315
How DOS Uses the Environment   318
Hands On   320
Review   322
Answers   322
Advanced Concepts   322
Key Terms   327

20

The DOS Redirection Operators   **329**

The Output Redirection Operator   329
The Append Redirection Operator   332
Possible Problems When
Redirecting Output   334
The Input Redirection Operator   334
Combining Input and Output
Operators   339
Hands On   340
Review   341
Answers   342
Advanced Concepts   342
Key Terms   348

21

The DOS Pipe   **349**

Locating the Pipe Operator
on Your Keyboard   349
Understanding the DOS Pipe   350
Which Commands Can You Pipe?   352
Combining the Pipe and I/O
Redirection Operators   353
Pipe Operator Pitfalls   354
Hands On   355
Review   358
Answers   358
Advanced Concepts   359
Key Terms   363

22

Protecting Your Files with BACKUP and RESTORE   **365**

Understanding the Backup Process   366
Backing Up Your Entire Hard Disk   368
Performing Daily Backup
Operations   370
Using BACKUP to Back Up a Key
File or Directory   373
Restoring Backup Files to Your
Hard Disk   374
Restoring a Specific File or
Directory   375
Using Third-Party Backup Utility
Programs   376
Hands On   377
Review   379
Answers   379
Advanced Concepts   380
Key Terms   383

23

Advanced File Manipulation   **385**

Manipulating File Attributes with
ATTRIB   385
XCOPY's Extended Copy
Capabilities   389
Comparing Two Files with COMP   392
Comparing Files with FC   397

Adding and Replacing Selected Files
  with REPLACE   399
Review   407
Answers   407
Advanced Concepts   408
Key Terms   410

24

**Customizing Your System
with CONFIG.SYS   411**
Understanding the CONFIG.SYS
  Entries   411
Hands On   419
Review   422
Answers   422
Advanced Concepts   423
Key Terms   433

25

Using CHKDSK   435
Understanding CHKDSK   435
Using CHKDSK to Correct Disk
  Errors   442
Handling Other CHKDSK Errors   446
Using CHKDSK to Display File
  Names   446
Hands On   446
Review   447
Answers   447
Advanced Concepts   448
Key Terms   450

26

**DOS Pretender
Commands   451**
Disk Drive Identity Swapping with
  ASSIGN   451
Substituting a Drive Letter for a
  Directory Name with SUBST   453
Making DOS Think a Drive Is a
  Directory
  with JOIN   456
Hands On   457
Review   461
Answers   461

Advanced Concepts   462
Key Terms   463

27

**DOSKEY and DOS 5
Macros   465**
Using DOSKEY to Recall
  Commands   465
Hands On   470
Review   471
Answers   472
Advanced Concepts   472
Key Terms   478

28

DOS 5 Crisis Prevention   479
Retrieving Deleted Files with
  UNDELETE   479
Protecting Your Disk and Files with
  MIRROR   488
Recovering a Disk with
  UNFORMAT   492
Safe vs. Unsafe Format Operations   498
Hands On   499
Review   503
Answers   503
Advanced Concepts   504
Key Terms   506

29

Using DEBUG   507
Creating Simple COM Commands   507
Hands On   513
Review   516
Answers   517
Advanced Concepts   519
Key Terms   536

30

Another Look at Disks   537
Disk Volume Labels: LABEL and
  VOL   537
Comparing Two Floppy Disks with
  DISKCOMP   542

File Sharing and Large Disk
  Support with SHARE 543
Verifying Disk Writes with VERIFY 545
Salvaging a File or Disk with
  RECOVER 546
Hands On 547
Review 550
Answers 550
Advanced Concepts 551
Key Terms 552

31

Improving Your System Performance   553

Directory Considerations for
  Maximum Performance 553
File Considerations for Maximum
  Performance 556
Disk Considerations for Maximum
  Performance 556
System Considerations for
  Performance 557
Hands On 559
Review 560
Answers 560
Advanced Topics 561
Key Terms 563

32

Understanding DOS Memory Management   565

Understanding Memory Types 565
How We Use Extended and
  Expanded Memory 573
Viewing Your Memory Usage 576
DOS 5 Memory Management 579
Hands On 583
Review 588
Answers 588
Advanced Concepts 589
Key Terms 594

33

How DOS Actually Stores Files   597

The File Allocation Table 597
Directory Entries 600

DOS Stores the FAT and Root
  Directory at Fixed Locations 601
How FORMAT Works 602
How CHKDSK Works 603
Review 604
Answers 605
Advanced Concepts 606
Key Terms 607

34

ANSI.SYS   609

Installing ANSI.SYS 609
Escape Sequences 610
Controlling Screen Colors Using
  ANSI.SYS 613
Redefining Keys with ANSI.SYS 616
Creating ANSI.COM to Execute
  Escape Sequences 620
Hands On 621
Review 622
Answers 622
Advanced Concepts 623
Key Terms 626

35

Advanced Disk Topics   627

Understanding Disk Head Parking 627
Disk Sector Interleaving 630
Low-Level Formatting 632
Review 633
Answers 634
Advanced Concepts 635
Key Terms 635

36

Creating Simple Text Files with EDLIN   637

Getting Started with EDLIN 637
Hands On 645
Review 646
Answers 646
Advanced Concepts 647
Key Terms 657

37

The DOS 5 Editor, EDIT   659

Starting EDIT 659

Hands On 669
Review 670
Answers 670
Advanced Concepts 671
Key Terms 674

38

Support for International Users 675

Selecting a Code Page 675
Setting an International
  Configuration 676
Selecting a Symbol Set 678
Selecting a Keyboard Template 680
Preparing Code Pages for Use 682
Changing Code Pages with CHCP 685
Hands On 686
Review 690
Answers 690
Advanced Concepts 691
Key Terms 691

39

Using the DOS 4 Shell 693

Starting the DOS 4 Shell 693
Using the Shell's Built-in Utilities 696
Using the Shell's Online Help 701
Using the File System 702
Hands On 709
Review 711
Answers 712
Advanced Concepts 712
Key Terms 714

40

Advanced DOS 4 Shell Techniques 715

Adding a Program to the Main
  Group 715
Working with Groups 718
Hands On 721
Review 721
Answers 722
Advanced Concepts 722
Key Terms 724

41

Using the DOS 5 Shell 725

Starting the DOS 5 Shell 725
Displaying the Shell in Graphics
  Mode 728
Working with Directory Trees 729
Exiting the DOS Shell 730
Working with Files 730
Changing the Shell Display 742
Running Programs from the
  Program List 745
Using the Shell's Online Help 748
Hands On 748
Review 750
Answers 750
Advanced Concepts 751
Key Terms 753

42

Advanced DOS 5 Shell Techniques 755

Setting Your Screen Colors 755
Working with Program Groups 756
Working with Program Entries 759
Hands On 762
Review 762
Answers 762
Advanced Concepts 763
Key Terms 765

43

DOS System Commands 767

Customizing Your System Prompt 767
Enabling Extended CTRL-BREAK
  Checking 770
Using EXIT to Resume a Program 771
Online Help for DOS 5 Commands 772
Displaying Extended ASCII
  Characters with GRAFTABL 774
Invoking the BASIC Programming
  Language 775
Revisiting MODE 775
Hands On 784
Review 787
Answers 788
Advanced Concepts 788
Key Terms 793

44

Detecting and Correcting Disk Fragmentation   795

Understanding Fragmented Files   795
Correcting File Fragmentation   800
Fragmented Files Can Prevent
    Successful File Undeletion   802
Hands On   804
Review   804
Answers   804
Advanced Concepts   805
Key Terms   806

45

Disk Partitions and FDISK   807

Understanding Hard Disk Partitions   807
Using FDISK   810
Creating a Primary and an
    Extended Partition   813
Hands On   817
Review   817
Answers   818
Advanced Concepts   818
Key Terms   820

46

The History of DOS   821

Before DOS   821
DOS 1.0   822
Version 1.1   823
Version 2.0   823
DOS 3.0   824
Version 4.0   825
Version 5.0   825
Conclusion   826

Command Reference   827

APPEND   827
ASSIGN   830
ATTRIB   832
BACKUP   835
BREAK   841

CALL   842
CHCP   843
CHDIR   845
CHKDSK   849
CLS   856
COMMAND   857
COMP   859
COPY   864
CTTY   867
DATE   869
DEBUG   871
DIR   873
DISKCOMP   878
DISKCOPY   882
DOSKEY   887
DOSSHELL   890
ECHO   891
EDIT   894
EDLIN   895
EXE2BIN   899
EXIT   900
EXPAND   901
FASTOPEN   903
FC   905
FDISK   911
FOR   920
FORMAT   923
GOTO   933
GRAFTABL   935
GRAPHICS   937
HELP   940
IF   942
JOIN   945
KEYB   947
LABEL   952
LOADFIX   955
LOADHIGH   956
MEM   957
MIRROR   960
MKDIR   963
MODE   966
MORE   975
NLSFUNC   976
PATH   978
PAUSE   980
PRINT   982
PROMPT   986

QBASIC 989
RECOVER 990
REM 991
RENAME 993
REPLACE 995
RESTORE 999
RMDIR 1003
SELECT 1005
SET 1009
SETVER 1011
SHARE 1014
SHIFT 1016
SORT 1017
SUBST 1019
SYS 1021
TIME 1024
TREE 1026
TYPE 1028
UNDELETE 1029
UNFORMAT 1032
VER 1036
VERIFY 1037
VOL 1039
XCOPY 1040

A ——————————————

Exit Status Values 1045
BACKUP 1045
DISKCOMP 1045
DISKCOPY 1046
FORMAT 1046
GRAFTABL 1046
KEYB 1046
REPLACE 1047
RESTORE 1047
SETVER 1047
XCOPY 1048

B ——————————————

**ASCII and Extended ASCII
Character Sets 1049**

C ——————————————

**DOS 4 and DOS 5 Shell
Menu Maps 1053**

D ——————————————

**International Keyboard
Templates & Code Pages 1057**
Keyboard Layouts
Code Page Tables

E ——————————————

Installing DOS Version 4 1071
Installing DOS 4 on a New Disk 1071
Installing DOS 4 on a System
  Currently in Use 1072
Performing the Installation 1073
Restoring Your Disk's Previous
  Files 1079

F ——————————————

Upgrading to DOS 5 1081
Upgrading to Version 5.0 1081
Using the UNINSTALL Disks 1086

G ——————————————

Common Error Messages 1087

——————————————

Index 1097

Acknowledgments

Each time I look through the pages of this book, I can't help but feel deep gratitude to Osborne's team of talented editors, artists, designers, and proofreaders who spent countless weeks working with this book's manuscript and illustrations. Through their unselfish effort, they have dramatically improved this book's quality and correctness. Unfortunately, we can't list the names of everyone involved in this project. Please take a moment and look near the beginning of this book for a list of the individuals who worked on this book. The list of names is long, but if listed, their contributions would be much longer.

From this book's start, my goal was to produce the one book you could turn to with your DOS questions. The book achieves this goal, thanks to the efforts of Phil Schmauder, my best friend and source of technical expertise. Throughout the book's development, Phil spent countless hours at his keyboard dissecting DOS and was available at all hours to entertain questions while poring over this book's manuscript as its technical editor. I don't need a CD-ROM knowledge base as long as I have Phil's telephone number. Phil could answer or find the answer to every question I posed. Phil's technical expertise and willingness to share his knowledge is unsurpassed. I greatly appreciate his efforts and have tremendous respect for his abilities.

Every book has one key individual behind the scenes who really pulls things together, making the book possible. In this case, that person was Allen Wyatt, Osborne/McGraw-Hill's Director of Operations, and my very close personal friend. Allen was not only responsible for overseeing the book's editing and production, but he personally read each page, injecting not only his vast knowledge of DOS, but also book publishing. Allen works with one thought in mind: "Something is not done unless it's done right." I could not ask to work with a more professional individual, nor could I ask for a more supportive friend.

Introduction

Since DOS was first introduced in 1981, many books on DOS have flooded the bookstores, making it difficult for users to determine which DOS book is right for them. For the past ten years, I have been studying DOS and have written over a dozen books on DOS, from getting started with DOS, to advanced discussions on its inner workings. *DOS: The Complete Reference, Third Edition*, contains the facts, tips, and secrets I have collected on DOS since its release in 1981. It is the most thorough discussion on DOS available.

What DOS Versions are Discussed?

When software developers make changes to a program and release the updated program to users, they assign a version number to the software. Since its release in 1981, DOS has grown from version 1.0 to the recently released DOS 5.0. Along the way, the number of people using DOS has grown beyond 50 million.

DOS: The Complete Reference, Third Edition, discusses the commands used with every DOS version. Regardless of the DOS version you are using, this book contains the answers to your questions.

Who Should Use This Book?

There are over 50 million DOS users and no two have the same level of understanding. With that fact in mind, this book presents each topic beginning with the basics and then lets you advance into detailed discussion on a topic as you feel comfortable.

New DOS Users

Don't be intimidated by this book's size. Each chapter goes to great lengths to explain new concepts in a straightforward manner. I have included many illustrations to help you understand the topics easily, all of which contribute to the book's size.

Because all new DOS users have different backgrounds, each chapter begins with a new topic, and then explains how and when you would use it, as well as giving some helpful hints. A Hands On section (that lets you perform commands) follows the introductory discussion. In this way, you can't hurt your computer, or lose information it contains. Every chapter contains a Review section with a few questions on concepts I consider most valuable. (Don't worry, the Answer section follows the questions.) Use these questions, along with the handy Summary section found in most chapters, as your guide to the key points you should retain from the chapter.

Intermediate DOS Users

If you have worked with DOS for a while, this book will take you to power-user status. I have included the tricks and shortcuts you can use to make your time with the computer more productive. Several of the book's introductory chapters may be "old hat" to you by now. Read each of these chapter's Summary section and make sure you can answer the corresponding questions. If a topic is new to you, make sure you read the discussion on the topic within the chapter. Also, skim each chapter's Advanced Concepts section. Don't worry if you don't thoroughly understand the discussion. By the time you complete this book's latter chapters, you will have the foundation you need to master the Advanced Concepts.

Advanced DOS Users

If you are looking for a single book to which you can turn for all your DOS questions, you have the right book in your hands. In addition, you will find many more secrets and advanced techniques in each chapter's Advanced Concepts section. Much of this discussion will teach you the steps DOS performs behind the scenes, making your knowledge of DOS complete.

Companion Diskette Packages

As you work with DOS on a regular basis, there will be times you need details on a specific command or concept. To complement this book's text, we have made two diskette packages available. The *DOS Help* diskette package provides an on-line discussion of every DOS command, the command's format, tips, and examples of the command's use. *DOS Help* puts the answers to your DOS questions at your finger tips.

DOS: The Complete Reference Companion Diskette contains all the DEBUG script routines presented throughout this book, along with a collection of utility programs that you can use with the DOS pipe and I/O redirection operators, and within your DOS batch files.

If you are interested in either disk, see the order form following this Introduction.

Special Offer

One of the greatest frustrations users experience when working with DOS is forgetting a command. *DOS Help* is a software program you can copy to your hard disk that contains all of the answers to your DOS questions.

DOS Help displays a friendly menu that summarizes all the DOS commands. By highlighting a command with your arrow keys and pressing Enter, you can discover command specifics, view common examples of the command in use, and even read tips that make you more productive.

Every computer user should have a copy of *DOS Help!*

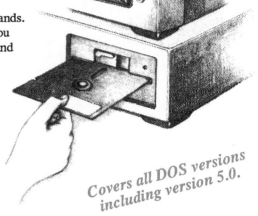

Covers all DOS versions including version 5.0.

As you examine different concepts throughout this book, you will run into cases where the commands DOS provides, don't give you all the capabilities you need. To help you better use your computer, we offer a disk containing several commands that DOS forgot. DOS the Complete Reference Companion Diskette contains the batch and DEBUG script files presented in this book, as well as several useful commands. Table 21-1 in Chapter 21 lists several of the commands you will find.

Ordering Information

Domestic Orders:

Please send *$24.95* (includes shipping and handling) to the address below. For fastest service, please send a money order or cashier's check. Please allow 2 to 3 weeks for delivery.

For companion Disk, please send *$9.95*. *(Includes Shipping & Handling)*

Foreign Orders:

Please send *$29.95* (USD, includes shipping and handling) to the address below. For fastest service, please send an international money order. Please allow 4 to 6 weeks for delivery.

For Companion Disk, please send *$12.95*. *(Includes Shipping & Handling)*

(Credit card orders not accepted)

- -

Name_____

Address_____

City_____ State_____ Zip_____

Country_____ Phone_____

Please send: _____   Copies of DOS Help $_____

                    _____   Companion Diskette $_____

Enclosed is my Check or Money Order For $_____

Please send your order with payment to:

Kris Jamsa Software, Inc.
P.O. Box 26031
Las Vegas, NV 89126

Getting to Know
Your Computer

Computers are incredibly powerful machines that affect almost every aspect of our lives. Computers work behind the scenes to control stoplights, to handle the millions of phone calls made each day, to control aircraft, and even to control the microwave oven you may have used to cook dinner. In fact, computers are so common, most of us take them for granted; until, that is, someone puts a personal computer on your desk.

This chapter takes a look at the different pieces that make up your computer. If you've never worked with a personal computer (PC for short) before, don't worry. Chapter 1 starts you off at square 1, and teaches you the fundamentals you'll use as the base for your learning throughout the remainder of this book.

Looking at Your Computer's Hardware

Your computer's hardware consists of its physical parts such as the keyboard, screen, printer, chassis, and, perhaps, mouse. Figure 1-1 illustrates the hardware parts common to most computer's today.

In general, the *keyboard* lets you type commands, letters, reports, or numbers. If you don't know how to type, don't worry. Typing on a computer's keyboard is much easier than using a typewriter, because you can quickly correct mistakes.

Your computer's *screen* (often called a monitor) displays a program's result, such as a graph, or the information you are currently typing, possibly a report or memo.

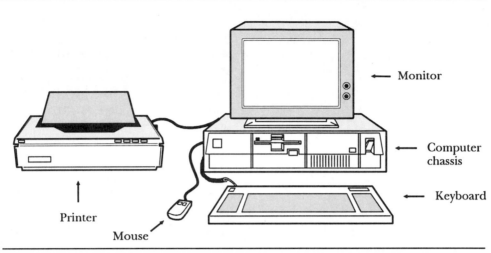

Figure 1-1.   Common hardware parts

Your computer screen works very much like a television, with its own on/off switch and brightness controls.

The *printer* lets you make printed copies of your letters, reports, spreadsheets, or even graphs of information. Like your monitor, the printer has its own on/off switch.

Your computer's *chassis* houses your computer's key electronic parts, such as its electronic memory and the microprocessor (often called the *CPU* or *central processing unit*). In addition, the chassis holds your computer's disk drives, which let you store information from one session at the computer to the next. As you will learn later in this chapter, most computers use two types of disks. A *hard disk* is a very fast nonremovable disk that can store very large amounts of information. *Floppy disks,* on the other hand are slower, removable disks with less storage capacity. Floppy disks let you exchange information between computers or load new programs on your hard disk.

Last, a *mouse* is a hardware device that simplifies your use of many programs, such as Microsoft Windows or the DOS shell provided with DOS versions 4 and 5. Using the mouse, you can often aim a mouse pointer, which appears on your computer screen, at different menu options to select them.

Table 1-1 briefly summarizes common hardware devices.

Connecting the Pieces

Most new users are introduced to a computer that is already up and running. If you buy a new computer, however, you will very likely have to set up the computer

Component	Name	Function
	Screen	Lets programs display meaningful results to you, and lets you view the information you type at the keyboard
	Keyboard	Lets you respond to a program's prompt for information, and lets you type in information for storage or processing
	Disk	Lets you store information from one computer session to the next
	Printer	Lets you obtain a printed copy of a program's result
	Mouse	Lets you move the cursor or pointer easily; lets you choose menu options or files by clicking on them
	Chassis	Houses your computer's central processing unit, memory, and other hardware boards. Also holds your computer's floppy and hard disk drives

Table 1-1.   Common Hardware Components and Their Functions

yourself. As you will learn in this section, setting up a computer is actually quite easy. In general, you will connect your keyboard, monitor, and printer to your computer's chassis, and then individually plug the chassis, monitor, and printer into a wall outlet.

To begin, your keyboard typically plugs into the back of your computer's chassis, as shown in Figure 1-2. Examine the keyboard's plug closely to make sure the pins line up with the holes in the chassis.

In a similar way, your monitor will plug into the back of the chassis. Typically, the back side of the chassis (back-right of the common chassis style pictured here, and back-top of the upright "tower" chassis style) will contain several different device

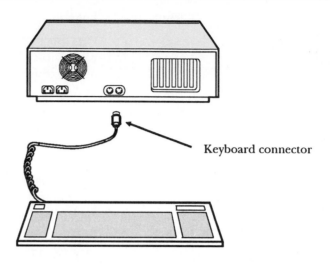

Figure 1-2.   *Keyboards typically plug into the back of your computer's chassis*

sockets called *ports.* Compare each port's connector to the plug at the end of your video cable, as shown in Figure 1-3.

In this same way, you must connect your printer cable to the back of your computer chassis, as shown in Figure 1-4.

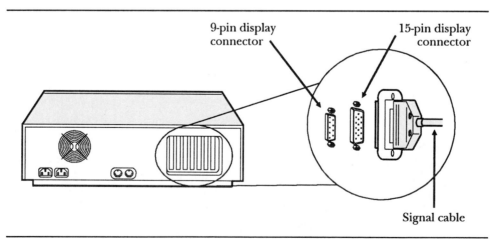

Figure 1-3.   *Match your video plug to one of the ports at the back of your computer (9-pin for CGA or EGA monitor, or 15-pin for VGA monitor)*

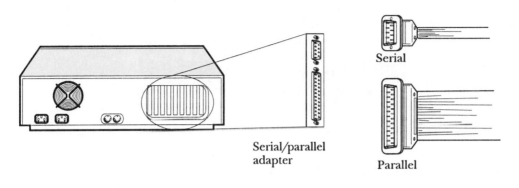

Figure 1-4.   Match your printer cable to one of the ports

Last, after you plug your chassis, monitor, and printer into a wall outlet, your system is ready to go!

Using a Surge Suppressor

As you can imagine, your computer contains thousands of sensitive electronic components. To protect your computer, a critical, yet often overlooked, item you should buy and use is a surge suppressor. A surge suppressor plugs into your wall outlet, and your computer equipment in turn plugs into the suppressor. The surge suppressor sits between your computer equipment and the electrical source to prevent a very large surge of electricity from damaging your computer. Such an electrical surge can be caused by lightning or even a faulty electrical transformer, either of which can occur several miles from your computer. Figure 1-5 shows three common type of surge suppressors.

Do not confuse surge suppressors with power strips that simply let you plug several devices into one outlet. A power strip does not protect the devices in any way, but might, in fact, create a possible hazard.

Surge suppressors range in price from $20.00 to $125.00. Typically, the primary difference between suppressors is the presence of individual on/off switches on the suppressor itself. Many suppressors will also filter phone lines, so you can protect your FAX or modem. Whichever suppressor you choose to buy, make sure it has an Underwriters Laboratory Approval.

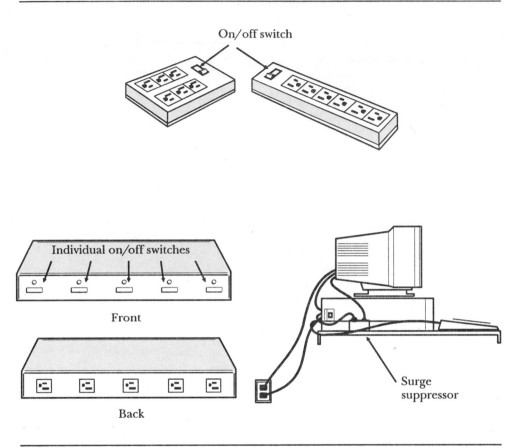

Figure 1-5.   *Common types of surge suppressors*

How Disks Store Information

Your computer is an electronic device and, as such, needs power to operate. The programs and information you are working with—a report you are typing with a word processor, or a spreadsheet, perhaps—reside in a temporary memory; when you turn off the computer, you lose the data that was there, unless you save it to a disk. Disks exist to let you store and retrieve information from one computer session to the next and to help you exchange information with other users. If you don't save information to disk before you turn off your computer, you will lose the information.

Disks are either nonremovable hard disks, which reside inside your computer's chassis, or removable floppy disks. Hard disks are much faster than floppies and

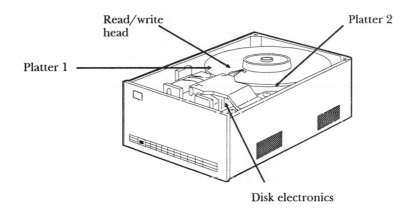

Figure 1-6.   Cutaway drawing of a hard disk

have much greater storage capacity. Hard disks reside in a sealed container. Figure 1-6 illustrates what you would find if you could open your hard disk.

Floppy disks come in two sizes, 5 1/4 and 3 1/2 inches. Your floppy disk drive only supports one of the two disk types; you can't interchange them.

Figure 1-7 illustrates the two floppy disk types and their drives.

The computer magnetically records information on your disk much like a tape recorder or VCR records songs or movies on tape. When you record a song on a cassette tape, you can play the song back immediately, a few days later, or even after months or years. Likewise, when you store information on a disk, you can access

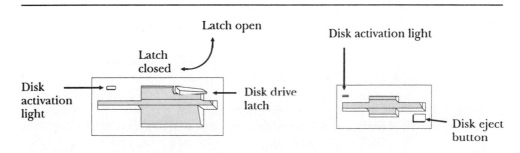

Figure 1-7.   5 1/4- and 3 1/2-inch floppy disks and their drives

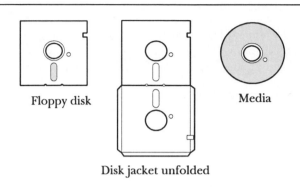

Floppy disk

Media

Disk jacket unfolded

Figure 1-8.   The inner construction of a 5 1/4-inch floppy disk

the information until you later erase it, or intentionally record other information over it. As a cassette tape only has space for a limited number of songs, your disk, too, has space restrictions.

If you look closely at a floppy disk, you will see portions of a circular plastic disk that looks like the same material as recording tape. The disk has a special coating onto which the computer can record information. Never touch the plastic disk. Doing so may damage the disk's surface and result in the loss of the information the disk contains. Figure 1-8 illustrates what you would find if you were to open up a 5 1/4-inch disk.

Floppy Disks in Detail

To better understand how a floppy disk works, you need to understand the disk's key components. Take out an unused 5 1/4-inch floppy disk (you don't want to endanger any data) and examine the disk as you read through the following discussion.

 The *disk envelope* is a protective paper sleeve that you can slide your disk into when it is not in use. Because the sleeve is only paper, it cannot protect the disk from damage or possible bending resulting from other objects set on top of the disk. The envelope's purpose is to protect the disk from dust and minor spills. You need to remove the disk from its envelope before you insert the disk into the drive. Get in the habit of always placing a disk immediately back into its envelope. 3 1/2-inch floppy disks do not require envelopes, because they are instead, surrounded by a protective hard-plastic cover.

The *disk jacket* of a 5 1/2-inch floppy is the dark cardboard-like covering that surrounds the flexible plastic disk. The jacket serves two purposes. First, the jacket gives you a way to pick up the disk. As discussed, if you touch the disk's plastic surface, you risk damaging the surface and losing the information the disk contains. Second, the jacket gives the disk the stiffness you need to insert the disk into the disk drive. Be careful never to bend the disk by trying to force it into the drive.

Read/write
opening

The disk's *read/write opening* provides your computer's disk drive with access to the disk's recording surface, which is like the recording tape in a cassette—very thin and flexible, thus the name "floppy." *Writing* is the process of recording information on the disk. *Reading*, on the other hand, is the process of accessing the information the disk contains. When you insert a floppy disk into a drive, the drive spins the floppy disk at about 300 revolutions per minute. If you listen closely to the drive, you may be able to hear the disk spinning. By spinning the disk surface past the read/write opening, your disk drive can access the entire recording surface much like a record album spins past the needle of a phonograph. Never touch the disk's surface at the read/write opening.

Disk hub

The *disk hub* is a reinforced ring at the center of the disk. When you place the disk into the drive, the disk drive actually "grabs" the disk at the hub to spin the disk. The hub provides your disk with additional strength. If your brand of floppy disk does not have a reinforced hub, you should consider purchasing a different brand of disk.

Index hole

The *index hole* is a small opening that some disk drives use to determine their current position on the disk. If you gently spin your unused disk inside the jacket, using the disk hub, you will eventually find a small hole in the disk. Using this hole as a point of reference, the disk drive can determine the disk's current position.

Write-protect
notch

The *write-protect notch* of a 5 1/2-inch floppy disk determines whether or not your disk drive can write or erase information to or from it. When the notch is exposed, the disk drive can read, write, or erase disk information. When the write-protect notch is covered, the disk drive can only read the information the disk contains. When you buy a box of floppy disks, the box should include a sheet of adhesive write-protect tabs like the one shown here:

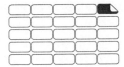

By peeling a tab off of the sheet and folding it over the write-protect notch, as shown here, you can prevent a disk from being written to or erased.

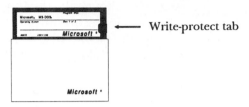

Write-protect tab

You should always write-protect the disks containing original copies of the software you purchase.

Disk shutter

The 3 1/2-inch disk does not permanently expose the disk's surface at a read/write opening. Instead, the disk has a metal shutter that the disk drive slides open to access the disk's surface. Using an unused (don't endanger any current data) 3 1/2-inch floppy, hold it so that you are looking at the front of the disk and the shutter is pointing upward, then slide the shutter to the left to expose the disk's surface, as shown below. As before, do not touch the disk's surface. When you release the shutter, it springs closed.

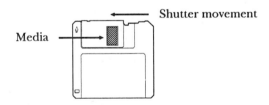

Shutter movement

Media

Drive spindle
Sector notch

Unlike the 5 1/4-inch floppy disk drives, which grab the disk's hub to spin the disk, 3 1/2-inch disk drives use a spindle mechanism. The drive uses the small square hole to spin the disk, and the larger hole to determine its current disk position (much like the 5 1/4-inch disk's index hole).

Write protect

The write-protect notch on a 3 1/2-inch disk has its own built-in sliding cover. By sliding the cover back and forth, you can quickly write-protect or unprotect a disk. When you can look through the small hole in the disk, the disk is write-protected, and the disk drive can only read information from the disk. When the hole is covered, the disk drive can read, write, and erase information.

Caring for Your Disk

Although floppy disks are very durable, they can be damaged, resulting in the loss of information the disk contains. Follow these rules for handling your disks and you will greatly reduce the chance of damage.

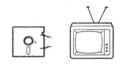 Your disk stores information by recording the information to the disk's magnetic surface. If you place a disk near a magnetic device, you risk inadvertently changing the disk's magnetized values. Many users ask if the X-ray machines at an airport can damage their disk. Airports claim no. Personally, I don't risk my key disks to such exposure.

 Users often have the bad habit of setting disks down on copiers, laser printers, or even next to TVs. Such powerful electronic devices can produce a magnetic flux capable of changing the information on your disk.

 Always place disks back into a disk envelope when you are not using them to protect them from dust, fingerprints, and minor spills.

A disk storage container provides your disk with additional protection from dust and spills. More importantly, if you begin the habit of always placing your disks in a storage container, you won't misplace a disk.

 Touching your disk's surface can damage the surface, resulting in the loss of stored information. Although most users never intentionally touch the disk's surface, they inadvertently do so by picking up the disk near its read/write opening.

 Chapter 12, "Fundamental Copy Operations," teaches you how to make identical copies of your key disks. You should always duplicate disks containing newly purchased software programs, using only the duplicates while storing the originals in a safe location.

 Smoke particles are one of the fastest ways to damage your disk's surface. The smoke particles not only collect on the disk, but inside the disk drive. Eventually these particles may scratch a disk, destroying the information the disk contains.

Exposing a disk to excessive cold or heat (direct sunlight) can cause the disk to expand or contract. Because the disk's surface contains millions of pieces of magnetized information, such changes in the disk's surface size can actually result in changes to the magnetized information. Many disk manufacturers recommend that the disks not be exposed to temperatures below 50 degrees or above 110 degrees Fahrenheit.

If you bend or crease a disk, the drive will no longer be able to spin the disk or correctly read the disk's surface. Users damage disks most often by forcing the disk into a drive.

Never write on a disk label attached to a floppy disk. The pressure from the pen tip can easily damage the plastic disk inside of the disk jacket. This is particularly true for 5 1/2-inch disks, whose jackets are not as rigid as their 3 1/2-inch counterparts. Instead, always write your disk label before attaching the label to a disk. If you must change a label, gently peel off the old label, or simply attach the new label over the top of it. If you have a light touch and use a felt-tip pen, you can safely write on the disk label attached to the disk.

Understanding Disk Sizes

Just as you purchase cassette tapes that let you store 60, 90, or 120 minutes of information, your computer disk also has fixed storage capacities. When you discuss computer storage capabilities, however, you don't speak in terms of minutes of storage, but rather you use the term *bytes*. For our purposes, consider a byte as a single character of information. The word "disk" uses four characters, for example, and would therefore require four bytes of storage. A single-spaced, typed sheet of paper typically contains 4000 characters or bytes. Depending on your disk type, the disk can store from several hundred thousand to over one hundred million bytes of information. In Chapter 4, "Getting Started with DOS Files," you will learn that DOS organizes the information you store on disk by grouping the information into files. All discussions about file sizes will be considered in terms of bytes.

To help you abbreviate your disk sizes, many users (and books) use the terms *k-bytes* (kilobytes) and *megabytes*. The letter "K" represents the word "kilo" or 1000. Actually, 1K is 1024 bytes, but round numbers are easier to visualize. A 360K-byte disk, for example, can store approximately 360,000 bytes. It is common to see kilobytes expressed as simply *Kb*. In a similar way, the term megabyte stands for a million (actually, 1,048,576) bytes. A 30-megabyte hard disk, for example, can store 30 million bytes. The term "megabytes" often appears as simply *Mb*.

As discussed earlier, floppy disks come in two sizes. When 5 1/4-inch disks were first introduced for the PC in 1981, each disk could store 160Kb (about 160,000 bytes). Likewise, the first 3 1/2-inch disk could store 720Kb. As disk technology has improved over the years, the disk's storage capacity has also increased. The increased capacity has resulted from the capability of disk drives to access both sides of a disk, and to store information closer (more densely) together. Table 1-2 describes the various 5 1/4-and 3 1/2-inch disk sizes that have emerged over the years.

The most commonly used disk sizes today are 360Kb and 1.2Mb on 5 1/4-inch disks, and 720Kb and 1.44Mb on 3 1/2-inch disks.

Looking at Disk Drives

Before your computer can access the information a disk contains, the disk must be in one of your computer's disk drives. For nonremovable hard disks, the storage disks actually reside within the drive itself. For floppy disks, on the other hand, you must insert the disk into a drive of the appropriate size. Figure 1-9 illustrates a 5 1/4- and a 3 1/2-inch disk drive.

When you insert a 3 1/2-inch disk into a drive, insert the disk so that the disk spindle is facing down and the shutter end of the disk enters the disk first. To insert a 5 1/4-inch disk, insert the disk with the label facing up, the end with the disk window going in first, and the end of the disk containing the label inserted last, as shown in Figure 1-10. If the disk does not have a label, insert the disk so that the

Disk Type	Size	Storage Capacity
5 1/4	160 Kb	163,840 bytes
5 1/4	180 Kb	184,320 bytes
5 1/4	320 Kb	327,680 bytes
5 1/4	360 Kb	368,640 bytes
5 1/4	1.2 Mb	1,213,952 bytes
3 1/2	720 Kb	737,280 bytes
3 1/2	1.44 Mb	1,457,664 bytes

Table 1-2.   Disk Storage Capacities

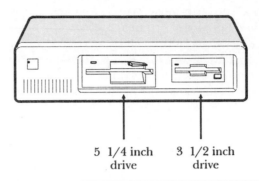

Figure 1-9.   *5 1/4- and 3 1/2-inch disk drives*

write-protect notch is on the left side of the disk and at the end of the disk inserted last.

After the 5 1/4-inch disk is safely in the drive, close the disk drive latch (Figure 1-11). Latch types for 5 1/4-inch disks differ a bit; most common are the rotary latch shown in Figure 1-7 and the overhead latch shown in Figures 1-10 and 1-11.

To remove the disk from the drive, open the drive latch and gently remove the disk. If you are using a 3 1/2-inch drive, press the disk eject button, as shown here:

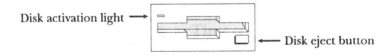

Note the small disk activation light on the front of your hard and floppy disk drives. Your computer illuminates this light whenever it is reading from or writing to a disk in the drive. Never turn off your computer or remove a disk while the disk activation light is on. If you do so, a critical disk operation may not complete, leaving your disk in an unusable state.

Disk Drives Have Single-Letter Names

Depending on your computer configuration, your computer will have one or more floppy disk drives and likely a hard disk. Each disk on your computer has a single-letter name. Your first floppy disk, for example, is drive A. Likewise, a hard disk is typically named drive C. If your computer has a second floppy drive, the drive is typically named drive B. A second hard disk might be named drive D. Figure 1-12 shows the name and location of common disk configurations.

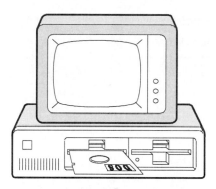

Figure 1-10. *Inserting a 5 1/4-inch floppy disk into the disk drive*

Understanding Software

When most users think about the computer's processing power, they picture the computer's hardware. As it turns out, hardware only provides half of the story. To perform useful work, your computer needs *software* to tell it what to do. Software is another name for computer programs. Popular computer programs include word processors, which let you type in reports and letters; spreadsheets, which let you

Figure 1-11. *After you place a 5 1/4-inch disk into the drive, you must close the drive latch*

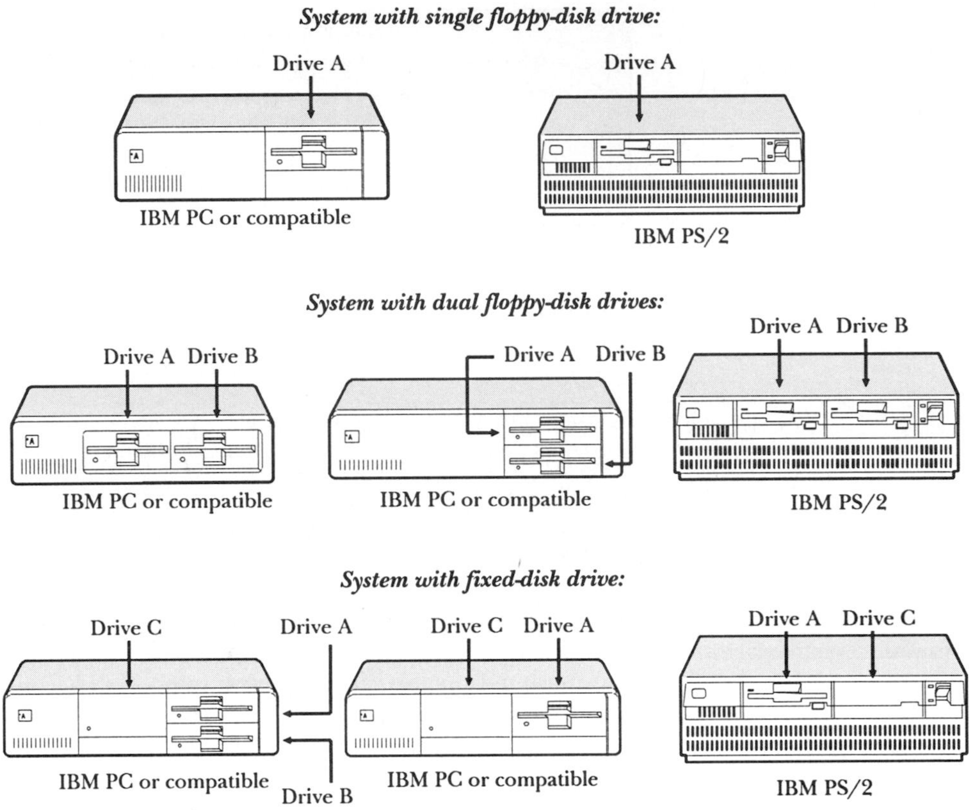

System with single floppy-disk drive:

Drive A   Drive A

IBM PC or compatible

IBM PS/2

System with dual floppy-disk drives:

Drive A Drive B   Drive A Drive B   Drive A Drive B

IBM PC or compatible   IBM PC or compatible   IBM PS/2

System with fixed-disk drive:

Drive C   Drive A   Drive C Drive A   Drive A Drive C

IBM PC or compatible   IBM PC or compatible   IBM PS/2
Drive B

Figure 1-12.   Common disk drive configurations and names

organize budgets and other numerical data; database programs, which help you organize information; graphics and drawing program; and even games!

A *computer program* is a list of instructions that tells your computer what to do. Without instructions, your computer's hardware will not do anything. A word processing program, therefore, is a list of computer instructions that lets you create, edit, and print documents. Computer software is stored on disks. When you buy a word processing program, for example, the program may require several disks. It's important to note that the disk *stores* software. The disk is not software. Just as a cassette tape stores music, the cassette tape is not music.

As you will learn in Chapter 3, "Issuing DOS Commands," you run a computer program by typing the program's name at the DOS prompt and pressing ENTER. DOS will then locate the program on your disk and load the program into your computer's fast electronic memory for execution.

Understanding DOS

Each time you turn your computer on, the computer loads a special program called the *operating system* into your computer's memory. After your computer loads it into memory, the operating system lets you run other programs and helps those programs use the hardware devices such as your disk and printer. In general, the operating system provides an interface between your application programs, such as a word processor or spreadsheet program, and your hardware. Figure 1-13 shows a diagram of this relationship.

DOS is the operating system for IBM PCs and PC-compatibles. In fact DOS stands for *Disk Operating System*. Without DOS, your computer cannot run other programs.

PC-DOS Versus MS-DOS

Many users become confused by the differences between PC-DOS and MS-DOS. Both names refer to DOS, your computer's disk operating system. The difference between the two lies in who supplies the product. PC-DOS is licensed by IBM for IBM Personal Computers. MS-DOS on the other hand, is licensed by Microsoft for PC-compatibles. For your purposes, it doesn't matter if you are using MS or PC-DOS. All of the commands presented in this book, unless explicitly stated, are supported by both versions.

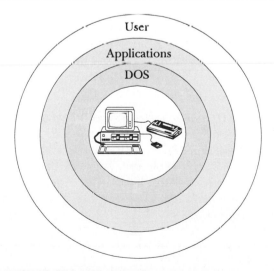

Figure 1-13.   *The DOS operating system provides the hardware interface to your application programs*

SUMMARY

Recording Information on Disk

Floppy disks are made from a flexible mylar plastic specially coated to let the computer magnetically record information on the disk's surface.

Hard disks, on the other hand, are typically made from inflexible, specially coated aluminum. Aluminum hard disks can use higher-precision devices that let the disks spin faster and store greater amounts of data.

Bytes, Kb, and Mb

Disk storage capacities and file sizes are expressed in bytes. A byte is a single character of information. To simplify the size expression for larger file and disk sizes, users use the terms Kb and Mb (pronounced kilobytes and Megabytes respectively). Kb is an abbreviation for about 1000 bytes. (Actually, it's 1024 bytes, but rounder numbers are easier to visualize.) Mb is an abbreviation for approximately one million (actually 1,048,576) bytes.

Disk Activation Light

Your computer illuminates the disk drive's activation light whenever the disk drive is operating. Never turn off your computer or remove a disk while the activation light is on. Doing so may damage your disk, destroying the information the disk contains.

Software

Software is computer programs. A program is a list of instructions for your computer to perform. Common software programs include word processors, spreadsheets, and database programs. Computer software is stored on disk. The disks only store software; the disks themselves are not software.

What Is DOS?

DOS stands for *Disk Operating System*. Each time your computer starts, the computer loads DOS from disk into memory. After DOS is in memory, it lets you run other programs. DOS, then, is a special program that virtually every IBM PC and PC-compatible uses. Like all programs, DOS initially resides on a disk. The rest of this book takes a detailed look at DOS, its commands, and DOS techniques you can use to make your time at the computer more productive.

Hands On

Using the disk drive figures presented in this chapter, determine your disk drive types (3 1/2 or 5 1/4) and whether or not you have a hard disk. In addition, determine your disk drive names (A, B, C, and so on). Use an unused floppy disk to experiment inserting and removing the disk into and out of the drive. If the disk is unlabeled, follow the guidelines specified in this chapter to ensure you are inserting the disk correctly.

Identify the disk's envelope, sleeve, jacket, index hole, write-protect notch, and disk hub. You might even consider sacrificing this disk by opening it up so you can examine the plastic disk.

Last, check if your computer is plugged into a surge suppressor. If not, you should strongly consider buying one.

Review

1. What is hardware?

2. What is software?

3. What is DOS?

4. How does a hard disk differ from a floppy disk?

5. Label the parts of the following floppy disks.

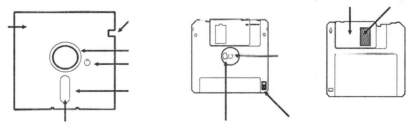

6. Label the disk drives shown in Figure 1-14 with their correct names.

7. What is a program? List several common programs.

8. What is write-protecting a disk?

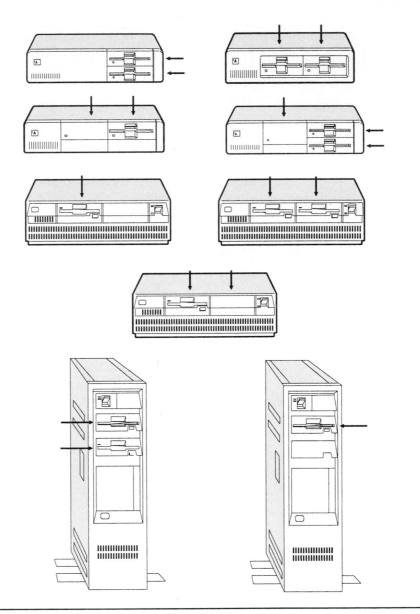

Figure 1-14. *Label the above disk drives with their correct names*

Answers

1. Hardware is your computer's physical parts, such as the keyboard, screen, chassis, and the electronic boards inside of each. Hardware, essentially, is the parts of the computer you can touch.

2. Software is computer programs that tell your computer's hardware what to do. Your word processor or spreadsheet are software. Software resides on disk. The disk itself is not software, it simply stores the software.

3. DOS stands for *Disk Operating System*. An operating system is a special program your computer loads into its electronic memory each time the computer starts. The operating system serves as your host while you work at the computer. In general, the operating system lets you run other programs, and use your computer's hardware.

4. Hard disks are nonremovable disks that reside inside the computer's chassis. Hard disk are much faster and can store much more information than removable floppy disks.

5. The following floppy disks are labeled like this:

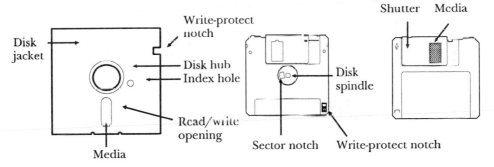

6. The disk drives shown in Figure 1-15 are labeled with their correct names.

7. A program is a list of instructions your computer performs. Software is another name for programs. Common programs include (but are not limited to) word processors, spreadsheets, computer games, and databases.

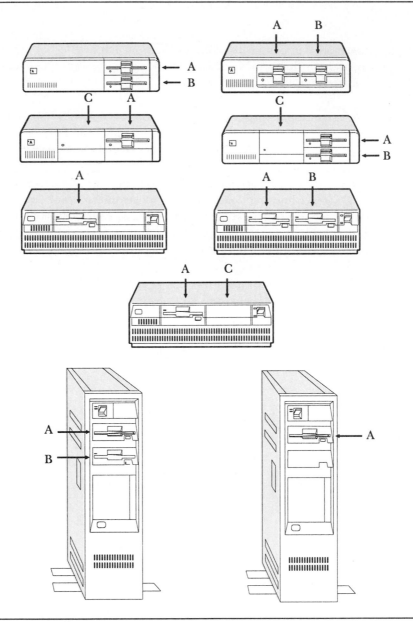

Figure 1-15.   Answer key for Review question 6

8. Write-protecting a disk prevents the disk drive from being able to record information on the disk. The drive can still read the information the disk contains, but it cannot add information to, or erase information from, the

disk. If you are using 5 1/4-inch floppy disks, you can write-protect the disk by placing a write-protect tab over the disk's write-protect notch. If you are using 3 1/2-inch floppy disks, you can write-protect a disk by sliding up the write-protect cover to expose a hole through the disk cover.

Advanced Concepts

All the discussion in the previous section centered on the computer's external hardware devices. In this section we'll take a look inside the chassis, identifying key components and terms along the way. Before we begin, it's important to note that if you choose to look inside your computer's chassis, don't touch or unplug anything you don't thoroughly understand. In other words, if it isn't broken, don't fix it.

The first step you must perform before opening your computer's chassis is to ensure that all of your hardware is unplugged. Next, remove the screws that hold the chassis cover on and slide the lid off. Figure 1-16 shows removal of one common type of chassis cover. Note that the lid should slide smoothly off the chassis. Never force the lid off the chassis; it may be stuck on one of your computer's internal cables.

As discussed, your computer's chassis houses your disk drives, power supply, controller boards, and CPU. The flat board covered with chips at the bottom of your computer is called the motherboard. Figure 1-17 illustrates the most common components you can easily identify within the chassis.

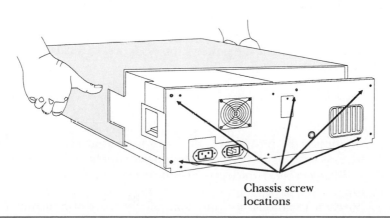

Chassis screw
locations

Figure 1-16.   *After you remove the screws*

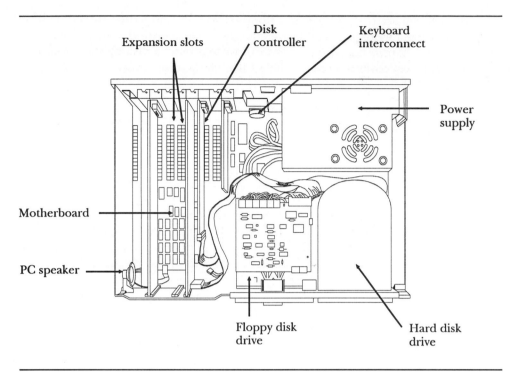

Figure 1-17.   *Common components inside the chassis*

Power Supply

The largest chassis component is the power supply, which distributes power to the computer's electronic components. The original IBM PCs used 65-watt power supplies. Most power supplies shipped today are 150 or 200 watts. In addition to distributing power, the power supply contains a fan to cool the computer's electronic components. If a computer fails to start, and you can't hear the fan whirring, the first item you should consider is the power supply. Figure 1-18 illustrates a typical power supply and interconnections.

Disk Drives

After the power supply, the next largest devices within your chassis are the disk drives. Each drive receives its power from the power supply and has a cable to a board called the disk controller, which provides the drive's interface to the computer (see Figure 1-19).

When you purchase a hard disk for your computer, you are obviously concerned with storage capacity. In addition, two other values can give you an indication of the

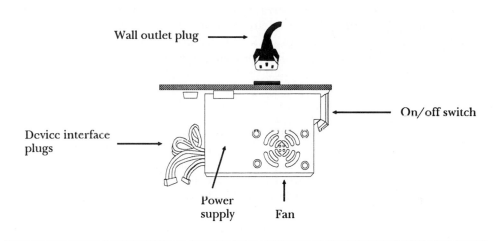

Figure 1-18.   *Typical PC power supply*

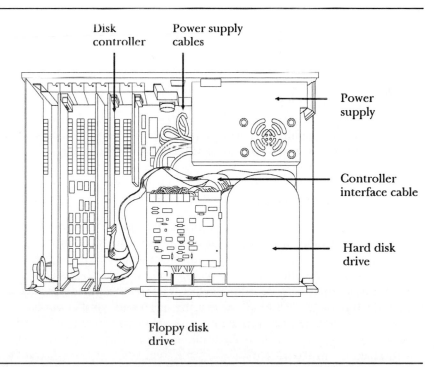

Figure 1-19.   *Each disk drive connects to the power supply and a disk controller*

disk's performance. First, the disk access time tells you how fast the disk head can move from one track to another. Second, the disk transfer time tells you how fast the disk can read or write information to or from the disk. Your computer retailer should provide these two values for each disk you are considering. Closely related to the disk's performance is the disk's controller type discussed next.

Disk Controller

The disk *controller* provides the interface between your computer and disk drive. In most cases, the controller is a hardware board that plugs into one of your computer's expansion slots; however, some controllers now reside on the actual drive. Four primary controller types dominate the industry. First, older systems use Shugart Technology or ST controllers such as the ST-506 or ST-412. For many years, ST controllers were the industry standard.

To increase storage capacity and performance while reducing the possibility of errors, disk controllers encode the information stored on the disk. When the controllers later read the information, they decode the data as necessary. To improve the performance of this encoding and decoding process, *ESDI*, or Enhanced Small Device Interface disks, have moved this encoding and decoding hardware off of the controller and placed it on the drive itself, which reduces bus traffic to the disk controller. When you buy an ESDI disk, you need to ensure that you have a compatible disk controller.

As briefly discussed, some controllers now reside on the drive itself. *IDE* or Integrated Drive Electronics controllers give computer manufactures and designers more available working space because the disk controller no longer requires an expansion slot, but rather, a small interface connector on the motherboard.

Last, many new personal computers have a very high speed I/O bus called the Small Computer System Interface or *SCSI* (pronounced "scuzzy"). The SCSI bus connects disk drives, tape drives, CD-ROMs and other devices to your system. Because the bus is highly specialized, it provides excellent performance. Before you purchase a SCSI drive you need to ensure that your system has a SCSI bus.

Expansion Slots and Cards

In the back (on the back-left corner in the models pictured) of your chassis you will find several hardware boards and possibly empty slots for more. Typically, your computer will have a disk controller card, additional memory, a video card, and one or more cards containing serial or parallel ports. Serial ports connect printers, a mouse, a modem, or other unique devices. The parallel ports typically only connect printers. Chapter 13, "Printing," covers the serial and parallel ports.

When you add new hardware to your system, you may need to install a board into one of the expansion slots. To do so, use a screwdriver to remove the metal slot cover, as shown in Figure 1-20.

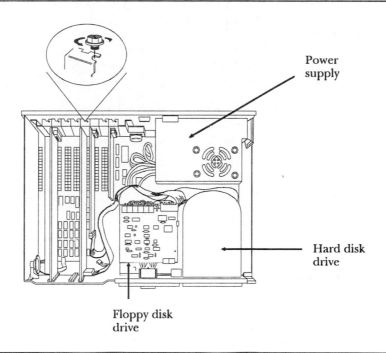

Power
supply

Hard disk
drive

Floppy disk
drive

Figure 1-20.   Removing an expansion slot cover

Place the cover in a safe storage location so you can later cover the slot should you ever remove a board. Next, gently slide the board into the guides as shown in Figure 1-21.

Make sure the board fits completely into the connectors attached to the motherboard. If you don't completely set the board into the slot, the computer will not be aware of the board's presence, or you may experience intermittent errors. Last, secure the board into the slot using the screw you removed with the slot cover.

Always handle computer boards gently during installation. Most boards contain sensitive electronic chips that you can easily damage. Also, make sure you don't loosen another board or cable during your board installation.

WARNING

Motherboard

Your computer's motherboard is the largest electronic board in the computer. The motherboard holds the computer's central processing unit (CPU), memory, math coprocessor, and other essential chips. In addition, the motherboard has the

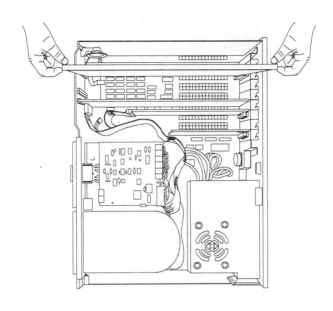

Figure 1-21.   *Sliding a board into the expansion slot*

connectors for all of your expansion boards and controllers. This row of interface connectors is the backplane. Figure 1-22 illustrates the motherboard for an 80386.

As you know, computers are categorized by their CPU type, such as 8086, 80286, 80386, and 80486. Table 1-3 describes the essential differences between these processor types.

Processor	Processor Size	Bus Size	Coprocessor
8086	16 Bit	16 Bit	8087
8088	16 Bit	8 Bit	8087
80286	16 Bit	16 Bit	80287
80386SX	32 Bit	16 Bit	80387SX
80386DX	32 Bit	32 Bit	80387DX
80486SX	32 Bit	32 Bit	80487SX
80486DX	32 Bit	32 Bit	Built-in

Table 1-3.   *Summary of CPU Types Found in the IBM PC and PC-Compatibles*

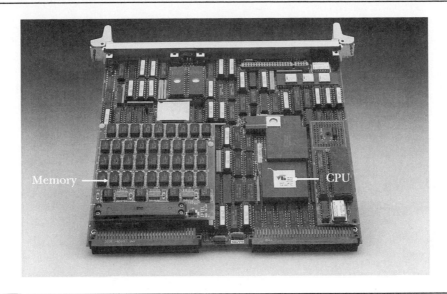

Figure 1-22. *An 80386 motherboard*

Key Terms

Bus   The common internal data channel used by the computer to transfer data to and from the CPU.

Hardware   The physical components that make up your computer, such as the keyboard, monitor, chassis, and printer, as well as the internal boards.

Software   Computer programs. Common software packages include word processors, spreadsheets, and database programs.

Byte   The computer's basic unit for data storage. For most purposes, a byte is a single character of information.

Kb   An abbreviation for kilobyte or 1,024 bytes.

Mb   An abbreviaton for megabyte or 1,048,576 bytes.

Operating System   The first program a computer runs, which provides the hardware interface for other application programs. DOS is your computer's operating system. DOS stands for *Disk Operating System.*

Chapter *2*

Getting DOS Started

Chapter 1 introduced you to your computer's hardware, such as the keyboard, monitor, and printer. At that time, you learned that your computer's hardware tells only half the story; software (computer programs) provides the second half. Before you can use your computer to run programs such as your word processor or spreadsheet, your computer must run a special program called the operating system. The operating system serves as your host while you work with your computer. In this chapter you will learn how to start DOS. Once DOS is running, you can type in DOS commands as discussed in Chapter 3.

Before You Begin

This chapter assumes you have already installed DOS on your hard disk, or your computer is floppy disk based and you will start DOS using a floppy DOS system disk. If you are planning on using your hard disk and you have not yet installed DOS on it, turn to Appendix E or F on installing DOS version 4 or 5, respectively. Once you have successfully installed DOS, continue your reading in this chapter.

Starting DOS from Floppy Disks

If your computer has DOS installed on a hard disk, continue your reading at the section titled "Turning On Your Computer." If you are starting DOS from floppy disks, which is a common practice for older PCs or laptop computers, you will need your DOS system disks. Typically, most floppy disk versions of DOS use two floppy disks, one labeled "Program Disk" and one labeled "Supplemental Programs," as shown in Figure 2-1

To start DOS from a floppy disk, insert the disk labeled "Program Disk" into drive A and close the disk drive latch as discussed in Chapter 1, "Getting to Know Your Computer." You are now ready to continue your reading with the next section.

Turning On Your Computer

If your computer has DOS installed on a hard disk, make sure drive A does not contain a floppy disk and the drive latch is open. As you will learn, your computer always looks to drive A first for a DOS disk, then examines your hard disk. If your floppy disk drive contains a disk other than DOS, your computer may not be able to start DOS.

As discussed in Chapter 1, your computer, monitor, and printer each have their own power cables and on/off switches. Make sure all three devices are plugged into working plugs. Next, individually turn on your monitor, computer, and printer. The order in which you turn the devices on does not matter.

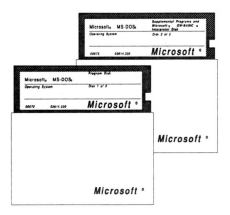

Figure 2-1.   *DOS system and supplemental programs floppy disks*

When you turn your computer on, you can hear it start to come to life as its internal fan begins to whir. Next, your monitor may display a sequence of increasing numbers as your computer examines its electronic memory. During this startup period, your computer examines many of its critical electronic components. Because your computer only performs these tests when you turn your computer on, the tests are collectively called a *power-on self-test*. Should one of the components fail its power-on test, your computer will likely display an error message you will need to write down and give to your computer repairperson.

If your computer successfully passes its power-on self-test, you will see drive A's disk activation light illuminate briefly as your computer searches drive A for a disk containing DOS. If drive A contains a DOS system disk, your computer will begin loading DOS from the floppy disk into your computer's electronic memory.

If drive A does not contain a floppy disk, your computer will load DOS from your hard disk. If the disk in drive A, or your hard disk contains DOS, your computer will successfully load DOS. If the disk does not contain DOS, your computer will display an error message (see the troubleshooting tips later in this chapter).

What DOS Will Display

Depending on your DOS version and system configuration, the actual information DOS will display may differ. In the simplest case, DOS will display characters similar to C> or A> called the *DOS prompt*. In this case, the letter "C" tells you DOS is using drive C, your hard disk. Likewise, the letter "A" informs you DOS is using the floppy disk in drive A.

Many times, DOS may ask you to set the system date and time before displaying its prompt. In such a case, DOS will prompt you for the date as follows.

```
Current date is Sun 06-02-1991
Enter new date (mm-dd-yy):
```

If DOS displays this prompt, simply press ENTER to continue, leaving the current date unchanged. If the date DOS displays is incorrect, don't worry. Chapter 3, "Issuing DOS Commands," teaches you how to set your computer's date. Next, DOS will prompt you to type in the system time, as shown in the following:

```
Current time is 6:04:32.32a
Enter new time:
```

Once again, simply press the ENTER key to continue leaving your computer's time unchanged.

DOS may display its user-friendly shell interface, or possibly Microsoft Windows. Figure 2-2 illustrates the DOS version 4 shell.

Chapters 39 and 40 discuss the DOS 4 shell in detail. If DOS displays this shell, hold down your keyboard's ALT key and press the F3 function key to exit the shell to the DOS prompt. Chapter 3 begins its discussion of DOS commands you issue at the DOS prompt.

If you are using DOS 5, DOS may automatically display the version 5 shell interface. Figure 2-3 displays the DOS 5 shell. If DOS displays this shell, press the F3 function key to return to the DOS prompt. Chapters 41 and 42 discuss the DOS 5 shell in detail.

Lastly, Figure 2-4 displays the Microsoft Windows interface. If your computer displays Windows, hold down the ALT key and press F to invoke the File menu. Next, type X to select the Exit option, to return to the DOS prompt.

Should your computer display a different program, exit the program to the DOS prompt.

Troubleshooting the DOS Startup

If your system does not successfully start DOS, use the following guidelines to identify the source of the problem.

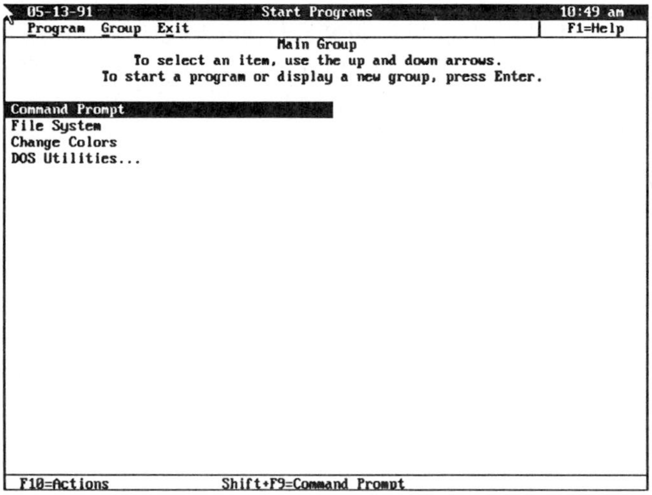

Figure 2-2.   *DOS 4 shell program*

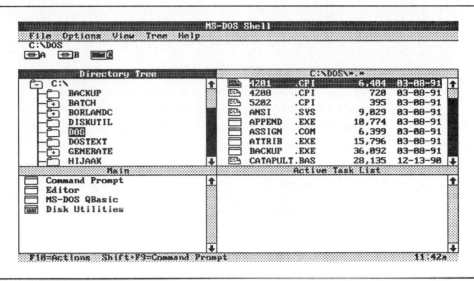

Figure 2-3.   DOS 5 shell program

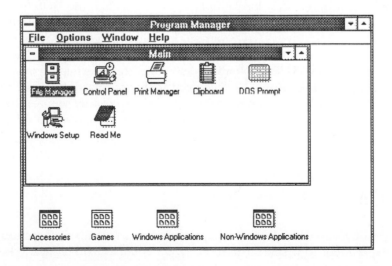

Figure 2-4.   Microsoft Windows interface

1. Make sure your computer and monitor are plugged into working outlets, and you have turned both on.

2. Can you hear your computer's internal fan whirring? If not, your computer very likely has a power supply problem that will require servicing.

3. Make sure your monitor's intensity level is adjusted correctly. Like a television, your monitor has a knob that lets you control the screen's brightness. If the intensity is set too low, your screen may be working but you simply can't see its contents.

4. Does your computer count up and display the amount of electronic random access memory? During the power-on self-test, most computers display a count of its working memory. If yours does not, the computer may be failing its self-test very early in the test sequence.

5. Does your computer illuminate drive A's disk activation light in search of DOS? As discussed, after your computer finishes its power-on self-test, the computer will first look for DOS on a floppy disk in drive A. If your computer does not, it is failing its self-test.

6. Does your screen display the following error message?

```
Non-System disk or disk error
Replace and strike any key when ready
```

   If so, you most likely have a floppy disk other than the DOS System Disk in drive A. If so, remove the disk and restart your computer. If you don't have a floppy disk in drive A, DOS was not installed correctly on your hard disk. If this is the case, you may need to start DOS using a floppy disk in drive A, use the DOS BACKUP command to save all of the information on your hard disk to floppy disks, install DOS correctly onto your hard disk, and lastly, use the DOS RECOVER command to restore the hard disk's original information from floppy. Should you need to perform these steps, have an experienced DOS user assist you.

Hands On

Beginning with Chapter 1, all of the chapters contain a "Hands On" section, which lets you experiment with several different DOS commands. For now, start DOS following the steps discussed. If DOS displays a shell or menu program similar to those discussed, exit the program to the DOS prompt.

Review

1. What is the purpose of the computer's power-on self-test?

2. The letters "DOS" stand for *Disk Operating System;* what does DOS do?

3. What is the DOS prompt?

4. How does the prompt A> differ from C>?

5. What is a shell program?

Answers

1. Each time you turn on your computer's power, the computer performs a series of diagnostic tests to ensure all of its electronic components are working properly. Although computers are very dependable, they do eventually wear out. The computer's self-test examines the key internal electronic components. Hopefully, if a component fails, your computer can display a message indicating the cause and location of its failure.

2. The DOS operating system serves as your host while you work at the computer. Operating systems provide your interface to the computer's hardware and let you run other computer programs such as your word processor or spreadsheet.

3. When you run programs at your computer, you type in the program's name and press ENTER. The DOS prompt is a series of one or more letters that DOS displays to inform you it is ready for you to type in commands. Typically, the DOS prompt contains the letter "A" for floppy disk systems (perhaps "A>") or the letter "C" for hard disk systems ("C>"). Regardless of the letters used, the DOS prompt is simply your notification that DOS is ready for you to issue commands.

4. The DOS prompt typically contains the letter that corresponds to the current disk drive. The A> prompt indicates that DOS is currently using floppy disk drive A. Likewise, the C> prompt indicates DOS is using the hard disk drive C. Chapter 6, "Getting Around Your Disk," examines using your computer's disk in detail.

5. A shell program is simply a menu-driven user-friendly interface that makes the computer easier to use. From within a shell program, users can run other programs, copy files, and perform many of the same tasks provided by DOS. Shell programs have grown in popularity due to their ease of use. DOS versions 4 and 5 provide shell interfaces that are described in Chapters 39 through 42.

Advanced Concepts

Although DOS is the most widely used operating system in the world, and millions of users start DOS every day, few users understand the DOS startup sequence. In this section we will examine this process in detail.

How Your Computer Finds DOS

As you know, each time you start your computer, your computer first looks for DOS on a floppy disk in drive A, regardless of whether or not your computer has a hard disk with DOS installed. Here's why.

First, hard disks are not shipped from the disk manufacturers with DOS installed, as they may supply drives to companies using other operating systems. Instead, the hard disk must be installed in a computer and formatted as a bootable disk. To format your hard disk, you need a way of initially starting DOS other than your hard disk. As such, your computer always looks first to drive A.

Second, although hard disks are very reliable, they eventually wear out or become damaged. Should your hard disk fail, you need a way to start your computer.

Last, users periodically inadvertently issue commands that delete or rename key files that DOS needs to start. By letting the user boot DOS from a floppy, the user can get DOS running and normally correct the error.

If you are using a hard disk, your computer must locate DOS on one of your hard disk partitions. As you will recall, during the DOS installation process, the FDISK command lets you divide your disk into one to four *partitions.* DOS views each partition as a unique disk drive. Assuming your hard disk has two partitions, DOS would access the first partition as drive C, and the second partition as drive D. Using FDISK, you must select one partition as the primary partition from which your computer will boot DOS. The first thing your computer must do when it tries to boot DOS from your hard disk is determine the primary DOS partition. To do so, your computer reads the disk's master boot record.

As part of its processing, the FDISK command writes information that describes the disk's partition to the very first sector of your disk. This information, called the master boot record, tells your computer where each partition begins and the partition's size. It also identifies the primary DOS partition, from which your computer will boot DOS. Figure 2-5 illustrates a disk with 2 partitions, as well as the master boot record.

Using the information it found in the master boot record, your computer locates the primary DOS partition and reads its first sector, the DOS boot record. As discussed, DOS views each partition as a unique disk. The DOS boot record describes the boot disk characteristics, such as the sector size, number of sectors, and so on. In addition, the boot record contains a small program the computer loads into memory to start the DOS boot process. Figure 2-6 illustrates the DOS boot record in relation to the disk's primary DOS partition.

Every bootable DOS disk has two hidden files. For MS-DOS, these two files are named IO.SYS and MSDOS.SYS. Likewise, PC-DOS names these files IBMBIO.COM and IBMDOS.COM. The function of the MS-DOS and PC-DOS files are the same. The following discussion uses the MS-DOS file names. The file IO.SYS contains software that builds upon your computer's basic I/O capabilities as provided in ROM. The file MSDOS.SYS contains the software that implements the DOS system services. DOS uses these services for a wide range of tasks such as reading and writing to disk, your printer, or even setting your computer's date and time. If these two files are not present, DOS will display the following error message.

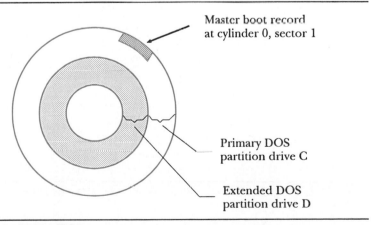

Master boot record
at cylinder 0, sector 1

Primary DOS
partition drive C

Extended DOS
partition drive D

Figure 2-5.   A two-partition disk

```
Non-System disk or disk error
```

Assuming the hidden files exist, DOS first loads the file IO.SYS into memory. In addition to containing the additional I/O services, IO.SYS contains a small system initialization program named SYSINIT. When SYSINIT is in memory DOS invokes it, and SYSINIT begins reading the file MSDOS.SYS from disk into memory. Next, SYSINIT searches the disk's root directory for the file CONFIG.SYS. SYSINIT uses the CONFIG.SYS entries to configure itself in memory. Last, SYSINIT locates and invokes the file COMMAND.COM, which contains all of the internal DOS commands as well as the DOS command processor responsible for displaying the DOS prompt and processing your commands. If SYSINIT cannot locate COMMAND.COM, the system startup will stop and DOS will display the following error message.

```
Bad or missing Command Interpreter
```

If this occurs, you may need to start DOS from a floppy disk and copy COMMAND.COM into your hard disk's root directory. Assuming SYSINIT finds and loads it, COMMAND.COM, in turn, searches your root directory for the file AUTOEXEC.BAT. If AUTOEXEC.BAT exists, COMMAND.COM will invoke it.

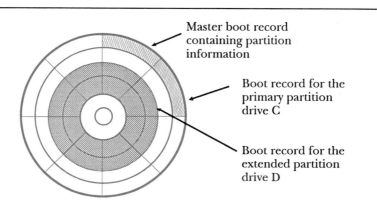

Master boot record containing partition information

Boot record for the primary partition drive C

Boot record for the extended partition drive D

Figure 2-6.   DOS boot record within the primary DOS partition

Otherwise, COMMAND.COM will invoke the familiar DATE and TIME commands completing the startup or boot process.

Key Terms

Booting DOS   Starting DOS. The process of loading DOS from disk into your computer's electronic memory.

Non-system disk   A disk that does not contain the files needed to start DOS.

System disk   A disk containing the DOS hidden files used to load DOS and the DOS command processor COMMAND.COM.

Disk partition   A portion of hard disk for use as a logical drive.

Primary DOS partition   The hard disk partition containing the system information used to start DOS.

DOS prompt   The characters DOS displays to indicate it is waiting for you to enter a command. Common DOS prompts include C> and A>.

Chapter 3

Issuing DOS Commands

In Chapter 2 you learned that after DOS successfully loads itself from disk into your computer's memory, it displays its *system prompt*, which indicates that DOS is ready for you to type in a command. In this chapter you will execute your first DOS commands. As you will learn, to improve its performance, DOS divides its commands into two types: internal commands, which are stored in your computer's fast electronic memory; and external commands, which are stored on disk. This chapter helps you understand why DOS does this, and how it affects the steps you must follow to execute each command type successfully.

Executing Your First DOS Commands

As discussed in Chapter 2, your system prompt may differ from the C> prompt used throughout this chapter. Because most DOS users today use the hard disk drive C, this chapter uses the drive letter within the prompt. If your system prompt differs, don't worry. The prompt will not change the way DOS executes the example commands. Don't worry if your prompt doesn't show the backslash either. You can learn more about the prompt in Chapter 10, "Directories."

To execute a DOS command, you type the command's name at the DOS prompt and press ENTER. DOS will execute the command, redisplaying its prompt after the command completes so you can type in your next command. First, if you simply press the ENTER key without typing a command name, DOS will redisplay its prompt:

```
C>    <ENTER>
C>    <ENTER>
C>
```

CLS Clears the Screen

As you work with DOS, your screen may periodically become cluttered with the output of your previous commands. The CLS command lets you erase or clear your screen contents. DOS abbreviates many of its commands to reduce your typing. CLS, for example, is an abbreviation for CLear Screen. To erase your screen's contents, type **CLS** and press ENTER.

```
C> CLS    <ENTER>
```

DOS will erase your screen's contents and redisplay its prompt in the upper-left corner of your screen (your screen's home position).

VER Displays the DOS Version Number

When Microsoft first released DOS in 1981, DOS initially had the version number 1.0. Over the years, as Microsoft has increased the capabilities DOS provides, they have released newer, more powerful versions of DOS. Each time the DOS developers release a new version, they increment the DOS version number. VER displays your DOS version number on the screen. To execute VER, type **VER** and press ENTER.

```
C> VER    <ENTER>
```

VER will respond by displaying the DOS version number. Under DOS version 3.3, VER will display the following.

```
MS-DOS Version 3.30
```

Likewise, under DOS 5, VER displays the version number:

```
MS-DOS Version 5.00
```

You must know your DOS version number. Some DOS commands are available under one version of DOS and not others. Likewise, many applications, such as your word processor or spreadsheet, may require a specific version of DOS. For the purposes of this book, however, unless you are explicitly told otherwise, you can assume the concepts discussed apply to every version of DOS.

Correcting a Mistyped Command

You have learned that, to execute a DOS command, you type the command's name at the DOS prompt and press ENTER. If, before you press ENTER, you notice that you have mistyped one or more letters in the command's name, you can correct the command using your keyboard's BACKSPACE key, shown on one common keyboard in Figure 3-1.

Suppose, for example, you mistyped the CLS command as "CKS" but have not yet pressed ENTER:

```
C> CKS_
```

When you press BACKSPACE, DOS will first erase the "S":

```
C> CK_
```

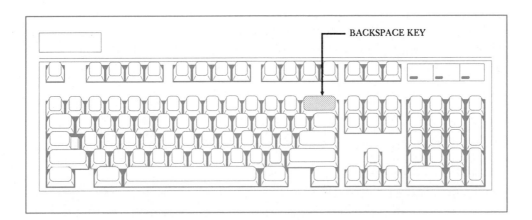

Figure 3-1.   Location of the keyboard's BACKSPACE key

By pressing BACKSPACE a second time, the "K" is erased.

```
C> C_
```

Next, retype the letters "L" and "S" and press ENTER:

```
C> CLS   <ENTER>
```

Upper- or Lowercase Letters

For consistency, all the command examples presented throughout this book use uppercase letters. DOS, however, does not care if you type your command names in upper- or lowercase letters, or a mixture of both. To DOS, the following three commands are all the same.

```
C> CLS   <ENTER>

C> cls   <ENTER>

C> cLs   <ENTER>
```

TIME Displays or Sets the System Time

You learned in Chapter 2 that, depending on your system configuration, DOS may ask you to set your system date and time when your system starts. If your system does not ask you to set the system time, you can use the TIME command to display the system time, and if necessary, set the correct time. Invoke TIME from the DOS prompt by typing **TIME**.

```
C> TIME   <ENTER>
```

TIME will display the current system time and prompt you to enter a new time:

```
Current time is  6:04:32.32a
Enter new time:
```

If you simply press ENTER, TIME will leave the current system time unchanged. Many users will invoke TIME throughout the day, simply to determine the current time.

By pressing ENTER at TIME's prompt for a new time, the current system time is left unchanged.

To set your current system time, you must invoke TIME from the DOS prompt, as before. When TIME prompts you to enter a new system time, you must type in the time desired, specifying hours and minutes in the form *HH:MM*. For example, you would type **10:30** for 10:30 AM.

DOS versions prior to version 4 use a 24-hour military clock, meaning you must add 12 to each hour after noon. 1:00 PM becomes 13:00. Likewise, 4:30 PM becomes 16:30. Table 3-1 provides standard times and their 24-hour equivalents.

The following TIME command, for example, sets the current system time to 4:30 PM (16:30).

```
C:\> TIME   <ENTER>
Current time is  6:04:32.32a
Enter new time: 16:30   <ENTER>
```

Likewise, this command sets the time to 8:30 AM.

```
C:\> TIME   <ENTER>
Current time is 16:30:33.12
Enter new time: 8:30   <ENTER>
```

If you are using DOS version 4 or later, DOS gives you an alternative to 24-hour military time and lets you instead append the letter "A" or "P" to your time to

Time	24-Hour Time	Time	24-Hour Time
12 Midnight	0:00	12 Noon	12:00
1:00 AM	1:00	1:00 PM	13:00
2:00 AM	2:00	2:00 PM	14:00
3:00 AM	3:00	3:00 PM	15:00
4:00 AM	4:00	4:00 PM	16:00
5:00 AM	5:00	5:00 PM	17:00
6:00 AM	6:00	6:00 PM	18:00
7:00 AM	7:00	7:00 PM	19:00
8:00 AM	8:00	8:00 PM	20:00
9:00 AM	9:00	9:00 PM	21:00
10:00 AM	10:00	10:00 PM	22:00
11:00 AM	11:00	11:00 PM	23:00

Table 3-1.   Standard Times and Their 24-Hour Equivalents

represent AM or PM. The following command uses this format to set the system time to 2:30 PM.

```
C:\> TIME   <ENTER>
Current time is  8:30:32.32a
Enter new time: 2:30P  <ENTER>
```

Correcting an Invalid Time

If you mistype the system time and enter an invalid time, TIME will display an "Invalid time" error message and prompt you to enter a correct time, as follows.

```
C:\> TIME   <ENTER>
Current time is  8:30:32.32a
Enter new time: 230P  <ENTER>

Invalid time
Enter new time:
```

Should the "Invalid time" message appear, make sure you are specifying the desired time in the form *HH:MM*.

Specifying a More Precise Time

All of the TIME command examples presented so far have only set the hours and minutes. TIME, however, lets you specify hours, minutes, seconds, and even hundredths of seconds. The complete format for the TIME command becomes the following: *HH:MM:SS.hh*, where *SS* represents seconds from 0 to 59 and *hh* represents hundredths of a second from 0 to 99. The following TIME command, for example, sets the system time to 11:59:59.99 AM.

```
C:\> TIME   <ENTER>
Current time is  8:30:32.32a
Enter new time: 11:59:59.99  <ENTER>
```

If you don't specify values for the seconds and hundredths of seconds, TIME uses the default value, zero.

DATE Displays or Sets the System Date

As was the case with the system time during startup, DOS may, depending on your system configuration, display the current system date and prompt you to enter a new date. The DATE command lets you display and set the current system date. To display the current system date, type **DATE** from the DOS prompt:

```
C> DATE    <ENTER>
```

DATE will display the current date and prompt you to enter a new date:

```
Current date is Sun 06-02-1991
Enter new date (mm-dd-yy):
```

To leave the date unchanged, simply press ENTER. To change the system date, type in the numeric representation of the desired date in the form *mm-dd-yy*, where *mm* is the current month from 1 to 12, *dd* is the day from 1 to 31, and *yy* is the last two digits of the year, such as 91 (optionally, you can include all four digits of the year). For example the following DATE command sets the system date to December 25, 1991.

```
C:\> DATE   <ENTER>
Current date is Sun 06-02-1991
Enter new date (mm-dd-yy): 12-25-91   <ENTER>
```

You must specify the month, day, and year. If you enter an invalid date, DATE will display an "Invalid date" message and prompt you to enter a new date:

```
C:\> DATE   <ENTER>
Current date is Sun 06-02-1991
Enter new date (mm-dd-yy): 25-12-91   <ENTER>

Invalid date
Enter new date (mm-dd-yy):
```

If this error message occurs, make sure you are specifying the date in the correct order, and that you are separating each field with a slash (/) or hyphen (-). The date format used throughout this book is *mm-dd-yy,* the format used in the United States.

If you have selected a different international system configuration using the CONFIG.SYS COUNTRY= entry, your date format may differ.

Note to Pre-DOS 3.3 Users

If you are using DOS version 3.2 or lower, the DATE and TIME commands do not permanently set the system clock on the IBM PC AT. Instead, each time your system starts you must use DATE and TIME to set the system clock. If you are using DOS 3.3 or higher, however, the date and time you set remain in effect until you change them at a future time. To set the system clock on a PC AT permanently under DOS 3.2 or lower, you can use the SETUP disk in your computer's Guide to Operations, which should have accompanied your computer.

Command-Line Parameters

You have learned that, to execute a DOS command, you type the command's name and press ENTER. The line of information you type before pressing ENTER is the *command line*. Many of the DOS commands you will use throughout this book let you specify additional information in the command line, such as a file name, or even the desired date or time.

You have learned that if you type **TIME**, TIME will display the current time and prompt you to enter a new time. If you want to set the time without viewing the current time, you can include the desired time in the command line, as shown here.

```
C> TIME  11:30   <ENTER>
C>
```

In this case, because your command line contains a valid time, TIME does not display the current time and prompt—it sets the system clock to time specified.

You can specify the desired date in the command line. For example, the following command sets the system date to October 31, 1991.

```
C> DATE  10-31-91   <ENTER>
C>
```

As before with TIME, DATE suppresses its display of the current date, as well as its prompt for a new date, because the command line contains a valid date.

External Versus Internal Commands

Before any program (or DOS command) can run, the program must first be stored in your computer's electronic memory. Each time you start your computer, for example, your computer must load DOS from disk into its memory chips before running DOS (see Figure 3-2).

Because DOS has so many commands, and your computer has a limited amount of electronic memory (or RAM), DOS only keeps a few of the smallest and most commonly used commands in memory at all times. DOS can execute these commands, called *internal commands*, without first having to load them from disk into memory. As a result, these commands run almost instantly. CLS, VER, DATE, and TIME are all examples of internal commands.

Most DOS commands, however, are *external commands*, which reside on disk. When you execute an external command, DOS must locate the command on disk and then load the command into memory before the command can run, as shown in Figure 3-3. All applications, such as word processors or spreadsheets, are external commands.

You may be wondering why you should care about the external and internal commands. The reason has to do with the steps you must follow to execute a command. Because internal commands are always in your computer's memory, you can execute an internal command at any time simply by typing the command's name. With external commands, however, DOS must locate the command on disk before the command can execute. Unfortunately, DOS, by default, only looks for the

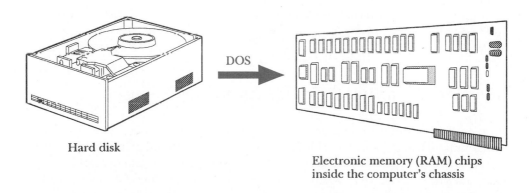

Hard disk

Electronic memory (RAM) chips inside the computer's chassis

Figure 3-2.   *Each time your computer starts, DOS is loaded from disk into the computer's fast electronic memory*

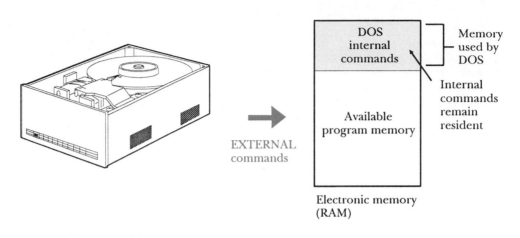

Figure 3-3. *To execute an external command, DOS must first load the command from disk into memory*

command in certain locations. In Chapter 4, "Getting Started with DOS Files," you will learn how DOS stores information on your disk using files. At that time, you will begin to understand why it is sometimes difficult for DOS to locate your external commands.

For now, however, simply be aware that internal DOS commands are always in your computer's memory once DOS is active, while external commands are located on disk. Before DOS can execute an external command, DOS must find the command on disk and load the command into memory.

Table 3-2 lists the internal DOS commands. Likewise, Table 3-3 lists the external DOS commands.

The "Bad command or file name" Message

If you mistype a command name and you have not yet pressed ENTER, you can correct the command using BACKSPACE. However, if you type an invalid command and press ENTER, DOS will try to locate the command you specified. For example, if you type **CKS** and press ENTER, DOS will try to locate a command named CKS. In this case,

Command	DOS Version	Command	DOS Version
BREAK	2.0 and later	IF	2.0 and later
CALL	3.3 and later	MKDIR (MD)	2.0 and later
CHCP	3.3 and later	PATH	2.0 and later
CHDIR (CD)	2.0 and later	PAUSE	1.0 and later
CLS	2.0 and later	PROMPT	2.0 and later
COPY	1.0 and later	REM	1.0 and later
CTTY	2.0 and later	REN	1.0 and later
DATE	1.1 and later	RMDIR (RD)	2.0 and later
DEL	1.0 and later	SET	2.0 and later
DIR	1.0 and later	SHIFT	2.0 and later
ECHO	2.0 and later	TIME	1.0 and later
ERASE	1.0 and later	TYPE	1.0 and later
EXIT	2.0 and later	VER	2.0 and later
FOR	2.0 and later	VERIFY	2.0 and later
GOTO	2.0 and later	VOL	2.0 and later

Table 3-2.   DOS Internal Commands

DOS won't find such a command and will display the "Bad command or file name" error message and a new prompt:

```
C> CKS   <ENTER>
Bad command or file name


C>
```

Get into the habit of reading and analyzing the error messages DOS displays. In this case, the words "Bad command" inform you that you have entered an invalid command name or the name of an external command DOS could not locate. The Command Reference section of this book examines the DOS error messages in detail and presents steps you should follow to resolve them.

Type **CKS** again and watch your disk's activation light. Each time you type in a command name, DOS first checks to see if the command name matches one of its internal commands, which reside in memory. If so, DOS executes the command. If not, DOS searches the disk for a matching external command. When you type **CKS** and press ENTER, you should see your disk's activation light illuminate briefly as DOS searches the disk for the command.

Command	DOS Version	Command	DOS Version
APPEND	3.2 and later	KEYB*xx*	3.0 to 3.2
ASSIGN	2.0 and later	LABEL	3.0 and later
ATTRIB	3.0 and later	LOADFIX	5.0
BACKUP	2.0 and later	LOADHIGH	5.0
CHDKSK	1.0 and later	MEM	4.0 and later
COMMAND	1.0 and later	MIRROR	5.0 and later
COMP	1.0 and later	MODE	1.0 and later
DISKCOMP	1.0 and later	MORE	2.0 and later
DISKCOPY	1.0 and later	NLSFUNC	3.3 and later
DOSKEY	5.0	PRINT	2.0 and later
DOSSHELL	4.0 and later	RECOVER	2.0 and later
EDIT	5.0	REPLACE	3.2 and later
EDLIN	1.0 and later	RESTORE	2.0 and later
EXE2BIN	1.1 to 3.3, 5.0	SELECT	3.0 and later
EXPAND	5.0	SETVER	5.0
FASTOPEN	3.3 and later	SHARE	3.0 and later
FC	MS-DOS 2.0 and later	SORT	2.0 and later
FDISK	2.0 and later	SUBST	3.1 and later
FIND	2.0 and later	SYS	1.0 and later
FORMAT	1.0 and later	TREE	2.0 and later
GRAFTABL	3.0 and later	UNDELETE	5.0
GRAPHICS	2.0 and later	UNFORMAT	5.0
JOIN	3.1 and later	XCOPY	3.2 and later
KEYB	3.3 and later		

Table 3-3.   DOS External Commands

Online Help in DOS 5

DOS, in version 5, will display a brief explanation about a command if you invoke it using the /? switch. The following displays information about the DATE command.

```
C:\> DATE  /?  <ENTER>
Displays or sets the date.

DATE [ date ]

Type DATE without parameters to display the current date setting
and a prompt for a new one. Press ENTER to keep the same date.
```

Using /? you can obtain a brief description of each DOS command. For more detailed online help on all versions of DOS, refer to the disk package advertised at the start of this book.

Hands On

To begin, press ENTER several times.

```
C>    <ENTER>
C>    <ENTER>
C>    <ENTER>
```

Next, use CLS to clear your screen display.

```
C> CLS   <ENTER>
```

Use VER to display the current DOS version number.

```
C> VER   <ENTER>
```

Repeat VER, but this time, misspell it as "VAR" without pressing ENTER.

```
C> VAR_
```

Use BACKSPACE to erase the letters "R" and "A" and correct the command.
   Next, use TIME to display the system time.

```
C> TIME   <ENTER>
```

If your system time is incorrect, set the correct time. Repeat the process with DATE.

```
C> DATE   <ENTER>
```

CLS

CLS is an abbreviation for CLear Screen. CLS erases your screen's current contents. When CLS completes, DOS redisplays its prompt in the upper-left corner of your screen. To invoke CLS, type **CLS** at the DOS prompt and press ENTER:

```
C:\> CLS <ENTER>
```

VER

VER is an abbreviation for VERsion. The VER command displays your DOS version number on the screen. DOS version numbers consist of two parts, a major and minor version number. Under DOS 5.0, for example, 5 is the major version number and 0 is the minor. When software developers release a new version of a program, the developers increment the major version number if a large number of changes to the program have been made. In the case of DOS, version 4 becomes version 5. If instead, the changes are only small updates or error corrections, the developers increment the minor version number. Using DOS once again, version 3.2 becomes version 3.3. To display your current version number, invoke VER, as shown here.

```
C:\> VER   <ENTER>
```

TIME

The TIME command lets you set or display the current system time. To set the system time, you must specify the hours and minutes of the desired time in the form *HH:MM*. If you are using DOS 3.3 or prior, you must use 24-hour military time. If you are using DOS version 4 or greater, you can simply append the letter "A" or "P" to your time to indicate AM or PM. The simplest way to invoke TIME is shown here:

```
C> TIME   <ENTER>
```

SUMMARY

DATE

The DATE command lets you set or display your computer's system date. To view the date without changing it, simply press ENTER in response to DATE's prompt for a new date. If you want to change the date, type in the month, day, and year in the form *mm-dd-yy*. The simplest way to invoke DATE is

```
C> DATE   <ENTER>
```

Review

1. How does an internal command differ from an external command?

2. What is the command line?

3. How do the following commands differ?

```
C> DATE   <ENTER>

C> date   <ENTER>
```

4. How do you determine the current DOS version?

5. What is the DATE command to set the system date to 12/25/91?

Answers

1. To increase your system performance, DOS provides two kinds of commands, internal commands and external commands. Internal commands include the smaller and commonly used DOS commands. Internal commands are so named because DOS keeps the commands in your computer's fast electronic memory whenever DOS is active. Because internal commands are stored in memory, DOS can execute them very quickly. External commands, on the other hand, reside on your computer's disk. External commands are larger,

less commonly used commands. When you execute an external command, DOS must locate the command on disk and then load the command into memory before executing it. All applications, such as your word processor or spreadsheet, are made up of external commands.

2. The command line is the line of information you type at the DOS prompt, before pressing ENTER, to execute a command. The command line may simply contain a command name, or it may contain additional information such as a disk drive letter, file name, or system date.

3. The commands are the same. DOS is not sensitive to the case of the letters.

4. Type the command **VER** at the prompt to display the current DOS version number.

5. You can set the system date two ways. First, simply invoke DATE and type in the date, as shown here.

```
C:\> DATE   <ENTER>
Current date is Sun 06-02-1991
Enter new date (mm-dd-yy): 12-25-91   <ENTER>
```

Second, you can include the date in DATE's command line:

```
C:\> DATE   12-25-91   <ENTER>
```

Advanced Concepts

External DOS commands have either the EXE or COM extensions. You may wonder why DOS just doesn't use one or the other. As it turns out, in addition to having different extensions, EXE (EXEcutable) and COM (COMmand) files have different internal formats and characteristics. DOS uses COM files for smaller commands (less than 64Kb). In addition, DOS has less freedom over where and how it loads COM files into memory. Because of these size and placement restrictions, however, DOS is able to load COM programs into memory faster than it can EXE programs. Unfortunately, the choice of whether a program becomes a COM or EXE file is made by the programmer when he or she creates the program. You can generally consider that a COM extension indicates a single command, while an EXE extension indicates an entire executable program.

Chapter 15, "Grouping Commands with Batch Files," discusses DOS batch files, in which several command calls can be lumped together. One of the rules you should follow when creating DOS batch files is never create a batch file with the same name as an existing DOS command. Assume, for example, that you create a batch file named CLS.BAT. When you type CLS to execute the batch file, DOS will instead execute its internal CLS command. Remember, DOS always searches its internal commands first for a matching command, then looks for an external command on disk.

If you assign the name of an external command to a batch file, such as FORMAT.BAT, the rule for determining whether DOS will execute the batch file or external command depends on which file DOS encounters first, FORMAT.COM or FORMAT.BAT. Avoid such confusion—don't use DOS command names for batch file names.

Key Terms

Internal command   A command that resides in memory whenever DOS is active. Examples of internal commands include CLS, DATE, and TIME. Because internal commands reside in memory, DOS can execute them very quickly.

External command   A command that resides on disk. Before an external command can run, DOS must first locate the command on disk and load it into memory. The majority of DOS commands are external commands. All applications, such as your word processor or spreadsheet, are made up of external commands.

Command line   To execute a DOS command, you type the command's name at the DOS prompt and press ENTER. The information you type at the prompt before you press ENTER is your command line. Many DOS commands let you specify additional information, such as a file name, in the command line.

Chapter 4

Getting Started with DOS Files

To save and retrieve information from one computer session to the next, you must store information on disk. DOS organizes the information you store on disk by letting you group related pieces of information into *files*. As you create letters, reports, and spreadsheets you will store each in its own file, much like you would place related information into a paper file in an office. Each file you create must have a unique name. You should choose meaningful names that describe the file's contents. In this chapter you will learn how to list the names of each file on your disk, as well as each file's size and the date and time the file was created. You will also examine several of the key DOS file names as well as rules you should follow when you name your own files.

A Directory Is a List of Related Files

As you work with different programs, such as a word processor, spreadsheet, or database, you will create files to store your information. To help you organize your files, DOS lets you separate the files into related lists called *directories*. In most cases, users will have a directory each for their word processing files, DOS command files, and any other application programs they are using. The best way to view directories on your disk is as drawers of a filing cabinet into which you place related files, as shown in Figure 4-1.

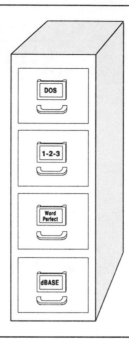

Figure 4-1.   *DOS lets you organize files using directories as you would use the drawers of a filing cabinet*

Unlike a filing cabinet, which has a fixed number of drawers, you can create a virtually unlimited number of directories on your disk. In Chapter 10, "Directories," you will learn how to create, select, and remove directories on your disk using the MKDIR, CHDIR, and RMDIR commands. For now, however, simply understand that a directory is a list of related files.

Using the DIR Command

As discussed, a directory is a list of related files. Depending on the different programs installed on your disk, your disk may already contain several directories. The DIR command lets you display a list of the files in a directory. DIR is an abbreviation for DIRectory. The simplest way to invoke DIR is to type **DIR** and press ENTER, as shown.

```
C:\> DIR <ENTER>
```

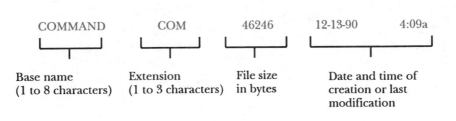

Figure 4-2.   *DIR displays each file's base name, extension, size, and date and time*
                stamps

DIR will display a list of file names on your screen. This list only contains files that reside in the current directory. As you will learn in Chapter 10, the current directory is conceptually similar to the filing cabinet drawer that is currently open. The directory listing will display file names and possibly names of other directories.

DOS *file names* consist of two parts, an eight-character *base name* and a three-character *extension*. The DIR command displays each file's base name, extension, size, and the date and time the file was created or last changed. Figure 4-2 illustrates a typical directory entry.

As discussed in Chapter 1, DOS refers to file and disk sizes in bytes. A byte, as you will recall, is a character of information.

Some of the entries DIR displays may use "<DIR>". DOS uses these letters to signify a directory. At a minimum, your hard disk should have a directory named DOS that contains the external DOS commands.

Understanding File Names and Extensions

Each file in a directory must have a unique name. DOS file names can use eight characters for the base name and three characters for the extension. The file name should be meaningful so it can help you determine the file's contents. The eight-character base name typically describes specific information about the file. The three-character extension specifies the file's general category. For example, for files containing letters you may use the extension LTR. Likewise, for reports, you might use RPT. Table 4-1 describes several commonly used file extensions.

In addition to the common file extensions listed in Table 4-1, DOS uses several file extensions to describe the different operating system files. Table 4-2 lists different DOS file extensions you may encounter.

File Extension	File Category
LTR	File containing a letter
MEM	File containing a memo
RPT	File containing a report
DAT	File containing numeric data
BAS	File containing a BASIC program
TXT	File containing word processing text document

Table 4-1.   Common User File Extensions

When you specify a DOS file name, you must separate the base file name and extension using a period, as shown in Figure 4-3.

By using all eight of the base name characters, you can produce meaningful file names that describe the file's contents. Table 4-3 illustrates several meaningful file names that describe each file's contents.

Do not overlook the importance of assigning meaningful names to your files. Although it is easy to use a file name such as A or B, such names certainly won't help you later recall the information the file contains.

File Extension	File Category
COM	File containing a DOS command
EXE	Executable file
SYS	DOS system file typically containing a device driver
BAT	DOS batch file containing a series of DOS commands
CPI	Code-page information file used to define international character sets
HLP	Contains help information
MOS	Contains DOS Shell mouse driver information (DOS 4)
CLR	Contains DOS Shell color infotmation (DOS 4)
MEN	Contains the initial DOS shell menu options (DOS4)
PRO	Contains printer profiles for the GRAPHICS command
INI	DOS Shell or Windows initialization values

Table 4-2.   File Extensions Commonly Used by DOS

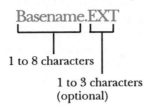

Figure 4-3.   *Separate a file's base file name and extension with a period*

Valid File-Name Characters

A file's base name can contain from one to eight characters—the three-character extension is optional. DOS lets you use the letters A through Z and the numbers 0 through 9 in your file names. In addition, your file names can include one or more of the following characters.

~ ! @ # $ ^ & ( ) - _ { } '

You can type in upper- or lowercase letters—for consistency, DOS always converts lowercase letters to uppercase. Using these characters, you can create file names similar to the following:

1991.TAX	PHONE#S.DAT	MAYSALES.$$$
MAY&JUNE.RPT	OUR-COST.SEP	PROFITS!.DAT

Understanding Date and Time Stamps

In addition to the file name and size, DIR displays the date and time each file was created or last changed. You can use a file's date and time stamps, to determine if you have the latest copy of a file, or to help you locate files you created or changed

File Name	File Contents
FORMAT.COM	File containing the external DOS FORMAT command
BUDGET.RPT	File containing the annual budget report
ANSI.SYS	File containing the ANSI device driver
IRS.LTR	File containing a letter to the IRS
CHAPTER4.TXT	File containing Chapter 4's word processing text

Table 4-3.   *Meaningful File Names and Extensions*

on a specific date. In Chapter 3, "Issuing DOS Commands," you learned how to set the system date and time using the DATE and TIME commands. DOS uses the system date and time when it assigns or updates a file's date and time stamps. If the system date or time is incorrect, so too will be the file's date and time stamps.

The only time DOS changes a file's date and time stamps is when the file's contents actually change. If a program views a file's contents, for example, the file's contents don't change, so DOS will not change the date and time stamps.

Determining the Number of Files and Available Disk Space

After DIR displays the entries in a directory, DIR displays a count of the number of files it displayed, the amount of disk space the files consume, as well as the amount of available disk space, as shown here.

```
90 file(s) 2236185 bytes
          16395328 bytes free
```

Many of the software packages you will purchase specify the minimum amount of free space your disk must contain before you can successfully install the file. Using the DIR command, you can quickly determine the amount of available disk space on your computer.

Listing Files in a Specific Directory

As discussed, a directory is a list of files. In Chapter 10 you will learn how to quickly move from one directory to another, as you would open and close drawers of a filing cabinet. For now, however, you can use the DIR command to list the files in your DOS directory. To do so, issue the following DIR command.

```
C:\> DIR \DOS <ENTER>
```

You must include the backslash (\) before the directory name. Make sure you use the backslash (\) and not a forward slash (/). In this case, DIR will list the files in the DOS subdirectory, as shown.

```
C:\> DIR \DOS <ENTER>

 Volume in drive C is DOS
 Volume Serial Number is 1661-AB75
 Directory of C:\DOS
```

```
.              <DIR>       10-16-90     4:44p
..             <DIR>       10-16-90     4:44p
EGA      SYS     4885  12-13-90     4:09a
DISPLAY  SYS    15682  12-13-90     4:09a
FORMAT   COM    32285  12-13-90     4:09a
ANSI     SYS     8868  12-13-90     4:09a
COUNTRY  SYS    13496  12-13-90     4:09a
HIMEM    SYS    11120  12-13-90     4:09a
KEYB     COM    14699  12-13-90     4:09a
HELP     EXE    11443  12-13-90     4:09a
EDIT     COM      413  12-13-90     4:09a
  :        :       :       :           :
  :        :       :       :           :
APPEND   EXE    10614  12-13-90     4:09a
ATTRIB   EXE    15732  12-13-90     4:09a
FIND     EXE     6642  12-13-90     4:09a
LABEL    EXE     8954  12-13-90     4:09a
RESTORE  EXE    38054  12-13-90     4:09a
SORT     EXE     6618  12-13-90     4:09a
SHELL    MEU     4588  10-06-88    12:00a
DOSUTIL  MEU     6660  10-06-88    12:00a
ASSIGN   COM     6271  12-13-90     4:09a
DRIVER   SYS     5384  12-13-90     4:09a
EGA      CPI    49068  12-13-90     4:09a
GRAPHICS COM    19374  12-13-90     4:09a
GRAPHICS PRO    21226  12-13-90     4:09a
JOIN     EXE    17614  12-13-90     4:09a
LCD      CPI    10703  12-13-90     4:09a
NLSFUNC  EXE     6924  12-13-90     4:09a
PRINTER  SYS    18760  12-13-90     4:09a
SUBST    EXE    18350  12-13-90     4:09a
COMMAND  COM    46246  12-13-90     4:09a
         90 file(s)   2236185 bytes
                     16387136 bytes free
```

Depending on your DOS version, the number of files the directory contains, as well as the actual file names, may differ. Listing the contents of the DOS directory in this way is conceptually similar to opening the filing cabinet drawer labeled "DOS" and listing the files the drawer contains, as shown in Figure 4-4.

If the file entries scrolled past you on the screen faster than you could view them, include the /P *switch* in the DIR command line, as follows.

```
C:\> DIR \DOS /P <ENTER>
```

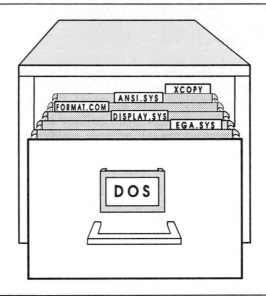

Figure 4-4.   *Listing the files in the DOS directory*

The /P switch directs DIR to temporarily suspend its output with each screenful of files until you press a key to continue. When you use the /P switch, DIR will prompt you with a message to press a key to continue, as shown here.

```
C:\> DIR \DOS /P <ENTER>
 Volume in drive C is DOS
 Volume Serial Number is 1661-AB75
 Directory of C:\DOS

 .             <DIR>      10-16-90    4:44p
 ..            <DIR>      10-16-90    4:44p
EGA      SYS    4885 12-13-90    4:09a
DISPLAY  SYS   15682 12-13-90    4:09a
FORMAT   COM   32285 12-13-90    4:09a
ANSI     SYS    8868 12-13-90    4:09a
COUNTRY  SYS   13496 12-13-90    4:09a
HIMEM    SYS   11120 12-13-90    4:09a
KEYB     COM   14699 12-13-90    4:09a
KEYBOARD SYS   24336 12-13-90    4:09a
```

```
MODE        COM      23313 12-13-90      4:09a
SETVER      EXE       9162 12-13-90      4:09a
SYS         COM      13200 12-13-90      4:09a
SELECT      HLP      28695 10-06-88     12:00a
SELECT      PRT       1329 10-06-88     12:00a
UNFORMAT    COM      17680 12-13-90      4:09a
DEBUG       EXE      20506 12-13-90      4:09a
DOSKEY      COM       5693 12-13-90      4:09a
EDLIN       EXE      12578 12-13-90      4:09a
Press any key to continue . . .
```

Take a close look at the file names in the DOS directory listing. Many of the files have the EXE or COM extension. Such files contain *external* DOS commands. As discussed in Chapter 3, DOS commands are either *internal* commands, which reside in your computer's fast electronic memory, or external commands, which reside on disk. When you execute an external command, DOS must first load the command from disk into memory before the command can execute.

Displaying the Directory Listing for a Specific File

In the previous section you learned how to display the directory listing for files in a specific directory by including the directory's name:

```
C:\> DIR \DOS <ENTER>
```

In this case, DIR will display the directory entry for every file in the DOS directory. If you want to display the directory entry for a specific file, include the file name in the directory command. For example, the following DIR command displays the directory listing for the file FORMAT.COM that resides in the DOS directory.

```
C:\> DIR \DOS\FORMAT.COM <ENTER>
```

In this case, DIR displays the following:

```
C:\> DIR \DOS\FORMAT.COM <ENTER>

Volume in drive C is DOS
Volume Serial Number is 1661-AB75
Directory of C:\DOS
```

```
FORMAT   COM    32285 12-13-90    4:09a
         1 file(s)    32285 bytes
                   16387136 bytes free
```

Conceptually, this DIR command is equivalent to opening the filing cabinet drawer labeled "DOS" and accessing the file labeled FORMAT.COM, as shown in Figure 4-5.

As you create more files on your disk, you will frequently use DIR in this manner to locate specific files.

Displaying a Wide Directory Listing

As discussed, the DIR command displays file base names, extensions, sizes, and the date and time stamps. If you only want file names and extensions, you can use the /W switch to direct DIR to display a wide directory listing with five file names across

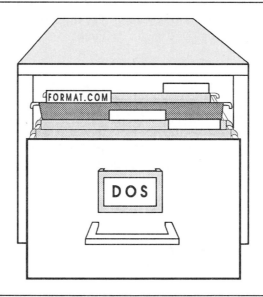

Figure 4-5.   Accessing the FORMAT.COM file

the screen. The following command uses /W to display the files in the DOS directory.

```
C:\> DIR \DOS /W   <ENTER>

 Volume in drive C is DOS
 Volume Serial Number is 1661-AB75
 Directory of C:\DOS

[.]            [..]           EGA.SYS        DISPLAY.SYS    FORMAT.COM
ANSI.SYS       COUNTRY.SYS    HIMEM.SYS      KEYB.COM       KEYBOARD.SYS
MODE.COM       SETVER.EXE     SYS.COM        SELECT.HLP     SELECT.PRT
UNFORMAT.COM   DEBUG.EXE      DOSKEY.COM     EDLIN.EXE      EMM386.EXE
FASTOPEN.EXE   SELECT.DAT     FC.EXE         FDISK.EXE      MEM.EXE
   :        :           :           :            :
   :        :           :           :            :
ASSIGN.COM     DRIVER.SYS     EGA.CPI        EXPAND.EXE     GRAFTABL.COM
GRAPHICS.COM   GRAPHICS.PRO   CATAPULT.BAS   NIBBLES.BAS    JOIN.EXE
LCD.CPI        NLSFUNC.EXE    PRINTER.SYS    SUBST.EXE      COMMAND.COM
        90 file(s)   2236185 bytes
                   16387136 bytes free
```

As you can see, using /W, you direct DIR to only display file names and extensions, suppressing each file's size and date and time stamp.

Hands On

Using the following DIR command, list the files in the current directory.

```
C:\> DIR <ENTER>
```

Note each file's base name, extension, size, and date and time stamp. Also note the amount of available space on your disk. As discussed, entries containing "<DIR>" are directories containing additional lists of file names. Note the directories that reside on your disk. The directory names should give you an indication of the different applications programs that are installed on your disk.

SUMMARY

Directories

To help you organize your files on disk, DOS lets you group files into lists called directories. DOS directories are conceptually similar to drawers of a filing cabinet, which also contain related files.

File Names

DOS file names have two parts, an eight-character base name and a three-character extension. When you specify a file name, you separate the base name and extension using a period. Your file names should be as meaningful as possible to help you understand the file's contents simply by examining the file name. The eight-character base name should provide specifics about the file, whereas the three-character extension should specify the file's type.

File Date and Time Stamps

For every file you create on your disk, DOS assigns a date and a time stamp. Each time you update a file's contents, DOS updates the file's date and time stamps using the current system date and time. Using the date and time stamps, you can determine if you have the most recent copy of a file. You can also search for files created on a specific day. If your system date and time is wrong, DOS will assign the wrong date or time to the file date and time stamp.

If the files in your directory scroll past you faster than you can read them, invoke DIR using the /P switch, as shown here.

```
C:\> DIR /P <ENTER>
```

Next, use the following DIR command to display the files in the DOS directory.

```
C:\> DIR \DOS <ENTER>
```

Next, using the /W switch, display the files in your DOS directory using a wide-directory format.

```
C:\> DIR \DOS /W <ENTER>
```

Last, use the following command to display the directory entry for the file DISKCOPY.COM that resides in the DOS directory.

```
C:\> DIR \DOS\DISKCOPY.COM <ENTER>
```

Review

1. How does a directory differ from a file?

2. How can you determine the amount of available space on your disk?

3. What are the probable contents of the following files?

   DIRSORT.BAT
   LABEL.COM
   BUDGET91.RPT
   BUSINESS.LTR

4. What is the purpose of a file extension?

5. How many characters can a DOS file name contain?

6. What is the purpose of DIR /W switch?

Answers

1. To organize the information you store on your disk, DOS lets you group related pieces of information into a file, much like you would use a paper file within an office. A directory, on the other hand, is a list of related files, similar to a filing cabinet drawer.

2. The last piece of information the DIR command displays is the number of files in the directory and the amount of available disk space.

```
90 file(s)   2236185 bytes
            16387136 bytes free
```

3. The probable contents of these files are as follows:

DIRSORT.BAT	A DOS batch file that sorts a directory
LABEL.COM	The LABEL command
BUDGET91.RPT	A report describing the 1991 budget
BUSINESS.LTR	A business letter

4. A DOS file name consists of two parts, an eight-character base name and a three-character extension. The file extension provides information on the file's type, such as a command (COM or EXE extension), a letter (LTR extension), or a report (RPT extension).

5. A DOS file name can have an eight-character base name and a three-character extension. You must separate the base name and extension with a period, as shown here: BASENAME.EXT.

6. The /W switch directs DIR to suppress its display of each file's size and date and time stamps, displaying instead only base names and extensions. Because the base names and extensions don't take up much space, DIR can display five file names per line.

Advanced Concepts

By default, the DIR command displays file entries in the same order the files appear in the directory listing. To obtain a sorted directory listing, users often *pipe* (redirect) the output of the DIR command into SORT, as shown here.

```
C:\SORTTEST> DIR | SORT <ENTER>
```

In this case, DOS will display the file entries by name in ascending order (A to Z), as shown here.

```
C:\SORTTEST> DIR | SORT <ENTER>
                 167342080 bytes free
      10 file(s)    13824 bytes
 Directory of C:\SORTTEST
 Volume in drive C is DOS
 Volume Serial Number is 1661-AB75
 .            <DIR>      03-03-91    8:22a
 ..           <DIR>      03-03-91    8:22a
```

```
AAAAAAAA AAA       5120 02-27-91    1:36p
BBBBBBBB BBB       2176 01-09-91    1:33p
CCCCCCCC CCC        640 02-22-91   11:23a
DDDDDDDD DDD       1024 11-08-90    1:22p
EEEEEEEE EEE        512 02-20-91   11:23a
FFFFFFFF FFF        896 02-04-91   10:20a
GGGGGGGG GGG        768 02-08-91    9:33a
HHHHHHHH HHH       2688 02-06-91    1:07p
```

Because of the sort order, the command displays the number of files in the directory and amount of available disk space before the file names.

If you sort the files in descending order using SORT's /R switch, the ordering becomes worse, as shown here.

```
C:\SORTTEST> DIR | SORT /R <ENTER>
HHHHHHHH HHH       2688 02-06-91    1:07p
GGGGGGGG GGG        768 02-08-91    9:33a
FFFFFFFF FFF        896 02-04-91   10:20a
EEEEEEEE EEE        512 02-20-91   11:23a
DDDDDDDD DDD       1024 11-08-90    1:22p
CCCCCCCC CCC        640 02-22-91   11:23a
BBBBBBBB BBB       2176 01-09-91    1:33p
AIBLAEEB              0 03-03-91    8:27a
AIBLAEDM              0 03-03-91    8:27a
AAAAAAAA AAA       5120 02-27-91    1:36p
..          <DIR>        03-03-91    8:22a
.           <DIR>        03-03-91    8:22a
 Volume Serial Number is 1661-AB75
 Volume in drive C is DOS
 Directory of C:\SORTTEST
        12 file(s)    13824 bytes
                  167342080 bytes free
```

If you examine the last lines (non-file name), you'll find each contains the lowercase letter "e." Using the FIND command /V switch, you can remove these lines from the output, cleaning up the sorted directory listing:

```
C:\> DIR | SORT /R | FIND /V "e" <ENTER>
```

If you use this command on a regular basis, you may simply want to place it into a batch file named DESCEND.BAT.

Just as there are times when you want to sort the directory by name, there may be times when you want to sort by size. The following command uses SORT's /+*n* column switch to display the directory listing sorted by size (beginning in column 13).

```
C:\> DIR | SORT /+13 | FIND /V "e"  <ENTER>
```

If you are using DOS 5, DIR provides several new command-line switches that give you tremendous flexibility.

Using the /O Switch to Specify a Sort Order

Under DOS 5, DIR's /O switch lets you specify the order in which you want DIR to display directory entries. The format of this switch is /O: *options*, where options are one or more of the entries specified in Table 4-4.

The following DIR command sorts the directory by name in reverse (Z to A) order.

```
C:\> DIR /O:-N  <ENTER>
```

Likewise, this command displays the files sorted by size.

```
C:\> DIR /O:S  <ENTER>
```

Option	Order
D	By date, oldest to newest
–D	By date, newest to oldest
E	By extension, A to Z
–E	By extension, Z to A
G	Group directories and display them before files
–G	Group directories and display them after files
N	By name, A to Z
–N	By name, Z to A
S	By size, smallest to largest
–S	By size, largest to smallest

Table 4-4.   *DOS 5 DIR /O Sort Options*

DIR lets you specify several options at one time. For example, the following DIR command groups directories, displaying the directories before files, and then displays the files sorted by extension.

```
C:\> DIR /O:GE <ENTER>
```

Experiment with combinations of the sort options, and you will agree they are very convenient.

Using the /A Switch to List Files by Attribute

By default, DIR displays all of the entries in the directory, regardless of the entry's attribute settings. Using the /A switch, the DOS 5 DIR command lets you restrict your directory listings to read-only files, hidden files, directories, and so on. The format of the /A switch is /A: *options*, where options are one or more of the entries specified in Table 4-5.

The following command uses the /A switch to display read-only files.

```
C:\> DIR /A:R <ENTER>
```

Likewise, the next command displays all hidden files in the root directory.

```
C:\> DIR /A:H \*.* <ENTER>
```

By combining options, this command displays files that are not read-only but do require archiving.

Option	Files Listed
A	Files with the archive attribute set
–A	Files with the archive attribute clear
D	Directories
–D	All files except directories
H	All hidden files
–H	All files not hidden
R	All read-only files
–R	All files not read-only
S	All files with the system attribute set
–S	All files with the system attribute clear

Table 4-5.   DIR File Attribute Options

```
C:\> DIR /A:-RA <ENTER>
```

The Rest of the DOS 5 DIR Switches

In addition to /A and /O, DOS 5 provides three additional DIR command switches.
First, the /S switch directs DIR to display the directory entries for files that reside
in subdirectories beneath the target directory. Using /S, the following DIR command lists the directory entry for every file on your disk.

```
C:\> DIR \*.* /S <ENTER>
```

The /L switch directs DIR to display the file names using lowercase letters. The
following command displays the files in the DOS directory in lowercase.

```
C:\> DIR \DOS /L <ENTER>

 Volume in drive C is DOS
 Volume Serial Number is 1661-AB75
 Directory of C:\DOS

 .               <DIR>      10-16-90    4:44p
 ..              <DIR>      10-16-90    4:44p
 ega      sys      4885 12-13-90    4:09a
 display  sys     15682 12-13-90    4:09a
 format   com     32285 12-13-90    4:09a
 ansi     sys      8868 12-13-90    4:09a
 country  sys     13496 12-13-90    4:09a
 himem    sys     11120 12-13-90    4:09a
   :        :        :        :         :
   :        :        :        :         :
 graphics pro     21226 12-13-90    4:09a
 join     exe     17614 12-13-90    4:09a
 lcd      cpi     10703 12-13-90    4:09a
 nlsfunc  exe      6924 12-13-90    4:09a
 printer  sys     18760 12-13-90    4:09a
 subst    exe     18350 12-13-90    4:09a
 command  com     46246 12-13-90    4:09a
     90 file(s)      2236185 bytes
                    16387136 bytes free
```

Last, the /B switch directs DIR to display only base file names and extensions, one file per line, suppressing the file size and date and time stamps. Again using the DOS directory, the output of DIR using the /B switch becomes the following.

```
C:\> DIR \DOS /B <ENTER>
EGA.SYS
DISPLAY.SYS
SYS.COM
MIRROR.COM
MORE.COM
RAMDRIVE.SYS
SHARE.EXE
SMARTDRV.SYS
UNDELETE.EXE
XCOPY.EXE
GRAFTABL.COM
   :
   :
GRAPHICS.COM
JOIN.EXE
LCD.CPI
NLSFUNC.EXE
PRINTER.SYS
SUBST.EXE
```

Note that the /B switch suppresses the display of the number of files and available disk space.

DIR lets you combine all of its switches. For example, the following command displays a lowercase directory listing of your entire disk, showing only the base names and extensions.

```
C:\> DIR \*.* /S /L /B <ENTER>
```

Take time now to experiment with the DOS 5 DIR command-line switches.

Key Terms

Directory A list of file entries used to organize your disk.

Base name   The eight-character name that precedes the extension in a DOS file name. A file's base name should describe the file's contents.

Extension   The three-character sequence following the base file name that indicates a file's type, such as a letter (LTR), report (RPT), or command (COM).

Date and time stamps   The date and time DOS assigns to a file that correspond to the date and time the file was created or last changed.

Chapter **5**

Understanding Your Keyboard

As you learned in Chapter 1, "Getting to Know Your Computer," your keyboard lets you type information into your computer. The information you type might be a DOS command, a letter you are creating with your word processor, or expenses you are entering into a spreadsheet. This chapter examines your keyboard and different keyboard techniques you can use to save time and reduce keystrokes. In addition, you will learn how to use your keyboard to cancel a command, and to restart DOS without having to turn your computer's power on and off.

Keyboards Have Four Major Sections

Since the introduction of the IBM PC in 1981, keyboard layouts have changed to provide more capabilities and increase your ease of use. Figure 5-1 illustrates two of the most common PC keyboard layouts.

Although these keyboards may differ in key layout, each contains four primary sections: the standard typewriter keys, the function keys, the numeric keypad, and the cursor-control keys.

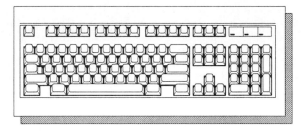

PC AT and PS/2 Keyboard

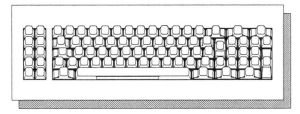

Original IBM PC Keyboard

Figure 5-1.   *Common keyboard layouts*

Standard Typewriter Keys

The vast majority of your keyboard is laid out in the same format as a typewriter. Such key layouts are often call "QWERTY" because they are based on the layout of the upper-left row of letter keys (see Figure 5-2).

Typing with a computer is much easier than typing on a typewriter because you can quickly correct mistakes using the BACKSPACE key (on some keyboards a long-stemmed left arrow directly above the ENTER key) discussed in Chapter 3, "Issuing DOS Commands."

There are two keys that appear on your keyboard, labeled CTRL (for "Control") and ALT (for "Alternate"), which don't appear on a typewriter. Note the location of these keys on your keyboard. You will use these keys in combination with other keys throughout this chapter.

Function Keys

Depending on your keyboard type, your keyboard will have keys labeled F1 through F10 (or possibly F12) called function keys. As you will learn, DOS as well as many of

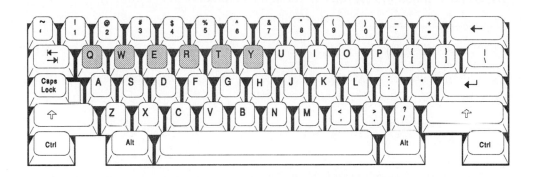

Figure 5-2.   *Keyboard using the standard typewriter layout, QWERTY key positioning*

your application programs, assigns unique functions to these keys. This section examines the three most widely used function keys under DOS—F1, F3, and F6.

Using the Function Keys to Repeat a Command

As you work with DOS, there will be many times when you need to repeat a command, or issue a slight variation of the previous command. As it turns out, each time DOS executes a command, DOS temporarily saves the command in case you want to repeat it. For example, assume you invoke the DIR command.

```
C:\> DIR <ENTER>
```

To repeat the command, you can type the command name once again, or you can instead press the F3 function key. When you press F3, DOS will immediately display the last command executed next to its prompt. To repeat the command, you can simply press ENTER. If you want to change the previous command slightly, you can. In the case of DIR, for example, you might want to add the /W switch. Likewise, if you misspell a command, you can redisplay the command using F3 and edit it using the arrow, BACKSPACE and INS insert keys.

Suppose, for example, that you have inadvertently misspelled the DOS command as "DSO":

```
C:\> DIR \DSO\FORMAT.COM <ENTER>
Path not found
```

Using the F3 function key, you can recall the command, as shown.

```
C:\> DIR \DSO\FORMAT.COM_
```

Using your keyboard's BACKSPACE key, you can erase the command to the point of the error:

```
C:\> DIR \D_
```

Next, you can type the "O" and "S" in the correct order:

```
C:\> DIR \DOS_
```

Last, pressing the F3 key a second time, you can display the remainder of the command:

```
C:\> DIR \DOS\FORMAT.COM_
```

Next, instead of transposing the letters "O" and "S," you simply forgot the "O":

```
C:\> DIR \DS\FORMAT.COM <ENTER>
Path not found
```

In this case, repeat the process of pressing F3 and using the BACKSPACE key to erase the command to the point of the error as shown.

```
C:\> DIR \D_
```

Because you need to insert a letter into the command, press the INS key. Next, type **O** and press F3 DOS will display the correct command.

```
C:\> DIR \DOS\FORMAT.COM_
```

The INS (insert) key works as a *toggle*. The first time you press the INS key, DOS enters *insert mode*, meaning DOS inserts the characters you type in front of the characters at the current position. The second time you press the INS key, DOS enters *overstrike mode*, meaning DOS will overwrite the characters at the current position.

Don't let insert and overstrike modes confuse you. Many word processors use INS. With DOS, the only time you need to concern yourself with the INS key is when you need to insert characters into a command you are editing with the function keys.

Similarly, there may be times when you need to delete a character from the middle of the previous command line. For example, suppose you have included an extra "O" in DOS:

```
C:\> DIR \DOOS\FORMAT.COM <ENTER>
Path not found
```

Using F3, you can recall the command. Next, using the BACKSPACE key, you can delete letters up to and including the extra "O":

```
C:\> DIR \DO_
```

Next, press the key labeled DEL ("Delete"). DOS will remove the current letter from the command buffer. When you press F3, DOS will append the remainder of the buffer resulting in the correct command:

```
C:\> DIR \DOS\FORMAT.COM_
```

As you have just found, pressing the F3 function key lets you quickly repeat or edit the entire previous command. In some cases, however, you may find it more convenient to display the letters of the previous command one letter at a time. The F1 function key lets you do just that.

Assume, for example, that you have just issued the following DIR command.

```
C:\> DIR \DOS\FORMAT.COM
```

Next, assume you want to simply execute the DIR command for the current directory. Each time you press the F1 function key, DOS will display a single letter of the previous command. In this case, by pressing the F1 function key three times, you can display the DIR command.

```
C:\> DIR_
```

Depending on the amount you need to edit the previous command, you may find using the F1 function key (or the right arrow, which serves the same purpose) is faster than using F3 in conjunction with the BACKSPACE key.

Copying Simple Files from Your Keyboard

In Chapter 4 you learned that DOS stores information on your disk in files. Using a word processor or the DOS editor, you can create your own files. In addition, if you are creating small, simple files, you can copy the file's contents directly from your keyboard. To begin, DOS assigns the device name CON (abbreviation for console) to your keyboard. Using the CON device name, the following COPY command directs DOS to copy into the file TEST.DAT input from your keyboard.

```
C:\> COPY CON TEST.DAT <ENTER>
```

When you invoke this command, DOS will advance the cursor to the start of the next line. Type the line shown and press ENTER.

```
C:\> COPY CON TEST.DAT <ENTER>
This is the file's first line. <ENTER>
The file only contains two lines. <ENTER>
```

As before, DOS will advance the cursor and wait for you to type the file's next line. You must tell DOS you are done entering information into the file. To do so, press the F6 function key. DOS will in turn display the letters "^Z" ("Control Z") as shown here.

```
C:\> COPY CON TEST.DAT <ENTER>
This is the file's first line. <ENTER>
The file only contains two lines. <ENTER>
^Z
```

DOS uses ^Z to indicate the end of a file. You can only generate this letter by pressing the F6 key, or by pressing the CTRL-Z key combination. When you press ENTER following the ^Z, DOS will create the file:

```
C:\> COPY CON TEST.DAT <ENTER>
This is the file's first line. <ENTER>
The file only contains two lines. <ENTER>
^Z <ENTER>
    1 File(s) copied

C:\>
```

Because it is commonly used to mark the end of a file you create from the keyboard, the F6 key is often called the *end-of-file* key. As you need to create small files, you may find copying the file's contents from the keyboard to be quite convenient. Beware—you can't change the contents of lines after you press ENTER. If you need to change (edit) the file's contents, use your word processor or the DOS editor.

Numeric Keypad

Every keyboard has a group of numeric keys that resemble the keys on a 10-key adding machine (see Figure 5-3).

DOS itself does not make extensive use of the numeric keypad. The keypad exists to simplify your entry of numbers when you enter data into a spreadsheet or some other application that requires the entry of many numbers. Your keyboard has a key labeled NUMLOCK. Before you can use the numeric keys to generate numbers, you may have to press NUMLOCK. As you will learn next, the numeric keypad also doubles as your cursor-control keys. The NUMLOCK key works as a toggle. The first time you press NUMLOCK, DOS selects the numeric keypad's number keys. The second time you press NUMLOCK, DOS selects the cursor-control keys. Most keyboards have a small light that indicates when NUMLOCK (meaning the numeric keys) is active.

Cursor-Control Keys

Depending on your keyboard type, your keyboard may have one or two sets of arrow keys, shown in Figures 5-3 and 5-4.

Figure 5-3.   The keyboard's numeric keypad

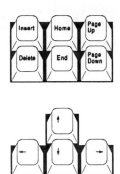

Figure 5-4.   Cursor-control keys

Outside of the DOS editor and the version 5 DOSKEY command (see Chapter 27, "DOSKEY and DOS 5 Macros,"), DOS doesn't make much use of the arrow keys. The arrow, or cursor-control, keys are used primarily by applications to let you traverse your word processing documents or spreadsheets.

If your keyboard only contains one set of arrow keys, you will need to use the NUMLOCK key as just discussed to toggle between the numeric keypad and the cursor-control keys.

Key Combinations

A *key combination* is a sequence of two or more keys you press to achieve a specific result. This section discusses the two most common key combinations. You will use the CTRL and ALT keys in combination with other keys to achieve differing results. For example, by holding down the CTRL key and pressing the C key, you can end a DOS command. Many DOS books and software manuals represent key combinations by listing the necessary keys separated by hyphens. For example, the letters CTRL-C represent the key combination you can use to end DOS commands. In the case of CTRL-C, you would first hold down the CTRL key, and then, while holding down CTRL, type C (resulting in both keys being depressed).

Using CTRL-C to End a Command

Should you inadvertently invoke the wrong DOS command, DOS lets you cancel the command using the CTRL-C key combination. For example, suppose you invoke the DISKCOPY command (see Chapter 12, "Fundamental Copy Operations") to copy the contents of one floppy disk to another blank floppy disk, only to find you don't have an unused floppy. DISKCOPY, unfortunately, will prompt you to insert the floppy disks into drives A and B, and then to press any key to continue.

```
C:\> DISKCOPY A: B: <ENTER>
Insert SOURCE diskette in drive A:

Insert TARGET diskette in drive B:

Press any key to continue . . .
```

Because you don't want DISKCOPY to continue, you need a way to end the command. Fortunately for you, the CTRL-C key combination directs DOS to cancel the current command. In this case, when you press CTRL-C at the DISKCOPY prompt, DOS will display ^C ("Control C") and will end the command, returning control to the DOS prompt:

```
C:\> DISKCOPY A: B: <ENTER>
Insert SOURCE diskette in drive A:

Insert TARGET diskette in drive B:

Press any key to continue . . .
^C

C:\>
```

Treat the CTRL-C key combination with extreme caution. If you use CTRL-C to end a command that updates one or more files on your disk, you may lose a portion of the file's contents. As a rule, you can generally end a DOS command using CTRL-C, but you should not use CTRL-C to end an application such as your word processor or spreadsheet. In fact, most applications won't let you do so. DOS also lets you use the CTRL-BREAK key combination to end commands, just as you would CTRL-C. If you try unsuccessfully to end a command using CTRL-C, try using CTRL-BREAK. Some commands may intentionally ignore CTRL-C but not CTRL-BREAK.

WARNING

Using CTRL-ALT-DEL to Restart DOS

In Chapters 18, "Automatic System Startup Commands with AUTOEXEC.BAT," and 24, "Customizing Your System with CONFIG.SYS," you will learn about two special files, AUTOEXEC.BAT and CONFIG.SYS, that DOS uses during its startup process. As you work with DOS, you will need to make changes to these two files.

Each time you make such a change, you need to restart DOS. Until now, your only way to restart DOS has been a *cold boot*, to turn your computer off and back on or press the Reset button. DOS, however, lets you do a *warm boot*, use the CTRL-ALT-DEL key combination to restart DOS. When you press CTRL-ALT-DEL, your screen will clear and your computer will reload DOS from disk, as if you had turned on your computer.

As a rule, only press the CTRL-ALT-DEL key combination when DOS is displaying its prompt. If you restart DOS while a program is updating a file or your disk, you may damage the file losing the information it contains.

Depending on the number of applications you use, you may eventually encounter a program that contains an error. When you run the program, your computer appears to freeze up and doesn't do anything. In such cases you may need to use CTRL-ALT-DEL to restart DOS. If DOS does not respond to CTRL-ALT-DEL, you will need to turn your computer's power off and back on, starting your computer's power-on sequence.

Hands On

From the DOS prompt, issue the following DIR command to display the files residing in the DOS directory.

```
C:\> DIR \DOS <ENTER>
```

When the DIR command is completed, press the F3 function key followed by ENTER to repeat the command.

Next, issue the following command, mistyping "CLS" as "CKS."

```
C:\> CKS <ENTER>
Bad command or file name
```

To correct the command, press F1, type L, and press F1 again. Press ENTER to execute the command.

You have learned that the CTRL-C key combination lets you end a command. In this case, invoke DATE.

```
C:\> DATE <ENTER>
```

Key Combinations

A key combination is a sequence of keys that you must hold down to achieve a specific result. Many books represent key combinations by separating the keystrokes with the hyphen (-). For example, the CTRL-C key combination instructs you to first hold down the CTRL key and then, while holding CTRL, press C.

F3 Function Key

Each time you execute a command, DOS temporarily saves the command in case you want to repeat or edit the command. Pressing the F3 function key at the DOS prompt directs DOS to display the previous command for editing or execution.

F1 Function Key

The F1 function key, like F3, lets you edit or repeat the previous command. Unlike F3, which displays the entire previous command at one time, F1 displays the command one letter at a time.

F6 Function Key

The F6 function key lets you indicate the end of the file you are copying from the keyboard. When you press F6, DOS will display its end-of-file marker, ^Z.

CTRL-C Key Combination

The CTRL-C key combination lets you end a DOS command. When you press CTRL-C, DOS will display ^C ("Control C") on your screen, ending the application and returning control to the DOS prompt.

CTRL-ALT-DEL Key Combination

The CTRL-ALT-DEL key combination lets you restart DOS. Use this key combination to restart DOS after you change the system startup files CONFIG.SYS and AUTOEXEC.BAT, or when your system hangs due to a program error.

When DATE displays its prompt for you to enter a new date, hold down the CTRL key and type **C**. DOS will end the command displaying ^C :

```
C:\> DATE <ENTER>
Current date is Wed 02-27-1991
ENTER new date (mm-dd-yy): ^C

C:\>
```

Creating short files directly from the keyboard is very convenient. Using the COPY command and the F6 function key, create the file NUMBERS.DAT, as shown here.

```
C:\> COPY CON NUMBERS.DAT <ENTER>
1 <ENTER>
2 <ENTER>
3 <ENTER>
4 <ENTER>
5 <ENTER>
^Z <ENTER>
    1 File(s) copied
```

As you will recall, you must press the F6 key or the CTRL-Z key combination to create the DOS end-of-file marker (^Z).

Using the DIR command, you can verify that the file exists on your disk:

```
C:\> DIR NUMBERS.DAT <ENTER>

 Volume in drive C is DOS
 Volume Serial Number is 1C56-17ED
 Directory of C:\

NUMBERS DAT     15 02-27-91  10:51a
    1 File(s)  17089920 bytes free
```

Likewise, using the TYPE command discussed in Chapter 8, "Fundamental File Operations," you can display the file's contents:

```
C:\> TYPE NUMBERS.DAT <ENTER>
1
2
3
4
5

C:\>
```

Use the following DEL command to erase the file from your disk.

```
C:\> DEL NUMBERS.DAT <ENTER>
```

Last, use the CTRL-ALT-DEL key combination to restart DOS. Your computer will follow the same sequence discussed in Chapter 2, "Getting DOS Started," with the exception that it won't execute its power-on self-test. If you are using a hard disk system, make sure you remove the floppy disk from drive A, if one is present, before you perform the CTRL-ALT-DEL key combination to restart DOS.

Review

1. What are the four sections common to all keyboards?

2. What is a key combination?

3. What is the function of the following key combinations?

   CTRL-C

   CTRL-ALT-DEL

4. How does the F1 function key differ from F3?

5. What is the function of the NUMLOCK key?

Answers

1. All keyboards share:

   Standard typewriter keys
   Function keys
   Numeric keypad
   Cursor-control keys

2. A key combination is two or more keys you hold down to achieve a specific purpose. DOS predefines several key combinations. The CTRL-C key combination, for example, directs DOS to cancel the current command. When you press the keys for a specific combination, you should hold down the keys in the order specified. For example, using CTRL-C, you should first hold down the CTRL key. Next, while you depress the CTRL key, press the C key.

3. The following key combinations have these functions:

   CTRL-C   Directs DOS to cancel the current command
   CTRL-ALT-DEL   Restarts DOS

4. The F1 and F3 function keys let you edit the previous command. The F1 function key retrieves the previous command a single letter at a time. The F3 function key, on the other hand, retrieves the entire command all at once.

5. The NUMLOCK key is a toggle that lets you select either the entry of numeric values or use of the cursor control keys using the numeric keypad. The first time you press NUMLOCK, your computer will use the numeric values. The second time you press NUMLOCK, your computer will activate the cursor control keys. Most keyboards have a small light that, when lit, indicates that you have selected the numeric keys.

Advanced Concepts

Much of the first section of this chapter dealt with using the F1 and F3 function keys to repeat or edit the previous command. If you are using DOS 5, DOS provides the very powerful DOSKEY command that lets you recall a list of your most recently used commands. The actual number of commands DOSKEY can track depends on the amount of memory you allocate for DOSKEY as well as the various length of each command. Chapter 27 looks at the DOSKEY command in detail. You may want to skip ahead to that chapter next.

The remainder of this chapter examines the function keys F2, F4, and F5, as well as the CTRL-S key combination. If you are interested in defining your own function keys, Chapter 34, "ANSI.SYS," discusses how to do so using the ANSI.SYS device driver.

Advanced Command-Line Editing

As you know, the F1 function key lets you copy a single letter of the previous command, while F3 copies the entire command line. Depending on the length of your command lines, you may find it faster to edit the previous command using the F2 or F4 function keys discussed here.

The F2 function key directs DOS to copy characters from the previous command line, up to, but not including, the character you type immediately after pressing F2.

For example, assume you have just issued the following DIR command.

```
C:\> DIR \DOS <ENTER>
```

Next, assuming you want to repeat the DIR command, but this time for the current directory, you can press F2 followed by the backslash character (\). DOS will copy the contents of the previous command, up to, but not including, the backslash resulting in the letters DIR:

```
C:\> DIR
```

The F4 function key directs DOS to copy the characters that include and follow the character you type immediately after pressing F4. After you type the desired letter, you must press F1 or F3 to perform the actual copy. Many users, for example, use the DIR command to search a directory for a specific command and then execute the command if it exists. The following command, for example, uses the DIR to search the DOS directory for the DOSKEY command.

```
C:\> DIR \DOS\DOSKEY <ENTER>
```

Assuming DIR successfully locates DOSKEY, you can quickly execute the command by pressing F4 followed by the backslash key (\) and F3. In this case, DOS will copy the characters including and following the first backslash:

```
C:\>   \DOS\DOSKEY_
```

As you have learned, the function keys F1 through F4 let you edit the previous command. If you realize you have made a mistake in the command you are currently typing, you can press F5 to edit the command using the other function keys. For example, assume you mistyped the FORMAT command as shown, but have not yet pressed ENTER.

```
C:\> FOMAT A:
```

If you press the F5 function key, DOS will display the @ character indicating it has copied the current command into the previous command buffer.

```
C:\> FOMAT A:@
```

You can then press the F1 key twice displaying the letters "FO":

```
C:\> FOMAT A:@
     FO
```

Next, press the INS key to inform DOS you need to insert a letter, type **R**, and press F3 to complete the command, as shown here.

```
C:\> FOMAT A:@
     FORMAT A:
```

When you press ENTER, DOS will invoke the command as desired.

Canceling a Command with ESC

As you have learned, you can terminate a command using the CTRL-C key combination. If, however, you have typed a command's name and realize you don't want to execute the command, you can press the ESC key. DOS will respond by displaying a backslash at the end of the command and moving the cursor to the next line, as shown here.

```
C:\> DISKCOPY A: B:\
    _
```

Assuming you are using a DOS version prior to DOS 5, the following example uses the ESC key to cancel the DISKCOPY command, and then invokes CLS to clear the screen.

```
C:\> DISKCOPY A: B:\
    CLS <ENTER>
```

Using ESC in this way, you don't have to erase the entire command using the BACKSPACE key. If you are using DOS 5, pressing ESC directs DOS to erase the current command, letting you type in the next command as if you had pressed F5 to edit the current command. Many applications use ESC to cancel menus or various options also. Locate the ESC key on your keyboard. Depending on your applications, you may use it quite frequently.

Using CTRL-S to Suspend Scrolling

Depending on your computer's speed, there may be times when DOS scrolls a program's output off the top of your screen faster than you can read it. In such cases, you can direct DOS to temporarily suspend scrolling by pressing the CTRL-S key combination. To resume scrolling, simply press a key.

Key Terms

Key combination   A sequence of two or more keys held down for a specific result.

Warm boot   The process of restarting DOS with the CTRL-ALT-DEL key combination.

Cold boot   The process of starting DOS by turning on your computer.

F2 **Function Key**

The F2 function key directs DOS to copy characters from the previous command line, up to, but not including, the first incidence of the character you immediately type after pressing F2. If the character specified does not exit in the previous command, DOS does not copy any characters.

F4 **Function Key**

The F4 function key directs DOS to copy all the characters from the previous command that include and follow the characters you type immediately after pressing F4. After you type the desired letter, you must press F3 to perform the actual copy. If the character specified does not exist, F4 copies the entire command.

F5 **Function Key**

The F5 function key directs DOS to copy the current command line to the previous command-line buffer for editing. When you press F5, DOS will display the @ character at the end of the current command line and then let you edit the command line using the other function keys.

ESC **Key**

The ESC key lets you cancel a command you have typed at the DOS prompt, but not yet invoked by pressing ENTER. When DOS encounters the ESC key, DOS will display the back slash (\) at the end of the command and redisplay its prompt for subsequent commands, as shown here.

```
C:\> DISKCOPY A: B:\
    ─
```

You must press ESC to cancel a command in this way. You cannot simply press the backslash key.

CTRL - S **Key Combination**

The CTRL-S key combination directs DOS to temporarily suspend output scrolling, letting you view a command's output on the screen. To resume scrolling, simply press any key.

Chapter 6

Getting Around
Your Disk

As you learned in Chapter 1, "Getting to Know Your Computer," all personal computers have at least one floppy disk drive, named drive A. In addition, most computers have a hard disk named drive C, and possibly a second floppy disk, drive B. The purpose of these disk drives is simply to let you access files stored on different disks. As you learned in Chapter 2, each time DOS starts, DOS selects the boot disk as its current (or default) drive. In most cases, your DOS prompt contains the drive letter corresponding to the current drive. The current drive is so named because, by default, it is the drive whose disk DOS will search for files and external commands unless you tell DOS to look elsewhere. In this chapter you will learn several different ways to access files stored on disks in drives other than the default.

Changing the Default Drive

The following discussion assumes you have a floppy disk that contains files in drive A, and that the drive latch is closed.

Your disk drives have single-letter names such as A, B, and C. When you specify a disk drive to DOS, you must place a colon after the disk drive name (such as "A:" or "B:"). To change from one drive to another, simply type the desired drive name (and colon) at the DOS prompt and press ENTER. The following command, for example, changes the default drive from C to A. Depending on the commands your computer executes when it starts, your prompt may differ slightly from those shown here. Don't be alarmed—in Chapter 10, "Directories," you will learn how to use the PROMPT command to modify your DOS prompt.

```
C:\> A:  <ENTER>

A:\>
```

Note that DOS immediately changes the system prompt to indicate the new default drive. If you issue a DIR command, DOS will display the files that reside on the disk in drive A.

```
A:\> DIR  <ENTER>
```

In other words, drive A is now the default drive. To change the default drive back to drive C, simply issue the following command.

```
A:\> C:  <ENTER>
```

If your computer has a floppy disk drive B, and the drive contains a floppy disk, you can select drive B as the default using the same technique.

Accessing a Drive's Disk Without Changing Default Drives

As you have learned, the DIR command lets you display a directory listing for the files in a directory. In the previous section you learned you can view a directory listing of the files on a different disk by first changing the default drive and then issuing the DIR command:

```
C:\> A:  <ENTER>
A:\> DIR  <ENTER>
```

The default drive is the drive that DOS uses unless you tell it otherwise. Most DOS commands let you include the desired disk drive letter in the command line. For example, the following DIR command directs DOS to perform a directory listing of the files stored on the disk in drive A.

```
C:\> DIR A: <ENTER>
```

You *must* include the colon after the drive letter. If you don't include the colon, DIR assumes you want to list the directory entry for a file named A. Because such a file probably does not exist on your disk, DIR will display an error message like the one below indicating it did not find the file.

```
C:\> DIR A <ENTER>

 Volume in drive C is DOS
 Volume Serial Number is 1661-AB75
 Directory of C:\

File not found

C:\>
```

Many of the DOS commands you will issue throughout the remainder of this book let you specify a disk drive in this way.

Accessing a File on Another Disk

In Chapter 4 you learned that the DIR command lets you list a directory entry for a specific file if you include the file name in DIR's command line, as shown here.

```
C:\> DIR FILENAME.EXT <ENTER>
```

If the file is on a disk other than the default, you can list the file's directory entry using this same technique by preceding the file name with the corresponding drive letter, as shown here.

```
C:\> DIR A:FILENAME.EXT <ENTER>
```

Do not place spaces between the disk drive specifier (A:) and the file name. When DIR examines its command line, DIR will look on drive A for the file specified. All the DOS file commands you will examine in this book support this drive-letter/file-name combination.

The Abort, Retry, Fail? Prompt

As you increase your use of floppy disk drives, you may inadvertently try to access a disk drive whose latch is not closed, or one that contains a floppy disk you have not yet prepared for use by DOS. (See Chapter 7, "Preparing Disks for Use," for information on the FORMAT command.) When such an error occurs, DOS will display an explanatory error message followed by the following prompt:

```
Abort, Retry, Fail?
```

DOS displays this prompt when it encounters an error it cannot resolve without user interaction. In this case, you must respond with the letter "A," "R," or "F," which correspond to each option. The Abort option directs DOS to end (abort) the command responsible for the error, and to redisplay the DOS prompt. Assume for example, you issue a DIR command for drive A, only to discover drive A does not contain a floppy disk:

```
C:\> DIR A: <ENTER>

Not ready reading drive A
Abort, Retry, Fail?
```

By selecting the Abort option, you can end the DIR command, and return to the DOS prompt.

```
C:\> DIR A: <ENTER>

Not ready reading drive A
Abort, Retry, Fail?A

C:\>
```

The Retry option, on the other hand, gives you an opportunity to correct the situation causing the error, so you can direct DOS to repeat, from the start, the operation that encountered the error without having to retype the command. In the previous example, you could insert a floppy disk into drive A as needed, and then type **R**, directing DOS to retry the directory operation.

The Fail option is the least-used option. Fail directs DOS to skip the operation that encountered the error and to continue the command's execution. In Chapter 9,

"DOS Wildcard Characters," you will learn how to copy several files from one disk to another. Assume that the disk you are copying from is an older floppy disk that is beginning to wear out. When DOS tries to read one of the files on the disk, the disk is so worn DOS can't read it. As a result, DOS will display its Abort, Retry, Fail? prompt to determine how you want to handle the error. Using the Fail option, you can direct DOS to fail the operation causing the error, but to continue trying to copy the remaining files.

Hands On

For the following discussion, place your DOS system disk in drive A and close the drive's latch. Issue the following DIR command.

```
C:\> DIR <ENTER>
```

Unless told to do otherwise, DOS uses the default drive. In this case, because drive C is the default, DIR displays a directory listing of drive C's files. Use the following command to change the default drive from drive C to A.

```
C:\> A: <ENTER>

A:\>
```

Next, repeat the DIR command.

```
A:\> DIR <ENTER>
```

Because drive A is now the default, DIR displays the directory listing for the files on the disk in it.

Repeat the DIR command, this time including drive C in the command line.

```
A:\> DIR C: <ENTER>
```

In this case, DIR displays a directory listing for drive C as specified instead of using the default drive.

Issue the following command to select drive C as the default.

SUMMARY

Changing the Default Drive

Every disk drive on your system has a single-letter name, such as A, B, or C. To specify a disk drive to DOS, type the drive letter followed by a colon and press ENTER. The following command, for example, changes the default drive from C to A.

```
C:\> A: <ENTER>
```

Accessing a Disk Other than the Default Drive

The current drive is the disk drive DOS uses by default to locate files and commands, unless you tell it to do otherwise. All the DOS disk commands let you specify the desired drive in their command line. For example, the following DIR command display's the files on the disk in drive A.

```
C:\> DIR A: <ENTER>
```

Accessing a File from Another Disk

Throughout this book, you will examine many DOS file manipulation commands that let you specify a file name in the command line. If the desired file is on a disk other than the default, simply precede the file name with a drive letter and colon, as shown in the following DIR example.

```
C:\> DIR A:FILENAME.EXT <ENTER>
```

Abort, Retry, Fail?

When DOS encounters a device-related error, such as an open disk drive latch or a printer off line, DOS will display the Abort, Retry, Fail? prompt to determine how you want to handle the error. The Abort option directs DOS to cancel the command causing the error and to return control to the DOS prompt. The Retry option directs DOS to repeat the operation after you have performed steps to correct the problem. Last, the Fail option directs DOS to fail the current operation, but to try to continue the command from the current point.

Issue the following command to select drive C as the default.

```
A:\> C:  <ENTER>
```

Next, open drive A's latch and issue the following command.

```
C:\> DIR A:  <ENTER>
```

Because DOS cannot access the disk in drive A, DOS will display its Abort, Retry, Fail? prompt. In this case, type **A** to end the DIR command, returning to the DOS prompt.

Repeat the DIR command. This time, when DOS displays the Abort, Retry, Fail? prompt, close drive A's latch, type **R**, and press ENTER. DOS will retry the DIR command and will succeed, because the drive is now ready for access.

Review

1. What is the default drive?

2. How do you change the default drive from A to B?

3. What is the function of the following command?

```
C:\> DIR B <ENTER>
```

4. Assuming drive C is the default, and the disk in drive A contains a file named READ.ME, what is the DIR command to display a directory listing for the file?

5. How does the Abort option differ from the Fail option in response to the DOS prompt to Abort, Retry, Fail?

Answers

1. The default or current drive is the disk drive whose disk, by default, DOS examines for the files and commands, unless you tell DOS to do otherwise. When you start your computer, DOS selects the drive it used to start as the default drive. Typically, the DOS prompt contains the drive letter that corresponds to the default drive (A> or C>).

2. To change the default drive, you simply type, at the DOS prompt, the letter of the desired drive followed by colon and ENTER.

```
A:\> B:  <ENTER>
```

3. Asking the function of the following command

```
C:\> DIR B <ENTER>
```

is a trick question. In this case, because the drive letter B is not followed by a colon (B:), DOS will search the current directory for a file named B. The correct DIR command to display the files on the disk in drive B is as follows:

```
C:\> DIR B:  <ENTER>
```

4. The DIR command to display a directory listing for the file, assuming drive C is the default, and the disk in drive A contains a file named READ.ME,   is:

```
C:\> DIR A:READ.ME  <ENTER>
```

5. The Abort option directs DOS to end the command that encountered the error and to return control to the DOS prompt. The Fail option, on the other hand, directs DOS to ignore the error, and if possible, to continue the command.

Advanced Concepts

As discussed in Chapter 1, different disk drives have different storage capacities. Depending on the age of your computer, you may want to upgrade to a newer, faster disk with increased storage capacity. If you are considering upgrading your disk drives, you need to also consider your disk controller card, as well as the disk's current power supply. Also, if you are adding a 3 1/2-inch drive to your system, you will need to upgrade to DOS version 3.2 as a minimum for 720Kb drives and version 3.3 for 1.44Mb drives.

Disk Controller

If you open your computer's chassis, you will find your disk drive connects to a board, as shown in Figure 6-1. This board is your disk controller card, which provides your computer's interface to the disk.

In general, the disk controller oversees every disk read or write operation.

In most cases, the disk controller is connected to both your hard and floppy disk. Before you buy a new disk, you need to ensure the disk is compatible with your existing controller. Depending on the age of your system, you may need to upgrade the controller as well.

If you have never installed a disk yourself, I advise you to have a trained technician do the upgrade for you. Chapter 1 discusses the various disk controller types in detail.

External Drives

An internal drive is a disk drive that resides within your computer's chassis. Depending on their computer's chassis size, some users can only add an external floppy drive. Many PS/2 users, for example, like to add a 5 1/4-inch floppy disk

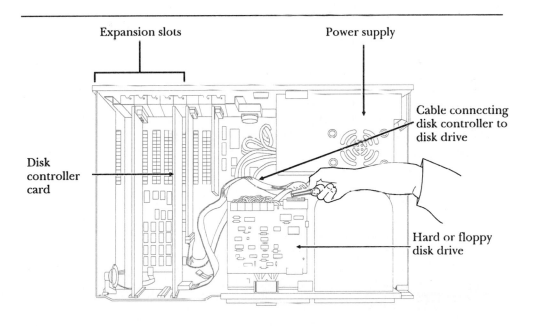

Figure 6-1.   Your disk connects to a controller card

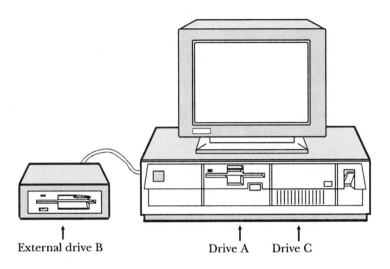

External drive B   Drive A   Drive C

Figure 6-2.   An external floppy disk drive

drive. Because the PS/2's chassis is so small, users must add an external drive. Figure 6-2 illustrates an external floppy drive.

To use an external floppy drive, you may need to install the DRIVER.SYS device driver, as discussed in Chapter 24, "Customizing Your System with CONFIG.SYS".

If DOS displays the following error message when you attempt to access an external floppy drive, you will need to use DRIVER.SYS.

```
C:\> DIR E: <ENTER>
Invalid drive specification
```

Key Terms

Default drive   The default (or current drive) is the disk drive DOS will search for files or commands unless you tell DOS to look elsewhere. The DOS prompt typically contains the drive letter of the default drive.

Disk drive specifier   Each disk attached to your computer has a unique single-letter name, such as A, B, or C. The disk specifier is the drive's single-letter name followed by a colon (A:).

Abort   To end a command.

Disk controller   The hardware device that provides the interface between a disk drive and the computer. The disk controller oversees all disk read and write operations.

External floppy disk drive   A floppy disk drive connected to your computer that resides outside of the computer's chassis.

Chapter 7

Preparing Disks for Use

The examples that appear throughout this book assume you are using DOS on a computer with a hard disk. As you work with DOS and other programs, you will need to copy files from floppy disks to your hard disk or vice versa. When you buy a box of floppy disks, the disk manufacturer has no idea whether you plan to use the disks on an IBM PC or compatible using DOS, an Apple computer, or even a Commodore. Before you can copy information to a floppy disk, you must first prepare the disk for use by DOS. This process of preparing a disk for use is *formatting*. In this chapter you will learn to use the FORMAT command to prepare a floppy disk for use.

FORMAT Is an External Command

You learned in Chapter 3 that DOS commands are either internal commands that reside in your computer's electronic memory, or external commands that reside on disk. Up to this point, we have been discussing internal commands. By contrast, FORMAT is an external DOS command residing in the file FORMAT.COM. Like the rest of the external DOS commands, FORMAT.COM is in the DOS subdirectory. This means that if you are using a floppy disk system and want to format a blank, the DOS disk with the file FORMAT.COM must be in the current drive when you issue the FORMAT command, not the blank disk. Use the following DIR command to display a directory listing for the file FORMAT.COM on your hard disk.

```
C:\> DIR \DOS\FORMAT.COM <ENTER>

 Volume in drive C is DOS
 Volume Serial Number is 1661-AB75
 Directory of C:\DOS

FORMAT   COM    32285 12-13-90  4:09a
      1 file(s)    32285 bytes
                16251968 bytes free
```

The Formatting Process

The best way to understand the format process is to visualize an unused disk as initially blank (see Figure 7-1).

The first stage of the format process divides your disk into circular *tracks* similar to the grooves in a record album as shown in Figure 7-2. Hard disk users refer to tracks as *cylinders*. The number of tracks on your disk depends on your disk type.

Next, FORMAT further divides each track into pie-shaped regions called *sectors*. When DOS stores a file on disk, it stores the file's contents into one or more sectors. Typically, most disk sectors store 512 bytes (or characters) of information. Figure 7-3 illustrates disk sectors.

Figure 7-1. *Picture an unused disk as blank*

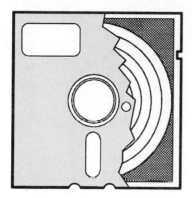

Figure 7-2.   FORMAT first divides your disk into circular tracks

The number of sectors per track also depends on your disk type. Table 7-1 details the number of tracks and sectors per track for common disk sizes.

Knowing your disk type, you can use Table 7-1 to determine the number of tracks per side and sectors per track. Using 512-byte sectors you can determine the amount of space a disk can store using the following equation.

Storage = (Number of sides) * (Tracks per side) * (Sectors per track) * (Sector size)

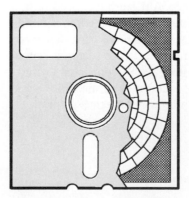

Figure 7-3.   FORMAT further divides each track into sectors

Disk Size	Tracks Per Side	Sectors Per Track
160 Kb	40	8
180 Kb	40	9
320 Kb	40	8
360 Kb	40	9
720 Kb	80	9
1.2 Mb	80	15
1.44 Mb	80	18
Hard disk (10 Mb)	306	17
Hard disk (20 Mb)	615	17

Table 7-1.   Tracks per Side and Sectors per Track for Common Disk Sizes

Using a 360Kb disk, for example, the disk's storage capabilities become the following:

Storage   =   (2) * (40) * (9) * (512)

          =   368,640 bytes

Not All Disk Sectors Are Capable of Storing Information

A disk drive stores information on a disk by magnetizing the information to the disk's specially coated surface. Although it is becoming less common, it is possible for sections of a disk's surface to be damaged, incapable of storing information. As part of its processing, FORMAT examines each disk sector to ensure that the sector is capable of storing information. If the sector is damaged, FORMAT marks the sector as unusable, preventing DOS from later trying to use the sector to store information. If FORMAT encounters damaged sectors, FORMAT will display a message describing the number of damaged sectors:

```
nnn bytes in bad sectors
```

The following summary informs you the disk has 5120 bytes of damaged sectors. Note that FORMAT has subtracted the number of damaged bytes from the total disk space to yield the disks available space.

```
362496 bytes total disk space
  5120 bytes in bad sectors
357376 bytes available on disk
```

Preparing a Floppy Disk for Use

The FORMAT command prepares a disk for use by recording on the disk information DOS will later use when you store files. As a result of its processing, FORMAT overwrites any existing information the disk may contain. Should you accidentally format the wrong disk, you normally cannot retrieve any of the information the disk previously contained. When you use FORMAT, take considerable care to prevent such accidental loss of information.

To begin, place an unused floppy disk in drive A. Next, issue the following FORMAT command to prepare the disk for use.

```
C:\> FORMAT A:  <ENTER>
```

FORMAT will prompt you to insert a new disk in drive A:

```
Insert new diskette for drive A:
and press ENTER when ready...
```

After you insert the unused disk in drive A and close the drive latch, press ENTER to continue the disk format operation. Depending on your DOS version, FORMAT will display the message:

```
Head:  n Cylinder:  nn
```

or the message:

```
nn percent completed.
```

As the format process continues, FORMAT will update the messages, informing you about how much of the disk it has formatted. When FORMAT completes, it displays the following message.

```
Format complete.
```

Again, depending on your DOS version, FORMAT may prompt you to type in a name for the disk, as shown here.

```
Volume label (11 characters, ENTER for none)?
```

A disk *volume label* is simply a disk name containing up to 11 characters. The label should help you better understand the files stored on the disk. Hard disk users can assign the disk label DOS to their hard disk. For a floppy disk, you might use a more specific label, such as REPORTS, WORKSHEETS, or MEMOS91, depending on the files you are storing on the floppy disk. If you don't want to assign a volume label, simply press ENTER.

Last, FORMAT will display a summary of the amount of disk space available on disk, as well as a prompt asking if you want to format additional disks.

```
362496 bytes total disk space
362496 bytes available on disk

 1024 bytes in each allocation unit
  354 allocation units available on disk

Volume Serial Number is 3703-10F3

Format another (Y/N)?
```

If you want to format additional disks, type Y and press ENTER. The format process will repeat, beginning at the prompt for you to insert a new disk into the drive. If you instead type N and press ENTER, FORMAT will end, and DOS will redisplay its prompt. In either case, the floppy disk in drive A is now ready for use by DOS.

Before you can understand the statistical information FORMAT displays, you need a better understanding of the actual processing FORMAT performs.

Formatting a Disk with Less Storage Capability than the Floppy Drive

In Chapter 1 you learned that although two disks are the same size, (both 5 1/4 inches or both 3 1/2 inches), the disks might not be able to store the same amount of information. When the original IBM PC was released in 1981, for example, a 5 1/4-inch floppy disk could store 163,840 bytes (160Kb). Today, 5 1/4-inch disks store up to 1,213,952 bytes (1.2Mb). A problem arises when users try to format an older, smaller-capacity disk in a newer higher-capacity disk drive. For example, if your computer has a 1.2Mb disk drive, FORMAT, by default, will try to format every disk you place into the drive as a 1.2Mb disk. Unfortunately, if you attempt to format a 360Kb disk using your 1.2Mb drive, the format will either fail or produce a disk with hundreds of unusable sectors. This same problem occurs when users try to format a 720Kb 3 1/2-inch disk in a 1.44Mb drive.

If you need to format a smaller capacity disk in a larger capacity drive, you must include switches in FORMAT's command line. In the case of the 360Kb disk in a 1.2Mb drive, you can specify the /4 switch:

```
C:\> FORMAT A: /4 <ENTER>
```

The actual format process is the same as that discussed earlier, with the only difference being FORMAT will use the correct disk size. If you need to format a 720Kb disk in a 1.44Mb drive, you can use the /F switch:

```
C:\> FORMAT A: /F:720 <ENTER>
```

For more information on FORMAT's disk-size switches, refer to the Command Reference at the end of this book.

Formatting Your Hard Disk

The majority of the discussion in this chapter has concerned formatting floppy disks, as opposed to hard disks. The reason for this is quite simple: There are only a few times when you would ever need to format your hard disk. The first occurs when you are upgrading to a higher version of DOS. The second occurs when you are experiencing hard disk errors, and the third occurs when you are correcting fragmented files, as discussed in Chapter 44.

As discussed, FORMAT *completely* overwrites the contents of the disk it formats. Regardless of why you are formatting your hard disk, always make sure you have completely backed up all the files the disk contains before performing the format.

Because an inadvertent format of your hard disk could be disastrous in terms of the information you could lose, FORMAT will display the following message, warning that you are about to format your hard disk, and prompting you to ensure that you really want to continue.

```
WARNING, ALL DATA ON NON-REMOVABLE DISK
DRIVE C: WILL BE LOST!
Proceed with Format (Y/N)?
```

 NOTE *Should you inadvertently format your hard disk, several software utility programs exist that may be able to recover portions of your disk. If you are using DOS 5, you may be able to recover your disk using the UNFORMAT command discussed in Chapter 28, "DOS 5 Crisis Prevention."*

Hands On

Locate an unused floppy disk and place the disk in drive A. Issue the following DIR command to ensure that the disk does not contain files you need.

```
C:\> DIR A: <ENTER>
```

If you have never formatted the disk, DOS will display a message similar to the following.

```
General failure reading drive A
Abort, Retry, Fail?
```

If this error message occurs, type A to abort the DIR command.

Next, issue this FORMAT command to prepare the disk in drive A for use.

```
C:\> FORMAT A: <ENTER>
```

/ SUMMARY /

DOS FORMAT Command

The FORMAT command lets you prepare a disk for use by DOS. To begin, FORMAT divides your disk into circular tracks, conceptually similar to the grooves in a record album. Next, FORMAT further divides each track into sectors. When DOS later stores a file on your disk, DOS will use one or more disk sectors.

FORMAT is a destructive command, meaning FORMAT will overwrite any existing information the target disk may contain. Should you inadvertently format a disk, you may be able to recover a portion of the disk's previous information using a third-party software utility or the DOS 5 **WARNING** *UNFORMAT command. Get in the habit of using DIR to examine the contents of every disk you intend to format. In so doing, you will greatly reduce the possibility of formatting a disk that contains needed files.*

If you are formatting a disk whose storage capacity is smaller than that of the disk drive, use either the /4 or /F switch, as discussed in this chapter.

If FORMAT prompts you to enter a volume label, type TESTDISK as follows.

```
Volume label (11 characters, ENTER for none)? TESTDISK
```

Last, note FORMAT's summary information to determine if the disk contains any damaged sectors. Disk quality has rapidly improved over the past few years to the point where bad disk sectors are rare. If several of your floppy disks format with damaged sectors, you should strongly consider purchasing a different brand of disk.

When the FORMAT command completes, use the following DIR command to display the contents of drive A. Note that DIR displays the disk volume name TESTDISK in its directory listing.

```
C:\> DIR A: <ENTER>
```

Review

1. Is FORMAT an internal or external DOS command?

2. List three operations FORMAT performs.

3. When do you need to use FORMAT's /4 and /F switches?

4. What is a volume label?

5. What is a bad sector?

Answers

1. FORMAT is an external DOS command that resides in the file FOR-MAT.COM.

2. The three operations FORMAT performs are as follows:

   - Divides your disk into tracks and sectors.

   - Identifies bad sectors and marks the sectors unusable for DOS.

   - Optionally assigns a disk volume label.

   The "Advanced Concepts" section of this chapter discusses several other functions FORMAT performs.

3. The FORMAT /4 option lets you format a 360Kb disk in a 1.2Mb disk drive. Likewise, using the /F option, you can format a 720Kb disk in a 1.44Mb drive. The only time you need to use the /4 or /F switches is when you are formatting a disk with less storage capacity than your disk drive.

4. A volume label is an optional 11 character name you can assign to your disk. Hard disk users can assign a name like DOS to their disk. For floppy disks, you might want to use names such as REPORTS, 123-DATA, or LETTERS, depending on the type of files the disk contains.

5. A bad or damaged sector is a sector on your disk that is not capable of storing information. Information is stored on a disk by magnetizing the information onto a specially coated surface. If the surface is scratched, or slightly damaged during manufacturing, the disk cannot store information in that sector. FORMAT will mark the sector as unusable.

Advanced Concepts

FORMAT, at a basic level, divides your disk into tracks and sectors. In addition, FORMAT defines, for the target disk, several key values that directly influence the amount of disk space files consume, as well as the number of entries you can store in a disk's root directory. Further, FORMAT lets you create bootable system disks.

Building a Bootable System Disk

For DOS to start, a disk must contain two hidden system files and the file COMMAND.COM. In the case of MS-DOS, the hidden files are named IO.SYS and MSDOS.SYS. DOS hides these files to prevent their inadvertent deletion.

For the DOS system startup process to locate these two files, DOS requires that the files occupy the first two root directory entries. The best time, then, to place these files on the disk is before the root directory contains any file or directory entries, immediately after the format operation completes.

By default, FORMAT does not place the hidden system files on each disk you format. Depending on your DOS version, these files can consume up to 70Kb of disk space. Since most users don't need to put DOS with every disk, placing the hidden files on each disk would consume disk space unnecessarily.

To build a bootable system disk using FORMAT, you must include the /S qualifier, shown here.

```
C:\> FORMAT A: /S <ENTER>
```

The format process will proceed as before. However, before completing, FORMAT will transfer the system files to the disk. FORMAT will then display, in its summary messages, a message indicating it has transferred the system files as well as the amount of disk space the system files consumed:

```
System transferred

Volume label (11 characters, ENTER for none)? TESTDISK

  362496 bytes total disk space
  118784 bytes used by system
  243712 bytes available on disk
```

Depending on your DOS version, FORMAT may not copy the DOS command processor (COMMAND.COM) to the target disk. As discussed in Chapter 2, DOS needs COMMAND.COM to boot. If FORMAT did not copy the file to the disk, do so using the COPY command.

```
C:\> COPY \DOS\COMMAND.COM A: <ENTER>
```

Every Disk Has a Boot Record

Whether you format a disk as a bootable system disk or not, DOS assigns the first sector on the disk for a *boot record*. The boot record contains specifics about the disk size, number of sectors, and so on. If the disk is bootable, the boot record contains a small software program that begins the DOS startup process. If the disk is not bootable, the boot record contains software that displays the following message when you try to boot from the disk:

```
Non-System disk or disk error
Replace and press any key when ready
```

Figure 7-4 illustrates the location of a boot record in the disk's first sector.

Reserving Space for the File Allocation Table

Chapter 33, "How DOS Actually Stores Files," examines in detail how DOS actually stores files on your disk. In that chapter you'll learn that DOS tracks the actual sectors used to store each file's sectors in a table called the *file allocation table* or *FAT*. DOS stores the file allocation table on your disk. Each time you perform a file operation, copying a file or executing an external command, for example, DOS uses the file allocation table to locate the file's sectors on disk.

In general, the file allocation table serves as your disk's road map. Because DOS stores the file allocation table on disk, you can imagine the impact of a disk error in one of the sectors containing the FAT. If DOS is unable to access the FAT, DOS would also be unable to locate any of the files on the disk. To prevent a single disk error from having such devastating effects, DOS typically stores two copies of the FAT on your disk. If DOS is unable to access the first copy of the FAT, DOS uses the second copy.

After FORMAT places the boot record as your disk, FORMAT places the file allocation tables on your disk. DOS stores the file allocation tables on your disk following the boot record, as shown in Figure 7-5.

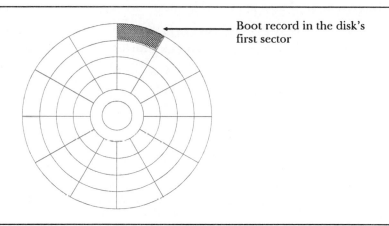

Figure 7-4. *The first sector of every disk contains a boot record*

Reserving Space for the Root Directory

Every DOS disk automatically starts with a root directory. Whether you format a disk as a system disk or not, one of the major functions FORMAT performs is the reservation of disk sectors for the root directory.

Each time you format a disk, FORMAT assigns sectors to serve as the root directory. The actual number of sectors DOS reserves for the root directory depends

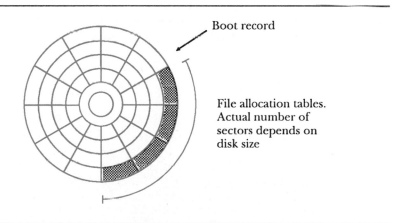

Figure 7-5. *DOS places the file allocation tables immediately after the boot record*

Disk Size	Root Directory Maximum Entries	Root Directory Sectors Reserved
160 Kb	64	4
360 Kb	112	7
720 Kb	112	7
1.2 Mb	224	14
1.44 Mb	224	14
Hard Disk	512	16 or 32

Table 7-2.   Number of Disk Sectors Reserved for the Root Directory

on your disk type. Table 7-2 defines the number of sectors DOS reserves for the root directory for each disk type.

FORMAT places the disk's root directory sectors immediately after the file allocation tables, as shown in Figure 7-6.

Each time you create a subdirectory or file, DOS allocates a 32-byte directory entry that contains the file or directory name, size, date and time stamps, and so on. Knowing the number of disk sectors FORMAT reserves for your disk as well as the disk sector size, you can determine the number of entries your root directory can store using the following equation.

Number of entries = Number of sectors * sector size / 32

Once FORMAT establishes the disk's root directory, DOS cannot increase the root's size. If you try to place more files or directories in the root than DOS can store, DOS will display the following error message.

```
File creation error
```

For most users, the number of entries the root directory supports is more than enough.

Understanding Allocation Units

If you examine the disk statistics FORMAT displays after it successfully formats a disk, you will find a size for allocation units, as shown here.

```
1024 bytes in each allocation unit.
 238 allocation units available on disk.
```

For simplicity, we typically say that DOS allocates disk sectors for your files. As the size of a file grows, DOS allocates additional sectors as required. Although DOS stores a file's contents in disk sectors, DOS actually reserves disk space for a file using groups of connected sectors called *allocation units* or *clusters*. The size of the allocation unit tells you the minimum number of bytes DOS can allocate for a file.

Assume for example, the allocation unit size is 2048 bytes (or four 512-byte sectors). Next, assume you want to store three files named SMALL, EXACT, and LARGE with the following sizes.

```
SMALL   1024 bytes
EXACT   2048 bytes
LARGE   3072 bytes
```

DOS will allocate and use clusters for each file, as in Figure 7-7.

Remember the allocation unit dictates the smallest amount of disk space DOS can allocate for a file. Although the file SMALL only has 1,024 bytes of information, DOS must still allocate a complete allocation unit for the file, or in this case, 2,048 bytes leaving 1,024 bytes unused. If the file size grows in the future, DOS will use the available space. If the file size never changes, the disk space will remain unused and inaccessible to other files.

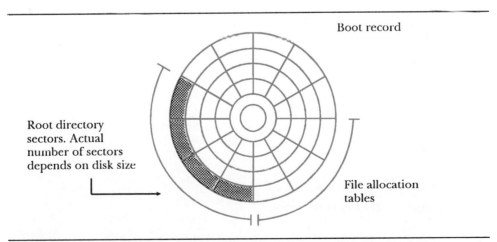

Boot record

Root directory
sectors. Actual
number of sectors
depends on disk size

File allocation
tables

Figure 7-6.   FORMAT places the root directory sectors immediately after the boot record and FAT

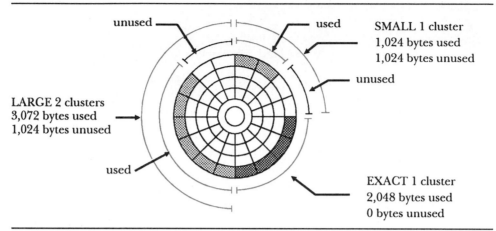

unused — used

SMALL 1 cluster
1,024 bytes used
1,024 bytes unused

unused

LARGE 2 clusters
3,072 bytes used →
1,024 bytes unused

used ◄

EXACT 1 cluster
2,048 bytes used
0 bytes unused

Figure 7-7.   DOS allocates disk space in clusters

As an example, perform a directory listing and note the amount of available disk space.

```
15 File(s) 102400 bytes free
```

Next, create the file ONE as follows:

```
C:\> COPY CON ONE
1 ^Z <ENTER>
     1 File(s) copied
```

In this case, the file only contains 1 byte of information. However, DOS must still reserve a complete allocation unit for the file resulting in 2,047 bytes of unused disk space. If you repeat the directory command, you will find DOS has decreased the amount of free disk space by an allocation unit, which in this example is 2,048 bytes.

```
16 File(s) 100352 bytes free
```

Why Does DOS Use Allocation Units?

Although using file allocation units appears to waste disk space, DOS has several reasons for using them. First, DOS keeps track of each file's data using the file allocation table. The FAT is a table of entries that tells DOS which clusters each file is using, as well as the available clusters, and the damaged clusters FORMAT marks as unusable. Assuming the file allocation table had to track disk sectors, a 60-megabyte disk, for example, would require 122,880 entries! Not only would the two copies of the FAT take up considerable disk space, the large number of table entries would become very time consuming for DOS to traverse, which would decrease your system performance. Second, in Chapter 44, "Deleting and Correcting Disk Fragmentation," you will learn how disk fragmentation can decrease your system performance. Disk fragmentation occurs when DOS stores a file's contents in locations across your disk, as opposed to consecutive storage locations.

Figure 7-8 illustrates two files. The first file's contents are stored in consecutive locations, while the second file's contents are spread out across the disk.

When DOS accesses the contiguous file, DOS can read the file's contents one sector after another. For the fragmented file, however, DOS must wait for disk to rotate each sector of the file under the disk read/write head. These rotational delays decrease your systems performance.

By reserving disk space for your files using clusters, DOS decreases the chance of disk fragmentation by grouping multiple sectors of the file together. Disk fragmentation is most common when a file's size increases because DOS may have to allocate additional disk space for the file. By using clusters, DOS can first allocate the unused portion of the cluster before having to look elsewhere on the disk for storage locations.

Chapter 33 examines how DOS stores files on disk, and how the file allocation table tracks the file locations. For now, simply understand that, no matter how hard you try, the allocation unit size determines the smallest amount of disk space DOS will reserve for a file. If you think you are saving disk space by creating several very small files, in reality you're not.

Formatting Under DOS 5

Chapter 28 discusses the UNFORMAT command in detail. In general, should you accidentally format the wrong disk, the UNFORMAT command may be able to retrieve the disk's information. Unless you tell FORMAT to do otherwise, by including the /U switch, FORMAT will perform a "safe format" of your disk. A safe format creates a new root directory and initializes the file allocation table. A safe format does not, however, overwrite the information that currently resides on the disk. In addition, before the safe format initializes the file allocation table and root directory, the safe format makes a copy of both, which it stores on the disk. Should

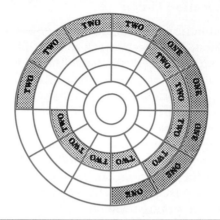

Figure 7-8.   A contiguous file (ONE) and a fragmented file (TWO)

you inadvertently format the wrong disk, UNFORMAT can use the information the safe format stores on the disk to retrieve the disk's previous information.

When you format a disk using DOS 5, FORMAT will check if the disk has been previously formatted and will display the following:

```
Checking existing disk format
```

If the disk has been previously formatted, FORMAT will save the information UNFORMAT needs to recover the disk, as follows.

```
Saving UNFORMAT information
```

By providing a safe format, DOS helps you protect your disks and files.

Key Terms

Disk formatting   The process of preparing a disk for use by a specific operating system.

Tracks   Circular divisions of your disk that DOS uses to locate specific disk sectors. Hard disk users often use the term cylinders instead of tracks.

Sectors   Storage regions on your disk. DOS stores your files in one or more sectors.

Allocation unit   The smallest amount of disk space DOS can allocate for a file. Allocation units are also called clusters.

Fragmented file   A file whose contents are stored in locations spread out across a disk. Fragmented files decrease system performance.

Volume label   An 11- character name you can assign to your disk. Volume labels aid in floppy disk organization.

Bad sector   A damaged disk sector, incapable of storing information.

File allocation table (FAT)   A table DOS uses to track the location of each file's contents as well as the available disk space and damaged sectors. The file allocation table is your disk's road map.

Chapter 8

Fundamental File Operations

DOS organizes information on your disk using files. Consider your disk files as if they were files stored in paper folders in an office. With paper files, you examine the file's contents, make copies of files, rename files as necessary, and discard the files when they are no longer needed. As you will learn in this chapter, DOS provides four fundamental file commands:

TYPE	View a file's contents
COPY	Make a duplicate of a file
RENAME	Change a file's name
DEL	Delete a file that is no longer needed

These four commands provide you with the key file-manipulation capabilities you will use every day. Because of their frequent use, all four of these commands are internal commands that DOS keeps in your computer's electronic memory at all times.

TYPE Displays a File's Contents

Just as you browse through the contents of paper files, so will you occasionally want to browse through files stored on disk. The TYPE command lets you display a file's contents, provided the file contains standard text (characters and numbers). For example, the following TYPE command displays the contents of a file named AUTOEXEC.BAT.

```
C:\> TYPE  \AUTOEXEC.BAT   <ENTER>
PATH C:\DOS;C:\DISKUTIL
PROMPT $P$G
```

Depending on the configuration of your system, the file contents of your AUTOEXEC.BAT may differ from those shown. If TYPE displays the "File not found" message, your disk may not yet have an AUTOEXEC.BAT file. Don't worry; you will create an AUTOEXEC.BAT file in Chapter 18, "Automatic System Startup Commands with AUTOEXEC.BAT".

You learned in Chapter 4, "Getting Started with DOS Files," that DOS files can store external commands, spreadsheets, word processing documents, and so on. TYPE cannot meaningfully display some of these on your screen. If you try to view the contents of a command file having the COM or EXE extension, for example, your computer will very likely beep and display unrecognizable characters on your screen. Likewise, if you use TYPE to view a file containing a word processing document, the file's contents may again be difficult to read. Word processors let you produce professional-quality documents by letting you align the left and right margins, type in boldface text, and so on. To accomplish these capabilities, word processors embed special characters within the document. One special character may turn on boldface, while another selects italics. Although these special characters are meaningful to the word processor, the characters confuse TYPE, resulting in unrecognizable output. In other words, if you create a file with your word processor, you'll have to use the word processor to view the file's contents.

The TYPE command displays text files, which are also called *ASCII files*. Examples of text files include batch files (with the BAT extension) that you will create in Chapter 15, "Grouping Commands with Batch Files."

If TYPE is unable to locate the file you specify, TYPE will display an error message:

```
C:\> TYPE  FILENAME.EXT
File not found

C:\>
```

If this error message appears, make sure you are spelling the file name correctly and that you are specifying the correct disk drive letter or directory name. If the file of interest resides on a different disk, simply precede the file name with a disk drive letter and colon. The following TYPE command, for example, would display the contents of a file on the disk in drive A.

```
C:\> TYPE  A:FILENAME.EXT   <ENTER>
```

COPY Duplicates a File's Contents

In an office, it is common to make copies of your paper files, either as a backup copy or to distribute to other users. These same scenarios hold true for the files you store on disk. To help you duplicate your disk files, DOS provides the COPY command. Before you begin, format an unused floppy disk as discussed in Chapter 7, "Preparing Disks for Use." Next, place the floppy disk in drive A. Using the COPY command, you will copy files from your hard disk to this floppy.

The COPY command copies the contents of a file in one location to another. To use COPY, therefore, you must specify the name of the file you want to copy, and where you want the file copy to go. As you learned in Chapter 7, the FORMAT command is an external command stored in the file FORMAT.COM. Like all your external DOS commands, FORMAT.COM is in the DOS directory. The following DIR command displays the directory entry for FORMAT.COM:

```
C:\> DIR  \DOS\FORMAT.COM   <ENTER>

 Volume in drive C is DOS
 Volume Serial Number is 1661-AB75
 Directory of C:\DOS

FORMAT    COM     32285 12-13-90    4:09a
      1 file(s)       32285 bytes
                   16497728 bytes free
```

Using the name \DOS\FORMAT.COM, the following COPY command copies the contents of the file FORMAT.COM to the floppy disk in drive A.

```
C:\ COPY  \DOS\FORMAT.COM  A:FORMAT.COM   <ENTER>
    1 File(s) copied
```

When you execute this COPY command, you will see your hard disk's drive activation light illuminate briefly as DOS reads the file's contents. Next, drive A's activation light will illuminate as DOS copies the file's contents to the disk. When COPY successfully completes, COPY will display a message indicating the number of files copied. Using the following DIR command, you can verify that the

COPY operation was successful by viewing FORMAT.COM in the directory listing for drive A.

```
C:\> DIR  A:   <ENTER>

 Volume in drive A has no label
 Volume Serial Number is 0340-0BFE
 Directory of A:\

FORMAT   COM     32285 12-13-90   4:09a
       1 file(s)        32285 bytes
                       329728 bytes free
```

If COPY is unable to locate the file specified, COPY will display an error message indicating it did not find the file:

```
C:\> COPY  FILENAME.EXT  A:FILENAME.EXT   <ENTER>
File not found
     0 File(s) copied

C:\>
```

If this error message appears, double-check the spelling of your file name. Also, make sure you are specifying the correct directory name for the file if necessary.

As shown in Figure 8-1, file copy operations specify the names of a *source file* to copy, and a *destination* or *target file* to which the copy is made.

In the previous examples, the source and destination file names were the same. When you copy files, COPY lets you use any destination name you like. For example, the following COPY command again copies the contents of the file FORMAT.COM to drive A. This time, however, the destination file name is FMAT.COM.

```
C:\> COPY  \DOS\FORMAT.COM  A:FMAT.COM   <ENTER>
         1 File(s) copied
```

A directory listing of drive A reveals entries for both copies of the file.

```
C:\> DIR  A:   <ENTER>

 Volume in drive A has no label
 Volume Serial Number is 0340-0BFE
```

```
Directory of A:\

FORMAT    COM      32285 12-13-90    4:09a
FMAT      COM      32285 12-13-90    4:09a
          2 file(s)        64570 bytes
                          296960 bytes free
```

If you specify only a drive letter for the destination of a file copy, COPY will use the source file's name. The following COPY command copies the contents of the file DISKCOPY.COM from the DOS directory to the disk in drive A.

```
C:\> COPY  \DOS\DISKCOPY.COM  A:  <ENTER>
        1 File(s) copied
```

Because the destination did not include a file name, COPY used the source name, as shown in Figure 8-2.

A directory listing of drive A reveals the file DISKCOPY.COM.

```
C:\> DIR  A:  <ENTER>

 Volume in drive A has no label
 Volume Serial Number is 0340-0BFE
 Directory of A:\

FORMAT    COM      32285 12-13-90    4:09a
FMAT      COM      32285 12-13-90    4:09a
DISKCOPY  COM      11393 12-13-90    4:09a
          3 file(s)        75963 bytes
                          284672 bytes free
```

Figure 8-1.   Each file copy operation has a source and destination file name

File copy operation: C> COPY DISKCOPY.COM A: <ENTER>

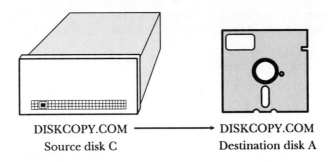

DISKCOPY.COM ──────────▶ DISKCOPY.COM
Source disk C   Destination disk A

Figure 8-2. *If the destination of a file copy operation does not specify a file name,*
COPY will use the source name.

 COPY is a destructive command. This means it will overwrite the contents of a file
whose name matches the destination file name of a COPY operation. For example, the
following command copies the file DISKCOPY.COM to drive A. The destination file
WARNING *name is FMAT.COM.*

```
C:\> COPY  \DOS\DISKCOPY.COM  A:FMAT.COM   <ENTER>
     1 File(s) copied
```

In this case, COPY performed the operation even though a file existed with the
same name as the destination file. The COPY command overwrote the previous
file's contents. If you perform a directory listing of drive A, you will find that the
file size of FMAT.COM matches the size of DISKCOPY.COM, indicating that
FMAT.COM was indeed overwritten.

```
C:\> DIR  A:   <ENTER>

 Volume in drive A has no label
 Volume Serial Number is 0340-0BFE
 Directory of A:\

FORMAT   COM     32285 12-13-90    4:09a
FMAT     COM     11393 12-13-90    4:09a
DISKCOPY COM     11393 12-13-90    4:09a
        3 file(s)      55071 bytes
                      305152 bytes free
```

In later chapters you will learn how to protect your files from being inadvertently deleted or overwritten in this way. For now, however, use the DIR command to determine if a file exists with the same name as the proposed destination file. If a file with the same name exists, choose a different destination name.

RENAME Changes a File's Name

Just as you must change the name of a paper file in your office when the name no longer reflects the file's contents, so it is true for your disk files. The RENAME command lets you rename an existing file. Because RENAME is used so frequently, DOS lets you abbreviate RENAME as REN. In order to rename the files you just copied to the floppy disk in drive A, select drive A as the current drive:

```
C:\> A: <ENTER>

A:\>
```

The format of the RENAME command is RENAME *OLDNAME NEWNAME*. The following RENAME command renames the file FMAT.COM as DCOPY.COM.

```
A:\> RENAME  FMAT.COM  DCOPY.COM  <ENTER>

A:\>
```

If RENAME is successful, RENAME completes, and DOS redisplays its prompt. RENAME does not display a message indicating success. You can verify that the rename operation was successful using DIR:

```
A:\> DIR  <ENTER>

 Volume in drive A has no label
 Volume Serial Number is 0340-0BFE
 Directory of A:\

FORMAT   COM     32285 12-13-90    4:09a
DCOPY    COM     11393 12-13-90    4:09a
DISKCOPY COM     11393 12-13-90    4:09a
        3 file(s)      55071 bytes
                      305152 bytes free
```

Do not confuse renaming a file with moving a file. RENAME will only change the name that appears in a directory listing. RENAME will not move a file from one drive or directory to another. If you try to rename a file from one disk to another, RENAME will display an error message as shown here:

```
A> RENAME  A:DISKCOPY.COM  C:   <ENTER>
Invalid parameter
```

Also, RENAME will not let you rename a file to a name that is already in use. If you try to do so, RENAME will display an error message telling you that a duplicate name exists in the directory:

```
A:\> RENAME  DISKCOPY.COM  FORMAT.COM   <ENTER>
Duplicate file name or file not found
```

If RENAME cannot locate the file you want to rename, RENAME will display this same message, indicating it did not find the file.

NOTE   *Do not rename any file on your disk until you are sure you understand the file's contents and use. Many of your applications programs expect to find files with specific names. If you rename such a file, the application may fail.*

DEL Deletes Files

In an office you can simply throw a file away when it is no longer needed. For files on your disk, you can delete files so DOS can reuse the disk space that previously held the file. The DEL command lets you delete a file from your disk. For example, the following command deletes the file DCOPY.COM of the current drive (in this case, A).

```
A:\> DEL  DCOPY.COM   <ENTER>

A:\>
```

Like RENAME, the DEL command does not display a message indicating its success. In this case, you can use DIR to verify the file DCOPY.COM has been deleted.

```
A:\> DIR   <ENTER>

 Volume in drive A has no label
 Volume Serial Number is 0340-0BFE
 Directory of A:\

FORMAT   COM     32285 12-13-90    4:09a
DISKCOPY COM     11393 12-13-90    4:09a
        2 file(s)       43678 bytes
                       317440 bytes free
```

Note that the amount of available disk space increases when you delete a file.

If you inadvertently delete the wrong file, there are third-party software packages you can use to retrieve the file's contents. If you need to undelete a file in this way, do not copy any files to the disk until you have successfully retrieved the file. If you are using DOS 5, you can use the UNDELETE command discussed in Chapter 28, "DOS 5 Crisis Prevention."

NOTE

If DEL cannot locate the file specified, DEL will display a "File not found" message:

```
A:\> DEL   FILENAME.EXT   <ENTER>
File not found
```

If the file you want to delete is on a different disk, simply precede the file name with the correct drive letter and a colon.

```
C:\> DEL   A:FILENAME.EXT   <ENTER>
```

Do not delete files from your disk whose contents or purpose you don't fully understand. If you delete a critical file, you may prevent an application from running, or even prevent DOS itself from being able to start.

NOTE

Hands On

Using the following COPY command, copy the file DISKCOPY.COM from the DOS directory to the floppy disk in drive A. If drive C is not the current drive, select drive C before you continue.

SUMMARY

The TYPE Command

The TYPE command lets you display a text file's contents on your screen. Text files contain only standard letters and numbers. The format of the TYPE command is as follows.

```
C:\> TYPE  FILENAME.EXT   <ENTER>
```

The COPY Command

The COPY command lets you duplicate a file's contents by copying the file to a new location. File-copy operations refer to the file you are copying as the source file. Likewise, the location you are copying the file to is the destination. The format of the COPY command is as follows.

```
C:\> COPY  SOURCE  DESTINATION   <ENTER>
```

The RENAME Command

The RENAME command lets you change the name of an existing file. Because of its frequency of use, DOS lets you abbreviate RENAME as REN. The RENAME command only renames a file within a directory, RENAME cannot move a file from one disk or directory to another. The format of the RENAME command is as follows.

```
C:\> RENAME  OLDNAME  NEWNAME   <ENTER>
```

The DEL Command

The DEL command lets you remove files from your disk when the files are no longer needed. When deleting a file, DOS makes the disk space the file contained available for reuse. Should you inadvertently delete the wrong file, you may be able to "undelete" the file using a third-party software package or the DOS 5 UNDELETE command. The format of the DEL command is as follows.

```
C:\> DEL FILENAME.EXT   <ENTER>
```

```
C:\> COPY  \DOS\DISKCOPY.COM  A:  <ENTER>
        1 File(s) copied
```

Use the DIR command to verify that the operation was successful.

```
C:\> DIR  A:  <ENTER>
```

Next, repeat the COPY command, but this time, name the target file DC.COM:

```
C:\> COPY  \DOS\DISKCOPY.COM  A:DC.COM  <ENTER>
```

Next, select drive A as the default drive.

```
C:\> A:  <ENTER>
A:\>
```

Now RENAME DC.COM as DCOPY.COM, using the command abbreviation REN.

```
A:\> REN  DC.COM  DCOPY.COM  <ENTER>
```

Use DIR to verify that the rename operation was successful.

```
A:\> DIR  <ENTER>
```

Note the amount of available space on your disk. Using DEL, delete the file DISKCOPY.COM

```
A:\> DEL  DISKCOPY.COM  <ENTER>
```

Using DIR, verify the file was deleted and that DOS has made the file's disk space available for reuse.

Last, use the following TYPE command to display the contents of the file CONFIG.SYS that resides on drive C.

```
A:\> TYPE  C:\CONFIG.SYS  <ENTER>
```

If TYPE displays the "File not found" message, don't worry; you will create a CONFIG.SYS file in Chapter 24.

Review

1. When can the COPY command result in the loss of information from your disk?

2. What file name does COPY use for the destination in the following COPY command, and why?

```
C:\> COPY \DOS\FDISK.EXE A:  <ENTER>
```

3. Why will the following command fail?

```
C:\> REN \DOS\FORMAT.COM A:  <ENTER>
Invalid Parameter
```

4. What is a text file?

5. How do the following commands differ?

```
C:\> RENAME OLDNAME.EXT NEWNAME.EXT  <ENTER>

C:\> REN OLDNAME.EXT NEWNAME.EXT <ENTER>
```

Answers

1. COPY is a destructive command, meaning COPY overwrites the contents of a file with the same name as the destination file when specified in a COPY command. For example, given the following COPY command,

```
C:\> COPY  SOURCE.EXT  DESTIN.EXT  <ENTER>
```

COPY will overwrite the contents of a file named DESTIN.EXT if such a file exists in the current directory. After COPY overwrites the file's contents, the information previously contained in the file is lost.

2. If you only specify a target drive letter as the destination of a file copy operation, COPY will duplicate the source file name for the destination file. In this case, COPY will create a file on drive A named FDISK.EXE.

3. The RENAME command will not move a file from one disk or directory to another. In this case, RENAME is used incorrectly in an attempt to move the file FORMAT.COM from the DOS directory on drive C to the disk in drive A. RENAME cannot perform such processing, and the command will fail.

4. A text file (sometimes called an *ASCII file*) is a file containing only standard letters and numbers. Examples of text files include DOS batch files. The TYPE command lets you view a text file's contents on your screen. Word processing documents and external command files contain non-standard characters that are meaningless to TYPE, and will appear on your screen as unrecognizable characters.

5. The commands are the same. Due to RENAME's frequency of use, DOS lets you abbreviate the RENAME command as REN.

Advanced Concepts

Using DOS *wildcard characters,* you can delete several files at one time. If you are using DOS 4 or later, you can include the /P switch in DEL's command line as shown here.

```
C:\> DEL *.EXT /P  <ENTER>
```

The /P switch directs DEL to individually display each file name and prompt you to determine if you want to delete the file. When you use /P, DEL will display the following prompt for each file.

```
FILENAME.EXT,   Delete (Y/N)?
```

An ASCII or text file is a file that contains standard characters and numbers. Depending on your application, there may be times when you need to combine two or more text files. For example, assume you have three files named START, MIDDLE, and END that contain the contents shown in Figure 8-3.

By placing the plus sign between file names, COPY lets you combine all three of these files into one file named WHOLE, as shown here.

```
C:\> COPY  START+MIDDLE+END  WHOLE  <ENTER>
```

In this case, WHOLE will contain the following.

```
C:\> TYPE  WHOLE  <ENTER>
UNLV      UNLV      UNLV
RUNNIN    RUNNIN    RUNNIN
REBELS!   REBELS!   REBELS!
```

The COPY command even lets you use wildcard characters in such operations. For example, the following command copies all the files with the DAT extension and then appends files with the TXT extension to create a file called LARGE.

```
C:\> COPY  *.DAT+*.TXT  LARGE  <ENTER>
```

Make sure you don't specify the name of the destination file as the last file name to copy. If you do, COPY tries to copy the file into itself and fails:

```
C:\> COPY  ONE+TWO  TWO  <ENTER>
Contents of destination lost before copy
```

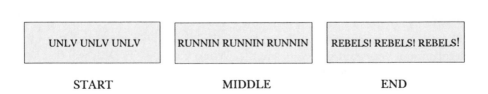

UNLV UNLV UNLV	RUNNIN RUNNIN RUNNIN	REBELS! REBELS! REBELS!
START	MIDDLE	END

Figure 8-3.   *Contents of the files START, MIDDLE, and END*

Many users ask when to use the plus sign in a file copy operation. The most common case is to add a line or two to a batch file. For example, assume you want to add the CLS ("clear the screen") command to the end of your AUTOEXEC.BAT file. Rather than spending time invoking an editor or word processor, you can quickly append a line by copying from the CON device (console) as shown here:

```
C:\> COPY  AUTOEXEC.BAT+CON  AUTOEXEC.BAT  <ENTER>
```

COPY will first copy AUTOEXEC.BAT's current contents, displaying the file's name. Next, DOS will display the word CON, indicating it is ready for you to type from the keyboard. In this case, simply type **CLS** and press F6 followed by ENTER:

```
C:\> COPY  AUTOEXEC.BAT+CON  AUTOEXEC.BAT  <ENTER>
AUTOEXEC.BAT
CON
CLS  <ENTER>
^Z  <ENTER>
        1 File(s) copied

C:\>
```

Abbreviating Directory Commands

Using the *.* wildcard combination, you can reference all of the files in a directory. For example, the following command displays a directory listing for the directory SUBDIR.

```
C:\> DIR  \SUBDIR\*.*  <ENTER>
```

However, by default, if you omit the wildcards, DIR will still display a directory listing of all the files in the directory.

```
C:\> DIR  \SUBDIR  <ENTER>
```

Most DOS commands default to the *.* wildcard combination if you specify only a directory. For example, the following COPY command will copy all of the files in the directory SUBDIR to drive A.

```
C:\> COPY  \SUBDIR  A:  <ENTER>
```

Likewise, the following DEL command will delete all of the files in SUBDIR.

```
C:\> DEL  \SUBDIR   <ENTER>
All files in directory will be deleted!
Are you sure (Y/N)?
```

By letting you abbreviate subdirectory names in this way, DOS saves you time and keystrokes.

Key Terms

Text file   A file containing only standard characters and numbers as opposed to embedded word processor characters or computer instructions. Text files are often called ASCII files.

Source file   The file whose contents a command will copy, display, rename, or delete.

Destination file   The file to which a source file's contents is being written or renamed.

Chapter 9

DOS
Wildcard Characters

In Chapter 8, "Fundamental File Operations," you learned how to copy, delete, rename, and display files. All the commands you issued in Chapter 8 worked with one file at a time. You can save time and typing in many cases by working with groups of files, for example, all the files with the LTR extension in a directory. In this chapter you will learn how to perform file operations on groups of related files using the two DOS *wildcard* characters, * and ?. DOS wildcard characters are so named, because like "wildcards" in a card game, which you can use as cards of your choice, wildcards in file names let DOS substitute letters to match groups of files. DOS wildcards quickly expand the number of files a command can manipulate at one time.

The * Wildcard

Wildcards help you match groups of files with similar names. In theory, wildcards let you specify character positions that DOS can ignore when trying to match file names. The *asterisk* wildcard (*) is the most powerful and most commonly used wildcard. When you place the asterisk in a file name, you tell DOS that you don't care about matching the characters that appear in the wildcard's position, as well as those that follow. The following DIR command, for example, uses the asterisk to list all the files in the DOS directory that have the COM extension.

```
C:\> DIR   \DOS\*.COM   <ENTER>
```

Under DOS 5, the command will display the following:

```
C:\> DIR   \DOS\*.COM   <ENTER>

 Volume in drive C is DOS
 Volume Serial Number is 1661-AB75
 Directory of C:\DOS

FORMAT   COM     32285 12-13-90    4:09a
KEYB     COM     14699 12-13-90    4:09a
MODE     COM     23313 12-13-90    4:09a
SYS      COM     13200 12-13-90    4:09a
UNFORMAT COM     17680 12-13-90    4:09a
DOSKEY   COM      5693 12-13-90    4:09a
MIRROR   COM     17193 12-13-90    4:09a
MORE     COM      2547 12-13-90    4:09a
DOSSHELL COM      4505 12-13-90    4:09a
TREE     COM      6764 12-13-90    4:09a
EDIT     COM       413 12-13-90    4:09a
MSHERC   COM      6947 12-13-90    4:09a
DISKCOMP COM     10428 12-13-90    4:09a
DISKCOPY COM     11393 12-13-90    4:09a
ASSIGN   COM      6271 12-13-90    4:09a
GRAFTABL COM     10053 12-13-90    4:09a
GRAPHICS COM     19374 12-13-90    4:09a
COMMAND  COM     46246 12-13-90    4:09a
        18 file(s)      249004 bytes
                     167493632 bytes free
```

The asterisk directs DOS to ignore the character position where the wildcard appears as well as all the character positions that follow. In this case, because the asterisk appears in the base name's first character position, DOS ignores the entire base name, matching all files that have the COM extension. When you use a wildcard character, DOS examines every file in the directory to determine if the file matches the wildcard. If the file matches, DOS uses the file entry. If the file does not match, DOS continues its search with the next file.

Using the same technique, the following command lists all the files in the DOS directory with the EXE extension:

```
C:\> DIR  \DOS\*.EXE   <ENTER>
```

By placing an asterisk in the second character position of the base name and one in the extension, you can list all the files in the DOS directory that begin with the letter "D."

```
C:\> DIR  \DOS\D*.*   <ENTER>
```

Under DOS 5, the command will display the following:

```
C:\> DIR  \DOS\D*.*   <ENTER>

 Volume in drive C is DOS
 Volume Serial Number is 1661-AB75
 Directory of C:\DOS

DISPLAY  SYS     15682 12-13-90    4:09a
DEBUG    EXE     20506 12-13-90    4:09a
DOSKEY   COM      5693 12-13-90    4:09a
DOSSHELL VID     15942 12-13-90    4:09a
DOSSHELL INI     17021 03-01-91    9:37p
DOSSHELL COM      4505 12 13 90    4:09a
DOSSHELL EXE    230388 12-13-90    4:09a
DOSSHELL GRB      4422 12-13-90    4:09a
DOSSWAP  EXE     18548 12-13-90    4:09a
DOSSHELL HLP    137646 12-13-90    4:09a
DRIVES   EXE     33011 01-16-89   12:00p
DOSHELP  HLP      5266 12-13-90    4:09a
DISKCOMP COM     10428 12-13-90    4:09a
DISKCOPY COM     11393 12-13-90    4:09a
DOSUTIL  MEU      6660 10-06-88   12:00a
DRIVER   SYS      5384 12-13-90    4:09a
        16 file(s)       542495 bytes
                      167489536 bytes free
```

In this case, the wildcard combination tells DOS you only care about the first letter of the file's base name. If you replace the extension with COM, DIR will display the following.

```
C:\> DIR   \DOS\D*.COM   <ENTER>

 Volume in drive C is DOS
 Volume Serial Number is 1661-AB75
 Directory of C:\DOS

DOSKEY   COM       5693 12-13-90    4:09a
DOSSHELL COM       4505 12-13-90    4:09a
DISKCOMP COM      10428 12-13-90    4:09a
DISKCOPY COM      11393 12-13-90    4:09a
        4 file(s)        32019 bytes
                    167485440 bytes free
```

Remember, once DOS encounters the asterisk within a file name, DOS ignores all the characters that follow. For example, consider the following DIR command.

```
C:\> DIR   \DOS\D*BUG.COM   <ENTER>
```

Because the asterisk wildcard appears in the second character position, DOS ignores all the characters that follow (in this case, DOS ignores "BUG"). As a result, DOS displays

```
C:\> DIR   \DOS\D*BUG.COM   <ENTER>

 Volume in drive C is DOS
 Volume Serial Number is 1661-AB75
 Directory of C:\DOS

DOSKEY   COM       5693 12-13-90    4:09a
DOSSHELL COM       4505 12-13-90    4:09a
DISKCOMP COM      10428 12-13-90    4:09a
DISKCOPY COM      11393 12-13-90    4:09a
        4 file(s)        32019 bytes
                    167481344 bytes free
```

Last, the following command displays all the files in the DOS directory.

```
C:\> DIR   \DOS\*.*   <ENTER>
```

The wildcard combination, in this case, tells DOS to ignore both the base name and extension. DIR, by default, does this anyway. As a result, the following DIR command is equivalent.

```
C:\> DIR  \DOS   <ENTER>
```

Using the * for Other Operations

The previous examples used the asterisk wildcard with DIR to illustrate how DOS uses the wildcard to let you select groups of files. Most of the DOS file manipulation commands you will use throughout this book support the DOS wildcards. In this section you will use the asterisk wildcard with COPY, RENAME, and DEL. To begin, place a formatted blank disk in drive A. Next, the following COPY command copies all the DOS commands that begin with the letter "D" with the COM extension to the disk in drive A.

```
C:\> COPY  \DOS\D*.COM  A:   <ENTER>
```

In this case, COPY will copy each matching file to drive A, displaying the file's name as it begins the copy operation:

```
C:\> COPY  \DOS\D*.COM  A:   <ENTER>
C:\DOS\DOSKEY.COM
C:\DOS\DOSSHELL.COM
C:\DOS\DISKCOMP.COM
C:\DOS\DISKCOPY.COM
        4 file(s) copied
```

As discussed in Chapter 8, if you don't specify a destination file name, COPY uses the source file name. A directory listing of drive A reveals that DOS has copied the files as desired.

```
C:\> DIR  A:   <ENTER>

Volume in drive A has no label
Volume Serial Number is 0340-0BFE
Directory of A:\

DOSKEY    COM       5693 12-13-90    4:09a
DOSSHELL COM       4505 12-13-90    4:09a
```

```
DISKCOMP COM       10428 12-13-90    4:09a
DISKCOPY COM       11393 12-13-90    4:09a
        4 file(s)          32019 bytes
                          327680 bytes free
```

In a similar way, this command copies to drive A all the files in the DOS directory that begin with the letter "A."

```
C:\> COPY  \DOS\A*.*  A:   <ENTER>
C:\DOS\ANSI.SYS
C:\DOS\APPEND.EXE
C:\DOS\ATTRIB.EXE
C:\DOS\ASSIGN.COM
        4 file(s) copied
```

The disk in drive A now contains the following.

```
C:\> DIR  A:   <ENTER>

Volume in drive A has no label
Volume Serial Number is 0340-0BFE
Directory of A:\

DOSKEY    COM      5693 12-13-90    4:09a
DOSSHELL  COM      4505 12-13-90    4:09a
DISKCOMP  COM     10428 12-13-90    4:09a
DISKCOPY  COM     11393 12-13-90    4:09a
ANSI      SYS      8868 12-13-90    4:09a
APPEND    EXE     10614 12-13-90    4:09a
ATTRIB    EXE     15732 12-13-90    4:09a
ASSIGN    COM      6271 12-13-90    4:09a
        8 file(s)          73504 bytes
                          283648 bytes free
```

Disks, like cassette or video tapes, do not have an unlimited amount of disk space. If, for example, you try to copy all the files from the DOS directory to the disk in drive A, the floppy disk will eventually run out of space. As a result, DOS will display the following error message:

```
Insufficient disk space
```

Should this error message occur, you can use DIR to determine the last file successfully copied and resume the copy operation with a new floppy disk. As you will learn in Chapter 23, "Advanced File Manipulation," the COPY command really doesn't give you an easy way to resume the copy operation at the last file copied. A better way to copy a large number of files to many floppy disks is to use the XCOPY command, presented in Chapter 23.

Select drive A as the default drive.

```
C:\>     <ENTER>

A:\>
```

Next, the following RENAME command renames all the files beginning with the word "DISK" (such as DISKCOPY and DISKCOMP), replacing "DISK" with the letters "FLOP" (yielding FLOPCOPY and FLOPCOMP).

```
A:\> REN  DISK*.*  FLOP*.*  <ENTER>
```

A directory listing of drive A reveals REN has successfully renamed the files.

```
C:\> DIR  <ENTER>

 Volume in drive A has no label
 Volume Serial Number is 0340-0BFE
 Directory of A:\

DOSKEY   COM     5693 12-13-90    4:09a
DOSSHELL COM     4505 12-13-90    4:09a
FLOPCOMP COM    10428 12-13-90    4:09a
FLOPCOPY COM    11393 12-13-90    4:09a
ANSI     SYS     8868 12-13-90    4:09a
APPEND   EXE    10614 12-13-90    4:09a
ATTRIB   EXE    15732 12-13-90    4:09a
ASSIGN   COM     6271 12-13-90    4:09a
        8 file(s)       73504 bytes
                       283648 bytes free
```

Likewise, the following command renames the file ANSI.SYS to ANSIFILE.SYS.

```
A:\> REN ANSI.* ANSIFILE.*  <ENTER>
```

In this case, the wildcard character tells DOS to leave the extension unchanged.

```
A:\> DIR   <ENTER>
 Volume in drive A has no label
 Volume Serial Number is 0340-0BFE
 Directory of A:\

DOSKEY   COM      5693 12-13-90    4:09a
DOSSHELL COM      4505 12-13-90    4:09a
FLOPCOMP COM     10428 12-13-90    4:09a
FLOPCOPY COM     11393 12-13-90    4:09a
ANSIFILE SYS      8868 12-13-90    4:09a
APPEND   EXE     10614 12-13-90    4:09a
ATTRIB   EXE     15732 12-13-90    4:09a
ASSIGN   COM      6271 12-13-90    4:09a
        8 file(s)       73504 bytes
                       283648 bytes free
```

You need to be careful using the DEL command with DOS wildcards. If you specify the wrong wildcard combination, you can inadvertently delete needed files from your disk. To reduce the possibility of inadvertent file deletions, you may want to first issue a DIR command using the wildcard combination you plan to use with DEL. By using DIR first, you can verify that DIR lists the files you really want to delete and no others.

The following command deletes all the files with the COM extension from the floppy disk. Make sure drive A is the default drive before you execute this command.

```
A:\> DEL *.COM   <ENTER>
```

A directory listing of drive A reveals DEL has successfully deleted the files.

```
A:\> DIR   <ENTER>

 Volume in drive A has no label
 Volume Serial Number is 0340-0BFE
 Directory of A:\

ANSIFILE SYS      8868 12-13-90    4:09a
APPEND   EXE     10614 12-13-90    4:09a
ATTRIB   EXE     15732 12-13-90    4:09a
        3 file(s)       35214 bytes
                       325632 bytes free
```

Because using the wildcard combination *.* with DEL can have a devastating effect on your files if you invoke it in error, DEL will first prompt you to verify you really want to delete all the files in the directory when you use *.* as shown here:

```
A:\> DEL *.*   <ENTER>
All files in directory will be deleted!
Are you sure (Y/N)?
```

If you are sure you are deleting the correct files, type **Y** and press ENTER, and DEL will delete the files. If you aren't sure, type **N** and press ENTER. Use DIR to verify the correct files will be deleted.

The ? Wildcard

As discussed, when DOS encounters the asterisk wildcard, it ignores the characters in the wildcard's position and all characters that follow. The *question mark* (?) wildcard gives you finer control over character matching. The question mark wildcard provides a one-for-one match. In other words, when DOS encounters the ? wildcard, DOS ignores only the character appearing in the same position as the wildcard. DOS still considers all the characters that follow the wildcard.

The question mark wildcard is less frequently used than the asterisk. The following examples illustrate its use. To begin, the following DIR command displays COM files in a DOS directory that begin with the letters "DISKCO."

```
C:\> DIR  \DOS\DISKCO??   <ENTER>

 Volume in drive C is DOS
 Volume Serial Number is 1661-AB75
 Directory of C:\DOS

DISKCOMP COM      10428 12-13-90    4:09a
DISKCOPY COM      11393 12-13-90    4:09a
        2 file(s)       21821 bytes
                    167514112 bytes free
```

In this case, the two question mark wildcards direct DIR to ignore the last two characters of the file name. Note that the DIR command does not include a file extension. By default, if you don't specify a file extension, DIR uses * to match all extensions.

This command tries to display the same two files, using only the letters "DISK" and a single question mark.

```
C:\> DIR  \DOS\DISK?  <ENTER>

 Volume in drive C is DOS
 Volume Serial Number is 1661-AB75
 Directory of C:\DOS

File not found
```

In this case, DOS displays the "File not found" message because the directory does not contain any five-letter file names that begin with the letters "DISK." Remember, the question mark wildcard only replaces a single character.

Last, this command displays the files in the DOS directory whose base names are only four characters or less.

```
C:\> DIR  \DOS\????  <ENTER>
```

Under DOS 5, the command will display

```
C:\> DIR  \DOS\????  <ENTER>

 Volume in drive C is DOS
 Volume Serial Number is 1661-AB75
 Directory of C:\DOS

.             <DIR>        10-16-90    4:44p
..            <DIR>        10-16-90    4:44p
EGA      SYS      4885 12-13-90    4:09a
ANSI     SYS      8868 12-13-90    4:09a
KEYB     COM     14699 12-13-90    4:09a
MODE     COM     23313 12-13-90    4:09a
SYS      COM     13200 12-13-90    4:09a
FC       EXE     18298 12-13-90    4:09a
MEM      EXE     22104 12-13-90    4:09a
MORE     COM      2547 12-13-90    4:09a
TREE     COM      6764 12-13-90    4:09a
EDIT     HLP     18431 12-13-90    4:09a
LINK     EXE     43988 10-06-88   12:00a
```

```
HELP     EXE     11443 12-13-90     4:09a
EDIT     COM       413 12-13-90     4:09a
COMP     EXE     13930 12-13-90     4:09a
FIND     EXE      6642 12-13-90     4:09a
SORT     EXE      6618 12-13-90     4:09a
4201     CPI      6404 12-13-90     4:09a
4208     CPI       720 12-13-90     4:09a
5202     CPI       370 12-13-90     4:09a
EGA      CPI     49068 12-13-90     4:09a
UMB      TXT     27574 12-13-90     4:09a
JOIN     EXE     17614 12-13-90     4:09a
LCD      CPI     10703 12-13-90     4:09a
        25 file(s)      328596 bytes
                    167514112 bytes free
```

The question mark results in a one-for-one match. In this case, a single letter matches, two letters match, three letters match, and finally, four letters match.

Hands On

Using the DIR command, list all files in the DOS directory with the EXE extension.

```
C:\> DIR  \DOS\*.EXE   <ENTER>
```

Next, change the command slightly to display the files with the SYS extension.

```
C:\> DIR  \DOS\*.SYS   <ENTER>
```

Next, list the files that begin with "C."

```
C:\> DIR  \DOS\C*   <ENTER>
```

By changing the command, you can display only files with the COM extension that begin with "C."

```
C:\> DIR  \DOS\C*.COM   <ENTER>
```

SUMMARY

* Wildcard

The asterisk wildcard helps you specify "don't care" character positions in file names so that DOS will match groups of files. When DOS encounters the asterisk, DOS ignores the characters in the position containing the wildcard as well as all the characters that follow it. The following command, for example, lists all the files in a directory with the BAT extension.

```
C:\> DIR *.BAT   <ENTER>
```

? Wildcard

The question mark wildcard lets you specify a single "don't care" position in file operations. When DOS encounters the question mark, DOS ignores only the character in the position containing the question mark. The following command, for example, lists files beginning with the letters DISKCO.

```
C:\> DIR DISKCO??   <ENTER>
```

Place an unused formatted disk in drive A. Next, issue the following command to copy all the files with the SYS extension from the DOS directory to drive A.

```
C:\> COPY  \DOS\*.SYS  A:  <ENTER>
```

Use the following DIR command to verify that the copy operation was successful.

```
C:\> DIR  A:  <ENTER>
```

Next, use the following command to copy the files from the DOS directory that begin with "F" to drive A.

```
C:\> COPY  \DOS\F*.*  A:  <ENTER>
```

Select drive A as the current drive.

```
C:\> A: <ENTER>

A:\>
```

Use the following RENAME command to rename the file FDISK.COM to F.COM.

```
A:\> REN FDISK.* F.*  <ENTER>
```

Use DIR to verify that the rename operation was successful.

```
A:\> DIR  <ENTER>
```

Next, delete all the files with the SYS extension.

```
A:\> DEL  *.SYS  <ENTER>
```

Using this same technique, delete all the files from the floppy disk.

```
A:\> DEL  *.*  <ENTER>
```

To prevent you from inadvertently deleting all the files in the directory, DEL will first prompt you with the following.

```
All files in directory will be deleted!
Are you sure (Y/N)?
```

To delete the files, type **Y** and press ENTER.

Review

1. What is a wildcard?

2. What command would list files in the DOS directory that begin with "B"?

3. What is the command to copy all the files with the SYS extension from the DOS directory to a disk in drive A?

4. How does the asterisk wildcard (*) differ from the question mark (?).

5. What is the function of the following command?

```
A:\> REN  FILENAME.*  F.*  <ENTER>
```

Answers

1. A wildcard is a symbol you can place within a DOS file name that directs DOS to ignore the symbol's position, and depending on the wildcard, the character positions that follow, to match groups of similarly named files. DOS supports the * and ? wildcards. Wildcards exist to help you perform file manipulation commands on groups of files.

2. The command to list the files in the DOS directory that begin with "B" is

```
C:\> DIR  \DOS\B*  <ENTER>
```

3. The command to copy all the files with the SYS extension from the DOS directory to a disk in drive A is

```
C:\> COPY  \DOS\*.SYS  A:  <ENTER>
```

4. The asterisk wildcard (*) directs DOS to not only ignore the character in the wildcard's position, but also the characters in all the positions following the wildcard. The question mark wildcard, on the other hand, directs DOS to ignore file name character positions on a one-for-one basis.

5. The command renames every file whose base name is FILENAME to the base name F, regardless of the file's extension.

Advanced Concepts

Most of the DOS commands support wildcard characters. For those that don't, you can create a batch file named WILD.BAT that lets you add wildcard support.

```
@ECHO OFF
REM WILD.BAT
REM Written By: Kris Jamsa
REM Function: Lets commands that aren't written to support
REM wildcard characters behave as if they were.
REM Format: WILD CommandName Parameters
REM Example: WILD TYPE *.BAT *.SYS

IF '%1'=='' GOTO NO_COMMAND
REM Save the desired command in the named parameter COMMAND
SET COMMAND=%1

REM Loop through the desired file names
:LOOP
  SHIFT
  FOR %%I IN (%1) DO %COMMAND% %%I
IF NOT '%1'=='' GOTO LOOP

REM No more files remain
GOTO DONE
:NO_COMMAND
ECHO WILD: Must specify desired command
:DONE
```

To use wildcards with the TYPE command, for example, you can invoke WILD as shown.

```
C:\> WILD TYPE *.BAT   <ENTER>
```

In addition to supporting wildcards, this batch file lets you place several file names in the command line, as shown here:

```
C:\> WILD TYPE \AUTOEXEC.BAT \CONFIG.SYS   <ENTER>
```

Because the batch file uses named parameters, it requires DOS version 3.3 or later. The batch file uses the FOR command to provide wildcard support and the SHIFT command to access multiple files.

If you don't want to create the batch file, or if you are not using DOS version 3.3 or higher, you can also combine the FOR command with TYPE from the command line, as shown here:

```
C:\> FOR %I IN (*.BAT) DO TYPE %I   <ENTER>
```

In this case, FOR behaves as it would within a batch file. Note, however, that when you invoke FOR from the DOS prompt, you only include one percent (%) sign before the variable name. The FOR command is discussed in detail in Chapter 17, "Getting the Most from Batch Files."

Key Terms

Wildcard   A character or symbol that DOS uses in matching groups of files. DOS supports the asterisk (*) and question mark (?) wildcards.

Chapter 10

Directories

In Chapter 4, "Getting Started with DOS Files," you found that DOS helps you organize files on your disk by grouping related files into lists called directories. As you learned to work with DIR and COPY, you made extensive use of files in the DOS directory. Almost every software program you buy will eventually have its own directory. In most cases, the installation program that places the program into your hard disk will create the directory for you. As you create your own files, however, it won't take long before you will want to organize them by creating your own directories. In this chapter you will learn how to create a directory using MKDIR, how to select a specific directory as the default using CHDIR, and how to use RMDIR to remove a directory when it is no longer needed.

The Root Directory

When you first format a disk, DOS creates a single directory on your disk called the *root directory*. The root directory is so named because all the directories you later create on your disk grow from the root, much like the branches of a tree. Conceptually, the root directory is much like a filing cabinet—you can put lots of files loose in the cabinet, or you can create drawers (directories)—or even smaller drawers (called subdirectories) with different names to put your files into to organize them. When you create a directory in the root to store specific files, you essentially label one of the filing cabinet drawers.

DOS uses the backslash character (\) to represent "directory" or "subdirectory." The backslash alone represents the root directory—since the root is the "home" immediately after the backslash. Using this symbol, the following DIR command lists the files and directories that reside in the root.

```
C:\> DIR  \   <ENTER>
```

Make sure you use the backslash character (\), and *not* the forward slash (/). Depending on the different applications programs on your disk, the number and names of directories in the root will differ. At a minimum, you will probably find a directory entry named DOS. In addition, you will probably see file entries for COMMAND.COM, CONFIG.SYS, and AUTOEXEC.BAT. As you will learn, DOS uses these three files each time DOS starts. As a rule, these are the only files you should have in the root directory. In other words, the root "filing cabinet" should contain primarily directories (drawers), not big piles of loose folders (files).

The Current Directory

You have learned that DOS lets you select one disk drive as the current or default drive that, unless you specify otherwise, DOS searches for external commands and files. In the same way, DOS lets you select one of your directories as the *current directory,* in which DOS searches unless you tell it otherwise.

Conceptually, selecting the current directory is equivalent to closing one drawer of a filing cabinet and opening another—when you ask for a file, DOS looks in the open drawer. By default, when your computer starts, the root directory is the current directory. To change the current directory, you must use the CHDIR command.

Tracking the Current Directory with the DOS Prompt

As you have learned, when you change the current drive, DOS changes its prompt to include the current drive letter. For example, watch how the prompt changes as you change the default drive from C to A.

```
C> A:   <ENTER>

A>
```

To help you keep track of the directory you are currently using, you can direct DOS to include the current directory as well as the current drive in the prompt. To do so, issue the following PROMPT command (PROMPT doesn't care about the case of the letters used).

```
C> PROMPT  $P$G   <ENTER>

C:\>
```

The backslash appears between the colon and the greater-than (>) character. This indicates that you are in the root directory of drive C. The PROMPT command is an internal DOS command that lets you define and customize the DOS system prompt, as you will learn in Chapter 43, "DOS System Commands." Although users sometimes get very creative with their prompts, I recommend using the prompt PG. The characters "$P " direct DOS to display the current drive and directory, while the characters "$G " direct DOS to display the greater-than character (>). As you will see, using this system prompt, you can easily determine the current directory.

CHDIR Changes the Current Directory

Changing the current directory is similar to opening a different drawer in a filing cabinet—DOS will look in the open drawer first. The DOS command to CHange DIRectories is CHDIR. The following, for example, selects the directory DOS as the current directory. The spaces after the command are optional; we will use two spaces for ease of reading and understanding.

```
C:\> CHDIR  \DOS   <ENTER>

C:\DOS>
```

Note how the system prompt changes to reflect the current directory. The backslash now has a name after it. If your prompt does not change, type **PROMPT PG** and press ENTER.

The DOS subdirectory is now the current directory. Unless you tell DOS to look elsewhere, DOS will look in this directory by default. For example, if you invoke the DIR command, DIR will display the list of external DOS commands among the files shown here.

```
C:\DOS> DIR   <ENTER>

 Volume in drive C is DOS
 Volume Serial Number is 1661-AB75
 Directory of C:\DOS
```

```
.                <DIR>       10-16-90    4:44p
..               <DIR>       10-16-90    4:44p
EGA      SYS       4885  12-13-90    4:09a
DISPLAY  SYS      15682  12-13-90    4:09a
FORMAT   COM      32285  12-13-90    4:09a
ANSI     SYS       8868  12-13-90    4:09a
 :        :         :         :          :
 :        :         :         :          :
NLSFUNC  EXE       6924  12-13-90    4:09a
PRINTER  SYS      18760  12-13-90    4:09a
SUBST    EXE      18350  12-13-90    4:09a
COMMAND  COM      46246  12-13-90    4:09a
        90 file(s)      2236185 bytes
                       16022592 bytes free
```

You may recall from before that, to list the files in the DOS directory, you had to specify the directory name DOS in the DIR command, as shown here.

```
C:\> DIR  \DOS   <ENTER>
```

The current directory then was the root directory, and you had to tell DOS explicitly to look elsewhere. Now, since you are in the DOS directory, you can simply execute the following command to display the directory entry for FORMAT.COM.

```
C:\> DIR  FORMAT.COM   <ENTER>

 Volume in drive C is DOS
 Volume Serial Number is 1661-AB75
 Directory of C:\DOS

FORMAT   COM      32285  12-13-90    4:09a
       1 file(s)       32285 bytes
                     167022592 bytes free
```

DOS locates FORMAT.COM because the file is in the current directory. Thus, you could copy the file to a disk in drive A, as follows.

```
C:\DOS> COPY  FORMAT.COM  A: <ENTER>
        1 File(s) copied
```

As you can see, by changing the current directory, you make it much easier to access files. To change from the DOS directory back to the root, you can use CHDIR as follows.

```
C:\DOS> CHDIR  \   <ENTER>

C:\>
```

Because CHDIR is so frequently used, DOS lets you abbreviate CHDIR as simply CD. Using the CD abbreviation, the following command selects the DOS directory as the current directory.

```
C:\> CD \DOS   <ENTER>
```

Now perform a directory listing. Before DIR displays the directory entries, DIR will display a line that tells you the corresponding directory name.

```
C:\DOS> DIR   <ENTER>

 Volume in drive C is DOS
 Volume Serial Number is 1661-AB75
 Directory of C:\DOS

 .              <DIR>      10-16-90   4:44p
 ..             <DIR>      10-16-90   4:44p
EGA      SYS     4885 12-13-90   4:09a
   :       :        :        :        :
SUBST    EXE    18350 12-13-90   4:09a
COMMAND  COM    46246 12-13-90   4:09a
        90 file(s)     2236185 bytes
                      16022592 bytes free
```

If you invoke the CHDIR command without including a directory name, CHDIR will simply display the current directory:

```
C:\DOS> CHDIR   <ENTER>
C:\DOS
```

If you include a drive letter, CHDIR will display the current directory for the drive specified:

```
C:\DOS> CD  A: <ENTER>
A:\
```

MKDIR Creates Directories

DOS directories exist to help you organize your files. When you install new software packages, most installation programs will create a unique directory for you. In some cases, however, you will need to create your own directories. The MKDIR (MaKe DIRectory) command lets you create directories on your disk. To begin, you can use MKDIR to create a directory named TESTDIR, as shown.

```
C:\> MKDIR  \TESTDIR  <ENTER>
```

Using the DIR command, you can be sure MKDIR created the directory:

```
C:\> DIR  \  <ENTER>

 Volume in drive C is DOS
 Volume Serial Number is 1661-AB75
 Directory of C:\

COMMAND   COM     46246 12-13-90    4:09a
AUTOEXEC  BAT       108 03-01-91    9:27p
CONFIG    SYS       102 03-01-91    9:27p
DOS          <DIR>      10-16-90    4:44p
DISKUTIL     <DIR>      10-16-90    4:55p
BATCH        <DIR>      01-28-91   10:13a
TESTDIR      <DIR>      03-03-91   10:47a
       7 file(s)      46456 bytes
                   16014400 bytes free
```

In this case, creating the TESTDIR directory in the root is conceptually similar to labeling a filing cabinet drawer "TESTDIR," as shown in Figure 10-1.

Using CD (the abbreviation for the CHDIR command), select TESTDIR as the current directory.

C:\> MKDIR \TESTDIR <ENTER>

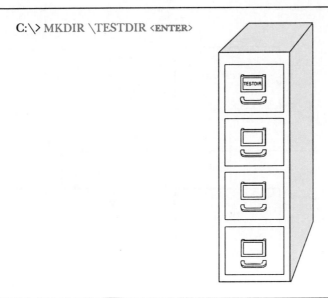

Figure 10-1. *Using MKDIR is similar to adding a new label to a filing cabinet drawer*

```
C:\> CD  \TESTDIR  <ENTER>
```

Using DIR, you can display the directory's contents:

```
C:\TESTDIR> DIR  <ENTER>

Volume in drive C is DOS
Volume Serial Number is 1661-AB75
Directory of C:\TESTDIR

.          <DIR>     03-03-91  10:47a
..         <DIR>     03-03-91  10:47a
    2 file(s)            0 bytes
               16010304 bytes free
```

Every directory you create has two predefined directory entries—"." and ".."—that advanced DOS users can use to simplify commands. For now, simply understand

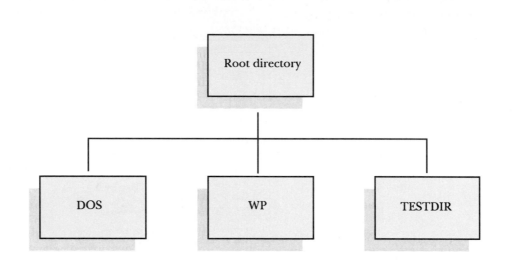

Figure 10-2   Directory tree for DOS, WP, and TESTDIR

that these two directory entries will automatically appear in every directory you create.

The directories on your disk are often referred to as a *directory tree* that grows from the root. Here's why. Assume, for example, your disk contains a DOS directory, a WordPerfect directory, (WP), and the TESTDIR directory you just created. Pictorially, your directory structure will appear similar to Figure 10-2.

As you work with your word processor, you may soon have many different letters, reports, and memos in the WP directory. To improve your file organization, you might create directories within WP named LETTERS, REPORTS, and MEMOS to store the corresponding files. When you create these directories, your directory tree grows, as shown in Figure 10-3.

Conceptually, these lower-level directories are equivalent to placing dividers within the WP drawer (see Figure 10-4).

As you work with your computer, you will use MKDIR to create directories to hold new software programs or to further organize existing directories.

MKDIR is so frequently used that DOS lets you abbreviate MKDIR as MD. Using MD, the following commands create three directories within TESTDIR.

```
C:\TESTDIR> MD   \TESTDIR\MEMOS      <ENTER>
C:\TESTDIR> MD   \TESTDIR\LETTERS    <ENTER>
C:\TESTDIR> MD   \TESTDIR\REPORTS    <ENTER>
```

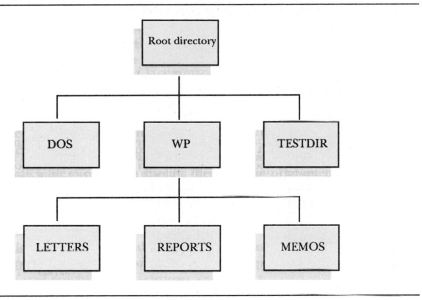

Figure 10-3.   *Using additional directories to organize WP*

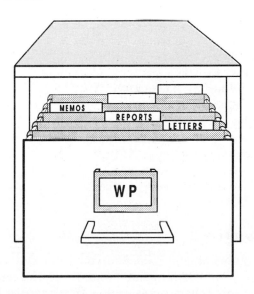

Figure 10-4.   *Dividing a directory for improved file organization*

A directory listing of TESTDIR reveals the three directories:

```
C:\TESTDIR> DIR   <ENTER>

 Volume in drive C is DOS
 Volume Serial Number is 1661-AB75
 Directory of C:\TESTDIR

.               <DIR>       03-03-91   10:47a
..              <DIR>       03-03-91   10:47a
MEMOS           <DIR>       03-03-91   10:51a
LETTERS         <DIR>       03-03-91   10:51a
REPORTS         <DIR>       03-03-91   10:51a
        5 file(s)            0 bytes
                    16098016 bytes free
```

Using CHDIR (CD), you can select the LETTERS directory:

```
C:\TESTDIR> CD  \TESTDIR\LETTERS    <ENTER>
```

A directory listing reveals that DOS has, as always, created the directory entries
"." and ".." within the directory.

```
C:\TESTDIR\LETTERS> DIR   <ENTER>

 Volume in drive C is DOS
 Volume Serial Number is 1661-AB75
 Directory of C:\TESTDIR\LETTERS

.           <DIR>       03-03-91   10:47a
..          <DIR>       03-03-91   10:47a
    2 file(s)            0 bytes
                16098016 bytes free
```

Naming Your Directories

As you should assign meaningful names to your files, the same is true for the
directories you create. Like DOS file names, your directories can have an eight-character base name and a three-character extension. In most cases, however, users only
use the eight character base name for directories. As you will recall from Chapter 4
the three-character extension indicates a file's type, which really isn't meaningful

with respect to directories. All the characters you can use in DOS file names are valid for DOS directory names.

RMDIR Removes Directories

As there are times when you no longer need a group of files stored in a filing cabinet, so the same is true for directories on your disk. The RMDIR (ReMove DIRectory) command lets you remove an unused directory from your disk. The directory must be empty (containing no files or directories) and must *not* be the current directory.

Using CHDIR, select the directory TESTDIR as the current directory.

```
C:\> CD  \TESTDIR   <ENTER>
```

Next, the following command removes the directory LETTERS from the directory TESTDIR.

```
C:\TESTDIR> RMDIR  \TESTDIR\LETTERS   <ENTER>
```

A directory listing reveals RMDIR has removed the directory:

```
C:\TESTDIR> DIR   <ENTER>

 Volume in drive C is DOS
 Volume Serial Number is 1661-AB75
 Directory of C:\TESTDIR

 .              <DIR>      03-03-91  10:47a
 ..             <DIR>      03-03-91  10:47a
 MEMOS          <DIR>      03-03-91  10:51a
 REPORTS        <DIR>      03-03-91  10:51a
        4 file(s)           0 bytes
                   167002112 bytes free
```

Due to its frequency of use, DOS lets you abbreviate RMDIR as RD. Using the RD abbreviation, the following command removes the directory MEMOS from the TESTDIR directory.

```
C:\TESTDIR> RD  \TESTDIR\MEMOS   <ENTER>
```

RMDIR will not let you remove the current directory or a directory containing files or directory entries. If, for example, you try to remove TESTDIR, RMDIR will display an error message similar to the following.

```
Attempt to remove current directory - \TESTDIR
```

Last, remove the directory REPORTS and then change to the root directory and remove the directory TESTDIR, as shown.

```
C:\TESTDIR> RD  \TESTDIR\REPORTS  <ENTER>
C:\TESTDIR> CD  \  <ENTER>
C:\> RD  \TESTDIR  <ENTER>
```

Hands On

Using the CHDIR command, select the DOS directory as the current directory.

```
C:\> CHDIR  \DOS  <ENTER>
```

Use the following DIR command to display the files in the directory.

```
C:\DOS> DIR  /P  <ENTER>
```

Note that DIR displays the directory name at the top of the directory listing.
   Next, use the following CD command to select the root directory.

```
C:\DOS> CD  \  <ENTER>
```

Using the DIR command, note the other directories in the root. Use CHDIR to move between each directory and the root.
   Next, using MKDIR, create the directory MUSIC, as shown here.

```
C:\> MKDIR \MUSIC  <ENTER>
```

Root Directory (\)

Every DOS disk begins with one directory called the root, within which you can store files and other directories. The root is so named because, like the branches of a tree, all the directories you later create on your disk to store files grow from the root. DOS uses the backslash character (\) to represent the root.

The CHDIR Command

The current directory contains the list of files and commands that DOS examines by default, unless you tell DOS to look elsewhere. The CHDIR command lets you change the current directory. In fact, CHDIR is an abbreviation for CHange DIRectory. Conceptually, changing the current directory is the same as closing one drawer of a filing cabinet and opening another. CHDIR is so frequently used that DOS lets you abbreviate CHDIR as CD. The following commands select the DOS directory as the current directory.

```
C:\> CHDIR \DOS   <ENTER>

C:\> CD \DOS   <ENTER>
```

If you invoke CHDIR without including a directory name, CHDIR will simply display the current directory.

The MKDIR Command

The MKDIR command lets you create directories on your disk to improve your file organization. In fact, MKDIR stands for MaKe DIRectory. As you work with DOS, you will make directories to hold new software programs and to improve your file organization by further dividing existing directories. Due to its frequency of use, DOS lets you abbreviate MKDIR as simply MD. The following commands create a directory named BUSINESS.

```
C:\> MKDIR  \BUSINESS   <ENTER>

C:\> MD  \BUSINESS   <ENTER>
```

SUMMARY

The RMDIR Command

The RMDIR command lets you remove a directory from your disk. In fact, RMDIR stands for ReMove DIRectory. Before you can remove a directory, the directory must be empty and cannot be the current directory. Due to its frequency of use, DOS lets you abbreviate RMDIR as RD. The following commands remove a directory named BUSINESS from your disk.

```
C:\> RMDIR  \BUSINESS  <ENTER>

C:\> RD  \BUSINESS  <ENTER>
```

Use DIR to verify the directory exists.

```
C:\> DIR  <ENTER>
```

Next, using the MD abbreviation, create the directories JAZZ and ROCK within MUSIC, as shown here.

```
C:\> MD  \MUSIC\JAZZ  <ENTER>
C:\> MD  \MUSIC\ROCK  <ENTER>
```

Use the following DIR command to display the directory entries.

```
C:\> DIR  \MUSIC  <ENTER>
```

Next, using RMDIR, remove the directories JAZZ and ROCK.

```
C:\> RMDIR  \MUSIC\JAZZ  <ENTER>
C:\> RMDIR  \MUSIC\ROCK  <ENTER>
```

Last, using the RD abbreviation, remove the MUSIC directory.

```
C:\> RD  \MUSIC  <ENTER>
```

Review

1. What is the current directory?

2. What is the root directory?

3. What are the directory entries "." and ".."?

4. Before DOS can remove a directory, what two conditions must be met?

5. Given a disk containing only the root directory, what commands must you execute to create the directory tree shown in Figure 10-5?

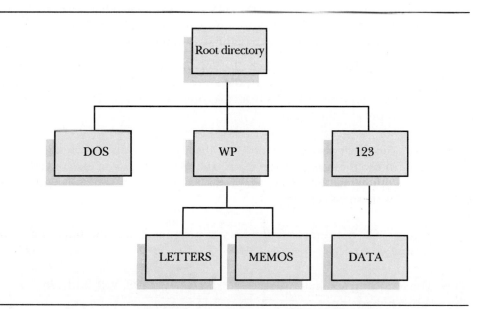

Figure 10-5. Adding new directories to the root directory

6. Given the directory tree in Figure 10-5, what commands must you execute to produce the directory tree shown here?:

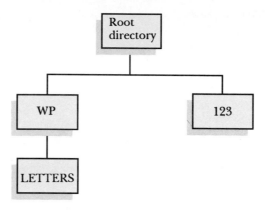

Answers

1. The current directory is the list of files and commands that, by default, DOS searches unless you tell DOS to look elsewhere. The current directory is conceptually the same as the open filing cabinet drawer.

2. Every DOS disk begins with one directory called the root. The root directory is so named because, like the branches of a tree, all the directories you will later create on your disk grow from the root. DOS uses the backslash character (\) to represent the root.

3. Every directory you create on your disk will have the entries "." and ".." You can use these as directory name abbreviations as you execute advanced DOS commands. For now, simply know that every directory you create contains these two entries.

4. Before DOS can remove a directory, it must be empty and must not be the current directory.

5. The following commands create the directories DOS, WP, and 123:

```
A:\> MKDIR \DOS
A:\> MKDIR \WP
A:\> MKDIR \123
```

Next, these commands create the lower-level directories:

```
A:\> MD \WP\LETTERS
A:\> MD \WP\MEMOS
A:\> MD \123\DATA
```

6. These commands remove directories from the directory tree in Figure 10-5, which results in the directory tree illustrated in Question number 6:

```
A:\> RMDIR \123\DATA
A:\> RMDIR \WP\MEMOS
A:\> RMDIR \DOS
```

Advanced Concepts

Although most users know they should use directories to improve their file organization, many users ask how many files each directory should contain. With the exception of the root directory, DOS directories can hold an almost limitless number of files. As the number of files in a directory increases, so will your difficulty in locating a specific file. In addition, the more files a directory contains, the more time DOS will need to perform directory search operations. In this way, long directory listings decrease your system performance.

If you are installing a large software program, you may not have any control over the number of files in the directory. If you are creating directories for your own files, however, you can control the number of files the directory contains. Chapter 44, "Detecting and Correcting Disk Fragmentation," which is on the subject of disk fragmentation, which occurs when a file's contents are stored in locations spread across your disk. Fragmented files decrease your system performance because DOS must wait for each sector of the disk containing the file to rotate past the disk's read/write head. It is possible for directories to become fragmented across your disk. When a directory becomes fragmented, every operation on that directory becomes time consuming, decreasing your system performance. The only way you can prevent directory fragmentation is to restrict the number of entries in a directory to an amount that only uses one disk allocation unit or cluster.

When you create a directory, DOS allocates a cluster to hold the directory entries. Each directory entry requires 32 bytes. Assuming your disk uses 2,048-byte clusters, a single cluster can hold 64 directory entries (2048/32). In this case, if the directory contains more than 64 entries, DOS must allocate a second cluster. In most cases, this second cluster will be located far from the first, and the directory will become fragmented, as shown in Figure 10-6.

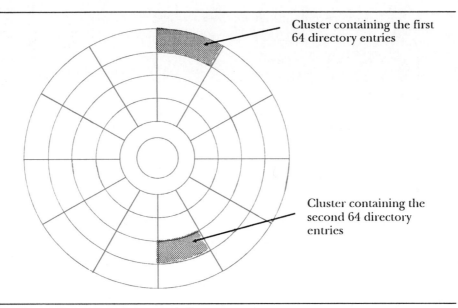

Figure 10-6.   *Creating a fragmented directory*

If you restrict the number of entries in your directory to an amount that fits in a cluster, the directory will never become fragmented. Using the CHKDSK command, you can determine your disk's cluster (allocation unit) size, as shown.

```
C:\> CHKDSK   <ENTER>

Volume DOS          created 10-16-1990 4:43p
Volume Serial Number is 1661-AB75

 200065024 bytes total disk space
     77824 bytes in 2 hidden files
    397312 bytes in 93 directories
  32583680 bytes in 1735 user files
 167002112 bytes available on disk

      4096 bytes in each allocation unit
     48844 total allocation units on disk
     40772 available allocation units on disk

    655360 total bytes memory
    578560 bytes free
```

Next, divide this amount by 32 to determine the number of directory entries a cluster can store. Use this value as a rule of thumb for determining the number of entries your directory should contain.

Protecting Private Directories

If you work in an office where your PC is accessible to other users, you may want to use an extended ASCII character to protect your directory from access by other users. In addition to the letters "A" through "Z" and the numbers 0 to 9, DOS lets you use extended ASCII characters in your file and directory names. Appendix B presents the entire ASCII and extended ASCII character sets.

In this case, you can use the extended ASCII value 255 to create a special blank character at the end of your directory name. To create this character, you must hold down the ALT key and keep it down while typing 255 with your keyboard's numeric keypad. You must use the keypad—it won't work with the number keys in the typewriter section.

For example, you can create a directory named PRIVATE that has the special blank character appended. To do so, type the following command but don't press ENTER.

```
C:\> MKDIR PRIVATE_
```

Next, hold down the ALT key, keep it down, and type 255. You must use the numeric keypad. When you release the ALT key, you will see the cursor move one position to the right indicating the blank character's presence.

```
C:\> MKDIR PRIVATE _
```

Press ENTER to create the directory. If another user examines your disk, the directory name will appear in a directory listing.

```
C:\> DIR \   <ENTER>

 Volume in drive C is DOS
 Volume Serial Number is 1661-AB75
 Directory of C:\

COMMAND  COM     46246 12-13-90    4:09a
AUTOEXEC BAT       108 03-01-91    9:27p
CONFIG   SYS       102 03-01-91    9:27p
DOS           <DIR>       10-16-90    4:44p
```

```
DISKUTIL      <DIR>        10-16-90    4:55
BATCH         <DIR>        01-28-91  10:13a
PRIVATE       <DIR>        03-03-91  10:47a
        7 file(s)          46456 bytes
                        16014400 bytes free
```

However, if the user tries to access the directory without including the special blank character, the command will fail. This even holds true for wildcard searches. PRIVATE*, P*, and PRIVATE? will all fail. Some menu or graphical interfaces, however, might allow access to the directory.

```
C:\> CHDIR  \PRIVATE <ENTER>
Invalid directory
```

When you need to access the files in the directory, you simply use ALT- 255 to append the special blank to the name as required.

Every Drive Has a Current Directory

If you ask most users "How many current directories are there?", most users will say one. Actually, there is a current directory for each disk drive. When DOS starts, the current directory for each drive is initially the drive's root directory. If you place a disk in drive A and use CHDIR to display to disk's current directory, CHDIR will display the root.

```
C:\> CHDIR  A:  <ENTER>
A:\
```

If you then change the current directory on drive C to DOS, drive A's current directory remains the root.

```
C:\> CHDIR  \DOS  <ENTER>
C:\DOS> CHDIR  A:  <ENTER>
A:\
```

As you can see, DOS keeps track of each disk's current directory. If you change the disks in a floppy drive, DOS automatically selects the root directory as the current directory if the new disk does not have a directory corresponding to the previous directory name.

Key Terms

Current directory   The list of files and commands that DOS searches by default, unless you tell DOS to look elsewhere.

Root directory   The first level in the directory tree from which all the rest of your directories grow.

Directory tree   The directory organization of your disk, beginning at the root directory, and growing outward, much like the branches of a tree.

Chapter 11

Getting the Most from DOS Directories

In Chapter 10 you learned that DOS directories help you organize the files you store on your disk. Using the CHDIR, MKDIR, and RMDIR commands, you were able to build and traverse directories. As you learned, your directories grow from an original directory called the root. In this chapter you will learn how to use the TREE command to display your disk's directory structure and optionally the files each directory contains, as well as the PATH command to simplify the execution of your commonly used commands. In addition, if you are using DOS 3.3 or later, you will learn how the FASTOPEN command can improve system performance. Last, this chapter takes a look at the "." and ".." directory abbreviations.

Displaying Your Directory Tree

The directories you create on your disk grow from the root directory much like the branches of a tree, as shown in Figure 11-1.

As you can imagine, after you work with DOS for some time, your directory structure can become very large and complicated. To help you track the directories on your disk, DOS provides the TREE command. TREE displays a "tree-like"

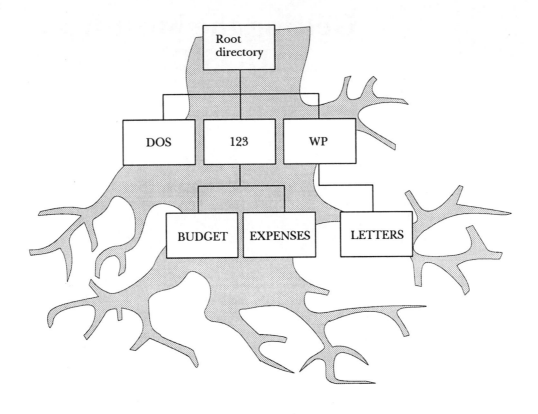

Figure 11-1.   *Your disk's directory structure forms your disk's directory tree*

representation of your directory structure. TREE is an external DOS command in the DOS directory. Use CHDIR to select the DOS directory and issue the TREE command:

```
C:\> CHDIR  \DOS   <ENTER>
C:\DOS> TREE  C:\   <ENTER>
```

DOS will display your disk's directories on screen. Assume, for example, that the disk in drive A contains the directory structure shown in Figure 11-2.

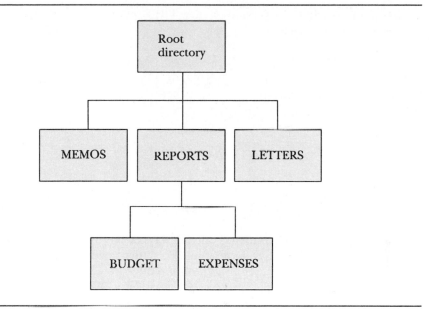

Figure 11-2.   *A simple directory structure*

Under DOS versions prior to 4, the output produced by the TREE command will be similar to the following:

```
C:\> TREE  A:   <ENTER>

DIRECTORY PATH LISTING
Path: \MEMOS
Sub-directories:  None

Path: \REPORTS
Sub-directories:  BUDGET
                  EXPENSES

Path: \REPORTS\BUDGET
Sub-directories:  None

Path: \REPORTS\EXPENSES
Sub-directories:  None

Path: \LETTERS
Sub-directories:  None
```

Beginning with DOS version 4, the TREE command uses a more pictorial representation, shown below.

```
C:\> TREE  A:  <ENTER>
Directory PATH listing
Volume Serial Number is 0315-1DC9
A:\
        ├─── MEMOS
        ├─── REPORTS
        │     ├──BUDGET
        │     └──EXPENSES
        └─── LETTERS
```

By default, the TREE command only displays directory names. If you include the /F switch, TREE will display all the files in each directory. Assume, for example, the directories on the disk in drive A contain the files shown in Figure 11-3.

Under DOS 4 or higher, using the /F switch with TREE results in the following:

```
C:\> TREE  A:  /F  <ENTER>
Directory PATH listing
Volume Serial Number is 0315-1DC9
A:\
        ├─── MEMOS
        │        JULY.MEM
        │        AUG.MEM
        │
        ├─── REPORTS
        │
        │        SUMMARY.RPT
        │
        │     ├─ BUDGET
        │     │     MONTHLY.RPT
        │     │
        │     └─EXPENSES
        │            JULY.EXP
        │            AUG.EXP
        │
        │
        └─── LETTERS
                 ALLEN.LTR
                 KENNA.LTR
```

Each of the previous TREE commands specified the root directory in the command line. In so doing, the commands directed TREE to display the disk's directory structure beginning at the root. If you simply invoke TREE without

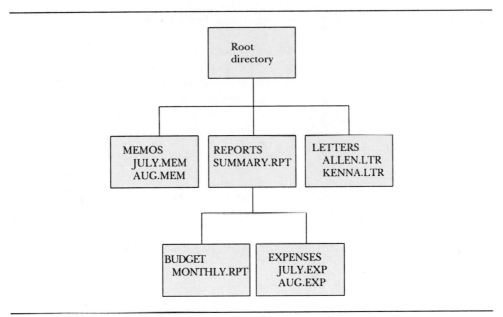

Figure 11-3.   *Directory tree with files*

specifying a directory, TREE will display only the directories that reside below the current directory.

Simplifying Execution of External Commands

You learned in Chapter 10, "Directories," that when you install a new software package on your hard disk, you typically create a unique directory to store the program. In most cases, to use the program, you will use CHDIR to select the directory containing the program's files. For example, to use the WordPerfect word processor, you would select the WP directory and invoke WordPerfect as shown.

```
C:\> CHDIR  \WP   <ENTER>
C:\WP> WP   <ENTER>
```

In this case, by selecting the WP directory before you begin, you keep your word processing files in one location.

In some cases, however, a directory may contain several commands you use so often, you don't want to select the directory each time you need to execute one of the commands. The DOS directory, which contains your external commands, is a good example of such a directory. Because of their frequent use, you don't want to have to select the DOS directory as the current directory each time you execute a DOS command.

As you have learned, to access files that are in a DOS directory, you have two choices. First, you can use CHDIR to select the file's directory and then reference the file by name. Second, you can access the file from any directory by specifying a complete directory path name to the file. The same two options apply to executing external DOS commands. If, for example, you want to execute the TREE command to display the directory structure, you can select the DOS directory and invoke TREE C:\ in the next command, as shown here.

```
C:\> CHDIR \DOS    <ENTER>
C:\DOS> TREE   C:\    <ENTER>
```

Second, you can specify a complete path name to the TREE command, invoking TREE from any directory, as shown here.

```
C:\> C:\DOS\TREE   C:\    <ENTER>
```

By specifying a complete path name to your external commands, you can execute your COM and EXE programs from any directory.

To execute your applications, such as your word processor or spreadsheet, you will normally use CHDIR to select the directory containing the program's files. To execute your commonly used DOS commands, however, repeatedly changing to the DOS directory could become quite time consuming. Fortunately, DOS provides the PATH command, which lets you tell DOS where it should look to find your commonly used external commands.

The PATH Command

Although your disk may contain many different directories, it's very likely only a few of the directories contain commands you use on a regular basis. If you don't tell DOS explicitly, by full path name, to look elsewhere, DOS only searches the current directory for external commands. If your file is in another directory, it is not found. To make it easier for you to execute your commonly used external commands, the PATH command lets you specify a list of directories you want DOS to automatically search each time it fails to locate an external command in the current directory. When issuing an external command in another directory that has been included in a PATH command, you don't have to supply a directory name or change to that directory—DOS will find the command and execute it. Most users, at a minimum, tell PATH to look in the DOS directory for DOS external commands. Issue the following PATH command to determine whether or not you have a command path defined.

```
C:\> PATH   <ENTER>
```

For most systems, DOS will display one or more directory names, as shown here.

```
C:\> PATH   <ENTER>
PATH=C:\DOS;C:\BATCH
```

If you don't have a command path defined, PATH will display a message stating so:

```
C:\> PATH   <ENTER>
No path
```

If your system doesn't have a command path defined, issue the following PATH command directing DOS to automatically search the DOS directory for your external commands.

```
C:\DOS> PATH   C:\DOS   <ENTER>
```

Next, select the root directory as the default.

```
C:\DOS> CHDIR   \   <ENTER>
```

Next, with the root directory as the default, issue the following TREE command.

```
C:\> TREE   C:\   <ENTER>
```

Although the external TREE command is in a different directory, DOS finds it and displays your disk's directory structure as desired. Here's why. Each time you execute a command, DOS first checks if the command specified is an internal command, such as CLS or DATE, that always resides in your computer's fast electronic memory. If the command is internal, DOS immediately executes it; otherwise, DOS searches the files in the current directory for a matching EXE or COM file. If DOS finds a matching external command, it executes it; otherwise, DOS checks to see if you have used PATH to define a command path. As discussed, the command path specifies one or more directories you want DOS to automatically search for a matching external command. In this case, using the command path,

DOS locates the TREE command in the DOS directory. As a result, DOS lets you execute TREE without regard for the current directory. The previous example assumed C:\DOS was the only directory in the command path. If your path contains several directories, DOS separates the directory names using semicolons, as shown here.

```
C:\> PATH   <ENTER>
PATH=C:\DOS;C:\BATCH
```

In this case, if DOS fails to locate an external command in the current directory, DOS will first search the directory DOS on drive C. If DOS finds a matching command, DOS will execute it; otherwise DOS will search directory BATCH. If DOS finds a matching command anywhere along the way, DOS executes the command, and the search is done. If DOS fails to locate a matching command in any of the directories, DOS will display an error message indicating this:

```
Bad command or file name
```

Figure 11-4 illustrates the steps DOS performs when you execute a command, starting with its search of internal commands, followed by commands in the current directory, and ending with its traversal of directories listed in the command path.

Changing the Command Path

PATH lets you change, display, and even remove the command path. In Chapter 18, "Automatic System Startup Commands with AUTOEXEC.BAT," you will learn about a special file named AUTOEXEC.BAT that you can use to specify commands you want DOS to automatically execute each time your system starts. You may already have an AUTOEXEC.BAT file in your root directory. Using the TYPE command, you can display the file's contents.

```
C:\> TYPE  \AUTOEXEC.BAT   <ENTER>
```

Most users determine two or three directories that contain their most commonly used commands and include those directory names in the command path. For example, the following PATH command directs DOS to look in the DOS, BATCH, and DISKUTIL directories.

```
C:\> PATH  C:\DOS;C:\BATCH;C:\DISKUTIL   <ENTER>
```

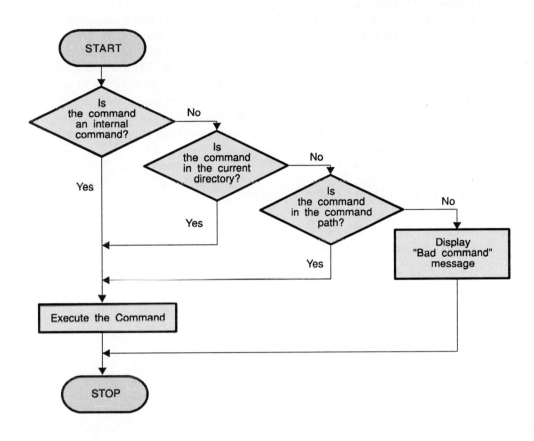

Figure 11-4.   The steps DOS follows to execute your commands

There are no spaces between directory names. Use the semicolon as shown to separate directory names. Note that each entry specifies drive C: before the directory name. If you don't include the drive letter, DOS will try to find the directories specified on the current drive. As long as drive C is the current drive, DOS will successfully locate the directories. However, if you change drives, DOS will look on the wrong drive for the directories and will be unable to locate the commands. Include drive letters in the command path.

By placing your PATH command in the AUTOEXEC.BAT batch file, you don't have to worry about setting your command path yourself. DOS will automatically set up your path for you each time your system starts. Chapter 18 discusses using PATH within AUTOEXEC.BAT.

Many software programs you buy direct you to include their directory in the command path. In most cases, the installation program you run to put the program on your hard disk will automatically update the PATH command in your AUTOEXEC.BAT file for you. It's a good idea to invoke PATH after you install a new program to determine if your command path has changed. You only want to include in the command path directories that contain commonly used commands. If your command path includes too many directories, your system will perform more slowly because DOS will spend a lot of time simply searching through directories.

Abbreviating Directory Names

In Chapter 10 you used MKDIR to create the subdirectories LETTERS, MEMOS, and REPORTS within TESTDIR using the following commands.

```
C:\> MD   \TESTDIR    <ENTER>
C:\> MD   \TESTDIR\LETTERS    <ENTER>
C:\> MD   \TESTDIR\MEMOS      <ENTER>
C:\> MD   \TESTDIR\REPORTS    <ENTER>
```

As you can see, each MKDIR (MD) command used complete DOS path names, beginning at the root directory. This amount of typing could become tedious after a while. As it turns out, DOS lets you simplify your directory paths by letting you access directories in the current directory without having to use a complete path name. Here's the rule to remember: Any time a directory is in the current directory, you can access the directory using only the directory name with no slash before the name.

For example, use CHDIR (CD) to select the root directory.

```
C:\DOS> CD \   <ENTER>
```

Assuming the TESTDIR directory exists, you can select TESTDIR using CHDIR as follows.

```
C:\> CD   TESTDIR   <ENTER>
```

Note the command does not include a slash before TESTDIR's name. Because the current directory was the root, and because TESTDIR resides immediately below the root, you can access the directory by name without the slash.

With TESTDIR as the current directory, issue the following CHDIR command to select the directory MEMOS.

```
C:\TESTDIR> CD   MEMOS   <ENTER>
```

Again, because the MEMOS directory is in the current directory, you can access the directory by name. You could have used the complete directory path name as shown here; however, doing so requires more typing.

```
C:\TESTDIR> CD   \TESTDIR\MEMOS   <ENTER>
```

Next, from the current directory, try to select the DOS directory by name only.

```
C:\TESTDIR\MEMOS> CD   DOS   <ENTER>
Invalid directory
```

In this case, CHDIR fails because the DOS directory does not reside in the current directory. To select the DOS directory, you must specify a complete path name, beginning at the root.

```
C:\TESTDIR\MEMOS> CD   \DOS   <ENTER>
C:\DOS>
```

The directory path provides DOS with the road map DOS should follow to locate a directory. If you are in doubt over whether you can abbreviate a directory or not, keep in mind that specifying a complete path name will always be correct.

The "." and ".." Abbreviations

You learned in Chapter 10 that every directory you create automatically has two directory entries "." and ".." as shown here.

```
C:\TESTDIR> DIR   <ENTER>
Volume in drive C is DOS
```

```
Volume Serial Number is 1661-AB75
Directory of C:\TESTDIR

.              <DIR>      03-17-91     10:22p
..             <DIR>      03-17-91     10:22p
LETTERS        <DIR>      03-17-91     10:23p
MEMOS          <DIR>      03-17-91     10:23p
REPORTS        <DIR>      03-17-91     10:23p
        5 file(s)              0 bytes
                     16761024 bytes free
```

These two directory entries actually serve as abbreviations for the current directory name and the name of the directory immediately above the current directory, which is the current directory's *parent*. Using CHDIR, select TESTDIR as the current directory. The single period (.) now corresponds to the current directory TESTDIR, while the double periods (..) correspond to TESTDIR's parent, the root. You can verify this with DIR. First, list the files in the current directory using the period:

```
C:\TESTDIR> DIR   .  <ENTER>

 Volume in drive C is DOS
 Volume Serial Number is 1661-AB75
 Directory of C:\TESTDIR

.              <DIR>      03-17-91     10:22p
..             <DIR>      03-17-91     10:22p
LETTERS        <DIR>      03-17-91     10:23p
MEMOS          <DIR>      03-17-91     10:23p
REPORTS        <DIR>      03-17-91     10:23p
        5 file(s)              0 bytes
                     16761024 bytes free
```

Next, list the files in the parent using the double periods (..):

```
C:\TESTDIR> DIR   ..  <ENTER>

 Volume in drive C is DOS
 Volume Serial Number is 1661-AB75
 Directory of C:\

COMMAND  COM      46246 12-13-90     4:09a
```

```
DOS          <DIR>        10-16-90    4:44p
DISKUTIL     <DIR>        10-16-90    4:55p
WS           <DIR>        10-18-90    9:25a
BATCH        <DIR>        01-28-91   10:13a
AUTOEXEC BAT        128  03-04-91    1:37p
CONFIG   SYS        128  04-04-91    2:44p
TESTDIR      <DIR>        03-17-91   10:22p
        8 file(s)     206377 bytes
                     16756928 bytes free
```

Using CHDIR, select the directory MEMOS.

```
C:\TESTDIR> CD   MEMOS   <ENTER>
```

When you change directories, DOS will update the abbreviations. In this case, the single-period abbreviation now corresponds to the current directory MEMOS, while the double periods correspond to TESTDIR (MEMOS' parent).

Use of the double-period abbreviation is most common. Using the double periods you can quickly move up one level in the directory tree:

```
C:\TESTDIR\MEMOS> CD .. <ENTER>
```

As you become more comfortable with directory operations, you may find these two abbreviations save you time and typing.

FASTOPEN Improves System Performance

Each time you access a file, whether to execute a program contained in an EXE or COM file or to open a word processing document, DOS must locate the file on your disk. As discussed, a directory is a list of file names, sizes, and date and time stamps. In addition, the directory contains the location on disk where the file begins.

To find a file, DOS must first read the directory, which also resides on disk. DOS then searches the directory for the file entry. Although hard disks are fast, their mechanical nature makes them much slower than your computer's electronic components. Depending on the size of your directory, the read and search operation may take considerable time. If you are using DOS 3.3 or higher, the FASTOPEN command can improve your system performance by reducing the amount of time DOS spends searching for the files you repeatedly use. Although your disk may contain thousands of files, you probably only use a small number of files on a regular basis—such as a word processing file, several key spreadsheets, or a set of database files. If you have a set of files you access often, FASTOPEN will improve your system performance.

FASTOPEN works by saving the name and location of each file you access. Assume, for example, you edit the file REPORT.TXT using your word processor. The first time you open the file, DOS will read and search the directory as discussed. When DOS locates the file, FASTOPEN will place the file's name and starting disk location in a list FASTOPEN stores in your computer's fast electronic memory. If you close the file to perform a different task and later reopen the file, DOS will first search FASTOPEN's list to see if the list contains the file's starting location. Because FASTOPEN's list is in your computer's fast electronic memory, this search only takes an instant. If FASTOPEN's list contains the file, DOS doesn't have to perform the slow directory-read-and-search operation.

FASTOPEN doesn't make every file open faster; FASTOPEN only improves performance when you are opening a file you recently accessed. However, because most users actually have a set of files they frequently use throughout the day, FASTOPEN will make a performance difference. If you are using DOS 3.3 or later on a hard disk, issue the following FASTOPEN command.

```
C:\> FASTOPEN  C:=50   <ENTER>
```

In this case, FASTOPEN will track the locations of up to 50 files. If you open more than 50 files throughout your computer session, FASTOPEN simply replaces older entries with more recently used files. FASTOPEN will track up to 999 files. However, because most users only repeatedly use a small number of files, tracking 50 files should be more than sufficient. In addition, each file FASTOPEN tracks consumes 32 to 48 bytes depending on your DOS version. If you create a large FASTOPEN list, you may simply waste memory. Because you can remove and insert floppy disks, FASTOPEN only supports hard disks.

If your computer has more than one hard disk, you can direct FASTOPEN to track files for both disks, as shown here.

```
C:\> FASTOPEN  C:=50  D:=50   <ENTER>
```

In this case FASTOPEN will track 50 files for drive C and 50 for drive D.

FASTOPEN uses a portion of your computer's available electronic memory to store its list and the software that searches the list for matching files. If you want to change the number of files FASTOPEN tracks, you must first restart your system. In Chapter 18, "Automatic System Startup Commands with AUTOEXEC.BAT," you will learn that most users place a FASTOPEN command in the special file AUTOEXEC.BAT so DOS automatically executes FASTOPEN each time your system starts. For more information on FASTOPEN, see the Command Reference at the end of this book.

SUMMARY

The TREE Command

The TREE command displays your disk's directory structure (or directory tree). To display all the directories on a disk, invoke TREE with the root directory symbol as shown here.

```
C:\>  TREE  \  <ENTER>
```

If you include the /F switch, TREE will list the files in each directory. If you don't specify a directory name in TREE's command line, TREE displays only those directories that are below the current directory.

The PATH Command

The PATH command lets you display, change, or remove your command path. The command path is a list of directories DOS automatically searches when it fails to locate an external command in the current directory. To search the command path, DOS begins with the first directory specified, followed by the second, until DOS finds a matching command or exhausts its directory list. Your command path should only include directories containing your commonly used commands, such as the DOS directory. Once you identify your commonly used directories, place an appropriate PATH command in the batch file AUTOEXEC.BAT discussed in Chapter 18. The following PATH command directs DOS to search drive C directories DOS and BATCH, in that order.

```
C:\> PATH  C:\DOS;C:\BATCH  <ENTER>
```

To display your current command path, invoke PATH with no parameters.

Abbreviating Directory Names

DOS uses directory path names as a road map to find your files and directories. Although you can always specify a complete directory path that begins at your disk's root directory, there may be times you can reduce the path names (and your typing). If the directory you desire is in the current directory, you can access the directory by name without placing a backslash character before the name. For example, assuming the directory LETTERS resides below the current directory TESTDIR, the following RMDIR commands are the same.

```
C:\TESTDIR> RD  LETTERS  <ENTER>

C:\TESTDIR> RD  \TESTDIR\LETTERS  <ENTER>
```

If the directory is not below the current directory, you must specify a complete path name.

"." and ".."

Each time you create a directory on your disk, DOS places the entries "." and ".." in the directory. These two entries are actually abbreviations. The single period abbreviates the current directory, while the double periods abbreviate the parent directory (the directory immediately above the current directory in the directory tree). Every directory on your disk except the root has a parent. Using directory abbreviations may save time and keystrokes.

The FASTOPEN Command

If you are using DOS 3.3 or later, the FASTOPEN command may improve your system performance by reducing the amount of time DOS spends locating commonly used files on your hard disk. FASTOPEN doesn't reduce the amount of time every time you open a file, just the times for files you have recently used. The following FASTOPEN command directs FASTOPEN to track up to 50 files on drive C.

```
C:\> FASTOPEN  C:=50  <ENTER>
```

Hands On

Issue the following PATH command to display the current command path.

```
C:\> PATH  <ENTER>
```

If your system does not have a command path defined, DOS will display the following message.

```
C:\> PATH <ENTER>
No path
```

Only if DOS displays the "No path" message, should you execute the following PATH command.

```
C:\> PATH   C:\DOS
```

If your system has a command path defined, note the directories DOS searches to locate your external commands, as well as the order in which DOS searches the directories.

If necessary, use CHDIR to select the root directory as the current directory and invoke the TREE command.

```
C:\> TREE    <ENTER>
```

Because your command path includes the DOS directory, DOS finds TREE although TREE.COM is in a different directory.

When TREE completes, invoke TREE including the /F switch to display the name of every file and directory on your disk. If the directory names scroll past you faster than you can read them, don't worry. You learned in Chapter 5, "Understanding Your Keyboard," that you can use F3 to repeat the command and, when you press ENTER, be ready with CTRL-S to suspend screen scrolling and CTRL-S again to resume scrolling. In Chapter 20, "The DOS Redirection Operators," you will learn how to use the MORE command to display a command's output a screenful at a time.

Next, use CHDIR to select the DOS directory.

```
C:\> CD   DOS    <ENTER>
```

Because the DOS directory is immediately adjacent to the root, you did not have to include the backslash before the directory name.

Next, using the period abbreviation, list the files in the current directory.

```
C:\DOS> DIR   .  <ENTER>
```

When the command completes, use the double periods to list the files in the parent directory.

```
C:\DOS>  DIR   ..  <ENTER>
```

Using the double periods with CHDIR, move one level up the directory tree.

```
C:\> CHDIR   ..  <ENTER>
```

Last, if you are using DOS 3.3 or later, issue the following FASTOPEN command.

```
C:\> FASTOPEN  C:=50  <ENTER>
```

Review

1. What is the command path?

2. What is the function of the following command?

```
C:\> PATH   C:\DOS;C:\BATCH   <ENTER>
```

3. How do the following commands differ?

```
C:\> PATH   C:\DOS;C:\BATCH   <ENTER>
C:\> PATH   \DOS;\BATCH   <ENTER>
```

4. How does the abbreviation "." differ from ".."?

5. When can you reference a directory by name without specifying a complete path name?

6. How does FASTOPEN improve your system performances?

Answers

1. The command path is the list of directories DOS searches to locate your external DOS commands when it fails to locate a command in the current directory. The PATH command lets you define your command path.

2. The command places the directories DOS and BATCH into the command path. If DOS fails to locate an external command in the current directory, DOS will first search the directory DOS for the command. If DOS locates the command, DOS will execute it, and the search ends. If DOS fails to locate the command, it will then search the directory BATCH.

3. The first command ensures DOS will look for the directories DOS and BATCH on drive C. The second command, however, directs DOS to look for the directories on the current drive. If drive C is the current drive, DOS will find the directories as desired. If a drive other than C is the default, DOS won't locate the directories, unless they also happen to be on the second disk.

4. The single period "." is an abbreviation for the current directory. The double ".." is an abbreviation for the current directory's parent (the directory that appears immediately above the current directory in the directory tree).

5. If the desired directory resides within the current directory, you can access the directory by name, without specifying a complete directory path.

6. If you are using DOS 3.3 or later, FASTOPEN lets DOS track the disk locations of your commonly used files. By default, when you access a file, DOS must read the directory from disk and search the directory to locate the desired file entry. Using the directory entry, DOS knows where the file begins on disk. If you repeatedly open the same set of files, FASTOPEN will keep track of where the files begin on disk, storing the information in a list in your computer's fast electronic memory. When you access a file, DOS first searches FASTOPEN's list of recently opened files. If DOS finds the desired file, DOS does not have to perform the slow directory-read-and-search. DOS will only find entries for recently opened files in FASTOPEN's list. Therefore, FASTOPEN improves the performance for files you open more than once during a user session, but not for every file you use.

Advanced Concepts

The PATH command lets you specify the list of directories in which you want DOS to search for your EXE, COM, and BAT files. DOS uses the command path when DOS fails to locate an external command. Using the command path, DOS lets you define default locations DOS should always search for commands. If you are using DOS version 3.2 or later, the APPEND command lets you define a data-file search path. Using APPEND, you can define a list of directories you want DOS to search each time DOS fails to locate a data file.

To better understand how APPEND works, create the following data file in the TESTDIR directory.

```
C:\TESTDIR> COPY  CON  UNLV.TXT   <ENTER>
UNLV Runnin Rebel Basketball!
^Z <ENTER>
        1 File(s) copied
```

Next, select the root directory as the default and issue this TYPE command.

```
C:\> TYPE  UNLV.TXT   <ENTER>
File not found
```

Because the data file is not in the current directory, TYPE cannot find the file, and the command fails. Using the following APPEND command, direct DOS to search the TESTDIR directory when it fails to locate a data file.

```
C:\> APPEND  C:\TESTDIR   <ENTER>
```

Next, from the root directory, repeat the previous TYPE command.

```
C:\> TYPE  UNLV.TXT   <ENTER>
UNLV Runnin Rebel Basketball!
```

Because DOS locates the file in the data-file search path, the command succeeds. DOS uses the data file search path restrictively. DOS will not, for example, delete a file it finds using the data-file search path. For example, if you try to delete a file named UNLV.TXT from the root directory, DOS will not delete the corresponding file in the TESTDIR directory. Depending on your DOS version, DOS will display an "Access denied" or "File not found" message:

```
C:\> DEL  UNLV.TXT   <ENTER>
File not found
```

Use of the APPEND command is much less common than PATH. However, if you have a program that only runs from a directory that contains specific files, you may be able to use APPEND to eliminate the directory restriction. For more information on APPEND, see the Command Reference at the end of this book.

Command-Path Tricks

The maximum number of characters your command path can contain is 121. Even though users should only include in their command path directories most likely to contain commonly used commands, users somehow manage to push the 121-character limit. Chapter 26, "DOS Pretender Commands," examines the SUBST command, which lets you substitute an unused disk drive letter for a directory name. For example, the following command abbreviates the DOS directory as drive E.

```
C:\> SUBST  E:  C:\DOS  <ENTER>
```

After you substitute a drive letter for a directory name, you can use the drive letter as you would the directory name. For example, the following DIR command uses drive E to list the files in the DOS directory.

```
C:\> DIR  E:  <ENTER>
```

If your command path has become excessively long, you may be able to reduce its length by substituting drive letters for the longer directory names. See Chapter 26 for more information on SUBST.

Key Terms

Directory tree   A name given to your disk's directory structure because the directories grow from the root directory much like the branches or root structure of a tree.

Command path   The list of directories DOS searches to locate your external commands. The PATH command defines your command path.

Parent directory   The directory above the current directory in the directory tree.

Data-file search path   The list of directories DOS searches to locate your data files. The APPEND command defines your data-file search path.

Chapter 12

Fundamental Copy Operations

In Chapters 10 and 11 you created and used DOS directories to organize your files. Because of the importance of this subject and its frequency of use, this chapter examines the steps you must follow to copy files from a hard disk to a floppy disk, or vice versa. Next, the chapter presents the DISKCOPY command, which duplicates an entire disk's contents. Using DISKCOPY, you can make working copies of the original floppy disks that accompany the software programs you buy. Once you copy the originals, store them in a safe place.

Copying Files from a Hard Disk to a Floppy Disk

No matter what programs you run on your computer, word processor, spreadsheet, or database, eventually you will need to copy one or more files from your hard disk to floppy, to exchange information with another user, or even as a backup. In fact, one of the most common questions DOS users ask is "What is the command to copy a file from a Lotus 1-2-3 directory to a floppy?"

You learned in Chapter 10 that when you use an application, such as Lotus 1-2-3 or WordPerfect, you will normally use CHDIR to change to the program's directory before you begin. If you want to copy a file from one of your applications, use CHDIR to go to the directory containing the file.

Next, place the floppy disk to which you want to copy the file in drive A. Use DIR to examine the floppy disk's current contents.

```
C:\123> DIR  A:   <ENTER>
```

If DOS displays the following error message, you must format the floppy disk for use, as discussed in Chapter 7.

```
General failure reading drive A
Abort, Retry, Fail?
```

If the floppy disk contains files, make sure your copy operation won't overwrite an existing file whose contents you need. Also note the amount of free disk space on the floppy. If the available disk space is less than the size of the file you want to copy, you'll need to use a different floppy disk.

If the disk has sufficient space, issue a COPY command that specifies your file name as the source file and drive A as the destination:

```
C:\123> COPY FILENAME.EXT  A:   <ENTER>
```

If you are copying several files, use a DOS wildcard if one can selectively copy the desired files. Otherwise, you may have to issue several COPY commands, one for each file.

Copying from a Floppy Disk to a Hard Disk

Copying files from a floppy disk to your hard disk essentially follows the steps just discussed. To begin, use CHDIR to select the directory to which you want to store the files.

Next, place the floppy disk containing the files to copy in drive A and issue the following DIR command.

```
C:\123> DIR  A:   <ENTER>
```

Examine the files on the floppy disk closely to make sure you won't overwrite existing files on your hard disk. If you accidentally overwrite a file's contents, you can't get the information back.

If you want to copy all the files on the floppy disk, you can use a wildcard combination, as shown here.

```
C:\123> COPY  A:*.*   <ENTER>
```

DOS will copy the files from drive A to your hard disk using each file's original name.

If you only want to copy selected files from the floppy disk, use a wildcard, if appropriate, or issue individual COPY commands for each file name, as shown here.

```
C:\123> COPY  A: FILENAME.EXT   <ENTER>
```

Whether you are copying files from your hard disk to floppy or vice versa, the copy operation becomes much easier if you select the correct directory before you begin.

DISKCOPY Copies an Entire Disk's Contents

One of the most important rules for working with your computer is never to use the original disks containing the software you buy. Instead, use the DISKCOPY command to duplicate the disk's contents, and place the original disk in a safe location.

DISKCOPY is an external DOS command in your DOS directory. Depending on the number and size of your floppy drives, the steps you will perform to copy a disk will differ slightly. Before you begin, however, use a write-protect tab, as discussed in Chapter 1 to protect the original floppy disks. If you are using 3 1/2-inch floppies, slide the write-protect cover into the write-protect position. As with COPY in Chapter 8, "Fundamental File Operations," DISKCOPY refers to the disk you are copying as the source and the disk you are copying to as the target.

The DISKCOPY command completely overwrites the existing contents of the target disk. Make sure the target disk does not contain needed information. If the target disk is unformatted, DISKCOPY will format the disk for you.

You might remember from Chapter 7, "Preparing Disks for Use," that your disk stores information in sectors on your disk's circular tracks, as shown in Figure 12-1.

DISKCOPY copies a source disk to the target sector by sector, track by track. Therefore, DISKCOPY requires the target disk to be exactly the same type of disk as the source—you can't use DISKCOPY to copy a 5 1/4-inch disk to a 3 1/2-inch disk.

Two-Drive DISKCOPY

If your computer has two floppy disk drives of the same size, place the source disk in drive A and the target in drive B as shown in Figure 12-2.

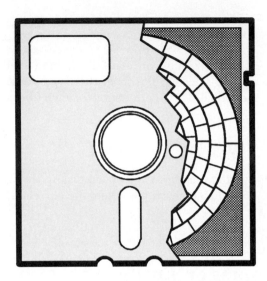

Figure 12-1.   *DISKCOPY copies the source disk's tracks and sectors*

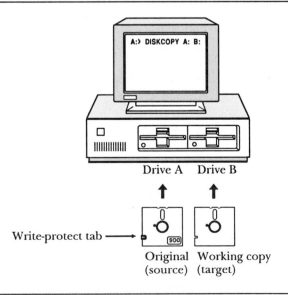

Figure 12-2.   *For two-drive DISKCOPY, place the write-protected source disk in drive A and the target disk in drive B*

Next, issue the following DISKCOPY command.

```
C:\> DISKCOPY  A:  B:   <ENTER>
```

DISKCOPY will display the following prompt to ensure that you have inserted the floppy disks in the drive.

```
C:\> DISKCOPY  A:  B:   <ENTER>

Insert SOURCE diskette in drive A:

Insert TARGET diskette in drive B:

Press any key to continue. . .
```

When you press a key you will see drive A's disk activation light illuminate as DISKCOPY reads the disk's contents. Next, drive B's disk activation light will illuminate as DISKCOPY writes information to the disk.

If the disk in drive B is unformatted, DISKCOPY will format the disk displaying the following message.

```
Formatting while copying
```

When DISKCOPY completes, it asks if you want to copy a second disk:

```
Copy another diskette (Y/N)?
```

Type N, and DISKCOPY will end, returning control to the DOS prompt. Remove the target disk and label it. Don't write on a label attached to the disk—write on the label *before* you detach it and put it on the disk.

One-Drive DISKCOPY

If your computer only has one floppy disk drive of a given size, you will need to perform a single-drive DISKCOPY operation. To do so, you will place the (write-protected) source disk in the drive for DISKCOPY to read, and then replace it with the target disk when DISKCOPY is ready to write. Depending on your disk size, you may have to exchange disks two or more times. Figure 12-3 illustrates the process of exchanging the source and target disks during a single-drive DISKCOPY operation.

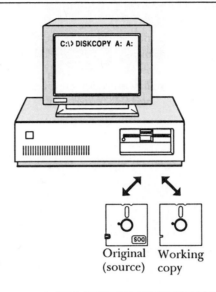

Original Working
(source) copy

Figure 12-3. *In single-drive DISKCOPY, you must exchange the source and target disks*
in the same drive

To perform a single-drive DISKCOPY, place the source disk in drive A and issue
the following command.

```
C:\> DISKCOPY  A:  A:  <ENTER>
```

DISKCOPY will display the following prompt to ensure that the source disk is in
drive A.

```
Insert SOURCE diskette in drive A:

Press any key to continue. . .
```

When you press a key to continue, you will see drive A's disk activation light
illuminate as DISKCOPY reads the disk's contents. When DISKCOPY is ready to
write information to the target disk, DISKCOPY will display the following prompt
for you to insert the target disk in the drive.

```
Insert TARGET diskette in drive A:

Press any key to continue. . .
```

Place the target disk in drive A and press any key to continue. As with double DISKCOPY, if the target disk is unformatted DISKCOPY will format it. Depending on your disk size, DISKCOPY may prompt you to exchange the disks again. When DISKCOPY completes, it will ask if you want to copy another disk. As before, type N to end DISKCOPY.

Hands On

Insert a floppy disk in drive A. If the disk is unformatted, use the FORMAT command to prepare the floppy for use, as discussed in Chapter 7. Use CHDIR to select the DOS directory as the current directory.

```
C:\> CD  \DOS  <ENTER>
```

Next, use the following COPY commands to copy the files DISKCOPY.COM, FORMAT.COM, and LABEL.COM to the disk in drive A.

```
C:\DOS> COPY DISKCOPY.COM  A:  <ENTER>
        1 File(s) copied

C:\DOS> COPY  FORMAT.COM  A:  <ENTER>
        1 File(s) copied

C:\DOS> COPY LABEL.COM  A:  <ENTER>
        1 File(s) copied
```

Whether you are copying files from the DOS directory or your 123 directory, the process is the same. Select the directory containing the desired files and then copy the files by name, as shown.

If you are still using the original disks that accompanied any of your software packages, use the DISKCOPY command to make working copies of each disk. Place the original disks in a safe location.

Review

1. Why can't you use DISKCOPY to copy a 5 1/4-inch disk to a 3 1/2-inch floppy?

2. When must you perform a single-drive DISKCOPY?

3. What are the commands to copy the files BUDGET.DAT and SALARY.DAT from the directory 123 to the floppy disk in drive A?

Answers

1. The DISKCOPY command duplicates a disk by copying the source disk track by track, sector by sector to the target disk. As such, both disks must have the same number of tracks and sectors.

2. If your computer only has one floppy drive of any given size and capacity, you must perform a single-drive DISKCOPY.

3. The commands to copy the files BUDGET.DAT and SALARY.DAT from the directory 123 to the floppy disk in drive A are

```
C:\> CHDIR  \123   <ENTER>
C:\123> COPY  BUDGET.DAT  A:  <ENTER>
C:\123> COPY  SALARY.DAT  A:  <ENTER>
```

Advanced Concepts

One of the most frustrating problems users experience when copying files from their hard disk to floppy occurs when the floppy disk does not have enough disk space to hold the files. When the floppy disk runs out of space, your screen will display the following message.

```
Insufficient disk space
```

The difficulty occurs in trying to resume the copy operation with the last file copied. If you have ever experienced this error, you know COPY does not provide you with an easy way to resume the copy operation with the last uncopied file.

For cases where you need to copy more files than a single floppy disk can hold, use the ATTRIB and XCOPY commands. Chapter 23, "Advanced File Manipulation," discusses them in detail. The following discussion provides you with a quick tip for copying a directory of files to floppy disk. To begin, select the directory containing the files you want to copy. Next, issue the following ATTRIB command to set each file's archive-required attribute.

```
C:\> ATTRIB  +A  *.*  <ENTER>
```

After the ATTRIB command completes, issue the following XCOPY command, which copies each file whose archive-required attribute is set.

```
C:\> XCOPY *.*  A:  /M  <ENTER>
```

Each time XCOPY successfully copies a file, XCOPY will clear the file's archive-required attribute. Eventually, the floppy disk will run out of space, and DOS will display the following message.

```
Insufficient disk space
```

Because XCOPY has been clearing the archive-required attribute for each file it successfully copies, you can easily continue the copy operation by inserting a new floppy disk in drive A and repeating the same XCOPY command.

```
C:\> XCOPY *.*  A:  /M  <ENTER>
```

XCOPY will resume the copy operation with the first file whose archive-required attribute is set. If the floppy disk fills again, insert a new floppy disk and repeat the XCOPY command until all of the files are copied.

Key Terms

Source disk   The disk containing required information.

Target disk   The disk to which a DOS command will copy information.

Chapter 13

Printing

No matter which applications (word processor, spreadsheet, or database) you use on your computer, you will eventually need to print information. Users call printed output *hard copy* because it is a physical copy of your information. In this chapter you will learn how to access your printer, not only from DOS, but from within your applications. In addition, you will examine several basic DOS printer capabilities, such as printing the contents of the current screen or writing a command's output to both the screen and printer at the same time.

Using Your Printer

Before you can use your printer, it must be attached to the back of your computer by a cable, plugged in, and turned on. In addition, most printers have a button labeled "On Line " or "ONLINE" or "Ready" that has a small light. When the light is on, your printer is "on the line," ready to accept data from the computer. When the light is off, the printer will ignore any information the computer sends it. The On Line button works like a toggle. Most printers begin on line when you first turn them on. Then the first time you press it, the printer goes off line. The next time you press it, the printer goes back on line. Figure 13-1 illustrates the common location of your printer's On Line button.

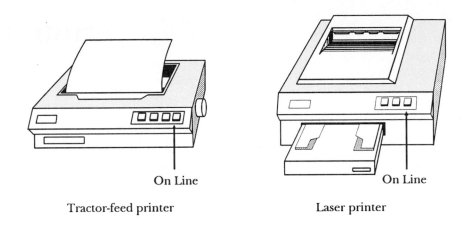

On Line   On Line

Tractor-feed printer   Laser printer

Figure 13-1.   Location of the printer's On Line button

Identifying Your Printer Type

Whatever your printer brand, your printer connects to a port at the back of your computer with a cable. The cable type and port used will differ, depending on whether your printer is a *parallel* or *serial* printer. You must know your printer type (parallel or serial) because the steps you must follow to access your printer from DOS will differ.

Serial and parallel printers differ in the number of wires they use to send data to your printer. Briefly, serial printers receive their information from the computer on one line. Parallel printers, on the other hand are receiving data on eight lines at the same time (in parallel). As you might expect, the parallel printers are the fastest. Since it has more data lines, a parallel connection needs more wires and pins than its serial counterpart. Don't be fooled by the number of pins in the plug, however; pins are often left unused. If you examine the cable that connects your printer to your computer, as well as the port on the back of your computer, you can determine if your printer is parallel or serial. Figure 13-2 shows what the ports on the back of your computer should look like.

Depending on your computer's hardware configuration, you may have from one to three parallel ports and one to four serial ports. Most systems, however, have at

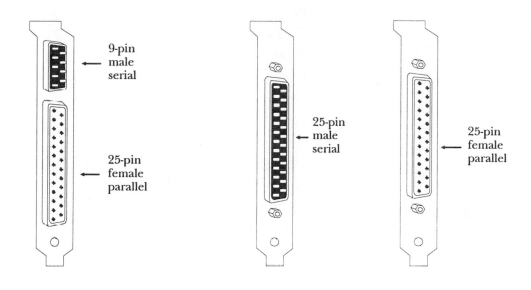

Figure 13-2.   Common parallel and serial printer ports

least one serial port and one parallel port. DOS assigns the names LPT1: through LPT3: to the parallel ports and COM1: through COM4: to the serial ports.

The Device Names PRN and AUX

Most computers have at least one parallel and one serial port. DOS assigns the name LPT1: to the first parallel port and COM1: to the first serial port. Typically, the only devices users attach to the computer's parallel ports are printers, and hence the letters "*LPT*" (*Line PrinTer*) in the port name. Serial ports, however, connect printers, mice, and modems. Because serial ports were initially used for communications with either modems or unique devices, DOS uses the letters "COM" (COMmunications) in the serial-port names.

In addition to the device names LPT*n* and COM*n* (the colon is optional), DOS lets you use PRN and AUX. Because most users have printers attached to the parallel port LPT1:, DOS lets you refer to this port as *PRN*. Likewise, because the serial port COM1: normally connects auxiliary devices, DOS lets you refer to the port as *AUX*.

Table 13-1 summarizes the DOS parallel and serial port names.

Device Name	Corresponding Port
LPT1:	First parallel port
LPT2:	Second parallel port
LPT3:	Third parallel port
PRN	First parallel port (same device as LPT1:)
COM1:	First serial port
COM2:	Second serial port
COM3:	Third serial port (DOS 3.3 and higher)
COM4:	Fourth serial port (DOS 3.3 and higher)
AUX	First serial port (same device as COM1:)

Table 13-1.   DOS Parallel and Serial Device Names

The Serial Port's Communication Settings

If your printer connects to a serial port, you have to make sure your printer and computer are using the same communication settings. If you are using a parallel printer, you don't have to worry about such matters.

If when you try to use your serial printer, nothing is printed or the hardcopy output contains unrecognizable or nonsense characters, your serial port's communication settings don't match your printer's. In such cases, you must refer to the documentation that accompanied your printer to determine the proper communication settings. Next, you must use the MODE command to assign those settings to the serial port. For example, the following MODE command assigns the proper communication settings for a HP LaserJet Series printer to the serial port COM1:.

```
C:\> MODE  COM1:96,N,8,1,P  <ENTER>
```

The actual MODE command you must execute depends on your specific printer brand. Chapter 43, "DOS System Commands," discusses the MODE command in detail.

Copying Files to Your Printer

In Chapter 8, "Fundamental File Operations," you learned how to copy a file from one location on your disk to another. You can also copy files to your printer using the COPY command. If you are using a parallel printer attached to LPT1:, you can use the following command to print the file CONFIG.SYS from your disk's root directory.

```
C:\> COPY  \CONFIG.SYS  PRN  <ENTER>
```

Since every COPY command has a source file and destination, CONFIG.SYS is the source and PRN (the printer) is the destination.

If you are using a serial printer attached to COM1:, the following command prints the file's contents.

```
C:\> COPY  \CONFIG.SYS  COM1:  <ENTER>
```

When the COPY command completes, you can eject the printed page from your printer by taking your printer off line and pressing its formfeed button. After the page ejects, make sure you place the printer back on line.

Printing the Screen

Depending on your application, there are many times when it is convenient to print a copy of the screen's contents. For example, assume you are running an application that generates an error message you don't understand. By printing the screen's contents you can get a copy of the error message to use later as a reference when you discuss the error.

To print the screen's contents, press the SHIFT-PRTSC ("print screen") key combination. When you do so, DOS will copy the current screen to your printer. As before, you will need to take your printer off line and press the formfeed button to eject the page.

Printing the Screen with a Serial Printer

By default, when you press SHIFT-PRTSC, DOS sends its output to the parallel port PRN (LPT1: by default). If you are using a serial printer, you must execute the following MODE command to direct DOS to print the screen contents to your serial printer.

```
C:\> MODE  LPT1:=COM1:  <ENTER>
```

When you do so, DOS will display the following message to indicate it is routing all output normally destined for LPT1: to COM1:

```
Resident portion of MODE loaded
LPT1: rerouted to COM1:
```

After you execute the MODE command, the SHIFT-PRTSC key combination will print the current screen using your serial printer. You only need to issue this MODE command once per user session. If you do this every session, you might consider putting this command into an AUTOEXEC.BAT file, so that it will execute automatically on startup (see Chapter 18, "Automatic System Startup Commands with AUTOEXEC.BAT," for more information).

Printing a Screen with Graphics

By default, the SHIFT-PRTSC key combination only supports screens of text, such as the output of the DIR command. If you want to print your screen contents when the screen contains a graphics image, such as a spreadsheet graph, and have it look like the screen does, you must first execute the GRAPHICS command.

The GRAPHICS command loads *memory-resident* software (software that remains in your computer's memory after the command completes) that helps DOS in printing a graphics image. GRAPHICS is an external DOS command that resides in the file GRAPHICS.COM.

The format of the GRAPHICS command is as follows

```
GRAPHICS [printer_type] [profile] [/R] [/B] [/LCD] [/PRINTBOX::id]
```

Items that appear within the left and right brackets are optional command-line entries. The *printer_type* option lets you specify your printer type. Table 13-2 lists the supported printer types.

The *profile* option specifies the complete directory path to a printer profile file that contains information about each of the supported printers listed in Table 13.2. If you don't specify a file name (and you probably won't), GRAPHICS uses the file GRAPHICS.PRO, which is in the DOS subdirectory.

The /R switch reverses the typical black-and-white color usage. By default, DOS prints white screen images as black and black screen images a white. The /R switch directs DOS to print black screen images as black, and white screen images as white.

The /B switch directs DOS to print the background images in color. This switch is only valid for the COLOR4 and COLOR8 printer types.

The /LCD option directs DOS to use the LCD screen aspect ratio. Many portable computers use LCD (liquid crystal display) screens.

Printer Type	Description
COLOR1	IBM color printer with a black ribbon.
COLOR4	IBM color printer with a red, green, blue, and black ribbon.
COLOR8	IBM color printer with a cyan, magenta, yellow, and black ribbon.
GRAPHICS	IBM Personal Graphics Printer, Prowriter, or Quietwriter.
GRAPHICSWIDE *	IBM Personal Graphics Printer with an 11-inch-wide carriage.
HPDEFAULT *	Any Hewlett-Packard PCC printer.
DESKJET *	Any Hewlett-Packard DeskJet printer.
LASERJET	Hewlett-Packard LaserJet printer.
LASERJETII *	Hewlett-Packard LaserJet Series II printer.
PAINTJET *	Hewlett-Packard PaintJet printer.
QUIETJET *	Hewlett-Packard QuietJet printer.
QUIETJET PLUS *	Hewlett-Packard QuietJet Plus printer.
RUGGEDWRITER *	Hewlett-Packard RuggedWriter printer.
RUGGEDWRITERWIDE *	Hewlett-Packard RuggedWriter Wide printer.
THERMAL	IBM Thermal printer.
THINKJET *	Hewlett-Packard ThinkJet printer.

Table 13-2. Printer Types Supported by GRAPHICS.COM. (* indicates DOS 5 printer support)

The /PRINTBOX option selects the size of the print box. The two valid print box IDs are STD (for STanDard size) and LCD (Liquid Crystal Display).

The following command invokes GRAPHICS for a Hewlett-Packard LaserJet II printer.

```
C:\> GRAPHICS  LASERJETII  C:\DOS\GRAPHICS.PRO  <ENTER>
```

The only time you must execute the GRAPHICS command is when you want to use the SHIFT-PRTSC key combination to print a screen containing graphics.

Sending Information to Both Screen and Printer

In some cases you may want DOS to send all the information it writes to the screen and printer. For example, you may want DOS to print a copy of your directory listing as it displays the file names on your screen. The CTRL-PRTSC key combination directs DOS to do just that. To begin, make sure your printer is on line. Next, press the CTRL-PRTSC key combination and then issue the DIR command. As DIR displays the file names on your screen, DOS also *echos* them to the printer, which prints them. When the DIR command completes, press CTRL-PRTSC a second time to turn off the printer echoing.

The CTRL-PRTSC key combination works as a toggle. The first time you press CTRL-PRTSC, DOS turns on printer echoing. The second time you press CTRL-PRTSC, DOS turns the printer echo off.

As before, if you are using a serial printer, you must first issue the following command before you can use CTRL-PRTSC.

```
C:\> MODE LPT1:=COM1:    <ENTER>
```

Telling Your Applications About Your Printer

Just as you must tell DOS where and what your printer is, so must you tell your applications. Normally, the program (word processor, spreadsheet, or database program) will ask you during its installation to identify your printer port. If you try to use your printer from within an application and nothing happens, make sure first that the printer operates properly from DOS. If not, you may need to specify the correct printer speeds for a serial printer using the MODE command. If you can use the printer from DOS, most applications have a setup or menu option that lets you specify your printer type and port. Refer to the documentation that accompanied the product for details.

Hands On

The following commands will differ slightly, depending on whether you are using a serial or parallel printer. If possible, examine your printer's cable to determine this. If you cannot tell, assume you have a parallel printer—most users do. If the printer commands fail to work, repeat the commands, following the steps for a serial printer.

Parallel and Serial Printers

Depending on the number of wires a printer uses to receive information from the computer, your printer is either a parallel or serial printer. Your computer can have one to three parallel devices and up to four serial devices depending on your DOS version. Parallel printers are the fastest and the most common. DOS assigns the names LPT1: through LPT3: to the parallel printer ports. Serial printers on the other hand, attach to the ports COM1: through COM4:.

Printing the Screen

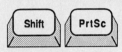

Press SHIFT-PRTSC to print the current screen contents. When DOS completes the screen copy, you can eject the page from your printer by taking your printer off line and pressing the formfeed button.

The GRAPHICS Command

By default, the SHIFT-PRTSC key combination correctly prints your screen contents when the screen contains only text data. To use the SHIFT-PRTSC key combination to print a graphics image, such as a spreadsheet graph, you must first issue the GRAPHICS command for your specific printer type.

Turning Printer Echo On and Off

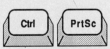

The CTRL-PRTSC key combination toggles printer echoing on and off. When printer echoing is on, DOS sends each character it displays on the screen to the printer also. CTRL-PRTSC, works as a toggle meaning the first time you press CTRL-PRTSC DOS enables printer echo. The second time you press CTRL-PRTSC , DOS turns printer echo off.

To begin, copy the contents of the file AUTOEXEC.BAT, which resides in your root directory, to your printer using one the following commands.

```
C:\> COPY \AUTOEXEC.BAT PRN <ENTER>
```

or

```
C:\> COPY  \AUTOEXEC.BAT  COM1: <ENTER>
```

If your serial printer prints meaningless characters, use the MODE command to define your port speed and settings as discussed earlier in this chapter.

When the COPY command completes, take your printer off line, and press the printer's formfeed button to eject the page. After the page ejects, place the printer back on line.

Next, if you are using a serial printer, issue the following MODE command.

```
C:\> MODE  LPT1:=COM1:  <ENTER>
```

Next, issue the following DIR command to list the files in the current directory.

```
C:\> DIR  /W  <ENTER>
```

When the DIR command completes, press SHIFT-PRTSC to print the current screen. When the operation completes, use the printer's formfeed button to eject the page.

Next, press CTRL-PRTSC to enable printer echo. Issue the following TREE command to print a copy of your disk's current directory structure.

```
C:\> TREE C:\  <ENTER>
```

When the TREE command completes, press CTRL-PRTSC once again to disable printer echoing. Issue the following DIR command.

```
C:\> DIR  \DOS\*.*  <ENTER>
```

Because you have disabled printer echoing, DOS does not print the command's output.

Review

1. Why do parallel port names begin with LPT?

2. Why do serial port names begin with COM?

3. What is the PRN device?

4. How does SHIFT-PRTSC differ from CTRL-PRTSC?

5. Why must serial printer users issue the following MODE command before they can use SHIFT-PRTSC and CTRL-PRTSC?

```
C:\> MODE  LPT1:=COM1:   <ENTER>
```

Answers

1. Parallel ports typically connect line printers to your computer. LPT is an abbreviation for Line PrinTer.

2. Serial ports commonly connect modems to your computer. A modem lets two computers communicate over telephone lines. COM is an abbreviation for COMmunication.

3. PRN is another name for LPT1, the first parallel port in your computer.

4. SHIFT-PRTSC directs DOS to print the screen's current contents. CTRL-PRTSC directs DOS to print each line of text it writes to your screen.

5. By default, DOS sends printer output to the parallel port LPT1:. If you want DOS to send the output to a serial port instead, you must use the MODE command.

Advanced Concepts

DOS lets you use one to three parallel ports (LPT1: through LPT3:) and up to four serial ports (COM1: through COM4:). When you buy a parallel or serial board, the manufacturer ships the board thinking it will be the first parallel or serial device in your computer (LPT1: or COM1:). If your computer has more than one parallel or serial device, you must tell each board its device name. If you have two serial ports, for example, you must tell one port to respond to the device name COM1: and the other board to respond to the device name COM2:. If you buy your computer with two or more ports already installed, you computer manufacturer has made sure each board knows its correct name. If you buy a second serial or parallel board and install the board yourself, you must tell the board its name.

Never work on your computer while it is plugged in. Depending on your board type, there are two ways to tell the board its name: DIP switches or jumpers. A *DIP switch* (Dual Inline Package) is a collection of two or more very small switches on the board. The switches look like miniature light switches (see Figure 13-3).

The manual that accompanies your board will include a page of the correct DIP switch settings for each device name. Each switch normally has an Off or On (possibly 0 or 1) label. Using the point of a pin, a small screw driver, or a bent paper clip, you can change the DIP switch settings. Never change a board's DIP switch settings without first writing down the original values.

A *jumper,* on the other hand, is a small connector that connects two or more pins. Figure 13-4 illustrates a jumper.

The manual that accompanied your board will contain jumper settings to select each device name. To change the jump, gently remove the jumper from the current pins. Next, carefully slide the jumper over the correct pins, taking care not to bend a pin. Again, never change a jumper before you note its original position. After you correctly set the board's switches or jumpers, close your computer's chassis, plug in your computer, and start DOS. Each board in your computer should now respond to its correct name.

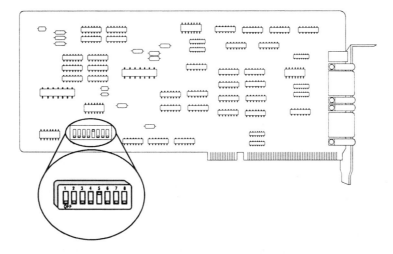

Figure 13-3.   DIP switches on a computer board

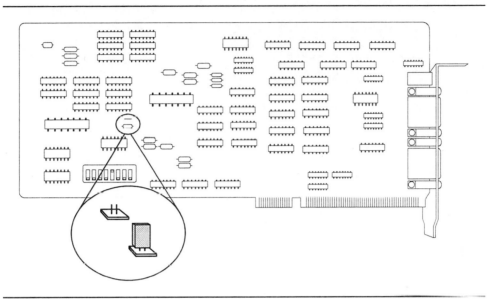

Figure 13-4. *A jumper connects two or more pins*

Key Terms

Serial device   A device such as a printer or mouse that connects to one of your computer's communication ports, such as COM1:. Serial devices send or receive information from the computer one bit at a time over a single wire.

Parallel device   A device, typically a printer, that connects to one of your computer's parallel ports, such as LPT1:. Parallel devices communicate with the computer eight bits at a time over eight wires and, thus, are faster than serial devices.

Modem   A hardware device that lets two computers communicate over standard telephone lines. Modem is an abbreviation for MOdulator/DEModulator.

Chapter 14

Getting the Most
from PRINT

In Chapter 13 you learned how to use basic DOS techniques to copy a file to your printer or to print your screen's current contents. If you have a word processor, you will normally want to use it to print your files due to the word processor's text formatting capabilities. There may be times, however, when you have several text files, or a large text file that doesn't require special formatting. Then you can use the PRINT command to print the file's contents. Using PRINT, you can perform other DOS commands while the file prints, essentially letting your computer perform two tasks at once.

Understanding PRINT

In Chapter 13, you copied a file's contents to your printer using the COPY command and either the device name PRN or COM1, as shown here.

```
C:\> COPY  \AUTOEXEC.BAT  PRN  <ENTER>
```

Although using COPY in this way can successfully print a file's contents, it has two shortcomings. First, in order to eject a page when COPY is completed, you must manually take your printer off line, press the printer's formfeed button, and place the printer back on line. Second, if you are copying a large file to the printer, the operation may take considerable time, leaving you unable to issue other commands until COPY completes.

To make it easier for you to print a large text file, or several smaller files, DOS provides the PRINT command. PRINT is an external DOS command in the DOS directory.

To print a text file using PRINT, invoke PRINT with the desired file name, for example:

```
C:\> PRINT  \AUTOEXEC.BAT  <ENTER>
```

PRINT does not know if you are using a parallel printer attached to the port LPT1 (also called PRN) or a serial printer attached to COM1. Therefore, the first time you invoke it, PRINT will display the following prompt, asking you which *list device* to use.

```
Name of list device [PRN]:
```

The "[PRN]" tells you PRINT's default device. If you simply press ENTER , PRINT will use PRN (LPT1:). If your printer attaches to a device other than PRN, such as COM1, you must type in the correct device name and press ENTER. If you are not sure to which device name your printer connects, simply press ENTER selecting PRN. If your printer fails to print the file, you will need to restart DOS and invoke PRINT using a different device name. Most users, however, will use parallel printers connected to PRN. PRINT only displays this device name prompt the first time you invoke it. After that, PRINT uses the device name specified until you restart DOS. If PRINT cannot locate the file specified, PRINT will display "File not found." Otherwise, PRINT will begin printing the file's contents, displaying the following message and returning control to the DOS prompt.

```
C:\AUTOEXEC.BAT is currently being printed
```

After PRINT finishes printing the file's contents, PRINT automatically ejects the last page of the file for you.

Although it's not obvious for small files whose contents PRINT can print quickly, PRINT actually returns control to the DOS prompt before it finishes printing the file's contents, unlike COPY. PRINT is unique among all of the other DOS commands in that PRINT lets DOS redisplay its prompt for other commands before it has finished its processing. While you execute other commands, PRINT continues printing your files until it is done.

Printing More than One File

PRINT is useful not only for printing a large text file, but also for printing several smaller files. To print multiple files, you can invoke PRINT several times, once for each file, or you can specify all the file names in one PRINT command. The following PRINT command, for example, prints the contents of the root directory text files AUTOEXEC.BAT and CONFIG.SYS.

```
C:\> PRINT  \AUTOEXEC.BAT  \CONFIG.SYS  <ENTER>
```

PRINT will begin printing the file AUTOEXEC.BAT displaying the following message.

```
C:\AUTOEXEC.BAT is currently being printed
C:\CONFIG.SYS is in queue
```

Because you told PRINT the desired list device the first time you invoked it, PRINT does not prompt you to do so now.

As you can imagine, your printer is only capable of printing one file at a time. PRINT, therefore, prints files in the same order you specify. In this case, PRINT begins printing AUTOEXEC.BAT first. If you direct PRINT to print several files, PRINT will start printing the first file and will place the remaining file names into a waiting list called a *queue*. As PRINT finishes one file, it begins printing the next file in the queue in a first-come, first-served basis. By default, PRINT lets you place up to ten files in the queue. If you need to queue more than ten files, you will need to invoke PRINT with the /Q switch as discussed in the "Advanced Concepts" section. Assuming your disk contains the files FIRST.DAT, SECOND.DAT, and THIRD.DAT, you can add the files to print queue, as shown here.

```
C:\> PRINT  FIRST.DAT  SECOND.DAT  THIRD.DAT  <ENTER>

  C:\AUTOEXEC.BAT is currently being printed
  C:\CONFIG.SYS is in queue
  C:\FIRST.DAT is in queue
  C:\SECOND.DAT is in queue
  C:\THIRD.DAT is in queue
```

You learned in Chapter 9, "DOS Wildcard Characters," that most DOS commands support the * and ? wildcards. PRINT is no exception. Using the * wildcard, the following command would print the files in the current directory with the BAT extension.

```
C:\> PRINT  *.BAT  <ENTER>
```

If you invoke PRINT without specifying a file, PRINT will display the name of file it is now printing as well as the files in the queue:

```
C:\> PRINT  <ENTER>

  C:\AUTOEXEC.BAT is currently being printed
  C:\CONFIG.SYS is in queue
  C:\FIRST.DAT is in queue
  C:\SECOND.DAT is in queue
  C:\THIRD.DAT is in queue
```

Canceling a File's Printing

PRINT quickly returns control to DOS before finishing the actual print job, letting you execute other commands. Because PRINT continues to work in the background while you execute other commands, PRINT ignores the CTRL-C keyboard combination that you usually use to end other DOS commands. If you want to cancel a file's printing, you must invoke PRINT again, using the /T or /C switches.

The /T switch directs PRINT to end the printing of the current file and to remove all files from the print queue. Assume, for example, your print queue contains the following files.

```
C:\> PRINT  <ENTER>

  C:\AUTOEXEC.BAT is currently being printed
  C:\CONFIG.SYS is in queue
  C:\FIRST.DAT is in queue
  C:\SECOND.DAT is in queue
  C:\THIRD.DAT is in queue
```

You can cancel the file printing by invoking PRINT using /T:

```
C:\> PRINT  /T  <ENTER>
PRINT queue is empty
```

In addition, this line will print on your hard copy:

```
All files canceled by operator
```

You should note that to improve their performance, most printers have their own electronic memories, called *buffers,* to which PRINT can send all or part of a file. If you use the /T switch to end a print job, your printer may still print several pages, depending on the size of its memory. PRINT, however, will not send any further information to the printer.

PRINT's /T switch directs PRINT to cancel the printing of all files. In many cases, you may simply want to remove a specific file from the print queue. PRINT's /C switch lets you do just that.

Assume, for example, your print queue contains the files ONE, TWO, THREE, FOUR, and FIVE:

```
C:\> PRINT   <ENTER>

  C:\ONE is currently being printed
  C:\TWO is in queue
  C:\THREE is in queue
  C:\FOUR is in queue
  C:\FIVE is in queue
```

Using the /C switch, the following command removes the file THREE from the print queue.

```
C:\> PRINT   THREE   /C   <ENTER>
```

PRINT will remove the file, displaying the queue's new contents:

```
  C:\ONE is currently being printed
  C:\TWO is in queue
  C:\FOUR is in queue
  C:\FIVE is in queue
```

When you use the /C switch, PRINT cancels the printing for the file whose name precedes the switch (including the one currently being printed), as well as those that follow it. The following command, for example, removes the files TWO and FOUR.

```
C:\> PRINT   TWO   /C   FOUR   <ENTER>
```

```
C:\ONE is currently being printed
C:\FIVE is in queue
```

Hands On

So that you have several files to print, use the COPY command to create the files BASEBALL.DAT, FOOTBALL.DAT, and HOCKEY.DAT, which contain the following team names.

```
C:\> COPY  CON  BASEBALL.DAT  <ENTER>
Red Sox    <ENTER>
Giants     <ENTER>
White Sox  <ENTER>
Cubs       <ENTER>
Blue Jays  <ENTER>
^Z  <ENTER>
        1 File(s) copied

C:\> COPY  CON  FOOTBALL.DAT  <ENTER>
Seahawks <ENTER>
Raiders  <ENTER>
Giants   <ENTER>
Bills    <ENTER>
^Z  <ENTER>
        1 File(s) copied

C:\> COPY  CON  HOCKEY.DAT  <ENTER>
Rangers <ENTER>
Kings   <ENTER>
Black Hawks <ENTER>
Maple Leafs <ENTER>
^Z  <ENTER>
        1 File(s) copied
```

Next, use the following command to print the file BASEBALL.DAT.

```
C:\> PRINT BASEBALL.DAT  <ENTER>
```

/ *SUMMARY* /

PRINT

The PRINT command lets you print one or more text files, while still using your computer to perform other commands. When you direct PRINT to print several files, PRINT will begin printing the first file while placing the remaining files in a waiting list called a queue. Each time PRINT finishes printing a file, PRINT automatically ejects the file's last page from the printer and begins printing the next file specified in the queue. PRINT, like the TYPE command, only supports text files. The following command prints a copy of the file AUTOEXEC.BAT.

```
C:\> PRINT \AUTOEXEC.BAT <ENTER>
```

PRINT, will prompt you for the printer device the *first* time it is invoked only:

```
Name of list device [PRN]:
```

If you are using a parallel printer connected to PRN, press ENTER. If your printer attaches to a different port, such as COM1, type in the port name and press ENTER.

Next, print the other two files:

```
C:\> PRINT FOOTBALL.DAT HOCKEY.DAT <ENTER>
```

While PRINT is printing your files, issue the following DIR command.

```
C:\> DIR <ENTER>
```

As you can see, PRINT lets you issue other DOS commands while it does its work in the background.

Using the asterisk wildcard, print all the files with the DAT extension.

```
C:\> PRINT *.DAT <ENTER>
```

Next, using PRINT's /C switch, remove the file HOCKEY.DAT from the print queue.

```
C:\> PRINT  HOCKEY.DAT  /C  <ENTER>
```

Last, using the /T switch, remove all the files from the print queue and cancel the current print job. Examine the last page of the printout for the "All files canceled" message.

Review

1. How does the PRINT command differ from simply copying files to your printer using the following command?

```
C:\> COPY  FILENAME.EXT  PRN  <ENTER>
```

2. What is the PRINT command to print the two root directory files AUTOEXEC.BAT and CONFIG.SYS?

3. What does the "[PRN]" in PRINT's prompt for a list device mean?

```
Name of list device  [PRN]:
```

4. What is the print queue?

5. Assuming your print queue contains the following files, what is the PRINT command to cancel the file LARGE.DAT?

```
C:\> PRINT  <ENTER>

  C:\SMALL is currently being printed
  C:\MEDIUM is in queue
  C:\LARGE is in queue
```

Answers

1. Unlike COPY, the PRINT command returns control to the DOS prompt before it completes its processing. PRINT then shares control of the CPU with DOS, printing your file in the background while you are free to execute other commands. Second, when the PRINT command finishes printing a file's contents, it automatically ejects the file's last page from your printer.

2. The PRINT command to print the root directory files AUTOEXEC.BAT and CONFIG.SYS is

   ```
   C:\> PRINT  \AUTOEXEC.BAT  \CONFIG.SYS  <ENTER>
   ```

3. Letters appearing between left and right brackets normally indicate the default setting. In this case, the letters "PRN" tell you that if you simply press ENTER, PRINT will use the parallel port PRN. If your printer is attached to a port other than PRN, such as COM1, type in the correct device name and press ENTER.

4. A queue is a waiting list. A print queue is a list of files that are waiting to print. PRINT prints files in the same order they enter the queue. In other words, PRINT uses first come, first served.

5. The proper command to cancel printing of LARGE.DAT is

   ```
   C:\> PRINT  LARGE.DAT  /C  <ENTER>
   ```

Advanced Concepts

If you use the PRINT command on a regular basis, PRINT provides several additional command-line switches you can use to improve performance. As you will learn in this section, you can only use these switches the very first time you invoke PRINT.

PRINT Installs Memory-Resident Software

Before DOS can run a program, the program must reside in your computer's electronic memory. In most cases, when you execute a command DOS loads the command from disk and runs it. When the command completes, DOS makes the memory available for the next command.

Some DOS commands, however, don't run to completion in this manner. Instead, these commands remain in your computer's memory after DOS redisplays its prompt. In this way, the commands can periodically run to perform a specific task. Commands that remain in memory in this way are called *memory-resident commands*. Because such commands remain resident in memory after they return control to DOS, users often refer to them as *Terminate-and-Stay-Resident* commands, or simply *TSRs*.

The PRINT command is a memory-resident command, which explains why PRINT can continue to print your files in the background while DOS executes other commands. After you invoke PRINT, you can visualize your computer's memory as having portions allocated to DOS and PRINT, as well as a portion available for other commands you will execute (see Figure 14-1).

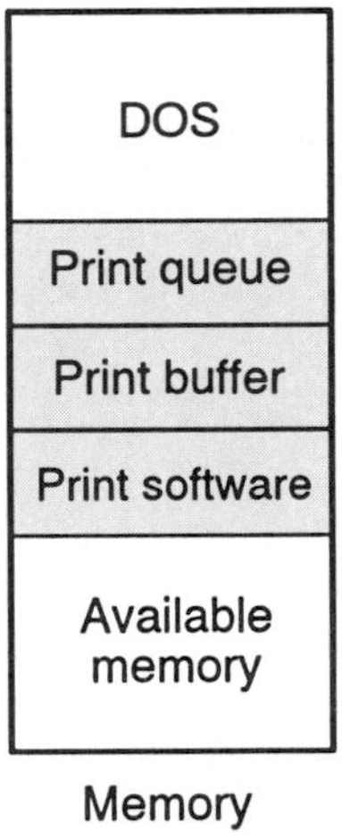

| DOS |
| Print queue |
| Print buffer |
| Print software |
| Available memory |

Memory

Figure 14-1.   *PRINT is a memory-resident command residing in a portion of your computer's electronic memory*

The switches discussed in the following section affect the way PRINT configures its memory-resident software. You can only use these switches the very first time you invoke PRINT—after that they "Stay Resident."

/Q Increases PRINT's Queue Size

By default, PRINT lets you place up to 10 files in the print queue. If you try to print more than 10 files at one time, PRINT will display a message indicating the print queue is full.

PRINT's /Q switch lets you increase or decrease the print queue size. To set the queue size, specify a queue size from 4 to 32 after /Q. The following command, then, selects a queue size of 32.

```
C:\> PRINT  /Q:32   <ENTER>
```

Use a colon to separate the desired queue size from "/Q". Don't arbitrarily use the queue size 32 if you don't think you will print that many files on a regular basis. Each queue entry consumes 64 bytes of available memory.

/B Increases PRINT's Buffer Size

To print a file's contents, PRINT reads a sector of the file from disk, prints the information, and then reads another sector, repeating this process for the entire file. Figure 14-2 illustrates this process. Each time PRINT reads a sector, PRINT places the sector into a memory buffer. By default, PRINT's buffer size is 512 bytes.

Compared to your computer's very fast electronic memory, your hard disk is very slow. If you use PRINT on a regular basis, you can improve PRINT's performance by increasing PRINT's electronic buffer size. PRINT lets you specify a buffer size from 512 to 16,384 bytes. You should increase the buffer size in multiples of 512 (1024, 1536, 2048, 4096, and so on). The following command, for example, directs PRINT to use a 4096-byte (4 Kb) buffer.

```
C:\> PRINT  /B:4096   <ENTER>
```

By increasing the buffer size, you increase the amount of information PRINT can read from your disk, and, in turn, reduce the number of slow disk operations PRINT must perform. A single-spaced, typed page will take about 4000 bytes. Use this value as your guide to determining how large a print buffer you need.

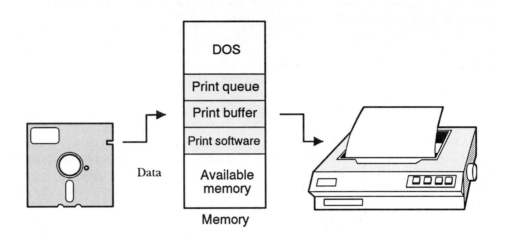

Figure 14-2.   PRINT reads a file's contents to a memory buffer, then prints it

/D Specifies the List Device

The first time you invoke PRINT, it will prompt you for a list device. PRINT's /D switch lets you specify the list device when you invoke PRINT. Then, PRINT will not prompt you for the list-device name. The following command directs PRINT to use the device PRN.

```
C:\> PRINT   /D:PRN   <ENTER>
```

If you are using a printer connected to the serial port COM1, use /D:COM1.

Giving PRINT More CPU Time

As discussed, PRINT is a memory-resident program that works in the background to print your files. When you use PRINT and issue other commands, your computer appears to perform two tasks at once. As it turns out, however, your computer is really letting PRINT work for a while, then your DOS command, then PRINT, and so on. Because your computer exchanges processing time between PRINT and your other commands so fast, the two commands appear to work at the same time.

Your computer achieves this illusion of running two commands at once by giving PRINT and DOS fixed time intervals (or *time slices*) in which to perform their work. This time interval is defined in terms of *CPU clock ticks,* which occur 18.2 times per second. In other words, the time interval lasts about 5/100 second. PRINT provides three switches that affect how often PRINT gets a turn and how long PRINT's turn lasts.

PRINT's /S switch determines how often PRINT gets to run. By default, PRINT does not get to run as often as the other DOS commands it is sharing the CPU with. The /S switch specifies the maximum number of clock ticks for which the other application can run before PRINT gets a chance. The default value for /S is 8 (4/10 of a second). You can specify values from 1 to 255 (1/20 second to 12 3/4 seconds). If you make the /S value too large, PRINT will not run as often—your files will still print, but they will take longer.

PRINT's /M switch specifies how long PRINT can keep the CPU each time PRINT gets a chance to run. The default value for /M is 2 (1/10 second). Using /M, you can give PRINT 1 to 255 clock ticks (1/20 second to 12 3/4 seconds). If you make the /M value too large, your other commands may become sluggish when PRINT is running.

Last, PRINT's /U switch specifies how long PRINT can wait for your printer if the printer isn't ready for more characters. Many older printers did not have very large built-in memory buffers to which PRINT could send characters. It was common for PRINT to be ready to send characters, but for the printer not to be ready to receive them. By default, PRINT will wait one clock tick for the printer to become available. If the printer remains busy, PRINT gives up its turn. PRINT's /U switch lets you increase the number of clock cycles PRINT can wait for the printer. For newer printers with large built-in memories, the /U switch normally isn't necessary. However, for older printers you might experiment with values of 8 or 16.

Placing a PRINT Command in AUTOEXEC.BAT

If you plan to make extensive use of PRINT, determine the switch settings that seem to give you the best performance. Next, place the corresponding PRINT command in your AUTOEXEC.BAT file so you don't have to worry about the switch details. Many users will place a command similar to the following in AUTOEXEC.BAT.

```
PRINT  /Q:16  /U:8  /M:32  /B:4096
```

Adding Files to the Print Queue

PRINT's /C switch lets you remove files from the print queue. When PRINT encounters the /C switch, PRINT cancels the file that precedes /C as well as all files that follow. In similar manner, the /P switch directs PRINT to add a file to the queue. The /P switch exists to let you add one or more files to the print queue in a command line that cancels one or more files using /C. For example, the following command cancels the files OLDONE and OLDTWO while adding the files NEWONE and NEWTWO.

```
C:\> PRINT  OLDONE  /C  OLDTWO  NEWONE /P  NEWTWO  <ENTER>
```

When PRINT encounters /P, PRINT will add to the queue the file name that precedes /P and all files that follow.

How Much Memory Does PRINT Allocate?

PRINT is a memory-resident program that allocates a portion of your computer's memory. Depending on your PRINT command-line switches, the amount of memory PRINT consumes will differ. To determine just how much memory your PRINT command uses, invoke either CHKDSK or the DOS 4 MEM command before you invoke PRINT and note the amount of free memory. Next, invoke your desired PRINT command. Repeat CHKDSK or MEM and note the amount of free memory. The difference between the two amounts is the amount of memory PRINT consumes.

Key Terms

Print queue   A list of files waiting to print.

List device   The printer device to which PRINT will send your hardcopy output.

Memory-resident software   A program that remains in your computer's electronic memory after returning control to the DOS prompt. Memory-resident software is also called terminate-and-stay-resident or TSR software. PRINT is a memory-resident software program.

Chapter 15

Grouping Commands
with Batch Files

Throughout Chapters 3 through 14, to execute a DOS command you type the command's name at the DOS prompt and press ENTER . When the command ends, DOS redisplays its prompt and waits for you to type the next command. Because you are in constant interaction with DOS, this process of executing a command, waiting for the command to complete, and executing the next command is called *interactive processing*. Interactive processing makes up the majority of the processing new DOS users perform. As you will learn in this chapter, you may save time and keystrokes by using DOS batch files.

A *batch file* is a file you create with your word processor or the DOS editor that contains the names of a "batch" of DOS commands to execute with one call. Batch files use the BAT extension. If you type the name of a batch file name at the DOS prompt and press ENTER, DOS will execute, in order, each of the commands the batch file contains. Because DOS automatically executes the batch file's commands on its own, you are free to work on other tasks away from your computer, as opposed to waiting at the keyboard just so you can type in the next command.

Creating Simple Batch Files

DOS provides batch files to make your computer easier to use. You might create a batch file to abbreviate a long or difficult command, for example, or to execute several commands you always execute as a group. In this chapter you will create several very small batch files. As you learn more about DOS batch capabilities in Chapters 16, "Decision-Making Batch Files," and 17, "Getting the Most from Batch Files," your batch files may grow from a few commands to very large collections, containing 10, 20, or even 50 or more commands. DOS batch files are very flexible and powerful tools. Many experienced DOS users are only now learning their true power.

Because the batch files presented in this chapter are quite short, you may find it easier and faster to copy the batch files directly from the keyboard. Before you create the batch files presented in this chapter, create a directory on your disk named BATCH, in which you can organize the files. Then make BATCH the current directory:

```
C:\> MKDIR  \BATCH  <ENTER>
C:\> CHDIR  \BATCH  <ENTER>
```

Next, the following COPY command creates a batch file named DATETIME.BAT that invokes the DATE and TIME commands.

```
C:\BATCH> COPY  CON  DATETIME.BAT  <ENTER>
DATE  <ENTER>
TIME  <ENTER>
^Z  <ENTER>
        1 file(s) copied

C:\BATCH>
```

From the DOS prompt, you can execute the batch file by typing its name:

```
C:\BATCH> DATETIME  <ENTER>
```

When you execute a batch file, DOS executes, in order, each command the batch file contains. In this case, DOS will first execute DATE displaying the following:

```
C:\BATCH> DATETIME  <ENTER>

C:\BATCH> DATE
Current date is Sun 03-17-1991
Enter new date (mm-dd-yy):
```

If your system date is correct, press ENTER to leave the date unchanged; otherwise, type in the correct date. When the DATE command completes, DOS will execute the TIME command:

```
C:\BATCH> DATETIME    <ENTER>

C:\BATCH> DATE
Current date is Sun 03-17-1991
Enter new date (mm-dd-yy):  <ENTER>

C:\BATCH> TIME
Current time is 11:16:23.67p
Enter new time:
```

Once again, type in the correct time or press ENTER to leave the current time unchanged. When the TIME command completes, the batch file has no more commands, and DOS redisplays its prompt.

Using an editor, edit the file DATETIME.BAT and insert a CLS command to clear the screen as soon as the batch file begins.

```
CLS
DATE
TIME
```

Again, from the DOS prompt, invoke DATETIME.BAT. As before, DOS will execute, in order, each of the commands the batch file contains.

DOS batch files exist to reduce your keystrokes and to eliminate the need for you to memorize long or difficult commands. Assume, for example, you typically use your computer to perform word processing in WordPerfect. Each time your system starts (you've established no command path, as discussed in Chapter 11, "Getting the Most from DOS Directories"), you use CHDIR to select the WP directory, and you then invoke WordPerfect using the WP command, as shown here.

```
C:\> CHDIR  WP  <ENTER>
C:\WP>  WP  <ENTER>
```

Using a DOS batch file named DOWP.BAT, for example, you can automatically execute both commands in only one step. In this case, DOWP.BAT would contain the following commands.

```
CHDIR  \WP
WP
```

To invoke the batch file, you would simply type **DOWP** at the DOS prompt.

```
C:\BATCH> DOWP   <ENTER>
```

If you are trying to help new users get started, you can eliminate many confusing intermediate-step commands such as CHDIR with DOS batch files.

Naming Batch Files

Like all your files, you should assign meaningful names to your batch files. A batch file's name should summarize the task the batch file performs. The previous examples used the meaningful names DATETIME and DOWP. Never give your batch files the same name as a DOS internal command. If you do, DOS will always execute the internal command, never getting to your batch file. If you give your batch file the name of an external DOS command, such as FORMAT or DISKCOPY, DOS will execute either the batch file or the external command, depending on which one DOS encounters first. In general, assigning a batch file the name of an external command is asking for confusion.

Disabling Command-Name Display

Invoke the batch file DATETIME.BAT and examine your screen. By default, when DOS executes a batch file command, DOS displays, or echos, the DOS prompt and the command name on your screen, as shown here.

```
C:\BATCH> DATETIME   <ENTER>

C:\BATCH> CLS                      ◄──── Screen clears after this
C:\BATCH> DATE                     ◄──── DATE command name
Current date is Sun 03-17-1991
Enter new date (mm-dd-yy): <ENTER>

C:\BATCH> TIME                     ◄──── TIME command name
Current time is 11:16:23.67p
Enter new time:
```

As your batch files become larger and more complex, displaying the command names in this way adds unnecessary screen clutter, which may confuse or intimidate a new user. By placing the ECHO OFF command as the first command in your batch file, you can disable command-name display, as shown here.

```
ECHO OFF
CLS
DATE
TIME
```

When you invoke DATETIME now, your screen will display the following.

```
C:\BATCH> DATETIME    <ENTER>

C:\BATCH> ECHO OFF
Current date is Sun 03-17-1991
Enter new date (mm-dd-yy):  <ENTER>
Current time is 11:16:23.67p
Enter new time:  <ENTER>
```

You may not see all this, because your screen will clear immediately after the ECHO OFF command executes. As you can see, DOS did not display the names of the DATE and TIME commands. However, DOS does display the command ECHO OFF. If you are using DOS version 3.3 or later, precede ECHO OFF with the @ ("at" sign) character, as shown here.

```
@ECHO OFF
CLS
DATE
TIME
```

The @ directs DOS to suppress the display of the current command's name.

Ending a Batch File

As you have learned, the CTRL-C keyboard combination lets you end DOS commands. If you press CTRL-C during a batch file's execution, DOS doesn't know if you want to end the current command or if you want to end the entire batch file. As a result, DOS displays the following prompt to find out.

```
Terminate batch job (Y/N)?
```

If you type Y, DOS will end the batch file, redisplaying the DOS prompt. If you instead type N, DOS will end the current command, continuing the batch file's execution with the next command in the batch file.

For example, invoke the DATETIME batch file. When DATE prompts you to enter a date, press CTRL-C. As discussed, DOS will prompt you to determine if you want to end the batch file or the current command:

```
C:\BATCH> DATETIME    <ENTER>
Current date is Sun 03-17-1991
Enter new date (mm-dd-yy): ^C

Terminate batch job (Y/N)?
```

Type Y to end the batch file. DOS will end the batch file, redisplaying the DOS prompt.

```
C:\BATCH> DATETIME    <ENTER>
Current date is Sun 03-17-1991
Enter new date (mm-dd-yy): ^C

Terminate batch job (Y/N)?Y

C:\BATCH>
```

Repeat this process, pressing CTRL-C at the DATE prompt. This time, respond to the DOS prompt to end the batch file by typing N to end the DATE command, but not the entire batch file. DOS will continue the batch file's execution with the TIME command, as shown.

```
C:\BATCH> DATETIME    <ENTER>
Current date is Sun 03-17-1991
Enter new date (mm-dd-yy): ^C

Terminate batch job (Y/N)?N
Current time is 11:16:23.67p
Enter new time:
```

Using PATH to Locate Commonly Used Batch Files

To help you organize your batch files, you should create a directory named BATCH. Place into the directory your most commonly used batch files. Next, using the PATH command discussed in Chapter 11, include the BATCH directory in your command path. In the simplest case, your path might become the following.

```
C:\> PATH  C:\DOS;C:\BATCH  <ENTER>
```

Display the current path before you change it to ensure you include all the necessary directories. As discussed in Chapter 18, "Automatic System Startup Commands with AUTOEXEC.BAT," the special batch file AUTOEXEC.BAT lets you specify a list of commands you want DOS to automatically execute each time your system starts. By including a complete PATH command in AUTOEXEC.BAT, you can simplify your command-path definition.

Three Commonly Used Batch Commands

Almost every batch file you will encounter uses the ECHO OFF command to disable command-name display during the batch file's execution. In addition to suppressing the display of command names, ECHO also lets you display messages to the user as your batch file executes. The following batch file, GREETING.BAT, uses ECHO to display the message "Hi, have a nice day!"

```
@ECHO OFF
ECHO Hi, have a nice day!
```

If you are using a DOS version earlier than 3.3, replace @ECHO OFF with an ECHO OFF and a CLS command. When you execute GREETING.BAT from the DOS prompt, your screen will display the following.

```
C:\BATCH> GREETING  <ENTER>
Hi, have a nice day!
```

The ECHO command serves two purposes. First, using ECHO OFF you disable command-name display. If you specify text other than OFF (or ON, which turns command-name display back on), ECHO will display the text as a message on your screen. As you increase your batch file knowledge, your batch files may eventually use ECHO to display menus such as the following.

```
              Menu

     F1 Start WordPerfect
     F2 Start Lotus 123
     F3 Run DBase IV
     F4 Quit to DOS
```

Placing Remarks in Batch Files

Your batch file name should summarize the processing the batch file performs. Even so, you should develop the habit of placing remarks in your batch files that better explain the task the batch file performs and why. If another user reads your batch file, the remarks will help the user understand each step the batch file performs. If you read the batch file yourself, the remarks serve to remind you why you created the batch file, along with the steps the batch file performs.

DOS provides the REM command to let you place remarks in your batch files. Using REM, you should include, at a minimum, your name, the date you created the batch file, and the function the batch file performs. The following batch file uses REM to describe the DOWP.BAT.

```
@ECHO OFF
REM DOWP.BAT - By Kris Jamsa 6-30-91
REM Function:  Let the user invoke WordPerfect in one step
CHDIR \WP
WP
```

When DOS executes your batch files, DOS ignores the lines containing REM, knowing the lines contain user documentation. Make sure you place your REM commands after the ECHO OFF command in your batch file, or DOS will display each command, cluttering your screen.

When your batch files are very short, you may wonder why the batch file needs remarks. If your batch files only contain two or three common commands such as CLS, DATE, and TIME, the batch file won't need a lot of explanation. You should still include lines describing who created the batch file, when, and why. When your batch files get longer and more complex, remarks are essential to your understanding of the batch file's processing. It only takes a few minutes to properly document your batch files. Those few minutes can save you a great deal of time when you later try to recall the steps the batch file performs.

Temporarily Suspending a Batch File

As your batch file complexity grows, you may need to perform a specific action, such as placing a floppy disk in a drive or turning on the printer, before the batch file can perform the next task. The PAUSE command temporarily suspends a batch file until the user presses a key to continue. PAUSE displays an optional message followed by a prompt for the user to press any key to continue.

```
[optional message]
Press any key to continue. . .
```

The optional message typically contains instructions for the user to perform a specific task. For example:

```
PAUSE Make sure your printer is on
```

When DOS encounters the above PAUSE command within a batch file, the screen will display the following:

```
PAUSE Make sure your printer is on
Press any key to continue. . .
```

When the user presses a key, DOS will continue the batch file's execution with the next command. In a different application, the PAUSE command might display a warning message, stating the batch file is about to delete files or perform some other critical operation. If the user doesn't want the batch file to continue, the user can press CTRL-C and end the batch file.

There is one problem with the PAUSE command; PAUSE does not work well with batch files using ECHO OFF. As discussed, the ECHO OFF command suppresses command-name display. Unfortunately, ECHO OFF also suppresses the PAUSE command's optional message. The following batch file, BATCOPY.BAT, for example, copies the batch files residing in the current directory to a floppy disk in drive A. The batch file intends to use the PAUSE command to prompt the user to place a formatted disk drive A.

```
@ECHO OFF
PAUSE Place a formatted disk in drive A
COPY  *.BAT  A:
```

What happens, however, is that the ECHO OFF command suppresses the PAUSE command's optional message. When you invoke BATCOPY, your screen will display the following.

```
C:\BATCH> BATCOPY
Press any key to continue. . .
```

Because ECHO OFF suppresses the message telling the user to place a disk in drive A, most users will simply press any key to continue, and the COPY command will fail. In this case, the easiest way to correct the problem is to remove the ECHO OFF command.

```
PAUSE Place a formatted disk in drive A
COPY  *.BAT  A:
```

Many times, however, a PAUSE command will appear in the middle of your batch file. The easiest way to correct the problem here is to use ECHO to display the desired message and PAUSE simply to prompt the user to press a key:

```
@ECHO OFF
ECHO  Place a formatted disk in drive A
PAUSE
COPY  *.BAT  A:
```

When you invoke this batch file, your screen will display the correct instructions.

```
C:\BATCH> BATCOPY   <ENTER>
Place a formatted disk in drive A
Press any key to continue. . .
```

Hands On

If you have not yet done so, use the MKDIR command to create a BATCH subdirectory. Select BATCH as the current directory.

```
C:\>      \BATCH  <ENTER>
C:\>      \BATCH  <ENTER>
```

SUMMARY

Batch Files

A DOS batch file is a file with the BAT extension that contains the name of one or more DOS commands. Like DOS commands, you execute DOS batch files by typing the batch file's name at the DOS prompt. When DOS encounters a batch file, DOS automatically executes, in order, the commands whose names the batch file contains. DOS batch files exist to save you time, keystrokes, and to eliminate your need to memorize long or difficult commands.

ECHO OFF

By default, DOS displays the DOS prompt and command name for each batch file command it executes. Using the ECHO OFF command, you can disable command-name display. Place the ECHO OFF command as the first command in your batch file. If you are using DOS 3.3 or later, precede ECHO with an "at" sign (@) character, @ECHO OFF.

```
ECHO OFF            @ECHO OFF
CLS                 DATE
DATE                TIME
TIME
```

(DOS 3.2 and earlier)   (DOS 3.3 and later)

Canceling a Batch File

As DOS lets you use CTRL-C to end a command, DOS also lets you cancel a batch file using CTRL-C. When you press CTRL-C during a batch file's execution, DOS doesn't know if you want to end the current command or if you want to cancel the entire batch file. As such, DOS displays the following prompt.

```
Terminate batch file (Y/N)?
```

If you type Y, DOS will cancel the batch file, redisplaying the DOS prompt. If you type N, DOS will end the current command, continuing the batch file's execution with the command that immediately follows.

/ SUMMARY /

The ECHO Command

The ECHO command lets your batch files enable or disable command-name display using ECHO OFF or ECHO ON. In addition, ECHO lets your batch files display messages to the user. Using the ECHO command, you can create menu-driven batch files, or even set your screen colors and key combinations, as discussed in Chapter 34, "ANSI.SYS."

The REM Command

The REM command lets you include explanatory remarks in your batch files that explain who wrote the batch file, when the batch file was written, and the function the batch file performs. REM is an abbreviation for "remark." When DOS encounters a REM command in your batch file, DOS ignores the command and continues the batch file's execution with the next command. Select a format that you like that explains who created the batch file, when, and why, and include the information after ECHO OFF in your batch files, for example:

```
@ECHO OFF
REM Written by:
REM Date written:
REM Function:
```

The PAUSE Command

The PAUSE command displays an optional message to the user and then suspends your batch file's processing until the user presses any key to continue. Using PAUSE, your batch file can display instructions or status messages to the user, pausing for a user response. If the user doesn't want the batch file to continue, the user can press CTRL-C to end the batch file. The following PAUSE command directs the user to place the printer on line.

```
PAUSE  Place your printer on line
```

When DOS encounters the PAUSE command in your batch file, your screen will display the following.

```
PAUSE  Place your printer on line
Press any key to continue. . .
```

Next, create the batch file WIDEDIR.BAT that clears your screen and then display your directory listing in a wide format using DIR's /W switch.

```
CLS
DIR /W
```

Invoke WIDEDIR from the DOS prompt, as shown here.

```
C:\BATCH> WIDEDIR   <ENTER>
```

Next, create the batch file HELLO.BAT that displays a personalized greeting.

```
@ECHO OFF
ECHO Hi, NAME
ECHO How are you today?
```

Replace *NAME* with your own name. Next create the batch file TREEPRT.BAT that contains the following.

```
@ECHO OFF
ECHO Turn your printer on line
ECHO Press Ctrl-PrtSc to print a directory tree
PAUSE
TREE C:\
ECHO Press Ctrl-PrtSc to disable printer echoing
```

Invoke the batch file TREEPRT, as shown here.

```
C:\BATCH> TREEPRT   <ENTER>
```

When your screen displays the prompt for you to press CTRL-PRTSC, do so to enable printer echoing, as discussed in Chapter 13, "Printing." DOS will in turn write the TREE command's output to your screen and printer. When the batch file completes, press CTRL-PRTSC again to disable printer echoing.

Execute the batch file TREEPRT again.

```
C:\BATCH> TREEPRT   <ENTER>
```

This time, when PAUSE displays the message to press any key to continue, press CTRL-C to end the batch file. DOS will display the following prompt.

```
Terminate batch file (Y/N)?
```

Type **Y** and DOS will end the batch file, redisplaying the DOS prompt.

Edit the batch file TREEPRT.BAT and use the REM command to comment the batch file:

```
@ECHO OFF
REM Written by: Kris Jamsa
REM Date written: 6-31-91
REM Function: Lets the user print and display the directory tree.

REM Prompt the user to enable printer echoing. Pause until the
REM user presses a key to continue.
ECHO Turn your printer on line
ECHO Press Ctrl-Prtsc to print a directory tree
PAUSE

REM Display the directory tree.
TREE C:\

REM Remind the user to disable printer echoing.
ECHO Press Ctrl-PrtSc to disable printer echoing
```

Review

1. What is a batch file?

2. How does ECHO OFF differ from @ECHO OFF?

3. List two uses of the ECHO command.

4. Create a batch file named JAN92.BAT that displays the calendar for January 1992, as shown here.

```
S    M    T    W    T    F    S
                    1    2    3    4
5    6    7    8    9   10   11
12   13   14   15   16   17   18
19   20   21   22   23   24   25
26   27   28   29   30   31
```

5. What is the purpose of the PAUSE command?

6. How does ECHO OFF affect PAUSE?

Answers

1. A batch file is a user-defined file with the BAT extension that contains the names of one or more DOS commands. You execute a batch file by typing its name at the DOS prompt. When DOS encounters the batch file, DOS will automatically execute each of the commands the batch file contains.

2. If you are using DOS 3.3 or later, you can precede a batch file command with the @ character ("at" sign) to suppress the display of the command's name when the batch file executes. If a batch file contains the ECHO OFF command, the batch file will display the following on your screen.

```
C:\BATCH> ECHO OFF
```

If the batch file uses @ECHO OFF instead, the command name and prompt is not displayed.

3. The ECHO command lets your batch files disable (ECHO OFF) and enable (ECHO ON) command-name display. In addition, ECHO lets your batch files display messages to the user.

4. The batch file named JAN92.BAT that displays the calendar for January 1992 is

```
@ECHO OFF
ECHO        S   M   T   W   T   F   S
ECHO                    1   2   3   4
ECHO        5   6   7   8   9   10  11
ECHO        12  13  14  15  16  17  18
ECHO        19  20  21  22  23  24  25
ECHO        26  27  28  29  30  31
```

5. The PAUSE command lets your batch file display a message to the user and temporarily suspend the batch file's execution until the user presses any key to continue. Most batch files use the PAUSE command to suspend processing when they need the user to perform manual processing, such as turning on the printer or inserting a disk.

6. The PAUSE command displays an optional user message followed by a message for the user to press any key to continue. If the batch file uses the ECHO OFF command, PAUSE's optional user message does not appear, and the user only sees the prompt to press any key to continue. As a solution, most batch files use ECHO to display PAUSE's optional message and PAUSE to suspend processing, as shown here.

```
@ECHO OFF
ECHO Place a disk in drive A
PAUSE
TREE A:
```

Advanced Concepts

If you are using DOS 5, the DOSKEY command discussed in Chapter 27, "DOSKEY and DOS 5 Macros," lets you create single-line macros that behave similarly to DOS batch files. DOSKEY macros, however, reside in RAM, which means DOS can execute the macros faster than it can execute your batch files. For more information on DOSKEY macros, turn to Chapter 27.

Using ECHO to Display Blank Lines

The ECHO command lets you disable command-name display and also write messages to the screen. As the complexity of your batch files increases, there may be times you want to improve your screen appearance by displaying blank lines. Unfortunately, using ECHO to display blank lines is harder than simply placing ECHO commands in a batch file, as shown here.

```
@ECHO OFF
ECHO Skip one line
ECHO
ECHO Skip two lines
ECHO
ECHO
ECHO DONE
```

By default, if you invoke ECHO without specifying ON, OFF, or a message, ECHO displays its current state of command-name display (either on or off).

```
C:\> ECHO    <ENTER>
ECHO is on
```

If you invoke the previous batch file, your screen will display the following.

```
C:\BATCH> SKIPLINE    <ENTER>
Skip one line
ECHO is off
Skip two lines
ECHO is off
ECHO is off
DONE
```

Rather than displaying blank lines as desired, the ECHO commands displayed ECHO's current status.

Depending on your DOS version, there are several techniques you can use to echo blank lines. First, the most commonly used method for echoing a blank line is to use a special extended ASCII blank character. As discussed in Chapter 10, "Directories," you create this special blank character by holding down the ALT key and typing 255 on your keyboard's numeric keypad. When you release the ALT key, DOS generates the blank character. You cannot generate this character using the spacebar. Most batch files that appear in books or magazines, represent this invisible character as ALT-255. For example, the previous batch file would appear as follows.

```
@ECHO OFF
ECHO Skip one line
ECHO ALT-255
ECHO Skip two lines
ECHO ALT-255
ECHO ALT-255
ECHO DONE
```

In addition to using ALT-255, many DOS versions let you place any one of the following characters immediately next to ECHO to produce a blank line:

[ ] + / \ ; , .

Using a period to produce blank lines, the previous batch file becomes the following.

```
@ECHO OFF
ECHO Skip one line
ECHO.
ECHO Skip two lines
ECHO.
ECHO.
ECHO DONE
```

Experiment with these characters using ECHO under your version of DOS.

Using Extended ASCII Characters

Appendix B lists all the extended ASCII characters, such as the ALT-255 special blank character. Using these extended ASCII characters, you can improve your batch file's screen output by boxing menus or messages, as previously shown.

Creating the box-drawing characters requires the same steps as creating the ALT-255 space character. Simply hold down the ALT key and type the extended ASCII value. Figure 15-1 illustrates the box-drawing characters and their corresponding values.

Using these characters, you can create BOX.BAT, as shown here.

```
@ECHO OFF
ECHO
ECHO     BOX
ECHO
```

Using ^G (CTRL-G) to Create Sound

PAUSE temporarily suspends a batch file's processing until you press a key. Unfortunately, if you have your back to the computer, the batch file may suspend for some time before you notice the prompt to press a key to continue. When you want the batch file to get the user's attention, you can echo the ^G character, which directs DOS to sound your computer's built-in bell. You can create the ^G character

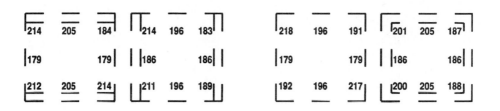

Figure 15-1.   Extended ASCII box characters and values

by holding down CTRL and pressing G. The following command creates a batch file named BELLS.BAT, which sounds the computer's speaker three times.

```
C:\BATCH> COPY CON BELLS.BAT   <ENTER>
@ECHO OFF   <ENTER>
ECHO ^G^G^G   <ENTER>
^Z   <ENTER>
        1 File(s) copied
```

By using your computer's bell in this way, your batch files can quickly notify the user of errors or other important events.

Key Terms

Batch   A group of one or more. In the case of DOS batch files, a batch is one or more related commands.

Batch file   A user-defined file with the BAT extension that contains the names of one or more DOS commands. When you type a batch file's name at the DOS prompt, DOS executes, in order, each of the commands the batch file contains.

Interactive processing   The process of executing a command, waiting for the command to complete, and then typing the next command to repeat the cycle.

Chapter 16

Decision-Making Batch Files

In Chapter 15, "Grouping Commands with Batch Files," you learned DOS batch files can save you time and keystrokes by letting you place one or more long or difficult commands into a file with the BAT extension. Like DOS commands, you execute your batch files by typing the batch file's name at the DOS prompt. When DOS encounters the batch file, DOS automatically executes all the commands the batch file contains. In Chapter 15, DOS executed batch file commands, in order, beginning with the first command in the batch file and ending with the last. Depending on your application, there may be times you'll want the batch file to execute one set of commands and not another. For example, assume you are writing a batch file that helps a new user get started with WordPerfect. If the user invokes the batch file from a directory other than WP, the batch file may need to perform additional CHDIR commands, or it may want to display a message to the user explaining how to use CHDIR to select the WP directory before starting WordPerfect. To perform such "custom" processing, your batch files must be able to make decisions on their own.

In this chapter you'll learn how to build decision-making batch files using the IF command. In addition, you'll learn how to expand your batch file's capabilities by letting the user provide information to the batch file such as a desired file name or directory. Chapter 15 illustrated the convenience of batch files. This chapter introduces their true power.

The IF Command

The IF command provides your batch files with decision-making capabilities. In general, the IF command lets your batch files ask DOS if a specific condition is met. If so, the IF command executes a corresponding DOS command. The general format of the IF command is

IF *CONDITION DOS_COMMAND*

The IF command supports three different conditions. The first condition lets your batch file test whether a specific file exists; the second determines whether the previous batch file command was successful; the third condition tests whether two words or phrases are the same. Table 16-1 briefly presents the IF command's three condition types.

Regardless of the condition type, the IF command performs the same processing. If the condition is true, IF executes the command that follows. If the condition is not true, IF does not execute the command and the batch file continues its processing with the next command.

IF EXIST Tests for Files

As your batch files become larger and more complex, they should behave intelligently. For example, a batch file should not use TYPE to display a file that doesn't exist. Likewise, a batch file that copies files from one directory to another should not overwrite existing files. Using the IF EXIST command, your batch files can find out if a specific file exists and act accordingly. For example, the following batch

Condition	Purpose	Example
IF EXIST	Tests if a file exists on disk	IF EXIST AUTOEXEC.BAT TYPE AUTOEXEC.BAT
IF ERRORLEVEL	Tests the success level of the previous batch command	IF ERRORLEVEL 1 GOTO SUCCESS
IF STR==STR	Tests if two character strings are the same	IF '%1'=='A' GOTO ASCENDING

Table 16-1. *The IF Command's Three Condition Types*

file IMPTROOT.BAT uses the TYPE command to display the contents of AUTOEXEC.BAT and CONFIG.SYS, which reside in your startup disk's root directory. Each time you start DOS, the DOS startup software searches the root for these two important files and uses their contents to customize itself in memory for your particular configuration.

```
TYPE   \AUTOEXEC.BAT
TYPE   \CONFIG.SYS
```

The problem with this batch file is that it assumes the files exist. If the files are present, the batch file successfully displays their contents. However, if one or both of the files don't exist, the TYPE command will fail, displaying the "File not found" error message.

```
C:\BATCH> IMPTROOT   <ENTER>

C:\BATCH> TYPE   \AUTOEXEC.BAT
File not found

C:\BATCII> TYPE   \CONFIG.SYS
File not found
```

To correct this possible problem, include the IF EXIST command:

```
IF EXIST  \AUTOEXEC.BAT  TYPE  \AUTOEXEC.BAT
IF EXIST  \CONFIG.SYS  TYPE  \CONFIG.SYS
```

As before, if either file exists, its contents are displayed. However, if a file does not exist, the IF command will not execute the corresponding TYPE command. Instead, the batch file's execution continues with the next command. Figure 16-1 uses a flowchart to illustrate the process.

To understand the flowchart, simply follow the direction of the arrows out of each condition box. If the condition is true, follow the arrow labeled "Yes." Likewise, if the condition is not true, follow the arrow labeled "No."

The NOT Operator

Just as there are times when you want IF to perform a command when a condition is true, so there may also be times you want IF to perform a command when a condition is false. For example, the IF EXIST command lets your batch file determine whether a file exists, and if so, to process accordingly. Many batch files, however, may want to perform specific processing when a file does not exist. In such cases, your batch files can use the logical operator, NOT.

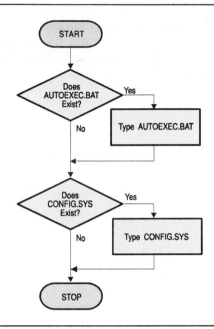

Figure 16-1.   *Charting IMPTROOT.BAT's possible execution paths*

The NOT operator follows the word "IF" and precedes the condition:

IF NOT *CONDITION DOS_COMMAND*

In general, NOT directs IF to perform the command specified when the condition is false (NOT true). In the case of IF EXIST, the NOT operator directs IF to execute the command if the file specified does not exist.

The following batch file, CHECKFOR.BAT, searches the root directory for three files, AUTOEXEC.BAT, CONFIG.SYS, and NOMATCH.EXT. Using IF EXIST and IF NOT EXIST, the batch file displays a message that states whether or not each file is present.

```
@ECHO OFF
IF EXIST \AUTOEXEC.BAT  ECHO Found AUTOEXEC.BAT
IF EXIST \CONFIG.SYS ECHO Found CONFIG.SYS
IF EXIST NOMATCH.EXT ECHO Found NOMATCH.EXT
IF NOT EXIST \AUTOEXEC.BAT  ECHO No such file: AUTOEXEC.BAT
IF NOT EXIST \CONFIG.SYS ECHO No such file: CONFIG.SYS
IF NOT EXIST NOMATCH.EXT ECHO No such file: NOMATCH.EXT
```

The batch file's first three IF commands test whether the file exists. The last three IF commands use the NOT operator to test whether the file does not exist. Assuming your root directory has the files AUTOEXEC.BAT and CONFIG.SYS, but not NOMATCH.EXT, your screen will display the following when you execute CHECKFOR.BAT.

```
C:\BATCH> CHECKFOR    <ENTER>
Found AUTOEXEC.BAT
Found CONFIG.SYS
No such file: NOMATCH.EXT
```

If you want your batch file to perform one command when a condition is true and another command when the condition is false, your batch file will need two IF commands, one of which uses the NOT operator.

A batch file that copies one file to a different disk or directory should not overwrite an existing file. For example, the following batch file CHECK1ST.BAT copies the files AUTOEXEC.BAT and CONFIG.SYS to a disk in drive A. The batch file only copies the files if they don't exist on drive A. If a file exists, the batch file displays a message stating that the disk already contains the file.

```
@ECHO OFF
IF EXIST A:AUTOEXEC.BAT ECHO AUTOEXEC.BAT exists on drive A
IF EXIST A:CONFIG.SYS ECHO CONFIG.SYS exists on drive A
IF NOT EXIST A:AUTOEXEC.BAT COPY \AUTOEXEC.BAT A:
IF NOT EXIST A:CONFIG.SYS COPY \CONFIG.SYS A:
```

Figure 16-2 uses a flowchart to illustrate the batch file's decision making.

All the examples presented so far, only execute one command when a condition is true or fails. In Chapter 17, "Getting the Most from Batch Files," you will learn how to use the GOTO command to execute several commands for one condition and several other commands for a different condition.

IF ERRORLEVEL Tests for Success

As your batch files increase in size, there will be times when you only want the batch file's execution to continue if the previous command was successful. In addition to displaying error messages on your screen, many DOS commands provide DOS with an exit status value that indicates whether or not the command was successful. Using the IF ERRORLEVEL command, your batch files can test this status value and process accordingly.

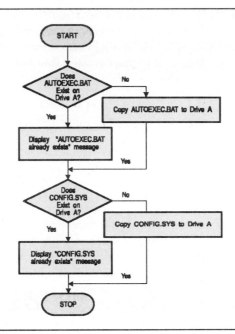

Figure 16-2. *Charting CHECK1ST.BAT's execution paths*

For example, in Chapter 12, "Fundamental Copy Operations," you learned that DISKCOPY copies the contents of one floppy disk to another. When DISKCOPY completes, DISKCOPY returns one of the status values listed in Table 16-2 to DOS.

If, for example, you have a batch file that uses DISKCOPY, you can place IF ERRORLEVEL commands immediately after the DISKCOPY command to determine whether DISKCOPY was successful and then process accordingly.

IF ERRORLEVEL lets your batch files test for a specific exit status value. Like IF EXIST, the IF ERRORLEVEL command has a condition and a corresponding command DOS executes when the condition is true. For IF ERRORLEVEL, a

Status Value	Meaning
0	Successful disk copy operation
1	Recoverable disk read or write error
2	CTRL-C termination
3	Fatal disk read or format error
4SS	Invalid disk drive, syntax, or insufficient memory error

Table 16-2. *Exit Status Values Produced by DISKCOPY*

condition is true when the previous command's exit status value is *greater than or equal to* the value specified. For example, the following IF ERRORLEVEL command tests for an exit status value *greater than or equal to* 3.

```
IF ERRORLEVEL 3 DOS_COMMAND
```

In this case, if *DOS_COMMAND* exits with a status value of 3 or above, DOS will execute the command specified. Because IF ERRORLEVEL also considers exit status values *greater* than the value specified as successful, you need to take care in creating your batch files.

The following batch file, WRONGIF.BAT uses IF ERRORLEVEL incorrectly to determine whether DISKCOPY was successful.

```
@ECHO OFF
DISKCOPY A:  B:
IF ERRORLEVEL 0 ECHO Successful disk copy!
```

As you can see in Table 16-2, DISKCOPY returns the exit status 0 to DOS when it successfully copies a disk. Unfortunately, the batch file uses IF ERRORLEVEL incorrectly. Remember, IF ERRORLEVEL evaluates to true for any exit status value that is greater than or equal to the value specified—in this case, 0. In DISKCOPY, every possibility is greater than or equal to 0. No matter how DISKCOPY completes, the batch file will display the "Successful disk copy!" message. Verify this for yourself by creating and invoking the batch file. When DISKCOPY prompts you to press any key to continue, use the CTRL-C key combination to end the command. Although the batch file did not perform the disk copy operation, batch file displays a success message:

```
C:\BATCH> CHKDCOPY   <ENTER>
Insert SOURCE diskette in drive A:

Insert TARGET diskette in drive B:

Press any key to continue . . .
^C
Successful disk copy!
```

The best way to prevent this type of confusion is to combine two IF ERRORLEVEL commands. The first command tests whether the exit status value is greater than or equal to the desired value. The second command uses the NOT operator to test whether the exit status is NOT greater than the value. By combining the two IF commands, your batch file can test for an exact value. For example, to test for an exit status value of 0, your batch file would use the following.

```
IF ERRORLEVEL 0 IF NOT ERRORLEVEL 1 DOS_COMMAND
```

Likewise, to test for an exit status of 1, your batch file would use the following.

```
IF ERRORLEVEL 1 IF NOT ERRORLEVEL 2 DOS_COMMAND
```

Using two IF ERRORLEVEL commands each to test for exact values, the following batch file CHKDCOPY.BAT displays the correct message for each of DISKCOPY's possible exit status values.

```
@ECHO OFF
DISKCOPY A: B:
IF ERRORLEVEL 0 IF NOT ERRORLEVEL 1 ECHO Successful disk copy!
IF ERRORLEVEL 1 IF NOT ERRORLEVEL 2 ECHO Recoverable disk error
IF ERRORLEVEL 2 IF NOT ERRORLEVEL 3 ECHO User Ctrl-C termination
IF ERRORLEVEL 3 IF NOT ERRORLEVEL 4 ECHO Fatal disk read or format
IF ERRORLEVEL 4 ECHO Invalid disk drive, syntax, or memory error
```

If you cancel CHKDCOPY.BAT using CTRL-C, you will display the following.

```
C:\BATCH> CHKDCOPY    <ENTER>
Insert SOURCE diskette in drive A:


Insert TARGET diskette in drive B:


Press any key to continue . . .
^C
User Ctrl-C termination
```

Unfortunately, not all DOS commands provide exit status values your batch files can test. Appendix A, "Exit Status Values," lists the exit status values provided by DOS commands.

In Chapter 29, "Using DEBUG," you will learn how to create your own simple commands using the DEBUG command. Many of these commands will return exit status values your batch files can use. One such command, HOUR.COM, returns the current hour of the day. Using IF ERRORLEVEL and HOUR.COM, the following batch file, GREET.BAT, displays either the message "Good morning!", "Good afternoon!", or "Good evening!", depending on the current time.

```
@ECHO OFF
HOUR
IF ERRORLEVEL 0 IF NOT ERRORLEVEL 12 ECHO Good morning!
IF ERRORLEVEL 12 IF NOT ERRORLEVEL 18 ECHO Good afternoon!
IF ERRORLEVEL 18 ECHO Good evening!
```

As you work more with DOS, you will encounter many more simple commands like HOUR.COM you can put to work in your batch files.

Using IF to Compare Two Character Strings

A *character string* is a sequence of characters. The sequence might be a single letter, a word, a phrase, or zero letters (the null string). The third form of the IF command lets your batch files compare two strings and execute a command if the strings are equal. The IF command specifies the strings to compare by separating the strings with two equal signs.

```
IF  String1==String2 DOS_COMMAND
```

NOTE

The IF command only considers two strings as the same if the strings match letter for letter, including matching either upper or lower case. IF would not, therefore, consider the strings "ABC" and "abc" as the same. The best way to understand this form of the IF command is to use it with batch parameters, discussed next.

Passing Information to Your Batch Files

As you work more with DOS batch files, you will find that a batch file you created to simplify one task could simplify several others if you could only change the name of a file the batch file uses. For such cases, DOS lets you pass information to your batch files using *batch parameters*.

So far, each time you have executed a batch file, you have simply typed the batch file name. If you include additional information on the command, such as a file name or drive letter, DOS makes that information available to your batch file. A batch parameter, then, is simply a value you specify in the batch command line.

To access the parameters within your batch files, you use the symbols %1 through %9. DOS assigns the first parameter to %1, the second to %2, and so on. If you don't specify values for a parameter, DOS assigns the parameter the *null string* or empty string. Using the IF command, your files can test for a null string. DOS assigns the batch file name to the parameter %0.

The following batch file, SHOWALL.BAT, uses ECHO to display the values of the parameters %0 through %9.

```
@ECHO OFF
ECHO This batch file is %0
ECHO The parameters are %1 %2 %3 %4 %5 %6 %7 %8 %9
```

If you invoke SHOWALL with no parameters, your screen will display the following.

```
C:\BATCH> SHOWALL   <ENTER>
This batch file is SHOWALL
The parameters are
```

In this case, DOS assigns the null string to the parameters %1 through %9. If you instead invoke the batch file with the letters "A," "B," and "C," your screen will display the following.

```
C:\BATCH> SHOWALL  A  B  C   <ENTER>
This batch file is SHOWALL
The parameters are A B C
```

Figure 16-3 illustrates how DOS assigns the parameter values.

If you invoke the batch file with the letters "A" through "L," your screen will display the following.

```
C:\BATCH> SHOWALL  A  B  C  D  E  F  G  H  I  J  K  L   <ENTER>
This batch file is SHOWALL
The parameters are A B C D E F G H I
```

You can see that DOS has assigned values to the parameters %1 through %9. In Chapter 17 you will learn how to access the values not assigned to a parameter with the SHIFT command.

Now that you know how batch parameters work, you need to put the parameters to work. The following batch file, COLOR.BAT, uses the IF command to compare the value in %1 to several color names. If the batch file locates a match, it displays a message on your screen.

```
@ECHO OFF
IF '%1'=='BLUE' ECHO The color is BLUE
IF '%1'=='RED' ECHO The color is RED
IF '%1'=='GREEN' ECHO The color is GREEN
IF '%1'=='' ECHO No color specified
```

Remember, the IF command only considers two strings the same if the letters match in case. If you invoke COLOR.BAT with "Blue," the batch file will not find a match.

```
C:\BATCH> COLOR  Blue
C:\BATCH>
```

After DOS assigns %1 the value Blue, the batch file actually performs the following comparisons.

```
@ECHO OFF
IF 'Blue'=='BLUE' ECHO The color is BLUE
IF 'Blue'=='RED' ECHO The color is RED
IF 'Blue'=='GREEN' ECHO The color is GREEN
IF 'Blue'=='' ECHO No color specified
```

Take a close look at the following IF command.

```
IF '%1'=='' ECHO No color specified
```

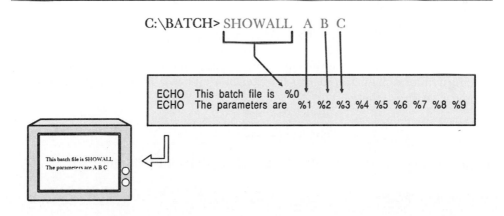

Figure 16-3.   Assigning A, B, and C to %1, %2, and %3

If you don't specify a parameter's value, DOS assigns the null string to the parameter. The two single quotes *with no space between* represent the null string. If %1 has no value, the IF command becomes the following.

```
IF ''=''  ECHO No color specified
```

Because the two null strings are the same, DOS executes the ECHO command.

When you compare strings using the IF command, you must make sure a string appears on both sides of the double equal signs. Assume, for example, you used the following IF command.

```
IF  %1==BLUE  ECHO  The color is BLUE
```

If the user does not specify a value for %1, the IF command becomes

```
IF  ==BLUE  ECHO  The color is BLUE
```

Because only one side of the double equal signs contains a string, DOS will display the following message informing you that the command violates the syntax or format of the IF command.

```
IF  ==BLUE  ECHO  The color is BLUE
Syntax error
```

To ensure that each side always has at least a null string, always surround the strings with single quotes, as shown here.

```
IF  '%1'=='BLUE'  ECHO  The color is BLUE
```

Some batch files achieve the result of ensuring that two strings are present by placing a unique character, such as the exclamation mark, next to the strings IF will compare, as shown here.

```
IF  %1!==BLUE!  ECHO  The color is BLUE
```

If the user specifies the value BLUE, the test becomes the following.

```
IF  BLUE!==BLUE!  ECHO  The color is BLUE
```

If the user doesn't specify a value for %1, the test is, at least, still valid.

```
IF  !==BLUE!  ECHO  The color is BLUE
```

SUMMARY

The IF EXIST command lets your batch files test whether a file exists, then process accordingly. The IF EXIST command specifies a file DOS is to search for and a command DOS executes if the file exists.

```
IF EXIST FILENAME.EXT DOS_COMMAND
```

Using the NOT operator, your batch file can execute a different command if the file does not exist.

```
IF NOT EXIST FILENAME.EXT DOS_COMMAND
```

IF ERRORLEVEL

The IF ERRORLEVEL command lets your batch files determine the success of the previous batch file command and process accordingly. IF ERRORLEVEL compares a command's exit status to the value specified. If the exit status is greater than or equal to the value, DOS executes the corresponding command. Otherwise, DOS continues the batch file's execution with the command that follows.

```
IF ERRORLEVEL value DOS_COMMAND
```

DOS exit status values cannot exceed 255.

IF *String1==String2*

The IF *String1==String2* command lets your batch files test whether two character strings are the same, and then process accordingly. The most common use of this form of the IF command is for testing batch parameters. For DOS to consider two strings as the same, the strings must match letter for letter. DOS does not consider an uppercase letter the same as its lowercase counterpart.

```
IF String1==String2 DOS_COMMAND
```

/ *SUMMARY* /

Batch Parameters

As DOS lets you pass file names and disk drive letters to your DOS commands, so the same is true for batch files. When you include additional information in your batch command lines, DOS assigns the first nine pieces of information to the batch parameters %1 through %9. Using these parameters, a batch file becomes more general and can support more than one application. In addition to %1 through %9, DOS assigns the batch file name to %0.

Although using a unique character in this way is valid, it is harder to understand than the pair of single quotes. At first glance, many users might think they needed to specify the color with an exclamation mark, such as "BLUE!", with perhaps puzzling results (BLUE!!==BLUE!).

If you create a batch file that uses batch parameters, use the IF command to ensure that the batch parameters are defined. In Chapter 17, you will create several powerful batch files that use batch parameters to specify file names and DOS wildcards. For now, simply recall that DOS assigns batch parameters to %1 through %9.

Hands On

If the BATCH directory is not the current directory, use CHDIR to select it. Next, create the following batch file TESTAUTO.BAT that tests if the file AUTOEXEC.BAT is in the root directory. If the file exists, the batch file displays the file's contents; otherwise, the batch file displays the message "\AUTOEXEC.BAT does not exist."

```
@ECHO OFF
IF EXIST \AUTOEXEC.BAT TYPE \AUTOEXEC.BAT
IF NOT EXIST \AUTOEXEC.BAT ECHO \AUTOEXEC.BAT does not exist
```

Next, create the batch file TESTFILE.BAT that uses the %1 batch parameter instead of AUTOEXEC.BAT to let the batch file support any file name.

```
@ECHO OFF
IF EXIST %1 TYPE %1
IF NOT EXIST %1 ECHO %1 does not exist
```

Invoke TESTFILE.BAT with the file name AUTOEXEC.BAT:

```
C:\BATCH> TESTFILE  \AUTOEXEC.BAT  <ENTER>
```

When you use the batch parameters %1 through %9, you need to use the IF command to test whether the parameter is defined. To understand why, invoke TESTFILE without a file name.

```
C:\BATCH> TESTFILE  <ENTER>
Bad command or file name
```

The test case will result in this error message because the first command line becomes

```
IF EXIST TYPE
```

which is a legal IF command that searches for a file named TYPE. Note, however, that the IF command does not provide a corresponding action if such a file exists. The second command line becomes

```
IF NOT EXIST ECHO DOES NOT EXIST
```

and DOS sees the word "DOES" as the bad command. Edit TESTFILE.BAT adding the following IF commands to test whether %1 is defined.

```
@ECHO OFF
IF NOT '%1'=='' IF EXIST %1 TYPE %1
IF NOT '%1'=='' IF NOT EXIST %1 ECHO %1 does not exist
```

Next create the batch file LISTPAR.BAT that displays each batch parameter, as shown here.

```
@ECHO OFF
ECHO %1
ECHO %2
ECHO %3
ECHO %4
ECHO %5
ECHO %6
ECHO %7
ECHO %8
ECHO %9
```

Experiment with LISTPAR.BAT, invoking it with 0, 3, 9, and 15 parameters.

Review

1. List three tests the IF command performs.

2. What is the purpose of the NOT operator?

3. How do the following IF commands differ?

   ```
   IF ERRORLEVEL 3 DOS_COMMAND
   IF ERRORLEVEL 3 IF NOT ERRORLEVEL 4 DOS_COMMAND
   ```

4. What is a batch parameter?

5. Create a batch file, DEFINED.BAT, that examines the batch parameters %1 through %3. If a parameter is defined, display the parameter's value. If the parameter is not defined, display an appropriate error message.

Answers

1. The IF command lets you test whether a file exists on disk, the previous command was successful, and two character strings are the same.

2. The NOT operator directs DOS to perform the command specified in an IF command when the corresponding condition is false.

3. The first IF command executes *DOS_COMMAND* if the previous command's exit status value is greater than or equal to 3. The second IF command only executes *DOS_COMMAND* when the previous command's exit status value is exactly 3.

4. A batch parameter is a value, such as file name or disk-drive letter the user includes in the batch file's command line. DOS assigns the first 9 batch parameters to the symbols %1 through %9 your batch files can use to access the parameter's value.

5. The batch file is:

   ```
   @ECHO OFF
   IF '%1'=='' ECHO %%1 has No value
   IF '%2'=='' ECHO %%2 has No value
   IF '%3'=='' ECHO %%3 has No value
   ```

```
IF NOT '%1'=='' ECHO %%1 is %1
IF NOT '%2'=='' ECHO %%2 is %2
IF NOT '%3'=='' ECHO %%3 is %3
```

When DOS encounters the double percent signs, such as %%1 or %%2, DOS will ECHO the string %1 or %2.

Advanced Concepts

As you have learned, batch parameters increase your batch file flexibility. If you are using DOS version 3.3 or higher, your batch files can use named parameters to access DOS environment entries. DOS environment entries have a name and value. Using the SET command, you can display the current environment:

```
C:\BATCH> SET    <ENTER>
PROMPT=$P$G
COMSPEC=C:\DOS\COMMAND.COM
PATH=C:\DOS;C:\DISKUTIL;C:\BATCH
```

As you will see in Chapter 19, the environment provides a place for you to store information for DOS, or as you will see, your batch files. A batch file *named parameter* is simply an environment entry whose name appears between percent signs, such as %PATH%.

When DOS encounters a named parameter in your batch file, DOS substitutes the parameter's corresponding environment value. If the parameter is not defined in the environment, DOS replaces the parameter with the null string. The following batch file, SHOWENV.BAT, uses the named parameters %PATH% and %PROMPT% to display your current command path and system prompt.

```
@ECHO OFF
ECHO Current path is %PATH%
ECHO Current prompt is %PROMPT%
```

Given the previous environment values, your screen will display the following when you invoke SHOWENV.BAT.

```
C:\BATCH> SHOWENV   <ENTER>
Current path is C:\DOS;C:\DISKUTIL;C:\BATCH
Current prompt is $P$G
```

As you can see, DOS substitutes the environment entry values as you desire. As you should always test batch parameters to ensure the parameters are defined, so should you test named parameters.

The following batch file modifies SHOWENV.BAT to test whether the named parameters %PATH%, %PROMPT%, and %BOOK% are defined.

```
@ECHO OFF
IF '%PATH%'=='' ECHO PATH is undefined
IF NOT '%PATH%'=='' ECHO PATH is %PATH%
IF '%PROMPT%'=='' ECHO PROMPT is undefined
IF NOT '%PROMPT%'=='' ECHO PROMPT is %PROMPT%
IF '%BOOK%'=='' ECHO BOOK is undefined
IF NOT '%BOOK%'=='' ECHO BOOK is %BOOK%
```

When you invoke this batch file, your screen displays the following.

```
C:\BATCH> SHOWENV   <ENTER>
PATH is C:\DOS;C:\DISKUTIL;C:\BATCH
PROMPT is $P$G
BOOK is undefined
```

Use the SET command to assign a value to BOOK. Generally SET, discussed in Chapter 19, allows you to assign a value to a name. Let's assign BOOK the name READER

```
C:\BATCH> SET BOOK=READER
```

and repeat the SHOWENV command. The batch file will display the entry's new value.

```
C:\BATCH> SHOWENV   <ENTER>
PATH is C:\DOS;C:\DISKUTIL;C:\BATCH
PROMPT is $P$G
BOOK is READER
```

As the complexity of your batch files increases, you will use named parameters to save and restore such information as the current directory, current drive, or command path. Chapter 17 shows you how you can save and later restore the current directory using named parameters.

Creating Y_OR_N.COM

The true power of the IF ERRORLEVEL command isn't its use with DOS commands, but rather commands you create yourself using DEBUG (discussed in Chapter 29). For example, the following DEBUG script file Y_OR_N.SCR creates a command named Y_OR_N.COM your batch files can use to get a yes or no user response.

```
N Y_OR_N.COM
A 100
MOV AH, 0
INT 16
MOV AL, 0
CMP AH, 15
JE  112
CMP AH, 31
JE  114
JMP 100
MOV AL, 1
MOV AH, 4C
INT 21
<ENTER>
R CX
18
W
Q
```

Create Y_OR_N.COM by redirecting the file's contents into DEBUG, as shown here.

```
C:\BATCH> DEBUG  <  Y_OR_N.SCR  <ENTER>
```

Y_OR_N.COM waits for the user to type either **Y** or **N**. If the user types **Y**, the command exits with the status value 1. IF the user types **N**, Y_OR_N exits with 0. Using the IF ERRORLEVEL command, your batch files can determine the user's response as shown here.

```
@ECHO OFF
ECHO Do you want to delete %1  (Y/N)?
Y_OR_N
IF ERRORLEVEL  1  DEL  %1
```

As you work with DOS batch files, you will collect a library of useful commands such as Y_OR_N.COM that increase your batch file flexibility.

Key Terms

Condition   A test producing a true or false result.

Exit status value   A value from 0 to 255 that states a command's level of success.

Batch parameter   Information that the user includes in the batch file command line the batch file can access using the symbols %1 through %9.

Named parameter   Under DOS 3.3 or later, an environment entry name surrounded by percent signs for which DOS substitutes the entry's value during the batch file's execution.

Chapter 17

Getting the Most from Batch Files

In Chapter 16, "Decision-Making Batch Files," you learned that, using the IF command and batch parameters, DOS batch files can become very powerful. Chapter 1, "Getting to Know Your Computer," defined a program as a list of instructions the computer is to perform. Although you may not have realized it, in Chapter 16 you became a batch file programmer. Not only did you provide DOS with a list of commands to perform, you used the IF command in many of your batch files so that they could make intelligent decisions about the processing they should perform. In this chapter you will round out your batch programming skills as you examine the remaining DOS batch commands.

Branching from One Location to Another Using GOTO

In Chapter 16 your batch files used the IF command to test for different conditions. When a condition was met, the batch file executed a specific command. In many cases, however, you will want your batch file to perform several related commands when a condition is met. To do so, you will group related commands, placing them at a specific location in your batch file. When the condition is met, your batch file will use the GOTO command to skip to the desired commands and then to the end of the batch file.

Until now, each batch has begun its execution at the first command at the top of the batch file, working its way through commands toward the bottom of the file. The GOTO command directs DOS to branch from one location in your batch file to another. The format of the GOTO command is GOTO *LABELNAME*.

A *label* is a name on a line in your batch file that serves as a marker or "landing site" for a GOTO jump. The first character of a label line is always a colon (:). This tells DOS that what follows on the line is a label name to be jumped to, not command to be executed. The following batch file, SKIPDIR.BAT, uses GOTO to branch to the label DONE.

```
@ECHO OFF
VER
GOTO DONE
DIR
:DONE
```

When executed, this batch file displays the current DOS version number and then ends. The batch file never executes the DIR command because the GOTO command branches, or jumps, past the command, as shown in the following:

```
@ECHO OFF
VER
GOTO DONE
DIR
:DONE
```

When you specify a label name in a GOTO command, don't include the colon in the command. You must, however, begin the label's line with a colon. When DOS encounters the colon, it knows the line contains a label instead of a DOS command. DOS does not care if your label name appears in the upper or lower case. The following batch file successfully executes, even though the GOTO command uses a lowercase label name.

```
@ECHO OFF
VER
GOTO done
DIR
:DONE
```

If you misspell a label name and GOTO can't find a match, the batch file will end immediately, and DOS will display the "Label not found" error message. DOS will not execute any batch file commands that follow an unfound GOTO.

Although batch label names can be virtually any length, DOS only uses the first eight characters of a label name. As a result, if your batch file uses two label names whose first eight characters are the same, DOS can't tell the difference between the two labels—GOTO will branch to the closest label. For example, the following batch file uses the labels PERFORM_END_OF_MONTH and PERFORM_END_OF_YEAR. If the value of %1 is MONTH, the batch file is intended to branch to PERFORM_END_OF_MONTH. Likewise, if %1 is YEAR, the batch file should branch to PERFORM_END_OF_YEAR.

```
@ECHO OFF
IF '%1'=='MONTH' GOTO PERFORM_END_OF_MONTH
IF '%1'=='YEAR' GOTO PERFORM_END_OF_YEAR
GOTO DONE
:PERFORM_END_OF_MONTH
ECHO Performing end of month processing
GOTO DONE
:PERFORM_END_OF_YEAR
ECHO Performing end of year processing
:DONE
```

The batch file doesn't work, however. Because DOS only uses the first eight letters of a label name, it can't tell the difference between PERFORM_END_OF_MONTH and PERFORM_END_OF_YEAR. Regardless of whether %1 contains "MONTH" or "YEAR," the batch file branches to the first occurrence of "PERFORM_" with unintended results. The following illustration shows this process.

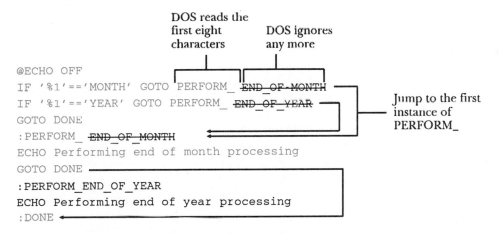

The previous batch file was the first to combine the IF and GOTO commands. When a condition is true, and you want a batch file to perform several commands, you group the commands at a specific location in the batch file and then let the batch file branch to them. For example, assume you are creating a batch file named

DOSHELP.BAT that contains online help for key DOS commands. To use the batch file, the user invokes DOSHELP.BAT with a command name, as shown here.

```
C:\BATCH> DOSHELP  DIR   <ENTER>
```

The batch file examines %1 and branches to a corresponding location within the batch file containing ECHO commands that describe the command. The following batch file implements the online help for the CLS, DIR, and VER commands.

```
@ECHO OFF
IF '%1'=='CLS' GOTO CLS
IF '%1'=='DIR' GOTO DIR
IF '%1'=='VER' GOTO VER
GOTO DONE
:CLS
ECHO CLS Command
ECHO Function: Clears the screen display.
ECHO Format: CLS
GOTO DONE
:DIR
ECHO DIR Command
ECHO Function: Displays a directory listing.
ECHO Format: DIR [file name] [switches]
GOTO DONE
:VER
ECHO VER Command
ECHO Function: Displays DOS version number.
ECHO Format: VER
:DONE
```

Note how the batch file first branches to the location containing the online help text. After the last ECHO command containing help text for the specific command completes, the batch file uses GOTO to jump to the end of the batch file. By combining the GOTO and IF commands, your batch files become very powerful.

Repeating a Command for a Set of Files

As you have learned, not all DOS commands support wildcards. For example, if you invoke TYPE using a wildcard, the command will fail.

```
C:\> TYPE *.BAT <ENTER>
Invalid filename or file not found
```

By creating a batch file that uses the FOR command, however, you can provide the wildcard support you desire. FOR is an internal command that lets you repeat a specific command for a set of files. Although you can execute FOR from the DOS prompt, FOR is most commonly used in DOS batch files. In general, you execute FOR with a set of file names and a command you want FOR to execute with each file. FOR will execute the command for the first file. When the command completes, FOR will execute the command for the second file, followed by the third, and so on for every file in the set. Consider the following batch file TYPE3.BAT, which uses FOR to display the contents of the files ONE, TWO, and THREE.

```
@ECHO OFF
FOR %%F IN (ONE TWO THREE) DO TYPE %%F
```

The characters %%F represent the FOR command's variable. As discussed, FOR repeats a command for a set of files. Each time FOR repeats the command, FOR assigns a new file name to its variable. FOR variable names can only be one character long. The word IN indicates that the set of files follows. You must place the set of files within parentheses. This example separates the files with spaces, but FOR lets you use commas or semicolons. The word DO indicates the command that FOR performs with each file that follows. In this case, FOR executes the TYPE command, displaying each file's contents.

The best way to understand how FOR works is to walk through a sample command. Using the previous batch file, FOR begins by assigning the file name ONE to %%F. When FOR executes the TYPE command, it uses the value of %%F, resulting in the command TYPE ONE. When the TYPE command completes, FOR assigns the file TWO to %%F and repeats this process. In this case, FOR executes the command TYPE TWO. Next, FOR will repeat the TYPE command using THREE. When the TYPE command completes, because FOR does not have any more files in its set, FOR ends.

One of FOR's most powerful features is that FOR supports DOS wildcards. Consider the following batch file, SHOWBAT.BAT, which invokes FOR using *.BAT as the set of files.

```
@ECHO OFF
FOR %%F IN (*.BAT) DO TYPE %%F
```

When FOR encounters a wildcard in its set of files, FOR expands the wildcard into the complete set of matching files. Taking this concept one step further, the following batch file, TYPEALL.BAT, uses the batch parameter %1 to define the set of files.

```
@ECHO OFF
FOR %%F  IN  (%1)  DO TYPE  %%F
```

If you invoke TYPEALL.BAT with a file name, such as AUTOEXEC.BAT, the batch file will display the file's contents. If you invoke TYPEALL.BAT using a wildcard, the batch file will display all matching files.

```
C:\BATCH> TYPEALL  *.BAT  <ENTER>
```

Last, if you invoke TYPEALL.BAT without specifying a file name, FOR encounters an empty set as soon as it starts. As a result, it ends without executing the TYPE command.

```
C:\BATCH>  TYPEALL  <ENTER>
C:\BATCH>
```

You can execute the FOR command from the DOS prompt. When you execute FOR from the DOS prompt, only precede the variable name with a single percent sign, as shown here.

```
C:\> FOR  %F  IN  (*.BAT)  DO  TYPE  %F  <ENTER>
```

Accessing More than Nine Batch Parameters

You learned in Chapter 16 that DOS lets you pass information to your batch files using batch parameters. DOS assigns the parameters to the symbols %1 through %9. If the user specified more than nine parameters, the batch files presented in Chapter 16 ignored the extras. To help your batch files use all the information the user includes in the command line, DOS provides the SHIFT command. In general, SHIFT moves each parameter one position to the left, discarding %0's value and moving the first unused parameter into %9, as shown here:

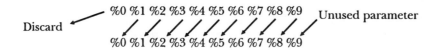

If no unused parameters are present, SHIFT assigns the null string to %9.

The following batch file, SHIFTONE.BAT, uses the SHIFT command to move the batch parameters one position to the left.

```
@ECHO OFF
ECHO %0 %1 %2 %3 %4 %5 %6 %7 %8 %9
SHIFT
ECHO %0 %1 %2 %3 %4 %5 %6 %7 %8 %9
```

If you invoke the batch file with the parameters A, B, and C, your screen will display the following.

```
C:\BATCH> SHIFTONE A B C   <ENTER>
SHIFTONE A B C
A B C
```

As you can see, each letter moved one position left. If you invoke the batch file with the letters A through L, your screen will display the following.

```
C:\BATCH> SHIFTONE A B C D E F G H I J K L   <ENTER>
SHIFTONE A B C D E F G H I
A B C D E F G H I J
```

As you can see, the batch file name has been shifted out of %0 and the letter "J" has been shifted into %9, as shown here:

In a similar way, the batch file SHIFTTWO.BAT uses ECHO to display the before, middle, and after of two SHIFT commands.

```
@ECHO OFF
ECHO %0 %1 %2 %3 %4 %5 %6 %7 %8 %9
SHIFT
ECHO %0 %1 %2 %3 %4 %5 %6 %7 %8 %9
SHIFT
ECHO %0 %1 %2 %3 %4 %5 %6 %7 %8 %9
```

As above, if you invoke this batch file with the letters "A" through "L," your screen will display the following.

```
C:\BATCH> SHIFTTWO A B C D E F G H I J K L   <ENTER>
SHIFTTWO A B C D E F G H I
A B C D E F G H I J
B C D E F G H I J K
```

For SHIFT to really be useful, your batch files need a way to use each parameter individually. The following batch file, SHIFTALL.BAT, combines the SHIFT and GOTO commands. The batch file examines the value of %1. If %1 contains the null string, the batch file ends. Otherwise, it echoes %1's value and performs a SHIFT. Using GOTO, the batch file loops back to the start and repeats this process. If you invoke the batch file with the letters "A" through "Z," the batch file will display each letter on its own line.

```
@ECHO OFF
:LOOP
IF '%1'=='' GOTO DONE
ECHO %1
SHIFT
GOTO LOOP
:DONE
```

A more useful version of this batch file might use the TYPE command to display the contents of multiple file names:

```
@ECHO OFF
:LOOP
IF '%1'=='' GOTO DONE
TYPE %1
SHIFT
GOTO LOOP
:DONE
```

In this case, you can invoke the new TYPEALL.BAT file with several file names, as shown.

```
C:\BATCH> TYPEALL \CONFIG.SYS \AUTOEXEC.BAT SHIFTONE.BAT   <ENTER>
```

Taking this batch file one step further, you can include the FOR command, discussed in the previous section, to expand any wildcard characters the command line may contain.

```
@ECHO OFF
:LOOP
IF '%1'=='' GOTO DONE
FOR %%F IN (%1) DO TYPE %%F
SHIFT
GOTO LOOP
:DONE
```

The batch file now supports multiple file names and DOS wildcards.

```
C:\BATCH> TYPEALL \CONFIG.SYS *.BAT SHIFTONE.BAT <ENTER>
```

Invoking One Batch File from Within Another

DOS batch files contain the names of one or more commands. When you invoke the batch file from the DOS prompt, DOS executes all the commands the batch file contains. All the commands in the batch file presented so far have been DOS commands. A batch file, can, however, execute another batch file as one of its commands. However, as you will see, executing one batch file from within another isn't as easy as simply including the second batch file's name. Depending on your version of DOS, to invoke a second batch file, your batch file must use the CALL command or COMMAND /C.

By default, when DOS ends a batch file, DOS returns control to the DOS prompt. Unfortunately, if you invoke a second batch file from the middle of a batch file, DOS redisplays the DOS prompt when the second batch file completes. As a result the commands that follow the second batch file's invocation never execute. When one batch file invokes a second, the second batch file is called a *nested batch file*.

For example, create the batch file NESTED.BAT, which contains the following ECHO commands.

```
ECHO In the batch file NESTED.BAT
ECHO All done here
```

Next, create the batch file NOEND.BAT, which contains the following.

```
@ECHO OFF
ECHO About to call the nested batch file
NESTED
ECHO Back from the nested batch file
ECHO Done!
```

As you can see, the third line of the batch file executes NESTED.BAT. When you invoke NOEND.BAT, your screen displays the following.

```
C:\BATCH> NOEND <ENTER>
About to call the nested batch file
In the batch file NESTED.BAT
All done here
C:\BATCH>
```

You can see that the NOEND.BAT batch file invokes NESTED.BAT. However, when NESTED.BAT ends, DOS redisplays its prompt. As a result, the last two lines in NOEND.BAT never execute.

To get a nested batch file to return control to the batch file that called it, you must invoke the nested batch file using CALL or COMMAND /C. In DOS 3.3 or higher, CALL is an internal command that lets one batch file invoke (or call) another. Using DOS 3.3 or later, change the batch file NOEND.BAT to the following.

```
@ECHO OFF
ECHO About to call the nested batch file
CALL NESTED
ECHO Back from the nested batch file
ECHO Done!
```

If you are using a DOS version older than 3.3, change the NOEND.BAT file to use COMMAND /C, as shown here.

```
@ECHO OFF
ECHO About to call the nested batch file
COMMAND /C NESTED
ECHO Back from the nested batch file
ECHO Done!
```

In either case, once you change NOEND.BAT, DOS will execute the nested batch file and then return control to the original batch file, letting the batch file complete. In this case, your screen will display the following.

```
C:\BATCH> NOEND   <ENTER>
About to call the nested batch file
In the batch file NESTED.BAT
All done here
Back from the nested batch file
Done!
```

The only time you don't need to use CALL or COMMAND /C to invoke a nested batch file is when you invoke the nested batch file as the last command. The nested batch file DOSSHELL is the last command called in the following batch file.

```
@ECHO OFF
PATH C:\DOS
PROMPT $P$G
DOSSHELL
```

You don't care that DOS won't return control in this case, because no commands follow the nested batch file. As a general rule, however, use COMMAND/C or CALL to invoke nested batch files.

Hands On

If your batch file misspells a label, and GOTO can't find a match, DOS immediately ends the batch file execution and displays the "Bad label" error message. Verify this by creating the batch file BADLABEL.BAT, as shown here.

```
@ECHO OFF
GOTO DONE
DATE
TIME
```

Execute BADLABEL from the DOS prompt:

```
C:\BATCH> BADLABEL   <ENTER>
```

Since there is no line labeled ":DONE", the batch file ends immediately after it encounters GOTO, never executing DATE or TIME.

When you use GOTO to create a loop, you need to make sure you give the batch file a way to end. The following batch file, INFINITE.BAT, uses GOTO, SHIFT, and

SUMMARY

GOTO

The GOTO command directs DOS to jump from one location in your batch file directly to another. The format of the GOTO command is

```
GOTO LABEL
```

LABEL is a unique name that appears on its own line in your batch file. The first character of the line must be a colon. When DOS encounters the colon, DOS knows the line contains a label and does not try to execute the line as a command. If your batch file does not have a label whose name matches the label specified in the GOTO command, DOS will end the batch file immediately and display an error message. Although your label names can essentially contain any number of characters, DOS only reads the first eight. If two labels in your batch file have the same first eight characters, your batch file will not behave as intended.

FOR

The FOR command lets you repeat a specific command for a set of files. FOR's format in batch files is as follows.

```
FOR %%F IN (FILES) DO DOS_COMMAND
```

The FOR command assigns a file from the set of files to its variable %%F and performs the command specified. When the command completes, FOR assigns the next file in the set to the variable. This process repeats until FOR uses every file in the set. If the set contains a DOS wildcard, FOR expands the wildcard into the matching file names. DOS lets you invoke FOR from DOS prompt as well as within batch files. If you invoke FOR from the DOS prompt, only precede FOR's variable name with a single percent sign.

SHIFT

The SHIFT command provides your batch files with access to more than the nine batch parameters DOS assigns to %1 through %9. When your batch

/ SUMMARY /

file executes SHIFT, DOS moves each batch parameter one position to the left, discarding the value of %0 and shifting into %9 the first unused parameter. If no unused parameters remain, DOS assigns %9 the null string. The format of the SHIFT command is simply SHIFT.

Nested Batch Files

A nested batch file is a batch file invoked by another batch file. When a batch file invokes a second batch file, you need to use the CALL command or COMMAND /C. If you don't DOS will return control to the DOS prompt when the nested batch file completes and the remaining commands in the original batch file never execute. CALL requires DOS 3.3 or later. The format of the CALL command is as follows.

```
CALL NESTED  OPTIONAL_PARAMETERS
```

ECHO to display each of the batch file's command-line parameters. Unfortunately, the batch file has the SHIFT and GOTO commands out of order.

```
@ECHO OFF
:LOOP
IF '%1'=='' GOTO DONE
ECHO %1
GOTO LOOP
SHIFT
:DONE
```

Invoke INFINITE.BAT with the parameters A, B, and C:

```
C:\BATCH> INFINITE  A  B  C  <ENTER>
```

Rather than displaying the parameters on individual lines, the batch file displays "A," jumps up to LOOP, and displays "A" again. Because GOTO is before SHIFT, the parameters never get shifted; %1 is never assigned the null string; and the file, therefore, never goes to DONE. The batch file enters a loop that never ends (an *infinite loop*).

```
@ECHO OFF
:LOOP        ←──────────────────────┐
IF '%1'=='' GOTO DONE                │
ECHO %1                              │
GOTO LOOP ───────────────────────────┘
```

Under DOS version 5, the DIR command, using the /B switch, will display each file name on its own line.

```
C:\BATCH> DIR  /B  <ENTER>
```

If you are using a DOS version older than 5, you can create the batch file DIR1LINE.BAT, shown here, to achieve the same effect.

```
@ECHO OFF
FOR %%F IN (%1) DO ECHO %%F
```

Using DIRLINE.BAT, you can display a directory for a single file or use a wildcard combination:

```
C:\BATCH> DIR1LINE  *.BAT  <ENTER>
```

In this case, FOR expands *.BAT into the set of matching files and then uses ECHO to display each file name on its own line.

Review

1. Why do batch label name lines begin with a colon (:)?

2. Use the GOTO command to create the batch file MULTIDEL.BAT, shown here, that lets you delete one or more files.

```
C:\BATCH>  MULTIDEL  ONE  TWO  THREE  <ENTER>
```

3. When must you use the CALL command or COMMAND /C? Why?

4. The IF command does not consider the uppercase letters the same as lowercase. The following batch file, COLORS.BAT, compares %1 to three colors RED, BLUE, and GREEN. If the user types the color in lowercase letters, the batch file doesn't match a color.

```
@ECHO OFF
IF '%1'=='BLUE' ECHO The color is BLUE
IF '%1'=='RED' ECHO The color is RED
IF '%1'=='GREEN' ECHO The color is GREEN
```

Use the FOR command to have the batch file support the entries RED, Red, red, BLUE, Blue, blue, GREEN, Green, and green.

Answers

1. When DOS encounters a colon as the first character in a batch file line, DOS knows the line contains a label and not a command. As a result, DOS makes a note of the label's position within the batch file, and DOS does not try to execute the line as a command.

2. One way to solve this is

```
@ECHO OFF
:LOOP
IF '%1'=='' GOTO DONE
FOR %%F IN (%1) DO DEL %%F
SHIFT
GOTO LOOP
:DONE
```

3. You must use either the CALL command or COMMAND /C to invoke another batch file from within the middle of a batch file. By default, when DOS finishes a batch file, DOS returns control to the DOS prompt. Unfortunately, if your batch file invokes another from within the middle of a list of commands and DOS returns control to the DOS prompt when the nested batch file completes, the commands that follow the batch file invocation will

never execute. If you are using DOS 3.3 or later, use the CALL command; otherwise, use COMMAND /C.

4. The new batch file would be:

```
@ECHO OFF
FOR %%F IN (BLUE Blue blue) DO IF '%1'=='%%F' ECHO BLUE
FOR %%F IN (GREEN Green green) DO IF '%1'=='%%F' ECHO GREEN
FOR %%F IN (RED Red red) DO IF '%1'=='%%F' ECHO RED
```

Advanced Concepts

One of the most common uses of GOTO is to create a menu-driven batch file. For example, the batch file MENU.BAT displays the following menu and waits for the user to press a key.

```
B A T C H    M E N U

D  Directory Listing
T  Set or Display TIME
V  Display DOS Version Number
Q  Quit to DOS
```

The batch file uses the command SCANCODE.COM that you'll create in Chapter 29 using DEBUG. SCANCODE returns an exit status value that corresponds to a key pressed.

```
@ECHO OFF
:MAIN_LOOP
CLS
ECHO B A T C H    M E N U
ECHO.
ECHO D  Directory Listing
ECHO T  Set or Display TIME
ECHO V  Display DOS Version Number
ECHO Q  Quit to DOS
:SCAN_LOOP
SCANCODE
IF ERRORLEVEL 32 IF NOT ERRORLEVEL 33 GOTO DIR
IF ERRORLEVEL 47 IF NOT ERRORLEVEL 48 GOTO VER
IF ERRORLEVEL 20 IF NOT ERRORLEVEL 21 GOTO TIME
```

```
IF ERRORLEVEL 16 IF NOT ERRORLEVEL 17 GOTO QUIT
GOTO SCAN_LOOP
:DIR
DIR
PAUSE
GOTO MAIN_LOOP
:VER
VER
PAUSE
GOTO MAIN_LOOP
:TIME
TIME
PAUSE
GOTO MAIN_LOOP
:QUIT
```

The batch file displays the menu and uses SCANCODE to wait for the user to press a key. If the key corresponds to one of the menu options, the batch file executes the corresponding commands and then uses GOTO to loop back to the menu display repeating this process. If the user presses an invalid key, the batch file uses GOTO to loop back to SCANCODE to get a valid key.

Saving and Restoring the Current Directory

As they increase in complexity, your batch files may change the current drive or directory or even create files during their processing. As a rule, your batch files should clean up after themselves, deleting their temporary files and restoring the original drive and directory.

If you are using DOS 3.3 or later, the following batch file SAVEDIR.BAT creates an environment entry named ORIG_DIR that contains the original directory. To use this batch file, you must create the file ORIG_DIR.DAT that contains the SET command shown here.

```
C:\BATCH> COPY  CON  ORIG_DIR.DAT   <ENTER>
SET ORIG_DIR=^Z   <ENTER>
         1 File(s) copied
```

You must place the end-of-file character (CTRL-Z) immediately next to the equal sign.

You learned in Chapter 10 that if you invoke CHDIR without a directory name, CHDIR displays the current directory. Using the DOS output redirection operator (>>), discussed in Chapter 20, you can append CHDIR's output to the SET command, creating a batch file that saves the current directory, as shown here.

```
@ECHO OFF
COPY \BATCH\ORIG_DIR.DAT  SAVEIT.BAT
CHDIR >> SAVEIT.BAT
CALL SAVEIT
DEL SAVEIT.BAT
```

The batch file copies your template file containing the partial SET command to a batch file named SAVEIT.BAT. Next, the batch file appends to SAVEIT.BAT's SET command, the name of the current directory, as redirected by CHDIR. Assuming your current directory was DOS on drive C, SAVEIT.BAT's SET command will now be SET ORIG.DIR=C:\DOS. Next, the batch file uses CALL to invoke SAVEIT.BAT, which in turn uses SET to define the ORIG.DIR environment entry. Because the batch file SAVEIT.BAT has performed its processing, the batch file deletes it, cleaning up after itself.

The following batch file, LISTTREE.BAT, invokes SAVEDIR.BAT using the CALL command. Next, the batch file selects the root directory and invokes the TREE command. When TREE completes, the batch file uses the named parameter, ORIG_DIR, from above, to restore the original directory.

```
@ECHO OFF
CALL SAVEDIR
CHDIR \
TREE
CHDIR %ORIG_DIR%
SET ORIG_DIR=
```

As you create your batch files, use techniques such as SAVEDIR to reduce the side effects of your more complex batch files.

Key Terms

Branch   To change the order in which a program or batch file is executed. In DOS batch files, branching (jumping) is accomplished through use of the GOTO command.

Label   A name in a batch file that GOTO can use as a marker to jump to when called. The first character on the line where the lavel appears must be a colon. This tells DOS that what is on the line is a label, not a command.

Nested batch file   A second batch file invoked by a batch file. To invoke nested batch files, you need to use the CALL command or COMMAND /C.

Automatic System Startup Commands with AUTOEXEC.BAT

You have seen that DOS batch files save you time and keystrokes while eliminating your need to memorize long or difficult commands. Using batch files, you can combine several related commands into one. As you work with DOS, you may find that you always perform several important commands each time your system starts, for example, defining the command path and system prompt or invoking the FASTOPEN command to improve your file access time. In this case, by placing the PATH, PROMPT, and FASTOPEN commands into a batch file, you can quickly perform all three steps with a single command.

You still have to call your setup batch file each time your system starts. It would be nice if you could tell DOS to automatically execute the batch file each time your system starts. As it turns out, you can. Each time DOS starts, it searches your startup disk's root directory for a special batch file named AUTOEXEC.BAT. If this batch file exists, DOS executes all the commands in it. In other words, DOS automatically executes your system startup commands.

If AUTOEXEC.BAT does not exist in the root directory, DOS executes the DATE and TIME commands. DOS uses the batch file name AUTOEXEC.BAT because it AUTOmatically EXECutes the commands in the BATch file. In this chapter you will examine several commands that users typically place in their AUTOEXEC.BAT file.

Common AUTOEXEC.BAT Commands

DOS provides the AUTOEXEC.BAT batch file to help you execute the commands you need to run each time your system starts. Table 18-1 lists several DOS commands users commonly place in their AUTOEXEC.BAT file.

Defining Your Command Path

You learned in Chapter 11, "Getting the Most from DOS Directories," that the PATH command lets you define the list of directories DOS searches for your external commands and batch files whenever it fails to locate the command in the current directory. At the very minimum, your command path should include the DOS directory, which contains your external DOS commands.

```
PATH C:\DOS
```

Depending on the applications you use on a regular basis, you may include additional directories, such as WINDOWS, 123, and WP (for WordPerfect), as shown here.

```
PATH C:\DOS;C:\WINDOWS;C:\123;C:\WP
```

By placing the PATH command in your AUTOEXEC.BAT file, DOS automatically sets up your command path each time your system starts. Only place directories that contain your commonly used commands in the command path. If you include

Command	Function
PATH	Defines the DOS command path
PROMPT	Defines the DOS prompt
FASTOPEN	Improves file access performance (DOS 3.3 or higher)
PRINT	Installs the PRINT commands memory-resident software
SET TEMP	Defines the disk and directory in which DOS creates its temporary files (DOS 5)
SET DIRCMD	Defines the default command-line switches for the DIR command (DOS 5)
SHARE	Provides additional support for large disks under DOS version 4, and file locking in network environments
DOSSHELL	Invokes the DOS shell user interface (DOS 4 or higher)

Table 18-1.   Common AUTOEXEC.BAT Commands

many directories, DOS will waste considerable time searching directories that are unlikely to contain your current command.

Defining Your System Prompt

In Chapter 10, "Directories," you used the following PROMPT command to display the current drive and directory within your system's prompt.

```
C> PROMPT  $P$G   <ENTER>
C:\>
```

Although you may choose to further customize your prompt, I strongly recommend that your prompt include the $P and $G entries to display the current drive and directory information. By placing the above PROMPT command in AUTO-EXEC.BAT, you can always easily determine the current directory because it will be displayed to you with each DOS prompt.

FASTOPEN Decreases File Access Time

If you are using DOS version 3.3 or later, the FASTOPEN command, discussed in Chapter 11, can improve your performance by reducing the amount of time your computer spends searching your disk for commonly used files.

By default, each time you run a program or open a file, be the file a letter, report or work sheet, DOS must search your disk to locate the file. Although your hard disk is fast, it is still mechanical, and thus much slower than your computer's electronic memory. FASTOPEN directs DOS to store, in your computer's fast electronics memory, the name and disk location of files as you access them. Each time you access a file, DOS searches FASTOPEN's list of recently used files to see if the file is among them. If the file is in the list, DOS immediately knows the file's disk location and does not have to send the disk drive head out searching the disk for the file. If the file is not present in the list, DOS must perform the slower, normal disk search.

The FASTOPEN command will not improve the access time for every file you access, only for the files you access more than once. The following FASTOPEN command directs DOS to track the names and disk location of up to 50 recently used files.

```
FASTOPEN  C:=50
```

You may specify FASTOPEN for more that one disk:

```
FASTOPEN  C:=50  D:=50
```

If you are using DOS 3.3 or later, you should include FASTOPEN in your AUTOEXEC.BAT file.

Installing a High-Performance Print Queue

Chapter 14, "Getting the Most from PRINT," discusses the PRINT command in detail and, in the "Advanced Concepts" section, presents several command-line switches that you can include the first time you invoke PRINT, which improve its performance. If you use the PRINT command on a regular basis, place the following command in your AUTOEXEC.BAT file.

```
PRINT  /B:4096  /D:PRN  /M:32  /U:8
```

The /B entry increases the print buffer from 512 bytes to 4096 bytes, meaning that DOS can give your printer bigger amounts of data at a time, and get on with its other business. The /D entry specifies which port to use. If your printer attaches to a serial port, replace PRN with the serial port name, such as COM1:. The /M entry increases the amount of time PRINT can keep the CPU from 2 ticks (1/10 second) to 32 ticks (1.4 seconds). The /U switch increases how long PRINT should wait (for an older, slower printer) from the default of 2 to 8 ticks. If you don't need some of these switches, you don't need to include them—if you don't use PRINT to print your files, you don't need to include this command in your AUTOEXEC.BAT file at all. Because PRINT only lets you specify these switches the first time you invoke it, placing the PRINT command in AUTOEXEC.BAT ensures the correct switches are in use each time your system starts.

Informing DOS 5 Where to Create Its Temporary Files

In Chapter 21, "The DOS Pipe," you will examine the *DOS pipe* operator, which lets one command's output become another command's input. For example, the following command displays a sorted directory listing by *piping* the output of the DIR command into SORT.

```
C:\> DIR  |  SORT  <ENTER>
```

To implement the pipe, DOS needs to create temporary files. By default, DOS creates these temporary files in your disk's root directory. Unfortunately, if your disk does not have enough disk space for the temporary files, the pipe operation will fail.

In DOS 5, you can tell DOS where to create these temporary files with the DOS 5 environment entry, TEMP. If you create an electronic-memory RAM drive

(Chapter 24, "Customizing Your System with CONFIG.SYS," discusses RAM drives in detail) with the RAMDRIVE.SYS device driver and then assign TEMP to point to the RAM drive, DOS can create the temporary files faster, which further improves your system performance. The following SET command assumes you have a fast RAM drive named E.

```
SET TEMP=E:
```

The TEMP environment entry is only used by DOS 5. If you are not using version 5, do not include such a SET command in your AUTOEXEC.BAT unless you know it is required by your applications software.

Specifying the DOS 5 DIR Command Attributes

Chapter 4, "Getting Started with DOS Files," examined the DIR command. At that time, you learned DIR displays a file's base name, extension, size, and date and time stamps. By default, DIR does not display the files in sorted order. If you are using DOS 5, however, DIR lets you specify a desired sort order.

The "Advanced Concepts" section of Chapter 4 describes the /O, /A, /S, and /L switches that you can use to customize your DOS 5 directory listing. As you experiment with these switches, you will eventually find a combination that you like best. Rather than forcing you to remember and type these switches each time you invoke DIR, DOS lets you define the DIRCMD environment entry. Each time you invoke DIR to display a directory listing under DOS 5, DIR searches the environment for an entry in the form DIRCMD=*SWITCHES*. If DIR finds the entry, DIR uses the switches specified. Placed in your AUTOEXEC.BAT, the DIRCMD entry lets you define the default format of your directory listing.

The following SET command creates a default format in which DIR is sorted by name and displayed in the lower case.

```
SET  DIRCMD=/O:N/L
```

Like TEMP, DIRCMD is only available under DOS 5.

Invoking the DOS Shell

DOS, in versions 4 and later, provides a user-friendly command shell that lets you work in a menu-driven environment. (Chapters 39 through 42 examine the DOS 4 and 5 shells in detail.) Many users who prefer to work from the DOS shell, as opposed to the command line, include the DOSSHELL command as the last command in their AUTOEXEC.BAT.

SHARE

Under DOS version 4, if you are using a hard disk partition larger than 32 megabytes, you need to install the SHARE command. Under DOS version 4, SHARE ensures that older programs using file control blocks (FCBs) don't destroy information on your disk. File control blocks are not compatible with the larger partition size. Therefore, many DOS 4 users place a SHARE command in AUTOEXEC.BAT to ensure the larger disk is supported when your system starts. However, for better memory utilization, you should use the CONFIG.SYS INSTALL= entry discussed in Chapter 24, "Customizing Your System with CONFIG.SYS."

DOSSHELL

Under DOS 4, DOSSHELL is a batch file and not an actual DOS command. As such, you should make DOSSHELL the last command in your AUTOEXEC.BAT file. As discussed in Chapter 17, "Getting the Most from Batch Files," when you invoke one batch file from within another without using CALL or COMMAND /C, the first batch file never regains control. If DOSSHELL is the last command in the batch file, you don't have to worry about AUTOEXEC.BAT regaining control; all of its work is already done.

A Sample AUTOEXEC.BAT

Depending on your own requirements, the actual commands that appear in your AUTOEXEC.BAT may differ from those shown here. The purpose of this file is to give you a sample format for creating your own AUTOEXEC.BAT file.

```
@ECHO  OFF
PATH  C:\DOS
PROMPT  $P$G
FASTOPEN  C:=50
PRINT  /B:4096  /D:PRN  /M:32  /U:8
DOSSHELL
```

AUTOEXEC.BAT and CONFIG.SYS

DOS only uses the AUTOEXEC.BAT batch file once—when your system starts up. For DOS to locate AUTOEXEC.BAT, it must reside in your startup disk's root directory.

In addition to AUTOEXEC.BAT, DOS uses a second user-defined file named CONFIG.SYS, which must also reside in the root. Chapter 24 discusses the CONFIG.SYS file in detail. You must understand the difference between these two files.

AUTOEXEC.BAT contains one or more *DOS commands* that DOS executes when your system starts. The CONFIG.SYS file contains single-line *system configuration entries* that tell DOS such information as the number of files it may need to open at one time. CONFIG.SYS entries are not DOS commands. The following TYPE command illustrates possible CONFIG.SYS entries.

```
C:\> TYPE  \CONFIG.SYS   <ENTER>
FILES=20
BUFFERS=25
DEVICE=C:\DOS\RAMDRIVE.SYS
```

These entries control how DOS CONFIGures itself in SYStem memory, hence the name CONFIG.SYS. Use DIR to examine the files in your root directory. Your root directory should have an AUTOEXEC.BAT file and CONFIG.SYS. Use TYPE to display the contents of each. AUTOEXEC.BAT will contain recognizable DOS commands. CONFIG.SYS, on the other hand, will contain single-line entries DOS uses during the startup process.

Change AUTOEXEC.BAT with Caution

AUTOEXEC.BAT is a very powerful tool. It runs powerful commands automatically each time your system starts. You need to be very careful when you make changes to AUTOEXEC.BAT. If you make an error, you could possibly prevent DOS from being able to boot your system. As a rule, always make a copy of AUTOEXEC.BAT before you make any changes. The following command, for example, copies AUTOEXEC.BAT to a file named AUTOEXEC.SAV.

```
C:\> COPY  \AUTOEXEC.BAT  \AUTOEXEC.SAV   <ENTER>
```

Should you make an errant entry or deletion to or from AUTOEXEC.BAT, you can reboot your system using a bootable DOS floppy disk and restore the original AUTOEXEC.BAT file from the saved one.

Keep in mind that the only time DOS uses AUTOEXEC.BAT is during system startup. If you make changes to AUTOEXEC.BAT, you will need to reboot to use the new AUTOEXEC.BAT.

SUMMARY

AUTOEXEC.BAT

Each time DOS starts, DOS searches your startup disk's root directory for a special batch file named AUTOEXEC.BAT. If AUTOEXEC.BAT exists, DOS executes each of the commands that the batch file contains. AUTOEXEC.BAT lets you specify commands you want DOS to automatically execute at system startup. If the file does not exist, DOS executes the familiar DATE and TIME commands.

Hands On

Using the TYPE command, display the current contents of your AUTOEXEC.BAT file.

```
C:\> TYPE  \AUTOEXEC.BAT   <ENTER>
```

So you have a backup copy of the file's current contents copy AUTOEXEC.BAT to AUTOEXEC.SAV, as shown here.

```
C:\> COPY  \AUTOEXEC.BAT  \*.SAV   <ENTER>
```

Next, using your word processor or the DOS text editor, you can edit AUTOEXEC.BAT. If you use a word processor, as discussed in Chapter 15, "Grouping Commands with Batch Files," you must edit batch files using ASCII or unformatted mode. Do not remove any commands from AUTOEXEC.BAT that you do not understand. If you would like, add commands to set your system prompt and define a command path. If you are using DOS 3.3 or later, include a FASTOPEN command to improve your system performance. If you are using DOS 5, consider adding SET commands for TEMP and DIRCMD. For more information on these two entries, see Chapter 19, "The DOS Environment."

If you make any changes to AUTOEXEC.BAT, reboot your system to put the changes into effect.

Review

1. How does AUTOEXEC.BAT differ from other batch files?

2. How does AUTOEXEC.BAT differ from CONFIG.SYS?

3. How can you distinguish between an AUTOEXEC.BAT entry and a CONFIG.SYS entry?

4. What does DOS do if the AUTOEXEC.BAT file does not exist?

5. How does DOS know you have made changes to AUTOEXEC.BAT so DOS can put the changes into effect?

Answers

1. Like all batch files, AUTOEXEC.BAT contains a list of DOS commands. AUTOEXEC.BAT is special because each time your system starts, DOS automatically searches your root directory for AUTOEXEC.BAT. If DOS locates the file, DOS executes all of the commands AUTOEXEC.BAT contains. If AUTOEXEC.BAT does not exist, DOS executes the familiar DATE and TIME commands.

2. DOS uses the files AUTOEXEC.BAT and CONFIG.SYS during system startup. However, DOS uses the files very differently. CONFIG.SYS is a user-defined file that contains single-line entries that let you customize DOS. Common uses of CONFIG.SYS are specifying the number of files DOS can open at one time, installing disk input and output buffers in memory to improve your system performance, and installing device driver software for RAM drives or unique hardware devices. AUTOEXEC.BAT, on the other hand, contains a list of commands you want DOS to execute each time your system starts. Common uses of AUTOEXEC.BAT include defining the command path, setting the system prompt, and invoking the DOSSHELL user interface.

3. AUTOEXEC.BAT entries are DOS commands. CONFIG.SYS entries are system configuration values.

4. If the file AUTOEXEC.BAT does not reside in the startup disk's root directory, DOS executes the DATE and TIME commands.

5. DOS does not know. The only time DOS uses AUTOEXEC.BAT is during system startup. If you make changes to AUTOEXEC.BAT, you will probably want to restart your computer. In some cases, you can simply invoke the new AUTOEXEC.BAT commands individually from the DOS prompt to achieve the same results.

Advanced Concepts

Many users understand that DOS uses both the CONFIG.SYS file and the AUTOEXEC.BAT file during system startup, but they are still not quite sure how DOS uses them and when. To better understand where AUTOEXEC.BAT and CONFIG.SYS fall into the DOS system startup process, the "Advanced Concepts" section of Chapter 3, "Issuing DOS Commands," discusses the DOS system startup process in detail. You may wish to review that section now.

Shielding AUTOEXEC.BAT from Software Installations

If you have worked with DOS for some time, you have probably experienced frustration when an application program's installation procedures overwrite your AUTOEXEC.BAT file. To prevent such a loss of your AUTOEXEC.BAT, consider creating a second batch file, perhaps called CUSTOM.BAT, that contains the commands you would typically place in AUTOEXEC.BAT. Next, within your AUTOEXEC.BAT file, only include the following command, which invokes your startup commands as desired.

```
CALL CUSTOM
```

Should a program's installation overwrite your AUTOEXEC.BAT file, you only lose this single command. If you are not using DOS version 3.3 or later, change the previous CALL command to COMMAND /C, as discussed in Chapter 17. After the installation is complete, check your AUTOEXEC.BAT file to insure it is consistent with CUSTOM.BAT; in other words, check that CUSTOM.BAT does not overwrite a needed command path entry.

Disabling AUTOEXEC.BAT

If DOS does not find AUTOEXEC.BAT, it executes the familiar DATE and TIME commands. If, for some reason, you don't want DOS to do either, you can disable the execution of AUTOEXEC.BAT using the CONFIG.SYS SHELL= entry discussed in Chapter 24. The SHELL= entry tells DOS the location of the command processor COMMAND.COM. Many users use SHELL= to direct DOS to use the copy of

COMMAND.COM that resides in the DOS directory; they can then remove the COMMAND.COM file from the root. Likewise, the SHELL= entry lets you increase your environment size. The following CONFIG.SYS entry directs DOS to use the COMMAND.COM file that resides in the DOS directory and to create an environment of 1,024 bytes.

```
SHELL=C:\DOS\COMMAND.COM  /E:1024  /P
```

If you omit the /P switch, DOS will not execute AUTOEXEC.BAT. Likewise, DOS will not execute DATE and TIME. DOS will simply display its system prompt.

Be careful if you do not include the /P switch. If you later execute the EXIT command, discussed in Chapter 43, "DOS System Commands," DOS will generate a "Bad or Missing Command Interpreter" error message, and your system will hang up. The only way to recover at that point is to reboot your computer.

Key Terms

AUTOEXEC.BAT   A unique user-defined batch file whose commands DOS automatically executes each time your system starts.

CONFIG.SYS   A unique user-defined file containing single-line entries (not commands) that direct DOS to configure itself in memory using the information you specify.

Chapter 19

The DOS Environment

Each time DOS starts, it reserves a section of your computer's memory it calls the *environment* to store information accessible to DOS commands and your applications. Typically, the information you store is specific to your own personal working environment, for example, the current command path and your system prompt.

In this chapter you will learn how to display the environment's current entries and how to add and remove entries. If you are using DOS 5, you will also learn how to use the environment to enhance the DIR command, as well as how to specify where DOS creates its temporary files.

The SET Command

The SET command lets you display, add, and remove environment entries. From the DOS prompt, issue the following SET command to display the environment's current contents.

```
C:\> SET    <ENTER>
```

Depending on your system configuration, the contents of your environment may differ from those of other users. At a minimum, your environment will probably contain a COMSPEC, PATH, and PROMPT entry:

```
C:\> SET   <ENTER>
COMSPEC=C:\DOS\COMMAND.COM
PATH=C:\DOS
PROMPT=$P$G
```

DOS environment entries have the form *NAME=Value*. In this case, COMSPEC has the value C:\DOS\COMMAND.COM, as shown here:

Adding an Environment Entry

In addition to letting you display the environment entries, the SET command lets you add environment entries. For example, the following entry creates an environment entry named BOOK and assigns it the value "DOS The Complete Reference."

```
C:\> SET  BOOK=DOS The Complete Reference  <ENTER>
```

Using the SET command, you can display the environment entry's current contents, ensuring that SET added the BOOK entry.

```
C:\> SET  <ENTER>
COMSPEC=C:\DOS\COMMAND.COM
PATH=C:\DOS
PROMPT=$P$G
BOOK=DOS The Complete Reference
```

SET always converts the entry name to uppercase letters, but leaves the entry's value in the upper- or lowercase letters you typed. If you assign an incorrect value to an entry, possibly mistyping it, simply repeat the command with the correct value. SET will overwrite the existing value. The following command overwrites the current value for the BOOK environment entry with "DCR Third Edition."

```
C:\> SET  BOOK=DCR Third Edition  <ENTER>
```

Using SET, you can display the environment's current contents to see that the former BOOK entry has been overwritten.

```
C:\> SET   <ENTER>
COMSPEC=C:\DOS\COMMAND.COM
PATH=C:\DOS
PROMPT=$P$G
BOOK=DCR Third Edition
```

Environment Space Is Not Unlimited

By default, DOS sets aside space for 160 bytes of environment information (256 bytes in DOS 5). If the number of entries in your environment exceeds this amount, DOS will try to expand the environment. If DOS cannot increase the environment's size, DOS will display the following error message.

```
Out of environment space
```

If this error message occurs, turn to "Increasing the Environment Size During System Startup" in the "Advanced Concepts" part of this chapter.

Removing an Environment Entry

Removing an environment entry is similar to adding an entry—you specify an environment entry name followed by an equal sign. The difference is that you don't specify a corresponding value—you set it equal to "nothing." The following command removes the BOOK entry.

```
C:\> SET   BOOK=   <ENTER>
```

Using SET, you can see the entry is gone:

```
C:\> SET   <ENTER>
COMSPEC=C:\DOS\COMMAND.COM
PATH=C:\DOS
PROMPT=$P$G
```

If you misspell an entry name or specify a nonexistent entry, SET does not display an error message. SET simply ignores the command.

How DOS Uses the Environment

In addition to the SET command, the PROMPT, PATH, and APPEND commands add entries to the DOS environment. Each time a command completes, for example, DOS searches the environment for a PROMPT= entry. If such an entry exists, DOS uses the entry's value to customize your system prompt. If the entry does not exist, DOS displays its default prompt, which contains only a drive letter followed by a greater-than sign (C>).

When DOS fails to locate a command as an internal command in memory, or as an external command or batch file in the current directory, DOS searches the directories specified in the command path. DOS uses the environment PATH= entry to determine which directories to search.

As you become more conversant with DOS batch files, you can create batch files that access environment entries to perform specific processing.

DOS 5 Environment Entries

If you are using DOS 5, DOS provides two special environment entries, TEMP and DIRCMD, that can increase your capabilities. As you will learn in Chapter 21, "The DOS Pipe," the DOS pipe operator lets you direct one command's output to become the input of a second command. For example, the following command uses the pipe operator (|) to display a sorted directory listing.

```
C:\> DIR | SORT <ENTER>
```

To implement the pipe operator, DOS actually creates temporary files in the root directory of your disk that exist while the command executes. If the current disk has limited available disk space, DOS may not be able to create the temporary files and the command will fail. The TEMP environment entry lets you tell DOS 5 where you want it to create these temporary files. For example, the following command assigns TEMP the value of the fast RAM drive E:

```
C:\> SET TEMP=E: <ENTER>
```

Because RAM drives use your computer's fast electronic memory, they are much faster than your mechanical disk drive. By directing DOS to create its temporary files on the RAM drive, the commands execute faster and reduce unnecessary wear on your disk. For more information on RAM drives, refer to Chapter 24, "Customizing Your System with CONFIG.SYS".

As discussed in Chapters 4, "Getting Started with DOS Files," and 18, "Automatic System Startup Commands with AUTOEXEC.BAT," the DOS 5 DIR command supports several additional command-line switches, as shown in Table 19-1.

The following DIR command, for example, displays a directory listing sorted by size, omitting directory names, with the file names and extensions in the lower case.

```
C:\> DIR  /A:-D  /O:S  /L   <ENTER>
```

Switch	Function
/A: *Attributes*	Displays only those files with the specified attributes:
	H Hidden files
	–H Exclude hidden files
	S System files
	–S Exclude system files
	D Directories
	–D Exclude directories
	A Files requiring archiving
	–A Files successfully archived
	R All read-only files
	–R Exclude read-only files
/O: *SortOrder*	Sorts the directory listing by one or more of the following orders:
	N Name, from A to Z
	–N Name, from Z to A
	E Extension, from A to Z
	–E Extension, from Z to A
	D Date and time, oldest to newest
	–D Date and time, newest to oldest
	S Size, smallest to largest
	–S Size, largest to smallest
	G Group, directories displayed before files
	–G Group, files displayed before directories
/S	Displays files in lower-level directories
/B	Displays only file names and extensions, one per line
/L	Displays file names and extensions in lower case

Table 19-1.   Command-line Switches Supported by the DOS 5 DIR Command

As you become more comfortable with the DIR command switches, you will eventually select several switches that best serve your needs. As you can imagine, having to type a complex series of switches each time you invoke DIR could become tedious very quickly. The DOS 5 DIRCMD environment entry lets you specify the options you want DOS to use by default each time you use DIR. The following SET command selects the settings used in the previous DIR command as the default.

```
C:\> SET  DIRCMD=/A:-D/O:S/L   <ENTER>
```

Once you define the DIRCMD entry, you no longer have to repeatedly type the switches. Under DOS 5, each time you invoke DIR to display a directory listing, DIR searches the environment entries for DIRCMD=. If a matching entry exists, DIR uses those switches to format the default directory listing.

Hands On

Using the SET command, display your current environment entries.

```
C:\> SET   <ENTER>
```

Next, create an entry called CHAPTER and assign it the value 19.

```
C:\> SET CHAPTER=19   <ENTER>
```

Use SET to display the environment's new contents. As discussed, to change an entry's value, simply invoke SET a second time specifying the desired value. In this case, change the CHAPTER entry to "Nineteen."

```
C:\> SET CHAPTER=Nineteen   <ENTER>
```

Use SET to display the entry's new value, and then remove the entry.

```
C:\> SET CHAPTER=   <ENTER>
```

SUMMARY

Displaying Environment Entries

The SET command displays the current environment entries. Environment entries have the form *NAME=Value*. To display the entries, execute the SET command:

```
C:\> SET   <ENTER>
```

Adding Environment Entries

To add an entry to the DOS environment, invoke SET with the environment name and value, as shown here.

```
C:\> SET EntryName=DesiredValue <ENTER>
```

SET will convert the entry name to uppercase letters, leaving the entry's value unchanged.

Removing Environment Entries

To remove an existing environment entry, invoke the SET command with the entry name followed by an equal sign but no value to the right of the equal sign.

If you are using DOS 5, direct DIR to display file name and extensions only, using lowercase letters by setting the DIRCMD entry as follows.

```
C:\> SET  DIRCMD=/B/L  <ENTER>
```

Experiment with different DIRCMD settings, invoking DIR each time until you determine the setting you prefer. Next, consider placing the corresponding SET DIRCMD command in your AUTOEXEC.BAT file so the setting is in place each time your system starts.

Review

1. What is the DOS environment?

2. What DOS commands place entries in the environment?

3. How do the following commands differ?

   ```
   SET BOOK=DOS The Complete Reference
   SET book=DOS The Complete Reference
   ```

4. How do you change an existing environment entry's value?

5. What is the purpose of the DOS 5 TEMP and DIRCMD environment entries?

Answers

1. Each time DOS starts, DOS allocates a portion of memory for the storage of system variables such as the command path and current system prompt. This area of memory is the DOS environment. Using the SET command, you can display, add, or remove environment entries.

2. The SET, APPEND, PROMPT, and PATH commands may add or update environment entries.

3. These two commands are the same. The SET command always converts an entry's name, in this case BOOK, to uppercase.

4. You change an existing environment entry's value by invoking SET with the entry name and desired value, as if you were setting the value for the first time.

5. The TEMP environment entry tells DOS where you want it to create its temporary files. The DIRCMD entry tells DIR the switches you want it to use by default. These switches let you specify the directory list sort order, whether the listing is in upper- or lowercase letters, and even which file types DIR displays.

Advanced Concepts

The "Advanced Concepts" section of Chapter 17, "Getting the Most from Batch Files," discussed how to access DOS environment entries from within your batch file using named parameters. To use named parameters, you must be using DOS 3.3 or later. In general, a named parameter is simply the name of an environment entry

entry surrounded by percent signs, for which a value is returned. For example, the following batch file displays the current value of the PATH entry.

```
@ECHO OFF
ECHO %PATH%
```

When DOS encounters letters enclosed by percent signs as it executes a batch file, DOS searches the environment for a matching entry, substituting the entry's value for the name. If the entry does not exist, DOS replaces the named parameter with the null string. The following batch file tests whether the named parameter BOOK is defined (not equal to the null string) and, if it is, displays BOOK's value. If the BOOK is undefined, the batch file displays a message saying so.

```
@ECHO OFF
IF '%BOOK%'=='' ECHO BOOK is undefined
IF NOT '%BOOK%'=='' ECHO BOOK's value is %BOOK%
```

Increasing the Environment Size During System Startup

As briefly discussed, by default DOS allocates either 160 or 256 bytes for the environment, depending on which version you use. If the total number of characters in all your environment entries exceeds the allocated amount, DOS attempts to increase the environment's size to accomodate them. If DOS has room to increase the environment's size, DOS does. If DOS cannot increase the environment size, the SET command fails, and DOS displays the following error message.

```
Out of environment space
```

To better understand why there are times when the environment can grow and times when it can't, you need to examine a simplified DOS memory map, shown here:

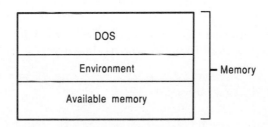

As you can see, the DOS environment resides in an area of memory next to the memory available for use. When the size of the environment exceeds the allocated space, DOS can increase the environment's size, as shown here:

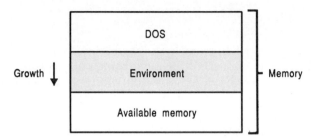

When you install memory-resident software, such as GRAPHICS, PRINT, or FASTOPEN, DOS uses a portion of the available memory, as shown here:

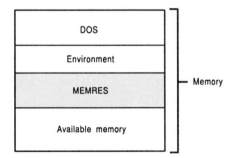

If DOS tries to increase the environment's size now, DOS fails because the memory-resident program is there.

If you experience the "Out of environment space" error message, you may be able to correct the problem by restarting DOS and issuing all of your SET commands before loading any memory-resident programs. If this technique fails, you can direct DOS to reserve more memory for the environment each time DOS starts by using the CONFIG.SYS SHELL= entry mentioned in Chapter 18 and discussed in detail in Chapter 24, "Customizing Your System with CONFIG.SYS".

One of the entries DOS always places in the environment is COMSPEC=, which tells DOS where to locate the command processor once the system is running. COMMAND.COM contains the software responsible for displaying the DOS prompt and executing the commands you enter. In addition, COMMAND.COM contains all the internal DOS commands. Each time your system starts, DOS loads the command processor into memory, as shown here:

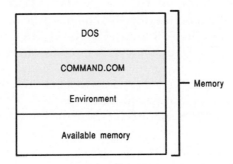

To make better use of your computer's memory, DOS divides the command processor into two parts—a *resident part*, which is always in memory, and a *transient part*, whose contents DOS can overwrite when it needs to execute a large program. The following illustration shows both the resident and transient portions of COMMAND.COM.

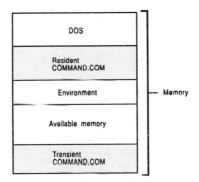

In the cases when DOS overwrites the transient portion of the command processor when a program executes, DOS must reload the command processor when the program completes. To do this, DOS reloads a portion of COMMAND.COM. The COMSPEC= environment entry tells DOS where to find COMMAND.COM. If DOS cannot locate COMMAND.COM, your system will hang and you must restart DOS. By default, COMSPEC= contains the drive letter and root directory of the boot disk, as shown here.

```
C:\> SET
COMSPEC=C:\COMMAND.COM
PATH=C:\DOS
PROMPT=$P$G
```

Most users have a copy of the file COMMAND.COM in their disk's DOS subdirectory and in the root directory. To eliminate the file duplication, many users will change their CONFIG.SYS and AUTOEXEC.BAT files to use the copy of COMMAND.COM in the DOS subdirectory so they can later delete the copy in the root.

The CONFIG.SYS SHELL= entry lets you tell DOS where to locate the file COMMAND.COM during the system startup process. To start DOS with the copy of CONFIG.SYS in the DOS subdirectory, use the following CONFIG.SYS entry.

```
SHELL=C:\DOS\COMMAND.COM /P
```

Should DOS later need to read the transient portion of COMMAND.COM back into memory, it locates COMMAND.COM using the COMSPEC= environment entry. Therefore, you must place a SET command in your AUTOEXEC.BAT that tells DOS to locate COMMAND.COM in the DOS subdirectory, for example:

```
SET COMSPEC=C:\DOS\COMMAND.COM
```

To summarize, DOS uses the CONFIG.SYS SHELL= entry during system startup and COMSPEC= environment entry after DOS is running to find COMMAND.COM.

As you will learn in Chapter 24, the CONFIG.SYS SHELL= entry lets you specify the value you want DOS to use for the COMSPEC environment entry, eliminating your need to use a SET command to assign a value to the entry. The following SHELL= entry tells DOS to locate COMMAND.COM in the DOS directory and to assign the DOS directory to COMSPEC.

```
SHELL=C:\DOS\COMMAND.COM C:\DOS /P
```

In addition to letting you move and use COMMAND.COM, the CONFIG.SYS SHELL= entry also lets you define the desired environment size. To specify an environment size, simply include with the SHELL= entry the /E switch, specifying the number of bytes desired, from 160 to 32,768. The following entry reserves an environment of 512 bytes.

```
SHELL=C:\DOS\COMMAND.COM /P /E:512
```

Using SET to Change Your Command Path or System Prompt

As you know, the PROMPT command defines your system prompt, and the PATH command defines your command search path. Both the PROMPT and PATH commands create environment entries. Since the SET command can change or remove any environment entry, you can change your system prompt or command path using SET. For example, the following command uses SET to change the current prompt to "What now?".

```
C:\> SET PROMPT=What now?   <ENTER>
What now?
```

Using SET to display the environment, you will see the new value for the PROMPT entry.

```
What now? SET   <ENTER>
COMSPEC=C:\DOS\COMMAND.COM
PATH=C:\DOS
PROMPT=What now?
```

To restore the prompt, you can use either the PROMPT or SET command.

```
What now?  SET PROMPT=$P$G   <ENTER>
C:\>
```

Although you will normally use the PROMPT and PATH commands instead of SET, you should know that SET can change any environment entry, no matter which command placed the entry into the environment originally.

Key Terms

DOS environment   An area of memory DOS reserves during system startup for the storage of such system variables as the current system prompt or command path.

Environment entry   A name and value combination stored in the DOS environment that takes the form *Name=Value*.

Transient command processor   The portion of the DOS command processor (COMMAND.COM) that DOS periodically overwrites during the execution of a large program. When this occurs, DOS must reload the software from disk.

Resident command processor   The portion of the DOS command processor that always remains resident in your computer's memory while DOS is active. A major task of the resident portion of the command processor is reloading the transient portion as necessary.

Chapter *20*

The DOS Redirection Operators

So far (except Chapter 13, "Printing"), each time you have executed a command, DOS has displayed the command's output to your screen. For most of your applications, displaying the output on the screen makes perfect sense. For some DOS commands, such as DIR, there may be times you would rather have DOS send the program's output elsewhere, perhaps to your printer or to a file. In this chapter you will examine the DOS output and append *redirection operators*. These operators are so named because they instruct DOS to redirect the output destination from the screen.

In addition to the output redirection operators, DOS provides an input redirection operator that lets a command get its input from a file, as opposed to the keyboard. The discussion of the DOS input redirection operator presents three new DOS commands: MORE, SORT, and FIND.

The Output Redirection Operator

By default, all DOS commands display their output to your screen. In some cases, however, you may find it more convenient for DOS to direct a command's output to the printer or to a file. The following command sends the output of the DIR command to your printer. Printing a directory listing in this manner provides an effective way to catalog the files on a disk.

```
C:\> DIR  >  PRN  <ENTER>
```

The greater-than symbol (>) is the *output redirection operator*. The following illustration shows the location of the output redirection key on your keyboard. You must press your keyboard's right or left shift key to access the greater-than character.

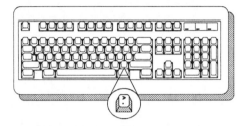

When DOS encounters the output redirection operator in a command line, DOS sends the output of the command specified on the left of the operator to the file or device specified on the right of the operator. In the previous example, DIR is the command whose output DOS redirects from the screen to PRN. DOS will print the directory listing in this case and will not display any of the directory listing to the screen.

Pictorially, you can visualize the output redirection process as shown in Figure 20-1.

Using the printer once again as the destination for redirected output, the following command prints the name of every file on your disk, including your disk's directory structure.

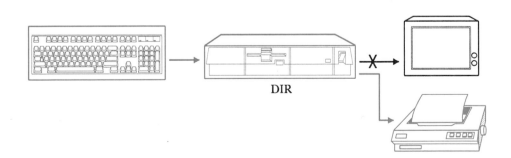

DIR

Figure 20-1.   *Redirecting the output of DIR from the screen to the printer*

```
C:\> TREE  C:\  /F  >  PRN  <ENTER>
```

As you can see, redirecting a program's output to the printer is very convenient when you need a hardcopy listing.

In some cases you may want to redirect a command's output to a file that you can later edit with your word processor or the DOS editor. To redirect a command's output to a file, place the file's name to the right of the redirection operator. The following command line, for example, redirects the output of the TREE command to the file TREE.DAT.

```
C:\> TREE  C:\  /F  >  TREE.DAT  <ENTER>
```

Pictorially, the redirection from the screen to the file TREE.DAT is shown in Figure 20-2.

The output redirection operator overwrites existing files with the same name as the file specified to the right of the output redirection operator. If you redirect the output of a DOS command to a file, and a file with the same name exists, DOS will overwrite the existing file's contents.

WARNING

Not All Commands Support Redirection

There are times when use of the output redirection operator makes obvious sense, such as printing a directory listing or the output of the TREE command. Most

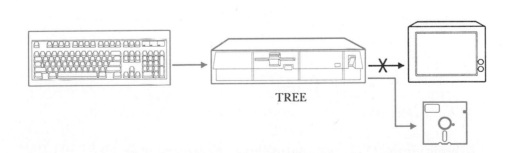

TREE

Figure 20-2.   Redirecting the output of TREE from the screen to the file TREE.DAT

applications (your word processor or spreadsheet), however, do not support I/O redirection. If you try to use output redirection with these commands, DOS will either ignore the redirection operator, or the command may fail, possibly causing your system to freeze up. Should you accidentally redirect such a command, first try to use the CTRL-C keyboard combination to cancel the command. If your system remains "hung up" you will need to use the CTRL-ALT-DEL keyboard combination to restart DOS or may even need to turn your computer off and back on.

The Append Redirection Operator

As you have learned, if you use the output redirection operator to route a program's output to a file, DOS will overwrite an existing file. The *append redirection operator* lets you redirect a command's output from the screen appending the output to the end of an existing file. DOS uses two greater-than signs for the append redirection operator (>>).

To better understand how the append redirection operator works, create the files START.DAT, MIDDLE.DAT, and END.DAT using your word processor, the DOS editor, or by copying the files from the keyboard. The first file, START.DAT, will contain

```
UNLV       UNLV       UNLV
```

with six spaces between each entry. The second file, MIDDLE.DAT, will contain

```
RUNNIN     RUNNIN     RUNNIN
```

with four spaces between entries. The last file, END.DAT, will contain

```
REBELS!    REBELS!    REBELS!
```

with three spaces between each. You can visualize these files as shown here:

UNLV UNLV UNLV	RUNNIN RUNNIN RUNNIN	REBELS! REBELS! REBELS!
START.DAT	MIDDLE.DAT	END.DAT

To begin use the TYPE command to display the contents of the file START.DAT:

```
C:\> TYPE  START.DAT  <ENTER>
UNLV        UNLV        UNLV
```

Using the append redirection operator, redirect the output of the TYPE command to the file ALLTHREE.DAT, as shown here.

```
C:\> TYPE START.DAT >> ALLTHREE.DAT.  <ENTER>
```

The append redirection operator attaches the redirected output to the end of an existing file. In this case, because the file ALLTHREE.DAT does not exist, the append redirection creates it.

Again redirecting the TYPE command, append the contents of the file MIDDLE.DAT to the file ALLTHREE.DAT:

```
C:\> TYPE MIDDLE.DAT >> ALLTHREE.DAT  <ENTER>
```

If you display the contents of the file ALLTHREE.DAT, you will find DOS has successfully appended the file's contents.

```
C:\> TYPE  ALLTHREE.DAT  <ENTER>
UNLV        UNLV        UNLV
RUNNIN      RUNNIN      RUNNIN
```

Next, the following command appends the last section of information to the file ALLTHREE.DAT.

```
C:\> TYPE END.DAT >> ALLTHREE.DAT  <ENTER>
```

Using the TYPE command to display the contents of ALLTHREE.DAT, the file's final contents has become the following.

```
C:\> TYPE  ALLTHREE.DAT  <ENTER>
UNLV        UNLV        UNLV
RUNNIN      RUNNIN      RUNNIN
REBELS!     REBELS!     REBELS!
```

Possible Problems When Redirecting Output

Redirection can be tricky. Not all commands support output or append redirection. Then, when you can perform output redirection, you can experience other errors that may be difficult at first to understand. First, if you are redirecting a program's output to your disk, you must ensure that your disk has adequate available space. If your disk runs out of space during a command's execution, DOS will display the following error message.

```
Insufficient disk space
```

Second, as you may remember from Chapter 1, "Getting to Know Your Computer," DOS cannot store information on a write-protected disk. If you try to redirect a command's output to a write-protected disk, DOS will display the following error message.

```
Write protect error writing drive A
Abort, Retry, Fail?
```

In Chapter 22, "Protecting Your Files with BACKUP and RESTORE," you will learn that DOS lets you protect a file from being accidentally deleted or overwritten by using the ATTRIB command to set the file to read-only. If you try to overwrite a read-only file using output redirection, or if you try to append additional information to the file, the command will fail and DOS will display an error message.

Last, a difficult redirection error to discover occurs when you redirect the output of a command that expects keyboard input. In Chapter 4, "Getting Started with DOS Files," you learned that the /P switch directs DIR to pause with each screenful of directory entries until you press a key to continue. If you redirect to the printer or a file, a DIR command that uses /P, DOS will also redirect the prompt for you to press a key to continue. As a result, the command won't complete. Instead, DIR will wait for you to respond to a prompt you can't see. Your system will appear to be hung up, and your screen will only display a blinking cursor. Should an error such as this occur, first try to cancel the command using the CTRL-C keyboard combination. If you cannot cancel the command, you will have to restart your system by pressing CTRL-ALT-DEL or by turning your computer off and then back on.

The Input Redirection Operator

You have learned that DOS writes a command's output to the screen display unless you tell it otherwise. In the same way, DOS, by default, gets a command's input from the keyboard. The *input redirection operator* lets you direct DOS to get a command's input from an existing file as opposed to the keyboard. DOS uses the less-than character (<) as the input redirection operator.

As you will learn, only a few DOS commands support input redirection. In this chapter, we will examine three commands specifically designed for input redirection: MORE, SORT, and FIND.

The MORE Command

The MORE command displays its input a screenful at a time, pausing with each screenful of information, for you to press a key to continue. Assume, for example, that you have a large text file named REPORT.DAT. If you try to display the file's contents using the TYPE command, the information may scroll past you on the screen faster than you can read it. Using the MORE command and input redirection, you can display the file's contents a screenful at a time, as shown here.

```
C:\> MORE   <   REPORT.DAT   <ENTER>
```

Each time MORE displays a screenful of information, MORE displays the following prompt giving you time to view the screen's contents.

```
-More-
```

If you want to view the next screenful of information, simply press any key. If you have seen enough, use CTRL-C to cancel the command. You can picture the input redirection to MORE as shown in Figure 20-3.

MORE is an external DOS command residing in the file MORE.COM.

The SORT Command

The SORT command lets you sort the contents of an existing file. For example, assume you have a file named PHONES.DAT that contains a list of names, addresses, and phone numbers, as shown here.

```
SMITH     ANDY       (602) 999-1212
JONES     ROBERT     (206) 888-3131
DAVIS     WALLY      (303) 332-2222
JAMSA     STEPHANIE  (702) 555-1212
SMITH     BETTY      (212) 223-9933
OLSON     TEDDY      (602) 331-4311
WHITE     KELLIE     (702) 555-1213
```

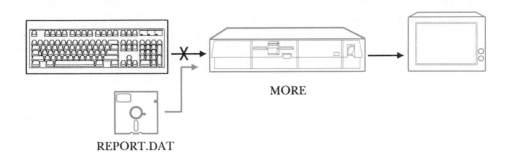

MORE

REPORT.DAT

Figure 20-3.   *Redirecting the input of MORE from the keyboard to the file REPORT.DAT*

Using input redirection and the SORT command, you can sort the file's contents by name, for example:

```
C:\> SORT  <  PHONE.DAT  <ENTER>
DAVIS      WALLY      (303) 332-2222
JAMSA      STEPHANIE (702) 555-1212
JONES      ROBERT     (206) 888-3131
OLSON      TEDDY      (602) 331-4311
SMITH      ANDY       (602) 999-1212
SMITH      BETTY      (212) 223-9933
WHITE      KELLIE     (702) 555-1213
```

By default, the SORT command sorts its input from lowest to highest based on the first letter of each line. You might, however, want to sort the file in descending order (highest to lowest), or sort the input on a character position other than the first character in each line. To let you achieve these capabilities, SORT provides two command-line switches, /R and /+n, described in Table 20-1.

Using the /R switch, the following command sorts the file PHONE.DAT by name in reverse order.

```
C:\> SORT  /R  < PHONE.DAT  <ENTER>
WHITE      KELLIE     (702) 555-1213
SMITH      BETTY      (212) 223-9933
SMITH      ANDY       (602) 999-1212
```

```
OLSON      TEDDY      (602) 331-4311
JONES      ROBERT     (206) 888-3131
JAMSA      STEPHANIE  (702) 555-1212
DAVIS      WALLY      (303) 332-2222
```

Likewise, assuming the phone numbers begin at column 22, the following command sorts the entries by phone number.

```
C:\> SORT  /+22  <  PHONE.DAT  <ENTER>
JONES      ROBERT     (206) 888-3131
SMITH      BETTY      (212) 223-9933
DAVIS      WALLY      (303) 332-2222
OLSON      TEDDY      (602) 331-4311
SMITH      ANDY       (602) 999-1212
JAMSA      STEPHANIE  (702) 555-1212
WHITE      KELLIE     (702) 555-1213
```

The SORT command is an external command residing in the file SORT.EXE.

The FIND Command

The FIND command lets you search redirected input, displaying only those lines containing a specific word or phrase. In other words, the command "finds" and displays each line that contains a specific word or sequence of words. Using the file PHONE.DAT, you can locate each entry for the last name Smith, as shown here.

```
C:\> FIND  "SMITH"  <  PHONE.DAT  <ENTER>
SMITH      ANDY       (602) 999-1212
SMITH      BETTY      (212) 223-9933
```

Switch	Function
/R	Performs a descending (reverse) order sort
/+n	Sorts the input based on column n

Table 20-1.   *SORT's Command-Line Switches*

Likewise, the following command locates each entry with the (602) area code.

```
C:\> FIND  "(602)"  <  PHONE.DAT  <ENTER>
SMITH      ANDY      (602) 999-1212
OLSON      TEDDY     (602) 331-4311
```

To increase your capabilities, FIND, like SORT, provides command-line switches described in Table 20-2.

The following command uses the /C switch to display a count of the number of entries in the file with the (206) area code.

```
C:\> FIND  /C  "(206)"  <  PHONE.DAT  <ENTER>
1
```

In a similar way, this command uses the /N switch to precede each line containing the name SMITH with its corresponding line numbers.

```
C:\> FIND  /N  "SMITH"  <  PHONE.DAT  <ENTER>
[1]SMITH     ANDY      (602) 999-1212
[5]SMITH     BETTY     (212) 223-9933
```

The FIND command is an external command residing in the file FIND.EXE. In Chapter 21, "The DOS Pipe," you will use FIND in conjunction with the DOS pipe operator.

Switch	Function
/C	Displays only a count of the number of lines containing the word or phrase
/I	Considers uppercase and lowercase letters equivalent (DOS 5 only)
/N	Precedes each matching line with its corresponding line number
/V	Displays the lines that *do not* contain the word or phrase

Table 20-2.   *FIND's Command-Line Switches*

SUMMARY

The Output Redirection Operator (>)

The output redirection operator (>) directs DOS to route a command's output from the screen display to a specified file or device. Most DOS commands support output redirection. If DOS redirects output to a file, it will overwrite a file with the same name. The following DOS command redirects the output of DIR from the screen to a printer.

```
C:\> DIR  >  PRN  <ENTER>
```

The Append Redirection Operator (>>)

The append redirection operator directs DOS to route a command's output from the screen display, and to instead, append the output to the end of an existing file. If the destination file specified on the right of the append redirection operator does not exist, DOS will create the file.

The Input Redirection Operator (<)

The input redirection operator directs DOS to get a command's input from an existing file, as opposed to the keyboard. DOS provides three commands that specifically support input redirection: SORT, which sorts the input; MORE, which displays it a screenful at a time; and FIND, which locates and displays lines with specified strings.

Combining Input and Output Operators

As you become more comfortable with DOS I/O redirection operators, you may use both operators within the same command line. The following command sorts the file PHONE.DAT and writes the output to the file SORTED.DAT.

```
C:\> SORT  <  PHONE.DAT  >  SORTED.DAT
```

In this case, SORT gets its input from the file PHONE.DAT and DOS redirects SORT's output to the file SORTED.DAT. Picture the redirection as shown in Figure 20-4.

Hands On

The following command uses output redirection to print a copy of the current directory structure.

```
C:\> TREE  C:\  >  PRN  <ENTER>
```

Next, this command redirects the output of the DIR command to the file FILES.DAT.

```
C:\> DIR  >  FILES.DAT  <ENTER>
```

Using the file FILES.DAT and the input redirection operator, the following command displays a sorted directory listing.

```
C:\> SORT  <  FILES.DAT  <ENTER>
```

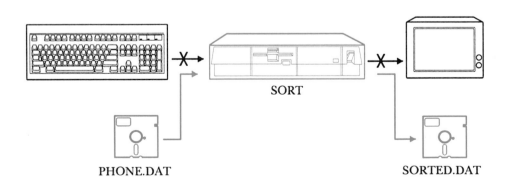

PHONE.DAT   SORTED.DAT

Figure 20-4.   *Combining the input and output redirection operators*

Using SORT's /R switch, sort the file in reverse order:

```
C:\> SORT  /R  <  FILES.DATE  <ENTER>
```

In a similar way, the following command uses FIND to locate and display only those lines containing the word <DIR>. In other words, all of the subdirectory names.

```
C:\> FIND  "<DIR>"  <  FILES.DAT  <ENTER>
```

Using FIND's /C switch, display a count of the number lines containing the word <DIR>.

```
C:\> FIND  /C  "<DIR>"  <  FILES.DAT  <ENTER>
```

Last, using FIND's /V switch, display the lines in FILES.DAT that don't contain <DIR>.

```
C:\> FIND  /V  "<DIR>"  <  FILES.DAT  <ENTER>
```

This gives you the capacity in a batch file, for example, to find all the files in a directory that are not SYS and deal with them accordingly.

Review

1. How does the output redirection operator differ from the append operator?

2. Use the output redirection to create the file TREE.DAT that contains the names of all directories and files on your disk.

3. Use the MORE command to display the file TREE.DAT a screenful at a time.

4. Use the FIND command to locate all the files listed in the file TREE.DAT that have the EXE extension.

5. Draw the pictorial representation of the following command.

```
C:\> FIND  ".COM"  <  TREE.DAT  >  PRN
```

Answers

1. The output and append redirection operators both redirect a command's output from the screen to a file or device. If you redirect a command's output to a file, and a file exists with the same name, the output redirection operator will overwrite the existing file's contents. The append redirection operator, on the other hand, will append the command's output to the file. If there is no existing file with the same name as the destination file, both the output and append redirection operators will create the file.

2. The output redirection to create the file TREE.DAT is

```
C:\> TREE  C:\  /F  >  TREE.DAT  <ENTER>
```

3. The MORE command to display the file TREE.DAT a screenful at a time is

```
C:\> MORE  <  TREE.DAT  <ENTER>
```

4. The FIND command to locate all the files listed in the file TREE.DAT with the EXE extension is

```
C:\> FIND  ".EXE"  <  TREE.DAT  <ENTER>
```

5. The pictorial representation of the command is shown in Figure 20-5.

Advanced Concepts

Many of the books and articles you will encounter that discuss the I/O redirection operators use the terms *standard input* and *standard output,* or their abbreviations *stdin* and *stdout.* Each time DOS executes a program, DOS assigns default devices for the program. By default, the keyboard is the program's source of input, or standard input device. Likewise, the screen display is the standard output device, as shown in Figure 20-6.

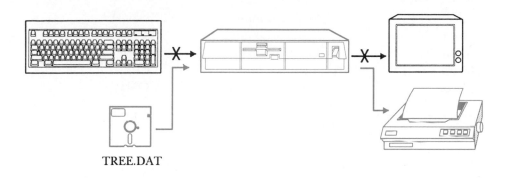

TREE.DAT

Figure 20-5.   Results of the command C:\> FIND ".COM" < TREE.DAT > PRN

When you use the redirection operators, DOS changes the devices associated with stdin or stdout.

In addition to stdin and stdout, DOS also assigns default devices for a program's printer (stdprn), destination for error messages (stderr), and auxiliary communications (stdaux). Table 20-3 defines these standard devices.

Understanding that DOS assigns these devices each time a program runs is important because these devices affect the number of files a program can open at one time. Each of these devices requires a *file handle*. By default, DOS provides 8 file handles to each program. Because these devices use up 5 of the handles, DOS only leaves your programs with three handles. Many applications (word processor, spreadsheet, or database) need to open several temporary files while they execute.

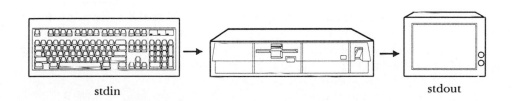

stdin   stdout

Figure 20-6.   The screen display is the standard output device

Device Name	Function	Default Device
stdin	Standard input	Keyboard
stdout	Standard output	Screen
stderr	Standard error	Screen
stdprn	Standard printer	LPT1:
stdaux	Standard auxiliary	COM1:

Table 20-3.   DOS Standard Device Names

If you do not provide enough file handles for the program to open its files, the program will fail.

The CONFIG.SYS file FILES= entry lets you specify the number of file handles DOS should provide for each program. At a minimum, you should set the value to 20.

```
FILES=20
```

Knowing that DOS will automatically use the first five handles, your program still has 15 handles available.

Chapter 2, "Getting DOS Started," discussed the DOS startup process in detail. At that time you learned DOS uses an initialization program named SYSINIT to perform much of its startup processing. As discussed, SYSINIT processes the CONFIG.SYS entries and then invokes COMMAND.COM, which in turn either invokes AUTOEXEC.BAT or DATE and TIME. Before SYSINIT invokes COMMAND.COM, however, SYSINIT opens the files stdin, stdout, stderr, stdaux, and stdprn. Many applications will specify the minimum number of file handles they require. Now you should be better able to understand why.

Redirecting Output to the NUL Device

In addition to the device names PRN, AUX, and LPT1, DOS also defines the device NUL for the nonexistent device. Using NUL, your batch files can discard output from commands that would otherwise clutter the screen. For example, the following batch file COPYMSG.BAT copies the contents of your AUTOEXEC.BAT and CONFIG.SYS files to files with the SAV extension.

```
@ECHO OFF
ECHO Backing up AUTOEXEC.BAT and CONFIG.SYS
COPY  \AUTOEXEC.BAT  \*.SAV
COPY  \CONFIG.SYS  \*.SAV
```

As you can see, the batch file uses the ECHO OFF command to suppress display of the command name as the batch file executes. When you invoke COPYMSG.BAT, your screen will display the following.

```
C:\> COPYMSG   <ENTER>
Backing up AUTOEXEC.BAT and CONFIG.SYS
        1 File(s) copied
        1 File(s) copied
```

Although the ECHO OFF command suppresses the display of command names, it does not eliminate the "File(s) copied" messages. However, the following batch file, NOMSG.BAT, discards the messages to the NUL device.

```
@ECHO OFF
ECHO Backing up AUTOEXEC.BAT and CONFIG.SYS
COPY  \AUTOEXEC.BAT  \*.SAV  >  NUL
COPY  \CONFIG.SYS  \*.SAV  >  NUL
```

When you invoke this batch file, your screen displays the following.

```
C:\> NOMSG   <ENTER>
Backing up AUTOEXEC.BAT and CONFIG.SYS
```

As you can see, the "File(s) copied" messages do not appear. As the complexity of your batch files increases, redirecting output to the NUL device can clean up your screen appearance considerably.

Building Batch Files on the Fly

As you work with DOS, you will eventually begin to build a library of batch files that you use on a regular basis. Depending on your application, there may be times when your batch file needs to invoke another, smaller batch file. For example, the following batch file SELERASE.BAT provides you with selective delete capabilities similar to the DOS 5 DEL/P command. When you invoke SELERASE.BAT with a list of file names or wildcards, SELERASE will prompt you individually for each file specified to determine if you want to delete that file. For example, the following command directs SELERASE to selectively erase all of the files in the current directory that have the BAK extension.

```
C:\> SELERASE  *.BAK   <ENTER>
```

In this case, SELERASE might display the following:

```
Delete FILENAME.BAK (Y/N)?
```

The following batch file implements SELERASE.BAT.

```
@ECHO OFF

REM Loop through the desired file names
:LOOP
  FOR %%I IN (%1) DO CALL DELETEIT %%I
  SHIFT
IF NOT '%1'=='' GOTO LOOP
```

The batch file uses the FOR and SHIFT commands to loop through all of the files specified in the command line. Using FOR, the batch file can support wildcards. The batch file uses a second batch file named DELETEIT.BAT that actually prompts you whether or not you want to delete the file, and if so, deletes it. The batch file DELETEIT.BAT contains the following.

```
ECHO Delete %1 (Y/N)?
Y_OR_N
IF ERRORLEVEL 1 DEL %1
```

As you can see, the batch files uses the Y_OR_N command that you created in Chapter 16, "Decision-Making Batch Files." You may recall that Y_OR_N waits for you to type either Y or N. If you type Y, the command exits with an error level of 1. If you type N, the command exits with an error level 0.

Although SELERASE.BAT is very useful, its use of the second batch file, DELETEIT.BAT, wastes disk space. Remember, every time DOS creates a file on your disk, DOS must allocate a cluster of disk space. In the case of DELETEIT.BAT, most of the cluster is unused. A better solution, therefore, is to let SELERASE.BAT create the batch file DELETEIT.BAT "on the fly" each time it executes and then delete the batch file before it completes.

Using the output and append redirection operators with the ECHO command, you can modify SELERASE.BAT to do just that.

```
@ECHO OFF

REM Build the batch file DELETEIT.BAT
ECHO ECHO Delete %%1 (Y/N)? > DELETEIT.BAT
ECHO Y_OR_N >> DELETEIT.BAT
ECHO IF ERRORLEVEL 1 DEL %%1 >> DELETEIT.BAT
```

```
REM Loop through the desired file names
:LOOP
  FOR %%I IN (%1) DO CALL DELETEIT %%I
  SHIFT
IF NOT '%1'=='' GOTO LOOP

REM Delete the temporary batch file
DEL DELETEIT.BAT
```

Take a close look at the following commands:

```
REM Build the batch file DELETEIT.BAT
ECHO ECHO Delete %%1 (Y/N)? > DELETEIT.BAT
ECHO Y_OR_N >> DELETEIT.BAT
ECHO IF ERRORLEVEL 1 DEL %%1 >> DELETEIT.BAT
```

The batch file SELERASE.BAT redirects ECHO's output to DELETEIT.BAT, building that batch file. Figure 20-7 illustrates how these commands actually build the batch file.

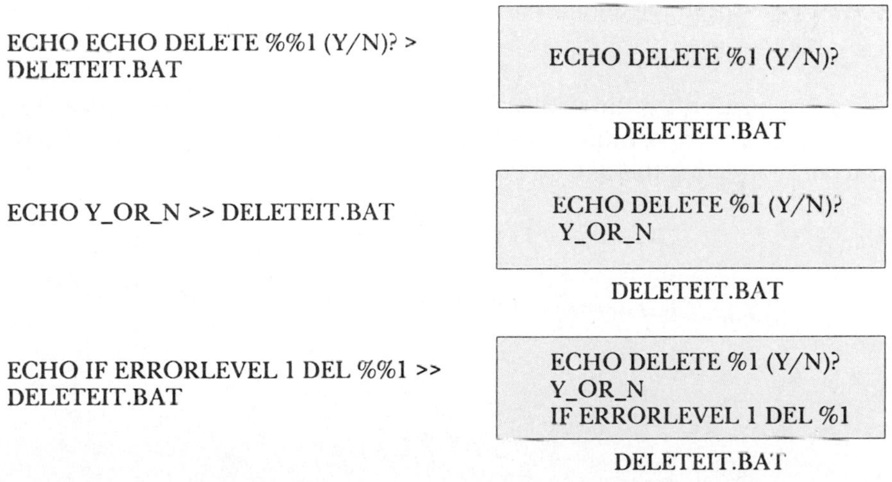

ECHO ECHO DELETE %%1 (Y/N)? >
DELETEIT.BAT

> ECHO DELETE %1 (Y/N)?

DELETEIT.BAT

ECHO Y_OR_N >> DELETEIT.BAT

> ECHO DELETE %1 (Y/N)?
> Y_OR_N

DELETEIT.BAT

ECHO IF ERRORLEVEL 1 DEL %%1 >>
DELETEIT.BAT

> ECHO DELETE %1 (Y/N)?
> Y_OR_N
> IF ERRORLEVEL 1 DEL %1

DELETEIT.BAT

Figure 20-7.   Using ECHO to build a batch file "on the fly"

Note the use of the double percent signs (%%1). As you know, when DOS encounters %1 within a batch file, DOS substitutes for %1 the value of the first batch parameter. In this case, however, we want DOS to ECHO the actual characters "%1". When DOS encounters the double percent signs, DOS only echoes one of them, leaving "%1" as desired.

If you have existing batch files that call other batch files in this way, you might consider changing the batch files to build their secondary batch files "on the fly."

Key Terms

I/O Redirection   The process of routing a program's source of input from the keyboard to an existing file, or directing a program's output from the screen display to a file or device. DOS provides the input (<), output (>), and append (>>) I/O redirection operations as well as the DOS pipe discussed in Chapter 21.

stdin   Abbreviation for the *standard input device*; by default, the keyboard. The input redirection operator lets you change stdin.

stdout   Abbreviation for the *standard output device*; by default, the screen display. The output and append redirection operators let you change stdout.

stdprn   Abbreviation for the *standard printer device*, which is LPT1:—you cannot change stdprn.

stdaux   Abbreviation for the *standard auxiliary device*, which is COM1:—you cannot change stdaux.

stderr   Abbreviation for the *standard error device*, which is the screen display—you cannot change stderr. Many programs write their error messages to stderr to prevent DOS from redirecting them.

Chapter 21

The DOS Pipe

In Chapter 20, "The DOS Redirection Operators," you learned how to use the DOS input (<), output (>), and append (>>) redirection operators to change a command's normal source of input (the keyboard) or output destination (the screen display) to or from a file. Using the redirection operators you were able to redirect a command's output to a temporary file for editing or to your printer. When you were done with these "temporary" files, you could delete them to clean up your disk.

In this chapter you will learn how to use the powerful DOS pipe operator (|), which combines the benefits and capabilities of both the input and output redirection operators. Using the pipe operator, you can route one command's output into another command's input.

Locating the Pipe Operator on Your Keyboard

Because many books print the DOS pipe operator differently, new users have difficulty identifying the pipe operator on their keyboard. Do not confuse the pipe operator (|) with the exclamation mark (!). The pipe operator typically shares the same key as the backslash key (\) you use in DOS directory names, as shown here:

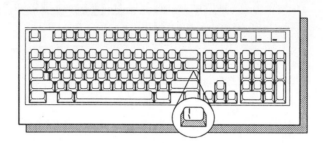

Hold down either the left or right shift key and then press this key to access the pipe operator. Depending on the book, magazine, or manual you are reading, the pipe character sometimes appears as two small vertical bars ¦ or a solid bar (|). In either case, both symbols refer to the pipe.

Understanding the DOS Pipe

The pipe operator redirects the output of one command into the input of another. For example, in Chapter 20 you used the SORT command to sort a file's contents. Using the pipe operator the following command redirects the DIR command's output to become the SORT command's input.

```
C:\> DIR  |  SORT  <ENTER>
```

Assume the directory contains the following files and subdirectories.

```
C:\SAMPLE> DIR   <ENTER>

 Volume in drive C is DOS
 Volume Serial Number is 1661-AB75
 Directory of C:\SAMPLE

 .              <DIR>     03-10-91    3:53p
 ..             <DIR>     03-10-91    3:53p
AAAAAAAA EXT         231 03-10-91    3:54p
BBBBBBBB EXT         128 03-04-91    1:37p
```

```
THIRD        <DIR>        03-10-91    3:53p
EEEEEEEE EXT        455 03-10-91    3:55p
DDDDDDDD EXT        128 03-04-91    1:37p
FIRST        <DIR>        03-10-91    3:54p
CCCCCCCC EXT         19 03-10-91    3:54p
SECOND       <DIR>        03-10-91    3:55p
       10 file(s)         961 bytes
                16403520 bytes free
```

The sorted directory listing then becomes the following.

```
C:\SAMPLE> DIR  | SORT   <ENTER>

                 16399424 bytes free
       10 file(s)         961 bytes
 Directory of C:\SAMPLE
 Volume in drive C is DOS
 Volume Serial Number is 1661-AB75
 .           <DIR>        03-10-91    3:53p
 ..          <DIR>        03-10-91    3:53p
 AAAAAAAA EXT        231 03-10-91    3:54p
 BBBBBBBB EXT        128 03-04-91    1:37p
 CCCCCCCC EXT         19 03-10-91    3:54p
 DDDDDDDD EXT        128 03-04-91    1:37p
 EEEEEEEE EXT        455 03-10-91    3:55p
 FIRST       <DIR>        03-10-91    3:54p
 SECOND      <DIR>        03-10-91    3:55p
 THIRD       <DIR>        03-10-91    3:53p
```

Pictorially, the pipe redirection operation is shown in Figure 21-1.

The pipe operator is a very powerful tool. By changing the previous SORT command to include the /R qualifier, you can quickly display the directory listing sorted in reverse (descending) order.

```
C:\> DIR  | SORT  /R   <ENTER>
```

Likewise, if your directory contains a large number of files, you can use the MORE command (discussed in Chapter 20) to view the files a screenful at a time:

```
C:\> DIR  | MORE   <ENTER>
```

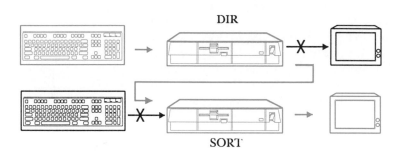

Figure 21-1.   Piping the output of DIR into the SORT command

Last, assuming that you only want to display the names of subdirectories that reside in the current directory, you can use the FIND command (Chapter 20) to display only those directory entries containing "<DIR>" :

```
C:\SAMPLE> DIR  |  FIND  "<DIR>"   <ENTER>
.            <DIR>      03-10-91   3:53p
..           <DIR>      03-10-91   3:53p
THIRD        <DIR>      03-10-91   3:53p
FIRST        <DIR>      03-10-91   3:54p
SECOND       <DIR>      03-10-91   3:55p
```

In this case, the FIND command does not display every line of input it receives. Instead, FIND only displays the lines with "<DIR>" in them. When the pipe operator redirects a command's output through a second command that examines its input and only displays or passes on specific lines, the second command is a *filter*. In general, a filter examines the pipe's contents and lets the data that meet a criteria continue while discarding the data that fail the criteria, as shown in Figure 21-2.

Which Commands Can You Pipe?

As was the case with the output redirection operator, you can use any command that writes its output to the DOS standard output device on the *input side* (left) of a pipe operation. Likewise, just as only a few commands support the input redirection operator (SORT, MORE, and FIND), only the same few commmands work on the *filter side* (right) of the pipe operator.

To help you make full use of the pipe, I have assembled a group of pipe utility commands that are available on disk (see the order form at the beginning of this

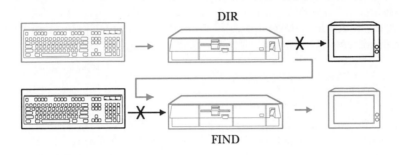

Figure 21-2. *Using the pipe operator with a filter*

book). Table 21-1 briefly summarizes some of the capabilities these commands provide.

Combining the Pipe and I/O Redirection Operators

In Chapter 20, you experimented with commands that use both the input and output redirection operators, as shown here.

```
C:\> SORT  <  \AUTOEXEC.BAT  >  PRN  <ENTER>
```

Routine	Function
TEE	Displays a program's output on the screen and also pipes the the output elsewhere.
LINECNT	Displays a count of the number of lines filtered
CHARCNT	Displays a count of the number of characters filtered
WORDCNT	Displays a count of the number of words filtered
FIRST	Displays the first *n* lines encountered
LAST	Displays the last *n* lines encountered
IFEXIST	Improves the IF EXIST command's pipe capabilities
IFSTR	Improves the IF STR== command's pipe capabilities

Table 21-1. *Pipe Commands Available with This Book's Companion Disk*

Just as DOS lets you use both the input and output redirection operators in the same command line, DOS also lets you combine them with the DOS pipe. For example, the following command pipes the output of the DIR command into SORT and then redirects SORT's output to the printer.

```
C:\> DIR  |  SORT  >  PRN  <ENTER>
```

Pictorially, the command's redirection is shown in Figure 21-3.

In a similar manner, the following command pipes the output of DIR into SORT, which in turn sorts the directory listing. Rather than displaying the sorted listing to the screen, DOS pipes SORT's output into MORE, which displays the sorted directory entries a screenful at a time.

```
C:\> DIR  |  SORT  |  MORE  <ENTER>
```

As before, pictorially, the redirection is shown in Figure 21-4.

In general, the only restriction to the number of pipe operators you can place in a single command is the 127-character limit on command length.

Pipe Operator Pitfalls

A difficult pipe error to detect occurs when you pipe the output of a command that prompts for user input and then waits for you to type in the input before it continues. When this occurs, your system will appear to hang up. Nothing will appear on the screen except for a blinking cursor. For example, as discussed in Chapter 4, "Getting

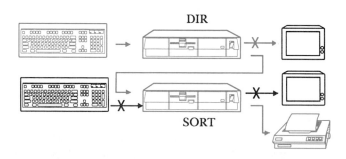

Figure 21-3.   *Combining the pipe and output redirection operators*

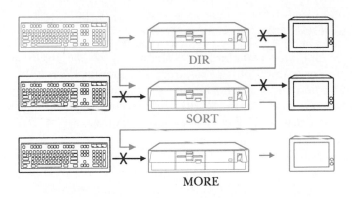

Figure 21-4.   Combining two pipe operations in the same command

Started with DOS Files," the DIR /P command directs DIR to pause with each screenful of file names, prompting you to press any key to continue. If you redirect DIR /P into the SORT command for example, your system may appear to hang because DIR is waiting for a keyboard response. Because DOS also redirects the prompt to press a key to continue into SORT, you may think the system is hung up. If this occurs, use CTRL-C to cancel the command. If your system remains frozen up, press CTRL-ALT-DEL to restart the system.

Hands On

The last two lines of the DIR command display include a count of the number of files in the directory listing and the number of bytes of available disk space.

```
     10 file(s)          961 bytes
                    16403520 bytes free
```

By piping the output of DIR into FIND, the following command displays only the number of files in the current directory as well as the available disk space.

```
C:\> DIR  |  FIND  "bytes"  <ENTER>
```

In this case, the FIND command works as a filter, discarding all input except the line containing the word "bytes." Actually, because DOS file names prior to DOS 5 (see Chapter 4 for DOS 5's /L lowercase switch) only appear in uppercase letters,

SUMMARY

DOS Pipe Operator (|)

The pipe operator combines the capabilities of the input and output redirection operators, letting you direct one command's output to become a second command's input. The following command pipes the output of the TREE command into the MORE command to display the disk's current directory structure (and files) a screenful at a time.

```
C:\> TREE  C:\  /F  |  MORE  <ENTER>
```

When the second command in the pipe operation selectively displays or discards lines of the piped input, the second command is called a filter.

---

you can reduce the previous command to only search for the lowercase letter "b," as shown here.

```
C:\> DIR  |  FIND  "b"  <ENTER>
```

As presented earlier, the following command uses the pipe operator to list the files in the current directory sorted in reverse order.

```
C:\> DIR  |  SORT  /R  <ENTER>
```

Unfortunately, because SORT cannot distinguish the file names from the additional directory information, the command's output may become messy:

```
C:\SAMPLE> DIR  |  SORT  /R  <ENTER>
THIRD         <DIR>       03-10-91    3:53p
SECOND        <DIR>       03-10-91    3:55p
FIRST         <DIR>       03-10-91    3:54p
EEEEEEEE EXT       455 03-10-91    3:55p
DDDDDDDD EXT       128 03-04-91    1:37p
CCCCCCCC EXT        19 03-10-91    3:54p
BBBBBBBB EXT       128 03-04-91    1:37p
AAAAAAAA EXT       231 03-10-91    3:54p
              <DIR>       03-10-91    3:53p
```

```
..              <DIR>       03-10-91    3:53p
 Volume Serial Number is 1661-AB75
 Volume in drive C is DOS
 Directory of C:\SAMPLE
       10 file(s)          961 bytes
                    16399424 bytes free
```

To eliminate the screen clutter, the following command uses two pipe operators. The first pipe operator obtains the sorted directory listing, while the second uses the FIND command to filter out all the lines not containing the lowercase letter "e." As it turns out, the lowercase "e" is found in each line except the lines containing a directory entry, provided you are not using the DOS 5 DIR /L switch to display directories in lowercase.

```
C:\> DIR  |  SORT  |  FIND  /V  "e"   <ENTER>
```

Given the previous directory contents, the command's output would become the following.

```
C:\> DIR  |  SORT  |  FIND  /V  "e"   <ENTER>
.               <DIR>       03-10-91    3:53p
..              <DIR>       03-10-91    3:53p
AAAAAAAA EXT      231 03-10-91    3:54p
BBBBBBBB EXT      128 03-04-91    1:37p
CCCCCCCC EXT       19 03-10-91    3:54p
DDDDDDDD EXT      128 03-04-91    1:37p
EEEEEEEE EXT      455 03-10-91    3:55p
FIRST           <DIR>       03-10-91    3:54p
SECOND          <DIR>       03-10-91    3:55p
THIRD           <DIR>       03-10-91    3:53p
```

As you can see, FIND restricted the output to only those lines not containing the lowercase e.

As you have just found, by piping the DIR command into SORT, you can display a directory sorted by name. There may be times, however, when you want to display the directory listing sorted by extension or file size. The SORT command, discussed in Chapter 20, lets you specify a column on which to sort the input data. The following command, for example, displays the directory entries sorted by extension (which begins in column 10).

```
C:\> DIR  |  SORT  /+10  |  FIND  /V  "e"   <ENTER>
```

Likewise, the following command displays the entries sorted by size (column 13).

```
C:\> DIR  |  SORT  /+13  |  FIND  /V  "e"  <ENTER>
```

By changing the previous command to include the output redirection operator, you can print the names of the files in the current directory sorted by size:

```
C:\> DIR  |  SORT  /+13  |  FIND  /V  "e"  >  PRN  <ENTER>
```

Review

1. What is the function of the pipe operator?

2. What restricts the number of pipe operators you can place in one command line?

3. Use the pipe operator and the FIND command to display only the names of files that reside in the current directory, discarding subdirectory names and other information (DOS 5 users, be aware of DIR /L).

4. What is a filter?

5. Pictorially represent the following command redirection.

```
C:\> SORT  <  \AUTOEXEC.BAT  |  MORE  <ENTER>
```

6. What is the function of the following command?

```
C:\> TREE  C:\ /F  |  FIND  ".BAT"  |  MORE  <ENTER>
```

Answers

1. The pipe operator combines the capabilities of the input and output redirection operators. In other words, the pipe redirects one command's output to become the input to another.

2. In general, the only restriction on the number of commands you can pipe together is the 127-character limit on the length of the command line. If you

are using the pipe with IF command, however, you can only use the pipe operator once.

3. The pipe operator and FIND command are used together to create the directory display like this:

```
C:\> DIR  |  FIND  /V  "<DIR>"  |  FIND  /V  "e"  <ENTER>
```

4. A filter is a command appearing to the right of a pipe operator that examines its input and selectively discards or passes on to the next program (or to the screen display) only those lines that meet the desired criteria.

5. The pictorial representation of the following command redirection is shown in Figure 21-5.

```
C:\> SORT  <  \AUTOEXEC.BAT  |  MORE  <ENTER>
```

6. The command displays the names and directory of each batch file on your disk a screenful at a time.

Advanced Concepts

As you have learned, the pipe operator lets you direct the output of one command to become the input of another. In general, the pipe operator combines the input

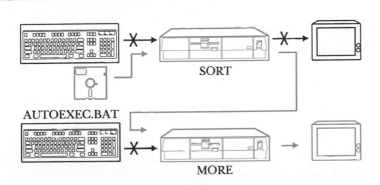

SORT

AUTOEXEC.BAT

MORE

Figure 21-5. *SORTed output of AUTOEXEC.BAT is piped to MORE, which displays it a screenful at a time*

and output redirection operations. For example, the following command uses the pipe to display a sorted directory listing.

```
C:\> DIR | SORT <ENTER>
```

In order to achieve the same result using the input and output operators you can create a temporary file named TEMP and redirect its output to SORT, as shown here.

```
C:\> DIR > TEMP <ENTER>
C:\> SORT < TEMP <ENTER>
```

When the SORT command completes, you can delete the temporary file.

```
C:\> DEL TEMP <ENTER>
```

You can see that the piped operation above performed in one command the steps that required 3 commands with the redirection operators.

To understand how DOS implements the pipe operator, you need to keep the notion of the *temporary file* in mind. When you use the pipe operator, DOS actually creates and deletes temporary files behind the scenes without your knowledge.

To illustrate that DOS creates these temporary files, issue the DIR command and note the amount of free disk space in bytes.

```
C:\> DIR <ENTER>
```

Next, issue the following command, which uses the pipe operator to filter out all the information in the directory listing except for the lines containing the amount of available disk space. Note that the amount of disk space differs, indicating DOS has allocated disk space during the pipe operation for use by the temporary files.

```
C:\> DIR | FIND "bytes" <ENTER>
```

When the command completes, repeat the DIR command and note that the free disk space again matches the original, indicating DOS has automatically deleted the temporary file at the completion of the pipe operation.

Depending on your DOS version, DOS may create the temporary file in the current directory or the root directory.

You should understand that the pipe operator creates temporary files for several reasons. First, if the current disk is write protected, DOS cannot create the temporary file, and the command will fail.

```
Write protect error writing drive A
Abort, Retry, Fail?
```

Likewise, if the current disk does not have enough disk space for the temporary files, or the root directory is full, commands using the pipe operator will fail.

```
Intermediate file error during pipe
```

Last, if you are using the pipe operator in a command that requires maximum processing performance, you might consider selecting a RAM drive as the default. Because of the RAM drive's fast speed, DOS can create the temporary file much faster, which helps the command complete sooner.

The DOS 5 TEMP Environment Entry

The DOS 5 TEMP environment entry, discussed in Chapter 19, "The DOS Environment," tells DOS where you want it to create its temporary files. Assuming, for example, you have a RAM drive E, the following command directs DOS to create its temporary files on the fast RAM drive.

```
C:\> SET  TEMP=E:  <ENTER>
```

Each time a DOS 5 command line includes a pipe operator, DOS searches the environment for a TEMP entry. If a such an entry exists, DOS creates the temporary files on the drive and directory specified. If the entry does not exist, DOS creates the temporary files in your disk's root directory. For more information on RAM drives, see Chapter 32, "Understanding DOS Memory Management."

Batch File Pipe Restrictions

In general, DOS only restricts the number of pipe operations you can perform in one command to the maximum command length of 127 characters. The only exception to the essentially unlimited use of pipe operators is when you combine the pipe with the IF command. IF, discussed in Chapter 16, "Decision-Making Batch Files," lets your batch files perform conditional processing. The following batch file

SORTIT.BAT examines the batch parameter %1. If %1 is "A", the batch file displays the directory listing in ascending order. Likewise, if %1 is "D," the batch file uses descending order.

```
@ECHO OFF
IF '%1'=='A' DIR | SORT
IF '%1'=='D' DIR | SORT /R
```

As you found in the directory sort examples presented in the start of this chapter, if you don't filter out the lines that don't contain file names using FIND, the directory listing displayed can become quite messy. As an initial solution to this problem, you might simply add the FIND command to the batch file, for example:

```
@ECHO OFF
IF '%1'=='A' DIR | SORT | FIND /V "e"
IF '%1'=='D' DIR | SORT /R | FIND /V "e"
```

Unfortunately, each time you execute the batch file, DOS will now display the "File creation error" message, and the batch file will fail (some DOS versions won't display the error message). The error occurs because when you use the IF command, DOS restricts you to only using the pipe operator once. To correct this situation, you must restructure your batch file to put the alternative uses into separate subroutines, as shown here. BAD_PARAM is for any keypress except "A" or "D."

```
@ECHO OFF
IF '%1'=='A' GOTO ASCENDING
IF '%1'=='D' GOTO DESCENDING
GOTO BAD_PARAM

:ASCENDING
DIR | SORT | FIND /V "e"
GOTO DONE

:DESCENDING
DIR | SORT /R | FIND /V "e"
GOTO DONE

:BAD_PARAM
ECHO Use A for Ascending or D for Descending
:DONE
```

Key Terms

Pipe operator (|) A command-line redirection operator that directs the output of one command to become the input of a second command. The pipe operator combines the capabilities of the input and output redirection operators.

Filter A command that appears in the command line to the right of the pipe operator whose purpose is to only output lines meeting a specific criteria, while discarding all others.

Chapter 22

Protecting Your Files with BACKUP and RESTORE

No matter how well you treat your computer, some of its parts will eventually wear out. If your hard disk fails, you may lose all the information the disk contains. Your only way of recovering your disk's previous contents is from backup copies stored on floppy disks. If you are using DOS 5, the DOS 5 crisis-prevention utilities UNDELETE and UNFORMAT, discussed in Chapter 28, "DOS 5 Crisis Prevention," may help you recover from a DOS command that accidentally destroys information on your disk. If you are not using DOS 5, many third-party software packages provide similar capabilities. Unfortunately, even the best file recovery utilities can't guarantee 100 percent recovery of your disk—you may still lose key information.

This chapter examines the BACKUP command, which copies your hard disk files to floppy disks for safe storage. Should your hard disk fail, or should an accidental DOS command such as FORMAT destroy the information on your disk, you can restore the backup copies of the damaged files from floppy disks. To fully protect your files, you need to perform backups on a regular basis. Using the BACKUP command-line switches presented in this chapter, you will find that your backup operations should only take a few minutes each day.

Understanding the Backup Process

Whether you use the BACKUP command or a third-party backup utility, the backup process is essentially the same. You will begin with a set of unused floppy disks. Depending on the amount of hard disk space in use and the size of your floppy disks, the number of floppy disks you'll need will differ. Chapter 25, "Using CHKDSK," discusses the CHKDSK command in detail. For now, invoke CHKDSK from the DOS prompt to determine the amount of space your hard disk is using.

```
C:\> CHKDSK   <ENTER>

Volume DOS         created Jul 24, 1990 8:23p
Volumn Serial Number is 166F-AD7B

 21309440 bytes total disk space
    53248 bytes in 3 hidden files
    47104 bytes in 12 directories
  4978688 bytes in 362 user files
    55296 bytes in bad sectors
 16175104 bytes available on disk

     2048 bytes in each allocation unit
    10405 total allocation units on disk
     7898 available allocation units on disk

   655360 bytes total memory
   527488 bytes free
```

Depending on your DOS version, the information CHKDSK displays may differ slightly.

To determine the amount of hard disk space in use, subtract the amount of available disk space from the amount of total disk space.

$$
\begin{array}{rl}
21{,}309{,}440 & \text{bytes total disk space} \\
-16{,}175{,}104 & \text{bytes available on disk} \\
\hline
5{,}134{,}336 & \text{bytes in use}
\end{array}
$$

Next, divide the amount of hard disk space in use by your floppy disk size. Table 22-1 describes the common floppy disk sizes.

Disk Type	Data Storage in Bytes
360Kb	362,496
720Kb	730,112
1.2 Mb	1,213,952
1.44Mb	1,457,664

Table 22-1.   Floppy Disk Storage Capacities

Using CHKDSK's previous output and 1.2Mb floppy disks, the number of floppy disks you would need to back up this disk becomes the following.

Number of 1.2Mb disks = 5,134,336 / 1,213,952
$$= 4.23$$
$$= 5$$

Different DOS versions let you direct BACKUP to format the floppy disks as part of the process. Unfortunately, using BACKUP to format the disks increases the amount of time your backup operation requires. Most users avoid performing backups if the operation takes too long. If you have enough formatted floppy disks available, backup operations proceed quite quickly.

Do not format your floppy disks using the /S switch. As discussed in Chapter 7, "Preparing Disks for Use," the /S switch directs FORMAT to copy the DOS startup files to the floppy disk. Since you won't be using your backup disks to boot DOS, placing these system files on the disk would consume disk space unnecessarily.

To back up your hard disk files, you will perform two types of backup operations. First, once a month you will back up your entire hard disk. This backup operation will copy every file on your hard disk to floppy disks. Depending on the size and number of files on your hard disk, this backup operation may take an hour or more. Because the complete hard disk backup operation takes so much time and uses so many floppy disks, you will only perform the complete disk backup once a month.

You should perform the second backup operation daily. This backup operation copies to floppy disks only those files you have created or changed that day. Because most users only create or change a few files each day, this second backup operation normally only takes one or two disks and a few minutes of your time. Many users won't perform these backup operations each day. However, by not backing up your files on a regular basis, you leave open a window for possible loss of files or key information.

When you complete your backup operation, you will have a collection of floppy disks that contain your file backups. For safety, place these disks into a floppy disk storage container. Such containers as the one illustrated below are inexpensive to buy and will protect the disks from dust and bending or folding. It is a good idea to have a separate box for backups only.

The BACKUP command is an external command that resides in your DOS directory. BACKUP's counterpart is RESTORE, also an external DOS command. Should you ever need to copy (restore) one or more files from your backup floppy disks, you will use the RESTORE command as discussed later in this chapter.

Backing Up Your Entire Hard Disk

You should get into the habit of backing up all the files on your hard disk once a month. When you successfully back up your entire hard disk, you can remove the current floppy disk backups from your disk storage container, replacing them with your new backup disks. You can now use the previous floppy disks for other operations. Before you begin, use the CHKDSK command as previously discussed to determine the number of floppy disks the backup operation will require. In DOS version 4 and later, if the floppy disks are not formatted, you can use the /F switch to direct BACKUP to format them. Using BACKUP to format the floppy disks increases the amount of time your backup operations require. For more information on /F, refer to the Command Reference at the end of this book.

A complete hard disk backup may require many floppy disks. Each time BACKUP fills a floppy, make sure you place a disk label on the floppy that specifies the disk contains files from a hard disk backup. The label should include the backup date, and the disk number, as shown in this example:

Monthly Disk Backup

July 1, 1991

Drive C

Disk 1 of 10

Use the following BACKUP command to back up your entire hard disk.

```
C:\> BACKUP  C:\*.*  A:  /S  <ENTER>
```

The command uses the asterisk wildcard to direct BACKUP to copy every file beginning in the root directory. The /S switch directs BACKUP to copy files in each directory below the directory specified. Because the command specifies the root directory and /S, BACKUP will copy your entire directory tree. Drive A, in this case, is the target drive to which it will copy the files.

BACKUP begins by prompting you to place the first backup floppy disk in drive A, then warns you that it will erase any files in the disk's root directory.

```
Insert backup diskette 01 in drive A:

WARNING! Files in the target drive
A:\ root directory will be erased
Press any key to continue . . .
```

Place your first backup floppy disk in drive A and press ENTER. BACKUP will respond with a message stating that it is backing up files to disk 1 in drive A. BACKUP will also display the name of each file it successfully copies to the floppy disk.

```
*** Backing up files to drive A: ***
Diskette Number: 01

\AUTOEXEC.BAT
\CONFIG.SYS
\COMMAND.COM
\DOS\ANSI.SYS
\DOS\CHKDSK.COM
```

Eventually the floppy disk in drive A will fill. BACKUP will display the following prompt for you to insert the second floppy disk into drive A.

```
Insert backup diskette 02 in drive A:

WARNING! Files in the target drive
```

```
A:\ root directory will be erased
Press any key to continue . . .
```

Remove the first floppy disk from drive A and place the disk in its disk envelope. Next, attach a label to the disk describing the disk's contents. Remember, never write on a label already attached to a disk. In doing so, you may damage the disk, destroying the disk's contents. Next, place the second floppy disk in drive A and press ENTER to resume the backup operation.

As each floppy disk fills, repeat the process of removing, labeling, and inserting new disks. When the backup operation completes, place these floppy disks in a safe storage location.

Performing Daily Backup Operations

Because backing up every file on your hard disk can consume so much time, BACKUP also lets you only back up those files you have created or changed since the last backup operation. These partial backup operations are called *incremental backups*. Because most users typically only change or create a few files each day, incremental backup operations are very fast. Here's how incremental backups keep your backup files up to date. Assume, for example, that on January 1 you perform a complete backup of your disk as previously discussed. BACKUP will produce a current backup of every file on your disk, as illustrated here:

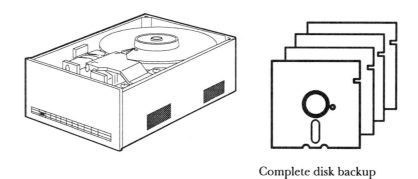

Complete disk backup

On January 2, you create the file NEW.DAT and change the contents of the files ONE.DAT and TWO.DAT. Because it only copies these three files, your incremental backup completes very quickly. Your backup disks now contain the files shown here:

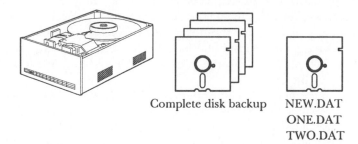

Complete disk backup   NEW.DAT
ONE.DAT
TWO.DAT

The complete disk backup copies every file on your disk, while the incremental backup copies new files and changes.

On January 3, you create two large files, BUDGET.DAT and EXPENSES.DAT. The first file fits on your first incremental backup disk, while the second is placed on a second backup disk.

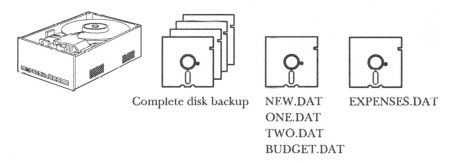

Complete disk backup   NEW.DAT   EXPENSES.DAT
ONE.DAT
TWO.DAT
BUDGET.DAT

You can see that, during the month, your number of incremental backup disks will grow.

On January 4, you change the contents of the file NEW.DAT. Your incremental backup will copy the file's contents, as shown here:

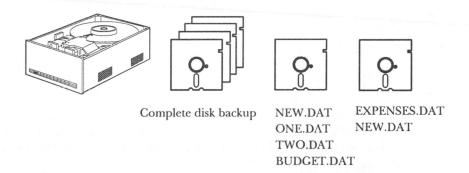

Complete disk backup   NEW.DAT   EXPENSES.DAT
ONE.DAT   NEW.DAT
TWO.DAT
BUDGET.DAT

Throughout the month, different versions of a file may be on several disks, depending on how often you change the file's contents and perform your backups.

By January 31, you will have the floppy disks from the complete disk backup, plus disks containing the incremental backups. As long as you perform backup operations at the end of each day, the most work you can lose due to a disk failure is the current day's files.

To perform incremental backup operations, the BACKUP command must be able to determine which files are new and which files you have changed. As you have learned, a directory is a list of file names, extensions, sizes, and date and time stamps. In addition, DOS keeps a byte of information for each entry, called the file's *attribute byte*. Each time you create a file or change a file's contents, DOS sets a value in the attribute byte called the *archive bit*. The archive bit tells DOS this file's current contents have not been archived or backed up to floppy disk with BACKUP. When you use BACKUP to perform an incremental backup operation, it examines every file's archive bit. If the bit is *set*, BACKUP knows the file needs archiving. As a result, BACKUP copies the file to the floppy disk. After the file is successfully copied to a floppy, BACKUP *clears* the archive bit.

The number of floppy disks your incremental backup requires depends on the number of files you have changed or created and their sizes. Use the following BACKUP command to perform an incremental backup.

```
C:\> BACKUP  C:\*.*  A:  /S  /A  /M  <ENTER>
```

As before, the wildcards and /S direct BACKUP to examine every file on your disk. The /M switch directs BACKUP to only copy those files whose archive attribute bit is set and to clear the archive attribute after it successfully backs up the file to floppy disk. The /A switch directs BACKUP to add these files to the end of the previous day's incremental backup disk.

In this case, BACKUP will prompt you to insert the last incremental backup disk in drive A.

```
Insert last backup diskette in drive A:
Press any key to continue . . .
```

If this operation is your first incremental backup of the month, place a formatted disk in drive A and press ENTER. If you have performed previous incremental backups, place the last disk you used in drive A and press ENTER. BACKUP will add files to the disk until no more disk space remains. Should a disk fill, BACKUP will prompt you to insert a new disk. Place a formatted disk in drive A and press any key to continue. Label your incremental backup disk to avoid confusion, as shown in this example:

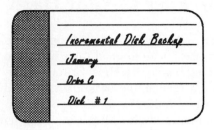

As you can see, by combining a complete system backup with daily or regular incremental backups, you keep your backups current. By the end of the month, you will have a large collection of disks. However, when you perform the next complete disk backup at the start of the following month, you can recycle the disks, repeating this process again. This way, you can limit the accumulation of backups to two months' worth.

Using BACKUP to Back Up a Key File or Directory

The previous backup commands assumed you want to back up your entire hard disk. There may be times, however, when you only want to back up one disk or directory. To do so, you invoke BACKUP specifying the directory name. For example, the following command backs up all the files in the DOS directory.

```
C:\> BACKUP  C:\DOS\*.*  A:  <ENTER>
```

The following command backs up all the files in the DOS directory with the COM extension.

```
C:\> BACKUP  C:\DOS\*.COM  A:  <ENTER>
```

Last, the following command backs up only the file FORMAT.COM from the DOS directory.

```
C:\> BACKUP  C:\DOS\FORMAT.COM  A:  <ENTER>
```

As you can see, BACKUP lets you get very specific about the files you want to back up. If you don't have time to back up your entire disk, you should make time to back up your key files or directories.

Restoring Backup Files to Your Hard Disk

Hopefully you will never have to restore files from your backup floppies to your hard disk. Because most users seldom need their backup copies, they tend to pay less attention to performing regular backups. Unfortunately almost like clockwork, when you quit performing regular file backups, either your disk will fail, or an inadvertent DOS command will destroy the files on your disk.

As the BACKUP command copies files from your hard disk to floppy, the RESTORE command copies backup files from floppy disks to your hard disk. Using RESTORE, you can copy every file on the backup disks or a specific file or directory back to your hard disk. To restore every file to your hard disk from the floppy disks in drive A, issue the following RESTORE command.

```
C:\> RESTORE  A:  C:\*.*  /S  <ENTER>
```

Drive A, in this case, is the drive into which you will place the disks containing the files to restore. The wildcards direct RESTORE to restore every file on the floppy disk. As before, the /S switch directs RESTORE to restore files to every directory below the directory specified.

NOTE   *The BACKUP command copies files to floppy disk using a unique storage format only it and RESTORE understand. Once you back up a file to floppy, the only way to place the backup copy back on to your disk is with RESTORE.*

When you issue the command above, RESTORE prompts you to insert the first backup disk into drive A.

```
Insert backup diskette 01 in drive A:
Press any key to continue . . .
```

After you place the disk in drive A and press ENTER, RESTORE will begin copying files from the backup disks to your hard disk, displaying the name of each file it successfully restores. If you are restoring your entire hard disk, begin with the first disk in your set of floppies from the complete disk backups. When RESTORE successfully restores all the files from the current floppy disk, it will prompt you to insert the next disk and press ENTER. After RESTORE successfully restores all the floppies, you must then repeat the RESTORE command to copy your incremental backups to the hard disk.

The two most common times you would perform a complete hard disk restore operation are when you have experienced a severe disk error losing all your files and when you are correcting disk fragmentation (the subject of Chapter 44). In most cases, you will use RESTORE to copy a specific file or directory of files as discussed next.

RESTORE will overwrite existing files on your hard disk with the files on the backup disk. If you have changed a file's contents and have not yet backed up your changes, RESTORE may overwrite the current file with the file's previous contents.

WARNING

Restoring a Specific File or Directory

Unless your hard disk fails or you can't recover from a disk format operation, you will normally use the RESTORE command to restore a specific file or directory. For example, assume your disk contained the directory LETTERS, within which you stored your correspondence, and you inadvertently delete the files in the directory. If you are using DOS 5, or a third-party disk utility program, you may be able to *undelete* the files. If you don't have an undelete program available, or if your undelete utility is unsuccessful, you'll need to restore your backup copies of the files. In this case, you don't want to restore your entire disk, just the directory LETTERS. To begin, place your first backup disk from the set of complete disk backup floppies in drive A and issue the following RESTORE command.

```
C:\> RESTORE  A:  C:\LETTERS\*.*  <ENTER>
```

RESTORE may have to examine several floppy disks before it locates the files to restore. To do so, RESTORE will prompt you to insert floppy disks into drive A as required. After RESTORE has examined your set of floppies from the complete disk backup, repeat the RESTORE command for your incremental floppies.

Although the process of examining every backup disk for matching files ensures RESTORE will locate the backup copies, you can easily see that looking at every backup disk could become quite time consuming. Luckily, if you are using DOS 3.3 or later, you can direct BACKUP to create a *log file* that lists which backup disks your files reside on. Using the backup log, you can quickly determine and select the disk containing the desired file or files and locate and restore the file much faster. If you are using DOS 3.3 or later, create a directory named BACKUP, in which you will store the backup log:

```
C:\> MKDIR  \BACKUP  <ENTER>
```

Next, when you invoke BACKUP to perform a complete disk backup operation, include the /L switch directing BACKUP to use the file BACKUP.LOG. If a file named BACKUP.LOG currently exists in the BACKUP directory, delete or rename the file.

```
C:\> BACKUP  C:\*.*  A:  /S  /L:C:\BACKUP\BACKUP.LOG  <ENTER>
```

Likewise, use /L when you perform an incremental backup.

```
C:\> BACKUP  C:\*.*  A:  /S  /A  /M  /L:C:\BACKUP\BACKUP.LOG
<ENTER>
```

Only delete or rename the BACKUP.LOG file before a complete disk backup. Your incremental backup operations will also log each file name in BACKUP.LOG as desired.

The backup log file contains each backup date and time as well as the disk number containing each file, for example:

```
4-08-1991  18:27:04
001  \CONFIG.SYS
001  \AUTOEXEC.BAT
001  \NETWORK\NETWORK.BAT
001  \NETWORK\NET4.COM
001  \NETWORK\NET5.COM
001  \NETWORK\IPX.COM
002  \BATCH\DATETIME.BAT
002  \BATCH\CLEANUP.BAT
002  \BATCH\AUTOEXEC.SAV
002  \DOS\ANSI.SYS
```

Using the log file, you can quickly locate and restore key files.

Using Third-Party Backup Utility Programs

Many DOS users buy third-party backup utility programs that provide a menu-driven interface and improved performance. If you choose to buy and use third-party backup software, you will essentially still perform complete disk backups as well as incremental disk backups. However, most third-party backup utilities let you select directories of files you don't want to back up because you can easily restore the corresponding files from your original disks. Whether you choose to use BACKUP and RESTORE or a third-party backup program, perform backup operations on a regular basis.

SUMMARY

Complete Disk Backup Operations

At the beginning of each month, you should back up every file on your hard disk to floppies. To do so, follow these steps:

1. Determine the number of floppy disks required using the CHKDSK command and Table 22-1.

2. Format the floppy disks using FORMAT.

3. Issue the following BACKUP command:

```
C:\> BACKUP  \*.*  A:  /S  <ENTER>
```

Incremental Backup Operations

Incremental backup operations direct BACKUP to copy only those files created or changed since the last complete backup operation. Because most users only create or change a few files each day, incremental backups take very little time. To keep your backups to date, perform the following BACKUP command on a regular basis.

```
C:\> BACKUP  C:\*.*  A:  /S  /A  /M  <ENTER>
```

Hands On

If you have never performed a complete disk backup or have not done so in some time, use BACKUP to do so now. To begin, use the CHKDSK command as discussed to determine the amount of disk space currently in use.

```
C:\> CHKDSK  <ENTER>
```

Using Table 22-1, determine how many floppy disks you will need to back up your disk. Next, format the number of disks specified. Use the following BACKUP command to backup all the files on your disk.

```
C:\> BACKUP  C:\*.*  A:  /S  <ENTER>
```

Correctly label each disk and place the disks into a disk storage container.

The best way to understand the BACKUP and RESTORE process is to try it. To begin, create the directory TESTINFO on your hard disk.

```
C:\> MKDIR  \TESTINFO  <ENTER>
```

Next, copy all files in your DOS directory with the SYS extension to this directory.

```
C:\> COPY  \DOS\*.SYS  \TESTINFO  <ENTER>
```

Next, back up the files in the TESTINFO directory to drive A.

```
C:\> BACKUP  C:\TESTINFO\*.*  A:  <ENTER>
```

When the BACKUP command completes, delete the files in the TESTINFO directory.

```
C:\> DEL  \TESTINFO\*.*  <ENTER>
```

Next, use RMDIR to remove the directory.

```
C:\> RMDIR  \TESTINFO  <ENTER>
```

With the disk containing the backup files in drive A, issue the following RESTORE command.

```
C:\> RESTORE  A:  C:\TESTINFO\*.*  <ENTER>
```

When RESTORE completes, the TESTINFO directory will be on your disk once again with its original files intact.

```
C:\> DIR  \TESTINFO  <ENTER>
```

Clean up your disk by deleting the files in the TESTINFO directory and remove the directory using RMDIR.

Review

1. How does a complete disk backup differ from an incremental backup?

2. What is an archive bit?

3. How does BACKUP use the archive bit?

4. What functions do the BACKUP command switches /S, /A, /M, and /L perform?

5. What is the purpose of a backup log?

Answers

1. A complete disk backup backs up every file on your disk. An incremental backup only backs up those files created or changed since the last BACKUP operation. You should perform a complete disk backup once a month and an incremental disk backup everyday.

2. In addition to the file's name, size, and date and time stamps, DOS stores an attribute byte for each file in the file's directory entry. One of the most commonly used attributes is the archive attribute. Each time you create or change a file, DOS sets the file's archive bit, indicating the file needs to be backed up to floppy. When BACKUP successfully backs up (or archives) the file, BACKUP clears the archive bit. When you perform an incremental backup operation, BACKUP only backs up those files whose archive bit is set.

3. Each time you perform either a complete disk or incremental backup operation, BACKUP clears the archive bit for each file it successfully backs up.

4. BACKUP command switches are as follows:

   /S Directs BACKUP to back up files contained in lower-level directories.

   /A Directs BACKUP to add backup files to an existing backup disk.

   /M Directs BACKUP to only back up those files whose archive bit is set.

   /L Directs BACKUP to log the names of each file it backs up as well as the disk number of the disk containing the file.

5. Over the period of a month, the number of floppy disks containing your complete disk and incremental file backups may become quite large. If you need to restore a file from your backup floppy disks, locating the disk containing the file can consume a lot of time. If you are using DOS 3.3 or later, BACKUP's /L switch lets you create a backup log, a file containing the name of each file, and the number of its corresponding backup disk. Using the backup log, you can locate the floppy disk containing the needed file much faster.

Advanced Concepts

The discussion in the previous section assumed you wanted to back up each file on your disk, or only those files whose archive attribute bit is set. To provide you with a little more control in choosing files to back up, the BACKUP command provides the /D and /T switches. The /D switch lets you specify a date, for BACKUP to refer to, only copying files created or changed on or after the date specified. For example, the following command backs up files created on or after July 4, 1991.

```
C:\> BACKUP  C:\*.*  A:  /S  /D:7-4-91  <ENTER>
```

In a similar way, the /T switch lets you specify a time. Users often combine the /T and /D switches like this.

```
C:\> BACKUP  C:\*.*  A:  /S  /D:7-4-91  /T:12:00  <ENTER>
```

Here, BACKUP will back up all files created after 12 noon on July 4, 1991.

As the BACKUP command provides switches to support date and time operations, so too does RESTORE. The /A and /B switches let you specify dates that control RESTORE's processing. The /A switch lets you specify a date for which RESTORE only restores files created or changed on or after the date specified. The /B switch works in just the opposite manner. Using /B, RESTORE only restores files created on or before the date specified. The following command restores the files on drive C created on or before August 1, 1991.

```
C:\> RESTORE  A:  C:\*.*  /B:8-1-91  <ENTER>
```

Similarly, the /E and /L switches let you specify earlier and later times. By combining these switches with /A and /B you can direct RESTORE to only restore files created on or before a specific time on a specific date. For a complete description of these date and time switches, turn to the Command Reference at the end of this book.

Although you might not use RESTORE's date and time switches on a regular basis, RESTORE provides the /P, /N, and /M switches, which you may find quite useful. RESTORE overwrites existing files on your disk, including files marked read-only, as discussed earlier in this chapter. The /P switch, however, directs RESTORE to display the following prompt before overwriting a read-only file.

```
WARNING! File FILENAME.EXT
is a read-only file
Replace the file (Y/N)?
```

/P also displays the following prompt if RESTORE detects that it is about to overwrite a file that was changed subsequent to backing up.

```
WARNING! File FILENAME.EXT
was changed after it was backed up
Replace the file (Y/N)?
```

Using the /P switch, you can reduce the possibility of RESTORE accidentally overwriting a needed file.

The /N switch provides an extra layer of protection by directing RESTORE only to copy those files that are no longer on your hard disk. In this way, RESTORE will not overwrite an existing file.

The /M option directs RESTORE to only restore those files changed since the last BACKUP operation. Assume, for example, your system crashes, leaving several files in a partially changed state. Using the /M option, you can quickly restore the disk to its state immediately following the last backup operation.

If you are using DOS 5, the /D switch directs RESTORE to display a list of matching files without actually restoring the files. For example, if you are trying to remember the name of a file containing a specific letter, you might use the /D switch as follows.

```
C:\> RESTORE  A:  C:\*.LTR  /S  /D  <ENTER>
```

Using BACKUP and RESTORE with Large Files

BACKUP and RESTORE use a unique storage format. One of the advantages this format provides is that BACKUP gives you a way of copying a file whose size is larger than your floppy disk. Assume, for example you need to give another user a copy of the file TWOMEG.DAT, which contains more than 2Mb of data. If you try to copy the file to a floppy disk, the floppy disk will run out of space:

```
C:\> COPY  BIGFILE.EXT  A:  <ENTER>
Insufficient disk space
       0 File(s) copied
```

Using the BACKUP command, you can copy parts of a file to different floppy disks.

```
C:\> BACKUP  TWOMEG.DAT  A:  <ENTER>
```

Later, using RESTORE, the other user can place the file on his or her hard disk.

```
C:\> RESTORE  A:  C:TWOMEG.DAT  <ENTER>
```

Using BACKUP and RESTORE in this way, you can copy large files without having to buy third-party data compression software.

Using BACKUP and RESTORE in Batch Files

To simplify the task of performing monthly and incremental backups, many users create the batch files MONTHLY.BAT and DAILY.BAT. The batch files use BACKUP's exit status values, defined in Table 22-2.

Exit Status	Meaning
0	Successful backup operation
1	No files found to backup
2	File sharing conflicts prevented a complete backup
3	User termination via CTRL-C
4	Fatal processing error

Table 22-2. BACKUP's Exit Status Values

The following batch file, MONTHLY.BAT, uses BACKUP to perform a complete disk backup. The batch file assumes you are using DOS 3.3 or later and that you have a directory named BACKUP for storing the backup log. If you aren't using DOS 3.3 or later, remove the /L switch from the BACKUP command, along with "C:\BACKUP\BACKUP.LOG" (the commands that save and rename the latest version of BACKUP.LOG).

```
@ECHO OFF
BACKUP C:\*.* A: /S /L:C:\BACKUP\BACKUP.LOG

IF ERRORLEVEL 0 IF NOT ERRORLEVEL 1 ECHO Successful backup
IF ERRORLEVEL 1 IF NOT ERRORLEVEL 2 ECHO No files to back up
IF ERRORLEVEL 2 IF NOT ERRORLEVEL 3 ECHO File sharing conflicts
IF ERRORLEVEL 3 IF NOT ERRORLEVEL 4 ECHO Ended by user Ctrl-C
IF ERRORLEVEL 4 ECHO Error in processing
```

In a similar way, the following batch file, DAILY.BAT, directs BACKUP to perform an incremental backup. If you aren't using DOS 3.3 or later, remove the /L switch and the BACKUP.LOG commands ("C:\BACKUP\BACKUP.LOG").

```
@ECHO OFF
BACKUP C:\*.* A: /S /A /M /L:C:\BACKUP\BACKUP.LOG

IF ERRORLEVEL 0 IF NOT ERRORLEVEL 1 ECHO Successful backup
IF ERRORLEVEL 1 IF NOT ERRORLEVEL 2 ECHO No files to back up
IF ERRORLEVEL 2 IF NOT ERRORLEVEL 3 ECHO File sharing conflicts
IF ERRORLEVEL 3 IF NOT ERRORLEVEL 4 ECHO Ended by user Ctrl-C
IF ERRORLEVEL 4 ECHO Error in processing
```

Last, there may be times you want to use RESTORE within your batch files. Table 22-3 describes RESTORE's exit status values.

Key Terms

Archival   A safe backup.

Complete disk backup   A backup operation that backs up every file on the hard disk to floppy.

Exit Status	Meaning
0	Successful file restoration
1	No files found to restore
3	User termination via CTRL-C
4	Fatal processing error

Table 22-3.   RESTORE's Exit Status Values

Incremental backup   A backup operation that copies only those files created or changed since the last backup.

Chapter 23

Advanced File Manipulation

In Chapter 8, "Fundamental File Operations," you learned the basic file operations COPY, RENAME, DEL, and TYPE that you now use on a daily basis. In Chapter 9 you learned how to use these commands with DOS wildcards. This chapter builds upon your knowledge presenting five more file-manipulation commands: ATTRIB, XCOPY, COMP, FC, and REPLACE. Although you may not use these commands on a daily basis, keep them in the back of your mind as you work with DOS. Each of these powerful commands provides capabilities that may save you considerable time and effort later.

Manipulating File Attributes with ATTRIB

A directory is a list of file names, extensions, sizes, and date and time stamps. In Chapter 22, you learned that each directory entry also contains an attribute byte that provides DOS with more information about the file. You also learned each time you create a file or change a file's contents, DOS sets the file's archive-required attribute, or archive bit, which tells DOS you have not yet backed up the file's new contents to another disk. By searching your directories for files with the archive bit set, the BACKUP command can selectively back up only those files created or changed since the last backup operation.

The ATTRIB command is an external command that lets you set or display file attributes. Using ATTRIB, you can set or clear a file's archive and read-only attributes. As discussed, the archive attribute specifies whether or not BACKUP should back up the file to floppy. A file's read-only attribute prevents DOS from changing, deleting, or overwriting the file's contents. If you are using DOS 5, ATTRIB also lets you set or clear a file's hidden and system attributes. The Advanced Concepts section discusses these two file attributes. Do not use ATTRIB to set or clear these attributes until you are very familiar with DOS and have thoroughly read and understand the discussion of their use.

Displaying File Attributes

ATTRIB sets and displays file attributes. To begin, display the attributes of the files in your DOS directory with the following command.

```
C:\> ATTRIB  \DOS\*.*   <ENTER>
```

ATTRIB will list each file name, preceding the file name with the letters "A" or "R" if the file's archive or read-only attributes are set.

```
C:\> ATTRIB  \DOS\*.*   <ENTER>
                C:\DOS\FORMAT.COM
                C:\DOS\SHARE.EXE
                C:\DOS\XCOPY.EXE
   A            C:\DOS\DOSSHELL.VID
                C:\DOS\DOSSHELL.INI
                C:\DOS\DOSSHELL.COM
   A            C:\DOS\DOSSHELL.EXE
   A            C:\DOS\DOSSHELL.GRB
   A            C:\DOS\DOSSWAP.EXE
   A            C:\DOS\EXE2BIN.EXE
```

The letter "A" states the file's archive bit is set. In this case, the letter "R" does not appear, indicating none of the files are read-only.

In DOS 5, ATTRIB will also display the letter "S" if the file's system attribute is set and "H" if the file is a hidden file.

In DOS 3.3 and higher, the /S switch directs ATTRIB to also process directories below the directory specified. For example, the following command directs ATTRIB to display the attributes for every file on your current (drive C) disk.

```
C:\> ATTRIB  \*.*   /S   <ENTER>
```

If the file names and attributes scroll past you faster than you can read them, use the DOS pipe operator discussed in Chapter 21 to display the command's output a screenful at a time using MORE.

```
C:\> ATTRIB \*.* /S | MORE <ENTER>
```

If you have recently performed a backup operation, note that only those files you have created or changed since the backup operation have their archive bit set.

Setting a File's Attributes

In Chapter 22 you learned each time BACKUP successfully backs up a file to another disk, BACKUP clears the file's archive bit. As you will learn, there are times when it is convenient to set or clear the file's archive bit yourself. To set a file's archive attribute, invoke ATTRIB with +A and the file name.

```
C:\> ATTRIB +A FILENAME.EXT <ENTER>
```

To clear a file's archive bit, use −A. The following ATTRIB command sets the archive bit of the files in your DOS directory.

```
C:\> ATTRIB +A \DOS\*.* <ENTER>
```

If you invoke ATTRIB to display the file attributes, ATTRIB will precede each file name with an uppercase "A."

```
C:\> ATTRIB \DOS\*.* <ENTER>
   A        C:\DOS\FORMAT.COM
   A        C:\DOS\SHARE.EXE
   A        C:\DOS\XCOPY.EXE
   A        C:\DOS\DOSSHELL.VID
   A        C:\DOS\DOSSHELL.INI
   A        C:\DOS\DOSSHELL.COM
```

In a similar way, the following ATTRIB command clears the archive bit of the files in the DOS directory.

```
C:\> ATTRIB -A \DOS\*.* <ENTER>
```

As you learned in Chapter 22, an incremental backup operation uses the archive bit to select the files to backup. If, for some reason, you want BACKUP to exclude one or more files, you can clear the file's archive bit manually using –A. Later in this chapter you will examine the XCOPY command, which provides extended capabilities for copying files. As you will learn, you can easily copy a directory of files to two or more floppy disks by combining ATTRIB and XCOPY.

A *read-only* file is a file whose contents DOS can read, but cannot change, delete, or overwrite. If you have files whose contents seldom change, setting the file to read-only protects it from being accidentally deleted or overwritten. All of your EXE or COM files, for example, are excellent candidates for read-only files because their contents never change.

The ATTRIB command lets you set one or more files to read-only using +R as shown here.

```
C:\> ATTRIB  +R  FILENAME.EXT   <ENTER>
```

To better understand how setting a file to read-only protects your files, create the file TEST.DAT.

```
C:\> COPY  CON  TEST.DAT  <ENTER>
This is a read-only test file. <ENTER>
^Z   <ENTER>
        1 File(s) copied
```

Using ATTRIB +R, set the file to read-only.

```
C:\>  ATTRIB  +R  TEST.DAT   <ENTER>
```

DOS can still use read-only files for TYPE and COPY operations, as they only read the file.

```
C:\> TYPE  TEST.DAT  <ENTER>
This is a read-only test file.
```

DOS cannot delete a read-only file. If you try, DOS displays the "Access denied" error message.

```
C:\> DEL  TEST.DAT  <ENTER>
Access denied
```

Likewise, if you try to overwrite the file's contents using COPY, the command will fail as shown here.

```
C:\> COPY  FILENAME.EXT  TEST.DAT  <ENTER>
Access denied - TEST.DAT
        0 File(s) copied
```

There may be times you want to change the file or delete the file when it is no longer needed. Using ATTRIB –R, you can remove the file's read-only attribute.

```
C:\> ATTRIB  -R  TEST.DAT  <ENTER>
```

When the file is no longer read-only, you can delete the file.

```
C:\> DEL  TEST.DAT  <ENTER>
```

The ATTRIB command lets you combine attribute settings in the same command. For example, the following command sets the files with the EXE extension in your DOS directory to read-only, while clearing the file's archive bit.

```
C:\> ATTRIB  +R  -A  \DOS\*.EXE  <ENTER>
```

XCOPY's Extended Copy Capabilities

Chapter 8 introduced the COPY command. Since then, you have used COPY as one of your fundamental DOS commands. As you work with DOS for some time, you will run into situations where COPY makes an operation more difficult than it needs to be. The most common case that frustrates users is copying a directory of files to multiple floppy disks.

Assume, for example, you want to copy the files in your DOS directory to floppy disks. If you are using 360Kb floppy disks, the copy operation will require several floppies. To begin the operation, invoke COPY as shown.

```
C:\> COPY  \DOS\*.*  A:  <ENTER>
```

COPY will begin copying files from the directory to your disk in drive A, displaying the name of the file it is currently copying. Eventually, your floppy disk will run out of space and COPY will display the "Insufficient disk space" error message.

```
C:\> COPY  \DOS\*.*  A:  <ENTER>
C:\DOS\EGA.SYS
C:\DOS\DISPLAY.SYS
C:\DOS\FORMAT.COM
C:\DOS\ANSI.SYS
C:\DOS\COUNTRY.SYS
C:\DOS\HIMEM.SYS
C:\DOS\KEYB.COM
C:\DOS\KEYBOARD.SYS
C:\DOS\MODE.COM
C:\DOS\SETVER.EXE
C:\DOS\SYS.COM
Insufficient disk space
        10 file(s) copied
```

In this case, COPY ran out of space when it tried to copy the file SYS.COM. To continue the file copying you insert a new disk in drive A. Here's where the trouble begins. COPY does not provide a way for you to continue the file copy operation with the last file copied. Your only option is to copy the files one by one, beginning with the first uncopied file.

If you are using DOS 3.2 or later, the XCOPY command extends the COPY command's capabilities providing you with more control over your file copy operations. For example, by combining XCOPY with the ATTRIB command, you can easily copy a directory of files to multiple floppy disks using XCOPY's /M switch.

The XCOPY /M switch directs XCOPY to behave much like the BACKUP command, copying only those files whose archive bit is set. When XCOPY successfully copies a file, XCOPY clears the archive-required bit. Using the /M switch in this way, XCOPY essentially places a bookmark at the last file copied. Should a floppy disk run out of space, you can insert a new floppy disk and repeat the XCOPY /M command. XCOPY will resume the copy operation with the first file whose archive bit is set, as desired.

To copy a directory of files using XCOPY /M, you must first set each file's archive bit. To copy the files in your DOS directory to drive A, for example, first set the file attributes using ATTRIB as shown here.

```
C:\> ATTRIB  +A  \DOS\*.*  <ENTER>
```

Next, invoke XCOPY using /M.

```
C:\> XCOPY  \DOS\*.*  A:  /M  <ENTER>
```

Like the COPY command, XCOPY will display the name of each file it is copying. As before, when the floppy disk fills, XCOPY will display the insufficient disk space message.

```
Insufficient disk space
        10 File(s) copied
```

When this occurs, insert a new floppy disk in drive A and repeat the same XCOPY command.

```
C:\> XCOPY  \DOS\*.*  A:  /M  <ENTER>
```

Because XCOPY has been clearing the archive bit of each file it successfully copies, XCOPY can pick up after the last file copied. Depending on the number of files in your directory, you may have to repeat the XCOPY command several times.

XCOPY provides the /S switch, which lets you copy files contained in directories below the directory specified. Using /S and /M, you might copy all the files in your WordPerfect directory, WP, and directories below WP with the following commands.

```
C:\> ATTRIB  +A  \WP\*.*  /S  <ENTER>
C:\> XCOPY  \WP\*.*  A:  /S  /M  <ENTER>
```

This book's Command Reference describes XCOPY in detail. Table 23-1 briefly describes XCOPY's switches.

Comparing Two Files with COMP

As you work with DOS for some time, it's not uncommon for two directories to contain files with the same name. If the files are ASCII files, you may be able to use TYPE or your word processor to determine if the files are the same. If you can't tell if the files differ, you can use the COMP command.

COMP is an external DOS command that compares the contents of two files. In its most general form, you invoke COMP with the two file names you want to compare, as shown here.

```
C:\> COMP   FILENAME.ONE   FILENAME.TWO   <ENTER>
```

COMP compares each file's contents byte for byte. If the files are exactly the same, COMP displays the following message.

```
Files compare OK
Compare more files (Y/N) ?
```

Switch	Function
/A	Copies only files whose archive attribute is set. Does not clear the attribute.
/D: *MM-DD-YY*	Copies only files created or changed on or after the date specified.
/E	Copies empty directories to the target disk (creates the directory). Use /E in combination with /S.
/M	Copies only files whose archive attribute is set. Clears the bit after successfully copying the file.
/P	Prompts you for each file individually to confirm you want to copy the file.
/S	Copies all directories below the directory specified.
/V	Verifies that each file was copied correctly.
/W	Prompts you to press a key to begin the copy operation, letting you first change disks.

Table 23-1.   XCOPY Command-Line Switches

To compare other files, type **Y** and press ENTER. COMP will prompt you to type in the next two file names. To return to the DOS prompt, type **N** and press ENTER.

If the files differ, COMP displays the byte number (or offset) of the first ten differences along with the corresponding byte values. Unfortunately, COMP displays these values using the *hexadecimal* or base 16 number system, as shown here.

```
Compare error at OFFSET 1A
File 1 = F3
File 2 = C2
```

Computer programmers use hexadecimal because it is convenient to represent the zero and one value combinations used by the computer. Most users, unfortunately, aren't conversant with hexadecimal. If you are using COMP to determine if two files are the same, you may not care about how the files differ, and you can ignore the hexadecimal values. If you want to know how the files actually differ, you can use the FC command, the next command discussed. If you are using DOS 5, COMP has become much more user-friendly.

Using COMP in DOS 5

As you have just learned, COMP's shortcoming is that COMP displays the offset and file differences as hexadecimal values. Under DOS 5, the /D switch directs COMP to display the differences as decimal values. Similarly, the /A switch directs COMP to display the values in ASCII.

Assume, for example, the files 0_TO_4.DAT and 0_TO_9.DAT contain the following.

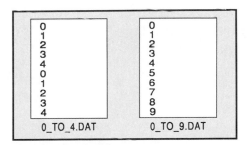

By default, COMP will display the following when you compare the files.

```
C:\> COMP  0_TO_4.DAT  0_TO_9.DAT  <ENTER>
Comparing 0_TO_4.DAT and 0_TO_9.DAT...
Compare error at OFFSET F
```

```
file1 = 30
file2 = 35
Compare error at OFFSET 12
file1 = 31
file2 = 36
Compare error at OFFSET 15
file1 = 32
file2 = 37
Compare error at OFFSET 18
file1 = 33
file2 = 38
Compare error at OFFSET 1B
file1 = 34
file2 = 39

Compare more files (Y/N) ?
```

As you can see, COMP displays the offsets and differences in hexadecimal.
Using the /D switch, COMP displays the following.

```
C:\> COMP  0_TO_4.DAT  0_TO_9.DAT  /D  <ENTER>
Comparing 0_TO_4.DAT and 0_TO_9.DAT...
Compare error at OFFSET F
file1 = 48
file2 = 53
Compare error at OFFSET 12
file1 = 49
file2 = 54
Compare error at OFFSET 15
file1 = 50
file2 = 55
Compare error at OFFSET 18
file1 = 51
file2 = 56
Compare error at OFFSET 1B
file1 = 52
file2 = 57

Compare more files (Y/N) ?
```

If you examine the ASCII chart in Appendix B, you'll find the decimal representations for the letters "0" to "9" are the values 48 to 57.

The /A switch, in this case, provides the most understandable output.

```
C:\> COMP  0_TO_4.DAT  0_TO_9.DAT  /A  <ENTER>
Comparing 0_TO_4.DAT and 0_TO_9.DAT...
Compare error at OFFSET F
file1 = 0
file2 = 5
Compare error at OFFSET 12
file1 = 1
file2 = 6
Compare error at OFFSET 15
file1 = 2
file2 = 7
Compare error at OFFSET 18
file1 = 3
file2 = 8
Compare error at OFFSET 1B
file1 = 4
file2 = 9

Compare more files (Y/N) ?
```

Note that even though you use /D on /A, COMP still displays the offset in hexadecimal. Using the /L switch, you can direct COMP to display the line number of each difference, as follows.

```
C:\> COMP  0_TO_4.DAT  0_TO_9.DAT  /L  <ENTER>
Comparing 0_TO_4.DAT and 0_TO_9.DAT...
Compare error at LINE 6
file1 = 30
file2 = 35
Compare error at LINE 7
file1 = 31
file2 = 36
Compare error at LINE 8
file1 = 32
file2 = 37
```

```
Compare error at LINE 9
file1 = 33
file2 = 38
Compare error at LINE 10
file1 = 34
file2 = 39

Compare more files (Y/N) ?
```

COMP does not consider upper- and lowercase letters as the same. Assume, for example, the files ABC.DAT and SMALLABC.DAT contain the following.

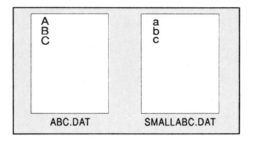

COMP considers the files' contents different.

```
C:\> COMP  ABC.DAT  SMALLABC.DAT  <ENTER>
Comparing ABC.DAT and SMALLABC.DAT...
Compare error at OFFSET 0
file1 = 41
file2 = 61
Compare error at OFFSET 3
file1 = 42
file2 = 62
Compare error at OFFSET 6
file1 = 43
file2 = 63

Compare more files (Y/N) ?
```

Using the /C switch, however, you can direct COMP to consider upper- and lowercase letters as the same.

```
C:\> COMP  ABC.DAT  SMALLABC.DAT  /C  <ENTER>
Comparing ABC.DAT and SMALLABC.DAT...
```

```
Files compare OK

Compare more files (Y/N) ?
```

Last, by default, COMP will not compare files whose sizes differ. If you try to compare files of different sizes, COMP displays the following error message.

```
C:\> COMP  SMALLABC.DAT  0_TO_4.DAT  <ENTER>
Comparing SMALLABC.DAT and 0_TO_4.DAT...
Files are different sizes

Compare more files (Y/N) ?
```

Using the /N: n switch, you can direct COMP to compare the first n lines of two files, even though their sizes may differ.

As you can see, COMP has come a long way under DOS 5. If you are not using DOS 5, you'll probably want to compare files using the FC command.

Comparing Files with FC

If you are using MS-DOS 2.0 or later, the FC command provides a more flexible file-comparison utility than COMP. FC is not available in IBM PC-DOS. You learned that COMP compares files on a byte-by-byte basis, displaying only the first ten differences between the files. Depending on the information in the files you are comparing, COMP could encounter ten differences in the first line and stop. FC, on the other hand, is much more flexible.

The general format of the FC command is

```
C:\> FC  FILENAME.ONE  FILENAME.TWO [switches]  <ENTER>
```

Use the following DIR command to determine if your DOS version has external command FC.EXE.

```
C:\> DIR  \DOS\FC.EXE  <ENTER>
```

If DIR displays the "File not found" message, your DOS version doesn't support the FC command, and you should continue your reading with the REPLACE command discussed next.

To better understand how FC works, create the files WORKDAYS.DAT and WEEKDAYS.DAT that contain the following.

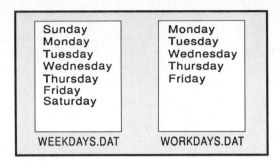

Next, compare the files using FC.

```
C:\> FC  WEEKDAYS.DAT  WORKDAYS.DAT    <ENTER>
```

As you can see, FC displays the lines in each file that differ, as opposed to the byte values and offsets displayed by COMP. In this case, you can quickly determine that the two files begin and end differently. Using the /N switch, you can display the actual line numbers that differ, as shown here.

```
C:\> FC  WEEKDAYS.DAT  WORKDAYS.DAT    <ENTER>
Comparing files WEEKDAYS.DAT and WORKDAYS.DAT
***** WEEKDAYS.DAT
    1:   Sunday
    2:   Monday
    3:   Tuesday
***** WORKDAYS.DAT
    1:   Monday
    2:   Tuesday
*****

***** WEEKDAYS.DAT
    7:   Saturday
***** WORKDAYS.DAT
*****
```

The FC command is very intelligent. Although the files begin with different days, FC recognizes that both files fall into the same pattern of days. Therefore, FC does not consider the file's contents as different, even though the days appear on different lines within the two files.

The Command Reference examines the FC command and each of its command-line switches in detail. If you are comparing ASCII files, FC is a very powerful utility. If you are comparing non-ASCII files to determine if the files are the same, you can use either FC or COMP. Table 23-2 briefly describes FC's command-line switches.

Adding and Replacing Selected Files with REPLACE

One of the difficulties you will experience when you begin using several different applications is keeping up with new releases of upgrades to your programs. If you are using DOS 3.2 or later, the REPLACE command may simplify your task. REPLACE is an external DOS command that lets you selectively add or replace files, typically from a floppy disk to your hard disk. As you will see, REPLACE provides

Switch	Function
/A	Directs FC to display only the first and last lines in a set of lines that differ, rather than the whole set.
/B	Directs FC to perform a byte-by-byte comparison similar to COMP.
/C	Directs FC to treat upper- and lowercase letters as the same.
/L	Directs FC to perform ASCII line-by-line comparisons. FC uses this mode by default except for files with the EXE, COM, OBJ, LIB, SYS, or BIN extensions, for which FC uses /B.
/LB n	Sets the number of consecutive lines that can differ before FC cancels the command. The default is 100.
/N	Directs FC to display line numbers for lines that differ in ASCII file comparisons.
/ *nnn*	Sets the number of consecutive lines that must match before FC considers the two files' contents in sync. Default is 2.
/T	Directs FC to not expand tabs into spaces.
/W	Directs FC to compress white space. If a file contains several blanks or tabs in succession, FC is to treat all the characters as one space or tab.

Table 23-2.   FC's Command-Line Switches

you with greater file control over simply copying the files. Assume, for example, you receive an upgrade to one of your programs that contains the following files.

```
C:\> DIR  A:   <ENTER>

 Volume in drive A has no label
 Volume Serial Number is 2C28-12E3
 Directory of A:\

MENU     COM    45056 01-01-80   12:08a
DATABASE EXE      128 04-10-91    4:53p
DATABASE DAT     2816 10-03-84   10:33p
        3 file(s)      48000 bytes
                      313344 bytes free
```

Assuming the program you are upgrading is in the directory SOMEPROG, you can invoke REPLACE to update the program using the files on drive A as follows.

```
C:\> REPLACE  A:*.*  \SOMEPROG   <ENTER>
```

In this case, REPLACE works much like the COPY command, simply copying the three files to the directory, as shown here.

```
C:\> REPLACE  A:*.*  \SOMEPROG   <ENTER>

Replacing C:\SOMEPROG\MENU.COM

Replacing C:\SOMEPROG\DATABASE.EXE

Replacing C:\SOMEPROG\DATABASE.DAT

3 file(s) replaced
```

Even though duplicate files waste disk space, there are times when users end up with an external command file in two or more directories. Using the /S switch, you can direct REPLACE to search every directory on your disk for files matching those on the replacement disk. Using /S in this way, REPLACE automatically replaces every copy of the original files on your disk.

```
C:\> REPLACE  A:*.*  C:\  /S   <ENTER>
```

Although automatically replacing every file on your disk in this way may seem convenient, it provides the chance of accidentally replacing the wrong file. To reduce the possibility of replacing the wrong file, invoke REPLACE using the /P switch. When you include /P, REPLACE will prompt you to confirm individually that you want to replace each matching file.

```
Replace  FILENAME.EXT ? (Y/N)
```

In some cases, you may only want REPLACE to copy to your hard disk those files on the replacement disk that aren't on your hard disk. The following command, for example, uses the /A switch to add to the SOMEPROG directory only those files on the replacement disks that aren't in the directory.

```
C:\> REPLACE  A:*.*  \SOMEPROG  /A  <ENTER>
```

Depending on the program you are upgrading, you may find REPLACE to be convenient. In some cases, the upgrade instructions may include the REPLACE command you should issue. The Command Reference examines REPLACE and its switches in detail. Table 23-3 briefly describes the REPLACE command-line switches.

Switch	Function
/A	Directs REPLACE to add only those files not found on the target disk. You can't use /A with /S or /U.
/P	Directs REPLACE to prompt you to confirm each file replacement or addition individually.
/R	Directs REPLACE to replace files marked read only. Without /R, the REPLACE command stops at the first read-only file.
/S	Directs REPLACE to search directories below the target directory for matching files.
/U	Directs REPLACE to replace only those files in the target directory that are older than the update files. Cannot be used with the /A switch.
/W	Directs REPLACE to wait for you to press a key before starting the replacement, giving you time to replace disks if necessary.

Table 23-3.   REPLACE Command-Line Switches

Displaying File Attributes

Every file on your disk has an attribute byte that contains the file's archive, read-only, system and hidden attributes. To display the file's current attribute settings, invoke the ATTRIB command with the file name, as shown here.

```
C:\> ATTRIB  FILENAME.EXT  <ENTER>
```

For versions before DOS 5, ATTRIB will display the letter "A" if the file's archive bit is set and "R" if the file is read-only. Under DOS 5, ATTRIB also displays the letter "S" for DOS system files and "H" if the file is hidden from the directory listing.

Setting File Attributes

The ATTRIB command lets you set or clear a file's archive and read-only attributes. If you are using DOS 5, ATTRIB also lets you set the file's hidden or system attributes. To set a file's attributes, invoke ATTRIB as shown here.

```
C:\> ATTRIB  [±Attribute] FILENAME.EXT  <ENTER>
```

where the following attributes apply:

+A   Sets a file's archive bit
−A   Clears a file's archive bit
+R   Sets a file to read-only
−R   Sets a file to read or write access

The XCOPY Command

The XCOPY command extends the capabilities of the COPY command letting you copy files whose archive attribute is set, files created or changed after a specific date, and files that reside in directories beneath the directory specified. The format of the XCOPY command is

```
C:\> XCOPY  SOURCE.EXT  TARGET.EXT  [switches] <ENTER>
```

The COMP Command

The COMP command compares two files byte by byte, displaying the location and corresponding byte values of the first ten differences. The format of the COMP command is as follows.

```
C:\> COMP  FILENAME.ONE  FILENAME.TWO  <ENTER>
```

If you are using DOS 5, COMP provides several command-line switches that greatly improve its capabilities.

The FC Command

If you are using MS-DOS 2.0 or later, the FC command provides a flexible file-comparison utility. Unlike COMP, which compares two files on a byte-by-byte basis, FC compares files line by line. The basic format of the FC command is

```
C:\> FC  FILENAME.ONE  FILENAME.TWO  [switches]  <ENTER>
```

The REPLACE Command

The REPLACE command helps you upgrade or replace files on your disk. Unlike COPY, which gives you less control over the files it copies, REPLACE lets you selectively add and replace files. REPLACE even lets you search your entire disk for files matching the upgrades. The format of the REPLACE command is

```
C:\> REPLACE  SOURCE  TARGET  [switches]  <ENTER>
```

Hands On

Using the following ATTRIB command, display the attributes of the files in the current directory.

```
C:\> ATTRIB  *.*  <ENTER>
```

Depending on your DOS version, DOS may precede the file names with the letters "A," "R," "H," and "S," based on the attributes set. Using the pipe operator and MORE, display the files a screenful at a time.

```
C:\> ATTRIB  *.*  |  MORE  <ENTER>
```

If you are using DOS 3.3 or higher, use the /S switch to display the attributes for every file on your disk.

```
C:\> ATTRIB  \*.*  /S  |  MORE  <ENTER>
```

Using the DOS output redirection operator, you can get a printed listing of the name of every file on your disk.

```
C:\>  ATTRIB  \*.*  /S  >  PRN  <ENTER>
```

It is good practice to set your files whose contents don't change to read-only. Use the following commands to set the EXE and COM files in your DOS directory to read-only.

```
C:\> ATTRIB  +R  \DOS\*.EXE  <ENTER>
C:\> ATTRIB  +R  \DOS\*.COM  <ENTER>
```

Now create the file DELETE.ME that contains the following.

```
C:> COPY  CON  DELETE.ME  <ENTER>
You can't delete read-only files  <ENTER>
```

```
^Z   <ENTER>
     1 File(s) copied
```

Next, use ATTRIB to set the file to read-only.

```
C:\> ATTRIB  +R  DELETE.ME   <ENTER>
```

Using DEL, try to delete the read-only file.

```
C:\> DEL  DELETE.ME   <ENTER>
```

When DEL fails, remove the file's read-only attribute and delete the file.

```
C:\> ATTRIB  -R  DELETE.ME   <ENTER>
C:\> DEL  DELETE.ME   <ENTER>
```

The most common use of the XCOPY command is to copy a directory of files to two or more floppy disks. In this case, you will use XCOPY to copy the files in your DOS directory to floppy disks in drive A. To begin, set each file's archive bit.

```
C:\> ATTRIB  +A  \DOS\*.*   <ENTER>
```

Next, with several unused formatted floppy disks in hand, issue the following XCOPY command.

```
C:\> XCOPY  \DOS\*.*  A:  /M   <ENTER>
```

As you will recall, the /M switch directs XCOPY to copy only those files whose archive bit is set. When XCOPY successfully copies a file, /M directs XCOPY to clear the file's archive bit. When the floppy disk fills, insert a second floppy disk in drive A and repeat the XCOPY command. Should you need to format additional floppy disks, do so. Because XCOPY uses the archive attribute as its bookmark, you can immediately issue XCOPY, or you can even issue the command tomorrow when you have more time. Because DOS stores the file attributes in the directory on disk, you can turn off your computer or issue other DOS commands, such as FORMAT, without affecting the file attributes.

Next, create the files XYZ.DAT and SMALLXYZ.DAT that contain the following.

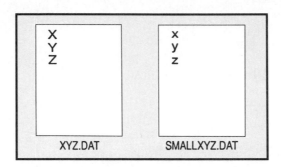

Next, issue the COMP command to compare each file's contents.

```
C:\> COMP  XYZ.DAT  SMALLXYZ.DAT  <ENTER>
```

Using Appendix B, look up the hexadecimal values displayed and you'll find the values correspond to the letters "xyz" and "XYZ." If you are using DOS 5, invoke COMP with the /A switch to display the differences as ASCII characters.

```
C:\> COMP  XYZ.DAT  SMALLXYZ.DAT  /A  <ENTER>
```

Repeat the command using the /C switch directing COMP to consider upper- and lowercase letters the same.

```
C:\> COMP  XYZ.DAT  SMALLXYZ.DAT  /C  <ENTER>
```

If you are using MS-DOS, issue the following command to determine if your DOS version supports FC.EXE.

```
C:\> DIR  \DOS\FC.EXE  <ENTER>
```

If the file is present, create the files ONETOTEN.DAT and NOSEVEN.DAT, which contain the following.

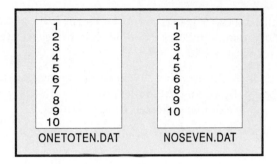

Next, issue the following FC command to compare each file's contents.

```
C:\> FC  ONETOTEN.DAT  NOSEVEN.DAT  <ENTER>
```

Repeat the command and include the /L switch directing FC to display the line numbers that differ.

```
C:\> FC  /L  ONETOTEN.DAT  NOSEVEN.DAT  <ENTER>
```

Delete the files with the DAT extension you created during this Hands On session.

Review

1. Where does DOS store file attributes?

2. What is a read-only file?

3. What files should you set to read-only?

4. How does FC differ from COMP?

5. List capabilities XCOPY provides that COPY does not.

Answers

1. DOS stores the file attribute byte in the file's directory entry.

2. A read-only file is a file whose contents DOS can read, as the source file in a TYPE or COPY command, for example, but whose contents DOS cannot change, delete, or overwrite.

3. You should set files whose contents very rarely change, such as EXE or COM files, to read-only. By setting these files to read-only, you reduce the chance of the files being accidentally deleted or overwritten.

4. First, not all DOS versions provide FC. In fact, IBM PC-DOS, does not provide FC at all.

    For most DOS versions, COMP compares two files displaying the first ten differences in hexadecimal. FC, on the other hand, provides a more meaningful file comparison. Under DOS 5, COMP supports several new command-line switches that improve its functionality.

5. XCOPY lets you copy files based on either the attribute bit being set or based on the date stamp. In addition, XCOPY lets you copy files residing in directories below the directory specified.

Advanced Concepts

Hidden files are files that exist on disk but don't appear in the directory listing. As discussed in Chapter 7, "Preparing Disks for Use," every time you create a bootable disk using FORMAT, DOS places two hidden files on the startup disk. DOS hides these files to prevent users from deleting or renaming them. If you are using DOS 5, the ATTRIB command lets you display hidden files and set files as hidden. Using ATTRIB, you can display hidden files in the root directory, as shown here.

```
C:\> ATTRIB   \*.*   <ENTER>
     SH        C:\IO.SYS
     SH        C:\MSDOS.SYS
   A           C:\COMMAND.COM
               C:\AUTOEXEC.BAT
               C:\CONFIG.SYS
```

If you work in an office where your computer is accessible to other users, you may want to hide a few of your files to protect them from other users. Be careful, however, to remember you have hidden the files. Should you later have difficulty removing a directory using RMDIR, its very likely the directory may still contain hidden files.

```
C:\> RMDIR  \DIRNAME  <ENTER>
Invalid path, not directory,
or directory not empty
```

Should this error message occur, invoke ATTRIB as follows.

```
C:\> ATTRIB  \DIRNAME\*.*  <ENTER>
```

If hidden files exist in the directory, ATTRIB will display them. The version 5 ATTRIB command also lets you set or clear a file's system attribute. DOS assigns this attribute to its two hidden root directory files. In general, you should not use the system attribute. Leave these attribute settings for use by DOS. You can achieve the same level of file protection and privacy using the hidden attribute.

Expanding DOS 5 Files

To reduce the number of installation disks, the DOS 5 update and installation disks store files in a compressed format. If you examine these disks using DIR, you will find several files with an underscore as the last letter of the extension, such as COMMAND.CO_ or FORMAT.CO_. These files are in compressed format. When you perform the DOS 5 upgrade or installation, the SETUP program automatically decompresses these files for you. Should you later accidentally delete a DOS file and you don't have the files backed up, you'll need to expand a copy of the compressed file yourself from the upgrade of the installation disk. The DOS 5 EXPAND command is an external command that lets you decompress a DOS 5 file. Assume, for example, you delete the file UNDELETE.EXE. Using the DIR, command to examine your upgrade of installation disks, you can find the disk containing the compressed file UNDELETE.EX_. Using EXPAND, you can decompress the file into your DOS directory, as shown here.

```
C:\> EXPAND  A:UNDELETE.EX_  \DOS\UNDELETE.EXE  <ENTER>
```

EXPAND supports DOS wildcards. If you need to locate several files, print a copy of the file PACKING.LST, which describes the contents of each floppy disk. PACKING.LST is not a compressed file. It resides on your upgrade disk number 1.

Key Terms

Hidden file   A file that exists on your disk but does not appear in the directory listing. You cannot accidentally delete or overwrite hidden files.

System file   A file whose system attribute is set, typically the files IO.SYS and MSDOS.SYS.

Read-only file   A file whose contents DOS can copy or display, but cannot delete, change, or overwrite.

Compressed file   A file stored in a special format to reduce the amount of disk space the file consumes. You must decompress a compressed file before you can use it. The DOS 5 EXPAND command decompresses the compressed files stored on the DOS 5 upgrade disks.

Chapter 24

Customizing Your System with CONFIG.SYS

In Chapter 18 you learned that each time your system starts, DOS searches the root directory for two files named CONFIG.SYS and AUTOEXEC.BAT. As you know, AUTOEXEC.BAT is a special batch file whose commands DOS automatically executes each time your system starts. The file CONFIG.SYS, like AUTOEXEC.BAT, is a file containing single-line entries you place into the file yourself. Unlike the entries in AUTOEXEC.BAT, the CONFIG.SYS entries are not DOS commands. Instead, each CONFIG.SYS entry defines a customization setting that helps DOS configure itself in memory for your specific requirements. In fact, the name CONFIG is an abbreviation for CONFIGuration. The SYS extension indicates that the file is a DOS SYStem file.

Understanding the CONFIG.SYS Entries

Depending on who installed DOS on your system, your root directory very likely already contains a CONFIG.SYS file. Use the following DIR command to determine if CONFIG.SYS exists.

```
C:\> DIR  \CONFIG.SYS  <ENTER>
```

If the file exists, use TYPE to display its contents.

```
C:\> TYPE  \CONFIG.SYS    <ENTER>
```

In most cases, your CONFIG.SYS file will contain BUFFERS, FILES, and possibly one or more DEVICE entries, as shown here.

```
BUFFERS=30
FILES=20
DEVICE=C:\DOS\ANSI.SYS
```

Every CONFIG.SYS entry is only one line in length. Table 24-1 briefly describes the CONFIG.SYS entries.

This chapter divides the CONFIG.SYS entries into two groups: those every user may need and those best suited for advanced DOS users.

To add or change a CONFIG.SYS entry you can use the DOS editor or your word processor. The only time DOS uses the CONFIG.SYS file is during system startup. Therefore, if you change or add a CONFIG.SYS entry, you must restart your system for DOS to use the new entry's value.

Table 24-1 lists 15 CONFIG.SYS entries. You do not need to use every entry in your CONFIG.SYS file. If you don't include one or more of the entries specified, DOS will use its own default values.

Using Disk Buffers to Improve Performance

Each time a program such as your word processor or spreadsheet reads information from a file, DOS reads one or more of the disk sectors holding the specified information from disk into an area of your computer's electronic memory called a *disk buffer*. DOS then transfers information from the disk buffer to the application's memory area as that program needs the information, as shown in Figure 24-1.

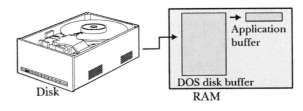

Figure 24-1.   *Information flows from disk to memory buffers, then to application's memory*

Entry	Function
BREAK	Enables or disables extended CTRL-BREAK checking at system startup.
BUFFERS	Defines the number of RAM disk buffers DOS can use to improve your disk performance.
COUNTRY	Defines a country-specific symbol set for international users.
DEVICE	Installs software support (a device driver) for a specific hardware device.
DEVICEHIGH	Similar to DEVICE, but places the device driver into reserved memory to make more conventional memory available for applications (DOS 5 only).
DOS	Directs DOS to use reserved and high memory to make more conventional memory available for applications (DOS 5 only).
DRIVPARM	Changes the parameters for a physical disk drive.
FCBS	Provides support for file control blocks (FCBs) used by old DOS programs running with SHARE installed.
FILES	Defines the number of files DOS can open at one time.
INSTALL	Loads one of four memory-resident DOS commands: KEYB, FASTOPEN, NLSFUNC, and SHARE.
LASTDRIVE	Defines the last drive letter from "E" to "Z" DOS can use for a logical disk drive.
REM	Lets you place comments within your CONFIG.SYS file (DOS 4 or later).
SHELL	Defines the location of the DOS command processor, typically COMMAND.COM.
STACKS	Provides additional RAM stack space to handle hardware interrupts.
SWITCHES	Forces an enhanced keyboard to generate scan code values corresponding to a conventional keyboard (DOS 4 or later).

Table 24-1.   CONFIG.SYS Entries

You may be wondering why DOS first places the information into the disk buffer. Here's why. For efficiency and performance, the smallest amount of information DOS can read from or write to disk is one sector (typically 512 bytes). As an example, assume you are running a database program that stores a simple mailing list. Each entry in this mailing list requires 64 bytes, as shown in Figure 24-2.

Name 20 bytes	Address 22 bytes	City 15 bytes	State 2 bytes	Zip code 5 bytes
Beth Arnold	2013 South 1st	Phoenix	AZ	85022
Ken Davis	Route 2 Box 3	Kent	WA	98032
Bill Jones	1531 South 9th	Medford	MA	02155
Alex Klause	1433 Rainbow	S. Spring	MD	20910

Figure 24-2.   A simple database with 64-byte entries

When you want to print a mailing label for the first database entry, the database program reads the entry from disk. When the database program asks DOS to read the entry, DOS must read and transfer a 512-byte sector from disk to memory. Because the size of each database entry is only 64 bytes, DOS actually transfers the first eight database entries from disk to memory (8 * 64 = 512 bytes), as shown in Figure 24-3.

Here's how disk buffers improve your system performance. Assume that after printing the mailing label for the first entry, you decide to print a label for the second. When the database program asks DOS to read the second entry from disk, DOS doesn't have to read the information from disk, because the entry is already in the disk buffer.

Although hard disks are becoming faster, they are still much slower than your computer's electronic memory. A general rule to follow is that reducing the number of disk input or output operations will improve a program's speed. Using the database example, if you decide to print mailing labels for the first eight entries, DOS only has to perform one slow disk read. Because the information was already in the disk buffer, DOS could very quickly provide the database program with entries 2 through 8.

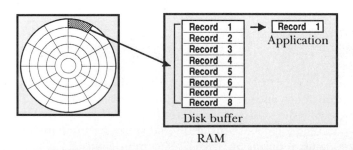

Figure 24-3.   The smallest unit of information DOS can transfer to or from disk is a sector

System Type	Buffer Recommendation
IBM PC XT (8088)	20
IBM PC XT (80286)	25
80386 computer	30
80486 computer	35

Table 24-2.   Recommended Buffer Settings for Various Computer Types

The CONFIG.SYS BUFFERS entry lets you specify the number of disk buffers you want DOS to use. To a point, the more buffers you provide, the better your system performance. Depending on your system configuration, the number of disk buffers you provide will differ slightly. Table 24-2 provides recommended buffer settings.

The following CONFIG.SYS entry directs DOS to use 30 disk buffers.

```
BUFFERS=30
```

Depending on your DOS version, you can use from 1 to 99 disk buffers. If you make the number of disk buffers too large, you will actually decrease your system performance for two reasons. First, each time DOS must read information from disk, DOS first checks to see if the data is present in a disk buffer, as shown in the following illustration.

System RAM	Default Buffer Settings
128Kb or less	2 for 360Kb disk 3 for disk larger than 360Kb
129Kb to 255Kb	5
256Kb to 511Kb	10
512Kb to 640Kb	15

Table 24-3.   Default Buffer Settings for Different System Configurations

If the number of disk buffers becomes too large, DOS will spend considerable time simply searching through the disk buffers. Second, each disk buffer requires 528 bytes of memory (512 bytes for the data, and 16 bytes for information DOS uses to locate the buffer). If you specify too many disk buffers, you may use up a considerable amount of memory an application may put to better use.

DOS provides default value settings for different CONFIG.SYS entries as required. Depending on your DOS version and available memory, the amount number of default buffers DOS uses will differ. In general, use the values shown in Table 24-3 to determine the default buffer settings.

Many applications, such as a database that reads a large number of entries or a word processor that reads a large document, will ask DOS to read one sector that the program will use, followed by a request to read the next sector. As you have learned, DOS stores a file on disk using groups of sectors that form allocation units. If a program asks DOS to read sector 100, for example, it is very likely the program will ask DOS to read sectors 101, 102, and 103.

If you are using DOS 4 or later, you can direct DOS to preread these sectors in anticipation of their later use. DOS refers to the process of prereading sectors as *read-ahead.* Using the CONFIG.SYS BUFFERS entry, you can direct DOS to preread from 1 to 8 sectors. The following CONFIG.SYS entry, for example directs DOS to use 30 disk buffers to allocate memory for 4 read-ahead buffers.

```
BUFFERS=30,4
```

Each read-ahead sector consumes a sector's worth of memory (typically 512 bytes). Last, if you are using DOS 4 and your system uses expanded memory, you can include the /X switch to direct DOS to store the buffers in expanded memory, freeing conventional memory for your applications. Chapter 32, "Understanding DOS Memory Management," discusses memory in detail.

NOTE *Many users install disk-caching software, which provides more efficient disk buffering than DOS buffers. If you are using disk-caching software such as the Windows or DOS 5 SMARTDRV.SYS, reduce the number of DOS disk buffers to 3.*

DOS Uses Disk Buffers for Output, Too

DOS not only uses disk buffers to reduce the number of disk-read operations, but also disk writes. Assume, for example, the database program discussed earlier wants to store the very first 64-byte mailing-list entry to disk. By default, DOS does not write a sector to disk until the sector is full, or the program tells DOS to flush all the buffers containing its data to disk. Buffer flushing normally only occurs when the program ends. Therefore, when the database program stores the very first entry, DOS actually just places the entry into an outgoing disk buffer, illustrated in Figure 24-4.

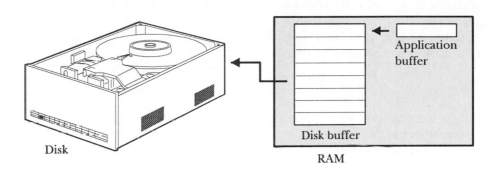

Figure 24-4. *DOS buffers disk output until the buffer is full or the program directs*
DOS to flush the buffer

DOS buffers the output data in this way because DOS assumes the program will eventually write more data to that sector. By buffering the output, DOS reduces the number of slow disk writes.

Unfortunately, should you turn off your computer before the program ends, or end the program using CTRL-C, the data in the disk buffer may never actually be recorded on disk. As a result, information you thought you stored is lost. To reduce the chance of DOS not flushing a buffer to disk, only turn off your computer when DOS is displaying its prompt.

Defining the Number of Files DOS Can Open at One Time

Just as the BUFFERS entry specifies the number of disk buffers DOS can use, the CONFIG.SYS FILES entry specifies the number of files DOS can open at one time. The default value for the FILES entry is 8; but as you will learn, you should use at least 20. Here's why.

In Chapters 20 and 21 you examined the input and output redirection operators. At that time you learned that DOS defines a default source for your program's input called stdin that DOS associates with your keyboard. You also learned that DOS provides default destinations for your command's output (stdout) error messages (stderr), printer output (stdprn), and auxiliary device (stdaux). To provide these input/output source and destinations, DOS automatically opens five files each time you run a program. Since the default setting for the number of files DOS can open is eight, and DOS automatically uses five of them to support I/O redirection, your programs are restricted, by default, to only opening three files. Very few programs can run if they are restricted to three files. If you are using a word processor, for example, the word processor needs to open the file you are editing, possibly a dictionary file used by the spell checker, a file of synonyms used by a built-in thesaurus, and possible font files. If you restrict the word processor to three files, it may not be able to run.

At a minimum, you should provide DOS with the ability to open up to 20 files at the same time using the FILES entry shown here.

```
FILES=20
```

DOS lets you specify up to 255 files. If you are using a large database program or several spreadsheets, the program's installation instructions may direct you to increase the number of files to 40 or 50. Because most programs don't open more files than this at one time, providing DOS with a larger number of handles will probably just waste memory. Each file entry you specify consumes about 64 bytes.

If the number of available files is too low, programs may display error messages telling you they could not open a file you know resides on disk. Should such messages appear, increase the number of available files and reboot your computer.

Beginning with version 2.0, each time DOS opens a file, for either read or write operations, DOS assigns a unique value to the file called a *file handle*. When your programs later read or write data to the file, the program uses the handle to identify the file to DOS.

Specifying International Symbol Sets

DOS is the most widely used operating system in the world. To help its international users, DOS lets users select their country's specific date, time, and currency formats, as well as the character set used to display letters on the screen and printer.

The CONFIG.SYS COUNTRY entry lets international users identify their country to DOS. Chapter 38 examines the capabilities DOS provides international users. For more information on the COUNTRY entry, turn to Chapter 38, "Support for International Users."

Placing Comments in Your CONFIG.SYS File

In Chapter 15, "Grouping Commands with Batch Files," you used the REM command to place comments (or REMarks) in a batch file to explain the batch file's processing. If you are using DOS 4 or later, DOS lets you place REM statements in your CONFIG.SYS file. While processing the CONFIG.SYS entries, DOS ignores any line that begins with REM, continuing with the next entry. Assume, for example, you have a spreadsheet program whose installation instructions direct you to set the FILES entry to 40. Using REM, you can explain the entry.

```
REM Provide file support for Lotus 123 V3.1
FILES=40
```

Should another user examine the contents of your CONFIG.SYS file, REM tells the user the reason for 40 file handles, reducing the chance that the user will change the entry.

Installing Software Device Drivers

By default, DOS provides software that lets you use your keyboard, screen, printer, and disks. When you add other hardware to your computer such as a mouse, plotter, scanner, or even a built-in FAX, you may need to install additional software that lets DOS communicate with the device. Because such software lets DOS control (or drive) the device, the software is called a *device driver*. To assist DOS, the device driver, like a program, must reside in your computer's memory.

The CONFIG.SYS DEVICE entry lets you install a device driver into memory. The format of the DEVICE entry is as follows.

```
DEVICE=C:\PATHNAME\FILENAME.EXT  [optional_parameters]
```

PATHNAME tells DOS the name of the directory containing the device driver file. If you don't specify a directory name, DOS only searches the root directory for the file. Rather than placing the device driver files in the root directory, use a complete path name that specifics the driver's original directory. As is the case with DOS commands, you don't need to type the brackets if you include an optional parameter. Most device driver files use the SYS extension to show they are system files. Use the following DIR command to list the device driver files provided by your DOS version.

```
C:> DIR  \DOS\*.SYS  <ENTER>
```

If you are using DOS 5, DOS also provides the device driver files SETVER.EXE and EMM386.EXE.

Table 24-4 defines the device drivers provided by different DOS versions. Most of the device drivers are examined in detail in chapters that best correspond to their use. For now, you need simply understand that a device driver is special software that lets DOS make use of a hardware device.

Hands On

BUFFERS, FILES, and DEVICE are the most common CONFIG.SYS entries. At a minimum, your CONFIG.SYS file should contain the following entries.

```
FILES=20
BUFFERS=30
```

Use the following DIR command to determine if your root directory has a CONFIG.SYS file

```
C:\> DIR  \CONFIG.SYS    <ENTER>
```

If the file exists, use TYPE to display its contents.

```
C:\> TYPE  \CONFIG.SYS    <ENTER>
```

Driver Name	Function
ANSI.SYS	Provides enhanced keyboard and video support (Chapter 34).
DISPLAY.SYS	Provides monitor code page (character set) switching for international users (Chapter 38).
DRIVER.SYS	Provides software support for external floppy disk drives.
EGA.SYS	Provides EGA video support for the DOS 5 task swapper (Chapter 42).
EMM386.EXE	Simulates expanded memory in DOS 5 systems containing only extended memory (Chapter 32).
HIMEM.SYS	Manages extended memory under DOS 5 (Chapter 32).
PRINTER.SYS	Provides printer code page (character set) support for international users (Chapter 38).
RAMDRIVE.SYS	Creates a fast electronic RAM drive (Chapter 32).
SETVER.EXE	Defines the version number DOS 5 should report when the specific commands ask DOS for the current version number (Chapter 43).
SMARTDRV.SYS	Creates a disk cache in expanded or extended memory (Chapter 32).
VDISK.SYS	Creates a fast electronic RAM drive similar to RAMDRIVE.SYS.
XMAEM.SYS	Provides expanded memory support for 80386 machines in PC DOS 4 (Chapter 32).
XMA2EMS.SYS	Provides expanded memory support for 80286 machines in PC DOS 4 (Chapter 32).

Table 24-4.   Device Drivers in Different DOS Versions

SUMMARY

BUFFERS

The CONFIG.SYS BUFFERS entry lets you specify the number of disk buffers DOS uses to increase your system performance. Compared to your computer's fast electronic parts, even your hard disk is very slow. By using disk buffers, DOS reduces the number of slow disk input and output operations it must perform. The following CONFIG.SYS BUFFERS entry allocates 30 disk buffers.

```
BUFFERS=30
```

FILES

The CONFIG.SYS FILES entry specifies the number of files DOS can open at one time. By default, DOS uses eight file handles, five of which are used for I/O redirection. At a minimum, you should use the FILES entry to specify 20 available files as shown here.

```
FILES=20
```

REM

The CONFIG.SYS REM entry lets you place comments throughout your CONFIG.SYS file that explain the values assigned to each entry. REM requires DOS 4 or later. When DOS encounters REM while processing your CONFIG.SYS entries, DOS ignores the line, continuing its processing at next entry. The following REM entry explains the BUFFERS entry.

```
REM Use minimal buffers due to caching with SMARTDRV.SYS.
BUFFERS=3
```

DEVICE

The CONFIG.SYS DEVICE entry lets you install a software device driver into your computer's memory. A device driver is special software that lets DOS use a hardware device. The software must reside in your computer's memory before DOS can use it. The following DEVICE entry loads the ANSI.SYS device driver from the DOS directory.

```
DEVICE=C:\DOS\ANSI.SYS
```

If the file does not exist, use your word processor or the DOS editor to create the file using the FILES and BUFFERS entries just shown.

Before changing the contents of your CONFIG.SYS file, always save a copy of the file's existing contents in a file named CONFIG.SAV, as shown here.

NOTE

```
C:\> COPY  \CONFIG.SYS  \CONFIG.SAV   <ENTER>
```

Should an added or changed CONFIG.SYS entry result in an error that prevents your computer from booting from hard disk, you can boot your computer using a bootable floppy disk in drive A, and then restore CONFIG.SYS's original contents using the file CONFIG.SAV. In fact, if you have not yet done so, make a copy of your CONFIG.SYS file right now. Also use the PRINT command to print the file's current contents, and place the hardcopy output in a safe location.

```
C:\> PRINT  \CONFIG.SYS   <ENTER>
```

If your current CONFIG.SYS file does not contain the BUFFERS or FILES entry, add the entries previously shown.

Remember, if you add or change CONFIG.SYS entries, you must reboot your computer for the change to take effect. The Advanced Concepts section examines the remaining CONFIG.SYS entries.

Review

1. How does CONFIG.SYS differ from AUTOEXEC.BAT?

2. When does DOS use the CONFIG.SYS entries?

3. What happens if your disk doesn't have a CONFIG.SYS file?

4. What is a disk buffer? How do disk buffers improve your system performance?

5. What is the purpose of the CONFIG.SYS FILES entry? Why are DOS programs restricted to only three files if you don't use the FILES entry?

Answers

1. Each time DOS starts, DOS searches your disk's root directory for the files CONFIG.SYS and AUTOEXEC.BAT. The CONFIG.SYS file contains single-

line entries that DOS uses to load itself in memory for your specific system configuration. If the file does not exist, DOS uses its own default values. CONFIG.SYS does not contain commands, but rather, single-line configuration entries. AUTOEXEC.BAT, on the other hand, is a special batch file with commands that DOS automatically executes at system startup. If AUTOEXEC.BAT does not exist, DOS invokes the DATE and TIME commands.

2. The only time DOS uses CONFIG.SYS is during system startup. If you make changes to CONFIG.SYS, you must restart your system to put the changes into effect.

3. If your system does not have a CONFIG.SYS file, DOS loads itself in memory using its own default configuration values. If your CONFIG.SYS file does not contain a value for each possible entry, DOS uses its default values.

4. A disk buffer is a region in your computer's fast electronic memory into which DOS reads information from disk. The smallest unit of information DOS can transfer to or from disk is a disk sector. Each time a program asks DOS to read information from disk, DOS reads at least one sector into a disk buffer. When the program asks DOS to read additional information, DOS first checks to see if the information is already in a disk buffer. If the information is in a buffer, DOS can quickly provide the information to the program without having to perform a slow disk read operation. By reducing slow disk reads, disk buffers improve your system performance.

5. The FILES entry defines the number of files DOS can open at one time. The default number is eight. Unfortunately, of these eight files, DOS uses five to support I/O redirection. As a result, unless your CONFIG.SYS file contains a FILES entry, DOS restricts your programs to three files. Most larger programs need more than three files to run.

Advanced Concepts

Although several of the CONFIG.SYS entries that appear in this section are simple to understand, they are presented in the Advanced Concepts section because they are less frequently used than the entries previously discussed.

Extended CTRL-BREAK Checking

As you know, DOS lets you end a command by pressing the CTRL - BREAK keyboard combination. When you run a command, DOS periodically checks to see if you have pressed either CTRL - BREAK or CTRL - C to end the command. By default, DOS only performs this checking when it reads a character from the keyboard, or when it writes a character to the screen, printer, or auxiliary port. If you have a program that doesn't perform these input or output operations on a regular basis, it may take DOS considerable time to recognize that you have pressed CTRL-BREAK.

Chapter 43 examines the BREAK command that directs DOS to perform extended CTRL-BREAK checking. Using BREAK, the following command turns on extended CTRL-BREAK checking.

```
C:\> BREAK  ON   <ENTER>
```

When extended CTRL-BREAK checking is on, DOS checks for a user-entered CTRL-BREAK after each DOS system service, such as a disk read or write. Because DOS checks for the CTRL-BREAK more often, DOS is likely to recognize and respond to your CTRL-BREAK sooner. Unfortunately, the amount of extra processing DOS must perform for extended CTRL-BREAK checking makes your system run slower.

As a rule, unless you are a programmer writing and testing programs, you should leave extended CTRL-BREAK checking off.

```
C:\> BREAK  OFF   <ENTER>
```

By default, DOS starts with extended CTRL-BREAK checking off. If you are a programmer and you want DOS to start with extended CTRL-BREAK checking on, you can place the following BREAK entry in your CONFIG.SYS file.

```
BREAK=ON
```

Specifying the Last Drive Letter

Chapter 26, "DOS Pretender Commands," examines how the SUBST command lets you abbreviate directory names using a logical disk drive letter. By default, DOS lets you use the drive letters A through E. If you create a drive letter greater than E, you must first use the CONFIG.SYS LASTDRIVE entry to specify the drive letter from A to Z of the last drive letter you intend to use. Chapter 45 examines FDISK, which lets you divide your hard disk into partitions. Using FDISK, you can further divide a disk partition into logical drives. When you create logical drives with FDISK, DOS automatically takes care of correct drive-letter assignments.

The following LASTDRIVE entry selects H as the last drive letter.

```
LASTDRIVE=H
```

If you aren't using logical drives, you don't need the LASTDRIVE entry. If you are using logical drives, only assign LASTDRIVE with the number of letters necessary. Each drive requires 80 to 96 bytes.

Providing File Control Block Support for Older Programs

The CONFIG.SYS FILES entry defines the number of file handles DOS can use to open files. Before version 2.0, DOS did not use file handles, but rather *file control blocks* or *FCBs*. If you are running a very old software program on a network or with the SHARE command loaded, and the program continually displays error messages when it tries to open files, you may need to provide additional file control blocks for the program. The CONFIG.SYS FCBS entry defines the number of file control blocks DOS should provide. The default value is 4. The format of the FCBS entry is as follows.

```
FCBS=MaxOpen,MaxNoClose
```

The *MaxOpen* value specifies the number of file control blocks DOS provides, from 1 to 255. If the older program is experiencing errors, experiment with values of 12 or 16. The *MaxNoClose* value specifies the number of file control blocks SHARE must not close. In some network configurations, DOS experienced problems when many files where opened using file control blocks that were never closed. By default, if four files are open using file control blocks, and a program tries to open a fifth, SHARE automatically closes one of the files. The *MaxNoClose* value specifies the number of file control blocks SHARE must leave open. The default setting is 0.

File control blocks existed long before disks larger than 32Mb. If you are using DOS 4, the SHARE command provides file control block support for disks larger than 32Mb. For more information on SHARE, see Chapter 30, "Another Look at Disks."

NOTE

Providing Support for Hardware Interrupts

As there are times throughout your day when you need to temporarily put one task aside so you can work on another, the same is true for DOS. When a device such as your disk finishes an I/O operation, the device interrupts DOS to request immediate attention. DOS in turn, puts aside its current task so it can handle the *device interrupt*. Because DOS must be able to later resume the task, DOS stores information about the first task in a memory location called a *stack*. Each time DOS receives an interrupt, DOS allocates one stack from the available stacks. Depending on your computer type and hardware, there may be times when so many interrupts occur in such a short period of time that DOS runs out of stack space. Should this occur, your system will halt, displaying the following error message.

```
Fatal: Internal Stack Failure, System Halted
```

If DOS runs out of stack space in this way, place a STACKS entry in your CONFIG.SYS. The STACKS entry directs DOS to allocate additional memory to support hardware interrupts. The format of the STACKS entry is as follows:

```
STACKS=NumberofStacks,StackSize
```

The only time you need to include the STACKS entry in CONFIG.SYS is when your computer hangs, displaying the "Fatal stacks" error. If this error occurs, experiment with different stack settings, beginning with

```
STACKS=8,512
```

Table 24-5 defines the number of stacks DOS uses by default for different computer types.

Try to keep the stack size as small as possible. The previous entry uses 4,096 bytes $(8 * 512 = 4,096)$.

Installing Memory-Resident Commands

Several DOS commands install memory-resident software. If you are using DOS 4 or later and the FASTOPEN, KEYB, NLSFUNC, or SHARE commands, you should use the CONFIG.SYS INSTALL entry to load the commands to make more efficient use of your computer's memory. The format of the INSTALL entry is as follows.

```
INSTALL=CommandName [optional_parameters]
```

For example, the following entry loads the FASTOPEN command.

```
INSTALL=C:\DOS\FASTOPEN.EXE   C:=50
```

Although the INSTALL entry makes efficient use of your computer's memory, it only supports these four DOS commands. Do not use INSTALL to load other memory-resident commands.

Computer Type	STACKS Entry
IBM PC, PC XT, Portables	0,0
All others	9,128

Table 24-5.   Default STACKS Entries

Making an Enhanced Keyboard Behave as a Conventional Keyboard.

Figure 24-5 illustrates a conventional and an enhanced keyboard.

If you are running an older program, the program may not support several of the enhanced keyboard's keys. Under DOS 4 and later the CONFIG.SYS SWITCHES entry lets you direct DOS to treat the enhanced keyboard as a conventional keyboard.

```
SWITCHES=/K
```

If you are using the ANSI.SYS device driver and SWITCHES /K, install the ANSI.SYS driver using the /K switch.

Changing Physical Drive Parameters

DOS supports two types of devices, character devices and block devices. Devices are classified as one type or the other, depending on how DOS sends or receives data to or from the device. Character devices such as your printer receive information a byte or character at a time. Block devices such as your disk receive information in groups (or blocks) of bytes. Beginning with DOS 3.2, the CONFIG.SYS DRIVPARM entry lets you change one or more block device characteristics. Most users won't

Standard keyboard

Enhanced keyboard

Figure 24-5.   *Standard and enhanced keyboards*

need to use DRIVPARM; however, using DRIVPARM, you may be able to change the characteristics of a drive to read a disk containing data in a unique format.

The format of the DRIVPARM entry is

```
DRIVPARM=/D:DriveNumber [/C] [/F:FormFactor] [/H:NumberofHeads]
    [/N] [/S:SectorsPerTrack] [/T:TracksPerSide] [/I]
```

DriveNumber specifies the drive's physical number from 0 to 25, where 0 corresponds to drive A, 1 to drive B, and 2 to C. /C indicates the drive provides change-line support. Each time you open and close a floppy disk drive, most floppy drives provide a signal to DOS telling DOS to check for a possible disk change. This signal is called a *change line*.

FormFactor is a unique value that specifies the device type. Table 24-6 defines the possible values of the form factor.

NumberofHeads specifies the number of read/write heads. The /N switch indicates the device is nonremovable. *SectorsPerTrack* and *TracksPerSide* specify the disk's sector layout. The /I switch indicates a 3 1/2-inch drive that is compatible with the existing drive controller. Use /I if your computer's ROM-BIOS does not support 3 1/2-inch disks.

If you don't specify a value for one of the DRIVPARM entries, DOS uses the device's existing value.

Customizing Your Command Processor

The file COMMAND.COM contains the DOS command processor, responsible for displaying the DOS prompt and executing the commands you type in. In addition, COMMAND.COM contains the internal DOS commands. By default, when you start your computer, DOS searches your disk's root directory for COMMAND.COM. The CONFIG.SYS SHELL entry lets you specify either a different command processor, or a location other than the root directory for the file. Most users use the SHELL entry to direct DOS to find COMMAND.COM in the DOS directory, so they can delete COMMAND.COM from the root directory. The format of the SHELL entry is as follows:

```
SHELL=\PATHNAME\FILENAME.EXT   [optional_parameters]
```

To direct DOS to locate COMMAND.COM in the DOS directory, the SHELL entry becomes

```
SHELL=C:\DOS\COMMAND.COM  /P
```

You must include the /P switch. If you don't, DOS will not execute the AUTOEXEC.BAT batch file or the DATE and TIME commands.

Form Factor	Device Type
0	160Kb, 180Kb, 320Kb, or 360Kb floppy drive
1	1.2Mb floppy drive
2	720Kb floppy drive
3	8-inch single-density floppy drive
4	8-inch double-density floppy drive
5	Hard drive
6	Tape drive
7	1.44Mb floppy drive
8	Optical drive (DOS 5)
9	2.88Mb floppy drive (DOS 5)

Table 24-6.   DRIVPARM Form Factor Values

You should note that if you use SHELL to locate COMMAND.COM in a directory other than the root, you must also update the COMSPEC environment entry to look for COMMAND.COM in the same location. As you will recall from Chapter 19, "The DOS Environment," DOS divides the command processor into two parts: a resident portion that always remains in RAM, and a transient portion whose contents DOS can overwrite when it executes large commands. When DOS overwrites the transient portion during a command's execution, DOS reloads it when the command ends. DOS uses the COMSPEC environment entry to locate COMMAND.COM so it can reload the transient portion. Depending on your DOS version, you have two ways of setting the COMSPEC entry. First, you can place the following SET command in your AUTOEXEC.BAT file.

```
SET COMSPEC=C:\DOS\COMMAND.COM
```

Depending on your DOS version, you can include COMMAND.COM's directory location in the SHELL entry,

```
SHELL=C:\DOS\COMMAND.COM  C:\DOS  /P
```

and DOS will automatically set the COMSPEC entry for you.

Increasing Your Environment Size

As you learned in Chapter 19, DOS initially allocates 160 bytes of memory for the environment. If you fill the environment, and have not installed memory-resident software, DOS will increase the environment size as needed. If DOS is unable to increase the environment size, it will display the following error message.

```
Out of environment space
```

Using the SHELL entry, you can increase the environment's starting size. The following entry reserves a 512-byte environment.

```
SHELL=C:\DOS\COMMAND.COM  /P  /E:512
```

DOS lets you use the /E switch to specify an environment size from 160 to 32,768 bytes.

Loading Error Messages into Memory

If you are using DOS 4 or later and running DOS from floppy disk, you may want to include the /MSG switch with your SHELL entry, which directs DOS to load its error messages into RAM.

By default, to reduce its memory use, DOS stores many seldom-used error messages on disk. Should DOS need to display one of those messages, DOS simply reads the message from disk. If you are using floppy disks, however, it may not be convenient for DOS to always look to disk to find these messages. The following SHELL entry uses /MSG to load the DOS error messages into RAM.

```
SHELL=COMMAND.COM  /P  /MSG
```

Memory Management Under DOS 5

If you are using DOS 5, the CONFIG.SYS DOS and DEVICEHIGH entries let you make very efficient use of your computer's conventional memory. Before you can fully understand how these entries work, you must understand conventional, reserved, and high memory areas. Chapter 32, "Understanding DOS Memory Management," examines DOS memory management in detail. The CONFIG.SYS DOS and DEVICEHIGH entries are presented at that time.

BREAK

The CONFIG.SYS BREAK entry lets you enable extended CTRL-BREAK checking at system startup. By default, DOS starts with extended CTRL-BREAK checking off. The BREAK command, presented in detail in Chapter 43, lets you turn extended CTRL-BREAK checking on and off as needed. The CONFIG.SYS entry selects the starting mode, on or off.

LASTDRIVE

The CONFIG.SYS LASTDRIVE entry lets you specify the drive letter of the last logical disk drive DOS is to recognize. The FDISK and SUBST commands create logical drives. The following LASTDRIVE entry directs DOS to recognize drives A through J.

```
LASTDRIVE=J
```

FCBS

The CONFIG.SYS FCBS entry provides support for older programs (typically before DOS 2.0) that use file control blocks to perform file input/output operations. If you are not using very old programs on a network or with SHARE active, you won't need to use the FCBS entry. If an older program experiences file errors, set the number of file control blocks to 12, as shown here.

```
FCBS=12
```

STACKS

The CONFIG.SYS STACKS entry directs DOS to allocate additional memory to handle hardware interrupts. The only time you need to use the STACKS entry is when your system hangs and displays the following message.

```
Fatal: Internal Stack Failure, System Halted
```

SUMMARY

Should this error message occur, experiment with the following entry.

```
STACKS=8,512
```

INSTALL

Under DOS 4 or later, the CONFIG.SYS INSTALL entry lets you load the following memory-resident DOS commands KEYB, NLSFUNC, FASTOPEN, and SHARE in a more efficient manner than if the commands were simply called. The following INSTALL command loads the SHARE command.

```
INSTALL=C:\DOS\SHARE.EXE
```

DRIVPARM

The CONFIG.SYS DRIVPARM entry lets you change the characteristics of a block device such as a disk or tape drive. Most users won't require DRIVPARM. The following entry configures a tape drive installed as drive E (physical device number 4).

```
DRIVPARM=/D:4  /H:1  /F:6  /T:20
```

SHELL

The CONFIG.SYS SHELL entry lets you specify the DOS command processor. By default, DOS uses the file COMMAND.COM, which resides in your disk's root directory. To eliminate duplicate copies of COMMAND.COM from their disk, many users use the SHELL entry to direct DOS to locate COMMAND.COM in the DOS directory. The following SHELL entry directs DOS to locate COMMAND.COM in the DOS directory.

```
SHELL=C:\DOS\COMMAND.COM /P
```

If you move COMMAND.COM from the root in this way, you must use the following SET command in your AUTOEXEC.BAT file to set the COMSPEC environment entry.

SUMMARY

```
SET   COMSPEC=C:\DOS\COMMAND.COM
```

The following SHELL entry includes the C:\DOS directory to automatically set the COMSPEC environment entry to the same.

```
SHELL=C:\DOS\COMMAND.COM   C:\DOS   /P
```

Key Terms

Buffer   A storage location. A disk buffer is a storage location in memory into which DOS reads disk sectors.

Read-ahead   The process of reading the next disk sector in anticipation of its use. Under DOS 4 or later, the CONFIG.SYS BUFFERS entry lets you specify the number of read-ahead buffers.

File handle   A unique value DOS 2.0 and higher assign to open files, that identifies the file.

File control block   A collection of information about an open file. Prior to DOS 2.0, DOS used file control blocks (FCBs) to access files. After 2.0, DOS uses file handles.

Stack   A storage location often used to store the computer's status so DOS can handle a device interrupt. Stacks are so named because should several interrupts occur in succession, DOS stacks its status on top of the previous status (like a stack of cafeteria trays). As DOS completes one interrupt, DOS removes the top item (status information) off the stack.

Chapter 25

Using CHKDSK

The more you use your computer, the more information you will store on your hard disk. This information may contain key budget data you produced with your spreadsheet or important reports or memos you created with your word processor. Should your keyboard, printer, or monitor quit working, you can replace it and quickly resume your work. If your disk fails, however, depending on the state of your file backups, you could lose a great deal of information.

Your hard disk is a mechanical device that will eventually wear out. In most cases, DOS will give you hints (in the form of disk read or write error messages) of your disk's impending doom. Rather than sit and wait for such error messages to appear, you can use the CHKDSK (CHecK DiSK) command to examine your disk's current health. If CHKDSK encounters disk errors or inconsistencies, it will display explanatory error messages on your screen. In many cases, CHKDSK can repair the error. In other cases, you may need to back up the files on the disk to floppies, format the disk, and then restore the files. Get into the habit of invoking CHKDSK on a regular basis to examine your disk.

Understanding CHKDSK

CHKDSK is an external DOS command that checks a disk's status. To examine the current drive, invoke CHKDSK as shown here.

```
C:\> CHKDSK   <ENTER>
```

To examine a drive other than the default, include the drive letter in CHKDSK's command line. The following CHKDSK command, for example, examines the floppy disk in drive A.

```
C:\> CHKDSK  A:   <ENTER>
```

Depending on your DOS version, the information CHKDSK displays may differ. Under DOS 3.3, for example, CHKDSK will display something like the following.

```
Volume DOS           created Jul 24, 1990 8:23p

 21309440 bytes total disk space
    53248 bytes in 3 hidden files
    47104 bytes in 12 directories
  4980736 bytes in 363 user files
    55296 bytes in bad sectors
 16173056 bytes available on disk

   655360 bytes total memory
   527488 bytes free
```

Under DOS versions 4 and 5, CHKDSK includes additional information describing the disk's allocation units, as shown here.

```
Volume DOS         created 03-29-1991 10:08a
Volume Serial Number is 1661-AB75

 200065024 bytes total disk space
     81920 bytes in 3 hidden files
    450560 bytes in 105 directories
  41267200 bytes in 1894 user files
 158261248 bytes available on disk

      4096 bytes in each allocation unit
     48844 total allocation units on disk
     38638 available allocation units on disk

    655360 total bytes memory
    510080 bytes free
```

As you learned in Chapter 7, "Preparing Disks for Use," the FORMAT command marks damaged sectors as unusable. If your disk contains damaged sectors, CHKDSK will include a line describing the number of bytes of bad sectors your disk contains.

```
1213952 bytes total disk space
868864 bytes in 27 user files
177152 bytes in bad sectors
167936 bytes available on disk

655360 total bytes memory
559776 bytes free
```

If CHKDSK discovers errors or inconsistencies, it will display a line similar to the following, where *n* is the actual number.

```
Errors found, F parameter not specified
Corrections will not be written to disk

n lost allocation units found in nn chains.
nnnn bytes disk space would be freed
```

If CHKDSK displays this error message, you will need to invoke CHKDSK a second time using the /F switch to correct the error, as discussed later in this chapter.

For now, examine each line of CHKDSK's output in detail.

Volume *VOLNAME*   created *mm-dd-yy HH: MM*

A volume label is a name you assign to your disk when you format the disk or use the LABEL command (discussed in Chapter 30, "Another Look at Disks") . If you have assigned a label to your disk, CHKDSK will display the label name and the date and time you assigned the label, for example:

```
Volume DOS        created 03-29-1991 10:08a
```

Volume Serial Number is *xxxx-xxxx*

If you are using DOS 4 or later, the FORMAT command assigns a unique serial number to your disk. Neither DOS nor any other application actually uses the serial numbers yet. However, for DOS 4 or later, CHKDSK, like DIR, will display the disk's serial number, if it exists.

```
Volume Serial Number is 1661-AB75
```

nnnnnn bytes total disk space

This line tells you the disk's total space, including unusable damaged sectors. When you buy a hard disk, the dealer describes your disk size in megabytes. A megabyte is 1,048,576 bytes. If you have a 30-megabyte disk, for example, you would expect your disk to have 31,457,280 total bytes. As it turns out, hard disks often contain more total bytes than guaranteed, which means it may have a megabyte or more than you expect when you actually format the disk.

nnnn bytes in *n* hidden files

For your computer to start DOS from your hard disk, your disk must contain the two hidden system files discussed in Chapter 7. In Chapter 23, "Advanced File Manipulation," you learned that under DOS 5, the ATTRIB command lets you hide files yourself for privacy and increased protection. This line of output describes the number of hidden files on your disk and the amount of disk space the hidden files consume. If you have assigned a volume name to your disk using FORMAT or the LABEL command (Chapter 30), DOS stores the volume name as a hidden file in the root directory, which may explain why CHKDSK displays three hidden files, as opposed to two.

```
81920 bytes in 3 hidden files
```

nnnnn bytes in *nn* directories

A directory is a list of file names, extensions, sizes, and date and time stamps. DOS stores directories on your disk. This output line tells you the number of directories your disk contains and the amount of disk space DOS must use to store the directory lists. As you will learn in Chapter 33, "How DOS Actually Stores Files," every file entry in a directory requires 32 bytes.

nnnnnn **bytes in** *nnn* **user files**

This line tells you the number of files on your hard disk and the amount of disk space the files consume. This does not include hidden files, whose contents CHKDSK has previously taken into account.

nnnn **bytes in bad sectors**

The FORMAT command marks damaged sectors as unusable to prevent DOS from trying to store information in the damaged disk locations. For older hard disks, bad sectors consuming 1 to 2 percent of the disk's space were not uncommon. Newer disks, however, typically format with no damaged sectors. If your disk's damaged sectors are less than 1 to 2 percent of your total space, don't be too concerned.

nnnnnn **bytes available on disk**

This line tells you the amount of disk space still available for use on your disk. If you subtract from the total disk space the number of bytes used for hidden files, directories, user files, and damaged sectors, the result should equal the amount of available disk space.

nnnnnn **total bytes memory**

As you know, your computer uses its electronic memory to run programs, and uses your disk to store information from one user session to the next. This line describes the amount of conventional electronic memory your computer contains. Chapter 32, "Understanding DOS Memory Management," examines the different memory types: conventional, extended, and expanded memory, for example. CHKDSK does not display statistics for these memory types. If you are using DOS 4 or later, you can display such information using the MEM command.

nnnnnn **bytes free**

This line tells you how much of your computer's electronic memory is available for program use. As you know, each time you start your computer, it loads DOS from disk into its electronic memory. Subtracting this line's value from the total memory tells you how much memory DOS and any other memory-resident programs you have loaded consume. Many applications will specify a minimum amount of memory they need to run. Using CHKDSK, you can ensure that you have enough available memory.

nnnn bytes in each allocation unit

If you are using DOS 4 or later, CHKDSK displays information about your disk's allocation units (clusters). As discussed in Chapter 7, "Preparing Disks for Use," FORMAT first divides your disk into concentric tracks, then further divides each track into pie-shaped storage units called sectors, as illustrated here:

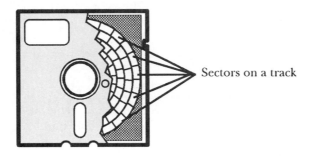

Sectors on a track

DOS stores information on your disk by recording the information in the disk sectors. For simplicity, users normally assume DOS stores a file's contents on disk a sector at a time. Actually, however, for performance and efficiency reasons, DOS reserves space for your files using groups of connected sectors called allocation units or clusters. Depending on your disk size, the number of sectors that make up an allocation unit will differ. Typically, most hard disks will use either four or eight sectors per allocation unit.

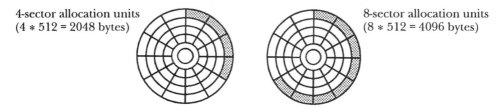

4-sector allocation units
(4 * 512 = 2048 bytes)

8-sector allocation units
(8 * 512 = 4096 bytes)

An allocation unit is the smallest amount of disk space DOS can reserve for a file. Depending on your file size, DOS may need to reserve one allocation unit or several. In most cases, a portion of the allocation unit remains unused. Figure 25-1 illustrates how DOS would store three files of 1, 1,024, and 2,048 bytes, respectively. Note the amount of unused space in each allocation unit.

Figure 25-1 illustrates that no matter how small your file size appears in the directory listing, DOS must still allocate a cluster of disk space to store the file. If you create several very small files, much of the allocation unit is unused. In Chapter

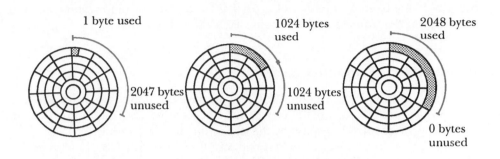

Figure 25-1.   Most files only use a portion of the allocation unit

44 you will better understand why DOS uses allocation units when you examine disk fragmentation. For now, keep in mind that creating several small files actually uses up more disk space than a large file containing the same information.

If your file size exceeds the size of an allocation unit, DOS reserves the number of allocation units required. Figure 25-2 illustrates how DOS might store two larger files.

If you are using DOS 4 or later, CHKDSK displays the disk's cluster size. If you are not using version 4, invoke either CHKDSK or DIR and note the amount of available disk space. Next, create a small file containing only a byte or two. Use DIR or CHKDSK once again to note the amount of available disk space. Rather than consuming the number of bytes listed in the file's directory listing, DOS has reserved

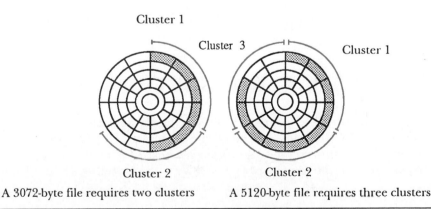

A 3072-byte file requires two clusters   A 5120-byte file requires three clusters

Figure 25-2.   DOS reserves the number of allocation units necessary

the number of bytes in an allocation unit. By subtracting the current number of bytes available from the number of bytes that were available before you created the file, you can determine the size of your disk's allocation units.

nnnn total allocation units on disk

If you are using DOS 4 or later, CHKDSK displays the total number of allocation units on your disk. If you are not using DOS 4 or later, you can determine this value by dividing your total disk space by the size of the allocation unit.

The allocation unit is the smallest amount of disk space DOS can allocate for a file. As a result, as your total disk space defines the size and number of files you can create on your disk, the total number of allocation units also defines the maximum number of files. For example, assume you have a 20 Mb hard disk, with 10,405 allocation units. If you wanted to store only files containing a single byte, your disk size would lead you to believe your disk can store 20 million 1-byte files. However, because each file requires a minimum of one allocation unit, the maximum number of 1-byte files the 20 Mb disk can store is 10,405, which happens to match the total number of disk allocation units.

nnnn available allocation units on disk

Again under DOS 4 or later, CHKDSK displays the number of available allocation units. If you are not using DOS 4 or later, you can determine this value by dividing your available disk space by your disk's allocation unit size.

As you work with DOS files, pay close attention to the amount of available space on your disk. Assume for example, you copy files to a floppy disk until the disk fills. If you perform DIR commands between each file copy, you will find the disk never has 5, 10, or 50 bytes of available disk space. Instead, the amount of available space is always a multiple of the allocation unit size: 2,048, 4,096, and so on. By remembering DOS always reserves disk space in allocation units, you can understand why copying a 5-byte file to a floppy disk that shows 2,048 bytes free fills the disk.

Using CHKDSK to Correct Disk Errors

CHKDSK examines your disk's current health and displays a summary of its findings on your screen. If CHKDSK encounters one or more of three specific errors, CHKDSK will display the error messages discussed next. Should one of the following error messages occur, you must invoke CHKDSK a second time, using the /F switch:

```
C:\> CHKDSK  /F   <ENTER>
```

After CHKDSK displays the error messages, CHKDSK will either automatically correct the condition or display a prompt asking you if you want to correct the error. Type **Y** and press ENTER to correct the error.

nnn lost allocation units found in *n* chains.
Convert lost chains to files (Y/N)?

You should only turn your computer off when DOS is displaying its prompt. Many applications, such as your word processor or spreadsheet, store information on disk. If you turn off your computer while a program is storing information to disk or has files open, only a portion of the information may actually get recorded, leaving your disk in an inconsistent state. A *lost cluster* (allocation unit) is information stored on your disk that does not belong to a file. Lost clusters typically occur when you turn off your computer while a program is running.

When CHKDSK encounters lost clusters, CHKDSK gives you a chance to store the clusters in files you can later edit using your word processor or the DOS editor. In some cases, the files may contain useful information. In most cases, however, you will simply delete the files using DEL to free up the disk space the lost clusters consumed.

When you convert lost clusters to files, CHKDSK creates the files in your root directory using the names FILE0000.CHK, FILE0001.CHK, and so on. The number of files CHKDSK creates depends on the number of *chains* of lost clusters. If CHKDSK finds one chain, CHKDSK will create one file. If CHKDSK encounters two chains, CHKDSK will create two files, and so on.

CHKDSK only converts lost clusters to files when you use the /F switch.

NOTE

After the files exist, select the root directory and use the TYPE command to display the file's contents:

```
C:\> TYPE  FILE0000.CHK  <ENTER>
```

If the file contains useful information, rename the file and store it in the proper directory. If the file contains unrecognizable characters, delete the file with DEL.

If you only turn off your computer from the DOS prompt, you greatly reduce the chance of lost clusters.

REMEMBER

FILENAME.EXT allocation error, size adjusted

As you know, each file's directory entry tracks the file's size in bytes. By dividing the file's size by the size of your disk's allocation units you can determine the number of disk allocation units the file requires. CHKDSK compares each file's size to the number of allocation units it finds for the file. In most cases, CHKDSK will find the number of allocation units is correct. However, if you have turned off your computer while a program is running, or used the CTRL-C keyboard combination to end a program that writes information to disk, CHKDSK may find an inconsistency. When this occurs, CHKDSK changes the file's directory entry size to match the number of allocation units found.

This error message normally implies you have lost data. If you can display the file's contents using TYPE or your word processor, do so and determine the amount of information lost. If the file contains a command, do not execute it. As you'll recall, a program is a list of instructions your computer executes. If the program now contains too few or too many instructions, running the program may destroy other information on disk. Copy the command from your original floppy or restore the file from your disk backups, as discussed in Chapter 22, "Protecting Your Files with BACKUP and RESTORE."

FILENAME.EXT is cross linked on allocation unit *nn*

DOS stores files on your disk using chains of clusters (allocation units). In Chapter 33 you will learn DOS uses a special table called the file allocation table or FAT to locate each file's clusters. As it examines your disk, CHKDSK makes sure two files aren't trying to use the same cluster. When two or more files think they own the same cluster, the files are *cross-linked*. Like before, cross-linked files typically occur when you turn off your computer when a program is running, or when you end a program that writes to disk by using the CTRL-C key combination.

Figure 25-3 illustrates two files, each containing three clusters. The figure includes a simple file allocation table that shows each file's clusters. For simplicity, the figure uses two-sector clusters.

Assume you were editing file ONE and you end the editing session using CTRL-C. As a result, DOS incorrectly updates the file allocation table, cross-linking the files on cluster 3, as shown in Figure 25-4.

In this case, file ONE thinks it owns clusters 2, 3, 4, and 7. Likewise, file TWO thinks it owns clusters 3, 4, and 7. Clusters 5 and 6 have become lost clusters, not belonging to any file. If you edit file ONE, the file will contain part of its original contents and part of file TWO's contents. Worse yet, if you delete file ONE, you will also delete part of file TWO. As you can see, cross-linked files are a nightmare.

The easiest way to correct cross-linked files is to invoke CHKDSK with the /F switch to first recover the lost clusters. Next, if you have backup copies of both files, delete the current copies and restore the current backups. If you don't have backup

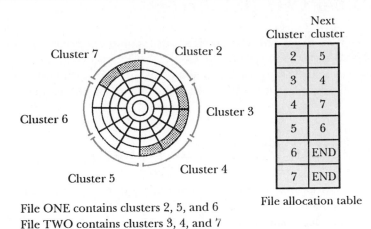

File ONE contains clusters 2, 5, and 6
File TWO contains clusters 3, 4, and 7

Figure 25-3. *Two files, each containing three clusters*

copies, turn to the Advanced Concepts section—you may still be able to rebuild the original files.

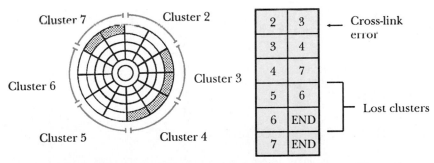

File ONE, due to cross-link, owns clusters 2, 3, 4, and 7
File TWO originally owned clusters 3, 4, and 7

Figure 25-4. *Files cross-linked on cluster 3*

Handling Other CHKDSK Errors

The previous section discussed CHKDSK's most common error messages. If CHKDSK displays other errors, turn to the Command Reference at the end of this book to find the corrective steps. By just making sure you turn off your computer only from the DOS prompt, you greatly reduce the chance of disk errors.

Using CHKDSK to Display File Names

To perform its processing, CHKDSK must read every directory on your disk. By invoking CHKDSK with the /V switch, you can direct CHKDSK to display the name of every file on your disk, as shown here.

```
C:\> CHKDSK   /V   <ENTER>

Volume DOS          created 03-29-1991 10:08a
Volume Serial Number is 1661-AB75
Directory C:\
C:\IO.SYS
C:\MSDOS.SYS
C:\COMMAND.COM
Directory C:\DOS
C:\DOS\EGA.SYS
C:\DOS\DISPLAY.SYS
C:\DOS\FORMAT.COM
C:\DOS\ANSI.SYS
```

Depending on your DOS version, you now have several ways to list all the files on your disk: DIR, TREE, ATTRIB, and CHKDSK.

Hands On

Invoke CHKDSK from the DOS prompt.

```
C:\> CHKDSK   <ENTER>
```

If you have not used CHKDSK before, don't be surprised if CHKDSK displays error messages about lost clusters. If these error messages occur, invoke CHKDSK again using the /F switch.

```
C:\> CHKDSK  /F   <ENTER>
```

Type **Y** when CHKDSK asks you if it should convert the lost cluster chains to files.

If you are using DOS 4 or later, note the size of your disk's allocation unit. Remember, every time you create a small file on your disk, CHKDSK reserves the number of bytes required for an allocation unit, not the actual file size.

Last, invoke CHKDSK using the /V switch to display the names of all the files on your disk.

```
C:\> CHKDSK  /V   <ENTER>
```

Review

1. What is an allocation unit?

2. When should you invoke CHKDSK?

3. What is the purpose of CHKDSK's /F switch?

4. What is a lost cluster? How do you correct lost clusters?

5. What is a cross-linked file? How do you correct cross-linked files?

Answers

1. An allocation unit is a collection of consecutive sectors. An allocation unit (sometimes called a disk cluster) defines the smallest amount of disk space DOS can allocate for a file.

2. You should invoke CHKDSK on a regular basis to examine your disk's current health. In fact, many users invoke CHKDSK from their AUTOEXEC.BAT to ensure CHKDSK executes on a daily basis.

3. If CHKDSK encounters errors it can correct, the /F switch directs CHKDSK to fix the errors. If you don't include the /F switch in the CHKDSK command line, CHKDSK will not correct the disk errors, regardless of how you respond to the various CHKDSK prompts.

4. DOS stores a file's information in one or more allocation units or clusters. A lost cluster is a cluster of information stored on your disk that does not belong to a file. Lost clusters typically occur when you turn off your computer while a program is running. If CHKDSK encounters lost clusters, CHKDSK will display a message showing the total number of allocation units in lost chains and the number of lost chains. Invoke CHKDSK with the /F switch to convert the lost clusters into files. CHKDSK will store each cluster chain in a root directory file with the name FILE*nnnn*.CHK (for example, FILE0000.CHK and FILE0001.CHK). Use TYPE or your word processor to display each file's contents. If the file contains useful information, rename the file and store the file in the proper directory. If the file contains unrecognizable characters, delete the file to free up the disk space the lost clusters consumed.

5. Like lost clusters, cross-linked files may occur when you turn off your computer while a program is running, or use the CTRL-BREAK keyboard combination to end a program that is writing to disk. The best way to correct two cross-linked files is to delete the files and restore your backup copies of the files. If backup copies are unavailable, and both cross-linked files contain text that you can easily distinguish, you may be able to rebuild the original files as discussed in the Advanced Concepts section.

Advanced Concepts

Chapter 33, "How DOS Actually Stores Files," examines in detail how DOS stores files on your disk. As you read through Chapter 33, consider the different steps CHKDSK actually performs, such as searching the file allocation table for clusters marked invalid by FORMAT, for lost clusters that don't belong to a file, and for cross-linked files. To perform this process CHKDSK must read each file's directory entry, locate the file's corresponding clusters in the file allocation table, and then compare the two for consistency. Considering your disk may contain a very large number of files, CHKDSK performs a lot of work in a very short time period.

How DOS Knows the Allocation Unit Size

Depending on your disk type, the size of your disk's allocation unit will differ. The question you should ask yourself is how DOS knows the correct allocation unit size. As discussed in Chapter 7, "Preparing Disks for Use," every time you format a disk, FORMAT uses the disk's first sector as a boot record. If you format the disk as bootable, the boot record contains a small program that begins the DOS startup process. If the disk is not bootable, the boot record contains a small program responsible for the following error message.

```
Non-System disk or disk error
Replace and strike any key when ready
```

In addition to these programs, your disk's boot record contains information about the disk, such as the sector size, total number of sectors, and the size of each disk allocation unit, as shown in Figure 25-5.

Using the boot record, DOS knows the disk's specifics.

Rebuilding Cross-Linked Files

Two files become cross-linked when one of the files thinks it owns one or more clusters actually owned by the other. The most common cause of cross-linked files is turning off your computer in the middle of a command, or using CTRL-C to end

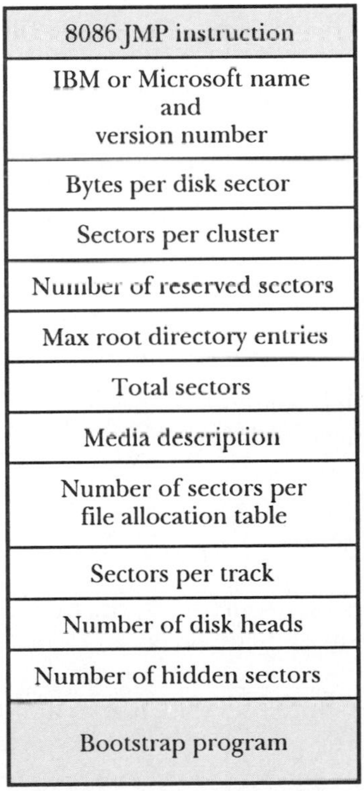

| 8086 JMP instruction |
| IBM or Microsoft name and version number |
| Bytes per disk sector |
| Sectors per cluster |
| Number of reserved sectors |
| Max root directory entries |
| Total sectors |
| Media description |
| Number of sectors per file allocation table |
| Sectors per track |
| Number of disk heads |
| Number of hidden sectors |
| Bootstrap program |

Figure 25-5.   Entries in the DOS boot record

a command that is writing to disk. Figure 25-4 illustrates two cross-linked files. The best way to correct cross-linked files is to delete the files and restore backup copies. If backup copies aren't available, and the files contain only text, you can rebuild the files by following the steps presented here.

First, when two files become cross-linked, you normally also have lost clusters. Using the /F switch, invoke CHKDSK to recover the lost clusters, as previously discussed.

Second, copy the currently cross-linked files to a new directory or floppy disk. Because DOS allocates unique clusters for the file copies, the files no longer share clusters. However, both of the new files will contain all the information in the cross-linked clusters. One file will be correct, one file will have the wrong clusters.

Next, delete the cross-linked files. Using the TYPE command or your word processor, determine which of the two new files contains the correct information and copy that file back to the current directory. Using your word processor or the DOS editor, edit the second file, removing the invalid information the file contains due to the previous cross-link.

Last, using your word processor, insert the previously lost clusters back into the file. The file is now correct, and you can copy its contents back to the current directory.

Delete the file FILE000n.CHK that contained the lost clusters, as well as the copies of the files you created in step 2. To rebuild files with cross-linked clusters, each file's contents must contain text you can easily distinguish. If you tried to edit two cross-linked command files, for example, each file would contain meaningless characters that prevent you from determining which information to delete and which information to add. For cross-linked command files, you have to rely on your backup copies.

Key Terms

Allocation unit   The smallest amount of disk space DOS can allocate for a file. Allocation unit sizes are multiples of your disk sector size, such as 512, 1,024, 2,048, or 4,096 bytes.

Cluster   A disk allocation unit.

Lost clusters   Disk clusters that contain information, but do not belong to a DOS file. Lost clusters are a result of a disk error.

Cross-linked files   Two or more files that, due to a disk error, think they own the same cluster or clusters.

Chapter 26

DOS Pretender Commands

Throughout this book you have used your hard disk drive C, the floppy drive A, and possibly drive B if your computer has two floppy disks. Because these disk drives physically connect to your computer, they are physical drives. This chapter examines the DOS *pretender commands* ASSIGN, SUBST, and JOIN. The commands are "pretenders" because they trick DOS into thinking one disk drive is another, a directory is actually a disk drive, or a disk drive is actually a directory.

DOS provides pretender commands to help you run older programs that only know about drives A and B, or older programs that don't support DOS subdirectories. Pretender commands also let you define *logical disk drives.* Like physical drives, you access a logical drive using a drive letter and colon. Unlike physical drives you can see and touch, logical drives correspond to a DOS directory or, in the case of RAM drives, an electronic location. For example, the logical drive E may correspond to the directory \WP\LETTERS. Once you define the logical drive E, you can use the drive letter instead of typing the entire directory name.

Disk Drive Identity Swapping with ASSIGN

The original IBM PC came with the floppy disk drives A and B. As such, many older applications were written to only use drive A or B. When the IBM PC XT first made hard disks available, many of these programs would not run on the hard disk. To help users run these older programs on their hard disk, DOS introduced the ASSIGN command. ASSIGN is an external command that lets you trick DOS into thinking one disk drive is another. Assuming a program only looks for its files on drive A, you can instruct DOS to direct all references for drive A to drive C with the following statement.

```
C:\> ASSIGN  A=C  <ENTER>
```

After you issue this command, DOS automatically uses drive C when a command references drive A. If the older program tries to open a file on drive A, DOS automatically uses drive C instead. For example, assume you issue the following DIR command.

```
C:\> DIR  A:  <ENTER>
```

Rather than displaying the files on the disk in drive A, DOS displays the files on drive C.

To remove the drive assignment, invoke ASSIGN without a command line.

```
C:\> ASSIGN  <ENTER>
```

A directory of drive A will now list the files on drive A as before.

ASSIGN lets you perform multiple drive assignments at one time. The following command, for example, assigns both floppy drives A and B to drive C.

```
C:\> ASSIGN  A=C  B=C  <ENTER>
```

As before, you remove the assignments by issuing any other assign command.

If you have a program that only looks to drive A for its files, your command sequence would be the following.

1. Use ASSIGN to assign drive A to drive C.

2. Run the program.

3. Use ASSIGN to remove the drive assignment.

If you are using DOS 5, you can use the /STATUS switch to display the current disk assignments as follows.

```
C:\> ASSIGN  /STATUS  <ENTER>
Original A: set to C:
```

Many DOS commands that perform low-level disk operations do not support logical disk drives and drive reassignments. Table 26-1 lists the commands you SHOULD NOT use with ASSIGN, SUBST, and JOIN. If you are using DOS 3.1 or later, Microsoft recommends that you use the SUBST command discussed next to perform your disk drive reassignments.

NOTE

Substituting a Drive Letter for a Directory Name with SUBST

Just as many older software programs didn't support disk drives other than A or B, many older programs didn't support DOS subdirectories. If you tried to use a directory path with such a program, the program would display an error message such as "File not found" or "Invalid file name." To let you use directories with such programs, DOS 3.1 introduced the SUBST command. SUBST is an external DOS command that lets you substitute a logical disk drive letter for a directory path.

The following command substitutes the logical drive letter E for the DOS directory.

```
C:\> SUBST  E:  C:\DOS  <ENTER>
```

Once you define a logical drive, you can use its drive letter as you would any disk drive. The following command, then, lists the files on drive E.

```
C:\> DIR  E:  <ENTER>
```

BACKUP	CHKDSK	DISKCOMP	DISKCOPY
FDISK	FORMAT	LABEL	MIRROR
RECOVER	RESTORE	SYS	UNFORMAT
UNDELETE			

Table 26-1. *Do Not Use These DOS Commands with ASSIGN, SUBST, or JOIN*

When DOS encounters the logical drive letter in this case, it automatically substitutes the corresponding directory path, and displays the files in the DOS directory.

```
C:\> DIR  E:  <ENTER>

 Volume in drive E is DOS
 Volume Serial Number is 1661-AB75
 Directory of E:\

 .               <DIR>       10-16-90    4:44p
 ..              <DIR>       10-16-90    4:44p
 EGA      SYS       4885 12-13-90    4:09a
 DISPLAY  SYS      15682 12-13-90    4:09a
 FORMAT   COM      32285 12-13-90    4:09a
 :        :          :        :         :
 PRINTER  SYS      18760 12-13-90    4:09a
 SUBST    EXE      18350 12-13-90    4:09a
 COMMAND  COM      46246 12-13-90    4:09a
        90 file(s)     2236185 bytes
                     15597120 bytes free
```

Drive E is called a logical disk because it does not physically exist inside your computer, only logically. Instead, DOS lets you use the logical disk, pretending such a drive exists.

If you invoke SUBST without a command line, SUBST will display the current drive substitutions.

```
C:\> SUBST  <ENTER>
E: => C:\DOS
```

If you select drive E as the current drive, you select the substituted directory as the current directory.

To remove a substitution, invoke SUBST with the logical drive letter and the /D switch, as shown here.

```
C:\> SUBST  E:  /D  <ENTER>
```

SUBST will not let you remove a drive substitution if the substituted drive is the current drive.

By default, drive E is the last drive letter DOS lets you use. If you need to assign a drive *letter greater than E, you must use the CONFIG.SYS LASTDRIVE entry discussed in Chapter 24, "Customizing Your System with CONFIG.SYS".*   **NOTE**

Although the DOS developers intended for SUBST to help users run programs that don't support directories, users commonly use SUBST to abbreviate long directory names.

Abbreviating Long Directory Names with SUBST

As you create new directories to organize your files, your directory tree will grow. Assume, for example, you constantly switch between the directories \WP\LETTERS\BUSINESS and \123\EXPENSES\1STQTR. You can see that repeatedly typing the long directory path names could become quite frustrating. Using SUBST, however, you can first assign the directory \WP\LETTERS\BUSINESS to drive E, as shown here.

```
C:\> SUBST  E:  \WP\LETTERS\BUSINESS  <ENTER>
```

Next, you can substitute drive F for the directory \123\EXPENSES\1STQTR.

```
C:\> SUBST  F:  \123\EXPENSES\1STQTR  <ENTER>
```

With your directories labeled as drives E and F, you can quickly switch between the two directories.

```
C:\> E:  <ENTER>
E:\> F:  <ENTER>
F:\>
```

Although you should only include directories most likely to include your external commands within the command path, many users often push PATH's 122-character limit. By assigning logical disk drive letters to the longer PATH entries, you can reduce your current path length, letting you add entries. When DOS examines the command path, DOS automatically substitutes the correct directory path for each drive letter. Remember, however, the more directories you include in your command path, the more time DOS must spend searching the directories.

As before, do not use SUBST with the DOS commands listed in Table 26-1.

Making DOS Think a Drive Is a Directory with JOIN

Between the ASSIGN, SUBST, and JOIN commands, users typically have the most difficulty understanding JOIN. The JOIN command is essentially the opposite of SUBST. JOIN lets you trick DOS into thinking a disk drive is a directory on the current disk.

To understand why you would want to join a drive to your directory tree, consider the DOSSHELL program. (Chapters 39 through 42 examine the DOS 4 and DOS 5 shells in detail.) The DOSSHELL provides a menu-driven interface to your directory structure and DOS commands. Each time you change the current drive, DOSSHELL reads all the files and directories on the selected disk and displays a directory tree. If you change drives on a regular basis, this constant reading of the directory structure not only becomes frustrating, but also consumes a lot of time. When you change directories, however, DOSSHELL doesn't read the directory tree.

Using the JOIN command, you can convince DOS that another commonly used drive is a directory, and can avoid the constant reading of the directory tree.

To use JOIN, you must first create an empty directory on your hard disk to which you will join the drive. In this case, you will join drive A to the directory A_DRIVE. Create the directory using MKDIR.

```
C:\> MKDIR  \A_DRIVE   <ENTER>
```

Next, use the following JOIN command to trick DOS into thinking drive A is actually the directory A_DRIVE.

```
C:\> JOIN  A:  \A_DRIVE   <ENTER>
```

Place a floppy disk that contains files in drive A. Next, issue the following DIR command.

```
C:\> DIR  \A_DRIVE   <ENTER>
```

Using the directory A_DRIVE, DOS will display the files on the floppy disk in drive A. Using CHDIR, you can select A_DRIVE as the current directory.

```
C:\> CHDIR  \A_DRIVE   <ENTER>
C:\A_DRIVE>
```

If you invoke the TREE command, it will include the directory A_DRIVE, as well as the files in the directory.

```
C:\> TREE   C:\   /F   <ENTER>
```

As you can see, DOS treats the disk in drive A as if the disk is part of the directory tree on drive C.

If you invoke JOIN without a command line, JOIN will display the drives it has joined, as well as the corresponding directories.

```
C:\> JOIN   <ENTER>
A: => C:\A_DRIVE
```

To remove the drive from the directory tree, invoke JOIN with the drive letter and /D switch.

```
C:\> JOIN   A:   /D   <ENTER>
```

Although you may not use JOIN for commands you issue from the DOS prompt, JOIN may improve the performance of different shell programs. As before, do not use JOIN with the DOS commands listed in Table 26-1.

Hands On

Place a floppy disk containing files in drive A. Issue the following DIR command to display the disk's contents.

```
C:\> DIR   A:   <ENTER>
```

Next, issue the following ASSIGN command directing DOS to route all references from drive A to drive C, and then reissue the DIR command.

```
C:\> ASSIGN   A=C   <ENTER>
C:\> DIR   A:   <ENTER>
```

ASSIGN

The ASSIGN command lets you redirect DOS from one disk drive to another. Some older programs only look for files on drive A or B. Using ASSIGN, you can trick these programs into using your hard disk. The following command directs DOS to use drive C for all references to drive A.

```
C:\> ASSIGN  A=C  <ENTER>
```

After you run the program, invoke ASSIGN without a command line to remove the drive assignments.

SUBST

The SUBST command was originally introduced to help you run older programs that don't support directories. SUBST lets you substitute a logical drive letter for a directory path. Today, most users use SUBST to abbreviate long directory names. The following command, for example, abbreviates a directory path with the logical drive letter E.

```
C:\> SUBST  E:  \WP\BUSINESS\MEMOS  <ENTER>
```

After you define the logical drive, you can use the drive letter in your commands as you would any disk drive. To create logical drives beyond the default drive letter E, such as drives F, G, and H, you must include a LASTDRIVE entry in your CONFIG.SYS file, as discussed in Chapter 24.

JOIN

The JOIN command lets you trick DOS into thinking another disk drive is actually a directory in your directory tree. Many shell programs perform extra processing when you change disk drives that the programs don't perform when you change directories. By using JOIN to convince DOS another drive is actually a directory, you can improve the shell's performance. You must join a disk drive to an empty directory. The following command, for example, joins drive A to the empty directory A_DRIVE.

SUMMARY

```
C:\> JOIN  A:  \A_DRIVE  <ENTER>
```

After you join a disk to a directory, you can access the files the disk contains using standard directory operations.

In this case, rather than displaying the files on drive A, DOS displays the files on drive C. If you are using DOS 5, invoke ASSIGN with the /STATUS switch.

```
C:\> ASSIGN  /STATUS  <ENTER>
```

Remove the drive assignment by invoking ASSIGN without a command line.

```
C:\> ASSIGN  <ENTER>
```

A directory listing of drive A displays, once again, the files on the floppy disk.

Next, issue the following SUBST command to substitute the logical drive E for the DOS directory.

```
C:\> SUBST  E:  \DOS  <ENTER>
```

Use the following DIR command to display a directory listing for drive E.

```
C:\> DIR  E:  <ENTER>
```

As you will see, DOS automatically substitutes the path C:\DOS for drive E, displaying your DOS files. Select drive E as the current drive and repeat the directory command.

```
C:\> E:  <ENTER>
E:\> DIR  <ENTER>
```

As you can see, DOS lets you use logical drives as you would any disk drive. Select drive C as the default and invoke SUBST to display the current substitutions.

```
E:\> C:   <ENTER>
C:\> SUBST   <ENTER>
```

Use the SUBST /D switch to remove the drive substitution.

```
C:\> SUBST   E:   /D   <ENTER>
```

Next, create the directory A_DRIVE using MKDIR.

```
C:\> MKDIR   \A_DRIVE   <ENTER>
```

Use the following JOIN command to attach the disk in drive A to the current directory tree.

```
C:\> JOIN   A:   \A_DRIVE   <ENTER>
```

Use the following DIR command to display the files on the disk in drive A.

```
C:\> DIR   \A_DRIVE   <ENTER>
```

Use CHDIR to select A_DRIVE as the current directory, and issue a DIR command.

```
C:\> CHDIR   \A_DRIVE   <ENTER>
C:\A_DRIVE> DIR   <ENTER>
```

Select the root directory as the current directory and issue the following TREE command.

```
C:\A_DRIVE> CHDIR   \   <ENTER>
C:\> TREE   /F   <ENTER>
```

As you can see, once you join a disk to a directory, you can access the disk's files using standard directory commands. Invoke JOIN without a command line to display the current joins.

```
C:\> JOIN   <ENTER>
```

Invoke JOIN using the /D switch to remove the directory join.

```
C:\> JOIN   A:   /D   <ENTER>
```

Last, using RMDIR, remove the directory A_DRIVE as shown.

```
C:\> RMDIR   \A_DRIVE   <ENTER>
```

Review

1. What is a logical disk drive?

2. What is a pretender command?

3. When would you use the ASSIGN command?

4. When would you use the SUBST command?

5. When would you use the JOIN command?

Answers

1. A logical disk drive is a drive that does not physically exist on your system, but that you can reference in your DOS commands. The SUBST command creates logical drives that correspond to existing directories. When you reference the logical drive letter, DOS automatically substitutes the corresponding directory name.

2. A pretender command is a command that tricks DOS into thinking one disk drive is another, a drive letter is actually a subdirectory, and a disk drive actually resides as a directory in the current directory tree. DOS provides three pretender commands: ASSIGN, SUBST, and JOIN.

3. Some very old software programs only let you use the floppy disk drives A and B. When you try to run these programs from your hard disk, the programs

still look for their data files on the floppy drive. The ASSIGN command lets you trick DOS into using the hard disk instead of the floppy drives.

4. Some older software programs do not support directory path names, but do let you include a drive letter before a file name (such as E:FILENAME.EXT). Using the SUBST command, you can trick the program into using the directory. When DOS encounters the logical disk drive, DOS will automatically substitute the correct directory path name. Most users, however, use SUBST to abbreviate long directory names.

5. Many menu-driven shell programs display a directory tree for the current disk letting you select files or directories from the tree using your keyboard or mouse. When you use the shell program to change default drives, the shell program will read the new drive's directory tree. Depending on the number of files on your disks and the number of times you change drives, this constant reading and rereading of directory trees can become quite tiresome. When you use these shell programs to change directories, however, the shell programs do not reread the directory tree. Using the JOIN command, you can trick DOS into thinking a disk drive is actually a directory in the current directory tree. In this way, you can reduce much of the extra processing shell programs perform.

Advanced Concepts

As you have learned, the SUBST command lets you create logical disk drives. If your computer only has a single floppy drive, DOS automatically creates a logical drive B to help you perform dual-floppy-disk commands.

By default, DOS assigns the drive letter A to your single floppy. However, if you use the drive letter B, in a DIR command for instance, DOS will prompt you to remove the current floppy disk and to insert the floppy disk you want to use in drive B, as shown here.

```
Insert diskette for drive B:
and press any key when ready.
```

DOS now considers your floppy disk as drive B until you explicitly reference drive A once again. At that time, DOS will prompt you to insert the disk you want to use for drive A.

```
Insert diskette for drive A:
and press any key when ready
```

Using the logical drive B, you may be able to successfully run an older program that wants to use both drives, although your computer only has a single floppy.

Key Terms

Logical disk drive   A disk drive that does not physically exist in your computer but that you define using the SUBST command. Logical drives help you abbreviate path names.

Pretender command   The name given to the ASSIGN, SUBST, and JOIN commands because they make DOS pretend that one disk is another, a drive letter is a directory name, or a drive exists as a directory on the current disk.

Chapter 27

DOSKEY and DOS 5 Macros

The discussion throughout the book to this point has related to all versions of DOS. For some commands, different DOS versions provided additional switches that improved the command's capabilities. This chapter and Chapter 28, "DOS 5 Crisis Prevention," present commands that are only available under DOS 5. If you are not using DOS 5, take a look at these chapters to get a feel for the advances DOS is making. This chapter presents the DOS 5 DOSKEY command, which remembers each command you enter, so you can quickly repeat them. In addition, DOSKEY lets you define single-line *macros*, which behave like one-line batch files, letting you abbreviate commonly used commands. Unlike DOS batch files stored on disk, DOSKEY macros reside in your computer's fast electronic memory, which means they execute very quickly.

Using DOSKEY to Recall Commands

In Chapter 5, "Understanding Your Keyboard," you learned how to quickly repeat the previous command by pressing the F3 function key. As you learned, each time you execute a command, DOS stores the command in a buffer you can access with the function keys F1 through F4. Although this *previous-command buffer* is convenient, it only lets DOS keep track of the one previous command. The DOS 5 DOSKEY command lets DOS track many commands. The actual number of commands

DOSKEY can track depends on the amount of memory you let DOSKEY use and the length (in characters) of the commands you execute.

DOSKEY is an external DOS command. The first time you execute the DOSKEY command, DOSKEY loads memory-resident software into your computer's memory. This software remains present in memory until you turn off your computer or restart DOS. When invoked from the DOS prompt, DOSKEY will display the following message, informing you that it has loaded its memory-resident software.

```
C:\> DOSKEY   <ENTER>
DOSKey installed.
```

By default, DOSKEY allocates 512 bytes of memory for a command buffer. Assuming the average length of your DOS commands is 10 characters, DOSKEY will let you track approximately the previous 50 DOS commands. Should your DOSKEY buffer fill, DOSKEY will discard the oldest command in the buffer to make room for the new command.

Invoke the DATE, TIME, VER, and CLS commands. Using the UP ARROW and DOWN ARROW keys, you can cycle through your list of previous commands. UP ARROW directs DOSKEY to display the command you invoked immediately before the command now displayed. Likewise, DOWN ARROW directs DOSKEY to display the command you invoked immediately after the command being displayed. When no more commands precede or follow the command now displayed, DOSKEY ignores the arrow keys.

In addition to cycling through your previous command list with UP ARROW and DOWN ARROW, DOSKEY lets you use the PGUP and PGDN keys. PGUP directs DOSKEY to display the oldest command in the previous-command buffer, and PGDN directs DOSKEY to display your most recently used command. Table 27-1 summarizes how DOSKEY uses these keys to traverse the previous-command buffer.

Using the arrow keys described in Table 27-1, you can cycle through your list of previous commands. When you only need to go back a few commands, using the arrows is very convenient.

As the number of commands in DOSKEY's previous-command buffer becomes large, locating the desired command with the arrow keys can consume more and more time. Fortunately, DOSKEY provides several faster ways to locate a command.

Key	Function
UP ARROW	Displays the command invoked before command now displayed
DOWN ARROW	Displays the command invoked next after displayed command
PGUP	Displays the oldest command name in the command buffer
PGDN	Displays the most recently used command name

Table 27-1.   The DOSKEY Traverse Keys and Their Functions

DOSKEY refers to the previous-command buffer as your *command history.* If you invoke DOSKEY using the /HISTORY switch, DOSKEY will display all the command names your previous-command buffer contains, as shown here.

```
C:\> DOSKEY /HISTORY  <ENTER>
DATE
TIME
VER
CLS
DOSKEY /HISTORY
```

To reduce your typing, DOSKEY lets you abbreviate the /HISTORY switch as simply /H.

```
C:\> DOSKEY /H  <ENTER>
```

If your previous-command buffer is large, DOSKEY lets you refer to commands by number. To begin, press F7, and DOSKEY will display your command history, preceding each command with its corresponding number.

```
1: DATE
2: TIME
3: VER
4: CLS
5: DOSKEY /HISTORY
6: DOSKEY /H
```

To select a command by number, press F9. DOSKEY will prompt you to type in the desired number as follows.

```
C:\> Line Number:
```

Type in the desired line number and press ENTER. In this case, if you type 4 and press ENTER, DOSKEY will display the CLS command.

```
C:\> CLS
```

DOS won't execute the command until you press ENTER. If you don't want to execute the command, press ESC. DOSKEY will erase the current command from your screen. As the number of characters in your commands becomes large, recalling commands in this way can be very convenient.

DOSKEY gives you one last way to recall a command. Simply type one or more letters of the command name and press F8. DOSKEY will then search the previous-command buffer, beginning with the letter or letters specified. For example, if you type V and press F8, DOSKEY will recall the VER command.

```
C:\> VER
```

As the number of commands in the previous-command buffer grows, two or more commands may begin with the letters specified. If you repeatedly press F8, DOSKEY will cycle through each of the matching commands.

If the number of commands in your previous-command buffer becomes unmanageably large, you can press ALT-F7 to discard the buffer's current contents: Once you empty the buffer in this way, the next command you invoke will become command number 1. Table 27-2 describes the DOSKEY function keys.

Editing a Previous Command

Once you recall the desired command, you can execute the command by pressing ENTER, or you can edit the command as you did in Chapter 5. When you recall a command, DOSKEY places the cursor immediately to the right of the command, so you can easily execute the command by pressing ENTER. To help you edit the

Function Key	Function
F7	Displays all command names in the buffer, preceding each with its corresponding number.
F8	Displays the first command name that matches the letters you typed immediately before pressing F8. If several command names match, repeatedly pressing F8 will cycle through the matching names.
F9	Prompts you to type in a command's number, as displayed by the F7 function key. If the number does not exist, displays the most recent command.
ESC	Removes the current command name, leaving only the DOS prompt.
ALT-F7	Discards the current buffer contents.

Table 27-2.   The DOSKEY Function Keys and Their Functions

command, DOSKEY lets you use several editing keys. RIGHT ARROW and LEFT ARROW let you move the cursor one character position to the right or the left. BACKSPACE backs over characters, rubbing them out. To delete characters, you can also move the cursor to the position of the character you want to delete and press DEL. To insert characters into the command, place the cursor in the position at which you want to insert the text. Press INS until DOSKEY displays a larger cursor indicating insert mode. Type in the desired characters.

In addition to RIGHT ARROW and LEFT ARROW, DOSKEY lets you move through the command a word at a time by holding down the CTRL key and pressing either RIGHT ARROW or LEFT ARROW. The CTRL - RIGHT ARROW key combination moves the cursor one word to the right, whereas CTRL - LEFT ARROW moves the cursor one word to the left. In addition, HOME moves the cursor to the command's first letter, and END moves the cursor to the end of the command. Table 27-3 summarizes DOSKEY's editing keys.

Other DOSKEY Switches

In addition to the /HISTORY switch, which lets you display the current contents of the previous-command buffer, DOSKEY supports four other switches: /BUFSIZE, /REINSTALL, /INSERT, and /MACROS.

DOSKEY's /BUFSIZE switch lets you specify, in bytes, the amount of memory you want DOSKEY to allocate for the previous-command buffer. By default, DOSKEY allocates 512 bytes. The larger you make DOSKEY's buffer, the more commands the buffer can store. For most users, a 512-byte buffer should be enough. If you make the buffer size too large, you may waste memory DOS could put to better use in another way. The minimum buffer size is 256 bytes. The following DOSKEY command selects a large buffer size of 1,024 bytes.

Key	Function
RIGHT ARROW	Moves the cursor one character position to the right
LEFT ARROW	Moves the cursor one character position to the left
CTRL-RIGHT ARROW	Moves the cursor one word to the right
CTRL-LEFT ARROW	Moves the cursor one word to the left
INS	Toggles insert mode on and off
DEL	Deletes the character at the current user position
HOME	Moves the cursor to the start of the command
END	Moves the cursor to the end of the command

Table 27-3.   The DOSKEY Editing Keys

```
C:\> DOSKEY  /BUFSIZE=1024  <ENTER>
```

Because DOSKEY loads memory-resident software and allocates the buffer the first time you invoke it, you must include the /BUFSIZE switch when you first invoke DOSKEY, or you must use the /REINSTALL switch discussed next.

In Chapter 14, "Getting the Most from Print," you learned that to change PRINT's memory-resident settings, you needed to restart DOS. If you decide you want to change DOSKEY's buffer size for example, you can restart DOS and invoke DOSKEY with the new buffer size, or you can specify the new buffer size and include the /REINSTALL switch as shown here.

```
C:\> DOSKEY  /REINSTALL  /BUFSIZE=640  <ENTER>
DOSKey installed.
```

The /REINSTALL switch directs DOSKEY to unload its current memory-resident software and reload itself using the new switch values. When you reinstall DOSKEY in this way, you discard the current contents of the previous-command buffer.

By default, when you edit a previous command you must first press the INS key to select insert mode. If you don't press INS, you will be in overtype mode, and will overwrite letters to the right of the cursor as you type. Depending on your preference, you can direct DOSKEY to automatically begin in insert mode so you don't have to press INS. To do so, invoke DOSKEY with the /INSERT switch.

```
C:\> DOSKEY  /INSERT  <ENTER>
```

As was the case with /BUFSIZE, you can only specify /INSERT the first time you invoke DOSKEY, or you must again use /REINSTALL.

The Advanced Concepts section discusses how to create DOSKEY macros, which are similar to single-line batch files. At that time, you will use DOSKEY's /MACROS switch to display your defined macros.

Hands On

If you have not already done so, invoke DOSKEY.

```
C:\> DOSKEY  <ENTER>
```

/ SUMMARY /

DOSKEY

The DOSKEY command lets you quickly recall your previous commands. DOSKEY provides a buffer in your computer's fast electronic memory that stores a list of your previously entered commands. Depending on the amount of memory you let DOSKEY allocate and the number of characters in each command, the actual number of commands DOSKEY can track will differ. Using your keyboard's UP ARROW and DOWN ARROW keys, you can quickly cycle through the list of commands.

Next, invoke the DIR, TIME, CLS, and DATE commands. Using the UP ARROW and DOWN ARROW keys, cycle through your list of previous commands. Press PGUP to display the oldest command in the buffer. Use PGDN to display the most recently used command. Next, use DOSKEY's /HISTORY switch to display your command history.

```
C:\> DOSKEY /HISTORY    <ENTER>
```

Repeat the command using the /H abbreviation.

```
C:\> DOSKEY /H    <ENTER>
```

Press the F7 function key to display the previous-command buffer, each command name preceded by its corresponding number. Select a command and use F9 to recall the command by number. Press ESC to remove the command name from the prompt.

Type **C** and press F8 to recall the CLS command. Type **D** and press F8. DOSKEY will highlight the DATE command. Press F8 again and DOSKEY will highlight DIR.

Last, press ALT-F7 to discard the current contents of the previous-command buffer.

Review

1. How many commands can the DOSKEY buffer store?

2. List three ways to recall a command with DOSKEY.

3. What happens when DOSKEY runs out of buffer space?

4. How does DOSKEY affect the behavior of the function keys F1 through F6?

5. What is a DOSKEY macro?

Answers

1. The number of commands DOSKEY can store depends on the amount of memory you allocate for DOSKEY's buffer, the number of characters in each command, and the number of DOSKEY macros you create. By default, DOSKEY uses a 512-byte buffer.

2. To recall a command with DOSKEY:

   a. Use the UP ARROW and DOWN ARROW to cycle through the previous-command buffer.

   b. Press F7 to show the number of each command in the previous-command buffer and then press F9, typing in the number of the desired command at DOSKEY's "Line Number:" prompt.

   c. Type the first few letters of the command name and then press F8.

3. DOSKEY will discard the oldest commands in the previous-command buffer to make space for new commands.

4. DOSKEY does not affect the behavior of the function keys F1 through F6. You can still use these function keys to edit the previous command that DOS buffers.

5. A DOSKEY macro is similar to a single-line batch file. Unlike batch files that reside on disk, DOSKEY macros reside in your computer's fast electronic memory, which means the macros execute faster than batch files.

Advanced Concepts

In addition to letting you quickly recall your previous commands, DOSKEY lets you define macros, which behave like single-line batch files. Like batch files, DOSKEY macros have a name. To execute the macro, you type the macro's name at the DOS prompt and press ENTER.

Unlike batch files that reside on disk, DOSKEY stores macros in your computer's fast electronic RAM. As such, DOS can execute macros very quickly because DOS doesn't have to first read the macro from the slower mechanical disk. Unlike batch files that can contain many lines of commands, DOSKEY macros are restricted to a single line.

Because DOSKEY stores macros in RAM, the macros are lost each time you turn off your computer or restart DOS. If you create several macros you frequently use, place corresponding DOSKEY commands in your AUTOEXEC.BAT to define the macros each time your system starts.

The following DOSKEY command creates a macro named HIST that executes the DOSKEY /HISTORY command.

```
C:\> DOSKEY  HIST=DOSKEY  /HISTORY  <ENTER>
```

After you define HIST, you can invoke the macro as follows.

```
C:\> HIST  <ENTER>
```

DOS will then execute the DOSKEY /HISTORY command as desired. DOSKEY macros take priority over DOS internal commands, external commands, and batch files by the same name. For example, the following DOSKEY command creates a macro named CLS that invokes the ECHO command to display the message "Clear screen is redefined."

```
C:\> DOSKEY  CLS=ECHO Clear screen is redefined.
```

If you invoke CLS from the DOS prompt, your screen will display the following.

```
C:\> CLS  <ENTER>
C:\> ECHO Clear screen is redefined.
Clear screen is redefined.
```

Because DOSKEY macros execute first, you may want to define macros for commands you don't want another user to access, such as FORMAT or DEL.

DOSKEY macros are not restricted to a single command, merely to a single line. For example, in Chapter 15, "Grouping Commands with Batch Files," you created the batch file DATETIME.BAT that cleared your screen display and then prompted you to enter the system date and time:

```
CLS
DATE
TIME
```

Because you can easily fit these three commands on one line, you can create a macro named DATETIME that issues all three commands as shown here.

```
C:\> DOSKEY  DATETIME=CLS  $T  DATE  $T  TIME  <ENTER>
```

DOSKEY uses the $T symbol to separate multiple commands that appear on one line. To invoke the macro, type DATETIME at the DOS prompt, as shown here.

```
C:\> DATETIME  <ENTER>
```

DOSKEY macros can also support command-line parameters and I/O redirection.

Accessing Command-Line Parameters

In Chapter 16, "Decision-Making Batch Files," you used the batch file parameters %0 through %9 to access command-line information. In a similar way, DOSKEY macros use the symbols $1 through $9. The following macro SHOWEM uses the symbols $1 through $9 to display its command parameters.

```
C:\> DOSKEY  SHOWEM=ECHO  $1  $2  $3  $4  $5  $6  $7  $8  $9
```

If you invoke SHOWEM with the letters "A," "B," and "C," your screen will display the following.

```
C:\> SHOWEM  A  B  C  <ENTER>
C:\> ECHO A  B  C
A  B  C
```

As was the case with DOS batch files, if you invoke the macro with more than nine parameters, DOSKEY ignores the extras.

```
C:\> SHOWEM  A  B  C  D  E  F  G  H  I  J  K  L  <ENTER>
C:\> ECHO  A  B  C  D  E  F  G  H  I
A  B  C  D  E  F  G  H  I
```

DOSKEY macros do not have a command like SHIFT that rotates parameters. Instead, if you want to access the entire command line, you must use the $* symbol, as shown here with the macro SHOWALL.

```
C:\> DOSKEY  SHOWALL=ECHO  $*  <ENTER>
```

Using the $* symbol, the following macro, TYPE, combines the TYPE command with FOR to support multiple file names and the DOS wildcards. Since a macro is higher in precedence than an internal command of the same name, it replaces the internal TYPE command.

```
C:\> DOSKEY  TYPE=FOR  %I  IN  ($*)  DO  TYPE  %I  <ENTER>
```

Using TYPE, you can display the contents of several files in succession.

```
C:\> TYPE  CONFIG.SYS  AUTOEXEC.BAT  <ENTER>
```

One DOSKEY macro cannot execute another. Therefore, when DOS encounters TYPE within the above FOR command, DOS correctly executes the internal TYPE command (not the macro), correctly displaying the file's contents.

Table 27-4 defines symbols you can use within DOSKEY macros.

Using I /O Redirection Operators

As you have seen, the commands your macros execute can be very complex as long as they all fit on one line. As you create more powerful macros, you may eventually want to include I/O redirection operators within the macro command. Using the I/O redirection operators, however, is more difficult than you might think. The goal of the following macro, PRINTDIR, is to redirect the output of the DIR command to the printer.

```
C:\> DOSKEY  PRINTDIR=DIR  >  PRN  <ENTER>
```

Unfortunately, when you execute this DOSKEY command, DOS assumes you want to redirect the output of DOSKEY to the printer, not the output of DIR.

Symbol	Meaning
$1 through $9	The macro's command-line parameters
$T	Separates multiple commands
$*	Represents the entire command line

Table 27-4.   *Symbols Supported by DOSKEY Macros*

If you want to use the I/O redirection operators within your DOSKEY macros, you must use the symbols $G for output redirection, $L for input redirection, GG for append redirection, and $B for the DOS pipe. Using the $G symbol, the following DOSKEY command correctly implements the PRINTDIR macro.

```
C:\> DOSKEY  PRINTDIR=DIR  $G  PRN  <ENTER>
```

In a similar way, the macro DIRONLY uses the DOS pipe to display only the directories in the current directory.

```
C:\> DOSKEY  DIRONLY=DIR  $B  FIND  "<DIR>"  <ENTER>
```

Table 27-5 summarizes DOSKEY's redirection symbols.
Using DOSKEY's /MACROS switch, you can display the defined macros.

```
C:\> DOSKEY  /MACROS  <ENTER>
SHOWEM=ECHO $1 $2 $3 $4 $5 $6 $7 $8 $9
SHOWALL=ECHO $*
TYPE=FOR %I IN ($*) DO TYPE %I
PRINTDIR=DIR $g PRN
DIRONLY=DIR $b FIND "$lDIR$g"
```

Macro Restrictions

Although DOSKEY macros are very powerful, they do have a few restrictions. First, DOSKEY stores macros in the same memory buffer it allocates for tracking your previous commands. If you create many macros, you may need to use DOSKEY's /BUFSIZE switch to increase the buffer size.

Symbol	Represents
$G	> DOS output redirection operator
$L	< DOS input redirection operator
GG	>> DOS append redirection operator
$B	| DOS pipe operator

Table 27-5.   *DOSKEY Macro I/O Redirection Symbols*

SUMMARY

DOSKEY Macros

A DOSKEY macro is similar to a single-line batch file. Like batch files, DOSKEY macros have names. You execute a DOSKEY macro by typing its name at the DOS prompt. Unlike batch files that reside on disk, DOSKEY macros reside in RAM, from which they execute very quickly. The format to create a DOSKEY macro is as follows:

```
C:\> DOSKEY   Name=Command [Parameters]   <ENTER>
```

Second, one DOSKEY macro cannot invoke a second macro. For example, the following macro, NESTED, tries to invoke the macro SHOWEM.

```
C:\> DOSKEY   NESTED=SHOWEM   <ENTER>
```

When you invoke NESTED, DOS will display the "Bad command" error message.

```
C:\> NESTED   <ENTER>
C:\> SHOWEM
Bad command or file name
```

Third, you can only invoke DOSKEY macros from the keyboard. If you reference a macro name within a batch file, for example, DOS will not locate the command.

How DOSKEY Works

DOSKEY loads memory-resident software, which captures the DOS keyboard interrupt, letting DOSKEY examine each keystroke before the DOS command processor, COMMAND.COM, gets a chance to. In most cases, DOSKEY simply passes the keys you type along to COMMAND.COM. If you press UP ARROW or DOWN ARROW however, DOSKEY's software takes over, recalling command names on your screen. Likewise, if you press ENTER to execute a command, DOSKEY looks at the command name before anyone else. If the name matches a macro, DOSKEY executes the macro's command(s). If the name does not match a macro, DOSKEY adds it to the command history and passes it along to COMMAND.COM. Because DOSKEY sees the command name before COMMAND.COM, you can redefine the internal DOS commands.

The only time DOSKEY gets to see command names is when they are typed at the keyboard. If you execute a batch file for example, DOSKEY does not get to see the command names, which explains why batch files can't successfully execute macros.

Key Terms

Previous-command buffer   The location in memory where the DOS 5 DOSKEY command stores the names of your previous commands.

Macro   A sequence of characters that, when entered at the keyboard as a command, DOS replaces with one or more different commands. Under DOS 5, the DOSKEY command provides macro support.

Chapter 28

DOS 5 Crisis Prevention

In Chapter 22 you learned the importance of backing up the files on your hard disk to floppies. In this chapter, you will examine the DOS 5 disk "crisis prevention" commands that let you rescue your files or disk after an inadvertent DEL or FORMAT command. Before you examine these commands keep one thing in mind: *There is no substitute for good disk backups.* Although the commands presented in this chapter may undelete files you have accidentally deleted or unformat your hard disk, the commands can't reproduce your files if your disk breaks. The DOS 5 UN-DELETE and UNFORMAT commands are very powerful and very convenient. Use these two commands to complement, not replace, your disk backups.

If you are using DOS 5, these crisis-prevention commands are a nice bonus. If you are not, several third-party software products exist that not only provide undelete and unformat utilities, but also other powerful utilities that will improve your system's disk and file performance.

Retrieving Deleted Files with UNDELETE

Chapter 4, "Getting Started with DOS Files," introduced the DEL command. Since then you have used DEL to delete a single file or, using wildcards, a group of files. As you have learned, you must use DEL with care to prevent the accidental deletion of needed files. In Chapter 22, "Protecting Your Files with BACKUP and RESTORE," you learned that if you accidentally delete a file, you can restore its contents—if you have good backups. If you are using DOS 5, the UNDELETE command lets you quickly undelete a recently deleted file.

To better understand how UNDELETE works, create the directory TESTDIR, and copy to the directory the DOS commands that begin with the letter "D."

```
C:\> MKDIR  \TESTDIR   <ENTER>
C:\> CHDIR  \TESTDIR   <ENTER>
C:\TESTDIR> COPY  \DOS\D*.COM   <ENTER>
```

The TESTDIR directory should contain the following.

```
C:\TESTDIR> DIR   <ENTER>

 Volume in drive C is DOS
 Volume Serial Number is 1661-AB75
 Directory of C:\TESTDIR

 .              <DIR>       03-17-91  10:22p
 ..             <DIR>       03-17-91  10:22p
DOSKEY   COM       5883 03-08-91    5:05a
DOSSHELL COM       4623 03-08-91    5:05a
DISKCOMP COM      10652 03-08-91    5:05a
DISKCOPY COM      11793 03-08-91    5:05a
        6 file(s)        32951 bytes
                      15248960 bytes free
```

Next, delete the file DOSKEY.COM.

```
C:\TESTDIR> DEL  DOSKEY.COM   <ENTER>
```

A directory listing of TESTDIR shows the file has been successfully deleted.

```
C:\TESTDIR> DIR   <ENTER>

 Volume in drive C is DOS
 Volume Serial Number is 1661-AB75
 Directory of C:\TESTDIR
```

```
.              <DIR>      03-17-91  10:22p
..             <DIR>      03-17-91  10:22p
DOSSHELL COM       4623 03-08-91   5:05a
DISKCOMP COM      10652 03-08-91   5:05a
DISKCOPY COM      11793 03-08-91   5:05a
        5 file(s)        26326 bytes
                     15220288 bytes free
```

To undelete the file, invoke UNDELETE, as shown here.

```
C:\TESTDIR> UNDELETE   DOSKEY.COM   <ENTER>
```

To undelete a file, you must perform two steps. First, UNDELETE will display the directory entry for a file that matches the file name or wildcard specified. The file name, however, begins with a question mark, instead of the original letter, as shown here.

```
C:\TESTDIR> UNDELETE   DOSKEY.COM   <ENTER>

Directory: C:\TESTDIR
File Specifications: DOSKEY.COM

    Deletion tracking file not found.

    MS-DOS Directory contains    1 deleted files.
    of those,   1 files may be recovered.

Using the MS-DOS Directory.

    ?OSKEY    COM     5883 03-08-91  5:05a  ...A  Undelete (Y/N)?
```

If the directory entry displayed corresponds to the file name you want to undelete, type Y.

Next, you must tell UNDELETE the first letter of the file name, as shown here.

```
Please type the first character for ?OSKEY  .COM: D

File successfully undeleted.
```

UNDELETE will now undelete the file. A directory listing of TESTDIR shows
DOSKEY.COM has been undeleted!

```
C:\TESTDIR> DIR    <ENTER>

 Volume in drive C is DOS
 Volume Serial Number is 1661-AB75
 Directory of C:\TESTDIR


 .            <DIR>      03-17-91   10:22p
 ..           <DIR>      03-17-91   10:22p
 DOSKEY   COM     5883 03-08-91     5:05a
 DOSSHELL COM     4623 03-08-91     5:05a
 DISKCOMP COM    10652 03-08-91     5:05a
 DISKCOPY COM    11793 03-08-91     5:05a
         6 file(s)       32951 bytes
                      15248960 bytes free
```

Now delete all four files in the TESTDIR directory.

```
C:\TESTDIR> DEL   *.*   <ENTER>
```

A directory listing of the directory reveals the directory is empty as shown.

```
C:\TESTDIR> DIR   <ENTER>

 Volume in drive C is DOS
 Volume Serial Number is 1661-AB75
 Directory of C:\TESTDIR

 .            <DIR>      03-17-91   10:22p
 ..           <DIR>      03-17-91   10:22p
         2 file(s)           0 bytes
                      15310400 bytes free
```

To undelete the files you have two choices. First, you can invoke UNDELETE
individually for each file, or you can use a wildcard.

```
C:\> UNDELETE  *.COM   <ENTER>
```

As before, UNDELETE will display a directory entry and ask you whether or not you want to undelete the entry.

```
C:\TESTDIR> UNDELETE  *.COM  <ENTER>

Directory: C:\TESTDIR
File Specifications: *.COM

    Deletion-tracking file not found.

    MS-DOS Directory contains    4 deleted files.
    Of those,   4 files may be recovered.

Using the MS-DOS Directory.

    ?OSKEY    COM     5883  3-08-91  5:05a  ...A  Undelete (Y/N)?
```

If you type **Y**, UNDELETE will prompt you to enter the file name's first letter.

```
    Please type the first character for ?OSKEY  .COM:
```

If you instead type **N**, UNDELETE will leave this entry deleted, continuing with the next file entry. To undelete all four files, respond with **Y** for each entry and type in the first letter of each file name.

How Can DOS Undelete a File?

When you delete a file, the file is gone. Right? Well, not exactly. When you delete a file using DEL, DOS does not actually erase the file's contents from disk right then. Instead, DOS makes the disk space that contains the file available for use by another file. When you delete one file and then create a second, DOS will very likely store the second file in one or more of the disk locations made available by the first file's deletion. When DOS stores the second file in these locations, DOS overwrites the first file's contents, just as you might record over a song on a cassette tape. Figure 28-1 illustrates this process.

If you accidentally delete a file and have not yet copied new information onto the disk, the file's original contents are still available. The UNDELETE command simply locates the file's original contents and rebuilds the file.

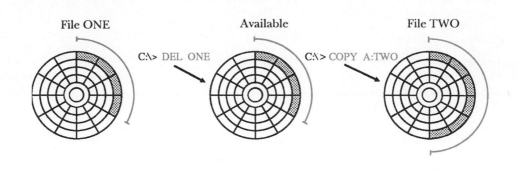

Figure 28-1.   *When you delete one file and create another, DOS may overwrite the deleted file's information*

NOTE   *If you accidentally delete a file, do not copy any information to your disk until you successfully use UNDELETE to undelete the file's contents. If you copy information to your disk, you will very likely overwrite the file's original contents, making the file impossible to undelete.*

Why Doesn't DOS Know the File Name's First Letter?

A directory is a list of file entries. When you create a file, DOS adds an entry to the directory list. When you delete a file, DOS no longer displays the file's directory entry, but DOS does not actually remove the entry from the directory list. Instead, like the file's disk space, DOS marks the file's directory entry available for reuse by the next file you create. DOS makes a directory entry available for reuse by replacing the first letter of the file name with a special character (σ). Assuming you delete the file DISKCOPY.COM, TESTDIR's directory entries become those shown in Figure 28-2.

When DOS searches a directory, to perform a DIR command for example, DOS ignores entries that begin with σ. UNDELETE, however, knows such entries correspond to deleted files. However, before UNDELETE can undelete the file, you need to tell UNDELETE what letter to use as the file name's first character.

Listing Files Available to Undelete

The /LIST switch directs UNDELETE to search the directory for deleted files, displaying the entries for files you can undelete. When you include /LIST, UN-DELETE only lists the files. It does not undelete them. The following command directs UNDELETE to list the files available to undelete.

```
C:\TESTDIR> UNDELETE  /LIST  <ENTER>
```

If you have deleted all four files in the example directory, UNDELETE will display the following.

```
Directory: C:\TESTDIR
File Specifications: *.*
    Deletion-tracking file not found.

    MS-DOS Directory contains    4 deleted files.
    Of those,   4 files may be recovered.

Using the MS-DOS Directory.

        ?OSKEY   COM     5883 03-08-91  5:05a   ...A
        ?OSSHELL COM     4623 03-08-91  5:05a   ...A
        ?ISKCOMP COM    10652 03-08-91  5:05a   ...A
        ?ISKCOPY COM    11793 03-08-91  5:05a   ...A
```

DOSKEY.COM	5883	03-08-91	5:05a	Attributes	Starting Cluster
DOSSHELL.COM	4623	03-08-91	5:05a	Attributes	Starting Cluster
DISKCOMP.COM	10652	03-08-91	5:05a	Attributes	Starting Cluster
σISKCOPY.COM	11793	03-08-91	5:05a	Attributes	**Starting Cluster**

Figure 28-2.   *DOS marks a directory entry as available by replacing the first character of the file name with* σ

Note the two lines that describe the number of deleted files in the directory and the number that can be recovered.

```
    MS-DOS Directory contains    4 deleted files.
    Of those,   4 files may be recovered.
```

UNDELETE determines the number of deleted files in the directory by counting the number of directory entries for which the first letter of the file name is σ. Next, UNDELETE checks to make sure each file's previous contents has not been overwritten by another file. If the file's entire contents are available, UNDELETE marks the file as recoverable. In this case, UNDELETE found four files, all recoverable.

Undeleting All Available Files at One Time

As you have learned, to undelete a group of files at one time, you must individually respond with **Y** to select the file and then type in the first letter of the file's name. UNDELETE's /ALL switch gives you a different way to undelete a group of files. When you include /ALL, UNDELETE automatically undeletes each matching file, without prompting you to confirm the file's selection or type in the file's first letter. Because UNDELETE must assign a letter to the file name's first character, UNDELETE automatically uses the # character. For example, assuming you have deleted the files in the TESTDIR directory, you can undelete all four files automatically as follows.

```
C:\TESTDIR> UNDELETE  /ALL   <ENTER>

Directory: C:\TESTDIR
File Specifications: *.*

    Deletion-tracking file not found.

    MS-DOS Directory contains    4 deleted files.
    Of those,   4 files may be recovered.

Using the MS-DOS Directory.

    ?OSKEY   COM     5883 03-08-91  5:05a  ...A

File successfully undeleted.
```

```
        ?OSSHELL COM      4623 03-08-91   5:05a   ...A

File successfully undeleted.

        ?ISKCOMP COM     10652 03-08-91   5:05a   ...A

File successfully undeleted.

        ?ISKCOPY COM     11793 03-08-91   5:05a   ...A

File successfully undeleted.
```

A directory listing reveals UNDELETE has assigned the # character to the first letter of each file name.

```
C:\TESTDIR> DIR   <ENTER>

 Volume in drive C is DOS
 Volume Serial Number is 1661-AB75
 Directory of C:\TESTDIR

.            <DIR>      03-17-91   10:22p
..           <DIR>      03-17-91   10:22p
#OSKEY    COM     5883 03-08-91    5:05a
#OSSHELL COM      4623 03-08-91    5:05a
#TSKCOMP COM     10652 03-08-91    5:05a
#ISKCOPY COM     11793 03-08-91    5:05a
         6 file(s)       32951 bytes
                    15257152 bytes free
```

After the files are undeleted, you can use the DOS RENAME command to assign the original file names.

Because each file name in a directory must be unique, UNDELETE will use one of the following characters for the file name's first character until the file name becomes unique:

#%$-0123456789ABCDEFGHIJKLMNOPQRSTUVWXYZ.

The UNDELETE command supports additional command-line switches you will examine later in this chapter, following the discussion of the MIRROR command.

Protecting Your Disk and Files with MIRROR

The MIRROR command is a memory-resident program that stores information UNDELETE can use to correctly undelete files. In addition, MIRROR stores information that assists UNFORMAT in unformatting your hard disk following an accidental FORMAT command. To begin, examine how MIRROR assists UN-DELETE.

The following illustration shows two files named ONE and TWO. As you can see, file ONE is stored on disk in nonconsecutive storage locations.

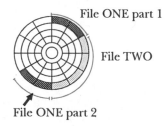

File ONE part 1

File TWO

File ONE part 2

Assume you accidentally delete both files. When you invoke UNDELETE to undelete file ONE, UNDELETE can determine from the file's size that file ONE requires two storage locations. UNDELETE can also determine from the file's directory entry, where the file's first location resides on disk. Unfortunately, UNDELETE doesn't know where the file's second location is. UNDELETE assumes the second location immediately follows the first, resulting in the file containing the disk locations shown here:

File ONE

Because UNDELETE has assumed file ONE's storage locations were consecutive, it has incorrectly merged file ONE's contents with what used to be those of file TWO.

If you examine file ONE's contents using TYPE or your word processor, you will very likely see the error. Unfortunately, because UNDELETE has assigned file TWO's previous contents to file ONE, UNDELETE now thinks file TWO's contents have been overwritten. If you try to undelete file TWO, UNDELETE will display a message telling you it can't undelete the file.

```
Starting cluster is unavailable. This file cannot be recovered
with the UNDELETE command. Press any key to continue.
```

Further, because UNDELETE undeleted enough disk locations to match file ONE's size, UNDELETE won't let you recover the other disk location that actually belongs to file ONE.

Fortunately, confusion over disk locations only occurs when a file is *fragmented*, meaning the file is stored in nonconsecutive disk locations. Most of the files on your disk are typically stored in consecutive locations, which means UNDELETE doesn't make these kind of mistakes very often. Chapter 44 discusses file fragmentation and ways you can correct it. For now, keep in mind fragmented files may prevent UNDELETE from successfully undeleting a file.

When you delete a file, DOS marks the file's directory entry as available by placing the character σ in the first letter of the file name. When you add a new file to your disk, DOS will use the first available directory entry for the new file. Therefore, if you delete a file and then create a second file, the second file may not overwrite the first file's disk locations, but it may overwrite the file's directory entry. If UNDELETE cannot locate a file's directory entry, UNDELETE cannot undelete the file, even though all of the contents may still be on disk. As you will learn in this section, the MIRROR command saves the directory entry and disk locations of files that you delete from your disk.

The MIRROR command assists UNDELETE by tracking the actual disk locations used by each file you delete from your disk. When you invoke MIRROR, it creates a hidden file in the root directory. When you delete a file from the disk, MIRROR stores specifics about the file that UNDELETE can use later to correctly undelete the file.

The following MIRROR command uses MIRROR's /T switch to install file-deletion tracking from drive C.

```
C:\> MIRROR  /TC  <ENTER>
```

MIRROR will load its memory-resident software, displaying the following message on your screen.

```
Creates an image of the system area.

Drive C being processed.

The MIRROR process was successful.

Deletion-tracking software being installed.

The following drives are supported:
Drive C - Default files saved.

Installation complete.
```

Depending on the number and size of the files you delete, MIRROR's hidden file will grow. To prevent this file from becoming so large it uses up space needed for other files, MIRROR restricts the number of file entries the file can hold, as well as the file's maximum size. Table 28-1 defines the default size restrictions MIRROR uses for each disk type.

MIRROR does not store the file's original information, just the disk location of the information. Using this information, UNDELETE can successfully undelete fragmented files.

NOTE

If you delete enough files to reach either the maximum number of entries or the maximum file size, MIRROR will discard the oldest information in the file to make room for new file deletion information.

If you copy files to your disk, the new files may overwrite the previous files' disk locations even though MIRROR's file-deletion tracking is active.

NOTE

If you find the number of entries MIRROR tracks in the delete file to be insufficient, you can specify a value up to 999 when you first invoke MIRROR. For example, the following command loads file-deletion tracking for drive C to support 500 entries.

```
C:\> MIRROR  /TC-500   <ENTER>
```

Because MIRROR loads memory-resident software, you must either restart DOS or unload MIRROR from memory with the /U switch if you want to change one of MIRROR'S settings.

Disk Type	Maximum Entries	Maximum Size
360Kb	25	5Kb
720Kb	50	9Kb
1.2Mb	75	14Kb
1.44Mb	75	14Kb
20Mb	101	18Kb
32Mb	202	36Kb
OVER 32Mb	303	55Kb

Table 28-1.   Maximum Number and File Restrictions for MIRROR's Deletion-Tracking File

Revisiting UNDELETE

When you use MIRROR to perform file-deletion tracking, UNDELETE has two ways to locate files. First, UNDELETE can search the directory for a matching entry and rebuild the file, assuming the file's contents are in consecutive locations. Second, and ideally, UNDELETE will use the information in MIRROR's file. By default, UNDELETE uses the deletion-tracking information, if it is available, as well as the information UNDELETE can determine by reading the directory. If you use the /LIST switch, UNDELETE lists the entries it can undelete without using MIRROR's file, as well as those entries for which it has deletion-tracking information.

```
C:\TESTDIR> UNDELETE  /LIST    <ENTER>


Directory: C:\TESTDIR
File Specifications: *.*

    Deletion-tracking file contains    4 deleted files.
    Of those,    4 files have all clusters available,
                 0 files have some clusters available,
                 0 files have no clusters available.

    MS-DOS Directory contains    4 deleted files.
    Of those,    4 files may be recovered.

Using the deletion-tracking file.

    DISKCOPY COM    11793 03-08-91  5:05a  ...A Deleted:  4-10-91 11:09a
    DISKCOMP COM    10652 03-08-91  5:05a  ...A Deleted:  4-10-91 11:09a
    DOSSHELL COM     4623 03-08-91  5:05a  ...A Deleted:  4-10-91 11:09a
    DOSKEY   COM     5883 03-08-91  5:05a  ...A Deleted:  4-10-91 11:09a
```

Depending on the files listed, there may be times you want UNDELETE only to undelete those files it knows about using DOS. To do so, invoke UNDELETE using the /DOS switch.

```
C:\> UNDELETE  *.*  /DOS   <ENTER>
```

Likewise, there may be times you want to only undelete those files for which file tracking is active. To do so, invoke UNDELETE with the /DT switch, and UNDELETE will undelete only those files listed in the file MIRORSAV.FIL.

```
C:\> UNDELETE  *.*  /DT  <ENTER>
```

Saving Disk Information for UNFORMAT

As briefly discussed, the MIRROR command supports both UNDELETE and UNFORMAT. Each time you invoke MIRROR, it records information about your disk's root directory, boot record, and file allocation tables in the root directory file MIRROR.FIL. Using this information, the UNFORMAT command can recover all or a portion of your disk following an accidental FORMAT command.

NOTE   *If you create or change files after running the MIRROR command, UNFORMAT may not fully recover your disk in the event of an accidental disk format. The more often you invoke MIRROR, the better your chances of UNFORMAT being able to fully recover your disk. At a minimum, you should invoke MIRROR each time your system starts by placing the MIRROR command in your AUTOEXEC.BAT file. If you want MIRROR to track file deletions (and most users should) invoke MIRROR from within AUTOEXEC.BAT, and be sure to include the /TC parameter.*

Recovering a Disk with UNFORMAT

In Chapter 7, "Preparing Disks for Use," you learned that formatting a disk destroys the disk's current contents. You may, however, be able to recover all or part of the disk's contents following an accidental format by using the UNFORMAT command.

NOTE   *UNFORMAT is a recovery command you should invoke only after an accidental disk format. Invoking UNFORMAT on a disk that does not need recovery may result in the loss of information. Do not execute the UNFORMAT commands presented in this section. Instead, examine the commands and note their functionality. You can refer to UNFORMAT any time in the future should an accident occur. For now, just execute the commands presented in the Hands On section.*

As was the case with UNDELETE, UNFORMAT can recover your disk using information it gets strictly from DOS or information contained in the MIRROR file MIRROR.FIL. One of the first problems users encounter when they accidentally format their hard disk is trying to find a floppy disk containing the UNFORMAT command. Before you continue reading, take out an unused floppy disk and format the floppy as a bootable floppy disk.

```
C:\> FORMAT  A:  /S  <ENTER>
```

When FORMAT completes, copy the file UNFORMAT.COM from the DOS directory to the floppy disk.

```
C:\> COPY  \DOS\UNFORMAT.COM  A:   <ENTER>
```

Label the disk as UNFORMAT and place the floppy disk in a safe location. Should you ever need to recover your disk, you can use the floppy disk to do so.

If you use the MIRROR file MIRROR.FIL, UNFORMAT can only recover your disk to the last saved state. UNFORMAT's /J switch directs UNFORMAT to examine your disk and verify that the information on your disk matches the information in the file MIRROR.FIL. The /J switch does not UNFORMAT your disk; it simply compares the disk to MIRROR's file.

```
C:\> UNFORMAT  C:  /J   <ENTER>
```

UNFORMAT will display a screenful of warning messages followed by the line "Just checking this time." to let you know an unformat operation will not take place.

```
Restores the system area of your disk by using the image file
created  by the MIRROR command.

   WARNING !!           WARNING !!

This command should be used only to recover from the inadvertent
use of the FORMAT command or the RECOVER command. Any other use
of the UNFORMAT command may cause you to lose data! Files
modified since the MIRROR image file was created may be lost.

Searching disk for MIRROR image.

Just checking this time. No changes written to disk.
```

The MIRROR command keeps two copies of your disk's system information, the latest copy (MIRROR.FIL) and the previous copy (MIRROR.BAK). Each time you invoke the MIRROR command, MIRROR renames the existing file MIRROR.FIL to MIRROR.BAK and copies the current disk information to the file MIRROR.FIL. When you invoke the UNFORMAT command, UNFORMAT locates these two files, displaying each file's creation date on your screen. UNFORMAT then asks you which file you want to use.

```
The last time the MIRROR or FORMAT command was used
was at 19:32 on 04-10-91.
The prior time the MIRROR or FORMAT command was used
was at 11:59 on 04-10-91.

If you wish to use the last file as indicated
above, press L. If you wish to use the prior
file as indicated above, press P. Press ESC
to cancel UNFORMAT.
```

If you want to use the latest copy, type **L**. To use the previous copy, type **P**. To exit UNFORMAT, press ESC.

If you are using UNFORMAT's /J switch to compare the disk's contents to the MIRROR file, and both match, UNFORMAT will display the following message.

```
The system area of drive C has been verified
to agree with the MIRROR image file.
```

If the disk's current contents don't agree with the MIRROR file, UNFORMAT will display the following message.

```
The system are does not agree with the
MIRROR image file.
```

If this message appears, invoke MIRROR to bring MIRROR's image file up to date.

If you need to UNFORMAT your hard disk and have used MIRROR on a regular basis, place the floppy disk you previously created that contains UNFORMAT into drive A and issue the following command.

```
A:\> UNFORMAT  C:  <ENTER>
```

As before, UNFORMAT will display its warning messages and prompt you to select the latest or previous version of the MIRROR file, or to press ESC to end the UNFORMAT operation.

```
Restores the system area of your disk by using the image file created
by the MIRROR command.

  WARNING !!            WARNING !!
```

```
This command should be used only to recover from the inadvertent
use of the FORMAT command or the RECOVER command. Any other use
of the UNFORMAT command may cause you to lose data!  Files
modified since the MIRROR image file was created may be lost.

Searching disk for MIRROR image.

The last time the MIRROR or FORMAT command was used
was at 19:32 on 04-10-91.
The prior time the MIRROR or FORMAT command was used
was at 11:59 on 04-10-91.

If you wish to use the last file as indicated
above, press L. If you wish to use the prior
file as indicated above, press P. Press ESC
to cancel UNFORMAT.
```

If you type either L or P, UNFORMAT will validate the MIRROR file, making sure the file is complete (although not necessarily current). UNFORMAT then asks you if you really want to update your disk's system area.

```
The MIRROR image file has been validated.

Are you sure you want to update the system area of
  your drive C (Y/N)?
```

To perform the UNFORMAT operation type Y. To end the operation type N. If you continue the operation, UNFORMAT will rebuild your disk displaying the following messages.

```
The system area of drive C has been rebuilt.

You may need to restart the system.
```

Perform a directory operation to examine your disk's root directory. Next, invoke CHKDSK to examine your disk's current structure. If CHKSDK reports several errors, invoke CHKDSK again, using the output redirection operator to write CHKDSK's output to your printer. The files CHKDSK lists may be damaged. You will need to restore the files from your backup disks. Invoke CHKSDK using the /F switch to correct the errors.

If you have never used MIRROR, or have not used it in a long time, you may be better off letting UNFORMAT rebuild your disk using the information it can get from DOS and ignoring the MIRROR file. UNFORMAT's /TEST switch lets you display the directories UNFORMAT will rebuild if UNFORMAT only uses information available from DOS. Like the /J switch, the /TEST switch only displays information to your screen about the unformat process, it does not actually unformat your disk. The following command uses UNFORMAT's /TEST switch to examine the directories UNFORMAT can rebuild.

```
A:\> UNFORMAT  C:  /TEST  <ENTER>
```

In this case, UNFORMAT will display a warning message telling you that unformatting without the MIRROR file may not completely recover your disk.

```
  CAUTION !!

This attempts to recover all the files lost after a
format, assuming you've not been using the MIRROR command. This
method cannot guarantee complete recovery of your files.
```

Remember, UNFORMAT is a *crisis* recovery program. If you accidentally format your disk, be grateful for any files UNFORMAT can recover—partial disk recovery is better than none.

Next, UNFORMAT will display additional messages describing the operation and a prompt asking you if you want to continue.

```
The search-phase is safe: nothing is altered on the disk.
You will be prompted again before changes are written to the disk.


Using drive C:

Are you sure you want to do this?
If so, press Y; anything else cancels.
```

Type **Y** to continue the text. UNFORMAT will display the message "Simulation only." letting you know it will not unformat the disk.

```
Simulation only.
```

Next, UNFORMAT will display a count of the number of files and directories it has located in the root.

```
Files found is the root: nn
Subdirectories found in the root: nn
```

UNFORMAT now begins searching your disk for directories, displaying the percentage of your disk it has examined as well as the number of directories found.

```
Searching disk...
 nn% searched, nn subdirectories found.
```

When UNFORMAT completes its search, it will display the directory paths of each directory it encountered, followed by a count of the number of files found.

```
Walking the directory tree to locate all files...
Path=C:\
Path=C:\DOS\
Path=C:\
Path=C:\BATCH\
    :       :
Path=C:\WP\LETTERS\

Files found: nnnn
```

UNFORMAT will now display a prompt asking you if you want to continue.

```
Simulation only.

Are you sure you want to do this?
If so, press Y; anything else cancels.
```

Type Y to continue, and UNFORMAT will list the fragmented files it encountered, telling you it can only recover a portion of the file. UNFORMAT will then prompt you to specify whether you want to delete the file or truncate (reduce) the file's size to only the recoverable information. To delete the file type D, and to truncate the file type T. Because the /TEST switch results in a *simulation* of the disk-rebuild process, you can type D or T for each file name displayed without actually affecting the file.

```
FILENAME.EXT  nnnn  12-25-90  8:30pm  ONLY  nnnn  bytes are
recoverable
Truncate or Delete this file?
```

After you respond to the delete or truncate prompt for each file, UNFORMAT will display the number of files it can recover, followed by a message indicating the operation is complete.

```
nnnn files recovered.

Operation completed.
```

If you want a hardcopy listing of the information UNFORMAT displays to your screen, invoke UNFORMAT with the /P switch.

```
A:\> UNFORMAT  C:  /TEST  /P  <ENTER>
```

If you have never invoked the MIRROR command, UNFORMAT will automatically rebuild your disk using only the information it can obtain from DOS. If your disk contains an old mirror file, you need to tell UNFORMAT not to use the file by invoking UNFORMAT with the /U switch.

```
A:\> UNFORMAT  C:  /U  <ENTER>
```

The /U switch directs UNFORMAT to perform a "DOS only" unformat operation that follows the exact same steps as the unformat operation shown using /TEST. This time however, UNFORMAT will update the disk.

Safe vs. Unsafe Format Operations

Under most versions of DOS, the FORMAT command, when formatting a hard disk, does not actually overwrite the contents of the disk it is formatting. Instead, FORMAT simply initializes the disk's root directory and file allocation tables such that the DOS considers the disk empty. Actually, the disk's previous information is still on disk, which explains how UNFORMAT can recover much of your disk following an accidental format operation. Because such format operations don't actually scrub the data off your disk, the operations are called *safe formats*.

Under DOS 5, FORMAT lets you perform safe formats on your hard disk and floppy disks. By default, each time you format a disk containing data, FORMAT attempts to record on the disk, information similar to that recorded by MIRROR that UNFORMAT can use to recover the disk. Note the message "Saving UN-FORMAT information" in the output of the FORMAT command shown here.

```
C:\> FORMAT  A: <ENTER>
Insert new diskette for drive A:
and press ENTER when ready...

Checking existing disk format.
Saving UNFORMAT information.
Verifying 360K
  nn percent of disk formatted
```

In most cases, you will want to perform safe formats. Not only do safe formats give you a chance to recover your information, they also execute faster than unsafe format operations because FORMAT only examines a small percentage of the disk.

In some cases you may have information on the disk you are formatting that you don't want another user to unformat and view. Using FORMAT's /U switch (DOS 5), you can direct FORMAT to completely overwrite a disk's existing data, making an unformat operation impossible. For more information on safe and unsafe format operations, see FORMAT in the Command Reference of this book.

Hands On

If you have not already done so, edit your AUTOEXEC.BAT file and include either the command MIRROR to save your disk's systems information or MIRROR /TC to also enable file-deletion tracking on drive C. Next, invoke MIRROR from the keyboard.

```
C:\> MIRROR  /TC  <ENTER>
```

Using MKDIR, create the directory TEST. Use CHDIR to select TEST.

```
C:\> MD  \TEST  <ENTER>
C:\> CD  \TEST  <ENTER>
```

UNDELETE

The UNDELETE command lets you undelete one or more accidentally deleted files. The format of the UNDELETE command is as follows:

```
C:\> UNDELETE  FILENAME.EXT  <ENTER>
```

UNDELETE supports the DOS wildcards.

NOTE   *If you accidentally delete one or more files, do not copy any files to or store any information on your disk until you use UNDELETE to undelete the file. If you overwrite the file's contents, UNDELETE cannot recover the file.*

MIRROR's File-Deletion Tracking

The MIRROR command installs memory-resident software that stores, in a root directory file, the directory entry and the disk locations of each file you delete from disk. Using this information, UNDELETE has a better chance of correctly undeleting a file.

NOTE   *To provide deletion tracking, MIRROR's memory-resident software must perform additional processing each time you delete a file. Depending on the size and number of files you are deleting from your disk, you may notice MIRROR's overhead when DEL takes longer to complete.*

Using MIRROR to Assist UNFORMAT

The MIRROR command stores information in the root directory file MIRROR.FIL that UNFORMAT can use to recover your disk following an accidental disk format. Specifically, MIRROR stores the current state of the disk's root directory and file allocation table. To improve the chances of UNFORMAT fully recovering your disk, you need to invoke MIRROR on a regular basis.

SUMMARY

UNFORMAT

The UNFORMAT command rebuilds a disk following an accidental disk format. If the file is present, UNFORMAT will use MIRROR.FIL (created by MIRROR) to rebuild your disk. If the file is not current, UNFORMAT can only recover a portion of your files. If the file does not exist, UNFORMAT will rebuild your disk using only information it can get from DOS. Using only DOS information to rebuild a disk is the least reliable method.

The best defense against an accidental disk format is regular disk backup
(see Chapter 22).

NOTE

Next, copy the files with the SYS extension from your DOS directory to TEST.

C:\TEST> COPY \DOS*.SYS \TEST <ENTER>

Using DIR, display the directory's contents.

C:\TEST> DIR <ENTER>

Delete the files beginning with the letter "A."

C:\TEST> DEL A*.* <ENTER>

Invoke UNDELETE with /LIST to display the recoverable files.

C:\TEST> UNDELETE /LIST <ENTER>

Use the following command to undelete the files.

C:\TEST> UNDELETE *.* <ENTER>

Next, delete all the files in the directory.

C:\TEST> DEL *.* <ENTER>

Use UNDELETE's /All switch to undelete all the files.

```
C:\TEST> UNDELETE  /ALL   <ENTER>
```

If you have MIRROR's file-deletion tracking enabled, UNDELETE will automatically undelete the files using each file's correct name. If not, UNDELETE will undelete the files using the # character for the first letter of the file name.

Use DEL to delete the TEST directory's files and RMDIR to remove the directory. Then use the FORMAT command to format an unused floppy disk and create the following directories on the floppy with MKDIR.

```
C:\> MD  A:ONE   <ENTER>
C:\> MD  A:TWO   <ENTER>
C:\> MD  A:THREE   <ENTER>
```

Use DIR to display the floppy disk's contents.

```
C:\> DIR  A:
```

Next, format the floppy disk, overwriting the disk's current contents.

```
C:\> FORMAT  A:   <ENTER>
```

When FORMAT completes, use DIR to verify that the disk is empty.

```
C:\> DIR  A:   <ENTER>
```

Next, invoke UNFORMAT to rebuild the floppy disk.

```
C:\> UNFORMAT  A:   <ENTER>
```

A directory listing of the disk will reveal the disk's original directories.

```
C:\> DIR  A:   <ENTER>
```

Review

1. What two steps does DEL perform when you delete a file?

2. What is file-deletion tracking?

3. How does MIRROR assist UNFORMAT?

4. When would you unformat a disk using only DOS information, as opposed to information in the file MIRROR.FIL?

5. What is stored in the file MIRROR.BAK?

6. What is the best defense against accidental file deletions or disk formats?

Answers

1. When you delete a file, DEL marks the disk locations that contained the file's contents as available for use by another file. Next, DEL marks the file's directory entry as available for reuse by assigning the character σ to the first letter in the file name. DEL does not actually erase the file's contents from your disk.

2. The MIRROR command provides file-deletion tracking, which records information about each file you delete, such as the file's directory entry and disk locations, in a hidden file in your disk's root directory. Using this information, UNDELETE is more likely to correctly undelete a file.

3. The MIRROR command records key information about your disk (the boot record, root directory, and file allocation tables) that UNFORMAT can use to rebuild your disk after an accidental FORMAT command. MIRROR places this information in the root directory file MIRROR.FIL.

4. If you have not invoked the MIRROR command in a long time, the information in the file MIRROR.FIL will be very obsolete. As such, you are probably better off letting UNFORMAT attempt to recover the disk using DOS data.

5. Each time you invoke MIRROR, it stores the disk's current boot record, root directory, and file allocation tables in the file MIRROR.FIL. In addition, MIRROR renames the previous contents of MIRROR.FIL as MIRROR.BAK (BAK stands for BAcKup), giving you a previous and current copy of the information UNFORMAT needs to recover your disk.

6. The best defense against accidental file deletions and disk formats is current backup disks.

Advanced Concepts

FDISK records your disk's partition information beginning at the first sector of your hard disk. This sector is called the master boot record. Each time you start your computer, the computer reads the master boot record to determine from which partition it should boot the operating system. Most DOS commands or programs cannot access the master boot record. However, if your computer encounters a virus, or you accidentally change the master boot record using FDISK, you can lose all the information the disk contains because the information describing the partition boundaries has been lost.

Using the MIRROR command, however, you can save the master boot record to a floppy disk. Should the partition table become damaged or corrupted, you can use UNFORMAT to restore the partition table information from floppy.

To begin, format an unused floppy disk and label the disk "Partition Information" (be sure to include the drive letter and date) as shown here:

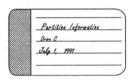

Next, invoke the MIRROR command using the /PARTN switch.

```
C:\> MIRROR  /PARTN  <ENTER>
```

MIRROR will display a message explaining that it will copy the master boot record to the file PARTNSAV.FIL on the floppy disk and then prompt you for the drive letter of the target disk, displaying drive A as the default.

```
Disk Partition Table saver.

The partition information from your hard drive(s) has been read.

Next, the file PARTNSAV.FIL will be written to a floppy disk.
Please insert a formatted diskette and type the name of the
    diskette drive.
What drive? A
```

Press ENTER to copy the partition table information to the floppy disk. When MIRROR completes, a directory listing of drive A reveals the file PARTNSAV.FIL.

```
C:\> DIR  A:  <ENTER>

 Volume in drive A has no label
 Volume Serial Number is 313C-1AF3
 Directory of A:\

PARTNSAV FIL     2048 04-10-91   7:48p
        1 file(s)        2048 bytes
                       360448 bytes free
```

As before, copy the UNFORMAT command to the floppy disk. Place the floppy disk in a safe location. Should you ever need to restore the partition table information, invoke UNFORMAT with the /PARTN switch.

```
A>   UNFORMAT  /PARTN   <ENTER>
```

UNFORMAT will display a prompt asking you to type the letter of the floppy disk containing the file PARTNSAV.FIL. UNFORMAT displays the drive letter A as the default.

```
A>   UNFORMAT  /PARTN   <ENTER>
Hard Disk Partition Table restoration.

Insert the diskette containing the file PARTNSAV.FIL
and type the letter of that disk drive.
What drive? A
```

After it reads PARTNSAV.FIL, UNFORMAT will display the date and time the partition table information was created, as well as information about your hard disks.

```
Partition information was saved by Mirror, 4-10-91  7:48pm

Old partition info for fixed disk #1 (DL=80h):

              Total_size      Start_partition  End_partition
     Type    Bytes  Sectors  Cyl Head Sector  Cyl Head Sector    Rel#
 ---------  ------- -------  --------------- ---------------    ------
| HUGE  Boot   191M  391168    0   1    1     814   14   32       32
```

Next, UNFORMAT will display your two options.

```
Options: Q - quit, take no action.
         1 - restore partition records for fixed disk #1.
Which option?
```

If you type Q, UNFORMAT will end the operation, returning to the DOS prompt. If you type 1, UNFORMAT will display a second prompt to verify that you really want to update the partition table.

```
Are you sure you want to do this?
If so, press Y; anything else cancels.
```

If you type Y, UNFORMAT will update the partition table and ask you to insert a bootable floppy drive in drive A.

```
Operation completed.

Insert a DOS boot disk in drive A and press ENTER to reboot....
```

Depending on the severity of the disk error that damaged your disk partition, you may not be able to boot from your hard disk. By booting DOS from floppy, you can use DIR and CHKDSK to examine your hard disk once your system successfully starts.

NOTE

If the partition table information stored on the file PARTNSAV.FIL does not correspond to your hard disk size, UNFORMAT will not use the file.

Key Terms

Deletion tracking   Information tracked under the DOS 5 MIRROR command about each file you delete from your disk.

Undelete   The process of rebuilding a file on disk previously deleted by DEL.

Unformat   The process of rebuilding a disk that has been accidentally formatted.

Chapter *29*

Using DEBUG

A program is a list of instructions that tell your computer what to do. When you execute a program, your computer performs each instruction, beginning with the first and ending with the last. Because programs are written by humans, who periodically make mistakes, the list of computer instructions isn't always correct. When this occurs, the errors may cause the computer to behave incorrectly. These errors are not the computer's fault. The computer is simply performing its given instructions. Computer programmers refer to program errors as *bugs*. The DEBUG command is a tool to help programmers remove bugs from their programs. The process of locating and removing program errors is called *debugging*.

Although the DEBUG command began as a programmer's tool, it is most used today by end users who use it to build simple commands. Programmers now use more powerful debuggers to assist them in locating program errors.

As you know, files with the EXE or COM extensions contain commands. These commands were created by programmers using programming languages such as C or Pascal. Using DEBUG you can create your own simple commands, even if you know nothing about programming. In this chapter, you will create several commands using DEBUG.

Creating Simple COM Commands

DEBUG lets you create COM files containing simple commands. To create a command, you need to provide DEBUG with the command's instructions. This chapter provides the instructions you'll need for each command. If you pick up almost any computer magazine, you'll find the instructions for other commands you can use DEBUG to create.

DEBUG is an external command in the DOS directory. The following example will use DEBUG to create a command named HELLO.COM that displays the message "Hello, world!" on your screen. To begin, invoke DEBUG with the file name HELLO.COM, as shown here.

```
C:\> DEBUG  HELLO.COM   <ENTER>
File not found
```

Because the file HELLO.COM does not yet exist, DEBUG displays the "File not found" message. DEBUG uses the hyphen as its command prompt. DEBUG commands are each one letter, possibly followed by additional parameters, such as a file name or memory location. To tell DEBUG you want to enter the command's instructions, type the command A 100 as shown below. Note that a hyphen remains at the beginning of the line with the command.

```
C:\> DEBUG  HELLO.COM   <ENTER>
File not found

_A 100
16C9:0100
```

DEBUG responds to your command by displaying a set of eight hexadecimal (base 16) numbers, separated by a colon. These numbers represent memory locations. You can ignore the first four numbers, which, depending on your DOS version, CONFIG.SYS entries, and memory-resident programs, will probably differ from those shown here. Pay attention to the four numbers following the colon. These four numbers should match the numbers shown in the examples. Because DEBUG was originally designed as a tool for programmers, DEBUG displays the memory locations as hexadecimal values.

DEBUG is now ready for you to type in the program's instructions. You will enter the instructions using symbols called *assembly language*. Because this chapter provides the program instructions, you don't need to understand assembly language itself. You can leave that chore to experienced programmers.

To begin, type the assembly language instruction MOV AH, 9 and press ENTER.

```
16C9:0100 MOV AH, 9   <ENTER>
16C9:0102
```

DEBUG will display a second memory address. Type in the instruction MOV DX, 10B as shown.

```
16C9:0100   MOV   AH, 9      <ENTER>
16C9:0102   MOV   DX, 10B    <ENTER>
```

Repeat this process until you have typed in the following instructions.

```
16C9:0100   MOV   AH, 9             <ENTER>
16C9:0102   MOV   DX, 10B           <ENTER>
16C9:0105   INT   21               <ENTER>
16C9:0107   MOV   AH, 4C            <ENTER>
16C9:0109   INT   21               <ENTER>
16C9:010B   DB    'Hello, world!$'  <ENTER>
16C9:0119
```

You have finished entering instructions. Press ENTER, and DEBUG will redisplay its hyphen prompt.

```
16C9:0100   MOV   AH, 9             <ENTER>
16C9:0102   MOV   DX, 10B           <ENTER>
16C9:0105   INT   21               <ENTER>
16C9:0107   MOV   AH, 4C            <ENTER>
16C9:0109   INT   21               <ENTER>
16C9:010B   DB    'Hello, world!$'  <ENTER>
16C9:0119         <ENTER>
-
```

You must now tell DEBUG the number of bytes of memory the assembly language instructions consume. To do so, type the command R CX. Remember, a hyphen stays at the beginning of the command line.

```
-R CX
```

DEBUG stores the command's length in a storage location called CX. The R command directs DEBUG to display CX's current value, and then to prompt you, using a colon to type in the new value. To determine the command's size, subtract the command's starting address from its ending address. In this case, the ending address is 0119 and the starting address is 0100. The command's size becomes 19 (0119-0100). Type 19 and press ENTER.

```
CX 0000
:19   <ENTER>
```

Next, use DEBUG's W command to write your command out to disk, storing it in the file HELLO.COM.

```
-W   <ENTER>
Writing 00019 bytes
```

Use the Q command to quit DEBUG, returning to the DOS prompt.

```
-Q   <ENTER>

C:\>
```

You can now execute your newly created command.

```
C:\> HELLO   <ENTER>
Hello, world!
```

If your command did not execute successfully, you may need to restart your computer using the CTRL-ALT-DEL key combination. Next, delete the file HELLO.COM and invoke DEBUG as before, typing in the DEBUG commands and assembly language instructions very carefully.

When you create a command using DEBUG, follow these steps:

1. Invoke DEBUG with the command name (C:> DEBUG *FILENAME*.COM).

2. Enter the instructions using the DEBUG command A 100.

3. Type in the assembly language instructions, pressing ENTER to return to DEBUG's hyphen prompt following the last instruction.

4. Use DEBUG's R CX command to tell DEBUG the command's size.

5. Use DEBUG's W command to write the command to disk.

6. Use DEBUG's Q command to quit DEBUG and return to the DOS prompt.

Using these six steps, the following example creates a command named BEEP.COM that sounds your computer's built-in speaker one time.

```
C:\> DEBUG BEEP.COM   <ENTER>
File not found

- A 100  <ENTER>
16C9:0100   MOV   AH, 2     <ENTER>
16C9:0102   MOV   DL, 7     <ENTER>
16C9:0104   INT   21        <ENTER>
16C9:0106   MOV   AH, 4C    <ENTER>
16C9:0108   INT   21        <ENTER>
16C9:010A  <ENTER>
- R CX  <ENTER>
CX 0000
: A  <ENTER>
- W  <ENTER>
Writing 0000A bytes
- Q  <ENTER>
```

By placing the BEEP command inside your DOS batch files, you can sound your computer's alarm to notify the user of key events.

```
@ECHO OFF
PAYROLL
BEEP
ECHO Payroll processing complete
ECHO Ready to print checks
PAUSE
PRTCHECK
```

DEBUG Script Files

To create the commands HELLO.COM and BEEP.COM, you invoked DEBUG and interactively typed in the DEBUG commands and assembly language instructions. The most common way to create commands using DEBUG, however, is to create a file that contains the information you would typically type at DEBUG's prompt. These files, called *script files*, typically have the SCR extension. Once the file exists, you can use the DOS input redirection operator to create the command as shown here.

```
C:\> DEBUG  <  FILENAME.SCR   <ENTER>
```

The following script file, HELLO.SCR, contains the information needed to create the command HELLO.COM.

```
N HELLO.COM
A 100
MOV  AH, 9
MOV  DX, 10B
INT  21
MOV  AH, 4C
INT  21
DB  'Hello, world!$'
<ENTER>
R CX
19
W
Q
```

The only line that should be new is the line containing DEBUG's N command to name the file. Note the line containing only <ENTER>. As you recall, you must specify a blank line after the command's last assembly language instruction. The line containing only <ENTER> does just that.

Using HELLO.SCR, you can create HELLO.COM using DEBUG and the DOS input redirection operator as shown here.

```
C:\> DEBUG  <  HELLO.SCR
```

Using your word processor or the DOS editor, create the script file HOUR.SCR that creates the command HOUR.COM, which returns the current hour of the day as an exit status value.

```
N HOUR.COM
A 100
MOV AH, 2C
INT 21
MOV AL, CH
MOV AH, 4C
INT 21
<ENTER>
R CX
A
W
Q
```

You may recall from Chapter 16, "Decision-Making Batch Files," that, using the IF ERRORLEVEL command, you can create a batch file named GREETING.BAT that displays a message based on the current time of day.

```
@ECHO OFF
HOUR
IF ERRORLEVEL 0 IF NOT ERRORLEVEL 12 ECHO Good morning!
IF ERRORLEVEL 12 IF NOT ERRORLEVEL 18 ECHO Good afternoon!
IF ERRORLEVEL 18 ECHO Good evening!
```

As the complexity of your batch files increases, you will find creating simple commands with DEBUG can be quite convenient.

Hands On

Using DEBUG interactively, create the command Y_OR_N.COM that waits for the user to type either Y or N. If the user types Y, the batch file returns the exit status value 1. If the user types N, the batch file displays the exit status value 0.

```
C:\> DEBUG Y_OR_N.COM    <ENTER>
File not found

-A 100    <ENTER>
2707:0100 MOV AH, 0     <ENTER>
2707:0102 INT 16        <ENTER>
2707:0104 MOV AL, 0     <ENTER>
2707:0106 CMP AH, 15    <ENTER>
2707:0109 JE 112        <ENTER>
2707:010B CMP AH, 31    <ENTER>
2707:010E JE 114        <ENTER>
2707:0110 JMP 100       <ENTER>
2707:0112 MOV AL, 1     <ENTER>
2707:0114 MOV AH, 4C    <ENTER>
2707:0116 INT 21        <ENTER>
2707:0118     <ENTER>
-R CX    <ENTER>
CX 0000
:18    <ENTER>
-W    <ENTER>
Writing 00018 bytes
-Q    <ENTER>
```

There may be times when you want AUTOEXEC.BAT to execute a specific command, and times you don't want the command executed, depending on your application. For example, you may or may not want AUTOEXEC.BAT to install memory-resident software, such as the DOS 5 DOSKEY command. Using Y_OR_N.COM, AUTOEXEC.BAT can prompt the user to determine whether to execute the command, as shown here.

```
ECHO Do you want to execute DOSKEY (Y/N)?
Y_OR_N
IF ERRORLEVEL 1 DOSKEY
```

Using your word processor or the DOS editor, create the file SCANCODE.SCR that returns the scan code corresponding to the key pressed by the user.

```
N SCANCODE.COM
A 100
INT 16
MOV AL, AH
MOV AH, 4C
INT 21
<ENTER>
R CX
8
W
Q
```

Using the DOS input redirection operator, create SCANCODE.COM as follows.

```
C:\> DEBUG  <  SCANCODE.SCR
```

Figure 29-1 displays the scan code values for each key. Using the scan code values, you can create the batch file MENU.BAT, which displays the following menu and waits for the user to press a key.

```
          M E N U

D  List directory files
C  Run CHKDSK
S  Sort directory listing
X  Exit to DOS
```

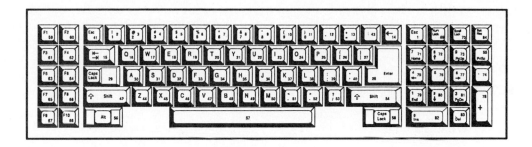

Figure 29-1.   Keyboard scan code values

Using SCANCODE.COM, the batch file determines the key pressed and proceeds accordingly.

```
ECHO OFF
:LOOP
CLS
ECHO          M E N U
ECHO.
ECHO D  List directory files
ECHO C  Run CHKDSK
ECHO S  Sort directory listing
ECHO X  Exit to DOS
:GET_KEY
SCANCODE
IF ERRORLEVEL 32 IF NOT ERRORLEVEL 33 GOTO DIR
IF ERRORLEVEL 46 IF NOT ERRORLEVEL 47 GOTO CHKDSK
IF ERRORLEVEL 31 IF NOT ERRORLEVEL 32 GOTO SORT
IF ERRORLEVEL 45 IF NOT ERRORLEVEL 46 GOTO EXIT
GOTO GET_KEY
:DIR
DIR
PAUSE
GOTO LOOP
:CHKDSK
CHKDSK
PAUSE
GOTO LOOP
:SORT
```

```
DIR | SORT | FIND /V "e" | MORE
PAUSE
GOTO LOOP
:EXIT
```

Review

1. What is a bug?

2. How do you determine the size of the following command?

```
C:\> DEBUG GETDAY.COM  <ENTER>
File not found

-A 100
16C9:0100   MOV AH, 2A <ENTER>
16C9:0102   INT 21     <ENTER>
16C9:0104   MOV AH, 4C <ENTER>
16C9:0106   INT 21     <ENTER>
16C9:0108
```

3. Using the following assembly language instructions, how would you use DEBUG to create the command SHOWLINE.COM?

```
MOV AH, 2
MOV SI, 82
MOV DL, [SI]
CMP DL, D
JZ 113
MOV AH, 2
INT 21
INC SI
JMP 105
MOV AH, 4C
INT 21
```

4. SHOWLINE.COM differs from ECHO because SHOWLINE does not write carriage return and linefeed characters, which advance the cursor to the next line. Change the batch file MENU.BAT to use SHOWLINE to prompt the user for an option.

5. Using the following assembly language instructions, create the DEBUG script file BOOT_DOS.SCR that reboots DOS.

```
MOV AX, 40
MOV DS, AX
MOV AX, 1234
MOV [72], AX
JMP FFFF:0
```

6. After the BOOT_DOS.SCR file exists, how can you use it to create BOOT_DOS.COM?

Answers

1. A bug is an error in a software program.

2. Subtract the starting address from the ending address (108 – 100 = 8). Assign this value to the CX register and write the command as shown.

```
-R CX
CX 0000
:8
-W
Writing 00008 bytes
-Q
```

GETDAY.COM returns, as an exit status value, the current day of the week. Sunday corresponds to the value 0, and Saturday corresponds to the value 6.

NOTE

3. Be sure to press ENTER at the end of each line shown in the following screen:

```
C:\> DEBUG SHOWLINE.COM   <ENTER>
File not found

-A 100   <ENTER>
2726:0100 MOV AH, 2       <ENTER>
2726:0102 MOV SI, 82      <ENTER>
2726:0105 MOV DL, [SI]    <ENTER>
2726:0107 CMP DL, D       <ENTER>
2726:010A JZ 113          <ENTER>
2726:010C MOV AH, 2       <ENTER>
2726:010E INT 21          <ENTER>
2726:0110 INC SI          <ENTER>
```

```
2726:0111 JMP 105        <ENTER>
2726:0113 MOV AH, 4C     <ENTER>
2726:0115 INT 21         <ENTER>
2726:0117      <ENTER>
-R CX          <ENTER>
CX 0000
:17            <ENTER>
-W             <ENTER>
Writing 00017 bytes
-Q             <ENTER>
```

4. The batch file would be changed as follows. Note the final ECHO command (with a period) to advance the cursor one line.

```
@ECHO OFF
:LOOP
CLS
ECHO        M E N U
ECHO.
ECHO D  List directory files
ECHO C  Run CHKDSK
ECHO S  Sort directory listing
ECHO X  Exit to DOS
SHOWLINE Enter choice:
:GET_KEY
SCANCODE
IF ERRORLEVEL 32 IF NOT ERRORLEVEL 33 GOTO DIR
IF ERRORLEVEL 46 IF NOT ERRORLEVEL 47 GOTO CHKDSK
IF ERRORLEVEL 31 IF NOT ERRORLEVEL 32 GOTO SORT
IF ERRORLEVEL 45 IF NOT ERRORLEVEL 46 GOTO EXIT
GOTO GET_KEY
:DIR
DIR
PAUSE
GOTO LOOP
:CHKDSK
CHKDSK
PAUSE
GOTO LOOP
:SORT
DIR | SORT | FIND /V "e" | MORE
```

```
PAUSE
GOTO LOOP
:EXIT
ECHO.
```

5. The script file would appear as follows.

```
N BOOT_DOS.COM
A 100
MOV AX, 40
MOV DS, AX
MOV AX, 1234
MOV [72], AX
JMP FFFF:0
<ENTER>
R CX
10
W
Q
```

6. Redirect the file BOOT_DOS.SCR into DEBUG using the DOS input redirection operator as shown here.

```
C:\> DEBUG < BOOT_DOS.SCR
```

Advanced Concepts

If you are an "old time" DOS user, you may use DEBUG extensively. Unfortunately, the size of this book prevents us from examining all of DEBUG's capabilities in detail. This section will briefly summarize each of DEBUG's commands. For the most part, DEBUG has remained unchanged over the past DOS versions. Table 29-1 lists the DEBUG commands.

The balance of this chapter summarizes each DEBUG command.

?

Function: Lists the available DEBUG commands.

Explanation: Displays a summary of the DEBUG commands and formats to your screen. This command requires DOS 5.

Command	Function
?	Displays a list of available DEBUG commands (DOS 5)
A	Lets you enter assembly language statements
C	Compares two memory areas
D	Displays a memory range
E	Enters data into a memory range
F	Fills a memory range with a specific value
G	Runs the command you are debugging from the current location to completion
H	Performs hexadecimal addition and subtraction
I	Displays the value in the port specified
L	Loads a file or disk sectors into memory
M	Copies a range of memory values from one location to another
N	Specifies the name of the file to be used with L and W commands
O	Writes a byte value to the port specified
P	Executes a loop, a repeated string instruction, a subroutine, or a software interrupt
Q	Quits a debugging session, returning control to DOS
R	Displays the contents of one or more registers, letting you change the register's value
S	Searches memory for the byte pattern specified
T	Executes the current instruction, displaying the register contents, the status flags, and the assembly language form of the instruction that DEBUG will execute next
U	Displays the assembly language representation for a range of memory values
W	Writes the current memory contents to the file specified by the N command
XA	Allocates a region of expanded memory (DOS 4 or later)
XD	Deallocates a region of expanded memory (DOS 4 or later)
XM	Maps expanded memory pages (DOS 4 or later)
XS	Displays the status of expanded memory (DOS 4 or later)

Table 29-1.   The DEBUG Commands

Example: The following ? command displays the DEBUG commands.

```
-?
assemble        A [address]
compare         C range address
dump            D [range]
enter           E address [list]
fill            F range list
go              G [=address] [addresses]
hex             H value1 value2
input           I port
load            L [address] [drive] [firstsector] [number]
move            M range address
name            N [pathname] [arglist]
output          O port byte
proceed         P [=address] [number]
quit            Q
register        R [register]
search          S range list
trace           T [=address] [value]
unassemble      U [range]
write           W [address] [drive] [firstsector] [number]
allocate expanded memory        XA [#pages]
deallocate expanded memory      XD [handle]
map expanded memory pages       XM [Lpage] [Ppage] [handle]
display expanded memory status  XS
```

A [*memory address*]

Function: Lets you enter one or more assembly language instructions.

Explanation: Using DEBUG's A command you can change a command's instruction or, if you are creating a custom command, type in a series of instructions.

The memory address specifies the command's location. When you create your own commands, use A 100. The hexadecimal value 100 corresponds to the value 256, which tells DEBUG to enter the command's first instruction immediately after the 255-byte program segment prefix, which contains DOS-specific information for the command, such as its command line.

Example: The following command creates a command named PRTSC.COM that prints your screen contents as though you pressed SHIFT-PRTSC.

```
C:\> DEBUG PRTSC.COM    <ENTER>
File not found

-A 100                    <ENTER>
2726:0100 INT 5           <ENTER>
2726:0102 MOV AH, 4C      <ENTER>
2726:0104 INT 21 <ENTER>
2726:0106
-R CX   <ENTER>
CX 0000
:6      <ENTER>
-W      <ENTER>
Writing 00006 bytes
-Q      <ENTER>
```

C *AddressRange StartingAddress*

Function: Compares the values stored in two or more memory locations, displaying differences.

Explanation: *AddressRange* specifies both a starting and ending address (or starting address and length) of the first memory range. *StartAddress* specifies only the starting of the second range. If you don't include segment addresses, DEBUG uses DS. DEBUG compares the corresponding byte of the first range with each byte of the second range. If the two byte values differ, DEBUG displays the addresses and differing values in the following format.

Address1 ByteValue1 ByteValue2 Address2

If DEBUG finds no differences, DEBUG simply redisplays its prompt.

Examples: The following command compares 7 bytes beginning at 0100 to 0106 and 0200.

```
-C   0100   0106   0200   <ENTER>
```

Because the command does not specify segment addresses, DEBUG uses DS. The following command compares the first 255 bytes (FF in hexadecimal) of the data segment to the extra segment.

```
-C  DS:0  LFF  ES:0  <ENTER>
```

D [*Address* [*NumberofBytes*]]

Function: Displays the values currently stored in a range of memory.

Explanation: DEBUG's D command directs DEBUG to display the values stored in a range of memory using the value's hexadecimal and ASCII representation. *Address* specifies the starting address of the first value to display. If you don't specify a segment address, DEBUG uses DS. If you don't specify the optional *NumberofBytes*, DEBUG displays 128.

DEBUG displays the memory dump as follows:

```
-D
2707:0100  59 58 86 C4 9E C3 8B 1E-02 96 4B 89 1E 02 96 A0   YX........K.....
2707:0110  97 03 0A C0 74 20 E8 06-00 B0 FF A2 34 00 F6 26   ....t ......4..&
2707:0120  F2 46 AC 8D 1E 08 96 FE-07 FE 0F 75 01 C3 FE 07   .F.........u....
2707:0130  E8 9A D5 75 01 C3 8B 1E-06 96 9F 4B 9E 89 1E 06   ...u,......K....
2707:0140  96 C3 8B 1E 04 96 9F 4B-9E 89 1E 04 96 E8 A1 FD   .......K........
2707:0150  E8 E4 BF 89 1E 06 96 C3-8B 1E 62 47 E8 BF BF 4A   ..........bG...J
2707:0160  8A E9 8A C7 0A C3 75 01-C3 43 8B F2 AC 8A C8 24   ......u..C.....$
2707:0170  7F 3C 0A 74 04 3C 0C 75-F6 8A C5 EB A6 9F 86 C4   .<.t.<.u........
```

If a byte value does not correspond to a printable ASCII character, DEBUG displays the value's ASCII representation as a period.

Examples: The following command displays the command's 255-byte program segment prefix.

```
-D  0  FF  <ENTER>
```

Likewise, the following command displays the next 128 bytes of the data segment.

```
-D  <ENTER>
```

E *StartingAddress* [*DataValues*]

Function: Enters byte values into successive memory locations.

Explanation: *StartingAddress* specifies the first address into which you want to assign one or more bytes or ASCII values. If you do not include a segment address, DEBUG uses DS. The optional DataValues is one or more hexadecimal byte values separated by spaces, tabs, or commas, or an ASCII string enclosed by single or double quotes.

If you don't specify *DataValues*, DEBUG will display each memory location's current value followed by a period, letting you type in the desired value. If you press ENTER after typing the value, DEBUG updates memory and the command ends. If you instead press the SPACEBAR, DEBUG will update memory and display the byte value stored in the next memory location, letting you continue the update. DEBUG lets you enter up to eight values on one line.

If you type in an invalid value, DEBUG will ignore it.

Examples: The following command assigns the ASCII string "DOS Book" to the memory location 100 relative to data segment.

```
-E  100  'DOS Book'
```

Likewise, the following command lets you enter byte values for a sequence of memory locations beginning at location 100.

```
-E  100
```

DEBUG will display location 100's current value followed by a period.

```
-E 100
2707:0100  44.
```

Type in the location's value and press ENTER to end the command or the SPACEBAR to enter a byte value in location 101.

F *AddressRange DataValues*

Function: Fills a range of memory with the value or values specified.

Explanation: *AddressRange* specifies the starting and ending address of the memory range to fill. The *DataValues* are one or more hexadecimal byte values separated by spaces, commas, or tabs or an ASCII character string enclosed by single or double quotes. If the number of data values is smaller that the range of memory, DEBUG repeatedly uses the values until the memory range is full.

Example: The following command fills a CGA screen with the word "DOS" using the ASCII values 44, 4F, and 53 for the letters "D," "O," and "S" and 20 for a space.

```
-F B800:0 4000 44,7,4F,7,53,7,20,7  <ENTER>
```

G [=*StartingAddress*] [*BreakPoint1*[... *BreakPoint10*]]

Function: Executes the current command either to completion or to an address specified.

Explanation: When you debug a program, you typically try to divide your program into pieces you can individually verify as working or containing a bug. A *breakpoint* is a location within the program at which you want execution to stop, so you can examine either memory or the current register values. When you stop a program's execution using DEBUG, you need a way to get the program restarted. DEBUG's G (Go) command lets you do just that.

If you don't specify a breakpoint, DEBUG will run the program until it successfully completes, at which time DEBUG display's the message "Program terminated normally," or DEBUG will run the program until the program fails.

The =*StartingAddress* value specifies the address of the instruction at which you want DEBUG to begin the program's execution. If you don't specify a starting address, DEBUG uses the current value of the CS and IP registers.

A breakpoint is an address at which you want DEBUG to stop the program's execution. If you don't specify a breakpoint, DEBUG tries to run the program to completion. If you specify a breakpoint, DEBUG only stops the program's execution if the program attempts to execute the instruction stored at the breakpoint's address. DEBUG lets you specify up to ten breakpoints. If you don't specify a segment address, DEBUG uses CS.

Examples: The following command directs DEBUG to run the program from the current address in CS and IP to completion.

```
-G   <ENTER>
```

This command restarts the program from address 100.

```
-G  =100   <ENTER>
```

Last, this command resumes the program's execution while setting three break-points.

```
-G  200  300  400  <ENTER>
```

H *HexValue1 HexValue2*

Function: Displays the sum and difference of two hexadecimal numbers.

Explanation: Because DEBUG works in hexadecimal, determining the correct hexadecimal values to use for offsets or sizes can be difficult.

DEBUG's H command adds and subtracts two hexadecimal values, displaying first the sum, then the difference. DEBUG's H command is convenient for determining the size of simple commands you interactively create using DEBUG.

Example: The following command displays the sum and difference (in hexadecimal) of the values 9 and 8.

```
-H  9  8  <ENTER>
0011  0001
```

The hexadecimal value 11 corresponds to the decimal value 17.

I *PortAddress*

Functions: Displays the byte value stored at the specified port address.

Explanation: Your computer exchanges information with hardware devices in one of two ways: First, the computer uses specific memory locations to address the hardware, such as memory-mapped video output. Second, your computer uses ports assigned to specific hardware devices, each individually addressed from 0 to FFFF. DEBUG's I command reads the value currently stored in the port.

Example: The following I command reads the port 378, which contains the last character sent to the parallel printer.

```
-I 378  <ENTER>
0A
```

In this case the 0A indicates that the last character sent to the printer was a linefeed character.

L [*StartingAddress*]

or

L *StartingAddress DriveNumber SectorNumber SectorCount*

Function: Loads either a file or specific disk sectors into memory.

Explanation: The first form of DEBUG's L command loads a file into memory at the address specified. DEBUG loads the file previously specified by a N (name) command. If you don't specify a segment address, DEBUG uses CS. If you don't specify an address at all, DEBUG loads files with the COM extension at location 100 and files with the EXE at the memory location specified in the program's header information.

   The second form of DEBUG's L command loads one or more disk sectors. *StartingAddress* specifies the location at which DEBUG loads the first sector. If you don't specify a segment address, DEBUG uses CS. *DriveNumber* is a value from 0 to 25 where 0 corresponds to drive A and 25 corresponds to drive Z. *SectorNumber* specifies the first sector to load. *SectorCount* specifies the number of sectors.

Examples: The following commands select the file LABEL.COM and load the file into memory.

```
-N   LABEL.COM   <ENTER>
-L   <ENTER>
```

   Likewise, this command loads the drive C's (drive number 2) boot record (sector number 0) at location 100 and then displays the sector.

```
-L   100   2   0   1   <ENTER>
-D   100   <ENTER>
```

M *AddressRange TargetAddress*

Function: Copies the values in one range of memory to another.

Explanation: *AddressRange* specifies the starting and ending memory addresses (or starting address and length) for the range of memory to copy. If you don't specify a segment address, DEBUG uses DS. *TargetAddress* is the address of the starting location to which you want the data copied. If the two memory ranges overlap, DEBUG will copy the data correctly.

Example: The following command copies 32 (hexadecimal 20) bytes of data beginning at location 0 to location 100.

```
-M  0  20  100  <ENTER>
```

N *Filename.Ext [CommandLine]*

Function: Specifies the name of a file to be loaded by an L command or written to by W.

Explanation: The file name can include a drive letter and directory path. When you issue the N command, DEBUG builds a 255-byte program segment prefix (PSP) at locations 0 to FF. The optional *CommandLine* is information DEBUG places at the hexadecimal offset 80 within the PSP. This information could possibly include a file name or other command information you want to use during debugging.

Examples: The following command selects the file name TEST.COM.

```
-N  TEST.COM  <ENTER>
```

This command selects TEST.COM and specifies command-line information that appears at DS:80.

```
-N  TEST.COM  Command line information  <ENTER>
```

O *PortAddress ByteValue*

Function: Outputs a byte value to a hardware port.

Explanation: Your computer exchanges information with hardware devices in one of two ways: First, the computer uses specific memory locations to address the hardware, such as memory-mapped video output. Second, your computer uses ports assigned to specific hardware devices, each individually addressed from 0 to FFFF. DEBUG's O command writes a value to the port specified. Use the DEBUG O command with caution. If you write the wrong value to a port, or write to the wrong port, you may hang your system.

Example: The following O command writes the value 61 to the port 378, which is the parallel port data register.

```
-O 378 61 <ENTER>
```

In this case the hexadecimal representation of a lowercase "A" is placed in the printer output register. Additional port output commands would be required to actually transfer the character from the adapter to the printer.

P [=*StartingAddress*][*InstructionCount*]

Function: Directs DEBUG to proceed through a loop, repeated string instruction, subroutine, or software interrupt.

Explanation: When searching for errors, programmers often use DEBUG to step through instructions one at a time. If you know that the next, possibly time-consuming, instruction is not the cause of the error, you can direct DEBUG to proceed through the instruction located at *StartingAddress* in one step, or until the number of instructions specified by *InstructionCount* have executed.

If you don't specify a segment address for *StartingAddress*, DEBUG uses CS. If you don't specify an instruction count, DEBUG uses the value 1. Using DEBUG's P command is very convenient for bypassing all of the instructions that correspond to INT 21.

Examples: The following command directs DEBUG to proceed through the current instruction.

```
-P  <ENTER>
```

The next command directs DEBUG to proceed through the software interrupt at address 112.

```
-P  =112   <ENTER>
```

Q

Function: Quits DEBUG, returning control to the DOS prompt.

Explanation: Q ends your debugging session. If you are using DEBUG to create simple commands, make sure you first write the command's instructions to a file on disk.

Example: The following command exits DEBUG to DOS.

```
-Q    <ENTER>
```

R [*RegisterName*]

Function: Displays the contents of one or more registers, letting you change the register's contents.

Explanation: *RegisterName* is the two-letter name of one of the 8086 registers or the single-letter Flags register.

AX BX CX DX SP BP SI DI
DS CS SS ES IP PC F

The Flags register F contains the current processor status codes. DEBUG displays the following status code symbols:

OV	Overflow flag set
NV	No overflow
UP	Direction up for string operations
DN	Direction down for string operations
EI	Interrupts enabled
DI	Interrupts disabled
NG	Negative sign
PL	Positive sign
ZR	Zero result
NZ	Nonzero result
AC	Auxiliary carry
NA	No auxiliary carry
PE	Even parity
PO	Odd parity
CY	Carry
NC	No carry

If you specify a *RegisterName*, DEBUG will display the register's current value and then prompt you (using a colon) to enter a new value. If you press ENTER at the colon prompt, DEBUG will leave the register's value unchanged.

If you invoke R with the Flags register F, DEBUG will display the status codes followed by a hyphen.

```
-R F   <ENTER>
NV UP EI PL NZ NA PO NC
-
```

To change one or more status codes, simply type the new setting or settings separated by spaces after the hyphen.

Examples: The following command displays the current register values.

```
-R   <ENTER>
AX=0000  BX=0000  CX=0000  DX=0000  SP=FFEE  BP=0000  SI=0000  DI=0000
DS=2707  ES=2707  SS=2707  CS=2707  IP=0100   NV UP EI PL NZ NA PO NC
2707:0100 0000        ADD     [BX+SI],AL                      DS:0000=CD
```

The following command assigns the CX register the value 5.

```
-R   CX   <ENTER>
CX  0000
:5   <ENTER>
```

The next command sets the overflow flag.

```
-R   F   <ENTER>
NV UP EI PL NZ NA PO NC
-OV   <ENTER>
```

S *AddressRange ByteValues*

Function: Searches memory for a byte pattern matching the values specified.

Explanation: *AddressRange* specifies either the starting and ending addresses for the range of memory DEBUG is to search, or the starting address and the number of bytes to search. To specify an address and a length, precede the second value with the letter "L." For example, L10 directs DEBUG to search 16 bytes (10 is the hexadecimal representation for the value 16). If you don't specify a segment address for the starting address, DEBUG uses DS. If you don't specify a segment address for the ending address, DEBUG uses the same segment address as the first value.

The *ByteValues* are one or more byte values separated by spaces, commas, or tabs or a character string enclosed by single or double quotes.

Each time DEBUG finds a match to the pattern, DEBUG will display the segment and offset address of the first matching byte.

Examples: Give the following command to search the 64Kb data segment for the "PATH=" string:

```
- S   O   FFFF   'PATH='   <ENTER>
```

Likewise, the next command searches the first 255 bytes of the data segment for the same string.

```
- S   O   LFF   'PATH='   <ENTER>
```

T [=*StartingAddress*] [*InstructionCount*]

Function: Executes the number of instructions specified displaying the contents of the CPU registers and status flags after each instruction.

Explanation: To debug programs, programmers must often "single-step" through the program, executing an instruction and then examining registers and memory to verify the instruction was successful. This process of single-stepping through a program is called *tracing*. The DEBUG T command lets you trace one or more instructions.

StartingAddress is the address of the instruction at which you want the program trace to begin. If you don't specify an address, DEBUG uses the address in CS and IP. *InstructionCount* specifies the number of instructions DEBUG should execute. If you don't specify an instruction count, DEBUG uses the value 1.

To suspend scrolling of a program trace, press CTRL-S; to cancel the program trace, use CTRL-C.

Examples: The following command traces the current instruction.

```
- T   <ENTER>
AX=0000   BX=0000   CX=20FA   DX=0000   SP=0080   BP=0000   SI=0000   DI=0000
DS=2726   ES=2726   SS=2971   CS=2930   IP=0012     NV UP EI PL NZ NA PO NC
2930:0012 8CC0            MOV     AX,ES
```

Likewise, this command traces five instructions.

```
-T   5   <ENTER>
```

Last, this command traces three instructions, beginning at location 100.

```
-T   =100   3   <ENTER>
```

U [*AddressRange*]

Function: Displays the byte values in a range of memory in their assembly language representation.

Explanation: DEBUG's U or unassemble command displays a range of memory values as assembly language instructions. The U command lets you quickly examine a program's instructions, several instructions at a time. *AddressRange* specifies a starting and an ending address for the memory range to unassemble, or a starting address and byte length. If you don't specify a starting address, DEBUG uses the address in CS and IP. If you don't specify a segment address, DEBUG uses CS. If you don't specify an ending address or byte length, DEBUG unassembles 32 bytes of memory. To specify a byte length, place the letter "L" before the second value. For example, L10 directs DEBUG to unassemble 16 bytes (10 is the hexadecimal representation of 16).

Examples: The following command unassembles the range 100 to 110.

```
-U   100   110   <ENTER>
```

The following command unassembles eight bytes, beginning at DS:00.

```
-U   0   L8   <ENTER>
```

W [*StartingAddress*]

or

W *StartingAddress   DriveNumber   SectorNumber   SectorCount*

Function: Writes the contents of a memory range to a file specified by a previous L command, or writes a range of memory directly to disk sectors.

Explanation: The most common use of DEBUG's W command is to write the instructions to a file of a simple command you have created with DEBUG. *StartingAddress* is the memory address of the first byte DEBUG is to write to disk. If you don't specify a starting address, DEBUG uses CS:0100.

DEBUG uses the register combination BX:CX to determine the number of bytes to write. Note: Before you issue a W command, make sure BX and CX contain the correct length values. For small files (less than 64Kb), BX will be 0.

DEBUG's W command also lets you write directly to specific disk sectors. *DriveNumber* is a value from 0 to 25, where 0 corresponds to drive A and 25 corresponds to drive Z. *SectorNumber* is the first sector to be written, and *SectorCount* specifies the number of sectors to be written.

WARNING

The slightest mistake when writing to disk sectors may render your disk unusable, losing all the information the disk contains. If you must write to a disk sector, do so with extreme caution.

Example: The following command writes the memory range beginning at CS:0100 to the file previously named with a DEBUG N command. The number of bytes to write must be stored in BX:CX.

```
-W   <ENTER>
```

XA [*PageCount*]

Function: Allocates a specified number of expanded memory pages.

Explanation: See Chapter 32, "Understanding DOS Memory Management," for a discussion on expanded memory. *PageCount* specifies the number of 16Kb pages DEBUG is to allocate. If sufficient pages are available to meet the allocation request, DEBUG will display the hexadecimal value of the memory handle created. Otherwise, DEBUG will display an error message.

Example: The following command allocates 2 expanded memory pages.

```
-XA  2   <ENTER>
Handle created = 0004
```

XD [*Handle*]

Function: Deallocates the expanded memory pages that correspond to the memory handle specified.

Explanation: See Chapter 32 for a discussion on expanded memory. *Handle* is the hexadecimal value of the handle value displayed by DEBUG's XA command. If you specify an invalid handle number, DEBUG will display an error message. If the handle number is valid, DEBUG will display a message stating the handle (and its corresponding memory) was deallocated.

Example: The following command deallocates the memory corresponding to handle 0004.

```
-XD  0004  <ENTER>
Handle 00004 deallocated
```

XM *LogicalPage PhysicalPage Handle*

Function: Maps the logical page number specified to a physical page number.

Explanation: See Chapter 32 for a discussion on expanded memory. *LogicalPage* is a page number relative to the *Handle* specified. *PhysicalPage* is an actual page number within expanded memory. If the page numbers and handle specified are valid, DEBUG will display a message indicating the mapping was successful. Otherwise, DEBUG will display an error.

Example: The following command maps logical page 1 of handle 0004 to physical page 1.

```
-XM  1  1  0004  <ENTER>
Logical page 01 mapped to physical page 01
```

XS

Function: Displays the current status of expanded memory.

Explanation: See Chapter 32 for a discussion on expanded memory. XS displays the physical page addresses and the number of allocated pages.

Example: The following command displays the current expanded memory status.

```
-XS   <ENTER>
```

Key Terms

Bug   An error within a program that prevents the program from correctly executing.

Debug   The process of removing errors from a program.

Debugger   A software program that helps programmers debug their programs.

Debug script file   A text file, typically with the SCR extension, containing the DEBUG commands and assembly language instructions needed to create a small COM command.

Chapter 30

Another Look at Disks

Throughout the first 29 chapters of this book, you have made extensive use of floppy and hard disks. In this chapter you'll round out the remaining DOS disk commands: LABEL, VOL, DISKCOMP, SHARE, VERIFY, and RECOVER.

Disk Volume Labels: LABEL and VOL

A disk volume label is a name you assign to a disk. Each time you issue a DIR command, DIR displays your disk name, as in the following directory listing.

```
C:\> DIR  <ENTER>

 Volume in drive C is DOS
 Volume Serial Number is 168C-5277
 Directory of C:\

COMMAND   COM     47867 03-08-91    5:05a
DOS          <DIR>       10-16-90    4:44p
DISKUTIL     <DIR>       10-16-90    4:55p
    :          :            :          :
BACKUP       <DIR>       03-22-91    2:27p
CONFIG   SYS       256 04-20-91    9:55a
AUTOEXEC BAT       256 04-20-91    9:55a
       12 file(s)      412796 bytes
                     14820608 bytes free
```

If the disk does not have a label, DIR displays the following line instead.

```
Volume in drive C has no label
```

Users most commonly assign disk volume labels to floppy disks. Consider the following scenario. Each month you copy the contents of the four spreadsheet files BUDGET.DAT, EXPENSES.DAT, PAYROLL.DAT, and SALARY.DAT to floppy disk. A directory listing of the disk in drive A reveals the following files.

```
C:\> DIR  A:  <ENTER>

 Volume in drive A has no label
 Volume Serial Number is 2C27-0ECF
 Directory of A:\

 BUDGET   DAT    40832 07-18-91  12:08p
 EXPENSES DAT    18944 07-18-91   3:27p
 PAYROLL  DAT    40576 07-16-91   2:22p
 SALARY   DAT    44800 07-21-91   8:23a
         4 file(s)     145152 bytes
                       216064 bytes free
```

In this case, the disk does not have a volume label. Assume that you give the disk to another user who consolidates data from several months to create year-to-date summaries. Before the user places your floppy disk into the drive, the user can look at the label attached to the disk to determine the month to which the files correspond. Once the user places the disk into the disk drive, the file names for one month look just like the names for another. Should the user forget which month's disk is in drive A, the user must remove the disk and look at the label. Using a disk volume label, however, such as JUNE, JULY, or AUGUST, the user can quickly determine the file's month using the DIR command.

```
C:\> DIR  A:  <ENTER>

 Volume in drive A is JULY
 Volume Serial Number is 2C27-0ECF
 Directory of A:\

 BUDGET   DAT    40832 07-18-91  12:08p
 EXPENSES DAT    18944 07-18-91   3:27p
 PAYROLL  DAT    40576 07-16-91   2:22p
 SALARY   DAT    44800 07-21-91   8:23a
```

```
     4 file(s)       145152 bytes
                      216064 bytes free
```

Assigning a Disk Volume Label

In Chapter 7, "Preparing Disks for Use," you learned FORMAT lets you assign a disk volume label after it successfully formats a disk.

```
Format complete.

Volume label (11 characters, ENTER for none)?
```

If you have a formatted disk that contains information, you can use the LABEL command to assign a disk volume label. LABEL is an external DOS command that resides in the DOS directory. If you include a drive specifier in LABEL's command line, LABEL will assign the volume label to the disk specified. If you don't specify a disk, LABEL uses the default drive.

The following LABEL command assigns a volume label to the disk in drive A.

```
C:\> LABEL  A:   <ENTER>
```

LABEL will display the disk's current volume label and possibly the disk's serial number depending on your DOS version. LABEL will then prompt you to type in the disk's new volume name.

```
C:\> LABEL  A:   <ENTER>

Volume in drive A has no label
Volume Serial Number is 168C-5277
Volume label (11 characters, ENTER for none)?
```

Disk volume names can contain up to 11 characters. DOS lets you use in your disk volume labels the letters of the alphabet and numbers, as well as the following characters:

```
   !    @    #    %    _    -    {    }    $    '    `    ~
```

In DOS 4 and later, you can use spaces within the name.

This command assigns the disk label AUGUST.

```
C:\> LABEL  A:  <ENTER>

Volume in drive A has no label
Volume Serial Number is 168C-5277
Volume label (11 characters, ENTER for none)? AUGUST  <ENTER>
```

If your label contains invalid characters, LABEL will display an error message and prompt you to type in a correct volume name.

```
Invalid characters in volume label
Volume label (11 characters, ENTER for none)? AUGUST  <ENTER>
```

If you assign the wrong disk label, invoke LABEL again and retype the label name. If you want to delete the current disk label, press ENTER at LABEL's prompt for a new volume label. LABEL will ask you if you want to delete the current label.

```
Volume label (11 characters, ENTER for none)? <ENTER>
Delete current volume label (Y/N)?
```

To delete the label, type Y and press ENTER. If you type N and press ENTER, LABEL will leave the current disk label unchanged.

If you include the label name in the command line, LABEL will use the label specified without prompting you for one. The following command assigns the disk volume label OCTOBER to the disk in drive A.

```
C:\> LABEL  A:OCTOBER  <ENTER>
```

Because the command line contains the disk label, LABEL assigns the disk label as desired and returns control to the DOS prompt.

Displaying a Disk Volume Label

As you just learned, the DIR command displays the disk volume label before each directory listing of files. Likewise, the CHKDSK command displays the disk label and the date and time you assigned the label.

```
C:\> CHKDSK   <ENTER>


Volume DOS          created 04-21-1991 8:46a
Volume Serial Number is 168C-5277

 200065024 bytes total disk space
     81920 bytes in 3 hidden files
    462848 bytes in 108 directories
  44699648 bytes in 2034 user files
 154820608 bytes available on disk

      4096 bytes in each allocation unit
     48844 total allocation units on disk
     37798 available allocation units on disk

    655360 total bytes memory
    562688 bytes free
```

In addition, the internal DOS command VOL displays the disk volume label for the disk specified. If you don't include a disk drive specifier in VOL's command line, VOL displays the volume label for the current disk.

```
C:\> VOL   <ENTER>

Volume in drive C is DOS
Volume Serial Number is 168C-5277
```

If the disk does not have a label, VOL displays the following.

```
Volume in drive A has no label
Volume Serial Number is 168C-5277
```

This command uses VOL to display the volume label for the disk in drive A.

```
C:\> VOL   A:   <ENTER>
```

Comparing Two Floppy Disks with DISKCOMP

For many years after DOS was released in 1981, most users had floppy disk-based systems. It was very common for users to copy the contents of the floppy disk in drive A to the floppy disk in drive B using DISKCOPY, as discussed in Chapter 12, "Fundamental Copy Operations."

After completing a DISKCOPY operation, users would invoke the DISKCOMP command to ensure the DISKCOPY operation was successful. The DISKCOMP command compares two floppy disks track by track, sector by sector, and byte by byte, displaying any differences it encounters in the following format.

```
Compare error on
side n, track n
```

If the two disks contain the same contents DISKCOMP displays the following.

```
Compare OK
```

The following command compares the floppy disk in drive A to the disk in drive B.

```
C:\> DISKCOMP  A:  B:  <ENTER>
```

DISKCOMP will prompt you to place the first disk in drive A and the second disk in drive B.

```
Insert FIRST diskette in drive A:

Insert SECOND diskette in drive B:

Press any key to continue...
```

When you press any key, DISKCOMP will perform the disk comparison.

When DISKCOMP completes, it will ask you if you want to compare additional disks.

```
Compare another diskette (Y/N) ?
```

If you type **Y** and press ENTER, DISKCOMP will prompt you to place disks into drives A and B, repeating the comparison process. If you type **N**, DISKCOMP will end, returning control to the DOS prompt.

DISKCOMP only compares floppy disks of the same size and capacity. You cannot use DISKCOMP to compare a 5 1/4-inch floppy to a 3 1/2-inch floppy.

If your computer only has a single floppy drive, simply specify the same drive letter as the second drive in DISKCOMP's command line.

```
C:\> DISKCOMP  A:  A:  <ENTER>
```

DISKCOMP will prompt you to insert either the first or second disk as required.

DISKCOMP only supports floppy disk drives. If you reference drive C, or only specify one floppy disk letter in the command line, DISKCOMP will display the following error message.

```
C:\> DISKCOMP  <ENTER>

Invalid drive specification
Specified drive does not exist
or is non-removable
```

File Sharing and Large Disk Support with SHARE

If your computer is connected to other computers over a local area network, there may be times when two or more users try to use the same file at the same time. If you aren't connected to a local area network, but instead use a program such as Windows or the DOS 5 shell (using the task swapper) to run several programs at the same time, two of the programs may simultaneously access the same file.

The SHARE command, introduced with DOS 3.0 loads memory-resident software that manages file sharing. Assume, for example, the program is reading the contents of a file, while another program is trying to update the file. Depending on the timing of the two operations, the program reading the file could get part of the old information and part of the new.

To prevent such conflicts, SHARE lets a program lock a file or part of the file for exclusive use. When the program is finished with its operation, the program unlocks the file so another program can use it. The format of the SHARE command is as follows:

SHARE   /F: *NumberofBytes*   /L: *NumberofLocks*

When a program locks a file, SHARE records information about the file such as its path name and the region locked to a table in memory. Each locked file requires 11 bytes plus the length of the file's path name, up to 64 bytes. SHARE's /F switch lets you specify the number of bytes SHARE should allocate for the table. For most users, the default size of 2,048 bytes is large enough.

SHARE's /L switch lets you specify the number of locks required. SHARE's default value is 20.

If your computer is connected to a local area network, your network administrator can tell you if you need to invoke SHARE. If you don't need to use SHARE, don't use it. SHARE's memory-resident software examines every file's read or write operation to prevent sharing conflicts. This examination requires processing time and, thus, slows down your programs.

One of the most common uses of SHARE is to correct a situation that arises under DOS 4 when you are using disk partitions larger than 32Mb.

DOS 4 was the first major DOS version to support disk partitions larger than 32Mb. When users with disk partitions larger than 32Mb started their systems under DOS 4, their screens would display a warning message about loading SHARE for large media.

Many users ignored the warning message and did not invoke the SHARE command. In fact, many users never experienced any adverse effects. These users where the lucky ones that never ran an older DOS program that accessed files using a file control block (FCBS), discussed in Chapter 24, "Customizing Your System with CONFIG.SYS".

Before version 2.0, DOS used file control blocks to access files. Older programs that use FCBS to access files, therefore, don't know about DOS 4's support of partitions larger than 32Mb. When one of these older programs ran on a large partition, the program might read and write disk information to the wrong locations. One disk write could destroy a file, directory, or even the file allocation table that tells DOS where each of your files reside on disk.

The DOS 4 SHARE command solves this FCBs problem. Because it is almost impossible to tell which programs use file control blocks, DOS 4 users with large disk partitions that don't invoke SHARE are playing "Russian Roulette" with their files.

If you are using DOS 4 and are using SHARE, place the following INSTALL entry in your CONFIG.SYS file to load the SHARE command.

```
INSTALL=C:\DOS\SHARE.EXE
```

DOS 5 corrects this problem and does not require you to install SHARE.

Verifying Disk Writes with VERIFY

When you copy a file to disk, or a program stores information to disk, DOS transfers the data to disk a sector at a time. In general, DOS directs the disk controller (hardware) to store the information in a specific sector location. The disk controller then actually oversees the information recording. By default, DOS assumes the disk controller correctly records the data on disk. In rare instances, however, the disk, due to a damaged surface area or hardware malfunction, may not record the data correctly. However, such disk storage errors are rare.

The VERIFY command lets you enable *disk verification*, which checks the information stored on disk to make sure the information was stored correctly. To enable disk verification, issue the command VERIFY ON as shown here.

```
C:\> VERIFY  ON  <ENTER>
```

You can think of disk verification as the reading of the information written to disk followed by a comparison to the original data. If the data recorded on disk matches the original, the write operation was correct. If the data on disk does not match the original, DOS knows an error occurred. In most cases, the disk controller, not DOS, performs the actual data verification.

The additional processing required to perform disk verification will decrease your system performance. Because disk recording errors are rare, most users should only turn disk verification on before key file copy or backup operations.

To turn disk verification OFF, invoke VERIFY as follows.

```
C:\> VERIFY  OFF  <ENTER>
```

If you invoke VERIFY without stating on or off, VERIFY will display its current state.

```
C:\> VERIFY  <ENTER>
VERIFY is off
```

Disk verification is useful when you copy key files or when you perform disk backup operations. To eliminate the need to explicitly turn disk verification on and off each time you copy key files, both COPY and XCOPY provide a /V switch, which turns disk verification on for only the duration of the copy operation. For more information on /V see COPY and XCOPY in the Command Reference at the end of this book.

NOTE

Salvaging a File or Disk with RECOVER

DOS stores your file contents on disk in sectors. Although such instances are rare, it is possible for a disk sector to become damaged, preventing your access to the file's information. When such an error occurs, DOS will display a disk read error message on screen, normally followed by the prompt "Abort, Retry, Fail?".

The RECOVER command lets you restore a portion of a file's contents, up to the damaged sector. For example, the following illustration shows a file containing a damaged sector.

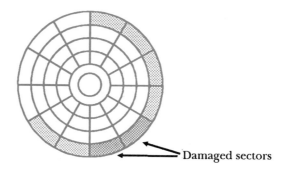
Damaged sectors

Using RECOVER, you can copy the file's contents up to the point of the damaged sector. To salvage a file using RECOVER, invoke RECOVER with the file name as shown here.

```
C:\> RECOVER   FILENAME.EXT    <ENTER>
```

RECOVER will rebuild the file up to the point of the bad sector; information beyond the bad sector will be lost.

In some cases, a damaged sector may prevent DOS from accessing the entire disk. Should such an error occur, invoke RECOVER with the disk drive letter, as shown here.

```
C:\> RECOVER   A:   <ENTER>
```

RECOVER will examine the disk and attempt to salvage as many files as it can. RECOVER will place the files it salvages in the disk's root directory, naming them FILE0000.REC, FILE0001.REC, and so on. A directory listing of a recovered disk might appear as follows:

```
C:\> DIR  A:   <ENTER>


 Volume in drive A has no label
 Volume Serial Number is 374A-0FF8
 Directory of A:\
FILE0001 REC       1024 04-21-91   10:19a
FILE0002 REC      35840 04-21-91   10:19a
FILE0003 REC      30720 04-21-91   10:19a
FILE0004 REC      46080 04-21-91   10:19a
FILE0005 REC       1024 04-21-91   10:19a
FILE0006 REC       7168 04-21-91   10:19a
FILE0007 REC      40960 04-21-91   10:19a
FILE0008 REC      26624 04-21-91   10:19a
        8 file(s)     189440 bytes
                      173056 bytes free
```

Use RECOVER as a last resort to salvage a file or disk. Never invoke RECOVER with a disk or file that is not damaged; doing so may destroy the information the file or disk contains. Do not rely on RECOVER. Instead, make sure you have current backup files. RECOVER does not undelete files.

NOTE

Hands On

Place a formatted floppy disk in drive A and issue the following LABEL command.

```
C:\> LABEL   <ENTER>
```

When LABEL prompts you for a volume label name, type CHAPTER-30.
   Use the following DIR command to display the label name.

```
C:\> DIR  A:   <ENTER>
```

Next, use VOL to display the label as follows.

SUMMARY

LABEL

The LABEL command assigns an 11-character disk volume label to the disk drive specified. The volume label is a name that helps you tell one disk from another. The following LABEL command assigns the disk volume label DOS to drive C.

```
C:\> LABEL  C:DOS   <ENTER>
```

VOL

The VOL command displays a disk's 11-character volume name. If you don't specify a disk drive, VOL displays the volume label for the current disk. The following VOL command displays the volume label for the current disk.

```
C:\> VOL   <ENTER>
```

DISKCOMP

DISKCOMP compares two floppy disks, track by track, sector by sector, and byte by byte. If the disks differ, DISKCOMP will display the side and track numbers that differ. If the disks are the same, DISKCOMP will display the "Compare OK" message. The following DISKCOMP command compares the floppy disk in drive A to the disk in drive B.

```
C:\> DISKCOMP  A:  B:  <ENTER>
```

SHARE

SHARE loads memory-resident software that provides file-sharing support for local area networks or users running several programs that may share the same files at the same time.

Under DOS 4, the SHARE command provides file control block support for disk partitions larger than 32Mb. If you are using DOS 4 and disk partitions greater than 32Mb, invoke SHARE using the CONFIG.SYS INSTALL entry as follows.

```
INSTALL=C:\DOS\SHARE.EXE
```

SUMMARY

VERIFY

VERIFY lets you turn disk verification on and off. In rare instances, the information DOS tells the disk controller to store on disk does not get recorded correctly. In most cases, the recording error is due to a hardware malfunction. When disk verification is on, every sector written to disk is compared to the original data to ensure the data match. Although this extra checking ensures the integrity of your data, it requires additional processing, which decreases your system performance.

Because such disk errors are rare most users should only enable disk verification before key file copy or disk backup operations.

RECOVER

RECOVER lets you salvage a portion of a damaged file or disk. You should use RECOVER only as a last resort. If you invoke RECOVER with a file or disk that is not damaged, RECOVER may destroy the information the disk or file contains.

```
C:\> VOL  A:   <ENTER>
```

Depending on your DOS version, CHKDSK may display the disk label, as well as the date and time the label was assigned.

```
C:\> CHKDSK  A:   <ENTER>
```

Next, invoke LABEL as follows to change the disk's label to DISKINFO.

```
C:\> LABEL  A:DISKINFO   <ENTER>
```

Using the following VERIFY command, display the current state of disk verification as follows.

```
C:\> VERIFY
```

By default, disk verification should be off. If your system has disk verification on, check your AUTOEXEC.BAT for the VERIFY command. Because disk recording errors are so rare, enabling disk verification for all operations only reduces your system performance.

Last, if you are using DOS 4 and disk partitions larger than 32Mb, make sure you use the CONFIG.SYS INSTALL entry to invoke the SHARE command.

Review

1. What is a disk volume label?

2. List three commands that display the disk volume label.

3. What is the difference between DISKCOPY and DISKCOMP?

4. Why does DOS 4 require the SHARE command?

5. What is disk verification?

Answers

1. A disk volume label is an 11-character disk name. The FORMAT and LABEL commands let you assign a volume label to a disk.

2. DIR, CHKDSK, LABEL, and VOL all display the disk volume label.

3. DISKCOPY copies the contents of one floppy disk to another. DISKCOMP compares the contents of one floppy disk to another.

4. DOS 4 was the first major DOS version to support disk partitions larger than 32Mb. Unfortunately, many very old programs that used file control blocks to access files were not compatible with the larger disks. When such a program ran, the program could incorrectly write information to any disk location, overwriting existing files, directories, or even the file allocation table.

5. Although it is rare, it is possible for the disk controller to incorrectly record information on disk due to a damaged disk surface area or a hardware malfunction. Disk verification is the process of comparing the information recorded on disk to the original data. If the information matches, the disk operation was successful. If the information differs, the disk controller can repeat the operation, recording the data correctly. VERIFY lets you enable and disable disk verification. Because such disk recording errors are rare, most users leave disk verification disabled to reduce system overhead. As a

rule, you only need to enable disk verification before backup or key file copy operations.

Advanced Concepts

Although the entry does not actually show up in directory listings or output of ATTRIB, TREE, or other DOS commands, DOS actually stores the disk volume label in a root directory entry. As you will learn in Chapter 33, "How DOS Actually Stores Files," every directory entry contains 32 bytes of information. In the case of a disk volume label, the file name and extension fields provide storage for the label's 11-character name, and the date and time fields record when you assigned the label.

Under DOS 5, DOS also records the volume label in the disk's boot record.

Assuming you assign the label name DOS to your hard disk, the directory entry storing the volume name will be similar to the label shown here:

DOS			12-25-90	12:44 PM	Volume
Name	Extension	Reserved	Date	Time	Attributes

A Closer Look at File Control Blocks

In Chapter 24 you learned that older (before DOS 2.0) versions of DOS use file control blocks (FCBs) to perform file input and output operations. In this chapter you learned that, if you are using partitions under DOS 4 larger than 32Mb and have not invoked SHARE, programs using FCBs can destroy the information on your hard disk. Beginning with DOS 2.0, DOS began using file handles to track open files instead of file control blocks. Figure 30-1 illustrates a file control block.

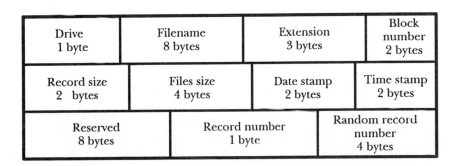

Drive 1 byte	Filename 8 bytes	Extension 3 bytes	Block number 2 bytes
Record size 2 bytes	Files size 4 bytes	Date stamp 2 bytes	Time stamp 2 bytes
Reserved 8 bytes	Record number 1 byte	Random record number 4 bytes	

Figure 30-1.   A file control block

As you can see, the file control block contains information about the file such as its name, size, date and time stamps, as well as record and block numbers that DOS uses to keep track of its current position in the file. Note the file control block does not contain directory path information. DOS versions before 2.0 did not provide directory support. When version 2.0 introduced directories, DOS had to maintain its current support for file control blocks, while providing a way to access files in directories. The solution came in the form of file handles, used by all DOS programs today. A file handle is an index into a table of values DOS maintains about the currently open files.

Unfortunately, until users throw away all the older programs based on FCBs, file control blocks will continue to be a nuisance.

Key Terms

Volume label   An 11-character name assigned to a disk.

Disk verification   The process of comparing the data written to disk to the original information to verify no recording errors occurred.

Chapter 31

Improving Your System Performance

It doesn't take most users very long before they want their system to run faster. Unfortunately, it's difficult to trade in your existing computer each time a faster, more powerful machine comes along. What you can do, however, is make sure your system is configured for maximum performance. This chapter examines DOS commands and concepts that relate strictly to improving your computer's performance. In most cases, the discussion will be brief, giving you a reference to another chapter that describes the concept in detail. Your computer represents a large investment of your time and money. This chapter will help you get the most results from that investment.

Directory Considerations for Maximum Performance

Each time you run a program or use a file, DOS must search your disk to first locate the directory containing the file or program. Then DOS must read the directory from disk into memory to search for the file's corresponding directory entry. Using the directory entry, DOS can determine where the file resides on disk and can then read the file from disk as required. Depending on your directory structure, the number of files in each directory, your command path (see PATH) or data-file search path (see APPEND), the amount of time DOS spends searching your disk for a program or file can become considerable. If you consider the number of times throughout the day you run programs or open files, the overhead resulting from repeated directory searches can become quite time consuming. Here are three steps you can take to reduce directory search overhead.

First, if you are using DOS 3.3 or later, the FASTOPEN command directs DOS to remember the starting location on disk of your recently used files. Assume, for example, you repeatedly edit the file BUDGET.RPT throughout the day. Each time you open the file, DOS must search the directory list to find the file's entry, so DOS can determine where the file starts on disk. To search the directory, DOS must locate the directory on disk, read the directory from disk into memory, and then search each entry until the file is found. FASTOPEN eliminates this directory searching overhead by placing the file's name and starting location in a table in your computer's fast electronic memory. When you open a file or execute an external command, DOS first checks FASTOPEN's table of entries to see if it can locate the file without having to perform the slow directory search. If the file is not in the table, DOS searches for the file on disk. After DOS locates the file, it places its name and location in FASTOPEN's table to be referenced when you access the file after that.

FASTOPEN will not decrease the time required to open every file on your disk, just those files you use more than once. Most users will find the following FASTOPEN command improves their system performance.

```
C:\> FASTOPEN  C:=50  <ENTER>
```

In this case, FASTOPEN will track your last 50 open files. FASTOPEN lets you track up to 999 files. Using a large value such as 999, however, will consume a considerable amount of your computer's memory. Remember, the goal of using FASTOPEN is not to track every file you open on your disk, but rather, the files you use on a repeated basis. If you are using DOS 4, use the CONFIG.SYS INSTALL entry to load FASTOPEN's memory-resident software. If you are using DOS 5, use the LOADHIGH command to load FASTOPEN into reserved memory.

One reason directory searches consume so much time is the number of files in the directory. DOS directories, discussed in Chapter 10, "Directories," help you organize your files. To use directories most effectively, you need to keep the number of files in any directory to a manageable number. If you have installed a third-party program such as a word processor or spreadsheet, you may not have control over the number of files in the directory. However, if you are creating directories that contain your own files, you can control the number of files in the directory by further organizing the files into subdirectories.

To determine the maximum number of files to which you should ideally restrict your directories, you need to know your disk's cluster size. DOS allocates disk space to files and directories using consecutive groups of sectors called clusters or allocation units. If you are using DOS 4 or later, the CHKDSK command displays your disk's allocation unit size. For hard disks, the allocation units are typically 2,048 or 4,096 bytes. Each directory entry consumes 32 bytes. For best performance, you should restrict the number of files in a directory to the number of entries that will fit in a disk cluster.

For a cluster size of 2,048, you should not exceed 64 files (2,048 / 32=64). Likewise, for 4,096-byte clusters, restrict your directories to 128 files. If you place more files into the directory than will fit in one cluster, DOS must allocate a second cluster for the directory. This second directory cluster will very likely be fragmented (see Chapter 44, "Detecting and Correcting Disk Fragmentation"), decreasing your system performance with every directory search operation.

As you have learned, the PATH command makes it very easy for you to execute external commands by letting you specify directories within which DOS will automatically search for commonly used commands. As a rule, you should only place the names of directories that are likely to contain commonly used commands in your command path. Otherwise, DOS may spend considerable time searching directories that are unlikely to contain the current command. In addition, put the directories containing your most commonly used commands (such as the DOS directory) at the beginning of the command path. Also, keep in mind that if the directory in your command path is fragmented because it contains a large number of files, your system performance will decrease every time DOS searches the directory for a command. If you are using APPEND to define a data-file search path, the same concepts apply.

The more files a directory contains, the longer it will take DOS to search the directory's contents. Depending on your DOS version, your DOS subdirectory may contain several commands you may never use. For example, the following files are used only by international DOS users:

COUNTRY.SYS	KEYB.COM	KEYBOARD.SYS
NLSFUNC.EXE	DISPLAY.SYS	EGA.CPI
4201.CPI	4208.CPI	5202.CPI
LCD.CPI	PRINTER.SYS	

If you don't need to use the international commands you can delete these files or move them into a directory below DOS. In addition, the DOS directory may contain several files with the BAS extension, which contains samples of BASIC programs. If you don't plan on using BASIC, you can delete those files or move them to a lower-level directory. If you take time to better organize the directories in your command path in this way, you will improve your system performance.

If you are not sure what function a command performs, or the contents of a specific file, do not move or delete the file.

File Considerations for Maximum Performance

In general, the biggest single factor that affects the performance of file-manipulation commands is fragmentation. A fragmented file is a file whose contents are spread out across your disk. Fragmentation occurs as a natural result of creating, deleting, and enlarging the files on your disk. If your programs seem to start slowly, or your data files in a word processing document or spreadsheet load slowly, your files may be fragmented. Chapter 44 discusses ways to identify and correct fragmentation.

When you use the DOS pipe operator (discussed in Chapter 21) to redirect one command's output to become a second command's input, DOS creates temporary files in your disk's root directory. If you are using DOS 5, you can use the TEMP environment variable to direct DOS to create the files in a different location, ideally on a fast RAM disk. Chapter 32, "Understanding DOS Memory Management," discusses RAM disks in detail and describes how to create a RAM disk using the RAMDRIVE.SYS device driver. If your computer has extended or expanded memory, use the memory to create a RAM disk and then use the SET command to assign TEMP to point to the RAM disk. If your computer doesn't have extended or expanded memory, creating a RAM disk in this way may consume memory your programs could put to better use.

Disk Considerations for Maximum Performance

Chapter 35, "Advanced Disk Topics," discusses disk interleaving, a process that changes the order of sectors stored on your disk to improve the timing coordination between your disk controller and computer. If your computer is not fast enough to keep up with your disk, your system performance will suffer because your disk will repeatedly have to wait for disk sectors to complete an extra revolution before the computer is ready to receive them. This extra rotational delay can have a big performance impact. Unfortunately, to correct the disk's interleave, you will need to purchase a third-party disk utility. DOS does not provide the capability to determine and set the correct interleave value for your computer and disk.

Because disks are mechanical, they are much slower than the computer's electronic components. One of your goals, therefore, is to reduce disk operations whenever possible. In Chapter 24, "Customizing Your System with CONFIG.SYS," you learned that the CONFIG.SYS BUFFERS entry lets you specify the number of buffers DOS should place in memory to reduce disk input and output operations. By increasing the number of available disk buffers, you can reduce the number of disk read operations DOS must perform. Each time an application asks DOS to read information from disk, DOS first checks its disk buffers to see if the information has already been read. If so, DOS can provide information to the program without having to perform a slow disk read operation. For more information on the correct number of disk buffers you should use, see Chapter 24.

Because DOS stores files on disk in groups of sectors called clusters, it is very likely that if a program asks DOS to read a file's first sector, the program will soon ask DOS to read the sectors that immediately follow. Beginning with DOS 4, the CONFIG.SYS BUFFERS entry lets you specify the number of sectors DOS can read in advance into a memory buffer. Should a program later request the sectors, DOS already has the sectors in memory, eliminating the need to perform another disk read operation. If you are using DOS 4 or later, and you are not using the SMARTDRV.SYS disk-caching software, use the BUFFERS entry to enable disk read-ahead operations.

The SMARTDRV.SYS device driver (discussed in Chapter 32) installs a high-performance disk cache in your computer's extended or expanded memory. The disk cache provides a larger buffer and better performance than do DOS disk buffers. If your computer has extended or expanded memory available, install the SMARTDRV.SYS device driver. When you install disk-caching software you should reduce the number of DOS disk buffers and eliminate DOS sector read-ahead just discussed.

There are rare instances when the disk does not correctly record information on disk. Using the VERIFY command (discussed in Chapter 30, "Another Look at Disks"), you can enable disk verification, which instructs the disk to check to make sure the information was recorded correctly. Because such disk errors are rare, leaving disk verification enabled results in unnecessary checking on every disk write, thus decreasing your overall system performance. Using the following VERIFY command, you can determine if disk verification is enabled (on) or disabled (off).

```
C:\> VERIFY  <ENTER>
VERIFY is off
```

If your system reports that verification is ON, check your AUTOEXEC.BAT file for a VERIFY ON command, and if such a command exists, remove it.

If you need to perform a file copy for critical data, the COPY and XCOPY commands both support the /V switch, which enables disk verification for the duration of the command. If you enable disk verification before your backup operations, remember to disable it when the backups are completed.

System Considerations for Performance

Chapter 32 examines DOS memory management in detail. In general, most larger applications will run faster given more memory because the programs can create larger buffers and keep more information in memory, rather than the slower disk. If you are using DOS 5, DOS gives you many ways to effectively manage your computer's memory to make more memory available to your applications. In addition to looking at DOS 5 memory management, Chapter 32 examines extended and expanded memory and explains why extended memory provides better performance.

In Chapter 43, "DOS System Commands," you will learn the MODE command can improve keyboard responsiveness. To begin, hold down a key on your keyboard and note the amount of time DOS waits before it repeats the character for the key depressed. Next, issue the following MODE command.

```
C:\> MODE  CON:  RATE=32  DELAY=1  <ENTER>
```

Hold down the same key once again and note the difference in your keyboard's responsiveness.

As discussed briefly in Chapter 24 with respect to the CONFIG.SYS BREAK entry and again in Chapter 43 with respect to the BREAK command, extended CTRL-BREAK checking is the process of increasing the number of times DOS checks for a user-entered CTRL-BREAK to end a command. By default, DOS checks for a CTRL-BREAK each time it writes to your screen, printer, or auxiliary device (COM1) or when it reads from your keyboard or auxiliary device. Because some programs don't perform these input and output operations often, it may take DOS considerable time to acknowledge a CTRL-BREAK. When you enable extended CTRL-BREAK checking, DOS will check for a CTRL-BREAK every time it performs a function such as opening a file, reading or writing to disk, or even returning the current system date or time to a program. Because DOS tests for CTRL-BREAK more often, DOS will recognize and respond to a CTRL-BREAK much sooner. Unfortunately, because DOS now spends more time testing for a CTRL-BREAK, DOS spends less time letting your programs run. As a result, your system performance decreases.

Unless you are a programmer who is developing and testing programs, you should leave extended CTRL-BREAK checking disabled. Using the following BREAK command, determine the state of extended CTRL-BREAK checking.

```
C:\> BREAK  <ENTER>
BREAK is off
```

If your system has extended CTRL-BREAK checking ON, check your CONFIG.SYS for a BREAK=ON entry, or AUTOEXEC.BAT for a BREAK ON command. If you find either, remove the entry from the file and issue the BREAK OFF command.

Hands On

If you are using DOS 3.3, place a FASTOPEN command in your AUTOEXEC.BAT
file. Most users will find tracking 50 files is sufficient.

```
FASTOPEN C:=50
```

If you are using DOS 4, use the CONFIG.SYS INSTALL entry to load FASTOPEN
as discussed in Chapter 24.

```
INSTALL=C:\DOS\FASTOPEN.EXE   C:=50
```

If you are using DOS 5, place the following LOADHIGH command in your
AUTOEXEC.BAT.

```
LOADHIGH C:\DOS\FASTOPEN.EXE   C:=50
```

Next, issue the following PATH command to display the current command path.

```
C:\> PATH   <ENTER>
```

For each directory specified in the command path, ask yourself if the directory really
contains commands you use on a regular basis. If the answer is no, edit your
AUTOEXEC.BAT file and update the PATH command. If you use APPEND to
define a data-file search path, ask yourself the same question.

Next, again examine the directories in the current command path. For each
directory, ask yourself if there are files you can move from the directory into a lower
directory to reduce the number of files DOS must compare while searching through
the command path.

Last, use CHDIR to select your commonly used directories and then issue the
following CHKDSK command to examine the files for fragmentation.

```
C:\DIRNAME> CHKDSK   *.*   <ENTER>
```

If a file is fragmented, CHKDSK will display the following message.

```
FILENAME.EXT Contains n non-contiguous blocks
```

If CHKDSK only displays a few fragmented files, don't worry. However, if a large percentage of your files are fragmented, you may want to turn to Chapter 44 and learn how to correct the fragmentation.

Review

1. Given a disk with 4,096-byte clusters, what is the maximum number of files you would ideally like a directory to contain? Why?

2. FASTOPEN improves system performance by tracking the disk locations of your commonly used files. If a setting of 50 FASTOPEN table entries is good, why isn't 999 better?

3. Why does a large number of entries in the command path decrease system performance?

4. Which is preferable, DOS BUFFERS or a SMARTDRV.SYS cache? Why?

5. How do fragmented files decrease system performance?

Answers

1. To determine the number of entries you should place in a directory, divide the disk's cluster size by 32 (the number of bytes in a directory entry). For a 4,096-byte cluster, the ideal number of directory entries is 128. If you store more than 128 directory entries, the directory will require two or more clusters, very likely becoming fragmented, which will decrease your system performance on every directory operation.

2. FASTOPEN's table of directory entries is not without cost. Each entry FASTOPEN tracks requires 48 bytes of memory. If you created a FASTOPEN table for 999 entries, you would quickly consume almost 48Kb of memory, perhaps better used by a different program. In addition, the larger FASTOPEN's table becomes, the longer it will take FASTOPEN to search the table, decreasing your system performance. The goal of FASTOPEN is to track your most commonly and recently used files. Very few users reuse 999 files on a regular basis.

3. If the number of entries in your command path is large, DOS must spend considerable time searching each directory for external commands and batch files. You can reduce this overhead some by placing the directories most likely to contain commonly used commands at the start of the command path.

4. If you have extended or expanded memory, the SMARTDRV.SYS cache will provide better performance. First, it uses intelligent software to reduce the cache buffer searching time. Second, because it resides in your computer's extended or expanded memory, it does not consume conventional memory better used by an application.

5. A fragmented file is a file whose contents are in clusters spread out across your disk. Fragmented files decrease system performance because they increase rotational disk delays and increase the number of disk head seek operations required to access the file.

Advanced Topics

You learned in Chapter 28, "DOS 5 Crisis Prevention," that each time you delete a file, DOS does not actually erase the file's contents from disk; rather, DOS marks the file's directory entry and disk clusters as available for reuse by another file. Assume, for example, a directory on your disk contains the files ONE, TWO, and THREE. The directory contents might contain the entries shown here:

ONE	1024	7-04-91	12:01P
TWO	2048	7-04-91	12:02P
THREE	3072	7-04-91	12:03P

If you later delete file TWO, DOS will mark the file's directory listing entry as available for reuse by setting the first character of the file name to the character σ, as shown here:

ONE	1024	7-04-91	12:01P
σWO	2048	7-04-91	12:02P
THREE	3092	7-04-91	12:03P

If you later create the file FOUR in the directory, DOS will reuse the first available directory entry as shown in here:

ONE	1024	7-4-91	12:01P
FOUR	2048	7-5-91	12:04P
THREE	3092	7-4-91	12:03P

Next, assume you have a directory containing 30 files with the LTR extension and you delete the files. Like before, DOS marks each directory entry as available for reuse as shown in Figure 31-1. If you delete a large number of files, your directory will contain many entries marked available for reuse.

The problem with having these unused entries in the directory is every time DOS searches the directory, DOS has to search through these unused entries. If you never create additional files in the directory, these entries will remain unused, and as a continual source of directory search overhead.

If you are using DOS 5, you can use the following UNDELETE command to determine the number of unused directory entries.

```
C:\> UNDELETE  *.*  /DOS  /LIST  <ENTER>
```

FILENAME.ONE	1024	7-4-91	12:01P
FILENAME.TWO	2048	7-4-91	12:02P
σNE.LTR	1024	7-4-91	12:01P
σWO.LTR	2048	7-4-91	12:02P
σHREE.LTR	3092	7-4-91	12:03P
.	.	.	.
.	.	.	.
.	.	.	.
σHIRTY.LTR	30720	7-4-91	12:30P
FILENAME.THR	3092	7-4-91	12:03P

Figure 31-1.   Unused directory entries available for reuse

If you want to get rid of the unused entries, use the following BACKUP command to backup the files in the directory to floppy.

```
C:\DIRNAME>  BACKUP  *.*  A:  /S  <ENTER>
```

When the backup operation completes, delete the files and subdirectories from the directory. Next, use RMDIR to remove the directory itself. Next, use MKDIR to create the directory once again and CHDIR to select the directory. Using the following RESTORE command you can restore the directory and its files, minus the unused entries.

```
C:\DIRNAME>  RESTORE  A:  *.*  /S  <ENTER>
```

Key Terms

Performance   The effectiveness of your computer's hardware and software.

Chapter 32

Understanding DOS Memory Management

As computer programs become more powerful and complex, the list of instructions needed to implement the programs has become very large. In fact, many programs are quickly outgrowing the 640Kb memory limits of the IBM PC. This chapter examines the different solutions that help you squeeze the most information into your computer's memory. In particular, you will learn the differences between, and how to use, conventional, reserved, and high memory. In addition, this chapter fully explains extended and expanded memory. If this book has a most difficult chapter, this may be it. However, if this book has a most valuable chapter, this one is definitely in the running. The figures in this chapter are worth more than a thousand words, so pay close attention to them.

Understanding Memory Types

There are three primary memory types used by the IBM PC and PC-compatibles. To begin, most computers have up to 640Kb of conventional memory, which is your computer's primary memory. Typically, DOS and your programs reside in this memory area. Using CHKDSK, you can display the amount of conventional memory in your computer.

```
C:\> CHKDSK   <ENTER>

Volume DOS         created 04-21-1991 8:46a
Volume Serial Number is 168C-5277

 200065024 bytes total disk space
     81920 bytes in 3 hidden files
    462848 bytes in 108 directories
  44785664 bytes in 2036 user files
 154734592 bytes available on disk

      4096 bytes in each allocation unit
     48844 total allocation units on disk
     37777 available allocation units on disk

    655360 total bytes memory
    562688 bytes free
```

When the IBM PC was first released in 1981, computers typically had 64Kb to 256Kb of conventional memory. As memory became more affordable, the amounts grew to 512Kb and then to 640Kb. Depending on your computer's age, the amount of conventional memory will fall somewhere in the range 64Kb to 640Kb.

When your computer starts, DOS loads itself into the lower part of conventional memory. If you install memory-resident programs, DOS places the programs in the next available lower memory areas. The amount of memory that remains determines the largest program your computer can run. This illustration shows the conventional memory layout.

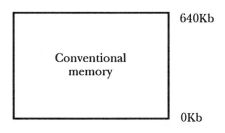

Although conventional memory cannot exceed 640Kb, the original IBM PC can address up to 1 megabyte of memory. If you subtract 640Kb from 1Mb, you'll find the PC has a 384Kb gap between the end of conventional memory and the highest memory location the IBM PC could access. As shown in Figure 32-1, your computer uses a portion of this memory to interface to your video display and a portion for the ROM-BIOS routines, leaving a portion of the 384Kb region unused.

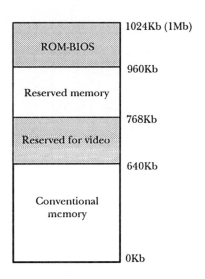

Figure 32-1.   How your computer uses the 384Kb region above conventional memory

Expanded Memory

Although a portion of the 384Kb region above conventional memory was unused, the region wasn't large enough to be of much use on its own. However, it didn't take hardware developers very long to figure out a way to use this small memory region to access memory outside of the PC's 1Mb limitation. *Expanded memory* combines hardware memory boards and powerful software called an *EMM driver* to expand the amount of memory DOS can use from 640Kb to up to 32Mb!

Here's how the EMS software works. There are two major versions of EMS software, LIM EMS version 3.2 and version 4.0. For simplicity, the initial discussion is based on version 3.2. Later in this chapter, you will learn how version 4.0 differs.

First, the EMS software uses a 64Kb region of memory in the reserved memory above 640Kb and below 1Mb. As shown in Figure 32-2, the expanded memory software divides this region into four 16Kb regions, called *page buffers*.

Next, when you run a program that supports expanded memory, the program is loaded into conventional memory, and its data is loaded into the memory on the expanded memory board. Such data might include a very large spreadsheet. The program must divide its data into 16Kb sections called *pages*, as shown in Figure 32-3.

When the PC needs to access data contained in an expanded memory page, the expanded memory software maps the address of a 16Kb page containing data to an address of one of the page buffers that the PC can access. For example, when the program first starts, the expanded memory driver maps the page of data from

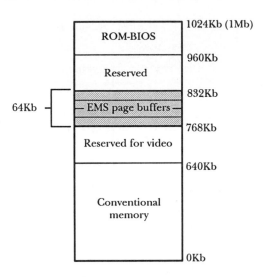

Figure 32-2.   *The expanded memory software uses a 64Kb region in the reserved memory region above 640Kb*

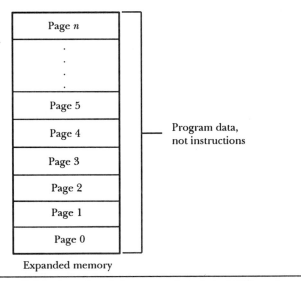

Figure 32-3.   *A program divides its expanded memory data into 16Kb regions called pages*

expanded memory into a page buffer as shown in Figure 32-4. Note that the expanded memory software does not move the data, but rather, performs memory address manipulation behind the scenes to make the data addressable to the PC.

Assuming the program uses data in pages 1, 2, 3, and 4, the page buffers will map the pages shown in Figure 32-5.

Assuming the program then uses page 5, the expanded memory driver changes the address mapping from one of the pages in the page buffer so it can map page 5's address, as shown in Figure 32-6.

To understand how expanded memory works, you need to remember that the original IBM PC could not access memory above 1Mb. To the PC, expanded memory is not addressed like standard memory. Instead, the PC knows there are 64Kb of memory (containing four 16Kb pages) it can access. The memory itself resides on an expanded memory board. The job of the expanded memory driver is to map information contained in the expanded memory into the page frame.

The advantage of expanded memory is that it lets the original IBM PC break the 640Kb boundary. The disadvantages of expanded memory are that not all programs support it, and those that do may execute slowly because of the continual time consuming address mappings required to map different pages in and out of the page buffers.

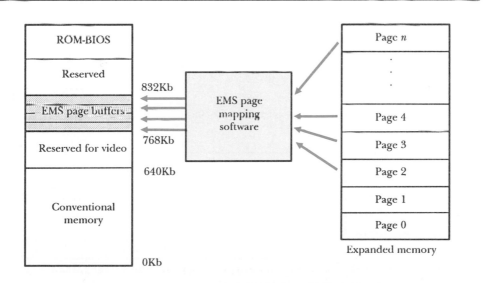

Figure 32-4. *The expanded memory software maps pages of expanded memory into the page buffers the PC can access*

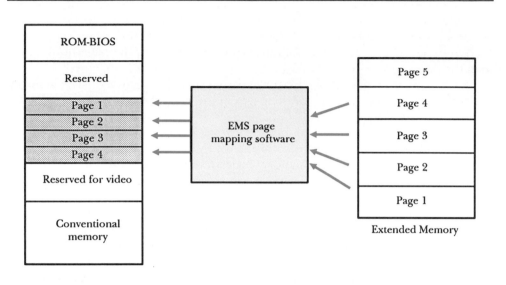

Figure 32-5.   *The page buffers can hold up to four pages at one time*

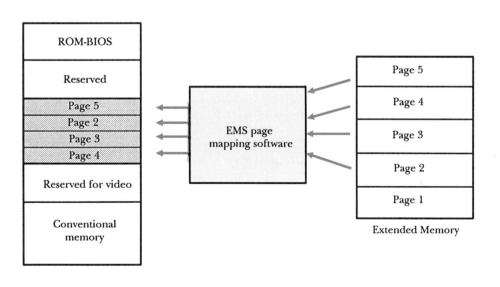

Figure 32-6.   *As a program executes, the expanded memory software changes address mapping to access different pages*

To use expanded memory, you will need an expanded memory board (or a board that simulates expanded memory) and a device driver for the board. You must install the device driver using the CONFIG.SYS DEVICE entry discussed in Chapter 24, "Customizing Your System with CONFIG.SYS". The device driver should be on a floppy disk that accompanies your memory board from the manufacturer.

The companies that initially drove the expanded memory development are Lotus, Intel, and Microsoft (LIM). The expanded memory boards and software you buy should meet the LIM expanded memory specifications (LIM EMS).

How LIM EMS Version 4.0 Differs   LIM EMS version 3.2 supported four fixed-size 16Kb page frames. The maximum amount of expanded memory a program could access using version 3.2 was 8Mb. The page frames had to map to a memory location above 640Kb.

LIM EMS 4.0 removed many restrictions of page size and page location found under version 3.2. To maintain compatibility with version 3.2, EMS 4.0 requires four fixed-size 16Kb page frames. After that, version 4.0 lets you create any number of page frames of any size, letting the pages map to any memory location. In addition, version 4.0 increases the amount of expanded memory a program can access to 32Mb. EMS version 4.0 also includes many capabilities required in a multitasking environment.

Extended Memory

Although expanded memory broke the IBM PC's 640Kb memory restriction, the overhead of mapping pages in and out of the page buffers left hardware developers looking for a more efficient way of accessing memory above 1Mb. When IBM introduced the PC AT (80286) in 1984, they also introduced the notion of *extended memory*. Like expanded memory, extended memory combines hardware and software to access program data stored in memory above 1Mb. The 80286 can use up to 16Mb of extended memory. If you have money to burn, the 80386 and 80486 can access up to 4 gigabytes (4 billion bytes) of extended memory!

The original IBM PC (8088) cannot use extended memory. To use extended memory, you must be using an 80286, 386, or 486.

NOTE

Because extended memory does not swap pages in and out of page buffers that reside below 1Mb, extended memory is much faster than expanded memory. The best way to view extended memory is as one large storage location, as shown in Figure 32-7.

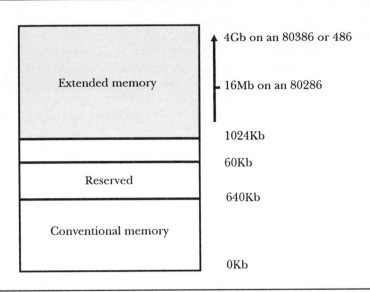

Figure 32-7.   Extended memory is one large memory region that resides above 1Mb

When you run a program written to use extended memory, DOS loads the program into conventional memory. The program in turn, loads its data into extended memory, as shown in Figure 32-8.

When the program needs to access data stored in extended memory, the extended memory software lets the program access the data directly, without the page mapping done by expanded memory.

Extended memory requires a software device driver that lets DOS use the memory. In many cases, a device driver on floppy disk will accompany your extended memory board. If you are using DOS 5 or Microsoft Windows 3.0, the device driver HIMEM.SYS provides DOS access to extended memory. Using the CONFIG.SYS DEVICE entry, you can install the driver as follows.

```
DEVICE=C:\DOS\HIMEM.SYS
```

If you are not using DOS 5, change the directory path to WINDOWS, as shown here.

```
DEVICE=C:\WINDOWS\HIMEM.SYS
```

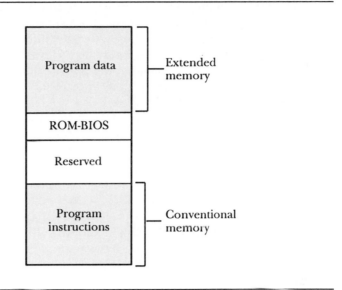

Figure 32-8.   DOS loads programs that support extended memory into conventional memory; the program, in turn, loads its data into extended memory

How We Use Extended and Expanded Memory

Although extended and expanded memory let DOS break the 640Kb boundary, both techniques have a big limitation. In most cases, you can only store a program's data above 1Mb. The program's instructions must still reside below 1Mb. The 80286, 386, and 486 have two modes of operation. Under DOS, these computers run in *real mode*, which means program instructions must reside below 1Mb. Under other operating systems such as OS/2, UNIX, or even Microsoft Windows (running in 386 Enhanced mode) your computer runs in *protected mode*, which lets a program's data and instructions reside in extended memory.

Unfortunately, because DOS runs in real mode, program instructions must reside below 1Mb. Even if your computer has a large amount of extended memory, many applications still don't take advantage of it. Therefore, users most commonly use extended and expanded memory for large disk buffers called disk caches or for fast electronic RAM drives, discussed next.

Creating a RAM Drive

If you have unused memory available, either conventional, expanded, or extended, DOS lets you use the memory to create an electronic *RAM drive*. Because RAM drives reside in your computer's fast electronic memory, they are many times faster than a mechanical hard disk. When you create a RAM drive, DOS assigns to the drive the first unused drive letter, such as D or E. Because of their tremendous speed, many users use RAM drives to store temporary files. However, because they store files in your computer's electronic memory, the information RAM drives contain is lost when you turn off your computer's power or restart DOS. RAM drives, therefore, are best suited for temporary files.

The RAMDRIVE.SYS device driver lets you install a RAM drive. To install the device driver, you must use the CONFIG.SYS DEVICE entry. The format of RAMDRIVE.SYS is

```
DEVICE=C:\DOS\RAMDRIVE.SYS [[DiskSize SectorSize]
   [DirectoryEntries]] [/A|/E]
```

DiskSize specifies the size of the disk in kilobytes. If you don't specify a value, the default size is 64Kb. RAMDRIVE.SYS lets you specify a size from 16 through 4,096Kb (4 megabytes). *SectorSize* specifies the RAM drive's sector size. The default sector size is 512 bytes. RAMDRIVE.SYS lets you specify sector sizes of 128, 256, or 512 bytes. *DirectoryEntries* specifies the number of files and directories the RAM drive can store in its root directory. Like all disk drives, RAM drives restrict the number of files you can store in the root directory. By default, the RAM drive's root directory can hold 64 entries. RAMDRIVE.SYS lets you specify from 2 to 1,024 entries.

By default, RAMDRIVE.SYS creates the RAM drive in conventional memory. The /E switch directs RAMDRIVE.SYS to create the RAM drive in extended memory. Likewise, the /A switch directs RAMDRIVE.SYS to use expanded memory.

The following CONFIG.SYS entry creates a 64Kb RAM drive in conventional memory.

```
DEVICE=C:\DOS\RAMDRIVE.SYS
```

When you start your computer, your screen will display a message similar to the following, possibly using a different disk drive letter or disk size.

```
Microsoft RAMDrive version n.nn virtual disk D:
    Disk size: 64k
    Sector size: 512 bytes
    Allocation unit: 1 sectors
    Directory entries: 64
```

To access the drive, use the drive letter D, as shown here.

```
C:\> DIR  D:  <ENTER>
```

Likewise, the following entry creates a 512Kb RAM drive in extended memory.

```
DEVICE=C:\DOS\RAMDRIVE.SYS  512   /E
```

DOS 5 uses the TEMP environment entry, discussed in Chapter 19, "The DOS Environment," to determine where it should create its temporary files during I/O redirection operations. By assigning TEMP to your fast RAM drive, you can improve your system performance.

The information stored in a RAM drive is lost when you turn off your computer or restart DOS. If you need the files the RAM drive contains, make sure you copy the files back to your hard disk or floppy before you turn your computer off.

REMEMBER

Before you can install a RAM drive into extended or expanded memory, the corresponding memory-management software must already be active. Place the RAMDRIVE.SYS DEVICE entry in CONFIG.SYS after the DEVICE entry for your extended memory or expanded memory device driver.

NOTE

Creating a Disk Cache

In Chapter 24, "Customizing Your System with CONFIG.SYS," you learned how disk buffers improve your system performance by reducing the number of disk I/O operations DOS must perform. As you also learned in Chapter 24, each disk buffer consumes 528 bytes of conventional memory. Depending on your DOS version, or if you are using Microsoft Windows, the SMARTDRV.SYS device driver lets you install disk-caching software into extended or expanded memory.

A *disk cache* is a very large disk buffer. Each time DOS needs to perform a disk read, DOS just searches the disk cache for the data. Disk caches have several advantages over DOS disk buffers. First, because disk caches reside in extended or expanded memory, they don't use conventional memory that DOS can use to hold program instructions. Second, disk caches can be very large, up to 8Mb. Last, most disk-caching software is very specialized and executes very fast. To install a disk cache, you must use the CONFIG.SYS DEVICE entry to load SMARTDRV.SYS. The format of SMARTDRV.SYS is

```
DEVICE=C:\DOS\SMARTDRV.SYS  [InitialCacheSize]
  [MinimumCacheSize]  [/A]
```

InitialCacheSize specifies the starting cache size in kilobytes, from 128Kb to 8192Kb (8 megabytes). The default cache size is 256Kb. Depending on your memory and cache usage, it is possible for some programs to reduce the cache size.

MinimumCacheSize specifies the smallest size in Kb a program can reduce the cache. For example, using Microsoft Windows, you can use SMARTDRV.SYS to create a very large disk cache. Should Windows later need to put unused portions of the cache to use, Windows will reduce the cache size. The default value is 0. By default, SMARTDRV.SYS installs the cache in extended memory. The /A switch directs SMARTDRV.SYS to use expanded memory instead.

The following CONFIG.SYS entry installs a 256Kb disk cache in extended memory.

```
DEVICE=C:\DOS\SMARTDRV.SYS
```

When you start your computer, your screen will display a message similar to the following.

```
Microsoft SMARTDrive Disk Cache version 3.13
    Cache size: 256K in Extended Memory
    Room for 16 tracks of 32 sectors each
    Minimum cache size will be 0K
```

Likewise, the following entry creates a 128Kb disk cache in expanded memory.

```
DEVICE=C:\DOS\SMARTDRV.SYS 128    /A
```

Because expanded memory must swap pages to access the cache, an extended memory disk cache will have better performance.

NOTE *Before you can install disk-caching software into extended or expanded memory, the corresponding memory-management software must be active. Place the DEVICE entry for SMARTDRV.SYS in CONFIG.SYS after the entry for the memory-management device driver.*

If you install a disk cache, reduce the number of DOS disk buffers to 3, as shown here.

```
BUFFERS=3
```

Viewing Your Memory Usage

CHKDSK displays statistics about your conventional memory usage. If you are using DOS 4 or later, the MEM command displays detailed information about conventional, expanded, and extended memory usage. When you invoke MEM under DOS 4, your screen will display output similar to the following.

```
C:\> MEM   <ENTER>

   655360 bytes total memory
   655360 bytes available
   521440 largest executable program size

  1441792 bytes total extended memory
  1441792 bytes available extended memory
```

Under DOS 5, MEM displays

```
C:\> MEM   <ENTER>

   655360 bytes total conventional memory
   655360 bytes available to MS-DOS
   606480 largest executable program size

   917504 bytes total EMS memory
   524288 bytes free EMS memory

  1441792 bytes total contiguous extended memory
        0 bytes available contiguous extended memory
   928768 bytes available XMS memory
        MS-DOS resident in High Memory Area
```

The first three lines provide information about your conventional memory usage. The lines that follow summarize your expanded and extended memory usage.

To help programmers, MEM provides the /PROGRAM and /DEBUG switches. Software device drivers and memory-resident programs remain present in your computer's memory until you turn off your computer or restart DOS. If you include the /PROGRAM switch, MEM will display the memory address and size of each program or software driver.

```
C:\> MEM   /PROGRAM   <ENTER>

   Address      Name        Size      Type
   - - - - - -  - - - -     - - - -   - - - -
   000000                   000400    Interrupt Vector
   000400                   000100    ROM Communication Area
```

```
000500                          000200      DOS Communication Area

000700      IO                  000A60      System Data

001160      MSDOS               0013D0      System Data

002530      IO                  008B50      System Data
               HIMEM            0004A0        DEVICE=
               EMM386           0020D0        DEVICE=
               SMARTDRV         005140        DEVICE=
                                000820        FILES=
                                000100        FCBS=
                                000200        BUFFERS=
                                0001C0        LASTDRIVE=
                                000740        STACKS=
00B090      MSDOS               000040      System Program

00B0E0      COMMAND             000940      Program
00BA30      COMMAND             000400      Environment
00BE40      MEM                 000080      Environment
00BED0      MEM                 0176F0      Program
0235D0      MSDOS               07CA10      — Free —
09FFF0      SYSTEM              028010      System Program

0C8010      IO                  001210      System Data
               SETVER           000190        DEVICE=
               ANSI             001060        DEVICE=
0C9230      MSDOS               016DC0      — Free —


    655360 bytes total conventional memory
    655360 bytes available to MS-DOS
    606480 largest executable program size

   1441792 bytes total contiguous extended memory
         0 bytes available contiguous extended memory
    928768 bytes available XMS memory
           MS-DOS resident in High Memory Area
```

If you use the /DEBUG switch, MEM also displays the location and size of the internal device drivers provided by DOS.

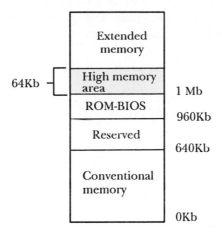

Figure 32-9.   *Under DOS 5, you can load DOS into the high memory area (the first 64Kb of extended memory)*

DOS 5 Memory Management

Each time your system starts, DOS loads itself into conventional memory. If you are using DOS 5, you can direct DOS to load part of itself into the high memory area that is the first 64Kb of extended memory, as shown in Figure 32-9.

By loading DOS into the high memory area, you free up additional conventional memory for your programs. To load DOS into the high memory area, you must do the CONFIG.SYS DOS entry as follows.

```
DOS=HIGH
```

NOTE *Before you can load DOS into the high memory area, the extended memory-management software must be active. Place the DOS entry in CONFIG.SYS after the entry that installs the extended memory device driver.*

The 384Kb memory area above conventional memory and below 1Mb is often called *reserved memory.* As you saw earlier, expanded memory makes use of 64Kb of this area. Under DOS 5, you can use portions of reserved memory for software device drivers and memory-resident DOS commands called upper memory blocks (UMBs). To use reserved memory, you must have a 386 or 486 computer and then include UMB in the CONFIG.SYS DOS entry, as shown here.

```
DOS=UMB
```

The UMB entry does not actually use reserved memory. It simply tells DOS you will later use it with the CONFIG.SYS DEVICEHIGH entry or the LOADHIGH command.

UMB is an abbreviation for *upper memory block* (a 64Kb region in reserved memory). By using reserved memory for software drivers or memory-resident commands, you free up conventional memory. The following CONFIG.SYS entry tells DOS you will later use reserved memory, and you want DOS to load itself in high memory.

```
DOS=UMB,HIGH
```

If you aren't using extended memory, you can direct DOS to load itself in conventional memory, while telling DOS you will later use reserved memory as shown here.

```
DOS=UMB,LOW
```

Last, if you use NOUMB, DOS will not let you later use reserved memory.

In Chapter 24 you learned the CONFIG.SYS DEVICE entry installs a software device driver. DOS places the corresponding software into conventional memory. Under DOS 5, the CONFIG.SYS DEVICEHIGH entry lets you install a device driver into reserved memory. Before you can use DEVICEHIGH, your CONFIG.SYS must contain entries similar to those shown here.

```
DEVICE=C:\DOS\HIMEM.SYS
DEVICE=C:\DOS\EMM386.EXE  NOEMS
DOS=UMB
DEVICEHIGH=C:\DOS\ANSI.SYS
```

In this case, DOS will try to load the ANSI.SYS device driver discussed in Chapter 34 into reserved memory. The HIMEM.SYS driver provides extended memory support. The EMM386.EXE device driver provides access to the reserved memory. The NOEMS parameter tells DOS you don't want the driver to simulate expanded memory.

 Do not try to install the HIMEM.SYS or EMM386 device drivers in reserved memory; these drivers must reside in conventional memory.

WARNING

The Advanced Concepts section of this chapter examines the EMM386.EXE device driver in detail. The CONFIG.SYS entries presented here are only for use on 386 and 486 systems that use only extended memory.

If you want DOS to also load itself into high memory, change the DOS entry to include HIGH, as shown here.

```
DOS=UMB,HIGH
```

If DOS does not have enough memory reserved to hold the driver software, DOS will load the driver in conventional memory as if you had used a DEVICE entry instead of DEVICEHIGH.

In Chapter 24 you learned that the CONFIG.SYS INSTALL entry lets you load four specific memory-resident DOS commands efficiently into memory. Under DOS 5, the LOADHIGH command lets you load memory-resident programs into reserved memory. LOADHIGH is not a CONFIG.SYS entry, it is an internal DOS command.

To determine the conventional memory usage and the amount of available upper memory, invoke MEM using the /CLASSIFY switch, shown here.

```
C:\> MEM   /CLASSIFY    <ENTER>

Conventional Memory :

  Name                Size in Decimal        Size in Hex
  - - - - - - - - -   - - - - - - - - - - - - - - - -   - - - - - - - - - - - -

    MSDOS             14752       ( 14.4K)        39A0
    HIMEM              1184       (  1.2K)         4A0
    EMM386             8400       (  8.2K)        20D0
    SMARTDRV          20800       ( 20.3K)        5140
    COMMAND            3392       (  3.3K)         D40
    FREE             606624       (592.4K)        941A0

Total   FREE :       606624       (592.4K)

Upper Memory :

  Name                Size in Decimal        Size in Hex
  - - - - - - - - -   - - - - - - - - - - - - - - - -   - - - - - - - - - - - -

    SYSTEM           163840       (160.0K)        28000
    SETVER              400       (  0.4K)          190
    ANSI               4192       (  4.1K)         1060
    FREE              93632       ( 91.4K)        16DC0

Total   FREE :        93632       ( 91.4K)
```

```
Total bytes available to programs (Conventional+Upper) :
700256    (683.8K)
Largest executable program size :
606480    (592.3K)
Largest available upper memory block :
93632    ( 91.4K)

  1441792 bytes total contiguous extended memory
        0 bytes available contiguous extended memory
   928768 bytes available XMS memory
           MS-DOS resident in High Memory Area
```

Before you can use LOADHIGH, your CONFIG.SYS file must contain a DOS=UMB entry just as if you were using DEVICEHIGH. The following LOADHIGH command, for example, installs the FASTOPEN memory-resident software into reserved memory. If insufficient reserved memory is available, LOADHIGH will load the command into conventional memory.

```
C:\> LOADHIGH  FASTOPEN  C:=50  <ENTER>
```

DOS lets you abbreviate LOADHIGH as LH. If your AUTOEXEC.BAT loads memory-resident software, you may be able to load the software into reserved memory using LOADHIGH.

As you have learned, use of DEVICEHIGH and LOADHIGH to load device drivers and memory-resident programs into reserved memory frees memory for your programs. In some cases, a program's initial starting address may reside below 64Kb.

Some programs cannot execute below 64Kb and will display the "Packed file corrupt" error message when you execute them in this low memory region. If this error message occurs, use DOS 5 LOADFIX to direct DOS to load the program above 64Kb.

The format of the LOADFIX command is

```
LOADFIX ProgramName [parameters]
```

where *ProgramName* specifies the program you are trying to run, and *parameters* specifies the program's optional command-line parameters. You will not need to use LOADFIX unless you experience the "Packed file corrupt" error message.

Hands On

Because the DOS memory-management capabilities differ greatly between DOS 5 and other versions of DOS, this section is divided into two parts: one for DOS 5 users and one for DOS users of any other version.

DOS 5 Users

To begin, invoke the MEM command to determine your system's current conventional, expanded, and extended memory usage.

```
C:\> MEM   <ENTER>
```

Next, redirect MEM's output to your printer and print a copy of your CONFIG.SYS file.

```
C:\> MEM  >  PRN  <ENTER>

C:\> PRINT  \CONFIG.SYS  <ENTER>
```

If you are using an 80286, 386, or 486 computer that has extended memory, make sure you install the HIMEM.SYS device driver in CONFIG.SYS.

```
DEVICE=C:\DOS\HIMEM.SYS
```

Next, if you are not using an expanded memory driver other than EMM386.EXE, place one of the following DEVICE entries in CONFIG.SYS to enable access to reserved memory.

```
DEVICE=C:\DOS\EMM386.EXE  NOEMS
```

or

```
DEVICE=C:\DOS\EMM386.EXE  RAM
```

Use the NOEMS entry if you want access to the reserved memory, but don't want DOS to simulate expanded memory using a portion of your computer's extended memory. Use the RAM entry if you want access to reserved memory and you want to simulate expanded memory.

SUMMARY

Conventional Memory

Conventional memory is your computer's memory from 0 to 640Kb. When your computer starts, DOS loads itself into the lower portion of conventional memory. If you invoke memory-resident programs such as PRINT, DOSKEY, or a network driver, DOS loads the program into the next available location in conventional memory.

Expanded Memory

Expanded memory lets the original IBM PC (8088) break the 640Kb boundary. Expanded memory combines hardware memory boards and powerful software.

Expanded memory uses a 64Kb region immediately above conventional memory as a buffer for four 16Kb pages. When you run a program written to use expanded memory, DOS loads the program into the 640Kb conventional memory. The program then loads its data into the expanded memory area. The program divides its data into 16Kb pages. When the program needs to access data stored in a specific page, the expanded memory software brings the page from expanded memory into one of the 16Kb page frames. If the page frames are currently full, the expanded memory software maps one page out so it can map in another page.

Extended Memory

Extended memory is the memory above 1Mb in an 80286, 80386, or 80486 system. Extended memory combines hardware memory boards with a software device driver you must load using the CONFIG.SYS DEVICE entry. When you execute a program that uses extended memory, DOS loads the program into conventional memory. The program in turn loads its data into extended memory. When the program needs to use data stored in extended memory, the extended memory software lets the program access the data directly without the time-consuming mapping to a page buffer that occurs with expanded memory. As a result, extended memory is much faster than expanded.

RAMDRIVE.SYS

The RAMDRIVE.SYS device driver lets you install a RAM drive in your computer's fast electronic memory. After you create a RAM drive, you access

> ## SUMMARY

the drive using the drive letter RAMDRIVE.SYS displays on your screen, which is typically D or E. Because of their tremendous speed, RAM drives are very convenient for storing temporary files. Because RAM drives reside in your computer's electronic memory, the files on the drive are lost when you turn off your computer's power or restart DOS.

SMARTDRV.SYS

The SMARTDRV.SYS device driver installs a disk cache into extended or expanded memory. A disk cache works as a high-performance, large disk buffer. Because the disk cache resides in either extended or expanded memory, the cache does not consume conventional memory that DOS can use to run larger programs.

MEM

The MEM command displays information about your use of conventional, extended, and expanded memory. If you include the /PROGRAM switch, MEM will display the location and size of each program in memory. If you include the /DEBUG switch, MEM will also include the location of standard device drivers. Under DOS 5, the /CLASSIFY switch directs MEM to group programs by memory usage.

DOS=

The CONFIG.SYS DOS entry lets you direct DOS 5 to install itself in high memory. In addition, the DOS= entry lets you request a link to reserved memory DOS can later use to install a device driver or command in reserved memory using DEVICEHIGH or LOADHIGH.

DEVICEHIGH=

The CONFIG.SYS DEVICEHIGH entry directs DOS 5 to install a device driver into reserved memory, making more conventional memory available to DOS to use for other programs. To use the DEVICEHIGH entry, your CONFIG.SYS file must contain a DOS=UMB entry, and the EMM386.EXE driver must be installed. The following DEVICEHIGH entry installs the RAMDRIVE.SYS driver in reserved memory.

SUMMARY

```
DEVICEHIGH=C:\DOS\RAMDRIVE.SYS
```

If DOS does not have enough reserved memory to hold the driver, DOS will load the driver into conventional memory as if you had used the DEVICE entry.

LOADHIGH

The LOADHIGH command lets you load memory-resident software into the reserved area of memory above conventional memory and below 1Mb. Loading memory-resident software into reserved memory frees conventional memory for other programs. To use LOADHIGH, you must be using a 386 or 486, with the DOS=UMB entry in CONFIG.SYS and the EMM386.EXE device driver installed. If your computer does not have enough reserved memory available for the program, LOADHIGH will load the program into conventional memory. The format of LOADHIGH is

```
LOADHIGH CommandName [parameters]
```

LOADFIX

If you load DOS into high memory and load your device drivers and memory-resident programs into reserved memory, you may actually free up so much conventional memory that a program's starting address is actually below 64Kb. Unfortunately, some programs cannot execute in this address range and will display the "Packed file corrupt" message when you attempt to execute them. Using the DOS 5 LOADFIX command, you can instruct DOS to load the program into memory above the 64Kb address, resolving the problem.

Next, if you are using extended memory use the following entry to load DOS into high memory and to establish links to reserved memory.

```
DOS=UMB,HIGH
```

Next, if your CONFIG.SYS file uses DEVICE to load other device drivers, use the DEVICEHIGH entry to load the drivers into reserved memory.

Likewise, if your AUTOEXEC.BAT installs memory-resident commands, use LOADHIGH to load the commands into reserved memory.

Using the CTRL-ALT-DEL key combination, restart your system. When the system restarts, again redirect MEM's output to your printer and print the contents of CONFIG.SYS.

```
C:\> MEM  >  PRN   <ENTER>

C:\> PRINT  \CONFIG.SYS   <ENTER>
```

Compare your new memory usage using high and reserved memory to the original memory usage. Your new configuration should have more conventional memory available.

Use the following MEM command to display your computer's memory usage by program.

```
C:\> MEM /PROGRAM  |  MORE  <ENTER>
```

Extended or Expanded Memory DOS Users

If you are not using DOS 5 but you are using extended or expanded memory, you can improve your system performance by installing disk-caching software. Like DOS 5, Microsoft Windows provides the device driver SMARTDRV.SYS that installs a disk cache. If you are using extended memory, place a DEVICE entry similar to the following after the DEVICE entry that installs your extended memory driver.

```
DEVICE=C:\DOS\SMARTDRV.SYS
```

If the SMARTDRV.SYS driver resides in your WINDOWS directory, use the following entry.

```
DEVICE=C:\WINDOWS\SMARTDRV.SYS
```

If you are using expanded memory, include the /A switch. You should note that the previous SMARTDRV.SYS entries install a disk cache using the default size of 256Kb. Depending on your available memory, you may want to create a larger or smaller disk cache.

If you install a disk cache, reduce the number of DOS disk buffers in CONFIG.SYS to 3, as shown here.

```
BUFFERS=3
```

All DOS Users

Regardless of your DOS version or memory types, you may want to install a RAM drive using the RAMDRIVE.SYS device driver. If you are using expanded or extended memory, you can install the RAM drive outside of conventional memory using the /A or /E switches. If you don't specify one of these two switches, DOS will create the RAM drive in conventional memory.

The following CONFIG.SYS entry creates a 64Kb RAM drive in conventional memory.

```
DEVICE=C:\DOS\RAMDRIVE.SYS
```

 If you are using DOS 5, create a RAM drive and assign the TEMP environment entry to point at the drive. DOS will use the fast RAM drive for its temporary files, which **NOTE** *will improve the performance of your I/O redirection operations.*

Review

1. What is conventional memory?

2. What is extended memory?

3. What is expanded memory?

4. What is reserved memory?

5. What is high memory?

Answers

1. Conventional memory is your computer's memory from 0 to 640Kb. All computers use conventional memory. Most DOS programs run in conventional memory.

2. Extended memory is the memory above 1Mb available in the IBM PC AT (80286), 386, and 486 computers. To use extended memory, you must install an extended memory manager (device driver). The PC AT supports up to 16Mb of extended memory. The 386 and 486 support up to 4 gigabytes!

3. Expanded memory uses hardware and software to break the 640Kb boundary of the IBM PC (8088). The expanded memory software reserves a 64Kb region of the computer's reserved memory (see Question 4) for use as a page frame. DOS will load programs into conventional memory as always. The program itself can then access up to 16Mb of data stored in expanded memory. The expanded memory software maps references to a program's data (the address of the data) from the memory region called a bank that resides on the expanded memory board, into one of four page frames in reserved memory. If all four page frames are in use, the expanded memory software swaps the contents of one page frame back to the memory region above 1Mb to make room for the new page. Because of this continual swapping of pages, expanded memory is slower than conventional memory.

4. Reserved memory is the 384Kb area of memory above 640Kb and below 1Mb. The IBM PC uses a portion of reserved memory for video output and memory-mapped device I/O. Under DOS 5, using the CONFIG.SYS DEVICEHIGH entry and LOADHIGH command, you can install device drivers and commands into reserved memory, freeing up conventional memory for use by DOS.

5. High memory is the first 64Kb memory region above 1Mb. Under DOS 5, you can use the CONFIG.SYS DOS=HIGH entry to load DOS into high memory, freeing up conventional memory for program use.

Advanced Concepts

The previous discussion of HIMEM.SYS and EMM386.EXE presented only the driver's basic capabilities. This section presents each of the driver's parameters and switches.

HIMEM.SYS

HIMEM.SYS allows your programs to use extended memory. You must install HIMEM.SYS using a DEVICE entry in your CONFIG.SYS file before any other drivers that use extended memory, such as RAMDRIVE.SYS, EMM386.EXE or SMARTDRV.SYS.

The complete format of HIMEM.SYS is

```
DEVICE=C:\DOS\HIMEM.SYS [/HMAMIN=MinimumMemory]
        [/NUMHANDLES=HandleCount] [/INT15=Kb] [/MACHINE:nnnn]
        [/A20CONTROL:ON|OFF] [/SHADOWRAM:ON|OFF] [/CPU CLOCK:ON|OFF]
```

The /HMAMIN switch specifies the minimum amount of high memory in kilobytes a program must use before the program can use the high memory area. The default value is 0. The range of valid values is 0 through 63. By default HIMEM.SYS gives the high memory area to the first program that requests it. Using /HMAMIN, you may be able to reserve the high memory area for the desired program.

Programs allocate extended memory in variable-sized blocks. When a program allocates a block, HIMEM.SYS returns a unique value called a handle that the program must use each time it references the block. The /NUMHANDLES switch specifies the number of available handles from 1 to 128. The default value is 32. Each handle requires 6 bytes of conventional memory.

Programs can access extended memory using hardware interrupt 15H. The /INT15 switch specifies the size in Kb of a memory buffer HIMEM.SYS provides for the INT 15H interface. The default size is 0. Valid values range from 0 to 64Kb. The ROM-BIOS lets programs access extended memory using hardware interrupt 15. The extended memory BIOS interface occurs outside of the extended memory-management software. You only need to use /INT15 if a program uses the BIOS to access extended memory in this way.

To access the high memory area, you computer uses special software called the A20 handler, which handles memory address ("A" stands for address) references that use address line 20 (a memory reference above 1Mb). In most cases, HIMEM.SYS can correctly determine the computer's A20 value. If you are using one of the machines listed in Table 32-1, and HIMEM.SYS displays A20 error messages when you install it, include the /MACHINE switch to assist HIMEM.SYS.

The /A20CONTROL switch specifies whether or not HIMEM.SYS takes control of the computer's A20 handler. If you specify ON (the default setting), HIMEM.SYS will take control of the A20 line, if the computer has it on or off. If you specify OFF, HIMEM.SYS only takes control of the A20 line if it is initially off.

Your computer's BIOS is stored in read-only memory whose contents never change, even when your computer's power is off. Compared to RAM, this read-only memory or ROM is slow. Many computers will copy the BIOS from slower ROM to locations in the faster RAM. The /SHADOWRAM switch directs HIMEM.SYS to

Code	Number	Machine
AT	1	IBM PC AT
PS2	2	IBM PS/2
PT1Cascade	3	Phoenix cascade BIOS
HPVECTRA	4	HP Vectra A and A+
ATT6300PLUS	5	AT&T 6300 Plus
ACER1100	6	Acer 1100
TOSHIBA	7	Toshiba 1600 and 1200XE
WYSE	8	Wyse 12.5 MHz 286
TULIP	9	Tulip SX
ZENITH	10	Zenith ZBIOS
AT1	11	IBM PC AT
AT2	12	IBM PC AT (alternative delay)
CSS	12	CSS Labs
AT3	13	IBM PC AT (alternative delay)
PHILIPS	13	Philips
FASTHP	14	HPVECTRA

Table 32-1.   HIMEM.SYS A20 Handler Values

disable the use of shadow RAM to regain the memory for other uses. The ON value enables shadow RAM, while OFF disables it. Not all computers support shadow RAM. If your computer has less than 2Mb of RAM, HIMEM.SYS uses OFF by default.

In some cases, your computer's speed may slow down when you install HIMEM.SYS. The /CPUCLOCK switch lets HIMEM.SYS control the speed of your computer's system clock. When you specify ON, HIMEM.SYS can control the clock speed. The default setting is OFF.

EMM386.EXE

Depending on your applications, you may have a program that supports expanded memory and not extended memory. Using the EMM386.EXE driver, you can direct DOS to simulate expanded memory with a portion of your computer's extended memory, letting the program run. To use EMM386.EXE, you must be using a 386 or 486 computer. You must also install HIMEM.SYS before you can use EMM386.EXE.

The complete form of EMM386.EXE is as follows:

```
DEVICE=C:\DOS\EMM386.EXE  [ON|OFF|AUTO]  [Kb]  [W=ON|OFF]
     [Mnn |FRAME=Segment |/PSegment]  [PPage=Segment]
     [I=Range]  [X=Range]  [B=Segment]  [L=MinimumExtendedMemory]
     [A=AlternateRegisters]  [H=Handles]  [D=DMAKb]
     [RAM]  [NOEMS]
```

By default, EMM386.EXE uses the ON parameter, which keeps expanded memory support active. The AUTO parameter directs the driver to only provide expanded memory support when a program requests it. The OFF mode loads the driver but suspends it (makes it inactive), letting a program enable the driver support at a later time.

The Kb parameter specifies the amount of expanded memory desired from 16Kb to 32,768Kb (32Mb). The EMM386.EXE driver rounds the value specified down to a multiple of 16Kb. The default is 256Kb.

The W parameter provides support for the Weitek math coprocessor, which uses a 64Kb-block memory-mapped address space. If your system does not have a math coprocessor, you can omit this parameter. The default setting for W is OFF (no support).

Expanded memory uses a 64Kb region of your computer's reserved memory called the *page frame*. Depending on your hardware configuration, you may need to specify the base address of the page frame. The EMM386.EXE driver gives you several ways to specify the base address. First the M*nn* parameter uses one of the values specified in Table 32-2.

The FRAME and /P parameters let you explicitly state the segment address for the page frame. Using these two parameters you can select one of the base addresses listed in Table 32-2.

Using M, FRAME, AND /P, the following entries specify the same base address.

```
M5    FRAME=D000    /PD000
```

If you use the M, FRAME, or /P parameters, you define the base address for all four page locations. Thus, EMM386.EXE allocates a contiguous 64Kb memory region.

Using the P parameter, you can specify individual locations for each page. As before, the addresses you must use are in Table 32-2. To maintain compatibility with LIMS 3.2, pages 0, 1, 2, and 3 must be in contiguous memory locations.

The I parameter specifies a range of segment address values to be used for an expanded memory page. By default, the expanded memory software tries to determine which memory locations it can safely use to store pages. If you are aware of a safe region, you can use the I parameter to tell the expanded memory software.

The X parameter specifies a range of segment addresses to be excluded from storing extended memory pages. The X parameter has precedence over I, should ranges overlap. The following entry excludes the range C400H to C800H.

```
X=C400-C800
```

The B parameter specifies the lowest segment address EMM386.EXE can use for a page address from 1000H through 4000H. The default value is 4000H.

The L parameter specifies the amount of extended memory in Kb that must be available after you load EMM386.EXE. The EMM386.EXE driver will determine your expanded memory use by subtracting the extended memory size specified from the available extended memory.

To improve your performance during multitasking operations under Windows or the DOS 5 shell, you can specify the number of alternate register sets from 0 to 254. The default size is 7. Each alternate register set uses approximately 200 bytes of memory.

Like extended memory, when programs allocate blocks of expanded memory, the program receives a handle that uniquely identifies the block. By default, EMM386.EXE supports 64 handles. Using the H parameter, you can specify support for 2 through 255 handles.

Different block devices can use a special high-speed chip (instead of the CPU) to transfer data directly from the device into memory. This process of bypassing the CPU to transfer data into memory is *direct memory access* or DMA. To perform direct

Value	Base Segment	Value	Base Segment
1	C000H	8	DC00H
2	C400H	9	E000H
3	C800H	*10	8000H
4	CC00H	*11	8400H
5	D000H	*12	8800H
6	D400H	*13	8C00H
7	D800H	*14	9000H

*Table 32-2.   Page-Frame-Use Address Values. * Values 8000H through 9000H are only for computers with 512Kb of RAM*

access, the DMA chip needs a buffer to store the data that typically resides in the reserved memory. The D parameter lets you specify the amount of memory in kilobytes EMM386.EXE must reserve for direct memory buffers from 16Kb through 256Kb. The default size is 16Kb.

The EMM386.EXE driver lets you simulate expanded memory, and lets DOS load memory-resident programs and device drivers into reserved memory. If you want to simulate expanded memory and access reserved memory, use the RAM parameter. If you want to access reserved memory without simulating expanded memory, use NOEMS.

The following examples illustrate different uses of EMM386.EXE. The first entry simulates 256Kb (the default) of expanded memory.

```
DEVICE=C:\DOS\EMM386.EXE
```

The following entry includes a size 2048 to simulate 2Mb of expanded memory.

```
DEVICE=C:\DOS\EMM386.EXE  2048
```

This entry directs EMM386.EXE to place the page frame at location D000H.

```
DEVICE=C:\DOS\EMM386.EXE  FRAME=D0000
```

Last, this entry directs EMM386.EXE to simulate 512Kb of expanded memory and to provide access to reserved memory.

```
DEVICE=C:\DOS\EMM386.EXE  512  RAM
```

Key Terms

Conventional memory   The computer's memory from 0 to 640Kb.

Extended memory   The memory above 1Mb on an 80286, 386, or 486 computer.

Expanded memory   A memory-management technique that combines hardware and software to let the IBM PC (8088) break its 640Kb memory boundary. Expanded memory exchanges 16Kb blocks of memory from locations called banks that reside on the expanded memory board, into a page-frame buffer stored in reserved memory.

Reserved memory   The 384Kb memory region between 640Kb and 1Mb. The computer uses part of reserved memory for a video interface, part to communicate with other hardware devices, and optionally, a 64Kb region for expanded memory. Under DOS 5, the DEVICEHIGH CONFIG.SYS entry and the LOADHIGH command let you install device drivers and memory-resident commands into unused portions of reserved memory.

Chapter 33

How DOS Actually Stores Files

Throughout the previous chapters you have learned DOS stores your files in disk sectors. For efficiency, DOS groups sectors to form allocation units (clusters). You have learned a directory is a list of file names and related information such as file size, attributes (read-only, archive, hidden, and system), as well as the file's date and time stamp that tells you when the file was created or last changed. In addition, you have read brief discussions about the file allocation table (FAT) that serves as the road map DOS follows to locate the clusters belonging to each file. In this chapter you will see how all these concepts work together and will more fully understand the DOS file system. After you understand how DOS stores files, you can more efficiently use disk and file utilities to improve your system performance.

The File Allocation Table

DOS stores your files on disks in groups of sectors called clusters or allocation units. Depending on a file's size, the file may fit in a single cluster or may require many clusters. DOS tries to store a file's clusters in consecutive disk locations. In some cases, however, another file's cluster may prevent DOS from using consecutive cluster locations for a file, and the file becomes fragmented. The following illustration shows three files. The first file, ONE, fits in one cluster; the second, file TWO, resides in two consecutive clusters; while the third file, THREE, resides in three clusters dispersed across the disk. Each cluster may contain multiple disk sectors.

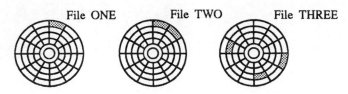

You learned when you examined CHKDSK in Chapter 25 that DOS divides your disk into a fixed number of clusters. Depending on your disk size, the number of clusters on the disk will differ. Table 33-1 lists the number of clusters available for several commonly used disk sizes. It should be noted that each cluster may contain multiple disk sectors.

As you have seen, DOS can store a file's contents on any unused cluster on your disk. To keep track of each file's clusters, DOS keeps a table on disk called the file allocation table. The file allocation table keeps track of every cluster on your disk, noting whether the cluster is in use, available for use, or has been marked unusable by FORMAT.

DOS uses the file allocation table to locate each file's clusters on disk, storing the list of cluster numbers that make up each file. Figure 33-1 illustrates a file that resides in clusters 2, 3, and 4. Using the file allocation table, DOS builds a chain of cluster numbers. If you look at the file allocation table entry for cluster 2, you'll find it contains the value 3, which corresponds to the next cluster in the file. Likewise, if you look at the entry for cluster 3, you'll find it contains the value 4, again the next cluster in the file. Cluster 4, in this case, is the file's last cluster. Within the file allocation table, DOS uses the hexadecimal value FFF8 to represent the end of file. You can see that the file resides in consecutive clusters.

Figure 33-2 illustrates a second file that again contains three clusters. In this case, however, the file is fragmented, having its data dispersed in clusters 3, 8, and 11. As before, however, you can trace the file's cluster map beginning at cluster 3, to cluster 8, and to the file's last cluster in cluster 11.

Disk Type	Number of Clusters
360Kb	354
720Kb	713
1.2Mb	2371
1.44Mb	2847
10Mb	2549

Table 33-1.   The Number of Clusters Available on Commonly Used Disk Sizes

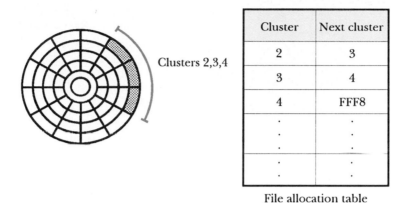

Cluster	Next cluster
2	3
3	4
4	FFF8
.	.
.	.
.	.

File allocation table

Figure 33-1.   *A three-cluster file with its corresponding file allocation table entries*

Last, Figure 33-3 illustrates a file that contains only one cluster (cluster 3). If you examine the file allocation table entry for cluster 3, you'll find it contains the hexadecimal value FFF8, indicating it is the last cluster in the file.

Note the file allocation table entries containing the value 0. DOS uses 0 to indicate an unused cluster. When you create a file on your disk or increase the size of an existing file, DOS searches the file allocation table for an entry with the value 0 and allocates the entry, placing it into the file's cluster chain.

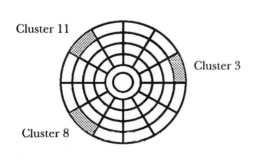

Cluster	Next cluster
3	8
.	.
.	.
.	.
8	11
.	.
11	FFF8

File allocation table

Figure 33-2.   *A fragmented file with its corresponding file allocation table entries*

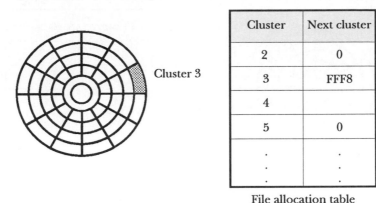

Cluster	Next cluster
2	0
3	FFF8
4	
5	0
.	.
.	.
.	.

File allocation table

Figure 33-3.   *A file containing only one cluster with its corresponding file allocation table entry*

When DOS needs to access a file's contents, either to copy, display, print, or even execute the file's contents, DOS follows the file's cluster chain in the same way you just have. In our case, however, the book told you each file's starting cluster. DOS, however, learns the file's starting cluster from the file's directory entry, discussed next.

Directory Entries

A directory is a list of file names and key information about each file. Each time you create a file on disk, DOS creates a directory entry for the file. Each directory entry contains 32 bytes of information, as shown here:

File name 8 bytes	Extension 3 bytes	Attribute 1 byte	Reserved by DOS 10 bytes	Time 2 bytes	Date 2 bytes	Starting cluster 2 bytes	File size 2 bytes

├─────────────────────── 32 bytes ───────────────────────┤

As you can see from the illustration, the directory entry stores the file's name, extension, size, and date and time stamps. In addition, the directory entry contains the file's first cluster number. By starting with this cluster value, DOS can locate the file's clusters by traversing the file allocation table.

DOS Stores Directories on Disk Just as Files

Each time you use MKDIR to create a directory, DOS creates a directory entry to store the directory name specified. To the user, the only difference between the directory and file entry is directory entries appear in directory listings with the letters "<DIR> " instead of a file size. To distinguish a file entry from a directory entry, DOS assigns directory entries a unique attribute value, just as it would assign a read-only, hidden, system, or archive attribute.

When MKDIR creates a directory, DOS allocates a disk cluster to store the directory entries. As the number of files in your directory list grows, DOS allocates additional clusters to hold the entries, updating the directory's cluster chain in the file allocation table. Figure 33-4 illustrates how DOS might store a directory on disk.

DOS Stores the FAT and Root Directory at Fixed Locations

The first sector on every disk contains the DOS boot record. If you have formatted the disk as a bootable system disk, the boot record contains a small program that begins the DOS startup process. If the disk is not bootable, the boot record contains a small program that causes your computer to display the following error message.

```
Non-System disk or disk error
Replace and strike any key when ready
```

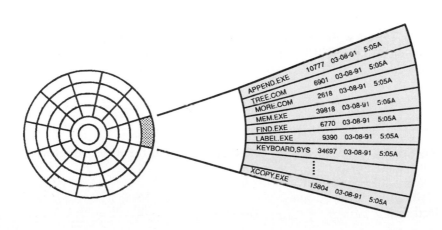

Figure 33-4.   *DOS stores directories on disk in one or more clusters, just as it stores files*

In addition to containing this small program, the boot record contains values that describe your disk size, root directory size, and cluster size.

Beginning in the sector immediately following the boot record, DOS stores the file allocation table (FAT). As you can imagine, because the file allocation table contains the road map DOS uses to locate your files on disk, a disk error causing damage to such a sector could have a devastating impact. To reduce the chance of lost information due to a disk error in the FAT, DOS stores two copies of the FAT on your disk. Should a disk error ever render the first file allocation table unusable, DOS can still access your files using the second FAT copy.

Following your file allocation table, DOS reserves several sectors on your disk to store the root directory. The number of sectors DOS reserves depends on your disk size. Table 33-2 defines the number of sectors DOS reserves for common disk sizes.

Knowing each disk sector contains 512 bytes, and each directory entry requires 32 bytes, you can calculate the maximum number of root directory entries as shown.

$$\text{Maximum root directory entries} = \frac{(\text{Root directory sectors}) \times (\text{Sector size})}{32 \text{ bytes per entry}}$$

The root directory is the only directory on your disk whose size is fixed. The disk space that follows the root directory is called data space. It is the disk space available for use by your files. Figure 33-5 illustrates the DOS disk layout.

How FORMAT Works

You learned in Chapter 7, "Preparing Disks for Use," that FORMAT prepares a disk for use by DOS. As you know, FORMAT examines your disk for bad sectors, and marks the bad sectors as damaged, preventing their use by DOS. To mark a sector as unusable, FORMAT places a special value in the file allocation table entry for the cluster associated with the damaged sector. For hard disks, FORMAT uses the hexadecimal value FFF7. Figure 33-6 illustrates a disk with damaged sectors in clusters 3 and 7. Note the file allocation table values for those entries. When DOS

Disk Size	Sectors Reserved for Root Directory
160Kb and 180Kb	4
320Kb, 360Kb, and 720Kb	7
1.2Mb and 1.44Mb	14
Hard disk	32

Table 33-2.   *Number of Sectors Reserved for Root Directory Entries*

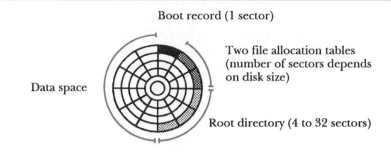

Figure 33-5. *Each disk contains a boot record, file allocation tables, a root directory, and data space*

is looking for disk space to store a file, DOS knows not to use clusters containing this value.

Before FORMAT prepares an unused disk for use, the disk is blank. FORMAT not only searches the disk for bad sectors, FORMAT builds the disk's boot record and the file allocation tables, as well as the root directory.

How CHKDSK Works

You learned in Chapter 25, "Using CHKDSK," that CHKDSK examines your disk's current health. CHKDSK performs a consistency check between the information

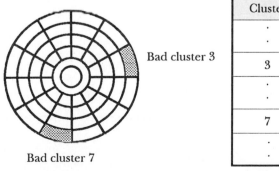

Figure 33-6. *FORMAT stores the value FFF7 in the file allocation table to indicate an unusable cluster*

stored about files in directory entries and the information stored in the file allocation table. To begin, CHKDSK reads a directory entry, noting a file's starting cluster and file size. Using the file allocation table entries, CHKDSK first makes sure the file size in the directory corresponds to the number of clusters it found. If the sizes differ, CHKDSK will truncate the file size displaying the message shown here.

```
Allocation error, size adjusted
```

Next, CHKDSK keeps track of which clusters each file believes it owns (which clusters CHKDSK found in the file allocation chain for the file). If two or more files believe they own one or more of the same clusters, the files are cross-linked as discussed in Chapter 25. When CHKDSK encounters cross-linked files, it displays a message similar to the following:

```
FILENAME.EXT is cross linked on Cluster n
```

Last, CHKDSK searches the file allocation table for clusters marked as in use, but not belonging to a file. As discussed in Chapter 25, CHKDSK calls such clusters "lost clusters." When CHKDSK encounters lost clusters, CHKDSK displays the following message, telling you the number of lost cluster chains and the amount of disk space the lost cluster chains consume.

```
nnn Lost allocation units found in n chains
nnn bytes disk space would be freed
Convert lost chains to files (Y/N)?
```

As you can see, CHKDSK performs much of its processing simply by comparing the file allocation table entries to the information recorded in directory entries.

Review

1. What is the file allocation table?

2. Given the following file allocation table and directory entries in Figure 33-7, mark the disk clusters in use by each file.

3. How does DOS find unused clusters?

4. How does FORMAT prevent DOS from using a damaged cluster?

Name	Size	Date	Time	Starting cluster
ONE	2048	8-1-91	6:01p	4
TWO	4096	8-1-91	6:02p	3
THREE	6144	8-1-91	6:03p	6

Cluster	Next cluster
2	0
3	5
4	FFF8
5	FFF8
6	7
7	8
8	FFF8

File allocation table

Figure 33-7.   Marking the disk clusters used by each file

5. A 360Kb disk can store 368,640 bytes of data. However, DOS uses portions of this disk to store the boot record, FAT, and root directory. How much disk space is actually available for files?

Answers

1. The file allocation table provides the road map DOS uses to locate files on your disk. To store a file on disk, DOS divides the file into one or more disk clusters. The file allocation table tracks the list of clusters that make up each file. DOS stores the file allocation table on disk immediately after the disk's boot record. To safeguard against a single disk error within the FAT's sectors preventing you from accessing your files, DOS stores two copies of the file allocation table on disk. If the first copy becomes damaged, DOS can use the second to access your files.

2. The disk clusters for the files are shown in Figure 33-8.

3. DOS assigns unused clusters with the value 0 within the file allocation table. When you create a file or increase an existing file's size, DOS searches the file allocation table for a cluster entry with the value 0.

4. FORMAT places the hexadecimal value FFF7 in the file allocation table for damaged clusters. When DOS searches the file allocation table for an available cluster, DOS knows not to use clusters marked by FORMAT as unusable.

5. The following screen shows the amount of space available for files using a 360Kb disk:

```
Boot record requires 512 bytes
File allocation tables require 2,048 bytes
Root directory requires 3,584 bytes

File space is left with 362,496 bytes
```

Advanced Concepts

As you have learned, one of the major problems arising from DOS assigning disk space to files using clusters is wasted space for small files. One of the largest offenders of wasted disk space is DOS batch files. If you count up the number of batch files on your disk and multiply the number of files by your disk's cluster size, you can determine how much space your batch files consume. If you are using DOS 3.3 or higher, use the following command to determine the number of batch files on your disk.

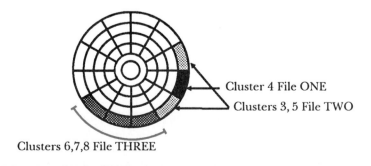

Cluster 4 File ONE

Clusters 3, 5 File TWO

Clusters 6,7,8 File THREE

Figure 33-8.   File cluster assignment

```
C:\> ATTRIB \*.BAT /S | FIND /C ".BAT" <ENTER>
```

If you have several batch files you don't use on a regular basis, you might consider merging the batch files and using either a menu or batch parameters to select a specific batch file from the resulting file. By merging files in this way, you can quickly free up disk space.

If you are using DOS 5, you might consider defining your commonly used smaller batch files as DOSKEY macros. To do so, you would place DOSKEY commands in your AUTOEXEC.BAT file, directing DOSKEY to define the macros each time your system starts. Using macros, you trade memory for disk space.

Key Terms

FAT   File allocation table.

File allocation table   A table containing the locations of each file's clusters, the location of damaged clusters marked unusable by FORMAT, and available clusters DOS can use to store additional information on disk.

Chapter 34

ANSI.SYS

In Chapter 24, "Customizing Your System with CONFIG.SYS," you learned the CONFIG.SYS DEVICE entry lets you install device driver software into memory. At that time you learned DOS provides several different device drivers, one of which, ANSI.SYS, lets you enhance your screen and keyboard capabilities. Because of its popularity and frequency of use, this chapter takes a detailed look at ANSI.SYS. Specifically, you will learn to use ANSI.SYS to set your screen colors, to redefine function keys, and to improve the output appearance of your DOS batch files.

Installing ANSI.SYS

ANSI.SYS is a device driver that resides in the DOS directory on your hard disk. Using your word processor or the DOS editor, add the following entry to your CONFIG.SYS file.

```
DEVICE=C:\DOS\ANSI.SYS
```

If you are using DOS 5 and have enabled access to reserved memory as discussed in Chapter 32, "Understanding DOS Memory Management," use the following DEVICEHIGH entry to load the ANSI.SYS driver.

```
DEVICEHIGH=C:\DOS\ANSI.SYS
```

Next, use the CTRL-ALT-DEL key combination to restart DOS, installing the ANSI.SYS device driver.

Escape Sequences

The ANSI.SYS driver lets you set screen colors, redefine keys, and position the cursor by writing unique character combinations to your screen. These character combinations begin with the ASCII *escape character* (ASCII value 27) and are called *escape sequences*. The escape character is a unique character that does not have a corresponding symbol that appears on your screen. Most books and magazines represent the escape character as Esc . Using the letters "Esc," we can represent the ANSI escape sequence Esc[44m that sets your screen background color to blue. In this case, the escape sequence contains the escape character immediately followed by a left bracket ([) and the characters "44m". This chapter presents many ANSI escape sequences. Each escape sequence will begin with the letters "Esc" and a left bracket ([).

Representing the Escape Character

In general, the ANSI device driver examines every character DOS writes to your screen display. When the ANSI driver encounters an escape character, the driver checks the characters that follow to see if they match one of its defined escape sequences.

To produce an ANSI escape sequence, you can use your word processor or the DOS editor to create a file containing the escape sequence, which you later display using the TYPE command.

```
C:\> TYPE  BLUEBACK.ESC  <ENTER>
```

Second, you can create a batch file that uses ECHO to write the escape sequence to your screen.

```
@ECHO OFF
ECHO Esc[44m
```

Your difficulty in using either of these techniques is entering the Esc character. When you are editing a text file or batch file, you can't just press the ESC key to generate the escape character. Instead, depending on your word processor, the steps you must perform will differ. If you simply type ECHO Esc[44m, ECHO will dutifully echo "Esc[40m" on screen. The following discussion teaches you how to create the batch file BLUEBACK.BAT which uses the ECHO command to write the ANSI escape sequence Esc[44m to your screen, setting your screen's background color to blue.

```
@ECHO OFF
ECHO Esc[44m
CLS
```

Creating Escape Sequences with EDLIN

Chapter 36, "Creating Simple Text Files with EDLIN," discusses the EDLIN command in detail. To create the Esc character using EDLIN, you must press CTRL-V (hold down the CTRL key and type V). Next, you must type a left bracket character. Issue the following command to create the file BLUEBACK.BAT:

```
C:\> EDLIN  BLUEBACK.BAT   <ENTER>
```

EDLIN will respond with the "New file" message and its asterisk (*) prompt.

```
New file
*
```

Type I and press ENTER to type in line 1, and then enter the batch file's first line as follows.

```
New file
*I   <ENTER>
        1:*@ECHO OFF <ENTER>
        2:*
```

Next, type ECHO followed by a space. To generate the ESC character, use the CTRL-V key combination, followed by a left bracket. Your screen will display "^V" as shown:

```
New file
*I   <ENTER>
        1:*@ECHO OFF <ENTER>
        2:*ECHO ^V[
```

You have now generated only the Esc character, you must complete the escape sequence by typing **[44m**.

```
New file
*I  <ENTER>
      1:  @ECHO OFF  <ENTER>
      2:  ECHO ^V[[44m
```

Press ENTER and type **CLS** for line 3.

```
New file
*I  <ENTER>
      1:*@ECHO OFF  <ENTER>
      2:*ECHO ^V[[44m  <ENTER>
      3:*CLS  <ENTER>
      4:*
```

The batch file is complete. Use the CTRL-C key combination to leave EDLIN's insert mode and the EDLIN E command to exit EDLIN to DOS.

```
New file
*I  <ENTER>
      1:*@ECHO OFF  <ENTER>
      2:*ECHO ^V[[44m  <ENTER>
      3:*CLS  <ENTER>
      4:*^C

*E  <ENTER>

C:\>
```

Your batch file is ready for execution.

```
C:\> BLUEBACK  <ENTER>
```

If your screen color does not change, make sure you have installed the ANSI.SYS device driver using CONFIG.SYS, and if necessary, restarted DOS. Next, delete the batch file and use EDLIN to create a second copy, making sure you type in the escape sequence exactly the same as just described.

Creating Escape Sequences with EDIT

Chapter 37, "The DOS 5 Editor, EDIT," examines the EDIT command in detail. To create an escape sequence using EDIT, press the CTRL-P key combination and then type P while holding the CTRL key down. EDIT will display a left arrow. Type in the rest of the escape sequence immediately next to the arrow.

Creating Escape Sequences with a Word Processor

If you are using a word processor to create the batch file, the steps you must follow to create the Esc character will differ. Under Microsoft Word, make sure your NUMLOCK key is on, and then hold down the ALT key and type *27 on the numeric keypad at the right of your keyboard.* When you release the ALT key, Word will display the Esc character as a left arrow.

In WordPerfect, like Microsoft Word, hold down ALT and type 27 on your keyboard's numeric keypad. WordPerfect will display the Esc character as a left-pointing arrow. If you are using a different word processor, refer to the documentation that accompanied the software. No matter which word processor you use, make sure you save the file as an ASCII file, not a word processing document file with special embedded formatting characters and symbols.

Controlling Screen Colors Using ANSI.SYS

When you use ANSI.SYS to set your screen color, the color will remain in effect while you issue commands such as DIR, TYPE, and CHKDSK from the DOS prompt. If you invoke a program such as your word processor or the DOS 5 EDIT command, the program will override your current screen color selection, using its own colors. If you don't like the program's colors, most programs provide an option that lets you select a color you like. When you exit the program to DOS, your ANSI color selection will resume.

The ANSI.SYS device driver provides foreground and background color values. As you just learned, the escape sequence Esc[44m lets you set your screen's background color to blue. By replacing the color value 44 with one of the values specified in Table 34-1, you can select a different background color.

Value	Background Color	Escape Sequence
40	Black	Esc[40m
41	Red	Esc[41m
42	Green	Esc[42m
43	Yellow	Esc[43m
44	Blue	Esc[44m
45	Magenta	Esc[45m
46	Cyan	Esc[46m
47	White	Esc[47m

Table 34-1.   *ANSI.SYS Background Color Values*

The following batch file, REDBACK.BAT, selects a red screen background.

```
@ECHO OFF
ECHO Esc[41m
CLS
```

ANSI.SYS also lets you set your screen's foreground color. Table 34-2 contains the ANSI.SYS foreground color values.

For example, the following batch file GREENFOR.BAT selects a green foreground color.

```
@ECHO OFF
ECHO Esc[32m
CLS
```

Value	Foreground Color	Escape Sequence
30	Black	Esc[30m
31	Red	Esc[31m
32	Green	Esc[32m
33	Yellow	Esc[33m
34	Blue	Esc[34m
35	Magenta	Esc[35m
36	Cyan	Esc[36m
37	White	Esc[37m

Table 34-2.   *ANSI.SYS Foreground Color Values*

Most users will select a foreground and background color combination they find most pleasing to work with. By separating the two color values with a semicolon, the ANSI.SYS device driver lets you select a foreground and background color in one escape sequence. The following batch file, WHITEBLU.BAT, selects a white background (47) and a blue foreground (34).

```
@ECHO OFF
ECHO Esc[47;34m
CLS
```

Controlling Screen Colors with PROMPT

There is one more way to control the screen colors with the Esc characters that you can use either in a predefined batch file (including AUTOEXEC.BAT) or interactively from the DOS prompt, namely through the PROMPT command. In Chapter 10, "Directories," you learned the letters PG direct PROMPT to use the current drive letter and directory name, followed by a greater-than symbol for your system prompt. In a similar way, $E directs PROMPT to generate the Esc character. The following PROMPT command chooses a black background and a magenta foreground.

```
C:\>PROMPT $E[40;35m$P$G   <ENTER>
```

You can see that the format of the color command from the "[" to the "m" is the same as above. Using the $E character, the next PROMPT uses the escape sequence Esc[44m to display your prompt on a blue background, and the escape sequence Esc[40m to display your other screen text on black.

```
C:\>PROMPT $E[44m$P$G$E[40m   <ENTER>
```

PROMPT is very useful for this purpose because you can type it right in from the DOS prompt and see the results immediately. It is limited in its use of escape characters to the colors, however. When you find a combination you like, you can include it in AUTOEXEC.BAT and other batch files. Be careful when typing. If you choose the same number twice, the foreground and background will be the same color—the characters you type will be invisible, and you may have to reboot DOS.

By combining ANSI escape sequences with the prompt metacharacters ($ character combinations) presented in Chapter 43, "DOS System Commands," you can create very unique custom prompts.

Redefining Keys with ANSI.SYS

The ANSI.SYS device driver enhances your screen and keyboard capabilities. As you have just learned, using ANSI.SYS you can select your screen's foreground and background colors. In this section, you will use ANSI.SYS to assign your commonly used commands to function keys and different key combinations.

Assume, for example, you use the following TREE command on a regular basis.

```
C:\> TREE   C:\   /F   <ENTER>
```

Rather than constantly retyping the command, you can use ANSI.SYS to assign the command to the F10 function key. Each time you press F10 at the DOS prompt, the ANSI.SYS driver will display the TREE command, letting you press ENTER to execute the command.

To assign a command to key using ANSI.SYS, you must know the key's unique scancode value the keyboard sends to DOS each time the key is pressed. For example, when you press the F10 function key, the keyboard sends DOS the value 0 followed by the value 68. Using these two values, the following batch file, F10TREE.BAT, assigns the TREE command to the F10 function key.

```
@ECHO OFF
ECHO Esc[0;68;"TREE C:\ /F"p
```

In general, you should assign commands to key combinations such as SHIFT-F10 or CTRL-F10 to avoid conflicts with other commands such as DOSKEY. Table 34-3 lists the scancode values for each key on your keyboard as well as the scan codes generated when you use the key in combination with SHIFT, CTRL, or ALT.

Using Table 34-3, the following batch file assigns the command DIR | MORE to the SHIFT-F10 key combination.

```
@ECHO OFF
ECHO Esc[0;93;"DIR | MORE"p
```

Figure 34-1 illustrates a 101-key keyboard.

If you have purchased an enhanced 101-key keyboard after buying your computer, the computer may not fully support some of the extended keys. If you experience difficulties when using the scan codes for the extended keys, and you are using DOS 4 or later, you can include the /K switch in the CONFIG.SYS DEVICE entry for ANSI.SYS to direct ANSI.SYS to ignore the extended keys.

```
DEVICE=C:\DOS\ANSI.SYS   /K
```

Key	Key only	Shift+Key	Ctrl+Key	Alt+Key
F1	0;59	0;84	0;94	0;104
F2	0;60	0;85	0;95	0;105
F3	0;61	0;86	0;96	0;106
F4	0;62	0;87	0;97	0;107
F5	0;63	0;88	0;98	0;108
F6	0;64	0;89	0;99	0;109
F7	0;65	0;90	0;100	0;110
F8	0;66	0;91	0;101	0;111
F9	0;67	0;92	0;102	0;112
F10	0;68	0;93	0;103	0;113
F11	0;133	0;135	0;137	0;139
F12	0;134	0;136	0;138	0;140
HOME	0;71	55	0;119	
UP ARROW	0;72	56	0;141	
PGUP	0;73	57	0;132	
LEFT ARROW	0;75	52	0;115	
RIGHT ARROW	0;77	54	0;116	
END	0;79	49	0;117	
DOWN ARROW	0;80	50	0;145	
PGDN	0;81	51	0;118	
INS	0;82	48	0;146	
DEL	0;83	46	0;147	
HOME*	224;71	224;71	224;119	224;151
UP ARROW*	224;72	224;72	224;141	224;152
PGUP*	224;73	224;73	224;132	224;153
LEFT ARROW*	224;75	224;74	224;115	224;155
RIGHT ARROW*	224;77	224;77	224;116	224;157
END*	224;79	224;79	224;117	224;159
DOWN ARROW*	224;80		224;145	224;160
PGDN*	224;81	224;81	224;118	224;161
INS*	224;82	224;82	224;146	224;162
DEL	224;83	224;83	224;147	224;163
PRTSC			0;114	
PAUSE/BREAK			0;0	
BACKSPACE	8	8	127	0;14
ENTER	13	13	10	0;28
TAB	9	0;15	0;148	0;165

*Indicates a gray key

Table 34-3.   Keyboard Scancode Values

Key	Key only	Shift+Key	Ctrl+Key	Alt+Key
A	97	65	1	0;30
B	98	66	2	0;48
C	99	67	3	0;46
D	100	68	4	0;32
E	101	69	5	0;18
F	102	70	6	0;33
G	103	71	7	0;34
H	104	72	8	0;35
I	105	73	9	0;23
J	106	74	10	0;36
K	107	75	11	0;37
L	108	76	12	0;38
M	109	77	13	0;50
N	110	78	14	0;49
O	111	79	15	0;24
P	112	80	16	0;25
Q	113	81	17	0;16
R	114	82	18	0;19
S	115	83	19	0;31
T	116	84	20	0;20
U	117	85	21	0;22
V	118	86	22	0;47
W	119	87	23	0;17
X	120	88	24	0;45
Y	121	89	25	0;21
Z	122	90	26	0;44
1	49	33		0;120
2	50	64		0;121
3	51	35		0;122
4	52	36		0;123
5	53	37		0;124
6	54	94	30	0;125
7	55	38		0;126
8	56	42		0;127
9	57	40		0;128
0	48	41		0;129
-	45	95	31	0;130
=	61	43		0;131
[	91	123	27	0;26
\	92	124	28	0;43
]	93	125	29	0;27
;	59	58		0;39
'	39	34		0;40

Table 34-3.   Keyboard Scancode Values (Continued)

Key	Key only	Shift+Key	Ctrl+Key	Alt+Key
, 44	60	0;51		
.	46	62		0;52
/	47	63		0;53
Keypad ENTER	13	13	10	0;166
Keypad /	47	47	0;149	0;164
Keypad *	42	42	0;150	0;55
Keypad -	45	45	0;142	0;74
Keypad +	43	43	0;144	0;78
Keypad 5	0;76	53	0;143	

Table 34-3. *Keyboard Scancode Values (Continued)*

The 101-key keyboard contains several duplicate keys, such as two HOME, PGUP, and PGDN keys. By default, DOS treats these keys as the same. If you want ANSI.SYS to assign one of these keys a character string as just discussed, and you are using DOS 4 or later, place the /X switch in the CONFIG.SYS DEVICE entry for ANSI.SYS, as shown here.

```
DEVICE=C:\DOS\ANSI.SYS   /X
```

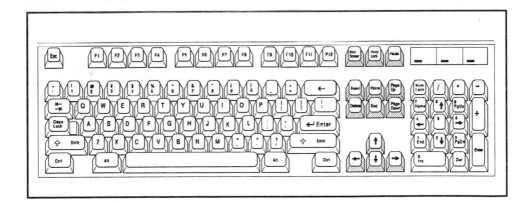

Figure 34-1. *A 101-key keyboard*

Creating ANSI.COM to Execute Escape Sequences

The previous examples have used the ECHO command within DOS batch files to write escape sequences. Once you learn how to generate the Esc character using your word processor or the DOS editor, creating such batch files is fairly easy.

In Chapter 29, "Using DEBUG," you learned how to use DEBUG script files to create custom commands. The following script file, ANSI.SCR, creates the command ANSI.COM that makes it easier for you to write escape sequences.

```
N ANSI.COM
A 100
MOV AH, 2
MOV SI, 82
MOV DL, 1B
INT 21
MOV DL, 5B
INT 21
MOV DL, [SI]
CMP DL, D
JZ 119
INT 21
INC SI
JMP 10D
MOV AH, 4C
INT 21
<ENTER>
R CX
1D
W
Q
```

Create the file ANSI.COM using the DOS input redirection operator, as shown here.

```
C:\> DEBUG < ANSI.SCR  <ENTER>
```

Using ANSI.COM, you can set your screen color to blue as follows:

```
C:\> ANSI 44m  <ENTER>
```

Likewise, you can assign the DIR command to the SHIFT-F1 combination as follows:

```
C:\> ANSI 0;84;"DIR"p   <ENTER>
```

So far, each time you have redefined a key to a commonly used function, pressing the key has only displayed the command name, forcing you to press ENTER to execute the command. If you include the carriage return character (ASCII 13) in the key's definition, DOS will automatically execute the command each time you press the key. The following command includes the carriage return character in the key definition, directing DOS to execute the DIR command each time you press SHIFT-F1

```
C:\> ANSI 0;84;"DIR";13p   <ENTER>
```

Hands On

Using your word processor, place a DEVICE or DEVICEHIGH entry in your CONFIG.SYS file and reboot DOS to load the ANSI driver, if you have not already done so.

Next, create the batch file YELLBLUE.BAT that selects a yellow screen background and a blue foreground.

```
@ECHO OFF
ECHO Esc[43;34m
CLS
```

If you don't know how to create the Esc character with your word processor, build the command ANSI.COM using the file ANSI.SCR, as previously discussed. Change the batch file to use ANSI.COM as follows:

```
@ECHO OFF
ANSI 43;34m
CLS
```

Using your ANSI.COM command, assign CHKDSK to the ALT-C key combination.

```
C:\> ANSI  0;46;"CHKDSK"p   <ENTER>
```

Using the ALT-C key combination and ENTER, invoke CHKDSK.

Next, change the previous escape sequence slightly using the value 13 (ENTER key) to direct ANSI.SYS to automatically execute CHKDSK when you press ALT-C without waiting for you to press ENTER.

```
C:\> ANSI  0;46;"CHKDSK";13p  <ENTER>
```

Review

1. When should you use DEVICEHIGH instead of DEVICE to install ANSI.SYS?

2. What is an escape sequence?

3. How do you generate the Esc character?

4. What is the function of ANSI.COM?

5. Use ANSI.COM to assign the CLS command to F10. Use the value 13 to direct ANSI.SYS to automatically execute the command without forcing you to press ENTER.

Answers

1. If you are using DOS version 5, and your CONFIG.SYS file contains the DOS=UMB entry and loads the EMM386.EXE device driver as discussed in Chapter 32, you can save conventional memory by directing DOS to load the ANSI.SYS device driver into reserved memory using DEVICEHIGH.

2. An escape sequence is a series of two or more characters, the first of which is the ASCII escape character (ASCII value 27). The ANSI.SYS device driver lets you use different escape sequences to set your screen attributes and to redefine keyboard keys.

3. If you are using EDLIN, press CTRL-V and then type [(a left bracket). If you are using EDIT, press CTRL-P and then press ESC. If you are using a word processor, refer to the documentation that accompanied your software to determine the steps you must perform to create an escape character.

4. ANSI.COM simplifies the process of writing ANSI escape sequences. Specifically, ANSI.COM writes the Esc character and left bracket. If you want to use ANSI.SYS to set your screen background color to blue, you need to generate

the escape sequence Esc[44m. Using ANSI.COM, you can issue the following command:

```
C:\> ANSI 44m
```

5. The command appears as follows:

```
C:\> ANSI  0;68;"CLS";13p  <ENTER>
```

Advanced Concepts

In the previous section you used ANSI.SYS to select screen colors and to define function keys. ANSI.SYS also lets you position the cursor to place output at specific screen locations, select a video display mode, and assign different text attributes.

Cursor Positioning with ANSI.SYS

In Chapter 29, "Using DEBUG," you created a batch file similar to the following that displayed a menu at the upper-left corner of your screen.

```
        M E N U

D  List directory files
C  Run CHKDSK
S  Sort directory listing
X  Exit to DOS
Enter choice:
```

To improve the menu's appearance you can change the batch file to display the menu in the middle of your screen. The "brute force" method of placing the menu at the middle of the screen is to use ECHO several times to write blank lines, and then to place spaces before each menu option to shift the options to the right.

A better solution, however, is to use ANSI.SYS to place the cursor at specific row and column positions on your screen, before the batch file writes each menu option. For example, the following ECHO command places the cursor at row 10, column 20 and then displays the message.

```
ECHO  Esc[10;20H  Row ten, column twenty
```

By default, screens use 25 rows of 80 columns. Using the row and column position escape sequence, the following batch file changes MENU.BAT slightly to display the menu at the center of your screen.

```
@ECHO OFF
:LOOP
CLS
ECHO Esc[10;30H         M E N U
ECHO <Alt+255>
ECHO Esc[12;30H D  List directory files
ECHO Esc[13;30H C  Run CHKDSK
ECHO Esc[14;30H S  Sort directory listing
ECHO Esc[15;30H X  Exit to DOS
ANSI 17;30H
SHOWLINE Enter choice:
:GET_KEY
SCANCODE
IF ERRORLEVEL 32 IF NOT ERRORLEVEL 33 GOTO DIR
IF ERRORLEVEL 46 IF NOT ERRORLEVEL 47 GOTO CHKDSK
IF ERRORLEVEL 31 IF NOT ERRORLEVEL 32 GOTO SORT
IF ERRORLEVEL 45 IF NOT ERRORLEVEL 46 GOTO EXIT
GOTO GET_KEY
:DIR
DIR
PAUSE
GOTO LOOP
:CHKDSK
CHKDSK
PAUSE
GOTO LOOP
:SORT
DIR | SORT | FIND /V "e" | MORE
PAUSE
GOTO LOOP
:EXIT
ECHO <Alt+255>
```

Table 34-4 describes the ANSI.SYS escape sequence for cursor positioning.

Selecting a Video Mode with ANSI.SYS

Although its use is uncommon, the ANSI.SYS device driver lets you select a video display mode. Table 34-5 lists the available display modes and their corresponding escape sequences.

Escape Sequence	Description	Example
Esc[*Row*; *Column*H	Places the cursor at the row; column position	Esc[10;20H
Esc[*Rows*A	Moves the cursor up the number of rows specified	Esc[5A
Esc[*Rows*B	Moves the cursor down the number of rows specified	Esc[4B
Esc[*Columns*C	Moves the cursor right the number of columns specified	Esc[20C
Esc[*Columns*D	Moves the cursor left the number of columns specified	Esc[15D
Esc[s	Saves the current cursor row and column position	Esc[s
Esc[u	Restores the cursor to a previously saved row and column position	Esc[u
Esc[2J	Clears the screen and moves the cursor to row 0	Esc[2J
Esc[K	Erases the characters from the current cursor position to the end of the line, leaving the cursor position unchanged	Esc[K

Table 34-4.   ANSI.SYS Cursor-Positioning Escape Sequences

Video Mode	Description	Escape Sequence
0	25x40 monochrome text	Esc[=0h
1	25x40 color text	Esc[=1h
2	25x80 monochrome text	Esc[=2h
3	25x80 color text	Esc[=3h
4	320x200 4-color graphics	Esc[=4h
5	320x200 monochrome graphics	Esc[=5h
6	640x200 monochrome graphics	Esc[=6h
7	Line wrap enabled	Esc[=7h
7	Line wrap disabled	Esc[=7l
13	320x200 color graphics	Esc[13h
14	640x200 16 color graphics	Esc[=14h
15	640x350 monochrome graphics	Esc[=15h
16	640x350 monochrome graphics	Esc[=16h
17	640x480 VGA 16-color graphics	Esc[=17h
18	640x480 VGA 16-color graphics	Esc[=18h
19	320x200 VGA 256-color graphics	Esc[=19h

Table 34-5.   ANSI.SYS Video Mode Escape Sequences

Assigning Text Attributes with ANSI.SYS

Earlier you learned how to use ANSI.SYS to set your screen's foreground and background colors. Using the red-background escape sequence, the following ECHO command displays a warning message to the user in red and one in black.

```
ECHO  Esc[31mWARNING!Esc[30mAbout to delete files.
```

In addition to letting you display text using different foreground and background colors, the ANSI.SYS device driver lets you use one or more of the text attributes listed in Table 34-6.

The following ECHO command uses blinking text for the word WARNING!

```
ECHO Esc[5mWARNING!Esc[0mAbout to delete files.
```

Setting Your Screen Size in DOS 5

If you are using DOS 5 and an EGA or VGA screen display, you can use the ANSI.SYS device driver and the MODE command, as discussed in Chapter 43, to specify the number of rows and columns on your screen. Not all of the software programs that you run will support these screen sizes and thus may bypass the ANSI.SYS device driver to use their own screen format.

Key Terms

Escape sequences   A series of two or more characters, the first of which is the ASCII escape character (ASCII value 27).

Attribute Value	Description	Escape Sequence
0	Attributes off	Esc[0m
1	Bold	Esc[1m
4	Monochrome underline	Esc[4m
5	Blink	Esc[5m
7	Reverse video	Esc[7m
8	Concealed black text on black background	Esc[8m

Table 34-6.   ANSI.SYS Text-Attribute Values

Chapter 35

Advanced Disk Topics

Because file and disk management are two of the most important functions DOS performs, this chapter looks at three important disk concepts: disk head parking, disk sector interleaving, and low-level formatting. By understanding these concepts, you can reduce your chance of damaging your disk, improve your disk performance, and appreciate corrective methods used when your disk experiences errors FORMAT can't correct.

Understanding Disk Head Parking

Your disk rotates past the disk drive's read/write head, as illustrated in Figure 35-1, providing access to every sector on the current track. When the disk drive needs to read or write information to a different track, the drive moves the read/write head in or out as required.

For floppy disks, the read/write head actually makes contact with the disk's surface. For hard disks, however, the read/write heads do not contact the disk's surface, but rather, float just above the disk's surface. The following illustration shows the separation distance between a hard disk surface and the read/write head using several very small objects as a comparison.

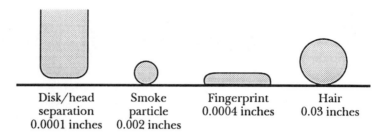

| Disk/head separation 0.0001 inches | Smoke particle 0.002 inches | Fingerprint 0.0004 inches | Hair 0.03 inches |

The hard disk spins past the read/write head at 3600 revolutions per minute (RPMs). If the read/write head accidentally makes contact with the disk's surface, possibly due to the computer being bumped or jarred, a *head crash* occurs. A head crash is generally accompanied by a loud scraping noise as the head scrapes off the disk's specially coated surface, splattering the fragments across the rest of your disk. When a disk head crash occurs, the information the disk contained will very likely be lost and you will probably have to purchase a new disk.

NOTE   *There are companies that can disassemble a disk that has experienced a crash, and possibly reconstruct portions of the disk's surviving data. This process is time consuming and very expensive. The best way to avoid loss of data is by performing regular disk backup operations, as discussed in Chapter 22, "Protecting Your Files with BACKUP and RESTORE."*

The first way to avoid disk head crashes is never to move your computer while the computer is on and the disk is spinning. When you power off your computer

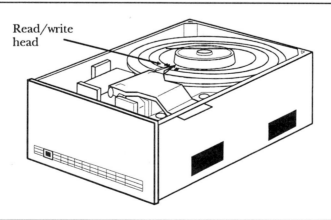

Read/write head

Figure 35-1.   *The read/write head moves in and out to access information on the rotating disk*

and the disk quits spinning, the disk head actually rests on the disk's surface. Because the disk is not moving, a head crash does not occur. When you turn your computer on, the disk drive raises the head off the disk's surface before the disk starts to rotate.

To provide better protection for your disk, many disk drives have a designated *landing zone* as shown in Figure 35-2. When you turn off your computer, the disk controller moves the read/write head above the landing zone before setting the head down on the disk's surface.

For earlier model disk drives that don't automatically move the read/write head to a landing zone, many DOS users use a *park utility* before turning off their computer. Most park commands move the read/write head to the disk's innermost track. If you don't have a disk park utility program, you can create a simple one using DEBUG, which was discussed in Chapter 29.

If you are using an IBM PS/2 computer, create the command PS2PARKC.SCR, shown here. This utility parks only the hard disk drive C.

```
N PS2PARKC.COM
A 100
MOV AH,19
MOV DL,80
INT 13
MOV AH,4C
INT 21
<ENTER>
R CX
A
W
Q
```

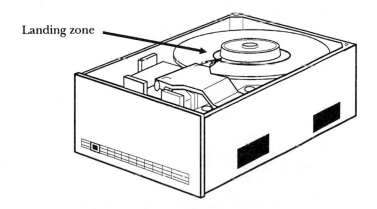

Landing zone

Figure 35-2.   *Many disk drives provide a designated landing zone, where the read/write head rests when the disk is powered off*

If you are using a computer *other* than a PS/2, create the utility PARKC.COM using the DEBUG script file PARKC.SCR, as shown here. This utility also only parks drive C.

```
N PARKC.COM
A 100
MOV AH,8
MOV DL,80
INT 13
JC  110
MOV AH,C
MOV DL,80
INT 13
JMP 117
MOV AH,9
MOV DX,11B
INT 21
MOV AH,4C
INT 21
DB 'Controller failed to respond correctly—heads not parked.$'
<ENTER>
R CX
55
W
Q
```

Before you turn off your computer, you can invoke one of these utility programs to move your disk's read/write head over a track that is unlikely to contain data.

Parking your disk head is simply the process of moving the head over a specific track. You can park your disk head any time the disk is not in use. The next time your computer uses the disk, the read/write head automatically moves from the parked track to the track desired.

These utility programs are quite simple. Just as there are many third-party software programs that undelete files or unformat disks, the same is true for park utilities. Some of the more powerful utilities install memory-resident software that monitors your disk activity, automatically parking the disk heads after periods of no use. If you have a third-party disk utility package, check to see if it provides a park command.

Disk Sector Interleaving

Your disk is divided into tracks, which are further divided into sectors. Depending on your disk size, the number of tracks and sectors per track will differ. By default, the sectors on each track are numbered sequentially, beginning with 1. This illustration shows tracks on a hard disk with sectors numbered 1 to 17.

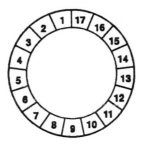

As you have learned, DOS stores your files using groups of consecutive sectors called *clusters*. Thus, when DOS reads one sector, it is very likely to immediately read the sector that follows. Assume, for example, DOS needs the information stored in sectors 1 and 2. To begin, DOS directs the drive to read sector 1. As discussed in Chapter 24, "Customizing Your System with CONFIG.SYS," the disk drive will transfer the data into a DOS disk buffer. Depending on the speed of your disk and computer, sector 2 may have already spun past the disk's read/write head before your computer is ready for it. As a result, you must wait for the sector to rotate past the read/write head once again—your computer may be unable to keep up with sequential sector reads.

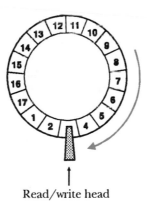

Read/write head

To correct this computer/disk timing problem, you can change the order sector numbers appear on your disk. In general, you specify a sector distance, called an *interleave*, between successive disk sectors. The illustration below shows a disk with a 2:1 (2 to 1) sector interleave, meaning sector 2 appears two sector positions from sector 1 and two sector positions from sector 3. By providing the interleave, you give your computer time to process the first sector before the second sector spins past the disk's read/write head.

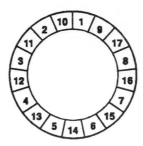

Likewise, the following illustration shows a 4:1 disk interleave, which might be needed for a slower computer.

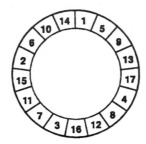

If your computer is very fast, a 1:1 interleave will provide the best performance.

DOS, unfortunately, does not provide a way of determining or setting your disk's ideal interleave. To do so, you will need a special third-party software program. If you are running database programs or using large spreadsheets that make extensive use of your disk, having the correct disk interleave will make a considerable performance improvement.

Low-Level Formatting

For simplicity, we have stated the FORMAT command prepares your disk for use by dividing the disk into tracks and sectors. For floppy disks, FORMAT performs this processing. For hard disks, however, a different program, called a *low-level format*, actually divides your disks into tracks and sectors. Most users don't know about low-level formats, however, because manufacturers typically perform the low-level format for you before they ship your computer.

The low-level format operation is actually performed by the disk controller that will eventually use the disk. If you order a new hard disk by mail order, for example, you may need to perform a low-level disk format of the disk yourself.

The low-level format performs three essential functions. First, it divides your disks into tracks and sectors. Second, the low-level format assigns your disk's sector interleave. Third, it lets you record bad disk locations, which the disk manufacturer identified when testing the disk. Typically, these bad blocks are recorded on a certificate attached to the outside of your hard disk's casing.

If you purchase a new hard disk and need to perform a low-level format yourself, you should receive documentation with your disk that explains the steps you should follow. In some cases, you will receive a floppy disk containing a low-level format program. In other cases, your disk controller will be built into its read-only memory (ROM), which you can access through DEBUG.

Do not perform a low-level format on a disk containing needed information. The low-level format will destroy the disk's contents.

NOTE

Because most users have hard disks that are already installed, low-level formatted, formatted for use by DOS, and containing files, you may be wondering why you need to be aware of low-level formatting. Over time, your disk may begin to experience disk read or write errors, as evidenced by an abundance of error messages. In such an event, you should immediately back up the disk, as discussed in Chapter 22. Next, your first corrective step should be reformatting the disk using the high-level FORMAT. If you continue to experience disk errors after reformatting, you may then need to try a low-level format operation. If you don't have a low-level program, many third-party software utilities provide one.

Review

1. What is disk head parking?

2. What is a disk head crash?

3. What is disk interleaving?

4. Using a 17-sector-per-track disk, draw a 3:1 disk interleave and a 5:1 disk interleave.

5. How does a low-level format operation differ from FORMAT.COM?

Answers

1. Disk head parking is the process of moving (seeking) the disk drive's read/write heads to a specific cylinder, typically the disk's innermost cylinder, to reduce the chance of the heads coming in contact with cylinders containing data. As a rule, you should park your disk heads before you turn your computer off.

2. A disk head crash occurs when your disk drive's read/write head comes in contact with the disk's surface, which is spinning at 3600 RPMs. When a disk head crash occurs, the read/write head will scrape off the disk's specially coated surface, destroying the information the disk contained. Disk head crashes occur most often when your computer is moved while turned on with the disks spinning.

3. Disk interleaving is the physical separation of sequentially numbered disk sectors on a hard disk to compensate for timing problems between the computer and disk. Using a 2:1 interleave, for example, sector 2 is placed two sectors from sectors 1 and 3. Likewise, sector 3 is two sectors from sector 4 and so on.

4. The 3:1 and 5:1 disk interleaves appear as follows:

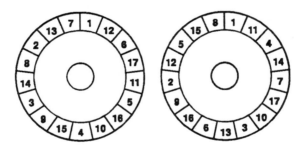

5. A low-level format performs a physical format of your hard disk, dividing the disk's surface into tracks and sectors recognizable by the disk controller. The low-level format also performs an analysis of the disk's surface to determine which areas are unusable. Using the information recorded on the disk by the low-level format, the FORMAT command performs a high-level or logical format of your hard disk, creating the structures DOS needs to store information on your disk, such as the boot record, file allocation tables, and root directory.

Advanced Concepts

Although the disk is divided into tracks and sectors, the disk controller still needs a way to identify specific sectors. To do so, the controller places header information before each sector that contains the sector's disk head (side) number, cylinder or track number, and sector address. In addition, this header can hold a sector-damaged flag stating the sector is unusable. The header ends with a CRC (cyclic redundancy check) value for error detection. The header information is followed by a small gap, which gives the controller time for the transition from reading to writing, and then the data. Following the data, the disk controller records error-corrective coding, information called ECC, that the controller can use, if necessary, to rebuild the sector's information when a disk error occurs. This information is followed by a small gap, which lets the controller change back to reading, then the following sector's header, as shown in Figure 35-3. The disk changes from reading to writing in this way because the only time sector headers are written to is during low-level formatting.

Key Terms

Cyclic redundancy check (CRC)   An error-detection protocol used when recording
information on a disk.

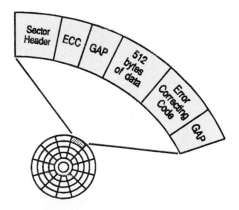

Figure 35-3.   *The disk controller uses header information to locate sectors on your disk*

Disk parking   The process of moving (often called seeking) the disk's read/write head to the innermost disk cylinder to reduce the chance of the disk head coming in contact with tracks containing data.

Disk crash   A problem occurring when the disk drive's read/write head comes in contact with the disk's rotating surface, scraping the disk surface and destroying the information it contains.

Sector interleaving   The process of separating sequentually numbered sectors to reduce sector misses when the computer can't keep up with the disk drive.

Low-level formatting   The physical formatting of the hard disk performed by the firmware or hard disk controller.

High-level formatting   The logical formatting of a disk by FORMAT to build the file allocation table and root directory.

Chapter 36

Creating Simple Text Files with EDLIN

When Microsoft first released DOS version 1.0 in 1981, they included a simple text editor called EDLIN. With EDLIN, users could create or edit simple batch files, or even simple memos. EDLIN was so named because it let users EDit one LINe of file at a time. If you have used a word processor to create and edit files, you can display the file's contents on your screen and move throughout the file using the PGUP, PGDN, and arrow keys. EDLIN, however, makes you work one line at a time.

If you are conversant with a word processor, you will probably never use EDLIN. If you are using DOS 5, it provides the more powerful EDIT command discussed in Chapter 37, "The DOS 5 Editor, EDIT." If you have only EDLIN, this chapter will teach you how to use EDLIN to create, and later change (edit), your files.

Getting Started with EDLIN

To create or edit a file using EDLIN, you must invoke EDLIN with the file name, as shown here.

```
C:\> EDLIN  FILENAME.EXT  <ENTER>
```

If you don't include a file name, EDLIN will display an error message telling you a file name is required.

```
C:\> EDLIN   <ENTER>
File name must be specified
```

The following command directs EDLIN to edit the batch file START.BAT, which will contain ECHO OFF, CLS, DATE, and TIME.

```
C:\> EDLIN   START.BAT   <ENTER>
```

Because the file does not exist, EDLIN displays the "New file" message, followed by its asterisk prompt.

```
C:\> EDLIN   START.BAT   <ENTER>
New file
*
```

The asterisk (*) is EDLIN's prompt for a command. EDLIN supports 14 single-letter commands, listed in Table 36-1.

To add text to a file, you must select EDLIN's insert mode with the I command. EDLIN will respond by displaying a line number and asterisk.

```
C:\> EDLIN   START.BAT   <ENTER>
New file
*I <ENTER>
       1:*
```

The first line of the batch file is @ECHO OFF. When you type the line and press ENTER, EDLIN displays a prompt for the file's second line.

```
C:\> EDLIN   START.BAT   <ENTER>
New file
*I   <ENTER>
       1:*@ECHO OFF <ENTER>
       2:*
```

Command	Function
?	Displays a list of EDLIN's available commands
A	Appends lines of a file from disk into memory to edit
C	Copies lines from one file location to another
D	Deletes lines from a file
E	Ends the editing session, saving the file's contents to disk and exiting to DOS
I	Enters EDLIN's insert mode to add lines to a file
L	Lists lines to the screen
M	Moves lines from one file location to another
P	Displays a page (typically 23 lines) on your screen
Q	Quits the editing session and returns to DOS without saving the file changes to disk
R	Replaces one word or phrase with another
S	Searches the file for a word or phrase
T	Moves lines from a second file into the current file

Table 36-1.   EDLIN Single-Letter Commands

If you mistype a line and you have not yet pressed ENTER, you can use BACKSPACE to correct the error. If you have already pressed ENTER, you'll have to exit EDLIN's insert mode and edit the line, as discussed later.

Repeating the process of typing a line of the file and pressing ENTER, the file's contents become the following.

```
C:\> EDLIN   START.BAT   <ENTER>
New file
*I <ENTER>
        1:*@ECHO OFF   <ENTER>
        2:*CLS         <ENTER>
        3:*DATE        <ENTER>
        4:*TIME        <ENTER>
        5:*
```

After you have typed in the last line of the file, you can leave EDLIN's insert mode by pressing CTRL-C. EDLIN will display the characters "^C" on your screen and redisplay its prompt.

```
C:\> EDLIN  START.BAT  <ENTER>
New file
*I <ENTER>
        1:*@ECHO OFF  <ENTER>
        2:*CLS        <ENTER>
        3:*DATE       <ENTER>
        4:*TIME       <ENTER>
        5:*^C
*
```

To save the file's contents and exit to DOS, use the E command. EDLIN will end your editing session, and DOS will redisplay its prompt.

```
C:\> EDLIN  START.BAT  <ENTER>
New file
*I      <ENTER>
        1:*@ECHO OFF  <ENTER>
        2:*CLS        <ENTER>
        3:*DATE       <ENTER>
        4:*TIME       <ENTER>
        5:*^C

*E <ENTER>

C:\>
```

Using the TYPE command, you can view the file's contents.

```
C:\> TYPE  START.BAT  <ENTER>
@ECHO OFF
CLS
DATE
TIME
```

Using PRINT, you can print a hard copy of the file.

```
C:\> PRINT  START.BAT  <ENTER>
```

In summary, to create a file using EDLIN, follow these steps.

1. Invoke EDLIN with the file name you desire.

2. Use EDLIN's I command to select insert mode.

3. Type in each line of the file followed by ENTER.

4. Press CTRL-C to exit EDLIN's insert mode.

5. Use the E command to save the file's contents and exit to DOS.

Editing an Existing File

The batch file START.BAT assumes you are using DOS version 3.3 or later and therefore includes the @ character before ECHO OFF. If you want to use this batch file on a system running a DOS version less than 3.3, you must edit the batch file to delete the @ character.

To change the batch file's contents, invoke EDLIN, specifying the file name as before.

```
C:\> EDLIN   START.BAT   <ENTER>
```

Because the file exists in this case, EDLIN does not display the "New file" message, but rather, a message indicating it loaded the entire file into memory, from the first line to the end of the file.

```
C:\> EDLIN   START.BAT   <ENTER>
End of input file
*
```

EDLIN only lets you edit one line of a file at a time. If you know the line number you want to change, you can simply type the line number and press ENTER. If you don't know the line number, use the EDLIN L command to list the file's contents with each line's corresponding line number, as shown here.

```
*L   <ENTER>
        1:*@ECHO OFF   <ENTER>
        2: CLS         <ENTER>
        3: DATE        <ENTER>
        4: TIME        <ENTER>
*
```

In this case, to edit line 1, you would type 1 and press ENTER. EDLIN will display the line's current contents, followed by a prompt for a new text.

```
*1 <ENTER>
        1:*@ECHO OFF
        1:*
```

If you press ENTER without typing anything else, EDLIN will leave the line unchanged, redisplaying its prompt.

To change the line's contents, you have several choices. First, you can simply type in the new line. Second, you can use the function keys F1, F2, F3, and F4 as discussed in Chapter 5, "Understanding Your Keyboard," to recall all or part of the previous line. Using the function keys, you can press DEL to delete the @ character and F3 to recall the rest of the line.

```
*1   <ENTER>
        1:*@ECHO OFF
        1:*ECHO OFF   <ENTER>
```

When you press ENTER, EDLIN will display its prompt and wait for your next command. In this case, using E, you can save the file's new contents and exit EDLIN, returning to DOS.

```
*E <ENTER>
```

If you use TYPE to display the file's contents, you will see that the @ character has been deleted from the new file as desired.

EDLIN Saves a Copy of the File's Previous Contents

Each time you edit a file and save the new changes to disk, EDLIN copies the file's previous contents to a file with the same base name and the BAK extension. In the case of START.BAT, EDLIN copied the file's original contents to the file START.BAK, as you can see in the following directory listing.

```
C:\> DIR  START.*

 Volume in drive C is DOS
 Volume Serial Number is 168C-5277
 Directory of C:\
```

```
START    BAK      29 05-03-91    3:18p
START    BAT      28 05-03-91    3:18p
         2 file(s)         57 bytes
                     15636864 bytes free
```

Should you decide, after editing a file, that you wish you hadn't made the changes, you can simply delete the current file and rename the file with the BAK extension to its original name.

Getting Around in Your File

As you learned, using EDLIN's L command, you can list the file's contents.

```
*L   <ENTER>
        1:*@ECHO OFF    <ENTER>
        2: CLS          <ENTER>
        3: DATE         <ENTER>
        4: TIME         <ENTER>
*
```

In this case, note that line 1 is followed by an asterisk, while the other lines aren't. EDLIN selects one line as the current line and identifies it with an asterisk. Many of EDLIN's commands will use the current line number if you don't tell EDLIN to do otherwise.

If you press ENTER at EDLIN's prompt, EDLIN will display the line following the current line, giving you a chance to edit the line's contents.

```
*   <ENTER>
        2:*CLS
        2:*
```

By pressing ENTER at EDLIN's prompt for a new line of the text, you leave the line's current contents unchanged. By repeatedly pressing ENTER, you can quickly traverse the file's contents.

```
*   <ENTER>
        2:*CLS
        2:*   <ENTER>
*   <ENTER>
        3:*DATE
```

```
        3:*  <ENTER>
*   <ENTER>
        4:*TIME
        4:*  <ENTER>
*
```

Inserting New Text at a Specific Location

Earlier you used EDLIN's insert mode to enter text into a new file. In some cases, you will want to insert one or more lines of text at a specific location in an existing file. To do so, include the line number before which you want the text inserted. For example, assume you want to change the batch file START.BAT so it invokes CHKDSK before the DATE command. The following I command directs EDLIN to insert text before line 3.

```
*3I   <ENTER>
```

EDLIN will enter insert mode, displaying a prompt for the text to insert at line 3.

```
*3I   <ENTER>
        3:*
```

In this case type **CHKDSK** and press ENTER. EDLIN will then prompt you for line number 4, at which point you should use CTRL-C to leave insert mode.

```
*3I   <ENTER>
        3:*  CHKDSK   <ENTER>
        4:*^C

*
```

Using the command 1L, you can direct EDLIN to list the file's contents beginning with line 1.

```
*1L   <ENTER>
        1:  ECHO OFF
        2:  CLS
```

```
        3:  CHKDSK
        4:*DATE
        5:  TIME
 *
```

As you can see, EDLIN inserted the line before DATE as you desired.

Hands On

The previous discussion taught you how to create a simple batch file using EDLIN. Although EDLIN is certainly far from a word processor, you can use EDLIN to create simple memos. Invoke EDLIN with the file name RICHARD.MEM.

```
C:\> EDLIN  RICHARD.MEM   <ENTER>
```

Using EDLIN's I command, select EDLIN's insert mode and type in the following memo.

```
*I    <ENTER>
        1:*Dear Richard,  <ENTER>
        2:*  <ENTER>
        3:*I really enjoyed getting together to watch the  <ENTER>
        4:*Rebel's game. We need to head down to Newport  <ENTER>
        5:*this summer to get away for a few days. Hope we  <ENTER>
        6:*can hit the beach!  <ENTER>
        7:*  <ENTER>
        8:*Kris   <ENTER>
        9:*^C

 *
```

Use CTRL-C to end insert mode and E to exit EDLIN to DOS saving the file's contents. From the DOS prompt print the memo using PRINT.

```
C:\> PRINT  RICHARD.MEM   <ENTER>
```

Next, invoke EDLIN once again with the same file. Using EDLIN's L command, list the file's contents. Next, insert the following line before line 7.

```
*7I  <ENTER>
        7:*  <ENTER>
        8:*Give me a call when you get to Vegas.
        9:*^C

*
```

Use CTRL-C to leave insert mode and the E command to exit EDLIN to DOS. Use the following DIR command to note EDLIN's backup copy of your file.

```
C:\> DIR  RICHARD.*  <ENTER>
```

Review

1. How does EDLIN differ from a word processor?

2. What is EDLIN's insert mode? How do you leave insert mode?

3. Why does EDLIN create a file with the BAK extension?

4. How does EDLIN's Q command differ from E?

Answers

1. EDLIN is a line editor, which means it only lets you work with one line of a file at a time. Word processors on the other hand, let you view you entire file on the screen, using your keyboard arrow keys to position the cursor throughout the file as you need to make changes and additions. In addition, word processors provide powerful text-formatting capabilities and let you bold, underline, and italicize key words.

2. To add text to a file using EDLIN, you must be in EDLIN's insert mode. EDLIN's I command selects insert mode. After you have inserted the desired

text, use the CTRL-C keyboard combination to leave insert mode back to the EDLIN prompt.

3. Each time you change a file's contents and save the changes using EDLIN's E command, EDLIN copies the file's previous contents to a file with the same base name, but with the BAK extension. Should you later decide you wish you had not made the changes to the file, the BAK file still contains the file's previous contents.

4. EDLIN's Q command quits an editing session, discarding the changes you have made to the file. EDLIN's E command exits the editing session, saving the editing changes to the file on disk.

Advanced Concepts

This section presents a summary of EDLIN's commands in a format similar to that used in Chapter 29, "Using DEBUG," for DEBUG. Before you examine the commands, however, you need to understand the different ways EDLIN lets you specify a range of lines.

EDLIN selects one line in the file as the current line. Because you may not always know the current line number, EDLIN lets you use the period instead. In a similar way, EDLIN lets you use the # character to represent the end of the file (the line after the last line of text).

Many EDLIN commands let you specify starting and ending line numbers separated by a comma. Using the period and # character, the following L command directs EDLIN to list the file's contents from the current line to the end of the file.

```
*.,#L   <ENTER>
```

In some cases you may want to specify a range of lines relative to the current line number. If you precede a number with a minus sign, –3 for example, EDLIN will use the line number 3 before the current line. If you precede a number with a plus sign, +4 for example, EDLIN will use the line 4 after the current line. Using the plus and minus offsets, the following command lists the lines in the range beginning three lines before the current line and ending five lines after.

```
*-3,+5L   <ENTER>
```

All the EDLIN commands that let you use a range of values support the period, # character, and plus and minus offsets.

?

Function: Displays a summary of EDLIN's commands.

Explanation: Under DOS 5, the question mark directs EDLIN to display a brief explanation of each command.

Example: The following command summarizes the available EDLIN commands.

```
*?
Edit line    line#
Append       [#lines]A
Copy         [startline],[endline],toline[,times]C
Delete       [startline][,endline]D
End          E
Insert       [line]I
List         [startline][,endline]L
Move         [startline],[endline],tolineM
Page         [startline][,endline]P
Quit         Q
Replace      [startline][,endline][?]R[oldtext][^Z newtext]
Search       [startline][,endline][?]Stext
Transfer     [toline]T[ drive:][path]filename
Write        [#lines]W
*
```

LineNumber

Function: Displays the line number and contents of line you want to see or edit.

Explanation: If you know the line number of the line you want to edit, you can simply type the line number at EDLIN's prompt and press ENTER. EDLIN will display the line's current contents followed by a second line at which you can edit the current line's contents by typing in a new line or using the DOS editing keys F1 through F5.

Example: The next command directs EDLIN to display line number 3 for editing.

```
*3    <ENTER>
        3:*Line three's current contents
        3:*
```

[*LineCount*]A

Function: Appends the number of lines specified to memory from disk when EDLIN was previously unable to load the file's entire contents into memory due to insufficient memory.

Explanation: If you are editing a very large file or have very little available memory, EDLIN may not be able to load the entire file into memory. When this occurs, EDLIN will not display its "End of input file" message when you first invoke it. Instead, EDLIN will simply display its prompt.

Should you need to edit part of the file that is not in memory, you can use EDLIN's W command to write part of the file back to disk to make room for you to append more information using the A command. By default, EDLIN will load as much of your file into memory as it can, with the exception that EDLIN will not use up more than 75 percent of the available memory. EDLIN leaves 25 percent of memory available to store changes or additions you make to the file.

Example: Assume you are editing a 2000-line file that can't fit into memory, so that EDLIN loads lines 1 through 1500. After you make changes to the earlier section of the file, you can use EDLIN's W command to write the first 500 lines back to disk and A to append the last 500 lines, as shown here.

```
*500W    <ENTER>
*500A    <ENTER>
```

[*StartLine*],[*EndLine*], *TargetLine*[,*Count*]C

Function: Copies one or more lines from one location in a file to another.

Explanation: *StartLine* specifies the first line in a range of lines to copy. If you don't specify a value, EDLIN uses the current line. *EndLine* specifies the line number of the last line in the range of lines to copy. Again, if you don't specify a line number,

EDLIN uses the current line. *TargetLine* specifies the line number within the file to which you want the lines copied. You must specify the target line number. *Count* is the number of times you want the information copied. If you don't specify a count, EDLIN uses the value 1.

Examples: The following command copies lines 1 through 5 to line 10.

```
*1,5,10C   <ENTER>
```

Because the command does not include a copy count, EDLIN only makes one copy. The following command copies the current line to line 10.

```
*,,10C   <ENTER>
```

NOTE   *Note that even though the command does not specify the optional start and stop line numbers, it still includes the commas. Last, this command copies lines 1 and 2 to the end of the file (#), three times.*

```
*1,2,#,3C   <ENTER>
```

[*StartLine*][,*EndLine*]D

Function: Deletes one or more lines from the file.

Explanation: *StartLine* specifies the line number of the first line in a range of line numbers you want to delete. If you don't specify a line number, EDLIN uses the current line. Likewise, *EndLine* specifies the line number of the last line in a range of lines to delete. Again, if you don't specify a line number, EDLIN uses the current line.

Example: The following command deletes the current line.

```
*D   <ENTER>
```

This command deletes lines 5 through 10.

```
*5,10D   <ENTER>
```

This command deletes the range of lines beginning five lines before, and three lines after the current line.

```
*-5,+3D   <ENTER>
```

E

Function: Ends the current editing session, saving the file changes to disk and returning control to DOS.

Explanation: After you have created your file or made your desired changes, the E command lets you save the changes to disk and exit EDLIN to DOS. If you are editing a file that existed on disk before you invoked EDLIN, E directs EDLIN to make a backup copy of the original file's contents, assigning the BAK extension to the new file. If you later decide you did not really want to make the changes, the BAK file contains the file's original contents.

If you want EDLIN to end your editing session and discard your changes, use Q instead.

Example: The following command ends the editing session, saving the file's contents to disk.

```
*E   <ENTER>
```

[*BeforeLine*]I

Function: Directs EDLIN to insert text into the file.

Explanation: To add lines of text to your file, EDLIN must be in insert mode. *BeforeLine* specifies a line number before which you want EDLIN to insert the text. If you don't specify a line number, EDLIN uses the current line. To append lines to your file, use the # character to specify the end of the file.

After you have typed in the desired text, use CTRL-C to exit insert mode.

Examples: The following command directs EDLIN to insert text before the current line.

```
*I   <ENTER>
```

Likewise, this command directs EDLIN to append lines to the end of the file.

```
*#I   <ENTER>
```

[*StartLine*][,*EndLine*]L

Function: Displays lines of the files preceded by their corresponding line numbers.

Explanation: The L command lets you list the contents of one or more lines. *StartLine* specifies the line number of the first line in a range of lines you want to display. If you don't specify a line number, EDLIN uses up to 11 lines before the current line. *EndLine* specifies the line number of the last line in a range of lines you want to display. If you don't specify a line number, EDLIN will display up to 24 lines from the starting line number, or possibly more if you are using the ANSI.SYS device driver to select 43-line EGA or 50-line VGA mode.

   If you specify a range of lines larger than the number of lines that fit on your screen (called a page), EDLIN will pause with each page and ask if you want to continue. If you answer Y, EDLIN will display the next page of text, otherwise if you answer N, EDLIN will end the L command redisplaying its prompt.

Examples: The following command displays up to a page of text, beginning (if possible) 11 lines before the current line.

```
*L   <ENTER>
```

This command lists lines 5 through 10.

```
*5,10L   <ENTER>
```

This command displays your entire file a page at a time.

```
*1,#L   <ENTER>
```

Each time your screen fills, EDLIN will display a prompt asking you if you want to continue.

[StartLine],[EndLine],TargetLineM

Function: Moves one or more lines from one location in the file to another.

Explanation: *StartLine* specifies the first line in a range of lines to move. If you don't specify a value, EDLIN uses the current line. EndLine specifies the line number of the last line in the range of lines to move. Again, if you don't specify a line number, EDLIN uses the current line. *TargetLine* specifies the line number within the file to which you want the lines moved. You must specify the target line number.

Examples: The following command moves lines 1 through 5 to line 10.

```
*1,5,10M   <ENTER>
```

Likewise the following command moves the current line to the end of the file.

```
*,,#M   <ENTER>
```

Although the command does not specify a starting or ending line, the command still includes the commas.

NOTE

[StartLine][,EndLine]P

Function: Displays one or more pages (screenfuls) of text.

Explanation: *StartLine* specifies the first line in a range of lines you want to display. If you don't specify a line number, EDLIN uses the current line. *EndLine* specifies the line number of the last line number in a range of lines you want to display. If you don't specify a line number, EDLIN displays a page of text beginning at the starting line number. By default, a page of text contains 24 lines. If you are using the ANSI.SYS device driver to select EGA 43-line or VGA 50-line mode, EDLIN's page size will differ.

If you specify a range of lines larger than a page, EDLIN will display a page and ask if you want to continue displaying pages. If you type **Y**, EDLIN will display the next page. If you instead answer **N**, EDLIN will end the page command and redisplay its prompt.

Each time EDLIN displays a page, EDLIN selects the line following the last line displayed as the new current line.

Examples: The next command displays a page of text beginning at the current line.

```
*P   <ENTER>
```

This command displays lines 100 through 300 a page at a time.

```
*100,300 P   <ENTER>
```

Each time your screen fills, EDLIN will display a prompt to determine whether or not you want to continue.

Q

Function: Quits the current editing session without saving changes to the file.

Explanation: There may be times after you view a file or make changes to a file that you decide to leave the file's original contents unchanged. EDLIN's Q command quits the current editing session, and returns control to DOS, discarding the changes to the file. When you invoke the Q command, EDLIN will display the following prompt to verify you really want to end the edit, discarding changes.

```
Abort edit (Y/N)?
```

If you type **Y**, EDLIN will end the editing session, discarding any changes to the file. If you type **N**, EDLIN will redisplay its prompt, continuing the editing session.

Example: The following command ends the current editing session, discarding changes to the file.

```
*Q   <ENTER>
```

[StartLine][, EndLine][?]R[OldString][^Z NewString]

Function: Replaces one word or phrase with another throughout your file.

Explanation: EDLIN's R command lets you quickly change or delete each occurrence of a word or phrase throughout your file. *StartLine* specifies the line number of the first line in a range of lines to which you want to restrict the replace operation. If you don't specify a line number, EDLIN will use the current line. *EndLine* specifies the line number of the last line to which you want to restrict the replace operation. If you don't specify a line number, EDLIN uses the end of the file.

The question mark directs EDLIN to display each occurrence of the word or phrase to replace, followed by the prompt "O.K.?" If you respond to the prompt by typing **Y**, EDLIN will replace the text; otherwise, if you respond with **N**, EDLIN will leave the text unchanged. In either case, EDLIN will continue the replace operation with the next matching word.

If you don't include the question mark, EDLIN will automatically replace every occurrence of the word or phrase, displaying the line number and contents of each updated line. The *OldString* specifies the word or phrase you want to replace. The ^Z indicates you must press the F6 (end-of-file) key to separate the old string from the new replacement string. *NewString* specifies the new word or phrase with which EDLIN replaces the old string. If you include the ^Z character after *OldString*, but don't specify a *NewString*, EDLIN will delete each occurrence of the old string. If you don't include the ^Z character after the *OldString*, instead simply pressing ENTER, EDLIN will replace each occurrence of *OldString* with the last string you specified for *NewString*.

If EDLIN cannot find the string to replace, EDLIN will display the message "Not found".

Examples: The following command directs EDLIN to automatically change each occurrence of "Mr" within the file to "Mr."

```
*1RMr^ZMr.  <ENTER>
```

Likewise, this command directs EDLIN to change each occurrence of the word "DOS" to "disk operation system", based on your **Y** or **N** response to EDLIN's "O.K.?" prompt.

```
*1?RDOS^Zdisk operating system   <ENTER>
```

Last, this command deletes each occurrence of the words "hard work".

```
*1Rhard work^Z   <ENTER>
```

[StartLine][, EndLine][?]S[String]

Function: Directs EDLIN to search for a word or phrase.

Explanation: When you edit large files, it is often convenient to search for a key word or phrase near the text location you want to edit. EDLIN's S command searches a file for a word or phrase and displays the line number and line of the phrase's first occurrence.

StartLine specifies the starting line number of a range of numbers to which you want to restrict the search operation. If you don't specify a line number, EDLIN uses the current line. *EndLine* specifies the line number of the last line in a range of numbers to which you want to restrict the search operation.

If you don't specify a value, EDLIN uses the end of the file. The question mark directs EDLIN to display the prompt "O.K.?" each time it locates a matching string to determine if you want to end or continue the search operation. If you respond to the prompt with **Y**, EDLIN will end the search operation. If you instead type **N**, EDLIN continues searching for the word or phrase. The string specifies the word or phrase for which EDLIN is to search. If you don't specify a word or phrase, EDLIN uses the word or phrase specified in the last search or replace operation. If EDLIN cannot find a matching word or phrase, EDLIN displays the message "Not found."

Examples: The following command searches the file for the first occurrence of the word "DOS".

```
*1SDOS    <ENTER>
```

The next command continues the search for the word or phrase used in the last search or replace operation.

```
*S    <ENTER>
```

The next command searches the entire file for the word DOS, directing EDLIN to continue the search until the word is not found, or the user answers **Y** to EDLIN's "O.K.?" prompt.

```
*1,?SDOS    <ENTER>
```

[BeforeLine]TFILENAME.EXT

Function: Inserts the contents of a second file at the line number specified.

Explanation: There are many times when you need to combine files. EDLIN's T command lets you merge a file before the line number specified. If you don't specify a value for *BeforeLine*, EDLIN uses the current line. *FILENAME.EXT* specifies the name of the file you want to merge. The file name can contain a drive letter and subdirectory path.

Examples: The following command merges the contents of START.BAT at the current line number.

```
*TSTART.BAT    <ENTER>
```

Similarly, the next command appends the contents of the file NOTES.TXT that resides on the disk in drive A to the end of the current file.

```
*#TA:NOTES.TXT    <ENTER>
```

[*LineCount*]W

Function: Writes the specified number of lines EDLIN was unable to load back to disk due to insufficient memory, to make memory available for you to append with EDLIN's A command.

Explanation: See EDLIN's A command.

If you don't specify a line count, EDIT writes lines back to disk until it is using only 75 percent of the available memory.

Example: See EDLIN's A command.

Key Terms

Editor   A software program that lets you create and later change (edit) a file's contents.

Screen editor   An editor that uses the entire screen to display a file's contents, and lets you traverse the file's contents using the arrows, PGUP, and PGDN keys, scrolling the file's text as necessary to display new text on the screen.

Line editor   An editor that restricts you to working with one line of a file at at time. EDLIN is a line editor.

Chapter 37

The DOS 5 Editor, EDIT

For almost a decade, EDLIN, the line editor discussed in Chapter 36, was the only tool DOS provided to users to create text and batch files. As you learned in Chapter 36, EDLIN is a line editor because it only lets you work with a single line of the file at a time. Starting with version 5, DOS provides EDIT, a full-screen editor. EDIT works much like a word processor, letting you view a file's contents on the screen, traversing from one position in the file to another using your keyboard's arrow and page keys.

This chapter takes a look at EDIT in detail. To begin, you will learn how to create, save, and print files with EDIT using either your mouse or keyboard. Next, you will learn how to customize EDIT's screen display and how to use EDIT's online help. In the Advanced Concepts section you will learn how to search a large file for key text, how to change text, and how to move text from one location in your file to another (cut and paste).

Starting EDIT

The simplest way to create a file using EDIT is to include the file name in EDIT's command line.

```
C:\> EDIT   FILENAME.EXT
```

If the file exists, EDIT will display the file's contents; if not, EDIT will display an empty editing window. Assume, for example, you want to create the simple batch file DATETIME.BAT, which contains the following commands:

```
@ECHO OFF
DATE
TIME
```

To begin, you would invoke EDIT as follows.

```
C:\> EDIT   DATETIME.BAT   <ENTER>
```

Because the file does not exist, EDIT displays an empty editing window, as shown in Figure 37-1.

Next, simply type the batch file's contents. The lines appear in the window, as in Figure 37-2.

To save the file's contents to disk, you must invoke EDIT's File menu. If you examine the top row of your screen, you'll find the names of five menus: File, Edit,

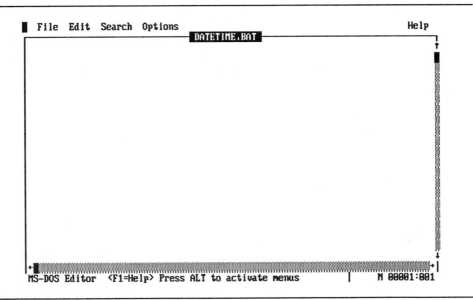

Figure 37-1.   *EDIT's empty editing window*

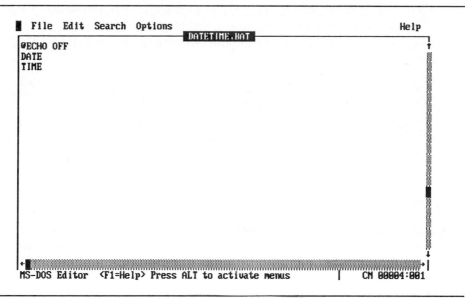

Figure 37-2.   Editing window showing the contents of DATETIME.BAT

Search, Options, and Help. If you hold down your keyboard's ALT key, EDIT will highlight the first letter of each menu's name. By typing one of these letters while ALT is depressed, you select the menu. To invoke EDIT's File menu, you would press ALT-F. If your computer has a mouse and you have installed the appropriate mouse device driver, EDIT will let you use your mouse to edit your file or to select a menu. To select EDIT's File menu, for example, position the mouse pointer at the word "File" and click the left button.

When you select the File menu, EDIT displays the following pull-down menu.

You can select a menu option by using your mouse to click on the option, or by pressing the key that corresponds to one of the highlighted letters.

Note the options that are followed by three periods (called ellipses). If you select one of these options, EDIT will display another menu or a prompt for additional information, such as a file name. In this case, to save the file's contents to disk, select the Save option either by clicking on the option with your mouse, by typing S, or by moving the menu highlight with your arrow keys to Save, and pressing ENTER. To exit EDIT after saving the file, returning to DOS, invoke the File menu (ALT-F) and select Exit. You can use DIR or TYPE at the DOS prompt to verify that the new file exists.

```
C:\> TYPE  DATETIME.BAT  <ENTER>
@ECHO OFF
DATE
TIME
```

Editing an Existing File

Assume you want to add the CLS command to DATETIME.BAT to clear your screen before displaying the current date. As before, invoke EDIT with the file name.

```
C:\> EDIT  DATETIME.BAT  <ENTER>
```

EDIT will display its editing window with the file's current contents. Using your keyboard's arrow keys, move the cursor to the first character on line 2. If you look at the lower-right corner of the edit window, you will notice a series of numbers separated by a colon, such as 00002:001. The first five digits tell you the current line number. The second three numbers tell you the current column. As your files become large, you can use these numbers to keep track of your current location within them.

Type **CLS** and press ENTER. EDIT will insert the command into your batch file. Invoke the File menu's Save option to save the file's contents. Next, use the File menu's Exit option to exit EDIT and go to DOS.

NOTE

EDIT supports insert and overstrike modes. In insert mode, EDIT inserts all text you type to the left of existing text. In overstrike mode, EDIT overwrites existing text with the text you type. Use the INS key to toggle between insert and overstrike mode.

Exiting EDIT Without Saving the Changes

There may be times when you want to discard the changes you have made to a file, or times when you forget to save your file before selecting the Exit option to leave

EDIT. If you invoke Exit without first saving your file changes, EDIT will display this dialog box, which asks you whether you want to save or discard the changes.

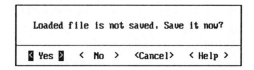

A *dialog box* is simply a way for a program to ask you for additional information (in other words, to carry on a dialog with you). In some cases dialog boxes will prompt you to type in a file name. In this case, the dialog box wants a Yes or No response. To select a dialog box option, either click on the option with your mouse, or press your keyboard's TAB key to highlight the option desired and then press ENTER. Depending on the dialog box's prompts, there may be times when you can select an option simply by typing the first letter of the option. In most cases, you can cancel a dialog box by pressing ESC.

If you select Yes to save the file's contents, EDIT will save your changes. If you select No instead, EDIT will discard all changes you have made since the last time you saved the file. In either case, EDIT will end, returning control to DOS.

Printing Your File

As you edit a large file, it is often convenient to print all or part of the file's contents without leaving the editor. EDIT's Print option, selected from the File menu, lets you do just that. When you select the Print option, EDIT will display this dialog box:

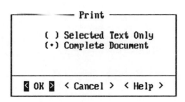

The Print dialog box lets you print part of a file (selected text) or the entire document. The Advanced Concepts section discusses how to select a specific part of the document. As before, use TAB to select OK (to begin printing) or Cancel (to return to the editor without printing).

Getting Online Help

Although EDIT does not provide the text formatting capabilities found in a word processor, EDIT has several powerful features. To help you use these features, EDIT provides built-in online help. There are two ways to invoke Help. First, you can press ALT-H. EDIT will display its Help menu.

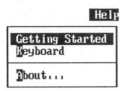

The Getting Started option provides information on using Help, menus, dialog boxes, and so on. This option splits your edit window in two, showing the help text in the top window and your file text in the bottom window, as in Figure 37-3.

To display help on a specific option, either press TAB to highlight the option and then press ENTER, or click on the option with your mouse. The Help menu's Keyboard option, for example, displays a window of help on keyboard-related topics, such as the keys you can use to scroll through your file, to select text, or to invoke menus.

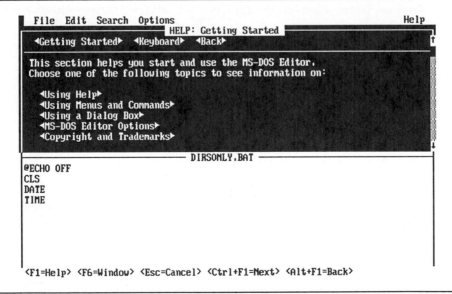

Figure 37-3.   *EDIT's online help divides your screen into two windows, one containing your file, and the other containing help text*

The second way to invoke Help is with the function keys. Note that the bottom line of your screen contains several key definitions. In general, you can press F1 at any time to get help on EDIT or help on an active dialog box. F6 lets you toggle between the Help window and the window containing your file. The ESC key cancels or ends the help session, removing the Help window from your screen. Pressing CTRL-F1 displays help on the next topic, letting you quickly traverse through several pages of help text. If you need to redisplay the previous Help screen, pressing ALT-F1 redisplays help text in the opposite order of your traversal. That is, pressing ALT-F1 lets you back up through through the previous 20 topics.

Use CTRL-F1 and ALT-F1 to view several pages of help text. Remember, you can end the help session at any time by pressing ESC.

Table 37-1 briefly describes keys you can use within EDIT's online help.

Getting Around Your Document

When your files are small, the easiest way to move from one location to another in a file is to use your keyboard's arrow and page keys. As your files become larger, however, EDIT provides faster ways to traverse them. Note the vertical and horizontal bars to the right of and below your edit window. These bars are *scroll bars*. As you use the arrow and page keys to move throughout your file, EDIT will move the dark markers along the bars to indicate your relative position in the file. When you are at line 1, column 1, the markers will appear at the top of the vertical scroll bar and at the left of the horizontal scroll bar. As you move down through your text, the dark marker will move down the vertical scroll bar. When you reach the bottom of your file, the marker will be at the bottom of the scroll bar. Likewise, as you move the cursor from left to right across columns that don't currently appear on your screen, EDIT will move the marker along the horizontal scroll bar. By observing the positions of the markers, you can easily determine your position within the file.

Key Combination	Function
TAB	Advances to next Help topic
SHIFT-TAB	Moves back to previous Help topic
Character	Moves to next topic beginning with *Character*
SHIFT-*Character*	Moves to previous topic beginning with *Character*
ALT-F1	Displays Help window for previously displayed topic
CTRL-F1	Displays Help window for next topic
SHIFT-CTRL-F1	Displays Help window for previous topic
F6	Toggles between Help window and file window
ESC	Ends the online help session

Table 37-1.   EDIT's Online Help Key Combinations

Key Combination	Function
ARROW KEYS	Move cursor one position
PGUP	Moves cursor up one text screen
PGDN	Moves cursor down one text screen
HOME	Moves cursor to beginning of line
END	Moves cursor to end of line
CTRL-LEFT ARROW	Moves cursor one word to the left
CTRL-RIGHT ARROW	Moves cursor one word to the right
CTRL-ENTER	Moves cursor to beginning of next line
CTRL-Q-E	Moves cursor to top line of window
CTRL-Q-X	Moves cursor to bottom line of window
CTRL-W or CTRL-UP ARROW	Scrolls text up one line
CTRL-Z or CTRL-DOWN ARROW	Scrolls text down one line
CTRL-HOME or CTRL-Q-R	Moves cursor to beginning of file
CTRL-END or CTRL-Q-C	Moves cursor to end of file
CTRL-PGUP	Scrolls text left one screen
CTRL-PGDN	Scrolls text right one screen

Table 37-2.   EDIT's Cursor-Movement and Text-Scrolling Key Combinations

If you are using a mouse, EDIT lets you quickly traverse the file by clicking on a scroll bar marker and *dragging* the marker to a new position on the scroll bar. To drag the marker, position the mouse pointer on the marker and hold the mouse button down while you pull the pointer to the new location; then release the mouse button. If you drag the marker slowly, you can see the text scrolling. If you drag the marker quickly, EDIT will scroll the text past you too quickly for you to read.

If you are not using a mouse, Table 37-2 describes keyboard combinations you can use to traverse your file.

Selecting an Existing File for Editing

The easiest way to edit a file is to invoke EDIT, specifying the file name in EDIT's command line. If you were finished editing one file and you wanted to edit another, it would be inconvenient to exit EDIT just so you could invoke EDIT using a different file name. To let you edit different files, the File menu's Open option lets you either type in the name of the file you want to edit, or select the file from a list of file names. When you invoke the Open option, EDIT displays the dialog box shown in Figure 37-4.

By default, EDIT displays only those files in the current directory with the TXT extension. If you know the name of the file you desire, you can type it in, or you can

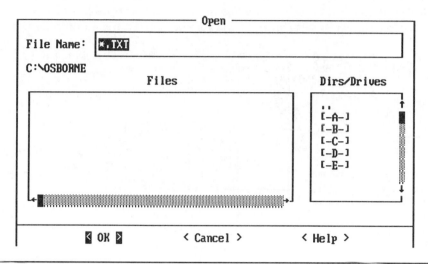

Figure 37-4.   EDIT's File Open dialog box

press TAB and your arrow keys to highlight and select the file from the list of names, provided the file is listed. If you want to display a different set of files, your batch files, for example, you can change *.TXT to *.BAT and press ENTER. Note the list of directory names that appears in the third box. By pressing TAB to select this box, you can use your arrow keys to highlight the desired directory and press ENTER to select the directory, displaying the list of files matching your file name specification in the file box.

After you select a file, press TAB to highlight the OK option and press ENTER. If you have made changes to your previous file and have not yet saved the changes, EDIT will display a dialog box asking you whether you want to save or discard the changes. If EDIT successfully opens the file you specify, it will display the file's contents in your editing window. If EDIT cannot open or locate the file, it will display a dialog box describing the error it has encountered.

Creating and Saving a New File

As you just learned, EDIT's File menu's Open option lets you open an existing file for editing without having to end and restart EDIT. In a similar way, the File menu's New option lets you create a new file. When you select New from the File menu, EDIT will display an empty editing window to hold your new file. If you have been editing a different file and have not yet saved the file's changes, EDIT will first display a dialog box asking you whether you want to save or discard the changes.

When you select the New option to create a new file, EDIT displays the name Untitled at the top of your window until you save the file's contents to disk. To save the file's contents to disk, invoke the File menu's Save As option. EDIT will display the dialog box shown here to prompt you for the desired file and directory name.

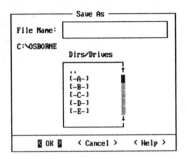

If you want to save the file in the current directory, type the file name and press ENTER. If you want to save the file in a different directory, you can either type in a complete path name or press TAB to select the directory list, then use your arrow keys to highlight the desired directory.

If the file name you specify matches an existing file, EDIT will display a dialog box informing you that a file with the name given exists and asking you if you want to overwrite the file's contents:

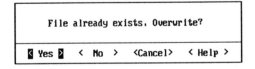

Unlike EDLIN and most word processors, EDIT does not create a backup file containing the file's previous contents when you save the file's new changes. If you overwrite an existing file, your file's previous contents are lost.

NOTE

Customizing EDIT's Screen Display

The Option menu's Display option lets you customize the foreground and background colors EDIT uses for your editing window, as well as letting you turn off the vertical and horizontal scroll bars to display an extra line and column of your file. When you select Display, EDIT displays the dialog box shown in Figure 37-5.

You can press TAB to toggle between the foreground and background color lists, and then use your keyboard's arrow keys to select different colors. EDIT displays a small box inside the dialog box that illustrates how text will appear in the editing window, based on your current color selections. When you are satisfied with your

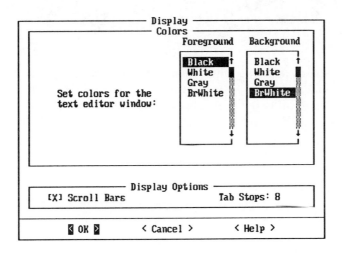

Figure 37-5.   Display options dialog box

color selection, select the dialog box's OK option. To leave the existing colors unchanged and cancel the dialog box, press ESC.

The Scroll Bars entry works as a toggle. If you highlight the entry and press SPACEBAR, EDIT will remove the X, telling you scroll bars will not be displayed. If you press SPACEBAR a second time, EDIT will redisplay the X, enabling scroll bars. The Tab Stops option lets you specify the column distances between tab settings. To change the default setting from 8, select the option and type in the new value desired.

Hands On

Using EDIT, create the following batch file DIRSONLY.BAT that displays only the names of directories within the current directory.

```
@ECHO OFF
REM Name: DIRSONLY.BAT
REM Function: Displays directories within the current directory
DIR | FIND "<DIR>"
```

To begin, invoke EDIT as follows:

```
C:\> EDIT  DIRSONLY.BAT  <ENTER>
```

When EDIT displays the Edit menu, type in the four commands. Use ALT-F to invoke EDIT's File menu, and use the Save option to save the file to disk. Invoke the File menu a second time and use the Print option to print the file's current contents.

Next, invoke the File menu and select the New option. EDIT will display an empty editing window. Type in the following commands into the file.

```
@ECHO OFF
REM Name:  NODIRS.BAT
REM Function: Displays only file names in the current directory
DIR | FIND /V "<DIR>"
```

Invoke EDIT's File menu and select the Save As option. When EDIT displays the dialog box prompt for a file name, type in NODIRS.BAT and press ENTER. Use the File menu's Exit option to end EDIT and return to DOS.

Review

1. How does EDIT differ from EDLIN?

2. What name does EDIT assign to the backup copy of your file's previous contents when you save new changes?

3. What is a dialog box?

4. What are scroll bars?

5. How do you invoke EDIT's online help?

Answers

1. EDIT is a full-screen editor that lets you view the file's contents on the entire screen, using a mouse or the arrow and page keys to traverse the file's

contents. EDLIN, on the other hand, only lets you work with one line of the file at a time. In general, EDIT behaves much more like a word processor than does EDLIN.

2. EDIT does not save a backup copy of your original file. If you edit a file and save the new contents using EDIT, the file's previous contents are lost.

3. A dialog box is a prompt for additional information, such as a file name or a user response to an error condition. EDIT uses dialog boxes to converse with the user.

4. To the far right of and immediately below the editing window, EDIT displays a vertical and a horizontal scroll bar. As you move throughout your file, EDIT moves a marker along each scroll bar to indicate your current position within the file. If the vertical marker appears near the top of the scroll bar, you are editing near the top of the file. If the horizontal marker appears near the left edge of the scroll bar, you are near the left side of your file. If you are editing the file using a mouse, you can drag the marker to a new position along the scroll bar to select a new position within the file.

5. You can invoke EDIT's online help using ALT-H to select EDIT's Help menu, or you can press F1 at any time to get help on a menu or dialog box, or to access EDIT's general Help facility.

Advanced Concepts

Using the key combinations in Table 37-2, or EDIT's scroll bars and your mouse, you can quickly traverse your files. In addition, EDIT's Search menu lets you specify a word or phrase you want to locate within your document. If EDIT successfully locates your selected text, it will place the cursor at the start of the text. In addition, the Search menu provides a Change option that lets you replace one word or phrase with another. If you invoke the Search menu using ALT-S, EDIT will display the following pull-down menu.

The Find option lets you specify a word or phrase to locate within your document. When you select this option, EDIT displays the Find Text dialog box, shown here:

```
┌─────────────────── Find ───────────────────┐
│ Find What: ┌───────────────────────────────┐ │
│            └───────────────────────────────┘ │
│                                              │
│   [ ] Match Upper/Lowercase    [ ] Whole Word │
├──────────────────────────────────────────────┤
│        ▓ OK ▓      < Cancel >     < Help >    │
└──────────────────────────────────────────────┘
```

To search a file for the word "Rebels!", for example, you would type **Rebels**! and press ENTER. If EDIT finds matching text, EDIT will advance the cursor to the first match. If the word does not exist in the file, EDIT will display a dialog box stating that it did not find a match.

By default, EDIT considers uppercase and lowercase letters the same. EDIT would consider "REBELS!" and "Rebels!" the same. If you want EDIT to perform a case-sensitive search, highlight the Match Upper/Lowercase option and press SPACEBAR. This option works as a toggle. When the X is present, EDIT performs case-sensitive matches. When the X is not present, EDIT considers uppercase and lowercase letters the same.

The Whole Word option is also a toggle. When no X is present, EDIT matches any occurrence of the word, even if the word forms part of a longer word. For example, EDIT would consider "Rebel" and "Rebels!" the same. If you select the Whole Word option, EDIT only matches occurrences of the word that are delimited by blanks, tabs, or other punctuation.

In many situations the text may appear several times throughout your file. The Search menu's Repeat Last Find option lets you quickly repeat the previous search without forcing you to type in the search string a second or third time. Note the "F3" that appears to the right of the option. F3 is a hot key for this option. You can press F3 at any time to repeat the last search operation without having to invoke the Search menu and select this option. Hot keys save you time and keystrokes.

The Search menu's Change option lets you replace one word or phrase with another. When you select this option, EDIT will display the dialog box shown here:

```
┌────────────────── Change ──────────────────┐
│ Find What: ┌───────────────────────────────┐ │
│            └───────────────────────────────┘ │
│ Change To: ┌───────────────────────────────┐ │
│            └───────────────────────────────┘ │
│                                              │
│   [ ] Match Upper/Lowercase    [ ] Whole Word │
├──────────────────────────────────────────────┤
│ ▓ Find and Verify ▓ < Change All > < Cancel > < Help > │
└──────────────────────────────────────────────┘
```

The Find What: option prompts you for the word or phrase you want to change. Type in the word or phrase and press TAB. The Change To: entry is the new word or phrase you want to use. Again, type in the word or phrase and press TAB. The

Find and Verify option directs EDIT to locate each matching word or phrase, and then to display a dialog box to determine whether you want to replace the match. The Change All option directs EDIT to automatically change each match without asking you for verification. As with all dialog boxes, you can cancel the Text Change dialog box at any time by pressing ESC.

Performing Cut-and-Paste Operations

Cutting and pasting is the process of moving text from one location in your file to another. To begin, you must select the lines of text you want to cut and paste. To select text, hold down a SHIFT key and press UP ARROW or DOWN ARROW (or PGUP and PGDN for large amounts or text). EDIT will display the selected text in reverse video. To select text using your mouse, move the mouse pointer to the beginning of the text. Next, hold down the left mouse button while you move the mouse. As before, EDIT will display the selected text in reverse video. After you select the text, you can invoke EDIT's Edit menu using ALT-E. EDIT will display the following menu options.

```
 Edit
┌─────────────────────────┐
│ Cut          Shift+Del  │
│ Copy         Ctrl+Ins   │
│ Paste        Shift+Ins  │
│ Clear             Del   │
└─────────────────────────┘
```

Note the available hot keys for each menu option. The Cut option removes the selected text from your file and stores the text in a location you can't view, called the clipboard. You use the Cut option when you want to move text from one location to another. The Cut option's counterpart is the Paste option, which copies the clipboard's current contents to the current cursor location in your file. To cut and paste text, you select the text to move, cut the text from the file to the clipboard, move the cursor to the location in the file where you want the text, and then paste the clipboard's contents into the file.

The Copy option copies selected text from the file to the clipboard without removing the text from the file. The Copy operation combines with Paste to let you duplicate text throughout your file.

Last, the Clear option simply deletes the selected text from your file without copying the text to the clipboard. When you use Clear to remove selected text, you can't get the text back.

EDIT does not provide a menu option to merge one file's contents into another. However, if you select all the text in one file and copy the text to the clipboard, you can then open a second file and paste the clipboard's contents into that file, merging the two files as desired.

NOTE

Key Terms

Screen editor   A text editor that lets you view and edit a file's contents on the entire screen, using your keyboard's arrow and page keys to traverse the file.

Cut and paste   The process of moving (cutting) text from one location in the file and placing the text (pasting) at a new location.

Scroll bar   A vertical bar at the right side of a window, or a horizontal bar at the bottom of a window, that displays a marker indicating your relative location within the file and that lets you quickly change locations within the file by dragging the marker to a new location on the scroll bar.

Dialog box   A box that a program displays to communicate with the user, either to obtain additional information, such as a file name, or to obtain a specific user response to a limited number of options.

Chapter 38

Support for International Users

Over the past few years, DOS use has been growing as rapidly in countries around the world as it has in the United States. To help international users work with their own character sets, keyboard templates, and symbol sets (date, time, and currency formats), DOS provides several "international commands." By default, DOS uses the United States configuration. If you are using DOS within the United States, and you don't need to correspond with international users using another country's character set, you can continue your reading with Chapter 39, "Using the DOS 4 Shell." If you are an international DOS user, you can finally customize your computer.

Selecting a Code Page

A *character set* is a collection of letters and punctuation symbols—in other words, a set of characters. Just as different countries use different languages, most countries have unique character sets. DOS refers to character sets as *code pages*. To let international users work with their own character sets, DOS provides support for many different code pages.

Code pages are similar in concept to typewriters that let you select a new set of letters by changing the typewriter ball:

When you tell DOS to change code pages, DOS, like the typewriter, will use the new character set. DOS provides support for six different code pages as listed in Table 38-1.

Appendix D presents all the characters in each code page. Take a moment to examine the code pages to determine the code page containing the character set you need. Most of the commands presented in this chapter require you to specify a code-page value (see Table 38-1).

Setting an International Configuration

To set up an international system, you have to perform several steps. Fortunately, once you determine the commands you need, you can place the commands and device-driver entries in your AUTOEXEC.BAT and CONFIG.SYS files and forget about them. Briefly, to set up an international system you must perform the following steps:

1. Select the country's symbol set using the CONFIG.SYS COUNTRY entry.

2. Install video code-page support with the DISPLAY.SYS device driver.

3. Install printer code-page support with the PRINTER.SYS device driver.

4. Optionally invoke the NLSFUNC command to define country-specific symbols and enable code-page switching.

5. Select the country's keyboard template using the KEYB command.

6. Load code-page support for the keyboard, screen, and printer using the MODE command.

Country	Code-Page Value
United States	437
Multilingual	850
Slavic	852 (DOS 5)
Portuguese	860
French Canadian	863
Nordic	865

Table 38-1.   Code Pages Supported by DOS

Loading Key Device Drivers

For DOS versions 3.3 and later, the DISPLAY.SYS and PRINTER.SYS device drivers, briefly discussed in Chapter 24, "Customizing Your System with CONFIG.SYS," provide code-page support for your video display and printer. The format of the DISPLAY.SYS device driver entry is

```
DEVICE=C:\DOS\DISPLAY.SYS CON[:]=(DisplayType[,[CodePage]
     [,CodePageCount]])
```

or for video devices supporting subfonts:

```
DEVICE=C:\DOS\DISPLAY.SYS CON[:]=(DisplayType[,[CodePage]
     [,(CodePageCount, SubfontCount)]])
```

DisplayType specifies your video display. You must specify one of the following types:

EGA (use for EGA and VGA systems)

LCD (liquid-crystal display for portables)

CGA

MONO

CodePage is one of the three-digit code-page values listed in Table 38-1. *CodePage Count* specifies the number of additional code pages your video system can support, from 0 to 6. For LCD systems the maximum value is 1. For EGA and VGA systems, the maximum value is 6. For CGA and MONO systems, the value is 0. *SubFontCount* specifies the number of font subsets your hardware supports for each code page. For EGA systems, the default value is 2. For LCD systems, the default is 1. Most users won't require subfonts.

The following DISPLAY.SYS entry loads code page 437 as the primary code page on an EGA (or VGA) system, specifying two additional code pages.

```
DEVICE=C:\DOS\DISPLAY.SYS  CON:=(EGA, 437, 2)
```

In a similar way, PRINTER.SYS device driver provides code-page support for parallel printers. The format of PRINTER.SYS is

```
DEVICE=C:\DOS\PRINTER.SYS  LPT n:=(PrinterType [,[CodePage]
    [,CodePageCount]])
```

LPT*n* specifies the printer port LPT1 through LPT3. *PrinterType* specifies one of the printers listed in Table 38-2.

As you can see, PRINTER.SYS restricts its code-page support to a select group of IBM printers. If your printer is not listed, your printer may be compatible with one of the three. Check your printer manual for details on code-page support. *CodePage* and *CodePageCount* as before, specify the primary code page, and maximum number of additional code pages the printer supports.

The following PRINTER.SYS entry installs code-page support for an IBM 4208 Proprinter.

```
DEVICE=C:\DOS\PRINTER.SYS  LPT1:=(4208, 437, 2)
```

Selecting a Symbol Set

Most countries have a unique date and time format, as well as unique currency formats. As briefly discussed in Chapter 24, the CONFIG.SYS COUNTRY entry lets you select an international symbol set. The format of the COUNTRY entry is

```
COUNTRY=CountryCode[,[CodePage] [,CountryInfoFile]]
```

Printer Type	Printer
4201	IBM 4201 or 4202 Proprinter
4208	IBM 4207 or 4208 Proprinter
5202	IBM 5202 Quietwriter III

Table 38-2.   Printer Types Supported by PRINTER.SYS

CountryCode is a three-digit number that identifies the desired country. Table 38-3 defines the country-code values, as well as the code-page values normally used for the country.

CountryInfoFile specifies the path name of the file containing the international symbol sets. Most users will use the DOS file COUNTRY.SYS.

To select the symbol set for Germany, for example, you would use the following CONFIG.SYS COUNTRY entry.

```
COUNTRY=049,850,C:\DOS\COUNTRY.SYS
```

Likewise, to select Finland you would use this entry.

```
COUNTRY=358,850,C:\DOS\COUNTRY.SYS
```

Country	Country Code	Code Page
United States	001	437 or 850
French Canadian	002	863 or 850
Latin America	003	850 or 437
Netherlands	031	850 or 437
Belgium	032	850 or 437
France	033	850 or 437
Spain	034	850 or 437
Italy	039	850 or 437
Switzerland	041	850 or 437
United Kingdom	044	437 or 850
Denmark	045	850 or 865
Sweden	046	850 or 437
Norway	047	850 or 865
Germany	049	850 or 437
Brazil	055	850 or 437
English (International)	061	437 or 850
Australia	061	437 or 850
Japan	081*	932* or 437
Korea	082*	934* or 437
Chinese (simplified)	086*	936* or 437
Chinese (traditional)	088*	938* or 437
Portugal	351	850 or 860
Finland	358	850 or 437
Arabic countries	785*	864* or 850
Israel	972*	862* or 850

Table 38-3.   *Country-Code Values and Code-Page Combinations (* indicates a symbol set or code page only available with special DOS versions)*

DOS 3.2 and Earlier

If you are using DOS 3.2 or earlier, only specify the country code in the COUNTRY entry. DOS did not use code pages or the COUNTRY.SYS file until version 3.3. Under DOS version 3.2, the following COUNTRY entry selects the German symbol set.

```
COUNTRY=049
```

Selecting a Keyboard Template

Just as each country has its own characters and symbol sets, most countries use a unique keyboard layout (called the *keyboard template*). Appendix D displays all the keyboard templates. Beginning with DOS version 3.3, the KEYB command loads memory-resident software that lets you select a keyboard layout. The format of KEYB is as follows:

```
KEYB KeyboardCode[,[CodePage][,KeyboardFile]][/E][/ID:nnn]
```

KeyboardCode is a unique two-letter code that identifies the desired keyboard template. Table 38-4 identifies the keyboard codes, code pages, and secondary identification values for cases where the country has two templates.

KeyboardFile is the complete path name to the file containing the keyboard templates, which is typically the file KEYBOARD.SYS. The /E switch informs DOS you are using an enhanced keyboard. The /ID switch lets you select one of two possible templates by specifying a secondary identification value.

The following KEYB command selects the German keyboard template.

```
C:\> KEYB  GR,850,C:\DOS\KEYBOARD.SYS  <ENTER>
```

KEYB does not force you to include a code-page value. If the code page has not yet been defined and you include the code-page value, the command will fail. The following KEYB command selects the German keyboard template without specifying the code-page value.

```
C:\> KEYB  GR,,C:\DOS\KEYBOARD.SYS  <ENTER>
```

If you are using DOS 4, use the CONFIG.SYS INSTALL entry to invoke KEYB as shown here.

```
INSTALL=C:\DOS\KEYB.COM  GR,850,C:\DOS\KEYBOARD.SYS
```

Country	Keyboard Code	Code Page	Secondary Identification
United States	US	437 or 850	103
French Canadian	CF	863 or 860	058
Latin America	LA	850 or 437	171
Netherlands	NL	850 or 437	143
Belgium	BE	850 or 437	120
France	FR	437 or 850	120, 189
Spain	SP	850 or 437	172
Italy	IT	850 or 437	141, 142
Switzerland German	SG	850 or 437	000
Switzerland French	SF	850 or 437	150
United Kingdom	UK	437 or 850	166, 168
Denmark	DK	850 or 865	159
Sweden	SV	850 or 437	153
Norway	NO	850 or 865	155
Germany	GR	850 or 437	129
Brazil	BR	850 or 437	
Portugal	PO	850 or 860	163
Finland	SU	850 or 437	153

Table 38-4. *International Keyboard Templates*

If you are using DOS version 5 and reserved memory, use the LOADHIGH command to install KEYB.

```
C:\> LOADHIGH C:\DOS\KEYB.COM  GR,850,C:\DOS\KEYBOARD.SYS  <ENTER>
```

If you invoke KEYB without specifying any parameters, KEYB will display information about the current keyboard template.

```
Current keyboard code: GR  code page: 850
Current CON code page: 850
```

If you have not yet prepared a code page for use using MODE, KEYB will display the following message.

```
KEYB has not been installed
Active code page not available from CON device
```

Command	Country
KEYBFR	French
KEYBGR	German
KEYBIT	Italian
KEYBSP	Spanish

Table 38-5.   Keyboard Template Commands Prior to DOS 3.3

Once you select a keyboard template you can switch between the default and current template using the CTRL-ALT-F1 and CTRL-ALT-F2 keyboard combinations. To select the default template press CTRL-ALT-F1. To select the new template press CTRL-ALT-F2.

DOS 3.2 and Earlier

KEYB was introduced with DOS 3.3. Before version 3.3, DOS provided individual commands for each keyboard template, as listed in Table 38-5.

Preparing Code Pages for Use

In Chapter 13, "Printing," you used MODE to redirect printer output of a parallel printer to a serial port. In Chapter 43, "DOS System Commands," you will use the MODE command to customize your serial ports, screen, and keyboard. In this section you will use MODE to prepare and select device code pages.

The MODE command lets you select a code page for use or prepare code pages for future use. To provide code-page support, DOS includes five files with the CPI (Code-Page Information) extension, as described in Table 38-6.

Preparing Device Code Pages

Before you can select a code page for use, you must prepare the device. Under DOS 4 and 5, the MODE command lets you prepare (download) code-page information for a device as follows:

```
MODE DeviceName  CODEPAGE  PREPARE=((CodePages) CodePageFile)
```

Under DOS 3.3 you only need one set of parentheses.

```
MODE DeviceName CODEPAGE  PREPARE=(CodePages) CodePageFile
```

Code Page File	Device Support
EGA.CPI	EGA
LCD.CPI	Liquid-crystal display (portables)
4201.CPI	IBM 4201 and 4202 Proprinter
4208.CPI	IBM 4207 and 4208 Proprinter

Table 38-6.   DOS Code-Page Support Files

DeviceName specifies the device you want to prepare for code-page use, either CON, LPI1, LPT2, or LPT3. The entries CODEPAGE and PREPARE tell MODE the operation you desire. MODE lets you abbreviate CODEPAGE as CP and PREPARE as PREP. *CodePages* tells MODE the code-page values the device may use, as described in Table 38-1. If you want MODE to prepare two or more code pages, separate the code-page values with commas. *CodePageFile* specifies the complete path name to one of the CPI files listed in Table 38-6.

Under DOS 4 and 5, the following command prepares the console device CON to use code pages 437, 850, and 860.

```
C:\> MODE CON: CP PREP=((437,850,860) C:\DOS\EGA.CPI) <ENTER>
```

Under DOS 3.3 an equivalent command is

```
C:\> MODE CON: CP PREP=(437,850,860) C:\DOS\EGA.CPI  <ENTER>
```

In DOS 4 and 5, the following MODE command prepares code pages for a 4201 Proprinter.

```
C:\> MODE LPT1: CP  PREP=((437,850)  C:\DOS\4201.CPI)  <ENTER>
```

In earlier versions, remove the second set of parentheses.

```
C:\> MODE LPT1: CP  PREP=(437,850)  C:\DOS\4201.CPI <ENTER>
```

If MODE cannot locate the CPI file, MODE will display the following error message.

```
Failure to access code page font file
```

If this error message appears, make sure you are specifying a correct path name to the CPI file.

If MODE successfully prepares the device, MODE will display the following.

```
MODE prepare code page function completed
```

Selecting Device Code Pages

After you prepare code pages for use, you can use the MODE CODEPAGE SELECT command to select a specific code page for use. The format of the command is as follows:

```
MODE   DeviceName CODEPAGE SELECT=CodePage
```

As before, *DeviceName* specifies the desired device, and *CodePage* is a three-digit code-page value. The following MODE command selects code page 850 for the CON device.

```
C:\> MODE CON CODEPAGE SELECT=850   <ENTER>
```

MODE lets you abbreviate SELECT as SEL. If MODE is successful, MODE will display the following.

```
MODE select code page function completed
```

If the code page specified has not yet been prepared for use, MODE will display the following error message.

```
Code page not prepared
```

Display Device Code-Page Information

After you prepare and select code pages, you may be interested in the current device configuration. Using the CODEPAGE /STATUS switch, you can display device code-page information as shown here.

```
C:\> MODE   CON   /STATUS   <ENTER>

Status for device CON:
------------
Columns=80
Lines=25

Active code page for device CON is 437
Hardware code pages:
  code page 437
Prepared code pages:
  code page 437
  code page 850

MODE status code page function completed
```

The MODE command lets you abbreviate /STATUS as /STA.

Refreshing a Code Page

When you prepare a device for code-page use, MODE downloads code-page information into the devices memory. If the device loses power, the code-page information is lost. Using the CODEPAGE REFRESH command, you can reinstate prepared code pages. The following MODE command, for example, refreshes the code pages previously prepared for LPT1.

```
C:\> MODE LPT1: CODEPAGE REFRESH   <ENTER>
```

MODE lets you abbreviate REFRESH as simply REF.

Changing Code Pages with CHCP

The DOS MODE command lets you select code pages for devices on an individual basis. Using the CHCP command, you can change code pages for your screen and printer in one step. Before you can use CHCP, you must invoke the NLSFUNC

(National Language Support FUNCtion) command. NLSFUNC lets you specify the directory containing the country-specific symbol-set file COUNTRY.SYS and enables code-page switching via CHCP.

If you are using DOS 3.3, invoke NLSFUNC as follows:

```
C:\> NLSFUNC  C:\DOS\COUNTRY.SYS  <ENTER>
```

If you are using DOS 4, invoke NLSFUNC using the CONFIG.SYS INSTALL entry shown here.

```
INSTALL=C:\DOS\NLSFUNC.EXE  C:\DOS\COUNTRY.SYS
```

Last, under DOS 5, use either INSTALL or the LOADHIGH command.

```
C:\> LOADHIGH  C:\DOS\NLSFUNC.EXE  C:\DOS\COUNTRY.SYS <ENTER>
```

After you invoke NLSFUNC, you can change code pages using CHCP. The format of CHCP is as follows:

```
CHCP  [CodePage]
```

CodePage is the three-digit value corresponding to a code page (see Table 38-1). If you don't specify a code page, CHCP will display the active code-page setting.

```
C:\> CHCP  <ENTER>
Active code page: 437
```

The following command activates code page 850. If you have not yet prepared a device for the code page specified, CHCP will display the following error message.

```
C:\> CHCP  850  <ENTER>
Invalid code page
```

Hands On

This section presents the steps you would follow to configure a system for use in Germany. Following these same steps, substitute your country's code page, country code, and keyboard template values.

DISPLAY.SYS

The DISPLAY.SYS device driver provides video code-page support for international users. DISPLAY.SYS lets you specify your video display type and hardware support for code pages. The following entry selects code-page support for an EGA (and VGA system).

```
DEVICE=C:\DOS\DISPLAY.SYS CON:=(EGA,437,2)
```

The value 437 specifies the primary code page, while the value 2 specifies the number of additional code pages supported.

PRINTER.SYS

The PRINTER.SYS device driver provides code-page support for a limited number of IBM printers. If your printer is not listed, check your printer documentation for code-page support. The following PRINTER.SYS entry loads code-page support for an IBM 4201 printer.

```
DEVICE=C:\DOS\PRINTER.SYS  LPT1:=(4201, 437, 1)
```

COUNTRY

The CONFIG.SYS COUNTRY entry lets you select an international symbol set. The symbol set defines the country's date and time formats, currency format, and collating order for sort operations. The following COUNTRY entry selects the French Canadian symbol set.

```
COUNTRY=002,C:\DOS\COUNTRY.SYS
```

KEYB

KEYB lets you select a international keyboard template. Once you select a template, you can switch between the default and new template using the following keyboard combinations.

SUMMARY

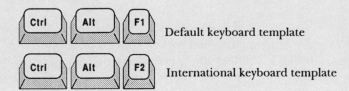

Default keyboard template

International keyboard template

The following KEYB command selects the Finnish keyboard.

```
C:\> KEYB  SU,850,C:\DOS\KEYBOARD.SYS    <ENTER>
```

MODE Code-Page Commands

Before a device can use code pages, you must prepare the device for code-page use. Using code-page font information stored in one of five CPI files, the MODE command lets you download code-page information to a device. The following DOS 5 MODE command, for example, prepares the console to use code pages 437 and 850.

```
C:\> MODE  CON: CP PREP=((437,850) C:\DOS\EGA.CPI)    <ENTER>
```

After you prepare a device for code-page use, you can select a specific code page using MODE's CODEPAGE SELECT command.

```
C:\> MODE  CON:  CP  SEL=850    <ENTER>
```

Last, using the /STATUS switch, you can display a device's code-page information as follows.

```
C:\> MODE  CON:  CP  /STA  <ENTER>
```

NLSFUNC and CHCP

The NLSFUNC command enables code-page switching by CHCP. The format of NLSFUNC is

SUMMARY

```
C:\> NLSFUNC  C:\DOS\COUNTRY.SYS  <ENTER>
```

When you select a code page using CHCP, DOS automatically selects the code page for all devices supporting code-page switching. To select code page 850 using CHCP, you would issue the following command.

```
C:\> CHCP  850  <ENTER>
```

Before you can select a code page for use with CHCP, you must first prepare the device for the code page using MODE.

First, load the DISPLAY.SYS device driver in CONFIG.SYS. The following entry assumes a VGA or EGA monitor.

```
DEVICE=C:\DOS\DISPLAY.SYS  CON:=(EGA,437,2)
```

Second, place a COUNTRY entry in CONFIG.SYS.

```
COUNTRY=049,437,C:\DOS\COUNTRY.SYS
```

If you are using one of the printers listed in Table 38-2, install the PRINTER.SYS device driver.

Next, invoke KEYB from within your AUTOEXEC.BAT file to select the German keyboard template.

```
KEYB  GR,437,C:\DOS\KEYBOARD.SYS
```

If you are using DOS 4 use the CONFIG.SYS INSTALL entry to load KEYB.

Again, from within AUTOEXEC.BAT or using the CONFIG.SYS install entry, invoke NLSFUNC.

```
NLSFUNC  C:\DOS\COUNTRY.SYS
```

Next, from within your AUTOEXEC.BAT file, invoke MODE to prepare the code page. Under DOS 4 and 5 use the following:

```
MODE  CON:  CODEPAGE  PREP=((437,850) C:\DOS\EGA.CPI)
MODE  CON:  CODEPAGE  SELECT=437
```

Under DOS 3.3, use the following.

```
MODE  CON:  CODEPAGE  PREP=(437,850) C:\DOS\EGA.CPI
MODE  CON:  CODEPAGE  SELECT=437
```

Using CTRL-ALT-DEL, restart your system in its international configuration.

Review

1. What is a code page?

2. What is an international symbol set?

3. What is a keyboard template?

4. What are CPI files?

5. How does selecting a code page using CHCP differ from using MODE?

Answers

1. A code page is a character set that contains letters, numbers, and punctuation symbols. DOS provides code-page (character-set) support for international users.

2. An international symbol set specifies a country's date, time, and currency formats, as well as collating sequences for sorting operations. The United States, for example, specifies dates as *MM-DD-YY*. In Germany, however, the date is specified as *DD.MM.YY*.

3. A keyboard template is the mapping of keys on the keyboard to letters, numbers, or symbols in the current character set (code page). To assist international users, DOS provides keyboard templates for each country.

4. CPI stands for code-page information. A file with the CPI extension contains code-page information for the device specified in the base name. For example, the file EGA.CPI contains code-page information for EGA (as well as VGA) monitors.

5. The CHCP command lets you change the code page used by the screen and printer in one step. The MODE command changes the code page for your devices one device at a time.

Advanced Concepts

As you know, the IBM PC lets you use ASCII and extended ASCII characters. Appendix B illustrates the extended ASCII character set. If you examine the code-page values in Appendix D, you will find the international character sets all reside in the range of extended ASCII characters (128 through 255). Depending on the age of your monitor, your monitor may not be able to display these characters clearly in different graphics modes. If your monitor has difficulty displaying such characters, you will need to invoke the GRAFTABL command discussed in Chapter 43. GRAFTABL loads memory-resident software that helps your computer display these characters correctly.

Key Terms

Code page   A character set containing letters, symbols, and numbers.

Code-page switching   The process of changing the character set a device uses to display output; remapping the keyboard for use with international symbols.

Chapter 39

Using the DOS 4 Shell

Throughout this book you have issued all your commands by typing the command's name and pressing ENTER from the DOS prompt. If you are using DOS 4 or later, DOS provides a menu-driven program called the DOS *shell*, from which you can issue DOS commands from menus and select files from a graphic directory by highlighting the file with your keyboard arrow keys or by clicking on the file using your mouse. The program is called a shell because it contains within it all the commands you need to work with DOS. This chapter gets you up and running with the DOS 4 shell. In Chapter 40 you will learn how to customize the shell by adding your own commands. If you are using DOS 5, Chapters 41 and 42 examine the DOS 5 shell in detail.

Starting the DOS 4 Shell

To start the DOS 4 shell program, type **DOSSHELL** and press ENTER.

```
C:\> DOSSHELL <ENTER>
```

If your AUTOEXEC.BAT file contains the DOSSHELL command, the shell will automatically start each time you turn on your computer. The DOS 4 shell will display the main menu shown in Figure 39-1.

The shell refers to this main menu as the Start Programs screen. From this screen you will later select and run (start) your DOS commands. The shell displays the

Figure 39-1. *The DOS 4 shell main menu*

current system date and time in the left and right corners of the top row or title bar. If the date or time is not correct, you can use the DATE and TIME commands to correct them or, as you will learn later in this chapter, you can select a Set Date and Time menu option directly from the shell's DOS Utilities menu. By taking advantage of such menu options, you will find the shell very easy to use. If your computer has a mouse connected, you can use the mouse to select menu options.

Immediately below the title bar is the shell's menu bar, which contains the Program, Group, Exit, and Help menu options. As you will learn in Chapter 40, "Advanced DOS 4 Shell Techniques," the Program and Group options let you customize the shell by adding your own set of commonly used commands to the main menu. To access one of the menu bar options, click on the option with your mouse; press F10 and press the letter of the menu option that appears underlined; or highlight the option using your arrow keys and press ENTER. When you select a menu bar option, the shell will display a pull-down menu similar to the following.

To select a menu option, click on the option with your mouse; press the letter in the option name that appears underlined; or highlight the option using your arrow keys and press ENTER. To cancel a menu without selecting an option, click your mouse on an area outside of the menu or press ESC. If a menu option appears dim, the option is not currently available. Chapter 40 examines the Program and Group options in detail. In this chapter you will examine Exit and Help.

Below the menu bar, the shell displays the Main Group menu. A *group* is a collection of related programs and commands, such as the DOS disk commands FORMAT, DISKCOMP, and DISKCOPY, or possibly your business commands, which may include your word processor, spreadsheet, and a database. When you select a group, the shell will display the program titles the group contains on a second menu, letting you quickly execute the program you desire. To select a group, double-click on the group name with your mouse, or highlight the name with your keyboard arrow keys and press ENTER. If the arrow keys don't move the Group menu highlight, press F10 to move the highlight from the menu bar back to the menu options. Also make sure your keyboard's NUMLOCK key is off, selecting the arrow keys instead of the numeric key pad.

Exiting the DOS Shell

Although you can run all your programs and perform all your tasks directly within the DOS shell, there may be times you want to end the shell permanently, or just temporarily to issue one or more commands from the DOS prompt. To end the shell permanently, press F3 or invoke the shell's Exit menu and select the Exit Shell option, as shown here.

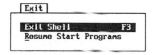

Note that "F3" appears to the right of the menu option. This represents a predefined *hot key* you can press at any time to select the option without having to go through the steps of invoking the menu and choosing the menu option.

When you exit the shell in this way, DOS removes the shell program from memory, redisplaying its prompt. To use the shell again, you must restart the shell with the DOSSHELL command.

If you only want to exit the shell temporarily, press SHIFT-F9 or select the Main Group's Command Prompt option. When you select this option the shell will display a DOS prompt, as follows.

```
When ready to return to the DOS SHELL, type EXIT then press Enter

Microsoft(R) MS-DOS(R) Version 4.01
              (C)Copyright Microsoft Corp 1981-1988

C:\DOS>
```

From the DOS prompt, issue the commands you require. When you are ready to return to the DOS shell, issue the EXIT command.

```
C:\> EXIT    <ENTER>
```

The shell will redisplay its menu, letting you continue your shell operations right where you left off.

WARNING   *Never turn off your computer or restart DOS when you have only temporarily exited the shell to DOS. If you have programs active within the shell with open files, changes to the files will be lost. As a rule, always exit permanently the shell to DOS using F3 before turning your computer off.*

Customizing Your Screen Colors

If you don't find the shell's current colors visually appealing, the shell lets you change them. From the Main Group options, select Change Colors. The shell will display the screen shown in Figure 39-2.

Using your keyboard's RIGHT ARROW and LEFT ARROW keys, you can cycle through the shell's various screen color combinations. If you are using a mouse, you can cycle through the colors by clicking on the right and left arrow keys that appear in the Change Colors box. When you find a color combination you like best, press ENTER to save the colors. If you decide you would rather leave the current color unchanged, press ESC. In either case, the shell will return you to the Main Group menu.

Using the Shell's Built-in Utilities

The shell's Main Group DOS Utilities option provides you with access to several commonly used DOS commands. The three periods (called ellipses) that follow the menu option indicate a second menu of options follow. When you select the DOS Utilities option, the shell displays the menu shown in Figure 39-3.

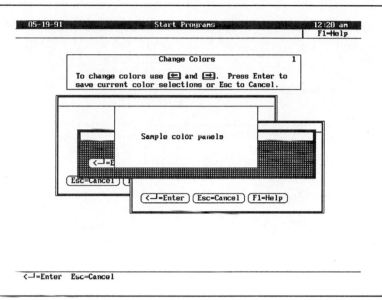

Figure 39-2. The Change Colors screen

Figure 39-2. The Change Colors screen

Figure 39-3. The DOS Utilities menu

Menu Option	DOS Command
Set Date and Time	DATE followed by TIME
Disk Copy	DISKCOPY
Disk Compare	DISKCOMP
Backup Fixed Disk	BACKUP
Restore Fixed Disk	RESTORE

Table 39-1.   *The DOS Utilities Menu Options and Their Corresponding DOS Commands*

Through these menu options, the shell provides you with access to the commands listed in Table 39-1.

In Chapter 40 you will learn how to add additional commands to this group. To issue a specific command, simply select the corresponding menu option. To return to the Main Group, press ESC.

Setting the System Date and Time

The shell displays the current system date and time at the top of your screen. If either the date or time is incorrect, you can correct them as follows. When you select the Set Date and Time option, the shell will first display the following dialog box, prompting you to type in a new date.

```
┌──────────────────────────────────────────┐
│      ▐ Set Date and Time Utility ▌        │
│                                           │
│        Enter new date ??-??-??            │
│                                           │
│        Parameters . . [        ]          │
│                                           │
│  (<─┘-Enter) (Esc-Cancel) (F1-Help)       │
└──────────────────────────────────────────┘
```

The shell displays a *dialog box* when it needs to get additional information such as a date or file name, or ask you to respond to a specific condition, such as a disk drive not ready. A dialog box, in other words, lets you communicate information to the shell (carry on a dialog). Type in the desired date in the form *mm-dd-yy* and press ENTER.

The shell will then display a second dialog box, prompting you for the new time:

```
┌──────────────────────────────────────────┐
│      ▐ Set Date and Time Utility ▌        │
│                                           │
│        Enter new time hh:mm               │
│                                           │
│        Parameters . . [        ]          │
│                                           │
│  (<─┘-Enter) (Esc-Cancel) (F1-Help)       │
└──────────────────────────────────────────┘
```

Type in the time desired in the form of *hh*:*mm* and press ENTER. If you decide you want to cancel the date and time operation, press ESC. The shell will remove the dialog boxes and return to the DOS Utilities menu. Otherwise, the shell will invoke the DATE and TIME commands, using the date and time you entered at each dialog box prompt as command-line parameters.

If you don't specify a date or time in the dialog box, the shell will invoke the command without a command line. In this case, you must specify the desired date and time as shown, just as if you had executed the date and time commands.

```
Current date is Thu 05-16-1991
Enter new date (mm-dd-yy):  06-21-91   <ENTER>
Current time is 11:04:31.12a
Enter new time:
```

Performing a Disk Copy or Disk Compare

The Disk Utilities menu Disk Copy option lets you perform a floppy disk copy operation. Selecting this option will display the Diskcopy Utility dialog box, shown in Figure 39-4, prompting you to enter the source and target drives.

If your computer has matching floppy disk drives A and B, press ENTER to copy the contents of the floppy in drive A to drive B. If you need to perform a single-drive disk copy, type in the drive letter of the desired drive twice (such as **A: A:**), and press ENTER. The shell will invoke DISKCOPY, discussed in Chapter 12, "Fundamental Copy Operations."

The Disk Compare menu option displays a dialog box very similar to Figure 39-4, letting you compare the contents of two floppy disks. As with the Disk Copy, type the desired drive letters and press ENTER. The shell will invoke the DISKCOMP command, discussed in Chapter 30, "Another Look at Disks."

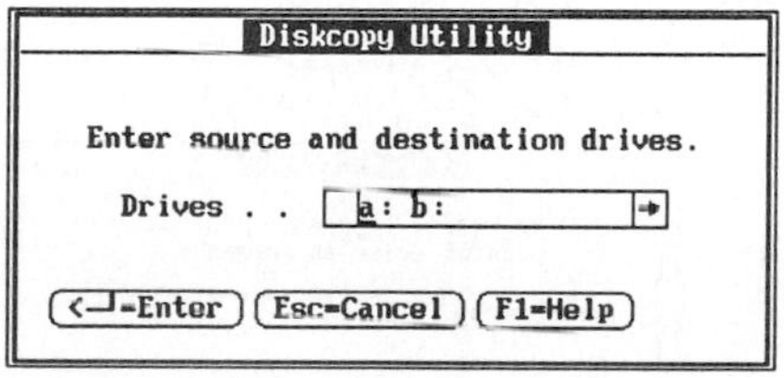

Figure 39-4.   The Diskcopy Utility dialog box for source and target drives

Performing a Backup or Restore Operation

The Disk Utilities menu Backup Fixed Disk option lets you back up the contents of your hard disk to floppy using the BACKUP command, discussed in Chapter 22, "Protecting Your Files with BACKUP and RESTORE." When you select this option, the shell will display the Backup Utility dialog box, asking you to enter the BACKUP command line.

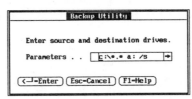

By default, the dialog box provides the command line you would use to perform a complete disk backup of drive C to floppy disk in drive A. To perform this backup, press ENTER, otherwise, change the command line as required. Chapter 40 teaches you how to add your own command to a group. At that time you might want to add an menu option that performs a daily backup.

The Restore Fixed Disk option uses the RESTORE command, discussed in Chapter 22, to restore your entire hard disk from floppies. When you select this option, the shell displays the Restore Utility dialog box, shown here:

```
┌──────────────────────────────────────┐
│          Restore Utility             │
│                                      │
│   Enter source and destination drive.│
│                                      │
│   Parameters . .  [a: c:\*.* /s  ▶]  │
│                                      │
│  (<─┘=Enter) (Esc=Cancel) (F1=Help)  │
└──────────────────────────────────────┘
```

By default, the Restore Utility dialog box provides a command line that completely restores the hard disk from the backup floppy disks in drive A. To restore only a specific file or set of files, change the command as appropriate and press ENTER.

Performing a Disk Format

The Disk Utilities menu Format option uses the FORMAT command discussed in Chapter 7, "Preparing Disks for Use," to format a disk for use by DOS. When you select this option, the shell displays the Format Utility dialog box, shown here:

```
┌──────────────────────────────────────┐
│          Format Utility              │
│                                      │
│        Enter drive to Format.        │
│                                      │
│   Parameters . .  [a:          ▶]    │
│                                      │
│  (<─┘=Enter) (Esc=Cancel) (F1=Help)  │
└──────────────────────────────────────┘
```

By default, the dialog box assumes you want to format the floppy disk in drive A. If you press ENTER, the shell will execute the FORMAT command. If you need to format a disk in a different drive, or need to use one or more of FORMAT's command-line switches, change the command line and press ENTER.

Canceling a Command

You can cancel each of the dialog boxes in the shell's DOS Utilities section by pressing ESC. Should you press ENTER to begin a command and decide you don't want the command to execute, press CTRL-BREAK. The shell will cancel the command, returning you to the DOS Utilities menu.

Using the Shell's Online Help

The shell provides a built-in help facility that explains different menu options and dialog boxes. For example, to display help text on the DOS Utilities group, highlight its menu option and press F1. The shell will display the online Help dialog box shown here:

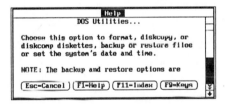

Using your keyboard arrow keys you can scroll through the help text. As you move through the text, the dialog box will move a slide that appears in the scroll box to the right of the box. By noting the slide's position, you can determine your relative location within the help text. If you are using a mouse, you can drag the slide up and down the scroll bar to scroll through the text. To drag the slide, aim the mouse pointer at the slide and press the mouse button. As you move the mouse, the slide will move. When the dialog box displays the desired text, release the mouse button.

To remove the help text, press ESC or click on the dialog box Cancel option. The F11 or Index option displays a list of topics covered by the online help. To display the index, click on the Index option using your mouse or press F11 (ALT-F1 if your keyboard does not have an F11 key). Next, scroll through the index until you find the desired topic, and press ENTER. F1 displays information about Help itself. F9 displays information about the shell's predefined keys.

Most of the shell menu options and dialog boxes provide online help that explain their processing. Get in the habit of using Help—you'll find it greatly increases your understanding of the shell.

Using the File System

The most powerful option in the Main Group menu is File System, which displays a directory tree of your disk and the files in the current directory, as shown in Figure 39-5.

The File System consists of four primary sections: a menu bar, available disk drive icons, the directory tree, and the file list. Using your keyboard's TAB key, you can quickly traverse from one section to the next. As in the shell's main menu, pressing F10 selects the menu bar. Pressing F3 or choosing the File menu Exit File System option returns control to the shell's main menu.

To select a different disk drive, click on the disk drive icon with your mouse; press CTRL and the letter of the desired drive; or select the drive icon section, highlight the drive with your arrow keys, and press ENTER. The shell will display the directory tree and files for the corresponding drive.

To change directories, click on the desired directory name, using the scroll bar to bring the directory name into view, if necessary. If you are using your keyboard, press TAB to select the directory tree and use the arrow keys to highlight the desired directory. When you press ENTER, the File System will display the files in the corresponding directory.

```
 05-19-91                    File System                 12:32 am
 File  Options  Arrange  Exit                           F1=Help
 Ctrl+letter selects a drive.
 ▣A  ▣B  ▢C

 A:\
      Directory Tree                          *.*
                                    ┌──────────────────────────────┐
 ✓A:\                               │ CHKDSK   .COM    17,787  10-06-88
                                    │ COMMAND  .COM    37,557  12-19-88
                                    │ DISKCOPY .COM    10,396  10-06-88
                                    │ DOSSHELL .BAT       179  05-18-91
                                    │ DOSUTIL  .MEU     6,660  10-06-88
                                    │ PCIBMDRV .MOS       263  10-06-88
                                    │ PRINT    .COM    14,131  10-06-88
                                    │ SHELL    .CLR     4,406  10-06-88
                                    │ SHELL    .HLP    66,527  10-06-88
                                    │ SHELL    .MEU     4,588  10-06-88
                                    │ SHELLB   .COM     3,894  10-06-88
                                    │ SHELLC   .EXE   153,055  10-06-88



 F10=Actions  Shift+F9=Command Prompt
```

Figure 39-5.   The File System window

Icon	Meaning
▤	Executable file: EXE, COM, or BAT
▨	Nonexecutable file

Table 39-2.   *File Icons Represent the Type of File*

Performing File Operations

If you examine the files in the file list, you will find the File system displays one of two kinds of icons next to the file name, depending on the file's type, as shown in Table 39-2.

The File System's File menu lets you copy, rename, move, delete, and change the attributes of one or more files. To use the File menu options, you must first select one or more files. To select a file, click on the file name with your mouse, press TAB to select the file list, or use the arrow keys to highlight a desired file and press the SPACEBAR. The File System will display the icon of each file you select using reverse video. To deselect a file, use the same process. Using the File menu Select All option you can quickly select all the files in a directory. Likewise, the Deselect All option cancels your current selections.

The File Systems Option menu File Options entry lets you enable file selections from multiple directories. Using this option, you can select several files from one directory, change directories, and select several more before performing the operation.

NOTE

If you invoke the File menu without first selecting a file, most of the menu options will appear dim, indicating they are unavailable.

Opening (Running) a File

The File menu Open option lets you run a command or batch file. To use the Open option, select an executable file (with the COM, EXE, or BAT extension). When you select Open, the File System will display a dialog box similar to the one shown here, letting you type in the program's command-line arguments.

```
┌──────────────────────────────────────────┐
│               ▐ Open File ▌               │
│                                           │
│  Starting program:  LABEL.COM             │
│                                           │
│  Associated file :                        │
│                                           │
│  Options. . [              ]  [→]         │
│                                           │
│                                           │
│   (<─┘=Enter) (Esc=Cancel) (F1=Help)      │
└──────────────────────────────────────────┘
```

If you highlight an executable file and press ENTER or double-click on an executable file with your mouse, the File System will automatically run the program, displaying the same dialog box. To cancel the program, press ESC or click on the dialog box Cancel option.

Printing One or More Files

If you select one or more files and the Print option still appears dim, you must exit the shell and invoke the PRINT command. Once PRINT is installed, you can use the Print option in the shell's File System. When you select the Print option, the File System will briefly display a dialog box informing you the file is either printing or being added to the print queue.

Associating a File Type with a Program

The File System lets you associate a file type (extension) with a specific program. Once you associate a file type with a program, the File System will automatically execute the program each time you double-click on a file with a corresponding extension, or highlight the file and press ENTER. For example, you might associate DOC extension files with your word processor.

To associate a program to a file type, select the desired program and choose the File menu Associate option. The File System will display a dialog box similar to the one shown below, which asks you for the file extensions to associate with the program.

```
┌──────────────────────────────────────────┐
│             ▐ Associate File ▌            │
│                                           │
│  Filename .  .:  WP.EXE        1 of   1   │
│                                           │
│  Extensions. . [DOC           ]  [→]      │
│                                           │
│                                           │
│                                           │
│   (<─┘=Enter) (Esc=Cancel) (F1=Help)      │
└──────────────────────────────────────────┘
```

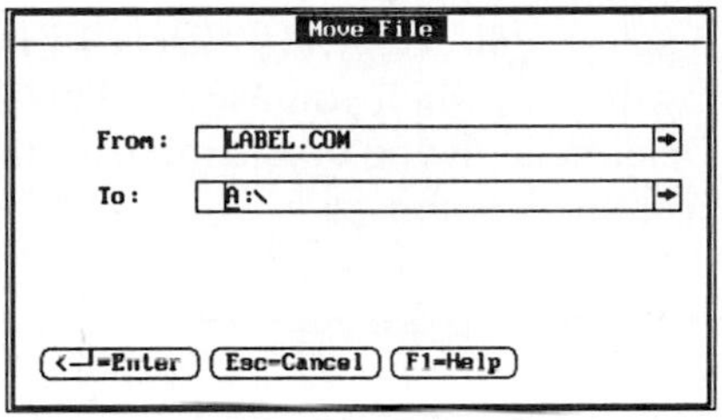

Figure 39-6. *The Move File dialog box*

Type in the three-letter extension that you want to associate with the program. If you want to associate multiple extensions, separate each extension with a space (up to 20 extensions).

Moving One or More Files

The File menu Move option lets you move one or more files from a directory to a different directory or disk drive. The Move option actually performs a copy operation followed by a delete. When you select the Move option, the File System will display a dialog box similar to the one shown in Figure 39-6, which prompts you for the target location. Type in the desired directory name or disk drive and press ENTER.

By default, the File System will not overwrite the contents of an existing file. If a file on the target disk matches the name of one of the files you are moving, the File System will display a dialog box asking you if you want to overwrite the existing file.

Copying One or More Files

The File menu Copy option lets you copy one or more files to a different drive or directory. Unlike the Move option, the files are copied and remain in the current directory. When you select the Copy option, the shell will display a dialog box very similar to Figure 39-6 that prompts you to type in the target drive or directory. As was the case with moving one or more files, the File System will not overwrite the contents of an existing file. If a file on the target disk matches the name of one of the files you are copying, the File System will display a dialog box asking you if you want to overwrite the existing file.

Deleting One or More Files

The File menu Delete option lets you delete the selected files or the current directory if no files are selected. To delete a directory, the directory must be empty, just as if you were using RMDIR. By default, when you use the File System to delete files, it automatically displays a Delete File dialog box, similar to the one shown here, for each selected file to confirm the deletion.

To delete the file whose name is displayed, select option 2. To leave the file on disk, select option 1.

Renaming One or More Files

The File menu Rename option lets you individually rename selected files or the current directory if no files are selected. When you select the Rename option, the File System will display a Rename File dialog box similar to the following, which prompts you for the desired name.

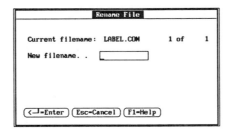

If you have selected several files, the File system will display this dialog box for each file. Like the RENAME command, the dialog box does not let you include a drive letter or directory in the new file name.

Changing One or More Files' Attributes

The File menu Change Attributes option lets you set or clear a file's Hidden, Read-only, and Archive attributes. When you select the Change Attributes option, the File System will first display a dialog box asking you if you want to change the file attributes all at once, or one file at a time. Next, the File System will display a Change Attribute dialog box, which prompts you to select the attributes desired.

To select an attribute, click on it with your mouse, or highlight the attribute and press the SPACEBAR. When you press ENTER or click on the Enter option, the File System will either update all the selected files, or only the current file, letting you select a different set of attributes for the next file.

Although hidden files do not appear in the DOS directory listing, the File System will display hidden files in its directory list.

NOTE

Viewing a File's Contents

Just as the TYPE command lets you view the contents of an ASCII file on your screen, the file menu View option lets you scroll through a file's contents. To use View, you must have one and only one file selected. When you select View, the File System will display the file's contents on your screen, letting you use the PGUP and PGDN keys to scroll through the file, as shown in Figure 39-7.

To view a file's hexadecimal and ASCII representation, press F9. View will display the hexadecimal values on the left side of your screen and the ASCII representation at the right. Press ESC to end the file viewing.

Creating a Directory

The File menu Create Directory option lets you create a directory within the current directory. When you select this option, the File System will display a Create Directory dialog box similar to the one shown here, which prompts you to enter the desired directory name.

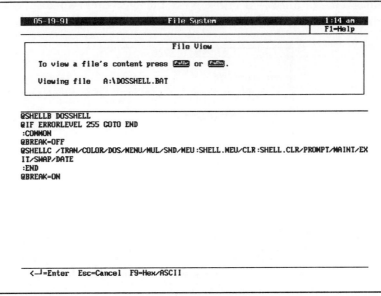

Figure 39-7.   *Displaying an ASCII file with File View*

Changing the Information the File System Displays

By default, the File System displays every file in the current directory, sorted by name. Using the Options menu Display Options entry you can change the types of files displayed as well as the sort order. When you select this option, the File System displays the Display Options dialog box shown here.

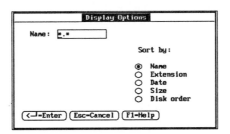

By changing the Name entry, you can change the file types displayed. For example, if you change the name to *.COM, the File System will display only those files with the COM extension. To change the sort order, click on the desired field with your mouse or press TAB and use your arrow keys to highlight the desired option.

Changing Confirmation Options

By default, the File System prompts you to confirm each file in a delete operation. Likewise, the File System asks you to confirm each move or copy operation that may overwrite an existing file. Using the Options menu File Options entry, you can disable these confirmations and enable file selections across multiple directories. When you select this option, the File System will display the File Options dialog box.

When an option's box contains an X, the option is selected. When the box is empty, the option is disabled. To select or disable an option, click on the options box with your mouse, or use your arrow keys to highlight it and press ENTER.

Arranging the Directory Tree

By default, the File System displays one directory tree and one file list. If you are performing file move or copy operations, it may be convenient to display both the source and target directories. Using the Arrange menu Multiple File List option, you can divide your screen in half to display two directory trees as shown in Figure 39-8.

When you display two directory trees, you can select different drives or directories within each tree by clicking on the drive or directory with your mouse or by pressing TAB to highlight the drive icons or directory tree desired, highlighting the desired drive or directory, and pressing ENTER.

The Arrange menu Single File List option restores the single directory tree and file list.

Last, the Arrange menu System File List option directs the File System to display the name of every file on your disk as a long alphabetized list. When you highlight a file, the File System will display specifics about the file and the directory containing the file and your disk, as shown in Figure 39-9.

Hands On

Using the DOSSHELL command, start the DOS 4 shell.

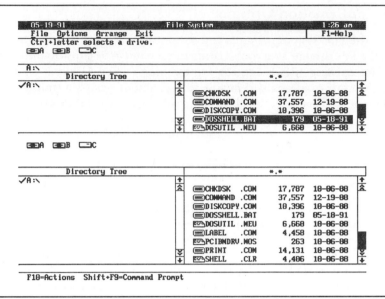

Figure 39-8.   *Displaying two directory trees and file lists*

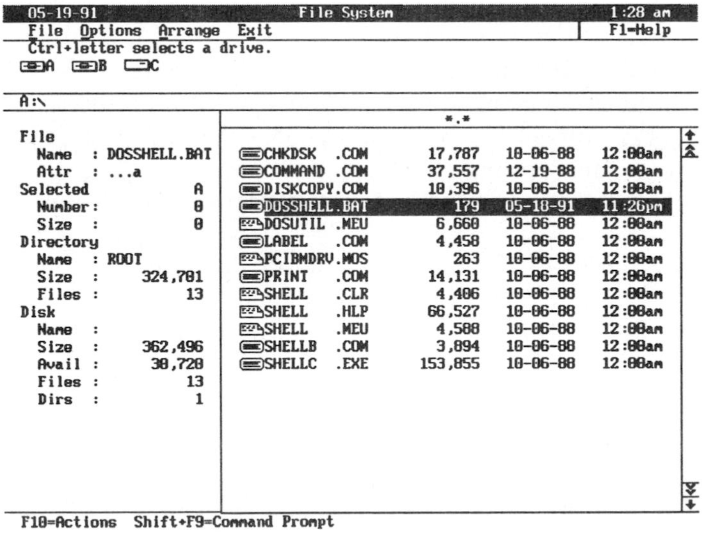

Figure 39-9.   *System File List information*

```
C:\> DOSSHELL   <ENTER>
```

Using your mouse or keyboard, select the Change Colors option and choose the color you find most appealing.

Next, select the Command Prompt option to temporarily exit the shell to DOS. At the DOS prompt, issue the DIR command.

```
C:\DOS> DIR   <ENTER>
```

Return to the shell using Exit.

```
C:\DOS> EXIT   <ENTER>
```

Select the DOS Utilities option and choose Set Date and Time. When the dialog box prompts you for the date and time, type in the correct date or time or press ENTER to leave the current settings unchanged. The shell will then invoke the DATE and TIME commands. After the commands complete, press ESC to return to the Main Group menu.

Select the File System option. Press the TAB key to advance from the menu bar to the disk drive icons, to the directory tree, to the file list, and back again. Using your mouse or keyboard, select the DOS directory. Select the file list and scroll through the DOS files. Next, select the root directory. Use your mouse or keyboard to select the file AUTOEXEC.BAT. Use the File menu View option to display the file's contents. Press ESC to end the viewing.

Select the Arrange menu and choose the System File List option. Use the arrow keys to examine the different files on your disk. Select the Arrange menu Multiple File List to view two directory trees. Select the root directory in the top tree and the DOS directory in the bottom.

Press F3 to return to the Main Group menu and F3 to exit the shell to DOS.

Review

1. What is a program group?

2. How does exiting the shell using F3 differ from exiting the shell using SHIFT-F9?

3. What is a dialog box?

4. How does a File System Move differ from a File System Copy?

5. What does it mean to associate a file type with a program?

Answers

1. A program group is a collection of related programs and commands, such as your business programs or DOS disk utility commands. Using program groups, you can organize your programs much as you would use a directory to organize files. When you want to run a program contained in the group, select the group and double-click on the program with your mouse, or highlight the program using your arrow keys and press ENTER.

2. F3 permanently exits the shell, removing the shell program from memory. You should use F3 at the end of the day to exit the shell before you turn off your computer. The SHIFT-F9 keyboard combination lets you temporarily exit the shell to the DOS prompt, leaving the shell program in memory. After you finish running the commands at the DOS prompt, you return to the shell by typing **EXIT** and pressing ENTER. The shell will resume right where you left off.

3. A dialog box is a framed region the shell displays prompting the user for a response. The dialog box may ask the user for the name of a file or for a simple yes or no response. The dialog box lets the shell communicate with the user, or carry on a dialog.

4. The move operation copies the selected files to the target directory, and if successful, deletes the files from the source. The copy operation on the other hand, copies the files to the target directory, leaving the original files in place on the source.

5. When you associate a file type (extension) with a program, the shell will automatically execute the program any time you select a file whose extension is associated with the program. Normally, the shell loads the selected file for use within the program. For example, you might associate files with the WKS extension to your spreadsheet.

Advanced Concepts

DOSSHELL is not a DOS command, but rather, a DOS batch file. If you place DOSSHELL in your AUTOEXEC.BAT file, make sure you place the command at the end of your batch file or use the CALL command to invoke it.

Switch	Function
/B	Specifies the size of the shell's File System buffer in Kb
/CLR	Specifies the file containing shell color selections, typically SHELL.CLR
/C01	Directs the shell to run in 16-color 640x350 EGA mode
/C02	Directs the shell to run in 2-color 640x480 VGA mode
/C03	Directs the shell to run in 16-color 640x480 VGA mode
/COLOR	Directs the shell to support the Change Colors menu option
/COM2	Informs the shell a serial mouse is connected to COM2, as opposed to COM1
/DATE	Directs the shell to display the system date and time
/DOS	Directs the shell to support the File System
/LF	Reverses the mouse select button from the left button to the right
/MAINT	Lets you change the menu structures and groups
/MENU	Directs the shell to support the Start Programs option. Without Start Programs, the shell automatically displays the File System
/MEU	Specifies the name of the file containing the Main Group menu options, typically SHELL.MEU
/MOS	Identifies the mouse device driver: PCMSDRV.MOS Microsoft serial mouse PCMSPDRV.MOS Microsoft parallel mouse PCIBMDRV.MOS IBM PS/2 mouse
/MUL	Directs the shell to use multiple File System buffers to improve performance
/PROMPT	Directs the shell to let you temporarily exit the shell to the DOS prompt
/SWAP	Directs the shell to save file and directory information to disk when it runs other programs, so it does not have to read the directory tree each time a command completes
/TRAN	Directs the shell to run in transient mode, only loading those sections of code it needs at this time, to make better use of memory
/TEXT	Directs the shell to run in text mode, as opposed to graphics

Table 39-3.   Shell Command-Line Switches

The following TYPE command displays a typical DOSSHELL.BAT file:

```
@C:
@CD C:\DOS
@SHELLB DOSSHELL
@IF ERRORLEVEL 255 GOTO END
:COMMON
@SHELLC /MOS:PCMSDRV.MOS/TRAN/COLOR/DOS/MENU/MUL
   /SND/MEU:SHELL.MEU/CLR:SHELL.CLR
:END
@BREAK=ON
```

The SHELLC command actually invokes the DOS shell program. The SHELLC command supports several switches. Table 39-3 briefly describes possible switches you may encounter.

Note the last command in the batch file shown enables extended CTRL-BREAK checking. For best system performance, remove the @BREAK ON command.

Key Terms

Click the mouse   To press and release the mouse button.

Double-click   To press and release the mouse button twice in quick succession.

Scroll bar   A vertical or horizontal bar, typically to the right or beneath a list or file, containing a small slide that moves along the bar as you scroll through the contents of your file. By dragging the slide with your mouse, you can quickly move to a specific location within the file or list.

Dialog box   A framed region on your screen within which a program displays one or more prompts for information from the user. The prompts may be for a file name, a yes or no response, or to select an item from a list. Dialog boxes give programs a uniform way to communicate with the user.

Chapter 40

Advanced DOS 4 Shell Techniques

In Chapter 39 you learned how to use the DOS 4 shell to run programs and how to use its File System to manage your files and directories. When you first start the shell, the Start Programs Main Group displays four command choices: Command Prompt, File System, Change Colors, and DOS Utilities. To make the best use of the shell, you will want to add other groups to this menu. In this chapter you'll learn not only how to create your own groups and how to add programs to each group, but also how to create dialog boxes that prompt the user for command-line inputs (while providing default values) and how to create online help for each program group you create.

Adding a Program to the Main Group

Initially, the Main Group contains three programs and the DOS Utilities group. If you have a program you use on a regular basis, you can add the program directly to the Main Group. For example, many users use the WordPerfect word processor. To add WordPerfect to the Main Group, select the Program menu, shown here.

Next, select the Add option. The shell will display the Add Program dialog box, shown in Figure 40-1.

"Title" is the menu title the shell displays in the group menu. The title can contain up to 40 characters. In the case of WordPerfect you might use the title "WordPerfect Version 5.1". "Command" is the command, or series of commands the shell should execute when the user selects this option. The command can contain up to 500 characters. If you want the shell to execute a series of commands, you must press F4 to separate each command. For example, to run WordPerfect, you might first issue a CHDIR command to change to a WordPerfect (WP) directory. To specify such a command, type **CD \WP**, press F4, and then type **WP**. Each time you press F4, the shell will display a double vertical line to indicate the command separation.

The Help Text option lets you specify up to 478 characters of online help information for the shell to display about the program when the user highlights the program entry and presses F1 for help. If you type in the text as sentences, the shell will automatically format the text to correctly display the text within a help dialog box. If you include one or more "at" signs (@), help will automatically perform a linefeed/carriage return each time it encounters the ampersand, letting you format the appearance of the help text.

Figure 40-1.   The Add Program dialog box

The Password option specifies a password of up to eight characters that the user must specify to use the program. If you don't correctly enter the password, you can't issue the program from within the shell. Don't rely on the password for security, however. In Chapter 39 you learned how to exit the shell using F3. By now you know how to locate program files within a directory and how to run the program from the DOS prompt, bypassing the shell. The password's primary usefulness is preventing another user from changing a group or program entry once you define it.

If you need to edit a previous dialog box field, click on the field with your mouse, or press TAB until the field is highlighted, then make your edits.

To add the program to the group press F2 or click on the Save option. The shell will display your program in its menu, as shown in Figure 40-2.

To run your new program, double-click on the program name with your mouse or use your arrow keys to highlight the program name and press ENTER. If you highlight the program and press F1, the shell will display your newly created online help.

Changing a Group Program Entry

There may be times after you add a program to a group when you need to change the program's entry, perhaps to add an additional command or to change the program's online help. To change an existing program entry, highlight the entry and select the Program menu Change option. The shell will display a dialog box very

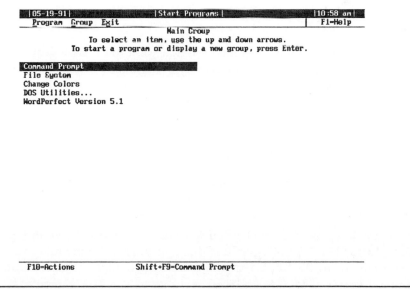

Figure 40-2. *WordPerfect added to the Main Group menu*

similar to the one shown in Figure 40-1 that lets you edit the entry. To edit a specific field, click on the field with your mouse or press TAB until the field is highlighted.

Removing a Program Name from a Group

Just as there will be times you add program names to a group, there may be times when you will want to remove a name. In the case of your WordPerfect entry, for example, you might want to combine the entry with several other programs, such as a spreadsheet, into a group called Business Programs. Using the Program menu Copy option, you can copy the WordPerfect program entry into the Business Programs group and then delete the entry.

To remove a program name from a group, highlight the program and select the Program menu Delete option. The shell will display the Delete Item dialog box shown here, asking you to confirm the program removal.

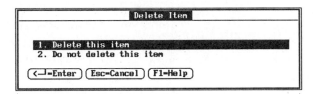

To delete the program select option 1 and press ENTER or click on the Enter option with your mouse.

Working with Groups

If you have several related programs, you may want to create a group to hold the programs, just as you would use a directory to organize your files. For example, to create a group named Business Programs, you would invoke the Group menu, shown here.

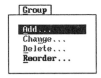

Select the Add option. The shell will display the dialog box shown in Figure 40-3.

As before, "Title" specifies the text that appears for the menu option. The title can contain up to 37 characters and should meaningfully explain the group's contents.

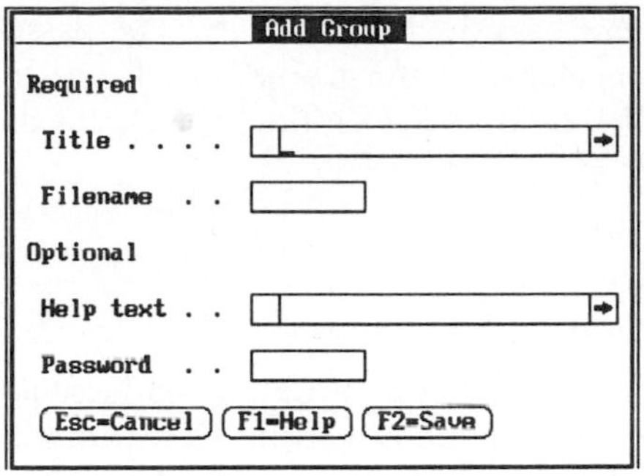

```
┌─────────────────[ Add Group ]─────────────────┐
│                                                │
│  Required                                      │
│                                                │
│   Title . . . .  ┌┌──────────────────────┐ →│ │
│                  └└──────────────────────┘    │
│                                                │
│   Filename  . .  ┌──────────────┐              │
│                  └──────────────┘              │
│  Optional                                      │
│                                                │
│   Help text . .  ┌┌──────────────────────┐ →│ │
│                  └└──────────────────────┘    │
│                                                │
│   Password  . .  ┌──────────────┐              │
│                  └──────────────┘              │
│   ┌ Esc=Cancel ┐ ┌ F1=Help ┐ ┌ F2=Save ┐      │
│   └────────────┘ └─────────┘ └─────────┘      │
└────────────────────────────────────────────────┘
```

Figure 40-3.   *The Add Group dialog box*

"Filename" specifies the eight-character file name within which the shell will store group information. In the case of your business programs, you could use the name BUSINESS. The shell automatically assigns the MEU extension to the file. The Help text lets you specify up to 478 characters of online help information for the shell to display in a dialog box when a user highlights the group and presses F1 for online help. The password entry specifies a password of up to eight characters that you

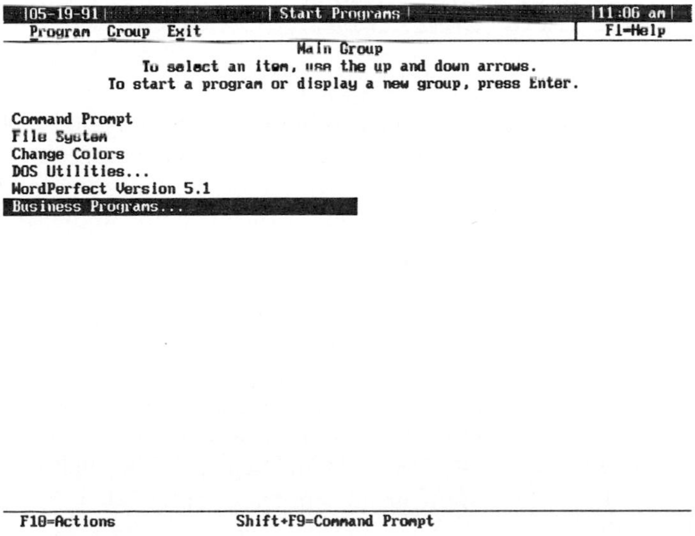

```
┌|05-19-91│──────────────│ Start Programs │─────────────│11:06 am │──┐
│ Program  Group  Exit                               │ F1=Help      │
│                          Main Group                                │
│            To select an item, use the up and down arrows.          │
│         To start a program or display a new group, press Enter.    │
│                                                                    │
│  Command Prompt                                                    │
│  File System                                                       │
│  Change Colors                                                     │
│  DOS Utilities...                                                  │
│  WordPerfect Version 5.1                                           │
│ █Business Programs...                                             █│
│                                                                    │
│                                                                    │
│  F10=Actions            Shift+F9=Command Prompt                    │
└────────────────────────────────────────────────────────────────────┘
```

Figure 40-4.   *Adding the Business Programs group*

must type before you can access the group. As discussed in the program entry section, do not rely on this password for security. The password is most useful to prevent another user from changing the group's characteristics or program entries. When you press F2 or click on the Save Option, the shell will add your new group, as shown in Figure 40-4.

Editing a Group

If you need to change a group's prompt or online help text after you add the group to the shell, highlight the group and select the Group menu Change option. The shell will display a dialog box similar to Figure 40-3 that lets you change the group's fields. To edit a field, click on the field with your mouse or press TAB until the field is highlighted. After your edit is complete, press F2 to save your changes.

Removing a Group

If you remove a set of programs from your disk, you will want to remove the corresponding group entry from the shell. To remove a group, highlight the group entry and select the Group menu Delete option. The shell will display the Delete Item dialog box, shown here, to confirm you really want to remove the group.

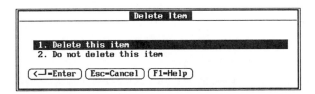

To delete this group, select option 1, otherwise select option 2. The shell will delete a group even when the group contains program entries.

In some cases, you may first want to copy one or more of the group's program entries to a different group before you remove the group from the shell menu.

Copying a Program Entry from One Group to Another

To copy a program entry from one group to another, select the group containing the entry and highlight the entry. Select the Program menu and select the Copy option. Next, select the group to which you want to copy the entry, displaying the group's current contents. Press F2 to perform the copy. The shell will display the program entry at the bottom of the group's previous entry list.

Rearranging Entries Within a Group

By default, the shell displays entries into the group in the same order as you originally added the entries. Ideally, you probably want your most frequently used entries at the top of the list. To move an entry to a new location, highlight the entry and select the Group menu Reorder option. Next, use your keyboard to highlight the desired location and press ENTER or click your mouse on the entry before which you want the selected entry placed. The shell will move the entry as desired. You can only move one entry at a time using this technique.

Hands On

Select the Group menu and choose the Add option. When the shell prompts you for a group title, type **Backup Operations**. Use the name BACKUP for the group file. For the help text, type in a few lines describing a complete system backup and a daily incremental backup, as discussed in Chapter 22. Do not include a password. Press F2 or click on the Save option to add the group.

Next, select the group. The shell will display the "Group is empty" message. Select the Program menu Add option. When the shell prompts you for a program title, use Daily Backup. For the command, use BACKUP C:*.* A:/S/A/M (as discussed in Chapter 22, "Protecting Your Files with BACKUP and RESTORE"). For the help text, describe an incremental backup to the floppy disk in drive A. Do not use a password. Press F2 or click on the Save option to add the program to the group.

Select the Program menu Add option again, this time creating an entry called Complete Disk Backup. Use the command BACKUP C:*.* A:/S. For the help text, discuss a complete disk backup operation. Do not specify a password. Press F2 or click on the Same option to add the program entry.

You can now perform daily or monthly backup operations from within the DOS shell. In the Advanced Concepts section, you will learn to create and display dialog boxes that prompt the user for command-line information.

Review

1. How can you distinguish a program entry from a group entry?

2. What information does the shell store in MEU files?

3. How do you direct the shell to perform a series of commands for a specific program entry?

4. When should you use a group entry as opposed to a program entry?

Answers

1. The shell indicates a group entry by displaying three periods (ellipses) to the right of the entry.

2. The shell stores the group's title, online help, password, and program entries within the group's MEU file.

3. Within the Add Program dialog box Command option, you can direct the shell to execute multiple commands for the program entry by typing a command name, pressing F4, and typing the next command. The F4 key is a command separator.

4. If you have a group of related programs you normally use together, such as a word processor, spell checker, and thesaurus, you should place the programs within their own group to better organize your menus.

Advanced Concepts

In Chapter 39, several of the program entries you selected displayed a dialog box requesting you to enter command-line information. When you add a program entry, the shell lets you use several predefined symbols within the entry's command box that result in a dialog box. Table 40-1 briefly describes each of these entries.

For example, assume you want to add the program entry View File, which prompts the user for a file name and displays the file's contents a screenful at a time using MORE. Your command line could use the following entries.

```
MORE < [/T"View a file" /I"Enter the name of the file to view"
  /P"File name:" /M"e"]
```

When the user selects your entry, the shell will display the dialog box shown here.

```
╔═══════════════════════════════════════╗
║              ▐ View a file ▌           ║
║                                        ║
║    Enter the name of the file to view  ║
║                                        ║
║     File name :[              ][→]     ║
║                                        ║
║  (<─┘=Enter) (Esc=Cancel) (F1=Help)    ║
╚═══════════════════════════════════════╝
```

When the user specifies an existing file name, MORE will display the file's contents. As soon as MORE completes, the shell redisplays the Group menu. The user may not have time to view the last screenful of information. To provide the

Entry	Function
/T"*Dialog box title*"	Specifies the text that appears in the dialog box title bar, up to 40 characters.
/I"*User instructions*"	Specifies text of up to 40 characters that appears below the title bar to assist the user.
/P"*Dialog box prompt*"	Specifies up to 20 characters of text as the dialog box prompt.
[%n]	Directs the dialog box to save user's response.
%n	Directs the dialog box to use a previously assigned parameter %1 through %10.
%D"*Default text*"	Specifies up to 40 characters of text to be the dialog box's default text.
%D"%n"	Directs the shell to use the value stored in a previously assigned parameter %1 through %10 as the default text.
/R	Directs the shell to remove the default text from the window when the user presses any key except an editing key.
/L"*length*"	Specifies the maximum number of characters.
/M"*e*"	Directs the shell only to accept a user response that specifies the name of an existing file.
/C"%n"	Directs the shell to save a parameter value %1 through %10 used in the previous command for use in this command.
/F"*path name*"	Directs the shell to ensure the file specified exists on disk. If the file does not exist, the shell sounds a bell and prompts user for a new file name.
/#	When used outside of brackets, directs shell to substitute /# with drive letter of the drive from which the shell was started.
/@	When used outside the brackets, directs the shell to substitute /@ with the path name from which the shell was started.

Table 40-1.   Shell Dialog Box Switches

user with a chance to view the output, use the F4 key to append the PAUSE command to your previous command line. When MORE completes, PAUSE will let you view the program's output, pressing any key to return to the Group menu.

In the Hands On section of this chapter, you created the Backup Operations group, placing within it program entries to perform a complete disk backup operation and an incremental backup. By creating a dialog box as just discussed, you might add a third program entry named Custom Backup that prompts the user for the files to back up with the following command.

```
BACKUP [/T"Custom Backup"/I"Enter the file to backup"
  /P"File name:" /M"e"] A:
```

Key Terms

Program group   A collection of related programs within the DOS shell.

Chapter 41

Using the DOS 5 Shell

Throughout this book, you have issued your commands from the DOS prompt or using DOS 5 batch files. Beginning with DOS 4, DOS introduced a graphical, menu-driven interface that lets you run programs or perform file operations by clicking on files with your mouse or by selecting menu options. Chapters 39 and 40 examined the DOS 4 shell in detail. This chapter gets you up and running with the DOS 5 shell. In Chapter 42 you will examine the shell's advanced features.

Starting the DOS 5 Shell

To start the DOS 5 shell, type DOSSHELL at the DOS prompt, just as you would execute any DOS command.

```
C:\> DOSSHELL <ENTER>
```

Many users place the DOSSHELL in their AUTOEXEC.BAT file to automatically start the shell each time their system boots. The shell displays the screen shown in Figure 41-1.

If your computer has a mouse, the DOS 5 shell lets you use the mouse to select files and programs. Before you invoke the shell, however, you must first install the mouse device driver that accompanied your mouse on floppy disk. Depending on your mouse driver, you may need to use a CONFIG.SYS DEVICE entry (for a driver

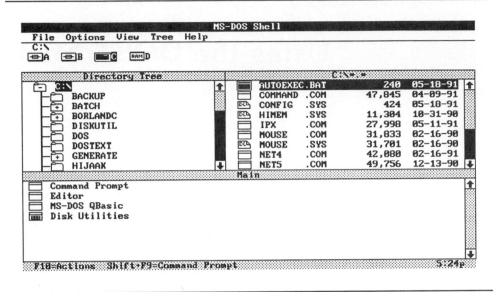

Figure 41-1.   The DOS 5 shell interface

such as MOUSE.SYS) or invoke a memory-resident program from within your AUTOEXEC.BAT file (for a program such as MOUSE.COM).

The DOS shell consists of several parts. The title bar appears at the top of your screen and contains the words "MS-DOS Shell." Immediately below the title is the menu bar, which contains the File, Options, View, Tree, and Help options. To activate a specific menu, click on the menu using your mouse, press F10 to select the menu bar, and type the letter of the desired menu option that appears underlined; you can also hold down ALT and type the first letter of the menu you desire. When you select a menu, the shell will display a pull-down menu as shown in Figure 41-2.

To select a menu option, click on the option with your mouse, type the letter appearing underlined in the option name or use the arrow keys to highlight the option and press ENTER. If a menu option appears dim, the option is not currently available. If the option is followed by three periods (called ellipses), the shell will display a dialog box when you select the option to request additional information. Several menu options work as toggles, meaning the first time you select the option, the shell enables an operation, and the second time you select the option, the shell disables the operation. For such options, the shell will display a diamond next to the option name when the operation is enabled. Several menus may display a key or key combination to the right of an option. These keys represent the option's hot key. You can press the combination to select the option without having to traverse the menu. If you choose not to select a menu option, press ESC or click the mouse outside of the menu.

```
File
┌─────────────────────────────┐
│ Open                        │
│ Run...                      │
│ Print                       │
│ Associate...                │
│ Search...                   │
│ View File Contents    F9    │
│                             │
│ Move...                F7   │
│ Copy...                F8   │
│ Delete...              Del  │
│ Rename...                   │
│ Change Attributes...        │
│                             │
│ Create Directory...         │
│                             │
│ Select All                  │
│ Deselect All                │
│                             │
│ Exit                 Alt+F4 │
└─────────────────────────────┘
```

Figure 41-2.   *The File menu*

The disk drive icons correspond to the drives from which the shell can access files or run programs. Depending on your computer's disk types, you may have one or more of the disk drive icons shown in Table 41-1.

To change drives, you can click on the desired icon with your mouse, hold down CTRL, and press the letter corresponding to the desired drive or repeatedly press TAB until the disk icons are selected and use your arrow keys to highlight the drive you desire and press ENTER.

The directory tree contains a graphical representation of the directory tree for the current disk. Using your mouse or keyboard arrow keys, you can select the

Icon	Disk Drive Type
▭A	Floppy disk drive
▭C	Hard disk drive
RAM D	RAM drive
NET F	Network drive

Table 41-1.   *The Disk Drive Icons*

current directory by selecting it from the directory tree. The File List displays the names of files that reside in the current directory. As you change directories, the shell updates the list of files. Using your mouse or keyboard arrow keys, you can select one or more files for file operations such as copying, deleting or renaming, or you can even run a program that appears in the list. Depending on the file's type, the shell will display one of the file icons listed in Table 41-2.

If you examine the directory tree and File List, you will find a vertical bar to the right of each called a scroll bar. If you traverse either list with your keyboard's arrow keys, a small slide will move up and down within the list indicating your relative position. If the slide is near the top of the scroll bar, you are near the top of the list. If the slide is near the bottom of the scroll bar, you are near the end of the list. If you are using a mouse, you can drag the slide up and down the scroll bar to traverse the list. To drag the slide, aim your mouse pointer at the slide and press the mouse button. With the button depressed, move your mouse to drag the slide. When the slide is in the desired position, release the mouse button.

The Main Group area contains program groups or programs you can execute by double-clicking on the program name or highlighting the name with your arrow keys and pressing ENTER. In Chapter 42, "Advanced DOS 5 Shell Techniques," you will learn how to add your own programs to the Main Group.

At the bottom of your screen the shell displays a status bar that defines commonly used key definitions and displays the current system time.

If you are using a mouse, you can click directly on disk icons, directories, file names, or programs within the Main Group. If you are using your keyboard, you can press TAB to move from one area on the screen to another, and then use your arrow keys to highlight the object, pressing ENTER to select it. If you need to move in the opposite direction, press SHIFT-TAB.

Displaying the Shell in Graphics Mode

If your monitor supports graphics but your shell does not match the shell displayed in the book, you are very likely running the shell in text mode. To select graphics mode, select the shell Options menu and choose the Display option. The shell will

Icon	File Type
⊟	Executable EXE, COM, or BAT file
🖻	Nonexecutable file

Table 41-2.   The File Icons

display a list of different video display options. Highlight the graphics mode option that best fits your monitor and press ENTER.

Working with Directory Trees

By default, the shell only displays the first level of your directory tree, in other words, the directories whose names appear within the root directory. If you examine the icons that appear next to the directory names, you will find some icons contain a plus sign, some a minus sign, and some are blank. The directories whose icon is blank do not contain additional directories. The directories whose icons contain a plus sign have additional levels of directories that are not currently displayed. A directory whose icon contains a minus sign has all of its next level directories visible.

Using your mouse or keyboard, you can select a directory and *expand* (make visible) or *collapse* (remove from view) one or more levels of directories beneath the directory.

Expanding the Next Level of Directories

The shell provides you with several ways to expand a directory to its next level of directories. First, you can click on the plus sign that appears in the directory's icon with your mouse. If you are with your keyboard, use your arrow keys to highlight the directory and press the plus sign or invoke the Tree menu and select the Expand One Level option. Note the plus sign to the right of the option indicating the option's hot key.

Expanding a Directory's Tree

To expand all the directories beneath a directory, click on the directory name with your mouse or use your arrow keys to select the directory. Next, type an asterisk (*). To expand your entire directory tree, you can select the root directory and type * or you can press the CTRL-* key combination, regardless of the current directory.

Collapsing a Directory's Branches

To collapse the branches beneath a directory, click on the minus sign that appears in the directory's icon or highlight the entry with your arrow keys and press the minus sign. The minus sign is the hot key corresponding to the Tree menu Collapse Branch option.

Exiting the DOS Shell

There are two ways to exit the DOS shell. First, if you are done using the shell and want to return to the DOS prompt, you can press ALT-F4 or select the File menu and choose the Exit option. DOS will remove the shell from memory. To use the shell again, you must reissue the DOSSHELL command.

At other times, you may only want to temporarily exit the shell to issue one or two DOS commands. Because you may have several programs active, each of which has open files, ending each program to quit the shell, only to restart the shell later, would be inconvenient and frustrating. Using SHIFT-F9, you can temporarily exit the shell to DOS, leaving your active programs unchanged. When you press this key combination, the shell will display the DOS prompt letting you issue commands. After you issue your last command, type EXIT to return to the shell.

```
C:\DOS> EXIT    <ENTER>
```

The shell will redisplay its screen, letting you resume your work right where you left off.

WARNING

Never turn off your computer or restart DOS when you have only temporarily exited the shell to DOS. If you have programs active within the shell with open files, changes to the files will be lost. As a rule, always exit permanently the shell to DOS using ALT-F4 before turning your computer off.

If while you have temporarily exited the shell to DOS, you created directories or files, your changes may not appear in the directory tree or File List when you later return to the shell. To update the directory list, select the desired directory and press CTRL-F5.

Working with Files

The shell File menu provides a series of options that let you print, move, copy, delete, or rename selected files. Before you can use these options, you must first select one or more files.

Selecting Files

Several file commands such as copy, print, or delete let you work with one or more files. To select one file with your mouse, click on the file name. To select one file with your keyboard, highlight the file's name with your arrow keys. Using either technique, the shell will display the selected file's icon in reverse video. If you inadvertently select the wrong file, click on the correct file or highlight the correct file with your keyboard arrow keys.

To select two or more files, the steps you must perform differ, depending on whether the files are a consecutive group or dispersed throughout the File List. To select a group of consecutive files with your mouse, click on the name of the first file in the list. Hold down SHIFT and click on the name of the last file in the list. The shell will display the entire group of files in reverse video. To select a group of consecutive files with your keyboard, use the arrow keys to highlight the first file in the group. Hold down SHIFT and use the arrow keys to highlight remaining files in the group.

To select two or more files that aren't consecutive, hold down CTRL while you click on each file. To select the files with your keyboard, use the arrow keys to select the first file you desire. Press SHIFT-F8. The shell will display the word "Add" in the status bar next to the current time. Use the arrow keys to highlight the second file desired. Press SPACEBAR to select the file. Repeat these steps to highlight and select the desired files. After all files are selected, press SHIFT-F8 again.

If you want to select all the files in the current directory, you can use the File menu Select All option. Likewise, to cancel your file selections, select the File menu and choose the Deselect All option.

Selecting Files from Different Directories

There may be times when you want to copy, move, or delete files that reside in different directories. By default, the shell only lets you select files from one directory at a time. Using the Options menu Select Across Directories option, you can enable and disable the selection of files from within one of several directories. When you enable this option you can select one or more files from the current directory, change directories, and then follow the procedure for selecting two or more nonconsecutive files. When the option is enabled, the shell displays a diamond next to the option name. When the option is disabled, the diamond is not displayed.

Running Programs

The shell provides several ways for you to run application programs and DOS commands. First, you can highlight a COM, EXE, or BAT file within the File List and press ENTER to execute the file. If you are using a mouse, you can double-click on the file name. Second, the shell lets you associate a file type (extension) with a specific program. For example, you might associate files with the DOC extension to your word processor. When you highlight an associated file and press ENTER or double-click on the file name, DOS will execute the associated program, loading the data file specified. The File menu Open option lets you run a highlighted program or the program associated with a highlighted file.

The File menu Run option lets you type in a command, just as you would from the DOS prompt. When you select the Run option the shell will display the Run dialog box.

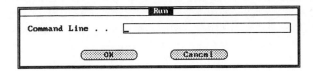

Type in the command name and its command-line arguments. The shell will run the command, displaying the command's output on its own screen. When the command completes, the shell will prompt you to press any key to continue before redisplaying the shell screen.

Last, as discussed later in this chapter, the shell lets you run programs by selecting the program from the Main Group that appears at the bottom of your screen.

Printing One or More Files

The File menu Print option lets you print one or more selected files. When you select this option, the shell will briefly display a dialog box informing you it has queued the files for printing. Before you can use the shell's Print option, you must first run the PRINT command, as discussed in Chapter 14, "Getting the Most from Print." If you have not yet run PRINT and you select the Print option, the shell will display the following dialog box telling you PRINT.COM has not been loaded and the files cannot print.

If this dialog box appears, exit the shell and invoke the PRINT command, as discussed in Chapter 14.

Associating a Program with a File Type

The shell lets you associate a file with a program. For example, you might associate TXT files with the DOS editor. When you later select the file, the shell will automatically run the associated program, loading the selected file. To associate a file type to a program, select a file of the desired type and invoke the File menu choosing the Associate option. The shell will display the dialog box shown in Figure 41-3, prompting you to type in the program name to which you want the files associated. Type in the complete path name to the program and press ENTER.

To remove an association at a later time, follow the same steps, removing the program name from the dialog box. If you select the program from which you want to dissociate files and then select the File menu Associate option, the shell will display a dialog box similar to the one in Figure 41-3, but that prompts you to enter the file type (extension) you want to dissociate from the program.

Searching Your Disk for Specific Files

If you misplace a file on your disk, you can use the File menu Search option to quickly locate it. When you select this option, the shell displays the Search File dialog box, prompting you to type in the name of the file to locate.

```
┌══════════════ Search File ══════════════┐
│                                          │
│ Current Directory is C:\                 │
│                                          │
│ Search for. .  [*.*        ]             │
│                                          │
│          [X] Search entire disk          │
│                                          │
│                                          │
│   ( OK )      ( Cancel )     ( Help )     │
└══════════════════════════════════════════┘
```

Type in the name of the desired file. The search operation fully supports the DOS wildcards. When you press ENTER or click on the OK option, the shell will begin searching your disk for matching files. If the search operation is successful, the shell will display the directory path to each matching file, as shown in Figure 41-4. From this matching list you can select one or more files for a file operation or to run a program. To return to the shell, press ESC.

```
┌══════════════ Associate File ══════════════┐
│                                             │
│  '.DOC' files are associated with:          │
│                                             │
│  [                                        ] │
│                                             │
│                                             │
│                                             │
│   ( OK )      ( Cancel )     ( Help )        │
└═════════════════════════════════════════════┘
```

Figure 41-3.   The Associate File dialog box

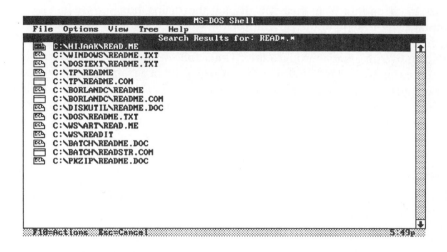

Figure 41-4.   Search File's list of matching files

Viewing a File's Contents

In Chapter 8, "Fundamental File Operations," you learned that the TYPE command lets you display an ASCII file's contents to your screen. Within the shell, you can use the File menu View File Contents option to page through a file. You can select one and only one file for display using the View option. When you select this option, the shell uses the full screen to display the file's contents, as shown in Figure 41-5. If the file is long, you can use PGUP and PGDN to traverse the file.

In addition to displaying a file's ASCII representation, the View option lets you examine the file's contents in its hexadecimal representation, displaying the hexadecimal values on the left side of the screen and the ASCII equivalents on the right. To switch between ASCII and hexadecimal display, select the Display menu ASCII and Hex options. To return to the shell, press ESC.

The View File Contents option will not let you change the file. To edit a file use the DOS editor or your word processor.

Moving One or More Files

The File menu Move option lets you move one or more selected files from one drive or directory to another. When you select the Move option, the shell will display the following dialog box, letting you view the names of the selected files and possibly add more, and prompting you to type in the target drive or directory.

```
┌───────────────────────■ Move File ■───────────────────────┐
│                                                            │
│                                                            │
│     From:   │PACKING.LST                              │    │
│                                                            │
│     To:     │C:\DOS_                                   │    │
│                                                            │
│                                                            │
│                                                            │
│          (  OK  )      ( Cancel )      ( Help )            │
│                                                            │
└────────────────────────────────────────────────────────────┘
```

To add or delete files to or from the list, click on the From box with your mouse or press TAB to highlight the box. Edit the file names as desired. Next, type in the name of the target drive or directory and press ENTER or click on the OK option with your mouse.

The shell will first copy the files to the new location and then delete the files. If the move operation will overwrite an existing file, the shell, by default, will display a dialog box similar to the one in Figure 41-6 asking you if you want to replace (overwrite) the existing file.

To replace the file click on the Yes option. To leave the existing file unchanged, click on the No option or press TAB to select No and press ENTER. To end the move operation, select Cancel.

```
┌──────────────────── MS-DOS Shell - PACKING.LST ────────────────────┐
  Display  View  Help
 ┌─ To view file's content use PgUp or PgDn or ↑ or ↓. ─────────────┐
 └──────────────────────────────────────────────────────────────────┘
Upgrade 360KB Distribution Disk Layout

DISK 1

autoexec.bat
command.co_
ega.sy_
format.co_
hdbkup.exe
io.sy_
msdos.sy_
setup.exe
setup.ini
uninstal.ex_
readme.1st


DISK 2
░░<→↑=PageDown░░Esc=Cancel░░F9=Hex/ASCII░░░░░░░░░░░░░░░░░░░░░░5:52p░░
```

Figure 41-5.   Viewing an ASCII file

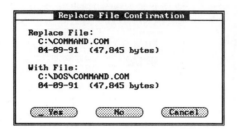

Figure 41-6.   The Replace File Confirmation dialog box

Copying One or More Files

The File menu Copy option lets you copy one or more selected files from one disk or directory to another. When you invoke the Copy operation, the shell will display a Copy File dialog box similar to the one shown here, which prompts you to type in the target drive or directory.

```
┌──────────────────── Copy File ────────────────────┐
│                                                    │
│                                                    │
│     From:   COMMAND.COM                            │
│                                                    │
│     To:     C:\DOS                                 │
│                                                    │
│                                                    │
│                                                    │
│       ( OK )        ( Cancel )        ( Help )     │
└────────────────────────────────────────────────────┘
```

As discussed in the Move File section, the shell lets you edit the names of the files selected for copying. Type in the target drive or directory and press ENTER or click on the OK option. If a selected file will overwrite an existing file on the Target drive or directory, the shell will display a dialog box similar to Figure 41-6 that asks you if you want to replace (overwrite) the existing file. As discussed in the Move File section, select Yes to overwrite the file, No to leave the existing file unchanged, and Cancel to end the Copy operation.

Moving or Copying Files by Dragging with the Mouse

In addition to using the File menu Copy and Move options, the shell lets you copy or move selected files to a different drive or directory by dragging the files with your mouse. To perform a copy, select the desired files and hold down your mouse select button, dragging the files on to the disk drive icon or target directory you desire. When you release the mouse button, the shell will display a dialog box asking you to confirm the file copy. To move one or more selected files, perform the same steps as above, but hold down ALT while you drag the files. When you release the mouse button, the shell will display a dialog box asking you to confirm the file move.

Deleting Files or Directories

The File menu Delete option lets you delete one or more selected files or remove an empty directory, similar to RMDIR. To remove an empty directory, select the directory within the directory tree and select the File menu Delete option. The shell will display a Delete Directory dialog box similar to one shown here, asking you to confirm the directory removal.

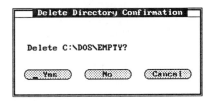

To remove the directory select Yes. To leave the directory on disk select No. Select Cancel to end the operation.

If you have selected more than one file for deletion, the shell will display a Delete File dialog box similar to the one shown here, letting you edit the list of selected files before beginning the delete operation.

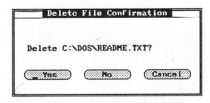

Select OK to continue the delete operation. By default, the shell will individually prompt you to confirm that you want to delete each selected file by displaying a Delete File Confirmation dialog box similar to the one shown here.

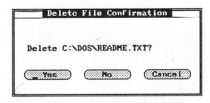

To delete the file, select Yes. To leave the file on disk, select No. If you have selected multiple files, you can end the delete operation by selecting Cancel.

Renaming One or More Files

The File menu Rename option lets you rename one or more selected files. When you select the Rename option, the shell will display a dialog box similar to the one shown here, prompting you for the desired file name.

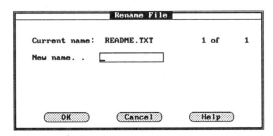

Type in the new file name you desire. Like the RENAME command, the shell's Rename option does not let you include a drive letter or directory path in the new file name. If you have selected several files to rename, the shell will repeat this dialog box for each file. If you look in the upper-right corner of the dialog box, you will find a count that tells you how many files you have renamed and how many files were originally selected.

Changing Attributes of One or More Files

Just as the ATTRIB command lets you set or clear a file's archive, read-only, hidden, and system attributes, so too will the File menu Change Attributes command. When you have selected several files and you choose this option, the shell will first display a dialog box as shown in Figure 41-7 asking you if you want to set attributes for selected files on an individual basis or if you want to set the attributes of all files at once.

Select option 1 or 2 as you desire. If you select option 2 to set all the files' attributes at one time, the shell will display the following dialog box that lets you select the attributes you desire.

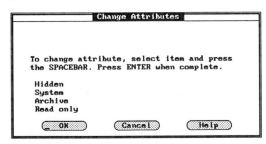

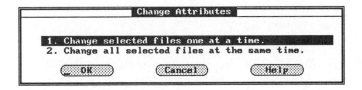

Figure 41-7.   *The Change Attributes dialog box*

To select or remove an attribute, click on the attribute with your mouse or highlight the attribute and press SPACEBAR. The shell will display a triangle to the left of attributes it will set and nothing to the left of attributes it will clear. Select OK to assign the attributes.

If you want to individually set each file's attributes, the shell will display a dialog box similar to the one shown in Figure 41-7, but containing a file name. Select the attributes desired and select OK to assign them. The shell will display the dialog box for each of the remaining files.

Creating a Directory

The File menu Delete option lets you remove empty directories from your disk. To add a directory, select the directory within which you want the new directory. Next, select the File menu and choose the Create Directory option. The shell will display a Create Directory dialog box similar to the one shown here, which displays the current directory and prompts you for the desired directory name.

```
╔═══════════════ Create Directory ═══════════════╗
║                                                 ║
║   Parent name: C:\DOS                           ║
║                                                 ║
║   New directory name. .  [           ]          ║
║                                                 ║
║                                                 ║
║        ( OK )      ( Cancel )     ( Help )       ║
╚═════════════════════════════════════════════════╝
```

Type in the directory name desired. Like the MKDIR command, the Create Directory option won't let you create a directory whose name matches an existing file or directory name.

Changing the Number and Order of Files Displayed

By default, the shell displays the name of every file in the directory. If you are primarily interested in files of a specific type, such as TXT or DOC files, select the Options menu and choose File Display Options. The shell will display a dialog box similar to the one shown here.

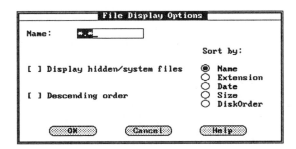

"Name" lets you type in the wildcard specification for the file type you want displayed. "Display hidden/system files" directs the shell to display files in the Files List whose system or hidden attribute is set. By default, the shell does not display these files. To enable the display of hidden and system files, click on the option box with your mouse or press TAB to select the option and SPACEBAR to set or clear the option. "Descending order" directs the shell to display the files sorted from highest to lowest. If the option is clear, the shell uses ascending order. If the option contains an X, the shell uses descending. "Sort by:" specifies the field by which the shell sorts the files. To select a field, click on the field with your mouse or press TAB to highlight the option with your arrow keys to select the desired field.

Enabling and Disabling Confirmation Dialog Boxes

By default, each time you delete a file, attempt to overwrite an existing file, or drag the mouse to move or copy a file, the shell displays a dialog box to confirm that you really want to perform the operation. Although these confirmations may prevent you from accidentally losing file information, they may slow down an experienced user who is very comfortable working with the shell. Using the Options menu Confirmation option, you can enable and disable these confirmation options. When you select this option, the shell displays the following dialog box.

The options whose boxes contain an X are enabled. To enable or disable an option, click on the option with your mouse or use your arrow keys to highlight the option and press SPACEBAR. Table 41-3 briefly describes each confirmation option.

Displaying File Specifics

The Options menu Show Information option directs the shell to display specifics about the currently selected file, the number of selected files, the current directory, and disk drive. When you select this option, the shell will display a dialog box similar to Figure 41-8.

"Name" specifies the last file selected. "Attr" specifies the file's attributes, where "a" corresponds to the archive attribute, "r" to read-only, "h" to hidden, and "s" to system. "Selected" specifies the disk drive from which you have selected the files, the number of files, and their combined size. Using this value you can determine if a target disk has enough space to hold the selected files prior to a copy or move operation. If you have selected files from two disks, the shell will display a two-column summary. "Directory" specifies the name of the current directory, the number of files the directory contains, and their total size. "Disk" specifies the volume label for the current disk, the size of the disk, the available disk space, and the number of files and directories.

Option	Confirmation
Confirm on Delete	Individually confirms each file deletion
Confirm on Replace	Confirms a move or copy operation that overwrites an existing file
Confirm on Mouse Operation	Confirms move or copy operations performed by a mouse drag

Table 41-3.   The Shell Confirmation Options

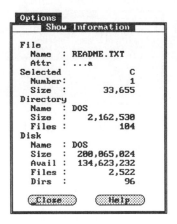

Figure 41-8.   *The Show Information dialog box*

Changing the Shell Display

By default, the shell displays a single directory tree and File List. If you are copying or moving files from one disk or directory to another, you may want to display two directory trees and File Lists. To do so, select the View menu Dual File Lists option. The shell will divide the screen in half, displaying two sets of disk drive icons, two directory trees, and two File Lists. Using the same steps you have used with one directory tree and File List, you can display two directory trees for the same disk or a different disk, as shown in Figure 41-9.

The View menu Single File List option directs the shell to use the entire screen for a single directory tree and File List, removing the Program List, as shown in Figure 41-10.

The View menu All Files option directs the shell to display an alphabetized listing of every file on your disk, displaying the specifics about the current file you would see if you selected the Options menu Show Information option previously discussed. Figure 41-11 illustrates the All Files option.

The View menu Program List option directs the shell to remove the directory tree and File List, expanding the Program List to full screen, as shown in Figure 41-12.

Last, the View menu Program/FILE LISTs menu directs the shell to restore its normal single directory tree, File List display with the Program List at the bottom of the display.

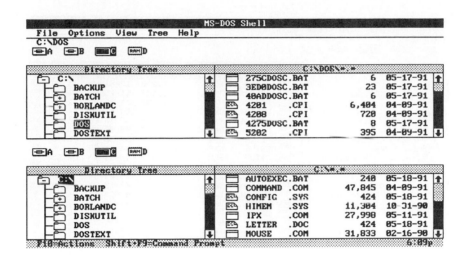

Figure 41-9.   *Viewing dual File Lists*

Figure 41-10.   *Viewing a single File List*

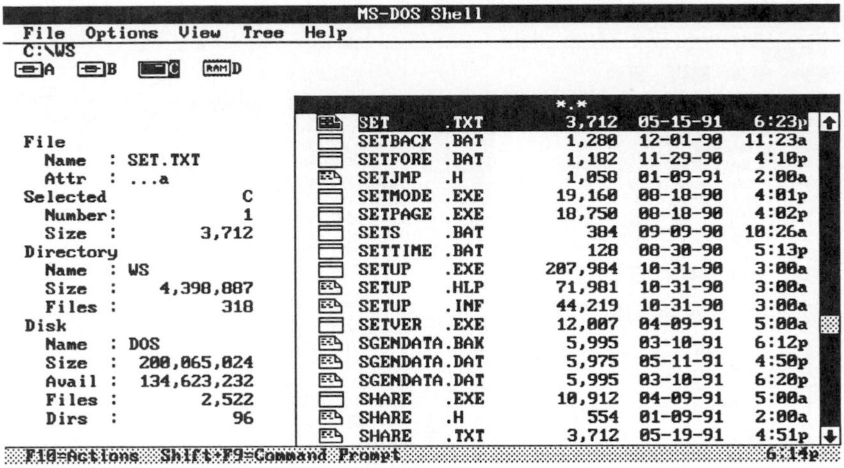

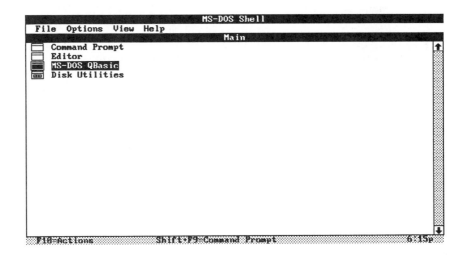

Figure 41-11.   *Viewing all the files on your disk*

Figure 41-12.   *Full-screen Program-List display*

Running Programs from the Program List

The Program List is a collection of programs and groups of programs (similar to a directory) from which you can quickly execute your commonly used commands. The shell provides three program entries and the Disk Utilities program group. In Chapter 42 you will learn how to add your own programs to this group.

To execute a program from within the Program List, you can double-click on the program or use your keyboard to highlight the program, pressing ENTER to execute it. The Command Prompt entry lets you temporarily exit the shell to DOS, as previously discussed. To return to the shell, you must issue the EXIT command. The Editor option invokes EDIT, the DOS full-screen editor discussed in Chapter 37. Likewise, the MS-DOS QBasic option invokes Microsoft's new QBasic interpreter, which lets you create and run your own programs written in BASIC. For more information on QBasic, turn to the Osborne/McGraw-Hill book *QBasic Made Easy*, 1991, by Don Inman and Bob Albrecht.

The Disk Utilities group is the most interesting menu option. You can distinguish a group entry from a program entry within the group using the icons shown in Table 41-4.

When you select the Disk Utilities group, the shell displays the following dialog box.

Copying a Disk

The Disk Utilities group Disk Copy option directs the shell to copy the contents of one floppy disk to another. When you select this option, the shell will display a Disk Copy dialog box similar to the following, prompting you to enter the source and target disk drives.

Icon	Entry Type
☐	Program Entry
▦	Program Group

Table 41-4.   The Program Icons

```
┌─────────────────────────────────────────────┐
│              ▐ Disk Copy ▌                    │
│  Enter the source and destination drives.     │
│                                               │
│  Parameters . . .    ▐a: b:▌                  │
│      ( OK )        ( Cancel )      ( Help )    │
└─────────────────────────────────────────────┘
```

If your system has two matching floppy drives, press ENTER to select the drive A and B defaults. If you need to perform a single drive operation, type in the same source and target drive letters (such as A: A:). When you press ENTER or click on the OK option, the shell will invoke the DISKCOPY command, as discussed in Chapter 12, "Fundamental Copy Operations."

Backing Up a Disk

The Disk Utilities Backup Fixed Disk option performs a complete backup of your hard disk, as discussed in Chapter 22, "Protecting Your Files with BACKUP and RESTORE." When you select this option, the shell will display the following dialog box, displaying the BACKUP command line.

```
┌─────────────────────────────────────────────┐
│            ▐ Backup Fixed Disk ▌              │
│  Enter the source and destination drives.     │
│                                               │
│  Parameters . . .    ▐c:\*.* a: /s▌           │
│      ( OK )        ( Cancel )      ( Help )    │
└─────────────────────────────────────────────┘
```

To back up your entire disk to floppies in drive A, press ENTER or click on the OK option. To perform an incremental backup operation or to select a different set of files, change the command line, as discussed in Chapter 22.

Restoring Fixed Disk Files

Just as the Backup Fixed Disk option performs a backup of your hard disk, the Restore Fixed Disk option lets you restore hard disk files from backup floppies. When you select this option, the shell displays the following dialog box that prompts you for the files to restore.

```
┌─────────────────────────────────────────────┐
│            ▐ Restore Fixed Disk ▌            │
│  Enter the source and destination drives.     │
│                                               │
│  Parameters . . .    ▐         ▌              │
│      ( OK )        ( Cancel )      ( Help )    │
└─────────────────────────────────────────────┘
```

Type in the RESTORE box's command line to restore from the backup floppies the files you desire, as discussed in Chapter 22.

Formatting a Disk

The Disk Utilities Quick Format and Format options let you format a disk for use by DOS. When you select the Quick Format option, the shell displays the following Quick Format dialog box that prompts you to enter the drive to quick format.

```
┌─────────────────────[ Quick Format ]─────────────────────┐
│                                                           │
│   Enter the drive to quick format.                        │
│                                                           │
│   Parameters . . .    ┌─────────────────────────────────┐ │
│                       │ a:_                             │ │
│                       └─────────────────────────────────┘ │
│        (   OK   )        ( Cancel )        (  Help  )      │
└───────────────────────────────────────────────────────────┘
```

To format a disk other than drive A, change the drive letter specified. If you want to create a bootable disk, add the /S switch. If you need to format a smaller capacity disk, include the /4 or /F switches.

The Format option displays a similar dialog box. The difference between the two options is Quick Format performs a quick disk format, only rebuilding the file allocation tables and root directory, whereas the Format option examines the disk for damaged locations. To perform a quick format, the disk must have been previously formatted. For more information on quick format refer to Chapter 7, "Preparing Disks for Use," or to the Command Reference.

Undeleting Files

The Disk Utility Undelete command lets you undelete one or more deleted files. When you select this option, the shell will display the following dialog box.

```
┌────────────────────────[ Undelete ]──────────────────────┐
│                                                           │
│   WARNING! This action may cause the permanent loss of    │
│   some deleted files.  Press F1 for more information.     │
│                                                           │
│   Parameters . . .    ┌─────────────────────────────────┐ │
│                       │ /LIST_                          │ │
│                       └─────────────────────────────────┘ │
│        (   OK   )        ( Cancel )        (  Help  )      │
└───────────────────────────────────────────────────────────┘
```

By default, the dialog box only lists files in the current directory that are available for undeletion. To actually undelete one or more files, specify the files to undelete, as discussed in Chapter 28, "DOS 5 Crisis Prevention."

Using the Shell's Online Help

The shell provides an extensive built-in online help system that explains the different menu commands, dialog boxes, and shell components. The shell provides several ways to invoke its online help. First, if you highlight a menu option or a section of the shell itself, such as a disk drive icon, you can press F1 to scroll through a dialog box of text about the topic. Second, many dialog boxes provide built-in help. If you don't understand how you should respond to a dialog box, press F1. Last, the Help menu lets you access help on several specific topics, as shown here.

Table 41-5 briefly describes the Help menu options.

When invoked, the shell's online help displays a help window similar to the one shown in Figure 41-13.

Using your keyboard arrow keys or dragging the scroll bar slide, you can view the information the window contains. As you scroll through the text, you will notice the window displays some text in reverse video or a different color. Such highlighted text indicates additional discussion about the topic. To view the additional text, double-click your mouse on the highlighted text or press TAB until the window highlights the text and press ENTER.

The Help window contains several options. The Close option ends the help session and removes the window. The Back button displays the previous help topic. The Keys option displays a list of related topics. The Index option redisplays Help's Index of topics, and Help displays help about the current dialog box.

Hands On

If the DOS shell is not currently running, invoke it.

```
C:\> DOSSHELL   <ENTER>
```

If your monitor supports graphics, and the shell is in text mode, use the Options menu Display option to select a graphics mode.

Option	Help Text
Index	Displays Help's main index letting you scroll through all the available help topics
Keyboard	Displays a list of predefined keys within the shell
Shell Basics	Discusses the fundamentals you must know to use the shell
Commands	Explains each of Help's menu options in detail
Procedures	Discusses the steps required to use such shell components as the File and Program lists
Using Help	Explains how to use the shell's online help
About Help	Displays Help's copyright notice

Table 41-5.   *The Help Menu Options*

Press TAB to traverse each of the shell sections. Highlight the root directory and press the asterisk hot key to expand your disk's entire directory tree. Using your mouse or keyboard, select different directories and watch the shell update the File List. Note the different icons the shell displays for each file type.

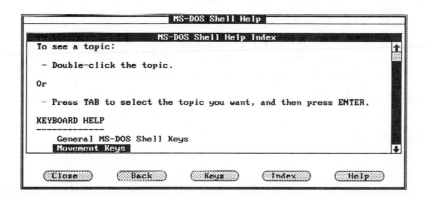

Figure 41-13.   *The Online help window*

Click the mouse on several of the minus signs that appear in different directory icons to collapse those directory branches.

Select the root directory. Highlight the CONFIG.SYS file and use the File menu View File Contents option to display the file's contents.

Next, select the View menu Dual File Lists option to display two directory trees and File Lists at the same time. Select the root directory as the current directory in the top tree and the DOS directory as the current directory in the bottom tree. Select the View menu All Files option to display an alphabetical list of every file on your disk. Use your arrow keys or mouse to scroll through the list. Use the View menu Program/File List option to restore the shell's standard display.

Press TAB to select the Program List and press ENTER to invoke the Command Prompt option (or click on the option with your mouse). The shell will let you temporarily exit to the DOS prompt. Invoke DIR. When the command completes, use EXIT to return to the shell.

```
C:\> EXIT   <ENTER>
```

Last, invoke the Help menu and choose the Index option. Take a few minutes to scroll through the shell's online help text. Press ESC or click on the Close option to exit Help. Press ALT-F4 to exit the shell, returning to the DOS prompt.

Review

1. How do you change disk drives within the DOS shell?

2. What does it mean to expand or collapse a directory branch?

3. How do you traverse from one shell section to another?

4. List two ways to copy files using the shell.

5. How do you select two or more files for a file operation?

Answers

1. You can change disk drives within the DOS shell by clicking on the icon of the drive you desire, by holding down CTRL and pressing the letter of the drive desired or by repeatedly pressing TAB to select the drive icon section, using your arrow keys to highlight the desired icon and pressing ENTER to select the drive.

2. By default, the shell only displays one level of the directory tree. When you expand a directory branch, you display the next level of a directory's tree. Likewise, when you collapse a directory branch, you remove the branch from view.

3. You can click on an item within the section you desire with your mouse, or you can repeatedly press the TAB key until the shell highlights the section.

4. To copy files using the shell, select the files with your mouse and keyboard and use the File menu Copy option or select the files you desire and drag the files with your mouse onto the directory icon to which you want the files copied, releasing the mouse button to complete the copy operation.

5. To select two or more consecutive files with your mouse, click on the name of the first file in the list. Hold down SHIFT and click on the name of the last file in the list.

   To select two or more consecutive files with your keyboard, use the arrow keys to highlight the first file in the group. Hold down SHIFT and use the arrow keys to highlight remaining files in the group.

   To select two or more files that aren't consecutive, hold down CTRL while you click on each file. To select the files with your keyboard, use the arrow keys to select the first file you desire. Press SHIFT-F8. The shell will display the word "Add" in the status bar next to the current time. Use the arrow keys to highlight the second file desired. Press SPACEBAR to select the file. Repeat these steps to highlight and select the desired files. After all files are selected, press SHIFT-F8 again.

   To select all the files in the current directory, use the File menu Select All option.

Advanced Concepts

As you have learned, DOS only lets you run one program at a time with the DOS 5 shell; however, you can start one program, such as your word processor, open a file, and temporarily suspend your word processor so you can run a second program, leaving the word processing session right where you left off. Using this technique, you can start several programs, switching between the programs as required. The DOS 5 shell refers to each program as a *task*, and the shell's *task swapper* lets you quickly switch between loaded programs. The number of programs you can load depends on their size and your available memory.

To enable task swapping, select the Options menu and choose the Enable Task Swapper option. The shell will display a diamond next to the option when task swapping is enabled.

Next, run your program. Press CTRL-ESC to return to the DOS shell. The shell will divide the Program List group in half, displaying an Active Task List. If you invoke several programs, your Active Task List may appear similar to Figure 41-14.

To select a program from the Active Task List, click on the program with your mouse or press the TAB key to highlight the list, use the arrow keys to highlight the desired program, and press ENTER.

To cycle through the active programs, press ALT-TAB. The shell will cycle through the active tasks, displaying each program's name in a title bar. To select a specific program, press ENTER.

To end an active task, select the program and end the program as you normally would. If a program hangs, select the Task List, highlight the program, and press DEL.

If you are using an EGA monitor and the shell does not correctly update your screen when swapping tasks, install the EGA.SYS device driver in your CONFIG.SYS file.

NOTE

To add a program appearing in the File List to the Active Task List, hold down SHIFT and double-click on the program or use your arrow keys to highlight the program and press SHIFT-ENTER. The shell will not run the program; rather, it will add the task to the active task list for selection.

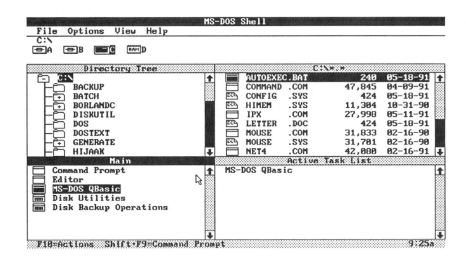

Figure 41-14.   The Active Task list

If you attempt to load more tasks than your memory can hold, the shell will display the following Program Error dialog box, indicating that it is unable to load the task.

As you work with the shell, you will find the task swapper is a very convenient way to switch between programs. Do not exit the shell until you first end your active tasks. If an active task has one or more open files and you do not end the task correctly, you may lose the information the files contain.

The task swapper does not perform multitasking—it does not run more than one program at a time. Instead, the task swapper lets you run one program at a time, remembering where you left off in the other programs so it can later resume their execution.

NOTE

Do not run disk utility programs with the task swapper. Such programs often read the current file allocation tables when they begin. If you start a disk utility, suspend it, and run a program that changes the file allocation table by creating or deleting files, you may later corrupt your disk, losing the information the disk contains when you resume the utility's execution.

WARNING

Key Terms

Task swapper   The program within the DOS 5 shell that lets you temporarily suspend one program so you can run another, letting you resume the original program's execution at a later time at the same point where you left off.

Chapter 42

Advanced DOS 5 Shell Techniques

In Chapter 41 you learned how to use the DOS 5 shell to perform file manipulation commands such as copy, move, rename, and delete. You also learned how to quickly traverse your directory tree or two different directory trees. In this chapter you will learn how to customize the DOS 5 shell by selecting screen colors and adding programs or program groups to the Program List. In the Advanced Concepts section, you will learn how to build custom dialog boxes the shell displays to prompt the user for command-line parameters when the user selects a specific program entry.

Setting Your Screen Colors

The shell provides eight different color settings you can select using the Options menu Colors option. When you select this option, the shell will display the following Color Scheme dialog box.

Using your arrow keys or mouse, highlight the color desired. If you want to see how the color will look before you select it, choose the Preview option. To select the color, select the OK option. If you decide to leave the existing color unchanged, press ESC or select the Cancel option.

Working with Program Groups

A program group is a collection of related programs, such as a word processor, spell checker, and thesaurus. If you have a program you use on a regular basis, you may simply want to add the program entry to the Main Group itself. However, if you have a set of related programs, you'll want to create a separate program group to organize your programs, much like you would store related files in a directory.

You might, for example, create a group named Disk Backup Operations that contains the command for a monthly backup and an incremental backup, as discussed in Chapter 22, "Protecting Your Files with BACKUP and RESTORE." To add the group, you would first select the shell's Program List. Next, invoke the File menu. When the Program List is selected, the options in the File menu change, as shown here.

```
┌─────────────────────────┐
│ File                    │
├─────────────────────────┤
│ New...                  │
│ Open            Enter   │
│ Copy                    │
│ Delete...         Del   │
│ Properties...           │
│ Reorder                 │
│                         │
│ Run...                  │
├─────────────────────────┤
│ Exit          Alt+F4    │
└─────────────────────────┘
```

Table 42-1 briefly describes each menu option.

Option	Function
New	Adds a new program or group entry to the current program group
Open	Displays the contents of the selected program group
Copy	Copies a program entry into a specific program group
Delete	Removes an empty program group from within the current group
Properties	Specifies the characteristics of a program or program group
Reorder	Moves a program or group entry within the Program Group menu
Run	Lets you run a command by entering the command name and its optional parameters
Exit	Quits the DOS shell

Table 42-1.   Shell File Menu Options When the Program List Is Selected

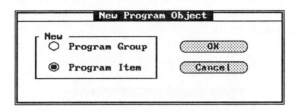

Figure 42-1.   The New Program Object dialog box with Program Item selected

To add a program group, select the File menu and choose the New option. The shell will display the New Program Object dialog box shown in Figure 42-1, asking you if you want to add a program entry or program group.

To add a program group, select the Program Group option and press ENTER or use your mouse to click on OK. The shell will display an Add Group dialog box, as shown in Figure 42-2, prompting you to type in the group specifics.

The Title option lets you specify a title containing up to 23 characters, which later appears within the group menu and as the group title bar when the group is open. The Help Text option lets you specify up to 255 characters of online help the shell will display about the group should you highlight the group and press F1. If you type in the text as sentences, the shell will later format the text to fit within the dialog box. If you want to control line breaks within the text, type ^m (insert the caret character (^) immediately followed by the letter "m") each time you want the shell to perform a carriage return and linefeed operation.

The Password option lets you specify a password up to 20 characters long that the user must type to access the group. Do not rely on the password as a security measure. As you learned in Chapter 41, pressing ALT-F4 lets the user exit the shell,

```
┌─────────────────■ Add Group ■─────────────────┐
│                                                │
│  Required                                      │
│                                                │
│    Title . . . .   ┌──────────────────────┐    │
│                    └──────────────────────┘    │
│  Optional                                      │
│                                                │
│    Help Text . .   ┌──────────────────────┐    │
│                    └──────────────────────┘    │
│    Password  . .   ┌──────────────────────┐    │
│                    └──────────────────────┘    │
│                                                │
│      ( OK )        ( Cancel )      ( Help )     │
│                                                │
└────────────────────────────────────────────────┘
```

Figure 42-2.   The Add Group dialog box

at which point the user can issue the commands from the DOS prompt. In general, the password is only useful to prevent another user from adding or deleting program entries within the group.

After you complete the group fields, press ENTER or use your mouse to click on the OK option. The shell will add the group, as shown here.

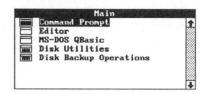

Editing an Existing Program Group

Should you later need to change a group's title, help, or password, highlight the group and select the File menu Properties option. If the group has a password, the shell will display a dialog box asking you to enter the password. If the password you enter is correct, the shell will display a dialog box similar to Figure 42-2 that lets you edit the group fields. To change a field, click on the field using your mouse, or press TAB to highlight the field. Next, edit the text as desired.

Removing a Program Group

If you delete the programs associated with a group from your disk, you will also want to remove the group entry from the Program List. To remove a program group, you must first remove each program entry within the group. Select the group and highlight an entry. Next, invoke the File menu and choose the Delete option. The shell will display the dialog box shown in Figure 42-3, asking you to confirm the deletion.

Select option 1 to delete the entry. Repeat this process for each program entry in the group. Next, press ESC to exit the program group to the next higher level. Select the File menu Delete option. The shell will display a dialog box similar to Figure 42-3 asking you to confirm the deletion. Select option 1 to delete the group. If the group has a password, the shell will prompt you to enter the password before removing the group.

Changing the Order of Group Items

For convenience, you probably want to place your most commonly used program and group entries at the top of the group list. To move an entry, highlight the entry and select the File menu Reorder option. Next, highlight the entry in the list before which you want to move the program or group and press ENTER. You must repeat this process for each entry you wish to move.

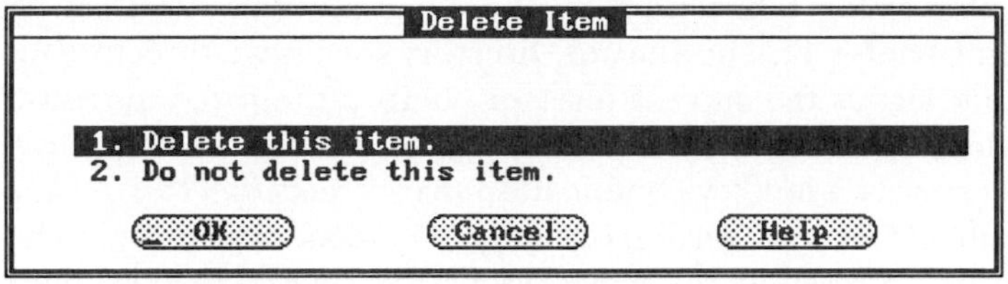

Figure 42-3.   The Delete Item dialog box

Working with Program Entries

To add a program entry to a group, select the desired group and invoke the File menu, choosing the New option. The shell will display the New Program dialog box, shown in Figure 42-1, asking you if you want to add a program or group item. Select the Program Item option. The shell will display the Add Program dialog box, shown in Figure 42-4, prompting you to enter the program item information.

The Program Title option lets you specify up to 23 characters that will appear in the group menu as the entry's title. Using the backup example, you might use the title Daily Backup. The Commands option lets you specify the command, or series of commands, the shell needs to issue when you invoke this option.

If the shell needs to perform two or more commands, such as first selecting a specific directory before running the program, separate each command with a semicolon. The commands can total up to 255 characters. If one of the commands is a DOS batch file, use the CALL command to invoke it. In the case of the incremental backup, you would simply enter the command BACKUP C:*.* A: /S /A /M, as discussed in Chapter 22. In the Advanced Concepts section you will learn

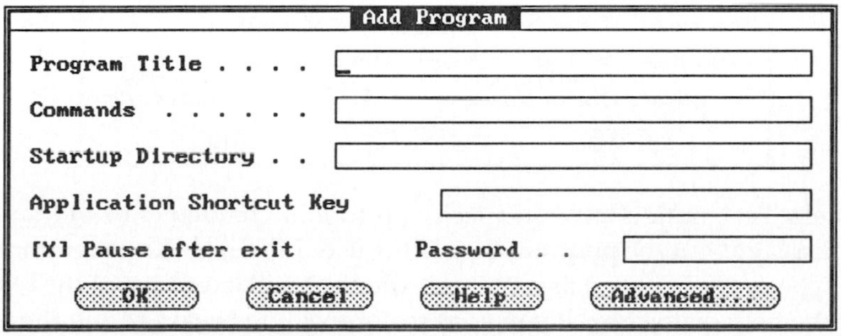

Figure 42-4.   The Add Program dialog box

how to direct the shell to display a dialog box of options when the program runs, similar to the dialog boxes used by the commands in the Disk Utilities group discussed in Chapter 41. The Startup Directory specifies a directory name you want the shell to select as the current directory before the program runs. If you don't specify a directory, the shell uses the current directory. The Application Shortcut key lets you specify a hot key combination that directs the Task Swapper discussed in the Advanced Concepts section of Chapter 41 to automatically select the program if the program is present in the active task list. To select a hot key, hold down SHIFT, ALT, or CTRL and press a key. If you press SHIFT and F10 for example, the dialog box will display the key as "SHIFT+F10". Do not use the following key combinations reserved by the shell:

CTRL-C	CTRL-[	SHIFT-CTRL-M	SHIFT-CTRL-[
CTRL-M	CTRL-5*	SHIFT-CTRL-I	SHIFT-CTRL-5*
CTRL-I	CTRL-H	SHIFT-CTRL-H	

* Indicates the numeric keypad number 5.

The Pause after Exit option directs the shell to display a message asking the user to press any key to continue when the program ends, before returning to the shell. With this option disabled, you may not be able to view the program's last screenful of output before your screen redisplays the shell. The Password option lets you specify a password up to 20 characters that the user must enter before runing the program. As is the case with program group passwords, do not rely on the password for security. Instead, only use a password to prevent a user from changing one of the program entry's properties.

For most programs, the information you specify in this dialog box will be enough to successfully run the program, and you can press ENTER or click on the OK option to place the entry in the Program List. If you want to specify online help text or the program's memory requirements, select the Advanced option. The shell will display the dialog box shown here.

The Help Text option lets you specify up to 255 characters of online help the shell will display about the program should the user highlight the program and press F1. If you type in the help text as sentences, the shell will later format the text to best fit within the help dialog box. If you want to control line breaks within the text, type

^m (insert a caret character immediately followed by the letter "m") each time you want the shell to perform a carriage return and linefeed operation.

The Conventional Memory KB Required option lets you specify the minimum amount of conventional memory, in kilobytes, the program requires before the Task Swapper can run the program. The default value is 128Kb. The XMS Memory Kb Required option lets you specify the minimum amount of extended memory the program must have before the Task Swapper can run it. The default value is zero. The XMS Memory Kb Limit specifies the maximum amount of extended memory, in kilobytes, the program can use. The default value is 384Kb, or the amount of the extended memory if the system has less than 384Kb.

When the Task Swapper changes from one active task to another, the Swapper must save the current task's screen display. The Video Mode option controls how much memory the Swapper must reserve to store the screen display. Unless you are using a CGA monitor, select text mode for all programs. If you are using a CGA monitor and the Task Swapper does not correctly restore your screen, select graphics mode.

By default, pressing ALT-ESC or CTRL-ESC directs the Task Swapper to either cycle through active tasks, or to display the active task list. If you have a program whose execution you don't want interrupted, select the Prevent Program Switch option. When you select this option, the only way to return to the shell when the program runs is to end the program.

The Task Swapper uses ALT-TAB, ALT-ESC, and CTRL-ESC to cycle through active tasks or to select the active task list. If your program also uses one of these key combinations, you must reserve the key for the program's use. When you reserve a key combination, the Task Swapper will not respond to that key combination when the program is running.

Changing a Program Group Entry

If you need to change a program entry's commands, online help, or an advanced option used by the Task Swapper, highlight the program entry and choose the File menu Properties option. The shell will display a dialog box similar to Figure 42-4. Change the fields required and select OK to save your changes.

Copying a Program Entry to a New Group

If accidentally you place a program entry in the wrong group, or later want to move an entry to a different group, highlight the entry and select the File menu Copy option. Next, display the group within which you want the item and press ENTER. The item will appear in the group's program list. Next, select the entry's original group and remove the entry with the File menu's Delete option. The shell will display a dialog box similar to Figure 42-3. Select option 1 to delete the entry.

Hands On

Select the Program List, invoke the File menu, and choose the New option. When the shell displays a dialog box prompting you to select a group or program item, select the Program Group item. For the group title, type in Disk Backup Operations. Within the Help Text option, type in a brief description of an incremental and complete disk backup, as discussed in Chapter 22. Select OK to add the group. Next, select your newly created group.

Invoke the File menu and choose the New option. When the shell displays a dialog box prompting you to select a group or program item, select the Program Item option. For the program title, type Daily Backup. For the command, type BACKUP C:*.* A: /S /A /M. Select OK to add the program entry.

Invoke the File menu and again choose New, selecting a second program item. For the program title, type Monthly Backup. For the command, type BACKUP C:*.* A: /S. Select the Advanced option and type in help text describing the complete disk backup. Select the OK option to remove the Advanced dialog box and OK a second time to add the program entry.

Highlight the Daily Backup option. Select the File menu and choose the Properties option. When the dialog box displays the option's current settings, select the Advanced option and add help text describing an incremental backup operation. Select OK to remove the Advanced dialog box and OK to save your changes.

You can now perform a complete disk or incremental backup operation directly from the Program List.

Review

1. When should you use a program group instead of a program entry?

2. With the exception of the Help Text option, when must you specify values for the program entry options that appear in the Advanced dialog box?

3. How can you change an existing program group or program entry?

Answers

1. If you have a set of two or more related commands, you should place the commands within a program group. If the shell's Program List is becoming cluttered, you should organize the programs into groups, much as you would use subdirectories to organize your files.

2. The only time you need to complete options in the Advanced dialog box for a program entry is when you need to specify the program's attributes to the Task Swapper, when you plan to run the program while the Task Swapper has other programs in memory.

3. To change an existing program or group entry, highlight the entry and select the File menu Properties option. The shell will display a dialog box that lets you edit the entry's fields.

Advanced Concepts

In Chapter 41, the programs in the Disk Utilities group displayed a dialog box requesting command-line information before they ran. For example, if you selected the Disk Copy operation, the shell displayed the Disk Copy dialog box.

```
┌──────────────────────■ Disk Copy ■──────────────────────┐
│                                                         │
│  Enter the source and destination drives.               │
│                                                         │
│  Parameters  .  .  .   ┌─────────────────────────────┐  │
│                        │ a: b:                       │  │
│                        └─────────────────────────────┘  │
│     ( ══ OK ══ )          ( ═ Cancel ═ )      ( ═ Help ═ ) │
└─────────────────────────────────────────────────────────┘
```

When you add your own program entries, the shell lets you design your own dialog boxes. To create a dialog box, you must reference a replaceable parameter %1 through %9 within the program entry's command line. For example, assume you are creating a program entry named Type File that uses the TYPE command to display the contents of the file the user specifies. Within the program's command, you would place the command TYPE %1, as shown here.

```
┌────────────────────────■ Add Program ■────────────────────────┐
│                                                               │
│  Program Title  .  .  .  .   ┌──────────────────────────────┐ │
│                              │ Type File                    │ │
│                              └──────────────────────────────┘ │
│  Commands   .  .  .  .  .  .  ┌──────────────────────────────┐ │
│                              │ TYPE %1_                     │ │
│                              └──────────────────────────────┘ │
│  Startup Directory  .  .   ┌──────────────────────────────┐   │
│                            └──────────────────────────────┘   │
│  Application Shortcut Key   ┌──────────────────────────────┐   │
│                            └──────────────────────────────┘   │
│  [X] Pause after exit      Password  .  .  ┌──────────────┐    │
│                                            └──────────────┘    │
│   ( ═ OK ═ )   ( ═ Cancel ═ )   ( ═ Help ═ )   ( Advanced... )  │
└───────────────────────────────────────────────────────────────┘
```

After you complete the entry's other fields and select OK, the shell will display the dialog box shown in Figure 42-5, prompting you to define the dialog box for use with %1.

The Window Title lets you specify up to 23 characters for the dialog box to display in its title bar. In this case, you might simply use the program entry name Type File.

The Program Information line lets you specify up to 106 characters of instructions that appear beneath the program title. The Prompt Message specifies an 18-character prompt the shell displays to the left of the box within which the user enters the information desired. In this case, you might use "Enter Filename." The Default Parameters option lets you specify the dialog box's default value. In the case of a disk operation, you might specify a drive letter or use the shell's predefined %L parameter, which corresponds to the parameter used the last time the user selected the program. In the case of a file operation, you use the shell's predefined %F value that uses the currently selected file. If you click on the Help option, the shell lets you type in online help text specific to this dialog box.

If your program's command line contains more than one replaceable parameter, the shell will display the dialog box shown in Figure 42-5, requesting you to design each box.

If the user later selects the Type File program entry with the file name AUTOEXEC.BAT selected, the shell will display the dialog box shown here.

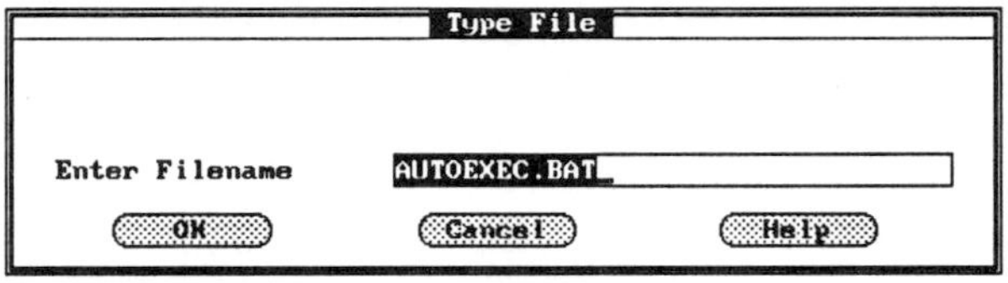

If a program requires several parameters, the shell will display the custom dialog box you created for each.

By creating dialog boxes and providing default values in this way, you can make running commands from within the DOS shell very straightforward.

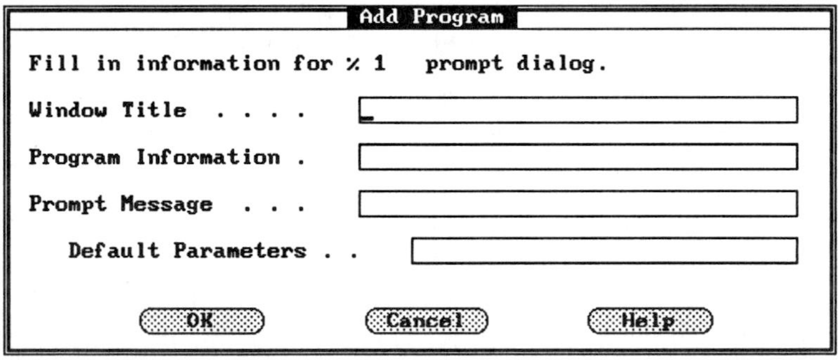

Figure 42-5.   Creating a custom dialog box

DOSSHELL.INI

Each time you make changes to the shell, such as confirmation settings, colors, or changes to program groups, the shell stores your changes in the file DOSSHELL.INI, which resides in the DOS directory. When you start the shell, the shell uses this file to establish your settings. DOSSHELL.INI is an ASCII file whose contents you can display, print, or even edit. Before you edit this file, however, make sure you make a copy of the file's original contents. By studying this file you can learn how to change several shell settings, as well as how to create your own color definition.

Key Terms

Replaceable parameter   A parameter value within a shell dialog box definition with the value %1 through %9, for which the user can specify the desired value when the shell displays the dialog box, prior to running a program.

Chapter 43

DOS System Commands

Throughout this book most of the chapters have combined DOS commands with discussion of a specific concept. For example, in Chapter 10, "Directories," you learned about DOS directories and the MKDIR, CHDIR, and RMDIR commands. Likewise, Chapter 32 was about DOS memory management and the corresponding DOS commands and CONFIG.SYS entries. This chapter presents several commands best described as DOS system commands, because the commands change the way DOS behaves. When you finish this chapter, the only command left to discuss is FDISK, which will be presented in Chapter 45.

Customizing Your System Prompt

In Chapter 10 you used the command PROMPT PG to set the system prompt to the current drive and directory followed by a greater-than sign. The symbols $P and $G are *metacharacters*; characters the PROMPT command translates to produce a result. In this case, PROMPT translates $P into the current drive and directory and $G into the greater-than symbol. The PROMPT command supports the metacharacters described in Table 43-1.

By default, DOS will display the current drive letter followed by a greater-than symbol for the prompt.

```
C>
```

Most users, however, place the PROMPT PG command in their AUTOEXEC.BAT file so that the system prompt will display the current drive and directory.

Depending on your preferences, you may want to change your prompt slightly, using the techniques discussed next. Regardless of the eventual prompt you select, I strongly recommend you include the $P metacharacter to display the current drive and directory.

The following command changes the system prompt to the current date, followed by a dollar sign.

```
C:\> PROMPT  $D$$   <ENTER>

Fri 06-28-91$
```

If you press ENTER several times, your system prompt will remain unchanged.

```
C:\> PROMPT  $D$$   <ENTER>

Fri 06-28-91$   <ENTER>
Fri 06-28-91$   <ENTER>
Fri 06-28-91$   <ENTER>
```

Metacharacter	Translation
$B	DOS pipe symbol |
$D	Current date
$E	ASCII escape character
$G	Greater-than symbol >
$H	Backspace character, which erases the previous character displayed by prompt
$L	Less-than symbol <
$N	Current disk drive letter
$P	Current drive letter and directory
$Q	Equal sign =
$T	CURRENT time
$V	DOS version
$$	Dollar sign $
$_	Carriage return and linefeed characters, which advance the cursor to the next line

Table 43-1.   The PROMPT Metacharacter Translations

Use the SET command to display the current environment settings.

```
Fri 06-28-91$   SET   <ENTER>
COMSPEC=C:\DOS\COMMAND.COM
PATH=C:\DOS;C:\DISKUTIL;C:\WINDOWS
PROMPT=$D$$
```

Each time it completes a command, DOS searches the environment for the PROMPT entry. If the entry exists, DOS uses it to assign the system prompt. If the PROMPT entry does not exist in the environment, DOS uses the default drive letter and greater-than symbol for the prompt.

Knowing that DOS searches the environment in this way, you actually have two ways to set the DOS prompt: using the PROMPT command or using SET PROMPT=.

If you invoke PROMPT without specifying a desired prompt, DOS selects its default PROMPT.

```
Fri 06-28-91$   PROMPT <ENTER>

C>
```

By combining the $D (date), $T (time), $_ (carriage return and line feed), $P (drive and directory) and $G (greater-than symbol), the following PROMPT command creates a prompt that spans three lines, displaying the date, time, current drive, and directory.

```
C> PROMPT   $D$_$T$_$P$G   <ENTER>

Fri 06-28-91
11:03:45.55
C:\>
```

In addition to letting you use metacharacters, PROMPT lets you include text in your prompt. The following PROMPT includes the words "Current Time," followed by the system time.

```
C:\> PROMPT Current Time $T

Current Time 11:04:33.63
```

In this case, the prompt includes minutes and seconds in the system time. Using the $H backspace character you can erase the minutes and seconds from the prompt, as shown here.

```
C:\> PROMPT Current Time $T$H$H$H$H$H$H   <ENTER>
```

Although such prompts can be entertaining, the most useful prompt is simply PG.

Enabling Extended CTRL-BREAK Checking

As you have learned, DOS lets you end commands and batch files by pressing the CTRL-C or CTRL-BREAK keyboard combinations. By default, each time DOS writes a letter to the screen, printer, or auxiliary device (COM1), or when it reads a letter from the keyboard or auxiliary device, DOS checks to see if you have pressed CTRL-BREAK to end the command. If you have, DOS ends the command and redisplays its prompt. If you have not pressed CTRL-BREAK, DOS continues the command's execution.

Depending on the commands you are running, considerable time may pass between the times DOS performs each one of these operations. After you press CTRL-BREAK to end the command, you'll have to wait until DOS acknowledges it. If the program never performs one of these operations, you will have to wait until the program ends.

The BREAK command lets you enable and disable extended CTRL-BREAK checking. When you enable extended checking, you increase the number of times DOS will check for a CTRL-BREAK. Actually, DOS will check for a CTRL-BREAK each time it completes any operation for the command, such as file input or output, or even a date or time operation. Because DOS checks for CTRL-BREAK more often, you'll have to wait less time for DOS to acknowledge your CTRL-BREAK and end the current command. Unfortunately, because DOS spends more time checking for CTRL-BREAK, it spends less time running your program. As a result, your programs will run slower and your system performance will decrease. Because this extended checking slows your system down, most users leave it disabled.

If you invoke BREAK with no command-line parameters, BREAK will display the current state of extended CTRL-BREAK checking (either on or off) as shown here.

```
C:\> BREAK   <ENTER>
BREAK is off
```

To enable extended CTRL-BREAK checking, invoke BREAK with the word ON as shown here.

```
C:\> BREAK ON   <ENTER>
```

DOS will then check for a CTRL-BREAK more often. To disable CTRL-BREAK checking, invoke BREAK with the word OFF as shown.

```
C:\> BREAK OFF   <ENTER>
```

Chapter 24, "Customizing Your System with CONFIG.SYS," discussed the CONFIG.SYS BREAK entry. By default, DOS starts with extended CTRL-BREAK checking turned off. Using the CONFIG.SYS BREAK entry, you can enable extended CTRL-BREAK checking as soon as the system starts. In general, the only users who might want to enable extended CTRL-BREAK checking are computer programmers who are writing and testing programs.

If you invoke BREAK and BREAK displays its status as already ON, check your CONFIG.SYS for a BREAK=ON entry, and your AUTOEXEC.BAT for a BREAK ON command. If either is present, remove it and restart your system. As a result, you will improve your system performance. If you want to enable extended checking before you run specific commands, do so, but then turn the checking off as soon as the command completes.

```
C:\> BREAK   ON   <ENTER>

C:\> SOMECOMM   <ENTER>

C:\> BREAK   OFF  <ENTER>
```

Using EXIT to Resume a Program

Many programs, such as a word processor or a shell interface like the DOS shell, let you temporarily leave the program to issue commands at the DOS prompt. Using the DOS 5 shell discussed in Chapter 41 as an example, pressing SHIFT-F9 lets you temporarily exit the shell to DOS.

Temporarily exiting a program to the DOS prompt is different than ending the program. When you end the program, you must first save your files. To use the program again, you must invoke it from the DOS prompt and reopen the files. When you temporarily exit a program to DOS, you leave things within the program just as they were—files that you have open can remain open. After you finish executing the commands you left the program to invoke, use the EXIT command to return to the program, right where you left off.

```
C:\> EXIT   <ENTER>
```

The only time you will normally use the EXIT command is to return back to a program after temporarily exiting to the DOS prompt.

WARNING

Do not turn off your computer or restart DOS before you return to the program, save your files, and end the program, returning to the DOS prompt. If you don't end the program correctly, you may lose changes you have made to files.

Online Help for DOS 5 Commands

Under DOS 5, you can get a brief summary of a command's function, parameters, and switches by invoking the command with the /? switch, as shown here.

```
C:\> XCOPY  /?    <ENTER>
Copies files (except hidden and system files) and directory
trees.

XCOPY source [destination] [/A | /M] [/D:date] [/P] [/S [/E]]
  [/V] [/W]

  source        Specifies the file(s) to copy.
  destination   Specifies the location and/or name of new files.
  /A            Copies files with the archive attribute set,
                    doesn't change the attribute.
  /M            Copies files with the archive attribute set,
                    turns off the archive attribute.
  /D:date       Copies files changed on or after the specified date.
  /P            Prompts you before creating each destination file.
  /S            Copies directories and subdirectories except empty ones.
  /E            Copies any subdirectories, even if empty.
  /V            Verifies each new file.
  /W            Prompts you to press a key before copying.
```

If you can't remember which command you need, you can type HELP at the DOS prompt. The HELP command will display each of the DOS commands and a one-line summary, as shown here.

```
C:\> HELP   <ENTER>
For more information on a specific command, type HELP command-name
APPEND    Allows programs to open data files in specified direc-
             tories as if they were in the current directory.
ASSIGN    Redirects requests for disk operations on one drive to
             a different drive.
ATTRIB    Displays or changes file attributes.
BACKUP    Backs up one or more files from one disk to another.
BREAK     Sets or clears extended CTRL-C checking.
CALL      Calls one batch program from another.
CD        Displays the name of or changes the current directory.
  :          :
  :          :
UNDELETE  Recovers files which have been deleted.
UNFORMAT  Restores a disk erased by the FORMAT command or restruc-
             tured by the RECOVER command.
VER       Displays the MS-DOS version.
VERIFY    Tells MS-DOS whether to verify that your files are writ-
             ten correctly to a disk.
VOL       Displays a disk volume label and serial number.
XCOPY     Copies files (except hidden and system files) and direc-
             tory trees.
```

The HELP command behaves like the MORE command. If you want to see the next screenful of commands, press any key; use CTRL-C to end the command.

In addition to listing each command, HELP lets you display help text for individual commands. For example, the following command displays help on the subject of COPY.

```
C:\> HELP  COPY   <ENTER>
Copies one or more files to another location.

COPY [/A | /B]  source  [/A | /B] [- source  [/A | /B] [- ...]]
  [destination  [/A | /B]] [/V]

  source      Specifies the file or files to be copied.
  /A          Indicates an ASCII text file.
  /B          Indicates a binary file.
  destination Specifies the directory and/or filename for the
                 new file(s).
  /V          Verifies that new files are written correctly.
```

```
To append files, specify a single file for destination, but
 multiple files for source (using wildcards or file1-file2-file3
format).
```

The information HELP displays is identical to what you would see if you invoke COPY using the /? switch. For a more complete online help for all versions of DOS, see the order form for the DOSHELP program described at the beginning of this book.

Displaying Extended ASCII Characters with GRAFTABL

As you have learned, your computer displays letters on the screen using the ASCII character set shown in Appendix B. In Chapter 15, "Grouping Commands with Batch Files," you learned how to use the extended ASCII characters to produce boxes and drop shadows, as shown here.

```
┌─────────────────────────────┐
│            Menu             │
│                             │
│    F1 Start WordPerfect     │
│    F2 Start Lotus 123       │
│    F3 Run DBase IV          │
│    F4 Quit to DOS           │
└─────────────────────────────┘
```

Chapter 38, "Support for International Users," examined the code-page settings international users can use to represent their country's character set. If you examine Appendix D, you will find DOS uses the extended ASCII values to represent the international character sets.

New video monitors have no difficulty displaying extended ASCII characters and international code pages. If you are using an older monitor, such as a CGA monitor in graphics mode for example, your monitor may have difficulty displaying extended ASCII characters. The GRAFTABL command loads memory-resident software to help such monitors display these characters. If your monitor displays the characters correctly, don't invoke GRAFTABL; its memory-resident software would use up memory unnecessarily.

Before DOS version 3.3, the format of the GRAFTABL command was simply GRAFTABL. Beginning with DOS 3.3, the command's format became

```
GRAFTABL   [CodePage] [/STATUS]
```

where *CodePage* specifies the international code-page value GRAFTABL will support.

437	United States
850	Multilingual
852	Slavic (DOS 5)
860	Portuguese
863	French-Canadian
865	Nordic

The /STATUS switch directs GRAFTABL to display the current *CodePage* selection.

The following command, for example, provides support for the extended ASCII character set (or U.S. code page).

```
C:\> GRAFTABL  437  <ENTER>
```

Remember, the only time you need to use GRAFTABL is when your monitor does not properly display the character set while operating in graphics mode.

Invoking the BASIC Programming Language

Computer programs are lists of instructions written in a programming language such as C, Pascal, or BASIC. To give you an opportunity to write and experiment with your own programs, every DOS version provides a command that lets you create, edit, and run your own programs using the BASIC programming language. Depending on your DOS version, your disk may contain a command named BASICA.COM, GWBASIC.EXE, or QBASIC.EXE in the DOS directory.

Under DOS 5, the command QBASIC.EXE provides a very powerful editor for creating, running, and debugging your BASIC programs. In addition, you may find several files in the DOS directory that contain the BAS extension. These files contain BASIC programs you can view and run.

For more information on GW-BASIC or QBasic, see the Osborne/McGraw-Hill books *GW-BASIC Made Easy* or *QBasic Made Easy*.

Revisiting MODE

In Chapter 13, "Printing," you may have used the MODE command to redirect printer output from the default PRN device to a serial device, such as COM1. In Chapter 38 you may have used the MODE command to prepare and select an international code page. In this chapter, you will examine the rest of MODE's capabilities using MODE for printer, video, and keyboard customization.

Customizing Your Printer Output

If you are using an Epson-compatible or IBM-compatible printer, you can use the MODE command to specify the character size and number of characters per line the printer will print. For DOS versions 3.3 and before, the format of the MODE command is as follows:

```
MODE  LPTn[:]  [CharactersPerLine] [,[LinesPerInch] [,Retry]]
```

Under DOS version 4 or later, the format of the command becomes the following:

```
MODE  LPTn[:]  [cols=CharactersPerLine] [lines=LinesPerInch]
  [retry=Retry]
```

CharactersPerLine specifies either 80 or 132 characters per line. By default, most printers use 80 characters per line and either wrap or ignore characters past column 80. If you specify 80 characters per line, MODE will discard (ignore) any characters appearing past column 80. *LinesPerInch* specifies the number of lines, either 6 or 8, the printer will print in a vertical inch on your page. The default setting is 6. If you select 8, your printed output becomes more condensed.

Retry specifies how DOS should react timeout errors when it tries to send information to a parallel printer and the printer is not ready. By default, MODE will wait for a period of time for the printer and then time out. Table 43-2 lists the valid retry options. These options are more meaningful to DOS than an end user.

When you specify a retry option, MODE will load memory-resident software that monitors the printer and its status.

NOTE   *The retry option P directs MODE to retry sending data to the printer until the printer accepts the data. If your printer is slow, it will eventually be ready for more data. If your printer experiences an error, MODE will remain in its continuous loop, trying to send data to the printer (apparently hanging your system) until you break the retry loop by pressing* CTRL-C .

The following command, for example, selects compressed print of 132 characters per column and 8 lines per vertical inch.

```
c:\> MODE  LPT1:  132,8   <ENTER>
```

To direct DOS to continuously retry printer operations until the operation is successful, include the *p* option, as shown here:

```
C:\> MODE  LPT1:  132,8,p   <ENTER>
```

If you are using DOS 4 or later, you can issue the same command as follows:

```
C:\> MODE  LPT1:  COLS=132  LINES=8  RETRY=P   <ENTER>
```

As discussed, not all printers let you set their printer attributes using MODE in this way. If your printer does not, your printer should support different escape sequences to achieve the same result. Refer to your printer documentation for more information.

Most newer programs provide built-in software to manage the printer, specify fonts, and so on. Using these programs, you probably won't need to use MODE to customize your printer. However, if a program has difficulty printing, you might experiment with MODE. In Chapter 34, "ANSI.SYS," you used escape sequences with the ANSI device driver to enhance your screen and keyboard capabilities. Most printers have a set of predefined escape sequences you can print to select various fonts, page layouts, and other printer attributes. For more information on printer escape sequences, refer to the documentation that accompanied your printer.

Using MODE to Set Your Keyboard's Response Rate

If you are using DOS 4 or later, MODE lets you set your keyboard's *typematic rate*, the rate at which DOS repeats a character if you leave the key depressed. The higher the value you assign to the typematic rate, the faster DOS repeats characters. Note: Not all keyboards support the typematic value. The format of this MODE command is as follows:

```
MODE  CON[:]   [RATE= RepeatRate DELAY=DelayTime]
```

Retry Option	Function
E	Returns an error status
B	Returns a busy status
P	Retries the operation until the printer accepts data
R	Returns a ready status
N or None	Takes no action

Table 43-2.   The Retry Options for Printer Timeout Errors

The CON device corresponds to your keyboard.

A *RepeatRate* value of 1 lets the keyboard repeat 2 characters per second, and the value 32 specifies 30 characters per second. By default, DOS uses a *RepeatRate* value of 20 (10 characters per second) for PC-AT keyboards and 21 (11 characters per second) for PS/2 keyboards. Table 43-3 lists the approximate characters per second for different *RepeatRates*.

DelayTime is a value from 1 to 4 that specifies the amount of time DOS will wait after you first press the key before it begins to repeat characters. Table 43-4 summarizes the delay settings.

For the fastest keyboard response, use the following command.

```
C:\> MODE  CON:  RATE=32  DELAY=1  <ENTER>
```

If your keyboard begins repeating keys you don't intend to repeat, try adjusting the delay value first to give your fingers a little more time to release the key.

Customizing Your Video Display

Depending on your video display type, the MODE command lets you specify the number of characters per row and number of rows per screen. Before DOS version 4,

Repeat Rate	Characters per Second	Repeat Rate	Characters per Second
1	2.0	17	8.0
2	2.1	18	8.6
3	2.3	19	9.2
4	2.5	20	10.0
5	2.7	21	10.9
6	3.0	22	12.0
7	3.3	23	13.3
8	3.7	24	15.0
9	4.0	25	16.0
10	4.3	26	17.1
11	4.6	27	18.5
12	5.0	28	20.0
13	5.5	29	21.8
14	6.0	30	24.0
15	6.7	31	26.7
16	7.5	32	30.0

Table 43-3. *Keyboard Typematic Repeat Rate Values and Their Corresponding Numbers of Characters Per Second*

Delay Time Value	Delay in Seconds
1	1/4 second
2 (default)	1/2 second
3	3/4 second
4	1 second

Table 43-4.   *Keyboard Typematic Delay Time Values and Their Corresponding Delays in Seconds*

the format to select a screen setting uses the MODE command followed by one of the display modes listed in Table 43-5.

The following MODE command, for example, selects 40 columns per row.

```
C:\> MODE  40   <ENTER>
```

To restore the screen to 80 columns, issue the following MODE command.

```
C:\> MODE  80   <ENTER>
```

Beginning with DOS 4, MODE lets you specify the number of columns and rows as follows:

```
MODE  CON[:]  [COLS=Columns]  [Lines=Rows]
```

Display Mode	Display Setting
40	40 characters per row
80	80 characters per row
BW40	Color disabled on a color adapter, 40 characters per row
BW80	Color disabled on a color adapter, 80 characters per row
CO40	Color enabled, 40 characters per row
CO80	Color enabled, 80 characters per row
MONO	Monochrome adapter, 80 characters per row

Table 43-5.   *Video Display Settings Supported by MODE*

The Columns value must be either 40 or 80. For CGA systems, the rows must be 25. For EGA, the rows can be 25 or 43. Last, for VGA systems, rows can be 25, 43, or 50. To set the number of rows using MODE, you must have previously installed the ANSI.SYS device driver, as discussed in Chapter 34, "ANSI.SYS".

The following command sets an EGA or VGA monitor to 43 rows.

```
C:\>  MODE   CON   LINES=43   <ENTER>
```

Similarly, this command sets a VGA monitor to 50 rows.

```
C:\>   MODE   CON   LINES=50   <ENTER>
```

If you are using an older monitor, you may need to shift characters to the left or right to view the characters on the screen. MODE lets you install memory-resident software that will automatically shift the characters. To shift characters to the left or right, use the following MODE command format.

```
MODE   DisplayMode,L|R[,T]
```

DisplayMode specifies one of the video adapter types listed in Table 43-5. The entry L|R specifies that you must select either the letter "L" to shift characters to left or "R" to shift characters to the right. The option T value directs MODE to display a test pattern of the values 0 through 9. The following example illustrates a right-shift operation.

```
01234567890123456789012345678901234567890123456789012345678 9
Do you see the leftmost 0 (Y/N)?
```

In this case, if you type N to MODE's prompt and you can see the leftmost 0, MODE will shift the letters to the right. When you eventually respond with Y, the MODE command will end MODE, loading memory-resident software that keeps the characters shifted until you turn off your computer or restart DOS.

Configuring Your Serial Port

You learned in Chapter 13 that your computer has one or more serial or parallel ports, as shown in Figure 43-1.

The parallel ports (LPT1, LPT2, and LPT3) normally connect a printer to your computer. The serial ports (COM1 through COM4) can connect printers, a mouse, or a modem, which lets your computer communicate with another computer over telephone lines.

In general, parallel devices send data over eight lines. A serial device, on the other hand, sends data over one line. Each ASCII character requires eight bits (or binary digits) to uniquely distinguish the character from another. Using the word "DOS," for example, the binary digits required to represent the three letters become

D	O	S
01000100	01001111	01010011

Because a parallel device can send data over eight lines at one time, each line sending a binary digit, your computer can send the word "DOS" to your printer as shown in Figure 43-2.

A serial device, on the other hand, can only send information over one wire, one bit at a time. Figure 43-3 illustrates how your computer would send the word "DOS" to a serial printer.

Because parallel printers can send more data at one time (in parallel), they are much faster than serial devices. If you look at a parallel or serial printer cable, however, you'll find that both cables contain many pins. In addition to the eight wires for data, parallel devices use wires to control the data transmission. For example, if your printer's memory buffer becomes full, it can use one of these wires to signal your computer to quit sending data until it is ready.

Although serial devices also have control wires available to them, most serial devices don't use them. Instead, your computer and the serial device agree how fast they will communicate, and how many bits of information they will exchange at one time. These values specify a *communication protocol*.

When you attach a printer to a serial port, the printer must know how fast and how much data the computer will send it. In most cases, the device determines the

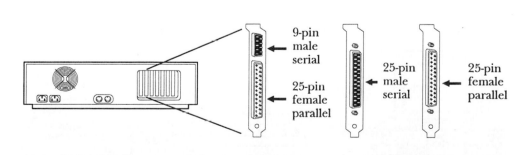

Figure 43-1.   *Your computer has one or more serial or parallel ports*

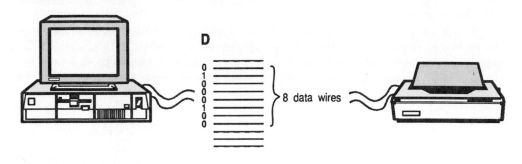

Figure 43-2.   *Parallel devices can send eight data bits at the same time over eight different wires*

protocol. Using the MODE command, you tell the serial port the protocol values to use. Before DOS 4, the format to set a serial port's communication parameters is

```
MODE COMn[:]   BaudRate[,Parity[,DataBits[,StopBits[,P]]]]
```

Beginning with DOS 4, the MODE command becomes

```
MODE COMn[:] [baud=BaudRate] [parity=Parity] [data=DataBits]
  [StopBits] [retry=Retry]
```

BaudRate specifies the speed at which the computer and the device will communicate in bits per second. Valid baud rates are 110, 150, 300, 600, 1200, 2,400, 4,800, 9,600, and 19,200 bits per second. MODE only requires you to specify the first two baud rate digits.

To help the computer or device recognize single bit errors, an extra parity bit is often sent immediately following the data bits. When the computer or device gets

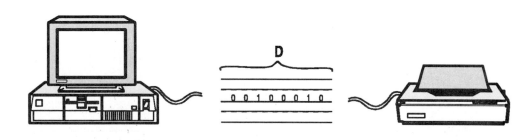

Figure 43-3.   *Serial devices send one bit of data at a time over one wire*

the data, it counts the number of binary digits that had the value 1. The result will either be an even or odd number. If the computer and device agree to use even parity, and the number of 1 digits is odd, a transmission error occurs. The same is true for odd parity and an even number of 1 digits. You must specify the letter "E" for even parity, "O" for odd parity, an "N" for no parity, "S" for space, and "M" for mark. Space parity always assigns the parity bit the value 0 while mark parity assigns the value 1. The default setting is even parity. The computer and device must agree on the amount of data to exchange at one time. *DataBits* value specifies the number of bits in each exchange that contain data. Valid values must be in the range 5 to 8. The default is 7.

After the data bits and parity, one or more stop bits indicate the transmission is done. Valid *StopBit* values are 1, 1.5, and 2. For 110 baud, the default number of stop bits is 2. For all other baud rates the default is 1. If you are familiar with data communications, you may notice MODE does not specify a start bit. DOS does not need one.

Last, the retry option specifies how MODE will handle device busy errors. Valid retry options are listed in Table 43-2.

Although using MODE to configure a serial port may seem difficult, the documentation that accompanies the device you are attaching to the serial port will contain the correct MODE command you will need to use. For example, the following MODE command configures the serial port COM1 for the settings needed by an HP LaserJet Series II printer.

```
C:\> MODE COM1 9600,N,8,1,p  <ENTER>
```

If you need to configure a serial port with MODE, place the command provided in the device documentation in your AUTOEXEC.BAT file and don't worry about the command after that.

Displaying a Device's Current Status

As you have learned, the MODE command lets you configure your printer, screen display, keyboard, and serial devices. Beginning with DOS version 4, you can use MODE /STATUS to display the current device settings. For example, the following MODE command displays the status of the serial port COM1.

```
C:\> MODE  COM1 /STATUS   <ENTER>

Status for device COM1:
-----------
Retry=B
```

If you don't specify a device name, as shown in the following, MODE will display the status of every known device.

```
C:\> MODE /STATUS   <ENTER>
```

Hands On

Using the BREAK command, determine if you currently have extended CTRL-BREAK checking enabled (on) or disabled (off).

```
C:\> BREAK   <ENTER>
```

If extended CTRL-BREAK checking is on, you can improve your system performance by turning it off. Make sure your CONFIG.SYS file does not have a BREAK=ON entry and your AUTOEXEC.BAT file does not turn extended checking on using BREAK ON.

Next, using the following PROMPT command, change your system prompt to display the current DOS version number followed by two blank lines, and then the current drive and directory followed by a greater-than sign.

```
C:\> PROMPT  $V$_$_$_$P$G   <ENTER>
```

Use the SET command to display the current environment entries.

```
MS-DOS Version 5.0


C:\> SET   <ENTER>
```

Note the PROMPT entry. Using SET, remove the entry.

```
MS-DOS Version 5.0


C:\> SET  PROMPT=   <ENTER>
```

PROMPT

The PROMPT command lets you customize your system prompt by combining text with one or more predefined metacharacters. The PROMPT command stores the current prompt in the PROMPT environment entry. Each time DOS completes a command, DOS uses the environment entry to assign the current prompt. If the PROMPT entry does not exist, DOS uses its default prompt of the current drive letter and greater-than symbol. The following PROMPT command directs DOS to display the current drive and directory.

```
C>   PROMPT  $P$G   <ENTER>
```

BREAK

The BREAK command lets you enable and disable extended CTRL-BREAK checking. By default, DOS checks for CTRL-BREAK each time it writes to the screen, printer, or auxiliary device, or when it reads from the keyboard or auxiliary device. When you enable extended CTRL-BREAK checking, DOS will check for a CTRL-BREAK each time it performs any function. Because extended CTRL-BREAK checking increases the number of times DOS checks for a CTRL-BREAK, DOS will recognize your CTRL-BREAK much sooner, ending the command. However, by enabling this extended checking, the amount of extra time DOS spends checking for a CTRL-BREAK decreases the amount of time DOS lets your program run. As a result, your programs run slower and your system performance suffers. To maximize your system performance, you should leave extended CTRL-BREAK checking using the following command.

```
C:\>  BREAK OFF  <ENTER>
```

EXIT

The EXIT command lets you return to a program such as the DOS shell after temporarily exiting the program to issue commands at the DOS prompt. So you don't have to save your files, and end the program only to later restart the program and reopen the files, many programs let you exit the program temporarily so you can issue commands at the DOS prompt.

When you are ready to resume the program's operation, invoke the EXIT command as shown here.

```
C:\> EXIT   <ENTER>
```

HELP

Under DOS version 5, the HELP command lets you display a list of the DOS commands and a one-line description of each. To view the Help command's primary list, invoke HELP as shown.

```
C:\> HELP   <ENTER>
```

In addition, if you include the command's name in the HELP command line, HELP lets you display information about specific commands. Using this technique, the following command displays help on UNDELETE.

```
C:\> HELP  UNDELETE   <ENTER>
```

GRAFTABL

Older video monitors are unable to correctly display the extended ASCII character set in certain graphics modes. The international code pages, for example, all use extended ASCII values. The GRAFTABL command loads memory-resident software to help the monitor correctly display these characters. If you are an international DOS user using the multilingual code page (850), you would execute the following command.

```
C:\> GRAFTABL  850   <ENTER>
```

Note that DOS displays its default prompt of the current drive followed by a greater-than symbol. Use the following PROMPT command to display the current drive and directory followed by a greater-than sign.

```
C>   PROMPT $P$G   <ENTER>
```

If you are using DOS version 5, issue the following HELP command to display a summary of the available commands.

```
C:\> HELP   <ENTER>
```

When HELP completes, invoke HELP with MODE to display information about the command.

```
C:\> HELP   MODE   <ENTER>
```

If you are using DOS 4 or later, hold down the D key and note how fast DOS repeats the character. Next, issue the following MODE command to maximize your keyboard typematic rate.

```
C:\> MODE   CON   RATE=32   DELAY=1   <ENTER>
```

Hold down the D key once again and note the keyboard's increase in responsiveness. If you are a fast typist, you might consider placing this command in your AUTOEXEC.BAT file.

Review

1. What is extended CTRL-BREAK checking?

2. How does the CONFIG.SYS BREAK entry differ from the BREAK command?

3. What is a metacharacter?

4. What is a typematic rate?

5. What is a serial communication protocol?

Answers

1. DOS lets you end most programs and batch files by pressing CTRL-BREAK. By default, each time DOS reads from the keyboard or auxiliary device or writes to the screen, printer, or auxiliary device, DOS checks to see if you have pressed CTRL-BREAK to end the program. If you have a program that does not perform one of these actions on a regular basis, it may take DOS considerable time before it acknowledges your CTRL-BREAK. Extended CTRL-BREAK checking extends the number of times DOS will check for a CTRL-BREAK. Using the BREAK command, you can enable and disable extended CTRL-BREAK checking. When extended checking is enabled, DOS will check for a CTRL-BREAK each time it completes an operation, which means DOS will recognize and respond to your CTRL-BREAK much sooner. Because DOS spends more time testing for CTRL-BREAK, your programs run less often, which decreases your system performance. Most users should leave extended CTRL-BREAK checking off.

2. The CONFIG.SYS BREAK entry and the BREAK command both let you enable and disable CTRL-BREAK checking. The CONFIG.SYS BREAK entry lets you specify the state of extended checking DOS will use from the moment your system starts. You can later override this initial setting using the BREAK command.

3. A metacharacter is a predefined character that follows a dollar sign character whose meaning the PROMPT command translates. For example, PROMPT translates the $P metacharacter into the current drive and directory.

4. The typematic rate controls how fast your keyboard will repeat a key when you leave the key pressed. Beginning with DOS 4, the MODE command lets you set your keyboard's typematic rate. The faster the rate, the faster DOS repeats keys, improving your keyboard's responsiveness.

5. Your computer and serial device must agree on the speed and data format they will use to exchange information. The communication protocol specifies such characteristics as the baud rate (speed), as well as the number of data bits, stop bits, and parity.

Advanced Concepts

This section completes the discussion of all the DOS commands with the exception of FDISK (Chapter 45). For more specifics on each DOS command, turn to the Command Reference at the end of this book.

Changing the Terminal Device

The CTTY command has been with DOS since version 1. It remains one of the least used commands. CTTY directs DOS to change its source of commands and output destination from your keyboard and screen to a terminal device attached to a serial port. The format of the CTTY command is as follows:

```
CTTY COMn[:] | CON | AUX | NUL | PRN | PRN | LPTn[:]
```

Assume, for example, you have a terminal or a custom hardware device attached to your computer's serial port COM1. Using the following CTTY command, you can direct DOS to use the terminal instead of your computer's screen and keyboard.

```
C:\> CTTY  COM1:  <ENTER>
```

Do not use the CTTY command unless you have a way to execute commands from the port specified. Otherwise, you will have to restart your system to continue.

If you use CTTY to access a terminal connected to a serial port, you can issue the following CTTY command from the terminal to restore normal keyboard and screen operations.

```
C:\> CTTY  CON  <ENTER>
```

Transferring System Files to a Target Disk

A bootable DOS disk contains the hidden system files IO.SYS and MSDOS.SYS, as well as the DOS command processor COMMAND.COM. The easiest way to create a bootable disk is using FORMAT /S. If a disk already contains files, however, you won't want to format the disk to make it bootable because doing so would destroy the information the disk contains. The SYS command lets you transfer the files DOS needs to boot to a target disk. For example, you can use SYS to update a disk containing the startup files for an older version of DOS to a newer version.

Depending on your DOS version, how SYS behaves will differ. Before you see how SYS differs, you need to understand the processing SYS performs. First, provided the target disk has sufficient disk space, SYS copies the files IO.SYS and MSDOS.SYS to the target disk. Your disk's boot record contains a small program that loads DOS into memory. Because this startup program must be small enough to fit in the boot record, it cannot be very complex, and thus requires the file IO.SYS to be the very first entry in your disk's root directory, immediately followed by the file MSDOS.SYS. If these first two directory entries are in use, the SYS command will fail under all DOS versions prior to DOS 4, displaying the following error message.

```
No room for system on destination disk
```

In addition, prior to DOS 4, the two files IO.SYS and MSDOS.SYS had to reside in consecutive disk locations at the start of your disk's data area, as shown in Figure 43-4.

If you examine the FORMAT command in the Command Reference section, you will find the /B switch directs FORMAT to reserve the directory entries and disk space for these two files on a disk, but not to place the files on the disk. In the early 1980s, some computer games that ran from floppy disks would direct you to restart your system for the programs to run. Due to licensing restrictions, the software companies could not ship DOS on their floppy disks. Instead, the companies would format the floppy disks using the /B switch to leave space for DOS. The companies could then copy their files to the disk. Before you could run the program, you would have to use SYS to copy the DOS system files to the disk to create a bootable disk.

Beginning with DOS version 3.3, the SYS command became a little more flexible. Version 3.3 eliminated the restriction that IO.SYS and MSDOS.SYS reside in consecutive locations at the start of the disk's data area. In DOS 4, if files already resided in the target disk's first two root directory entries, SYS moved the directory entries (provided the root directory had two unused entries) to make room for the IO.SYS and MSDOS.SYS entries.

To transfer system files prior to DOS version 4, the format of the SYS command is

```
SYS TargetDrive:
```

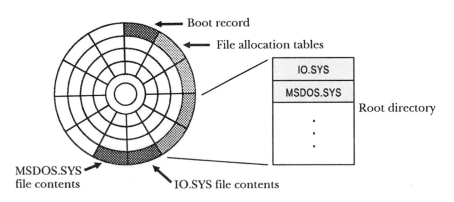

Figure 43-4.   *Older DOS versions not only required IO.SYS and MSDOS.SYS to be the first two root directory entries; the files had to occupy the first locations in the disk's data area, too*

Using this format, the current drive must contain the bootable system files SYS is to transfer. Beginning with DOS version 4, SYS lets you not only specify the target drive to which you want to transfer files, but also a source drive and directory containing the files to transfer.

```
SYS SourcePath:  TargetDrive:
```

If you don't specify a source drive and directory, SYS uses the root directory of the current disk by default.

The following SYS command transfers a copy of the DOS system files from drive C to the floppy disk in drive A.

```
C:\> SYS  A:   <ENTER>
```

Under DOS 4 or later, the following SYS command copies the DOS system files from the floppy disk in drive A to the floppy disk in drive B.

```
C:\> SYS  A:  B:  <ENTER>
```

In addition to IO.SYS and MSDOS.SYS, your hard disk must have a copy of COMMAND.COM before it will boot. The DOS 5 SYS command automatically copies the COMMAND.COM file to the target disk for you. If you are using a DOS version earlier than 5, you will need to copy the COMMAND.COM to the target disk.

Directing DOS 5 to Report a Specific Version Number

When many programs first start, they may ask DOS to tell them its version number. If, for example, a program needs a capability provided by DOS version 3.3 and you are running DOS version 3.2, the programs can display an error message and end. Unfortunately, if such a program has not yet been updated to know about DOS 5, the program may display the same error message and end just because the program is testing for version 3.3 or 4. To let you run such programs, the SETVER command lets you specify the version number you want DOS to report to the program when the program asks. In other words, you can trick the program into thinking it's running under a different DOS version.

Before you can use SETVER to provide version number reporting, you must load the file SETVER.EXE as a device driver using the CONFIG.SYS DEVICE or DEVICEHIGH entry.

```
DEVICE=C:\DOS\SETVER.EXE
```

Assume, for example, you have a program named V33ONLY.EXE that checks for DOS version 3.3 and ends if it encounters any other version. Using the following SETVER command, you can tell DOS to report the version number 3.3 when the program V33ONLY asks.

```
C:\> SETVER  V33ONLY.EXE  3.3    <ENTER>
```

SETVER will place information about V33ONLY.EXE in a table DOS reads each time it starts. SETVER will tell you it has added the new entry to the table, but that you have to restart your system for the table entry to take effect.

```
C:\> SETVER  V33ONLY.EXE  3.3    <ENTER>

WARNING - The application you are adding to the MS-DOS version
table may not have been verified by Microsoft on this version of
MS-DOS. Please contact your software vendor for information on
whether this application will operate properly under this ver-
sion of MS-DOS. If you execute this application by instructing
MS-DOS to report a different MS-DOS version number, you may lose
or corrupt data, or cause system instabilities. In that cir-
cumstance, Microsoft is not responsible for any loss or damage.

Version table successfully updated
The version change will take effect the next time you restart
your system
```

DOS provides several predefined entries for you. If you invoke SETVER without a command line, SETVER will display the current entries.

```
C:\> SETVER    <ENTER>
WIN200.BIN       3.40
WIN100.BIN       3.40
WINWORD.EXE      4.10
EXCEL.EXE        4.10
HITACHI.SYS      4.00
MSCDEX.EXE       4.00
REDIR4.EXE       4.00
NET.EXE          4.00
NET.COM          3.30
NETWKSTA.EXE     4.00
DXMA0MOD.SYS     3.30
BAN.EXE          4.00
```

```
BAN.COM           4.00
MSREDIR.EXE       4.00
METRO.EXE         3.31
IBMCACHE.SYS      3.40
REDIR40.EXE       4.00
DD.EXE            4.01
DD.BIN            4.01
LL3.EXE           4.01
REDIR.EXE         4.00
SYQ55.SYS         4.00
SSTDRIVE.SYS      4.00
ZDRV.SYS          4.01
ZFMT.SYS          4.01
TOPSRDR.EXE       4.00
```

When you later receive the DOS 5 upgrade for one of the programs, you can remove the entry from the table using the SETVER /DELETE switch, shown here.

```
C:\> SETVER  V33ONLY.EXE  /DELETE    <ENTER>

Version table successfully updated
The version change will take effect the next time you restart
your system
```

As you can see, SETVER again displays information telling you to restart your system for the change to take effect. To suppress the display of the system restart message, include the /QUIET switch when you delete entries from the table.

```
C:\> SETVER  V33ONLY.EXE  /DELETE  /QUIET   <ENTER>
```

Using SETVER, you can upgrade to DOS 5 and still use programs that only know about previous DOS versions.

Key Terms

Metacharacter   A special character preceded by a dollar sign whose value the PROMPT command translates to obtain a specific result. PROMPT translates the $D character into the current system date.

Typematic delay   The minimum amount of time a keyboard key must be depressed before DOS repeats the key's value.

Parallel communication   The communication between a computer and device using at least eight dedicated wires to transmit eight binary digits (one byte) of data at a time.

Serial communication   The communication between a computer and a device where one binary digit is transmitted at a time over a single wire.

Baud rate   The communication speed between a computer and a device, typically measured in bits per second.

Chapter 44

Detecting and Correcting Disk Fragmentation

If you are like most DOS users, it won't be long before you look for ways to make your system run faster. In Chapter 31 you looked at several DOS performance improvement techniques. Briefly mentioned in Chapter 31, "Improving Your System Performance," were the identification and correction of fragmented files. As you will learn in this chapter, a *fragmented* file is a file whose contents are stored in sectors dispersed across your disk. If your programs are taking longer to start, or your word processing or spreadsheet files are taking longer to load, the files on your disk may be fragmented.

Fragmented files occur as a natural result of creating, deleting, and enlarging files on your disk. Unfortunately, fragmented files not only decrease your system performance, but may also prevent successful file undeletions when you use either third-party software or the DOS 5 UNDELETE command.

Understanding Fragmented Files

As you have learned, DOS stores your file contents on disk in groups of sectors called disk clusters. A fragmented file is a file whose contents require several clusters, which reside on disk locations dispersed across your disk. Figure 44-1 illustrates two

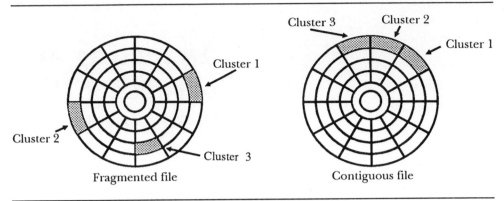

Figure 44-1.   *A fragmented file and a contiguous file*

files. The first file's contents are fragmented. The second file's contents are contiguous, meaning its clusters reside in consecutive storage locations.

Here's how fragmented files decrease your system performance. Your disk drive has a read and write head that reads the information stored on the disk or records new information as required. The disk drive can move the read/write head in and out to access different tracks on the disk. To access different disk sectors, the disk drive must rotate the disk past the read/write head. The following illustration demonstrates how the disk read/write head accesses the information stored on your disk by moving to the correct track and waiting for the desired disk sector to rotate past.

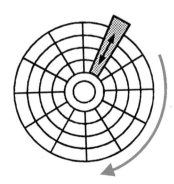

Unlike your computer's fast electronic memory, your disk drive is mechanical, meaning it physically moves. Compared to the speed of electricity, even the smallest physical movement is very slow. To improve your system performance, you need to reduce the amount of this physical disk head movement. Fragmented files, unfortunately, increase the amount of head movement and rotational delay.

Using the files in Figure 44-1, watch the steps DOS must perform to read each file's contents. To begin, the disk drive moves the read/write head to the outermost

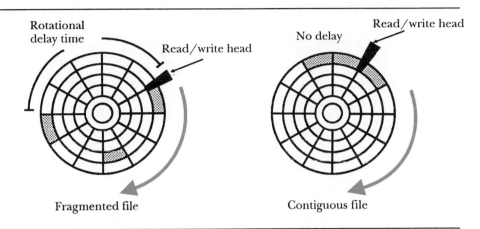

Figure 44-2.   Fragmented files cause rotational delays

track. When cluster 1 spins by the read/write head, the drive reads it. Next, using the contiguous file, the disk drive can immediately read the second cluster. For the fragmented file, however, the disk drive must wait for the disk to spin one half a revolution before it can read the second cluster, as illustrated in Figure 44-2.

To read cluster 3 of the contiguous file, the disk drive simply reads the next cluster. For the fragmented file, however, the disk drive must first move the read/write head to the correct track, and then wait for the cluster to spin by (see Figure 44-3).

What Causes Fragmented Files?

Fragmented files are a natural occurrence of using your disk to store files. Assume, for example, your disk contains two small files ONE and TWO, as shown here:

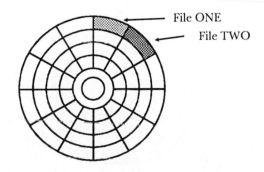

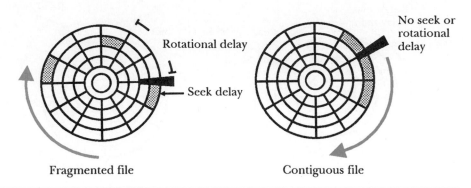

Figure 44-3.   *In the worst case, fragmented files cause disk head movement and rotational delays*

Assume you edit file ONE and increase its size by one cluster. Because file TWO is physically next to file ONE, DOS must use the next available cluster. As a result, file ONE becomes fragmented as shown here:

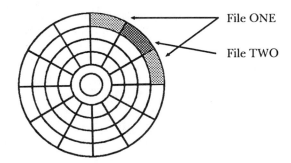

If you later increase the size of file TWO by one cluster, it too becomes fragmented.

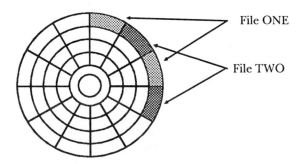

As you can see, fragmented files can occur quite easily. Fortunately, however, many of the files on your disk, such as EXE and COM files, don't change in size.

Therefore, if DOS can originally store the file's contents in consecutive storage locations, those files will never become fragmented.

When placing a file on disk, DOS does its best to store the file in consecutive storage locations. If DOS knows the file's size, it divides the size by the disk's cluster size to determine the number of clusters the file requires. DOS can then search the disk for a location with enough available consecutive clusters.

How to Detect File Fragmentation

If your programs are taking longer to start, or your data files take longer to load, check the directory for fragmented files using CHKDSK as shown here.

```
C:\> CHKDSK  *.*   <ENTER>
```

CHKDSK will examine every file in the directory for fragmentation. If CHKDSK encounters a fragmented file, it will display the following message.

```
C:\FILENAME.EXT
Contains nn non-contiguous blocks
```

A block is simply a cluster. Noncontiguous blocks are clusters stored in nonconsecutive locations.

CHKDSK only examines one directory of files at a time for fragmentation. To examine your entire disk, you must invoke CHKDSK individually for each directory or use a third-party disk utility. If you have a large file, you can use CHKDSK to examine the file for fragmentation as shown here.

```
C:\> CHKDSK  FILENAME.EXT  <ENTER>
```

If CHKDSK only displays a few file names as fragmented, don't be too concerned. If CHKDSK lists many files, you should correct the fragmentation using one of the techniques discussed next.

Correcting File Fragmentation

Depending on the number of fragmented files your disk contains, there are two ways to correct the fragmentation. First, when DOS copies a file to your disk, it tries to store the file in consecutive storage locations. If you are trying to eliminate fragmentation for a single file, you can first try copying the file to a different disk, deleting the file from the original, and then copying the file back from the second disk to the original disk. If DOS has enough consecutive clusters, it will use them, eliminating the fragmentation. If your disk is very full, however, the file's fragmentation can actually get worse when you copy the file back to your disk.

If your disk contains many fragmented files, or a file copy operation did not correct the fragmentation, you must use a third-party disk utility program or the BACKUP, FORMAT, and RESTORE commands discussed here to eliminate fragmentation.

To eliminate fragmentation using DOS, you must copy all the files on your disk to floppy, format your disk, and then copy the files back to your disk, as illustrated in Figure 44-4.

To begin, use the BACKUP command to perform a complete disk backup operation as discussed in Chapter 32, "Understanding DOS Memory Management."

```
C:\> BACKUP  C:\*.*  A:  /S  <ENTER>
```

If the backup operation does not successfully back up every file on your disk, do not continue! Instead, repeat the backup operation until it successfully completes.

WARNING

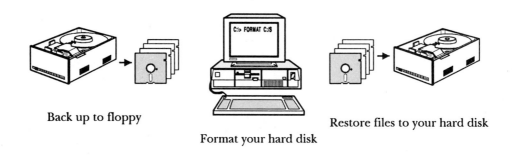

Back up to floppy

Format your hard disk

Restore files to your hard disk

Figure 44-4.   *To eliminate fragmentation using DOS, you must use BACKUP, FORMAT, and RESTORE*

After you back up the files on your disk, format a bootable floppy disk.

```
C:\> FORMAT  A:  /S  <ENTER>
```

If the disk does not contain COMMAND.COM, copy COMMAND.COM to the disk. Next, copy the RESTORE command to the floppy disk.

```
C:\> COPY  \DOS\RESTORE.*  A:  <ENTER>
```

Label the floppy disk RESTORE and place the floppy disk in a safe location. Next, issue the following command to reformat your hard disk.

```
C:\> FORMAT C:  /S  <ENTER>
```

When the format operation completes, place the floppy disk labeled RESTORE in drive A and issue the following RESTORE command, as discussed in Chapter 22, "Protecting Your Files with BACKUP and RESTORE."

```
A> RESTORE  A:  C:\*.*  /S  <ENTER>
```

After RESTORE places the files back onto your hard disk, the fragmentation is eliminated.

Using Third-Party Defragment Utilities

Although using the BACKUP, FORMAT, and RESTORE commands eliminates disk fragmentation, depending on your disk size, it can be a very time-consuming operation.

To simplify the elimination of file fragmentation, you can use one of many third-party utility programs. The advantage of using one of these programs over DOS is the utility programs don't need to copy files to floppies and can run on their own without your interaction. Depending on your disk size and number of files, these programs may take an hour or more to eliminate fragmentation. Because the programs can run unattended, however, you can run them at night before you go home. When you return to work, your files will be contiguous.

Fragmented Files Can Prevent Successful File Undeletion

If you are using DOS 5, the UNDELETE command lets you undelete accidentally deleted files. If you are not using DOS 5, you should upgrade to DOS 5 or purchase a third-party disk utility that provides file undelete capabilities. Your best disk and file protection, however, is current file backups, as discussed in Chapter 22.

If you are using a third-party undelete utility or the DOS 5 UNDELETE command, fragmented files may prevent successful file undeletion. Assume, for example, your disk contains the files shown here. In this case, file ONE is fragmented, while file TWO is contiguous.

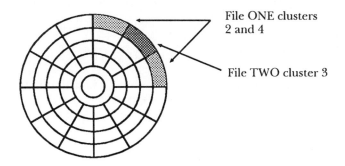

File ONE clusters 2 and 4

File TWO cluster 3

Assume you accidentally delete both files and you use UNDELETE or a third-party utility program to undelete the files. To begin, UNDELETE determines from file ONE's directory entry that file ONE requires two disk clusters. Also, from file ONE's directory entry, UNDELETE knows the file's starting cluster. Unfortunately, UNDELETE assumes file ONE is contiguous. As a result, UNDELETE assigns clusters 2 and 3 to file ONE, as shown here:

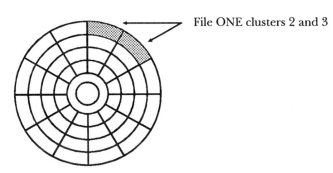

File ONE clusters 2 and 3

Because UNDELETE has incorrectly assigned cluster 3 to file ONE, you cannot use UNDELETE to undelete file TWO since UNDELETE knows another file has overwritten file TWO's contents. (File TWO's starting cluster is now in use by file

SUMMARY

Fragmented Files

A fragmented file is a file whose contents are stored in clusters spread out across your disk. Fragmented files decrease your system performance by increasing disk read/write head movements and disk rotation delays. File fragmentation is a natural occurrence of creating, deleting, and enlarging files on your disk. If your programs start slower, or your data files take longer to load, your files may be fragmented.

Using CHKDSK to Detect Fragmentation

If you include a file name or DOS wildcards in the CHKDSK command line, CHKDSK will examine the matching files for fragmentation. If a file is fragmented, CHKDSK will display a message informing you of the number of noncontiguous clusters the file contains. The following CHKDSK command searches the files in the WordPerfect directory WP for fragmentation.

```
C:\> CHKDSK  \WP\*.*  <ENTER>
```

Eliminating Fragmentation Using DOS

To eliminate file fragmentation using DOS, you need to back up the contents of your hard disk to floppy, format your hard disk, and then restore the files. Depending on your disk size and number of files, this three-step process may become quite time consuming. (To simplify defragmentation, you can use one of many third-party utility programs.)

ONE). The net result of the UNDELETE operation is that file ONE contains the wrong information, file TWO cannot be recovered, and file ONE's actual second cluster cannot be recovered.

If you use the MIRROR command's delete tracking, discussed in Chapter 28, "DOS 5 Crisis Prevention," UNDELETE may correctly recover fragmented files. For most undelete utilities, however, fragmented files pose a great difficulty.

For best performance and the best chance of undeleting files, check your disk for fragmented files, and eliminate the fragmentation on a regular basis.

Hands On

CHKDSK lets you examine a directory or file for fragmentation. The following CHKDSK command checks the files in the DOS directory.

```
C:\> CHKDSK  \DOS\*.*  <ENTER>
```

Using CHKDSK in this way, DOS examines the files in your most commonly used directories. If CHKDSK lists two or three files, don't worry. If CHKDSK lists a large number of files, it's probably a good time to buy and use a third-party unfragment utility or to perform a BACKUP, FORMAT, and RESTORE operation.

Review

1. What is a fragmented file? What are its symptoms?
2. How does fragmentation occur?
3. How can you identify fragmented files?
4. How can you correct fragmentation?

Answers

1. A fragmented file is a file whose contents are stored in sectors dispersed across your disk. When a program starts slowly, or a file (such as a word processing document or spreadsheet) takes a long time to load, the file may be fragmented.

2. Fragmentation is a natural result of creating, deleting, and increasing the size of files on your disk. You cannot prevent file fragmentation, you can only correct fragmentation once it occurs.

3. The CHKDSK command lets you examine the files in a directory for fragmentation. The following command, for example, checks the files in the root directory.

```
C:\> CHKDSK  \*.*  <ENTER>
```

4. Using DOS, you can correct fragmentation by performing a complete disk backup, format, and restore operation. An easier way to correct fragmentation is to use a third-party disk utility program.

Advanced Concepts

To fully understand how file fragmentation impacts your system performance, you need to break a disk read or write operation into individual parts and examine the time required for each.

Disk manufacturers often advertise their disk's average *access time*, in other words, the time to read or write a disk sector. Disk access time is made up of four parts: seek time, rotational delay, data transfer time, and controller overhead.

Seek time is the amount of time the controller takes to move the disk's read and write head to the desired track. Most disk manufacturers will advertise an average seek time based on bench mark programs, typically around 20ms (milliseconds).

Rotational delay is the amount of time the disk controller must wait for the desired sector to spin past. All hard disks will have this rotational delay. Hard disks all spin at 3600 RPMs (rotations per minute). To determine the average rotational delay, simply compute the amount of time required to spin the disk one half revolution, as illustrated in Figure 44-5.

Data transfer time is the amount of time required to transfer a sector of data to or from disk. Transfer rates of 2 to 4Mb per second are not uncommon.

Last, to read or write data, the disk controller must perform its own processing. This *controller overhead* typically takes only a few milliseconds.

Because the controller overhead and data transfer times are fixed and the disk rotation speed is always 3600 RPM, the only way to reduce the average disk access time is to reduce the number of seeks and rotations the disk drive must perform. By eliminating file fragmentation, you do just that.

$$\frac{3600 \text{ Revolutions}}{\text{minute}} \div \frac{1 \text{ minute}}{60 \text{ seconds}} = \frac{60 \text{ Revolution}}{\text{second}}$$

1   revolution = 0.0166 seconds

1/2 revolution = 0.00833 seconds or 8.3 ms

Figure 44-5.   Computing a hard disk's average rotational delay

Key Terms

Fragmented file   A file whose contents are stored in two or more disk clusters spread out across your disk.

Contiguous file   A file whose contents are stored in consecutive disk clusters.

Disk head seek   The process of moving the disk read/write head from one disk track to another.

Rotational delay   The amount of time the disk controller must wait for the desired sector to spin past the disk drive's read/write head.

Seek time   The amount of time required to move the disk head from the current track to the desired track.

Chapter 45

Disk Partitions and FDISK

There are four steps involved in preparing a hard disk for use by DOS. The first step involves telling your computer about your disk, its size, and its characteristics. If you are using an IBM PC AT or AT-compatible, this step involves running the SETUP program that accompanied your computer on floppy disk. If you are using a 386 or 486 computer, the SETUP program is typically built into the computer's read-only memory (ROM). In either case, the documentation that accompanied your computer should explain the SETUP process. Chapter 35, "Advanced Disk Topics," briefly discussed the second step, low-level formatting. In most cases, the computer manufacturer will perform this step for you. The third step is dividing your disks into one or more partitions using FDISK. This chapter examines the FDISK command and disk partitions in detail. As before, depending on your computer manufacturer, your disk may have been partitioned for you. The final step is formatting your disk using the FORMAT command, discussed in Chapter 7, "Preparing Disks for Use." If your computer was able to start DOS the first time you turned your computer on, all four steps have been performed for you.

Understanding Hard Disk Partitions

When the original IBM PC shipped in 1981, it did not support hard disks. When IBM released the PC XT, which supported hard disks, the disks were normally only

10Mb. For several years after the first hard disk was placed in a PC, the cost of hard disks kept their size in the 10- to 20-megabyte range. A user with a large budget could afford a 30Mb disk. Because hard disk sizes where typically 30Mb or less, DOS only supported hard disk sizes up to 32Mb.

Eventually, disk technology caught up with the rest of the PC industry, and disks larger than 32Mb became readily affordable. Unfortunately, the largest disk size DOS could support was 32Mb. To let users with disks larger than 32Mb use the entire disk, DOS 3.3 let the user divide the disk into sections, called *partitions*. The first partition became drive C; the second partition, drive D. FDISK lets you create from one to four partitions on your disk. DOS, however, will only use two partitions, one called the *primary partition*, from which you start DOS, and a second called the *extended partition*. If you are using a second operating system in addition to DOS, you might create a third or fourth partition to store the operating system's files. If you are only using DOS, you will only create two partitions at most, a primary DOS partition and an extended partition.

As you know, a hard disk contains hundreds of circular tracks (or cylinders). A partition is simply a collection of consecutive tracks, as illustrated in Figure 45-1.

Conceptually, a partition is a barrier DOS cannot cross, much like the partitions that separate traffic on a highway. A command that works on one partition, such as FORMAT or DEL, cannot affect information stored on a second partition.

Prior to DOS 4, disk partitions where restricted to 32Mb or less. DOS 4 increased the maximum partition size to 512Mb. Under DOS 5, partition sizes grew to a maximum size of 2Gb (gigabytes)!

The FDISK command partitions your disk. If you are only using DOS, you have two choices. First, provided your DOS version supports large partitions, you can use

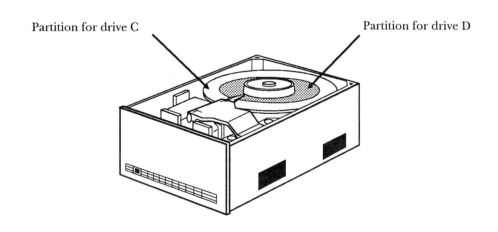

Figure 45-1.   Partitions divide your disk into distinct regions

your entire disk as a single partition. This is the easiest technique, also the most common. Second, you can use FDISK to divide your disk into two partitions, a primary DOS partition and an extended partition. Your primary DOS partition will become drive C. Your extended DOS partition will contain the rest of your disk (possibly more than 32Mb). Once you define your extended partition, you must further divide the partition into logical drives, each smaller than or equal to the largest partition size DOS supports. Figure 45-2 illustrates one hard disk with only partition C and a second hard disk with a primary and extended partition, for which the extended partition has been further divided into drives D, E, and F.

Other Reasons to Partition a Hard Disk

You can divide your disk in up to four partitions. However, DOS only lets you use two partitions, a primary partition and an extended partition. The remaining two partitions can be used for another operating system.

DOS is only one of several operating systems that run on the IBM PC or PC-compatibles. Some users, therefore, create a partition for DOS and a partition for a second operating system such as OS/2, UNIX, or XENIX (a version of UNIX developed by Microsoft). By separating the operating systems into different partitions, the user is free to boot and use any operating system without affecting another operating system's files in a different partition.

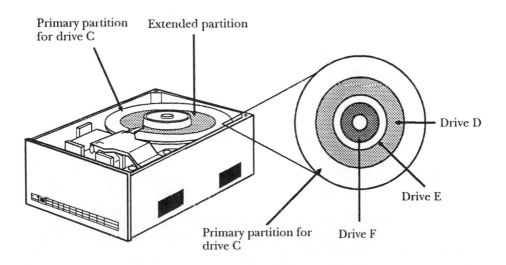

Primary partition
for drive C

Extended partition

Drive D

Drive E

Primary partition for
drive C

Drive F

Figure 45-2.   *A single partition disk and a disk with a primary and an extended partition, where the extended partition is further divided into the logical drives D, E, and F*

Using FDISK

If you can start your computer from your hard drive, your disk has been partitioned and formatted. If you cannot start your computer from hard drive, you may need to tell your computer about the hard drive using SETUP, and then partition and format the drive. In this case, you will need to first boot DOS using a bootable floppy disk.

Your hard disk may have already been partitioned for you. To determine if your disk has been partitioned, issue the following command.

```
A> DIR  C:   <ENTER>
```

If DOS displays the following message, your disk has not yet been partitioned.

```
Invalid drive specification
```

If instead, DOS displays one of the following error messages, your disk has been partitioned, but not formatted.

```
General failure reading drive C
Abort, Retry, Fail?
```

or

```
Invalid media type reading drive C
Abort, Retry, Fail?
```

Your disk has been partitioned, but not formatted.

If this message appears, place the disk containing the FORMAT command in drive A and issue the following command to format the disk.

```
A> FORMAT  C:   /S   <ENTER>
```

When the FORMAT command completes, your hard disk is bootable by DOS.

If your disk is unpartitioned, place the floppy disk containing the FDISK command in drive A and invoke FDISK.

```
A> FDISK   <ENTER>
```

If FDISK displays the following message, your computer does not know about your hard disk.

```
No fixed disk present
```

If this message (or one similar) occurs, you must invoke your computer's setup program to inform the computer about the disk. For IBM AT computers, the setup program typically resides on a floppy disk that accompanied your computer. For 386 and 486 systems, the setup is typically built into the computer's ROM. To access the built-in setup, you press a specific key, such as DEL, during the computer's power-on self-test. Whether you are using a setup program on disk or one built into your computer, the documentation that accompanied your computer will explain the steps you must follow to complete the setup operation.

The setup program accesses and modifies a special memory area of your computer called *CMOS*. The CMOS is a battery-powered chip that stores information about your computer, such as the number and type of disks.

Depending on whether you are using a large single partition or a primary and extended partition, the steps you must follow to partition your disk will differ.

Never use FDISK on a disk containing data. To partition a disk, FDISK overwrites portions of the disk, possibly destroying information you need. In DOS 5, if you inadvertently overwrite partition table information, you may be able to recover your disk provided you have used the MIRROR /PARTN command, discussed in Chapter 28, "DOS 5 Crisis Prevention."

NOTE

Creating One Large Disk Partition

Depending on your disk size and DOS version, you may only have to create one large partition that encompasses your entire disk. To begin, invoke FDISK from drive A.

```
A> FDISK   <ENTER>
```

FDISK will display the following menu of options.

```
                    FDISK Options

Current fixed disk drive: 1

Choose one of the following:
```

```
1. Create DOS Partition or Logical DOS Drive
2. Set active partition
3. Delete DOS Partition or Logical DOS Drive
4. Display partition information

Enter choice: [1]


Press ESC to exit FDISK
```

To create the DOS partition type **1** and press ENTER. Note that FDISK displays the default menu response between the left and right brackets. When you press ENTER to select option 1, FDISK displays the following menu.

```
          Create DOS Partition or Logical DOS Drive

Current fixed disk drive: 1

Choose one of the following:

1. Create Primary DOS Partition
2. Create Extended DOS Partition
3. Create Logical DOS Drive(s) in the Extended DOS Partition

Enter Choice: [1]

Press Esc to return to FDISK Options
```

To create the partition, select option 1 and press ENTER. FDISK will display the following screen, asking you to specify the partition's desired size.

```
          Create Primary DOS Partition

Current fixed disk drive: 1

Do you wish to use the maximum available size for a Primary DOS
partition and make the partition active (Y/N).............[Y]


Press Esc to return to FDISK Options
```

In this case, you want FDISK to use your entire disk for a partition. Type Y and press ENTER. FDISK will create the partition on disk, displaying the following message to tell you it will restart the system.

```
System will now restart

Insert DOS diskette in drive A
Press any key when ready...
```

Place your bootable DOS floppy disk in drive A and press any key to continue. When your system restarts, use FORMAT to prepare drive C as a bootable disk as follows.

```
A> FORMAT  C:  /S   <ENTER>
```

Creating a Primary and an Extended Partition

If your DOS version does not support partitions as large as your disk size, you must create a primary and an extended partition. Before you begin, you need to plan out how you want your disk partitioned. As briefly discussed, the extended disk partition can be any size. Within the extended partition you must divide the disk space into one or more logical drives, whose maximum size is less than the largest partition size DOS supports.

When you use a primary and an extended partition, your primary partition becomes drive C. Your extended partition can take on the drive letters D through Z (up to 23 logical drives!), depending on your partitioning.

If you make your partition or logical disk drive sizes too small, your drives will run out of disk space quickly. In addition, you may constrain the size of the largest file you can create.

As before, invoke FDISK from the floppy drive in disk A. FDISK will display its opening menu.

```
                    FDISK Options

Current fixed disk drive: 1

Choose one of the following:

1. Create DOS Partition or Logical DOS Drive
```

```
2. Set active partition
3. Delete DOS Partition or Logical DOS Drive
4. Display partition information

Enter choice: [1]

Press ESC to exit FDISK
```

Select option 1 to create a DOS partition. FDISK will display the following menu to determine if you want to create the primary or extended partition.

```
            Create DOS Partition or Logical DOS Drive

Current fixed disk drive: 1

Choose one of the following:

1. Create Primary DOS Partition
2. Create Extended DOS Partition
3. Create Logical DOS Drive(s) in the Extended DOS Partition

Enter Choice: [1]

Press Esc to return to FDISK Options
```

FDISK will not let you create an extended partition until after you create the primary partition. Select option 1 to create a primary partition. FDISK will display the following message, asking you if you want to use the largest possible partition.

```
            Create Primary DOS Partition

Current fixed disk drive: 1

Do you wish to use the maximum available size for a Primary DOS
partition and make the partition active (Y/N)............[Y]


Press Esc to return to FDISK Options
```

If you type **Y**, FDISK will create as big a primary partition as your disk will hold and your DOS version will support, display the following message, and restart when you press a key.

```
System will now restart

Insert DOS diskette in drive A
Press any key when ready...
```

After your system restarts, use the following command to prepare the primary partition for use by DOS.

```
A> FORMAT  C: /S  <ENTER>
```

Now you must create your extended DOS partition and define the corresponding logical drives. As before, invoke FDISK and select option 1 to create a DOS partition. When FDISK displays the following menu, select option 2 to create an extended partition.

```
           Create DOS Partition or Logical DOS Drive

Current fixed disk drive: 1

Choose one of the following:

1. Create Primary DOS Partition
2. Create Extended DOS Partition
3. Create Logical DOS Drive(s) in the Extended DOS Partition

Enter Choice: [1]

Press Esc to return to FDISK Options
```

FDISK will display a screen similar to the following that prompts you for the extended partition size.

```
           Create Extended DOS Partition

Current fixed disk drive: 1

Partition Status Type    Size in Mbytes    Percentage of Disk Used
  C:1          A    Pri DOS      30              50%

Total disk space is 60 Mbytes (1 Mbyte = 1048576 bytes)
```

```
Maximum space available for partition is 30Mbytes (50%)

Enter partition size in Mbytes or percent of disk space (%) to
create an Extended DOS Partition.........................[ 30]


Press Esc to return to FDISK options
```

Press ENTER to select the default partition size, which consumes the remainder of the disk. FDISK will display the following screen, telling you it has successfully created the partition.

```
                Create Extended DOS Partition

Current fixed disk drive: 1

Partition Status Type    Size in Mbytes    Percentage of Disk Used
  C:1         A   Pri DOS       30              50%
    2             Ext DOS       30              50%



Extended DOS Partition created

Press Esc to continue
```

You must further divide your extended partition into logical drives. Press ESC to continue, and FDISK will display a message telling you that no logical drives exist and prompting you to type in the size of the first drive.

```
Create Logical DOS Drive(s) in Extended DOS Partition

No logical drives defined

Total Extended DOS Partition is 30 Mbytes (1 Mbyte = 1048576
   bytes)
Maximum space available for logical drive is 30Mbytes (100%)


Enter logical drive in Mbytes or percent of disk space (%)..[30]

Press Esc to return to FDISK options
```

When you type in the size and press ENTER, FDISK will create the logical drive. Depending on the size of your extended partition, FDISK may prompt you for several logical drives. After you have defined all the logical drives, press ESC to return to FDISK's main menu and then ESC to return to DOS. As before, FDISK will display a message telling you the system will restart. Press any key to restart the system.

After the system successfully restarts, use the following format command to prepare the logical disk D for use by DOS.

```
C:\> FORMAT  D:   <ENTER>
```

Note the FORMAT command does not include /S. Because DOS only boots off the primary DOS partition, formatting the extended partitions as bootable disks would consume space unnecessarily for the DOS system files.

Hands On

If you don't need to partition your disk, there is no need for you to invoke FDISK. If you have worked with DOS for some time and have a current backup copy of your disk, you can invoke FDISK to determine the cylinders used for each of your disk partitions.

```
C:\> FDISK   <ENTER>
```

When FDISK displays its main menu, select option 4 to display partition information. FDISK will display information about your primary and extended partitions and then ask you if you want to view information about the logical drives. If you type Y, FDISK will display the starting and ending cylinder number for each logical drive along with the drive's size. Press ESC twice to return to DOS.

Review

1. What is a partition?

2. How many partitions can a disk have? How many of these partitions can DOS use?

3. What is a logical disk?

4. What are the four steps to prepare a hard disk for use?

5. What is the maximum primary partition size under the following DOS versions: 3.3, 4.0, 5.0?

Answers

1. A partition is a region of consecutive cylinders on your disk logically separated from the information stored on other partitions on the same disk.

2. A disk can contain up to four partitions. DOS lets you use two of these partitions, a primary DOS partition, and an extended partition.

3. If you create an extended partition on your disk, you must divide the extended partition into one or more logical disks. Your primary DOS partition will be drive C, and your first logical drive will be drive D. Because you only really have one hard drive, these additional (nonphysical) drives are called logical drives.

4. The four steps to prepare a hard disk are

    a. Inform your computer about the disk using SETUP.

    b. Perform a low-level format operation on the disk.

    c. Partition the disk using FDISK.

    d. Perform a high-level or logical disk format using FORMAT.

5. DOS 3.3 supports a maximum partition size of 32Mb, DOS 4.0 supports a maximum partition size of 512Mb, and DOS 5.0 supports a maximum partition size of 2Gb.

Advanced Concepts

There may be times when you want to change your disk's current partitions, for example, to upgrade to a version of DOS that supports larger partitions. To begin, back up your primary partition and logical drives to floppies. When the backup operation completes, invoke FDISK.

When FDISK displays its main menu, select option 3 to delete the DOS partitions. FDISK will display the following menu:

```
            Delete DOS Partition

Current fixed disk drive: 1

Choose one of the following:

1. Delete Primary DOS Partition
2. Delete Extended DOS Partition
3. Delete logical drive(s) in the Extended DOS Partition
4. Delete Non-DOS Partition


Enter choice: []
Press Esc to return to FDISK options
```

To begin, you must first delete your logical drives. Select option 3 and press ENTER. FDISK will display a screen containing information about each logical drive, followed by a prompt for the drive letter you want to delete. Type in the drive letter and press ENTER. FDISK will mark the drive as deleted and prompt you for the next drive letter. Repeat this process until no other logical disks exist. Press ESC to return to FDISK's main menu. Select option 3 again. FDISK will display a menu similar to the previous one. Choose option 2 to delete the extended partition. FDISK will display a warning message telling you the information on the partition will be lost and asking you to verify you want to continue. Type Y to delete the partition and press ENTER. FDISK will delete the partition. Press ESC to return to FDISK's main menu. Again select option 3. FDISK will display the previous main menu. Select option 1 to delete the primary DOS partition. As before, FDISK will display its warning that data will data be lost. Type Y and press ENTER to delete the partition. After FDISK deletes the partition, press ESC to return to FDISK's main menu. You can now create a new primary and, if necessary, a new extended partition using the techniques discussed earlier in this chapter.

Where FDISK Records Partition Information

As you have learned, every DOS disk has a boot record that it reads to determine the disk size and possibly to begin the DOS startup process. In addition, every hard disk contains a master boot record, which contains the disk's partition information, such as the starting cylinder for each partition. The master boot record starts at the disk's very first cylinder. The DOS boot record, on the other hand, starts at the beginning of the DOS partition, as illustrated in Figure 45-3.

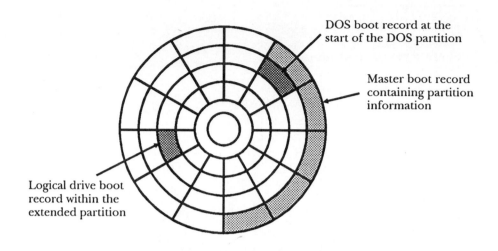

Figure 45-3.   *Every hard disk contains a master boot record that stores the partition information*

When you use FDISK to create or change disk partitions, FDISK updates the partition information stored in the disk's master boot record.

Key Terms

Partition   A region of consecutive, logically separated cylinders on a hard disk.

Primary partition   The disk partition used to boot DOS.

Extended partition   A technique introduced by DOS 3.3 to access disks larger than 32Mb. The extended partition could hold all the disk space unused by the primary partition. The extended partition was then further divided into logical disk drives, whose size could not exceed the maximum partition size defined by DOS.

Logical drives   Nonphysical disk drives. Your computer probably only has one hard drive. If you create an extended partition on the drive, you must further divide the partition into logical drives. Each of these drives receives a drive letter, such as D, E, F, all the way up to Z. Because your disk really doesn't have this many drives, these drives are called logical drives.

Chapter 46

The History of DOS

MS-DOS version 1.0 was originally released with the IBM PC in 1981. Since that time DOS has undergone many changes, becoming the most widely used operation system in the world. This chapter examines these changes in detail. If you are using DOS 5, you'll learn about many of the design decisions that led to DOS 5's development. If you are using a different version of DOS, you'll learn the differences between your DOS version and newer versions. If you really want to understand DOS, spend time reading this chapter. This information is presented at the end of this book because you now have the knowledge to understand fully and appreciate the discussion.

Before DOS

Although most users equate the term PC with the IBM PC or a PC-compatible originally introduced in 1981, the personal computer was actually in use throughout the 1970s. DOS is the operating system for the IBM PC and compatibles. Before DOS some computers used an interactive BASIC programming language for their operating system, while others used an operating system called CP/M, developed by Digital Research (the company who provides DR DOS).

Microsoft Corporation, the developers of MS-DOS, became a company in the late 1970s, when they developed programming languages such as BASIC for different microcomputers.

In 1980, IBM was designing the original IBM PC and asked Microsoft to develop several programming languages for their new computer. At this time CP/M was the operation system of choice and the leading candidate as the operating system for IBM's emerging computer. As Microsoft progressed in their design of languages and utilities for the IBM PC, they recognized that producing an operating system for the PC was a natural extension of their efforts. Unfortunately, they did not have enough time to develop an operating system from scratch. As a solution, Microsoft purchased, from the nearby Seattle Computer Products, 86-DOS, an operating system for the 8086 processor, which was very similar to the 8088 processor in the original IBM PC.

DOS 1.0

Using the 86-DOS operating system as its base, Microsoft developed MS-DOS version 1.0, the operating system released with the original IBM PC in 1981. Table 46-1 lists the commands provided in DOS version 1.0.

DOS 1.0 did not support tree-like (or hierarchical) directories. All file accesses where made through file control blocks, a technique borrowed from CP/M. DOS version 1.0 supported two types of executable files, COM and EXE. COM files used a format similar to CP/M executables and were restricted to 64Kb of memory for code, data, and stack space. In addition, version 1.0 introduced DOS batch files.

Because the original IBM PC normally shipped with only 64Kb to 256Kb, memory was a scare commodity. To reduce the amount of memory needed by the command processor (COMMAND.COM), version 1.0 divided the command processor into a resident section and a transient section whose contents DOS could overwrite during a program's execution. After each program ended, the resident section would examine the transient section, and if necessary, would load it from disk back into memory.

When Microsoft provided DOS to IBM, IBM used the name PC DOS to illustrate the close relationship to their IBM PC.

CHKDSK	DEBUG	ERASE	REM
COMMAND	DIR	FORMAT	REN
COMP	DISKCOMP	LINK	SYS
COPY	DISKCOPY	MODE	TIME
DATE	EDLIN	PAUSE	TYPE

Table 46-1.   DOS Commands Provided with Version 1.0

Version 1.1

In 1982, the second release of DOS, called MS-DOS version 1.25 by Microsoft and PC-DOS version 1.1 by IBM, provided support for double-sided disk drives. The initial single-sided floppy drives shipped with the original IBM PC could only access information stored on one side of the disk at a time. To reduce the number of disks required, users could buy disks called *flippies*. They could store information on one side of the flippy disk, take the disk out of the drive and "flip" it over to store information on the other. In addition to the support for double-sided disks, DOS 1.1 corrected some errors found in version 1.0 and provided the programmer's tool EXE2BIN.

Version 2.0

The original IBM PC was a floppy disk-based system, with floppy drives A and B. The original PC did not support hard disks, which, at the time, were very expensive. When IBM announced plans for the IBM PC XT, which contained a 10Mb hard disk, Microsoft had to develop a new file system for DOS. MS-DOS versions 1.0 and 1.1 did not support tree-like directories. For hard disks, however, such directories were a must.

Microsoft chose to develop a tree-like directory structure similar to the minicomputer UNIX operating system, whose popularity was beginning to grow at that time. Because file control blocks did not provide space for directory path names, Microsoft put file control blocks aside and based version 2.0 on file handles. A second benefit DOS obtained from file handles was the ability to perform I/O redirection (also a popular feature from UNIX).

By DOS version 2.0, the IBM PC was becoming very successful, and DOS was catching up with CP/M as the operating system of choice. Because of the PC's popularity, many hardware manufacturers developed PC-based products. To help these manufacturers integrate their products, MS-DOS 2.0 provided support for installable device drivers, providing the first CONFIG.SYS customization file. DOS version 2.0 contained many UNIX characteristics. UNIX, however, is a multiuser operating system that lets many users run several programs at one time.

To provide a very simple form of multitasking, version 2.0 provided support for memory-resident commands, such as GRAPHICS and PRINT.

Table 46-2 summarizes the commands added to DOS with version 2.0.

Following version 2.0, Microsoft released version MS-DOS 2.01, which provided support for international symbol sets. During this time, IBM was releasing its short-lived IBM PCjr computer. To support the PCjr, Microsoft developed PC-DOS 2.1 for IBM. Microsoft later combined these latest two DOS versions to produce MS-DOS 2.11. In late 1983, Microsoft released MS-DOS 2.25, which contained fixes to bugs and support for the extended ASCII character set.

ASSIGN	FC	MORE	SET
BACKUP	FDISK	PATH	SHIFT
BREAK	FIND	PRINT	SORT
CHDIR (CD)	FOR	PROMPT	TREE
CLS	GOTO	RECOVER	VER
CTTY	GRAPHICS	RESTORE	VERIFY
ECHO	IF	RMDIR (RD)	VOL
EXIT	MKDIR (MD)		

Table 46-2.   DOS Commands Introduced in Version 2.0

DOS 3.0

In 1984, IBM released its 80286 IBM PC AT, which used large 1.2Mb floppy drives and stored setup information about the computer in a CMOS chip. To support the PC AT, Microsoft released DOS version 3.0. The 1984 time period was the eve of computer networks. Although the widespread use of local area networks was still in the future, much of DOS version 3.0 was written with the future support for networks in mind. Table 46-3 lists the commands added to DOS in version 3.0

DOS support for local area networks arrived with version 3.1. Although DOS had replaced file control blocks with file handles in DOS version 2.0, programs still existed that used FCBs. To reduce the misuse of file control blocks in network programs, DOS 3.1 only let four file control blocks be open at one time. If a program opened a fifth, the network server or SHARE would close the oldest file control block. To provide support for additional file control blocks, DOS 3.1 added the CONFIG.SYS FCBS entry. In addition, DOS 3.1 introduced the JOIN and SUBST pretender commands.

In 1986, Microsoft released version 3.2, which provided support for 3 1/2-inch micro floppy disk drives. In addition, DOS version 3.2 introduced the REPLACE and XCOPY commands.

In 1987, IBM released its PS/2 line of computers. To support the PS/2, Microsoft released DOS version 3.3. In addition to supporting the PS/2, DOS 3.3 introduced five commands: CALL, APPEND, KEYB CHCP, NLSFUNC, and FASTOPEN.

ATTRIB	KEYB*xx*	SELECT
GRAFTABLE	LABEL	SHARE

Table 46-3.   DOS Commands Introduced in Version 3.0

DOS 3.3 was the most widely used and most popular version of DOS. In fact, many users today still run DOS 3.3 because they know it works well. The major shortcoming of version 3.3 is it only supports disk partitions up to 32Mb in size.

Version 4.0

In 1988, DOS version 4 was released to address the 32Mb disk partition-size restriction. Under version 4, disk partitions can contain up to 512Mb. In addition, DOS version 4 provided a menu-driven shell program that let users select files using menus or by pointing at a program or file and clicking the mouse. DOS version 4 also included the MEM command that let users not only display the contents of their computer's conventional memory, but also extended and expanded memory. In addition, version 4.0 updated several commands to make better use of memory.

The initial version of DOS 4 contained bugs and received poor reviews. To correct the bugs, Microsoft released version 4.01. Unfortunately, most users and many manufacturers had decided not to upgrade to DOS 4 by that time.

Version 5.0

Beginning in 1987, the personal computer revolution became the local area network revolution. Offices everywhere across the United States began connecting personal computers together to share information. It did not take long before user programs became so large, they had difficulty running within the 640Kb conventional memory limits imposed by DOS.

In some cases, users made use of expanded and extended memory. Unfortunately, many programs, including DOS, could not run in memory addresses above 640Kb.

In 1990, Microsoft had tremendous success with Windows, Microsoft's user-friendly interface. Under Windows, new users learned how to use their computer faster, and experienced users became more productive by running several programs at the same time.

Also in 1990, third-party disk utilities erupted into a several hundred million dollar annual market, selling "the utilities DOS forgot."

In 1991, Microsoft released DOS version 5.0, the result of a decade of improvements to the original 86-DOS.

DOS version 5 addresses memory restrictions by not only providing enhanced, extended, and expanded memory support, but also the ability to run DOS in high memory and to load device drivers and memory-resident commands into reserved memory.

DOSKEY	LOADFIX	MIRROR	UNDELETE
EDIT	LOADHIGH	SETVER	UNFORMAT
EXPAND			

Table 46-4.   DOS Commands Introduced in Version 5

DOS 5 also included a much more powerful menu-driven shell to replace the DOS 4 predecessor. In addition, version 5 lets users quickly recall previous commands and define memory-resident macros, which behave like small fast batch files.

To provide disk utilities to all users, DOS 5 provides commands that undelete files and rebuild a disk after an accidental disk format operation.

Last, to keep pace with the growth in hard disk sizes, DOS version 5 supports disk partitions up to 2 gigabytes!

Table 46-4 lists the commands introduced with version 5.

Conclusion

As you can see, DOS has evolved to support new computers, new hardware, and the ever-changing demands of users. It is impossible to expect one operating system to satisfy everyone's needs. DOS, however, continues to meet the demands of more than 50 million users and will continue to do so for some time. Just as DOS has come a long way since 1981, you have come a long way since you began Chapter 1. Congratulations on your journey, and may DOS be good to you.

Kris Jamsa

Command Reference

/ **APPEND** /

Defines a data-file search path

When DOS cannot find a data file as specified (or cannot find the file in the current directory), it searches to see if you have defined a data-file search path (a sequence of directories that DOS can follow to locate the data file). The APPEND command allows you to define disk drives and subdirectories to be included in this path, thus defining a *data-file search path* that DOS will use each time it fails to locate a file in the current directory or in a specified directory.

Format

```
APPEND [drive:][path] [;[drive:][path]...]
```

or

```
APPEND [/X][/E]
```

or

```
APPEND [;]
```

or, beginning with DOS 4

```
APPEND [/X:on|off] [/PATH:on|off]
```

drive: A disk drive that DOS is to include in the data-file search path.

path A DOS subdirectory to be included in the data-file search path.

... Indicates that the disk drive and subdirectories can be specified several times.

/X Aids in SEARCH-FIRST, FIND-FIRST, and EXEC options (see Notes).

/E Places an APPEND entry in the DOS environment in a manner similar to a PATH entry (see PATH). Therefore, the SET command can affect APPEND.

/X:on|off A DOS 4 or 5 switch that works much like the /X switch in previous versions of DOS. When you specify /X:on, the application can look in the appended directories for data files. When you specify /X:off, the application can only look in the current directory or the directory specified. You can abbreviate /X:on as simply /X.

/PATH:on|off   A DOS 4 or 5 switch that specifies that an application can search the appended directories for data files when the path name specified includes a drive and directory. If you specify /X:off, the application will search appended directories only if a filename is specified without a directory path. The default setting is /PATH:on.

Notes

APPEND is an external command that requires DOS 3.3 or later. If two files in the data path have the same name, APPEND will use the file it encounters first.

To reduce overhead with each file reference, place the directories that are most likely to contain data files first in your APPEND path. Each time it fails to locate a file in the current directory, DOS searches the first entry in your APPEND path. If it still doesn't locate your file in that directory, DOS searches the second, third, and so on. If your commonly used data files reside in the directories specified at the end of the APPEND command, DOS has to perform needless directory searches. These additional searches increase your system overhead. Not all commands use the data-file search path by default. Use the /X switch to increase the number of commands that use the data-file search path.

APPEND supports network drives and path names. If you use APPEND and ASSIGN, you must issue the APPEND command first. The /X:ON switch directs the following DOS system services to use appended directories:

System Service Number	Function
0FH	Open file
3DH	Open file handle
23H	Get file size
11H	Find first entry
4EH	Find first file
4FH	Find next file
4BH	Execute program

Examples

In the following example, if DOS cannot find the data file in the current directory, it will search the root directories on drives C, B, and A, in that order:

```
C:\> APPEND C:\;B:\;A:\   <ENTER>
```

In a similar manner, the following APPEND command directs DOS to search the directories \DOS, \UTIL, then \MISC, all of which reside on drive C.

```
C:\> APPEND C:\DOS;C:\UTIL;C:\MISC   <ENTER>
```

If you invoke APPEND without any command-line parameters, APPEND will display the current data-file search path.

```
C:\> APPEND   <ENTER>
```

To remove the current data-file search path, invoke APPEND with a semicolon.

```
C:\> APPEND ;   <ENTER>
```

Messages

APPEND/ASSIGN Conflict

You have issued the ASSIGN command before issuing the APPEND command. You must remove any disk drive reassignments before invoking APPEND.

APPEND/Top View Conflict

You are invoking APPEND while TopView is active. Terminate TopView and reissue the APPEND command.

No Append

The data-file search path is not currently in use.

APPEND already installed

The APPEND command has already been invoked. Once invoked, APPEND installs memory-resident software that handles your data-file search path processing. To modify the data-file search path, omit a disk drive specifier or subdirectory path that may precede the command name APPEND in the command line.

Out of environment space

You have very likely installed a memory-resident program (GRAPHICS, PRINT, or a third-party product) that prevents DOS from expanding the environment to store your new entry. If necessary, restart DOS and issue your APPEND command prior to invoking the memory-resident program. Remember, by using SHELL= in CONFIG.SYS, you can specify the desired size of your DOS environment. Last, you can simply invoke APPEND without specifying the /E switch.

ASSIGN

Routes disk drive references from one disk drive to another

Many older software packages look on drive A for data or overlay files. If you want to install such software on your hard disk, you must trick the software into looking on the hard disk for the files. ASSIGN lets you do this by routing disk drive references from one disk drive to another.

Format

```
ASSIGN [source_drive=target_drive [...]] [/STATUS]
```

source_drive   The drive letter of the disk from which I/O references are routed. A colon after the drive letter is optional.

target_drive   The drive letter of the disk to which I/O operations will be routed. A colon after the drive letter is optional.

...   Indicates that the command can be repeated several times.

/STATUS   Is a DOS 5 switch that lets you display the current drive assignments.

Notes

ASSIGN is an external command that requires DOS 2.0 or later. If you invoke ASSIGN without any command-line parameters, ASSIGN will restore its original disk drive assignments. In other words, invoking this command by simply typing **ASSIGN** restores the default assignments.

Most users should consider using the SUBST command instead of ASSIGN. Do not use an assigned disk with the BACKUP, DISKCOMP, DISKCOPY, FORMAT, JOIN, LABEL, MIRROR, PRINT, RESTORE, SUBST, UNDELETE, or UNFORMAT commands.

Microsoft recommends that, to ensure compatibility with future versions of DOS, you use the SUBST command instead of ASSIGN. If you use ASSIGN and APPEND, you must issue the APPEND command first.

The following ASSIGN and SUBST commands are functionally similar:

```
C:\> ASSIGN A=C   <ENTER>
C:\> SUBST   A:  C:\   <ENTER>
```

Examples

In the following example, DOS disk I/O operations that reference drive A are routed to the disk in drive C:

```
C:\> ASSIGN A=C   <ENTER>
```

If you invoke a command such as

```
C:\> DIR A:   <ENTER>
```

DOS will actually list the files contained on drive C, as shown here:

```
Volume in drive C has no label
Volume Serial Number is 1234-4321
Directory of  C:\MISC

HARDWARE        <DIR>      10-05-90    2:20p
SOFTWARE        <DIR>      10-05-90    2:24p
LEDGER          <DIR>      10-05-90    2:24p
        3 File(s)     1209344 bytes free
```

The following command illustrates that you can perform multiple disk drive assignments on one command line. In this case, DOS will route disk drive requests from either drive A or drive B to drive C:

```
C:\> ASSIGN A=C B=C   <ENTER>
```

Under DOS 5, you can use the /STATUS switch to display the current drive assignments.

```
C:\> ASSIGN /STATUS   <ENTER>
   Original A: set to C:
   Original B: set to C:
```

If you invoke ASSIGN without any command-line parameters, DOS will restore the original disk drive assignments:

```
C:\> ASSIGN   <ENTER>
```

ATTRIB

Displays or modifies a file's attribute byte

The ATTRIB command displays or modifies a file's attribute byte, which contains information about the file. Several DOS commands, such as BACKUP, RESTORE, and XCOPY, use a file's attribute to enable selective file processing. By using these commands in conjunction with ATTRIB, you can gain considerable file-processing control.

Format

```
ATTRIB [+A|-A] [+R|-R] file_spec [/S]
```

or, under DOS 5

```
ATTRIB [+A|-A] [+R|-R] [+S|-S] [+H|-H] file_spec [/S]
```

+A   Directs ATTRIB to set a file's archive bit (the bit used to identify the backup history of a file).

–A   Directs ATTRIB to clear a file's archive bit.

+R   Directs ATTRIB to set a file's read-only bit (the bit that only allows a file to be read and not written to).

–R   Directs ATTRIB to clear a file's read-only bit.

+S   Directs ATTRIB to set the file's system bit. This is a DOS 5 switch.

–S   Directs ATTRIB to clear the file's system bit. This is a DOS 5 switch.

+H   Directs ATTRIB to set the file's hidden bit. This is a DOS 5 switch.

–H   Directs ATTRIB to clear the file's hidden bit. This is a DOS 5 switch.

file_spec   The complete DOS file specification, including the disk drive and path name, of the file (or files) to be modified. ATTRIB supports DOS wildcard characters.

/S   Directs DOS to process all files in the subdirectories below the specified directory. This is a DOS 3.3 switch.

Notes

ATTRIB is an external command that requires DOS 3.0 or later. Every file on your disk has specific characteristics or attributes. The ATTRIB command lets you change a file's attributes. The read-only and archive attributes are the most common attributes users change. A read-only file cannot be overwritten or deleted by DOS. By setting the files on your disk whose contents don't change on a regular basis to read-only, you reduce the possibility of an errant DOS command destroying the file's contents. If you attempt to delete a file whose read-only bit is set, DOS will display the message "Access denied."

```
C:\> DEL FILENAME.EXT   <ENTER>
Access denied
```

If you really want to delete the file, you must first clear the file's read-only bit.

The archive attribute helps DOS determine which files on your disk need to be backed up. Every time you create a file or change an existing file's contents, DOS sets the file's archive attribute. The BACKUP command searches your disk for files whose archive attribute is set. After it successfully copies the file to a backup disk, BACKUP clears the file's archive bit. As you will see in the examples, you can use the archive bit in conjunction with XCOPY to copy files from your hard disk to floppy, resuming a copy operation with a second floppy disk when your first floppy disk runs out of space. Under DOS 5, you can set a file's system bit. The system attribute is normally reserved for the DOS hidden files that DOS uses each time the system starts. You should reserve its use for DOS.

Under DOS 5, you can set a file's hidden bit. A hidden file exists on your disk, but does not appear in a directory listing. By hiding a file, you prevent it from being inadvertently deleted or being viewed by another user who does not know the file exists. Be careful with the hidden file attribute—if you are not careful, you may misplace one or more files because you cannot later remember where you hid them.

Examples

In the following command

```
C:\> ATTRIB +R CONFIG.SYS   <ENTER>
```

ATTRIB will set the CONFIG.SYS file to read-only. This means that DOS cannot modify the file's contents. If you attempt to delete a read-only file, for example, DOS will display

```
Access Denied
```

If you do not specify an attribute switch,

```
C:\> ATTRIB *.*   <ENTER>
```

ATTRIB will display the current attributes of each file (in these examples, the files contain an archive designation):

```
A          C:\DOS\ANSI.EXE
A          C:\DOS\ATTRIB.EXE
A          C:\DOS\FDISK.EXE
A          C:\DOS\GWBASIC.EXE
A          C:\DOS\SUBST.EXE
A          C:\DOS\XCOPY.EXE
```

The BACKUP /M switch directs BACKUP to back up only those files modified since the previous backup (see BACKUP for more information on this command). By issuing the command

```
C:\> ATTRIB +A \*.* /S   <ENTER>
```

you can set the archive bit (the bit used to record the backup history of the file) of every file on disk, indicating that a backup is required for each. Similarly, the command

```
C:\> ATTRIB -A \*.* /S   <ENTER>
```

marks each file as being backed up.

You can use ATTRIB in conjunction with XCOPY to copy the entire contents of a fixed disk to floppy disks, still maintaining the original disk structure (see XCOPY for more information on this command). First mark all the files on disk as requiring a backup:

```
C:\> ATTRIB +A \*.* /S   <ENTER>
```

Next, simply invoke XCOPY.

```
C:\> XCOPY C:\*.* A: /S /M   <ENTER>
```

When the floppy disk fills, XCOPY displays a message stating that it is filled, then terminates. Insert a new floppy disk in the drive, then again repeat the XCOPY command. XCOPY will pick up with the first file marked needing archiving, resuming the process at the correct location. Repeat this process until XCOPY finds no files to copy.

Under DOS 5, the following command hides the file MY_NOTES.TXT.

```
C:\> ATTRIB +H MY_NOTES.TXT   <ENTER>
```

A hidden file will not appear in a directory listing. The DOS 4 and 5 shells provide the ability to view hidden files. If you try to remove a directory that appears empty, but get an error message that tells you the directory is not empty, the directory may contain hidden files.

Messages

Syntax error

Your command line contains an option other than ±A, ±R, ±S, or ±H.

BACKUP

Backs up one or more files to a new disk

Backs up (or copies) all of the files or the files you specify on your hard disk to floppy disks. Should you accidentally delete or overwrite the information on your hard disk, you can restore the files from the backup floppy disk, provided you perform backups on a regular basis.

Format

```
BACKUP source:[file_spec] target: [/A][/D:mm-dd-yy]
 [/L:log_file][/M][/S][T:hh:mm:ss][/F[:size]]
```

source: The source disk that contains the file (or files) to be backed up.

file_spec   The DOS path name (or names) for the file (or files) to back up. BACKUP fully supports wildcard characters.

target: The target disk to which copies are written.

/A   Directs BACKUP to append source files to files on the target disk.

/D: *mm-dd-yy*   Directs BACKUP to back up only files modified since the specified date.

/L: *log_file*   Places an entry for all the files in a specified log file. BACKUP.LOG is the default.

/M   Directs BACKUP to back up only files modified since the last backup.

/S   Directs BACKUP to back up all directories below the source directory.

/T: *hh:mm:ss*   Directs BACKUP to back up only files modified since the specified time. This switch requires DOS 3.3 or later.

/F   Tells DOS to format an unformatted disk. This switch requires DOS 3.3 or later. If you are using DOS 5, you can specify the size of the floppy disk BACKUP is to format using /F:*size*, where *size* is one of the following:

160	160K	160Kb			
180	180K	180Kb			
320	320K	320Kb			
360	360K	360Kb			
720	720K	720Kb			
1200	1200K	1200Kb	1.2	1.2M	1.2Mb
1440	1440K	1440Kb	1.44	1.44M	1.44Mb
2880	2880K	2880Kb	2.88	2.88M	2.88Mb

Notes

BACKUP is an external command that requires DOS 2.0 or later. The BACKUP command works closely with the operating system's directory entries to select specific files for backup. Note that DOS directory fields (information about each file that is listed in the directory) relate closely to switches included in the BACKUP command line (see the Format section for a complete list of these switches).

A 10Mb disk requires approximately 25 360Kb floppy disks or 8 1.2Mb disks for a complete backup. To determine the exact number of disks required to perform a backup, first use CHKDSK.

```
C:\> CHKDSK   <ENTER>

Volume DOSDISK    created 06-30-1991 9:46pm

21309440 bytes total disk space.
  206848 bytes in 90 directories.
13946880 bytes in 1694 user files.
   20480 bytes in bad sectors.
 7084032 bytes available on disk.

C:\>
```

The number of disks required is computed by means of this formula:

$$\text{Disks required} = \frac{(\text{Total disk space} - \text{available disk space})}{\text{floppy disk space}}$$

In this case, the equation becomes:

```
Disks required = (21309440  -  7084032)/1213952
               = 11.718
               = 12 (1.2Mb) floppy disks
```

If you use your computer, back up your files. If you are using floppy disks as opposed to a hard disk, use the DISKCOPY command to duplicate your original disks, thus creating working copies of the disk to use on a daily basis. Place your original disks in a safe location. If you are using a hard disk, backups are easy and fast. If you perform your backups on a regular basis, you will probably have to invest about five minutes a day to ensure that you have a complete system backup. However, if you don't perform backups regularly, when you finally perform them, your backups may take considerable time. If you are using DOS 3.3, the BACKUP log file can help you quickly locate which of your floppy disks contains a specific file you want to restore. The log file contains the date and time you performed the backup operation and the name of each file contained on each backup disk.

The BACKUP command exits with one of the following exit status values:

Exit Status	Meaning
0	Successful backup
1	No files found to back up
2	Sharing conflicts prevented some files from being backed up
3	User termination via CTRL-C
4	An error prevented system backup

Examples

The following command backs up all the files on drive C, including those in DOS subdirectories, to the floppy disk in drive A. In other words, the command performs a complete disk backup.

```
C:\> BACKUP C:\*.* A: /S   <ENTER>
```

The following command performs an incremental backup, backing up only those files you have created or changed since the last backup operation. Ideally, you should perform an incremental backup of your files at the end of each day.

```
C:\> BACKUP C:\*.*  A: /S /A /M   <ENTER>
```

The following command uses the BACKUP /A switch to add the file C:TEST.DAT to the files contained on the backup disk in drive A:

```
C:\> BACKUP C:TEST.DAT A: /A   <ENTER>
```

Finally, the next command directs BACKUP to back up only those files created since June 30, 1991:

```
C:\> BACKUP C:\*.* A: /S /D:6:30:91   <ENTER>
```

Messages

*** Backing up files to drive *n*: ***
Diskette Number: *n*

An informational message concerning the disk drive to which BACKUP is backing up files, along with the backup disk number that it is creating. You can use the disk number when labeling your backup disks.

*** Last file not backed up ***

BACKUP did not back up the last file displayed on the screen. This error normally occurs when the backup target disk becomes full. It occurs only when you are using a hard disk as a source disk.

Fixed backup device *n* is full

Your target drive for your BACKUP command is a hard disk. In this case, the disk has become full and BACKUP cannot continue.

Insert backup diskette *n* in drive *n*:
Press any key to continue . . .

BACKUP is prompting you to insert the backup disk number specified in the backup target drive. Once you have done so, press any key for BACKUP to continue.

Insert last backup diskette in drive *n*:
Press any key to continue . . .

Your BACKUP command line contains the /A switch, which directs BACKUP to add the files requiring a backup to the disk in the target drive. In this case, BACKUP is prompting you to place the last disk used in a backup operation into the specified drive. Once you do so, press any key to continue. Review the format of the BACKUP command and reissue the command.

Last backup diskette not inserted
Insert last backup diskette in drive *n*:
Press any key to continue . . .

The disk that you inserted in the BACKUP target drive is not the last disk you used for a BACKUP operation. Insert the correct disk and press any key to continue the backup.

Source and target drives are the same

The source and target disk drives that you have specified in your BACKUP command are the same disk drive. BACKUP does not support processing of this type. Reissue the BACKUP command, specifying a different disk drive as the target drive.

WARNING! Files in the target drive
***n:* root directory will be erased**
Press any key to continue . . .

BACKUP is warning you that if you continue with the BACKUP operation all of the files in the root directory of the target disk will be erased. Since you should be using newly formatted disks for your backup operations, this error message should be purely informational.

WARNING! Files in the target drive
C:\\BACKUP directory will be erased
Press any key to continue . . .

BACKUP is warning you that if you continue with the BACKUP operation all of the files in the \\BACKUP subdirectory of the specified hard disk will be deleted. Make sure that you no longer require the files in the directory before continuing.

WARNING! No files were found to back up

BACKUP either did not find any files requiring a backup, or it did not find any files matching the file specifications in your BACKUP command line.

Disk full error writing to BACKUP log file

Your BACKUP command line included the /L switch, directing BACKUP to create a log file. In this case, BACKUP ran out of disk space while trying to write to the log file. Press any key to resume the backup or press CTRL-C to end the backup, so you can correct the error.

Error opening log file

Your BACKUP command line contains the /L switch, directing BACKUP to create a log file. In this case, BACKUP encountered an error while trying to open the log file. Make sure you specify a correct path name to the log file you want BACKUP to create. Make sure an existing file with the same name is not a read-only file.

Invalid Date/Time

Your BACKUP command line contains either a /D (date) or /T (time) switch, and either the date or time specified is invalid. Repeat the BACKUP command specifying the date or time in the correct format.

Logging to FILENAME.EXT

Your BACKUP command line contains the /L switch, directing BACKUP to create a log file. BACKUP is simply displaying a message to tell you it is logging the backup to the file specified.

BREAK

Enables or disables DOS extended CTRL-BREAK checking

By default, DOS checks for a user-entered CTRL-BREAK when it completes keyboard, screen, and printer input or output operations. If you enable extended CTRL-BREAK checking (that is, enter a BREAK ON command), DOS will also check for a user-entered CTRL-BREAK when it completes services performed by the operating system, such as disk read or write operations.

Format

```
BREAK [ON | OFF]
```

ON   Enables extended CTRL-BREAK checking.

OFF   Disables extended CTRL-BREAK checking.

Notes

BREAK is an internal command that requires DOS 2.0 or higher. By using BREAK to enable extended CTRL-BREAK processing, you increase the amount of time that the system uses to complete operations, because DOS must check for a CTRL-BREAK upon completing each system service. Therefore, programmers may want to set BREAK to ON during program development. Most users, however, will leave the setting at the default BREAK OFF.

If you invoke BREAK without a command-line parameter, it will display the current state of processing, either ON or OFF.

By default, DOS boots with extended CTRL-BREAK checking turned off. To enable extended checking at system startup, place the entry

```
BREAK=ON
```

in the file CONFIG.SYS. If you want to enable extended checking right now, issue the BREAK ON command.

Examples

The following command enables DOS extended CTRL-BREAK checking:

```
C:\> BREAK ON   <ENTER>
```

Invoking BREAK without a command-line parameter causes BREAK to display the current state of extended CTRL-BREAK checking:

```
C:\> BREAK   <ENTER>
BREAK is on
```

Messages

Must specify ON or OFF

You have invoked the BREAK command specifying a command-line parameter other than ON or OFF. Reissue the command with either no command-line parameters (to display the current break setting), or with either the parameter ON (enable extended checking) or OFF (disable extended checking).

CALL

Invokes one batch file from within a second batch file

DOS has difficulty invoking one batch file from within a second batch file (see AUTOEXEC for a discussion of batch files). This is especially true when the invocation of a procedure appears in the middle of the batch file. If you must invoke a batch procedure from within a batch file (using a batch procedure within a batch file), the CALL command lets you do so.

Format

```
CALL BatchFile [argument [...]]
```

BatchFile   The name of the second batch file to invoke.

argument   One or more command-line parameters for the nested batch file.

Notes

CALL is an internal command that requires DOS 3.3 or higher. The batch file CALL invokes must include a complete path name or be in the current directory or a directory in the command path. Do not use I/O redirection with CALL. CALL supports recursion, meaning a batch file can call itself to perform a specific task. This command is similar to the function provided by using COMMAND /C within a batch file (see COMMAND).

Examples

As in the following example, CALL can be included in a batch file to invoke a nested procedure (that is "nested" or included within another batch command):

```
CLS
CALL MYPROC
DATE
```

The following batch file, SHOWLINE.BAT, uses CALL to recursively call itself to display its first ten command-line arguments.

```
@ECHO OFF
IF NOT '%1'=='' ECHO %1
SHIFT
IF NOT '%1'=='' CALL SHOWLINE %1 %2 %3 %4 %5 %6 %7 %8 %9
```

CHCP

Displays or changes the current code page

Each time DOS displays a character on the screen, DOS must first map the ASCII value of the character to a specific letter in a chosen character set. DOS uses code pages to map characters to letters.

Format

```
CHCP [code_page]
```

code_page   Specifies the desired code page. This parameter must have been previously prepared by the system as either the primary or secondary code page in CONFIG.SYS. Valid codepage entries include the following:

Code Page	Country
437	United States
850	Multilingual
852	Slavic (DOS 5)
860	Portuguese
863	French Canadian
865	Nordic

Notes

CHCP is an internal command that requires DOS 3.3 or higher. The CHCP command lets you temporarily set the desired code page for a device. If you intend to use the code page that you have specified on a regular basis, use the COUNTRY= entry in CONFIG.SYS. In so doing, your system will always start with the desired code page active.

DOS lets you use different character sets for your DOS session, thus offering international character support. To select an alternate code page (that is, a special character set), you must have previously issued the NLSFUNC command (see NLSFUNC). By entering a codepage value using CHCP, you can reassign an alternate character set to be used by DOS. If you invoke CHCP without a command-line parameter, CHCP will display the current code page.

The steps to use CHCP to change code pages are the following:

1. Install DISPLAY.SYS in CONFIG.SYS with the correct settings.

2. Optionally install PRINTER.SYS in CONFIG.SYS with the correct printer settings.

3. Run the NLSFUNC command. If you are using DOS 4, use the CONFIG.SYS INSTALL entry to load NLSFUNC. If you are using DOS 5, use the LOADHIGH command.

4. Optionally invoke KEYB to select the international keyboard template.

5. Use the MODE command to prepare the code page for use.

DOS provides several files with the CPI extension. These files contain codepage information for a specific device type.

Examples

The following command directs CHCP to select the Nordic code page. Remember, this code page must have been prepared for use by DOS on your system, via the MODE command.

```
C:\> CHCP 865   <ENTER>
```

To view the current code page, invoke CHCP without specifying a codepage value.

```
C:\> CHCP   <ENTER>
Active code page: 865
```

Messages

Code page *nnn* not prepared for system

Make sure you have installed the PRINTER.SYS and DISPLAY.SYS device drivers in CONFIG.SYS as required. Next, make sure you have issued the NLSFUNC command and prepared the code page for use via the MODE command.

File not found

CHCP could not find the file COUNTRY.SYS. Make sure that the file COUNTRY.SYS resides in the current directory or that you specify the location of this file when you invoke NLSFUNC.

No code page has been selected

This message is purely informational, telling you no code page has been selected yet. Use the MODE command to view the code pages that have been prepared.

CHDIR

Changes or displays the default directory

To organize your files, DOS lets you group related files into directories. The CHDIR command changes or displays the current directory name for a specified disk drive. Changing directories is similar to opening a new drawer of a filing cabinet to access different files.

Format

```
CHDIR [drive:][path]
```

or

```
CD [drive:] [path]
```

drive: The disk drive on which you want to set the current directory. If you omit this parameter, CHDIR will use the current drive.

path   The DOS path name for the current directory that you desire. If you omit the path, CHDIR will display the current directory.

Notes

CHDIR is an internal command that requires DOS 2.0 or later. All DOS disks begin with a single directory called the root directory. DOS uses the backslash \ to represent the root. Using the MKDIR command you can create directories on your disk, much as you would label drawers in a filing cabinet. The CHDIR command lets you select a specific directory (open a filing cabinet drawer). When you work within a specific directory, your commands typically only affect the files in the current directory. DOS maintains a current directory for each disk drive. For example, the current directory on drive C may be C:\DOS, while the current directory on drive A may be the root, A:\. Due to its frequency of use, DOS lets you abbreviate CHDIR as CD.

Each time you specify a DOS path name (the path that DOS follows to locate a file or command) for CHDIR, DOS will perform the following processing: If the path name is preceded with a slash (as in \SUBDIR) DOS will begin its search for the directory at the root (the directory in which the system begins operations at startup). However, if the path name does not begin with a slash (as in SUBDIR) the subdirectory must reside below the current default directory.

For every subdirectory that you create, DOS predefines two directory names:

.   Current default directory
..   Parent directory of the current directory

Verify this by performing a directory listing of a DOS subdirectory:

```
 Volume in drive C is DOSDISK
 Volume Serial Number is 1234-4321

Directory of C:\SUBDIR

 .   <DIR>       11-01-90   11:34a
 ..  <DIR>       11-01-90   11:34a
   2 File(s) 7182336 bytes free
```

If you issue the following directory command, DOS will display a directory listing of the current directory:

```
C:\> DIR .  <ENTER>

 Volume in drive C is DOSDISK
 Volume Serial Number is 1234-4321

Directory of C:\SUBDIR

.          <DIR>         11-01-90   11:34a
..         <DIR>         11-01-90   11:34a
      2 File(s)     7182336 bytes free
```

If you use the following command, the files in the parent directory are displayed:

```
C:\> DIR ..  <ENTER>
```

Always separate your files logically into DOS subdirectories. Once you have created several levels of subdirectories, however, it is not always easy to remember which directory you are currently using. Thus, use the following DOS prompt command

```
C> PROMPT $p$g  <ENTER>
```

which sets your DOS prompt to the current drive and directory. Note how your prompt changes as you change directories:

```
C> PROMPT $p$g       <ENTER>
C:\> CD DOS          <ENTER>
C:\DOS> CD \LOTUS    <ENTER>
C:\LOTUS>
```

Examples

Invoking CHDIR without a path name causes CHDIR to display the current directory:

```
C> CD
C:\SUBDIR
```

This command is valid with a disk drive letter, in this case displaying the current directory for drive A.

```
C> CD A:
A:\UTIL
```

The following DOS CHDIR command selects the \DOS\BATFILES directory as the current default directory for drive C:

```
C:\> CD \DOS\BATFILES    <ENTER>
```

You could actually issue this command as two separate commands, first selecting the subdirectory \DOS, like this:

```
C:\> CD \DOS    <ENTER>
```

and then selecting BATFILES:

```
C:\DOS> CD BATFILES    <ENTER>
```

Note the use of the leading backslash in the command

```
C> CD \DOS    <ENTER>
```

When the backslash is used, DOS looks for the subdirectory named DOS in the root directory of drive C. With the following command, however,

```
C:\DOS> CD BATFILES    <ENTER>
```

CHDIR will not look for the directory in the root, but in a subdirectory below the current directory (which is \DOS). If the command had been

```
C:\DOS> CD \BATFILES   <ENTER>
```

CHDIR would not have found the directory, because it would have looked in the root instead of in the current directory.

Messages

Invalid directory

The subdirectory (or a path in the directory) that you are specifying in the command does not exist. Recheck the spelling of the path, ensuring that it contains the necessary backslashes.

CHKDSK

Checks a disk's current status

CHKDSK examines your disk's file allocation tables and directory structures and reports errors and inconsistencies, giving you the opportunity to correct the errors.

Format

```
CHKDSK [drive:][path][file_name] [/F] [/V]
```

drive: The disk drive that CHKDSK is to examine.

path   A DOS subdirectory that contains files that CHKDSK is to examine for disk fragmentation.

file_name   The file name and extension of the file, or files, that CHKDSK is to examine for disk fragmentation. CHKDSK supports wildcard characters.

/F   Directs CHKDSK to fix errors found in a directory or FAT (file allocation table).

/V   Directs CHKDSK to display the names of all files on the disk.

Notes

CHKDSK is an external command supported by all DOS versions. It reports on the status of the following disk conditions:

- The amount of free, used, and corrupted disk space
- The number of hidden files
- The amount of free and used memory

Occasionally, as the normal day-to-day operations of a disk cause wear and tear on the storage media, files become corrupted and lose sectors. CHKDSK allows you to view and even repair such discrepancies. It is also possible for a DOS file to become fragmented, which means that the file's contents are dispersed in different locations on the disk. The problem with fragmented files is that they decrease the speed at which the system performs file I/O operations because the disk drive must rotate the disk several additional times to read the disk. The CHKDSK command displays information on fragmented files as well. Once your disk becomes severely fragmented, you should consider a system backup-format-restore operation (see BACKUP, FORMAT, and RESTORE).

CHKDSK does not work with JOINed or SUBSTed disks (see JOIN and SUBST).

If you are operating on a local area network, do not try to repair your disk. When DOS has files open (as may be the case with a network), DOS cannot correctly update the file allocation table (FAT), which is used by DOS to record disk sectors currently being used to store files, sectors that are available for file allocation, and sectors that are unusable because of media corruption.

By default, CHKDSK will only report disk errors—CHKDSK will not attempt to fix them. To write actual corrections to disk, use the /F switch.

At a minimum, you should issue CHKDSK

```
C:\> CHKDSK /F  <ENTER>
```

once a month to examine your hard disk. Although it is not common, DOS can periodically encounter errors when it writes information to disk. Depending upon the error, you may not realize that it has occurred. The CHKDSK command is your only tool for testing the "health" of your disk. If CHKDSK locates lost cluster pointers caused by an error, CHKDSK will display

```
nnn lost allocation units found in n chains.
Convert lost chains to files  (Y/N)?
```

If you respond with Y, CHKDSK will create one or more files containing the information referenced by the lost pointers. These files will be placed in your root directory and given the names FILE0000.CHK, FILE0001.CHK, and so on.

Use the TYPE command to examine the contents of these files. If they don't contain useful information, simply delete them.

Examples

The following command displays the state of the current disk:

```
C:\> CHKDSK   <ENTER>
```

The output might be

```
Volume DOS          created 05-20-1991 7:12p
Volume Serial Number is 1529-17E8

 104515584 bytes total disk space
     73728 bytes in 3 hidden files
    182272 bytes in 65 directories
  44589056 bytes in 2254 user files
  59670528 bytes available on disk

      2048 bytes in each allocation unit

     51033 total allocation units on disk
     29136 available allocation units on disk

    655360 total bytes memory
    492672 bytes free
```

If you specify a file specification or DOS wildcard characters, CHKDSK will report on disk fragmentation within the current directory.

```
C:\> CHKDSK *.*   <ENTER>
```

If fragmented files exist, CHKDSK will display

```
C:\FILENAME.EXT contains n non-contiguous blocks.
```

If CHKDSK discovers errors while examining your disk contents, it will display

```
Volume DOS         created 05-20-1991 7:12p
Volume Serial Number is 1529-17E8

Errors found, F parameter not specified
Corrections will not be written to disk

1 lost allocation units found in 1 chains.
2048 bytes disk space would be freed.
```

To direct CHKDSK to repair the error, use the /F switch:

```
C:\> CHKDSK /F   <ENTER>
```

Many users use CHKDSK to locate a file quickly. If you invoke CHKDSK with the /V switch, CHKDSK will display the name of every file on the disk:

```
C:\> CHKDSK /V   <ENTER>
```

Messages

Directory is joined

CHKDSK cannot process the subdirectory specified because the directory is joined to another DOS disk. CHKDSK cannot process a subdirectory that is joined. See JOIN.

Directory is totally empty, no . or ..

The subdirectory specified is probably damaged. In most cases, this error message is an indication of a severely damaged disk. If possible, back up the files on your disk immediately.

Disk error reading fat *n*

CHKDSK cannot read the file allocation table (FAT) specified. DOS tracks its files by recording which sectors are associated with a file in a table called the file allocation table that DOS stores on disk. To keep a single disk error from preventing DOS from accessing your files, DOS provides two identical file allocation tables. If one file allocation table becomes corrupted, DOS uses the second table. Should this error message occur, back up the files on your disk immediately. Use the FORMAT command to reformat your disk and RESTORE to place your files back on to the disk.

Disk error writing fat *n*

CHKDSK cannot write to the file allocation table (FAT) specified. DOS tracks its files by recording which sectors are associated with a file in a table called the file allocation table that DOS stores on disk. To keep a single disk error from preventing DOS from accessing your files, DOS provides two identical file allocation tables. If one file allocation table becomes corrupted, DOS uses the second table. In this case, DOS is telling you that it cannot write to the file allocation table. Back up the files from your disk immediately. Perform a disk FORMAT and RESTORE operation.

Insufficient room in root directory
Erase files in root and repeat CHKDSK

Your CHKDSK command line included the /F switch to convert lost clusters to files in the root. The root directory is full, and CHKDSK cannot continue converting the lost clusters until you make room in the root by copying files to another disk or directory. After you have made available directory entries, repeat the CHKDSK command to convert the remaining lost cluster chains.

Errors found, F parameter not specified
Corrections will not be written to disk

CHKDSK found errors while examining the disk specified. Since you did not place the /F switch in the CHKDSK command line, CHKDSK will not record its corrections to disk. In most cases, you will want to reissue the CHKDSK command, including the /F switch.

File allocation table bad drive *n*:

CHKDSK cannot access the file allocation table on the disk drive specified. DOS tracks its files by recording which sectors are associated with a file in a table called the file allocation table that DOS stores on disk. To keep a single disk error from preventing DOS from accessing your files, DOS provides two identical file allocation tables. If one file allocation table becomes corrupted, DOS uses the second table. In this case, DOS cannot access the file allocation table on the drive specified. Back up the files on your disk immediately. Use FORMAT to reformat your disk and RESTORE to place your files back on to the disk.

First cluster number is invalid, entry truncated
Has invalid cluster, file truncated

Either message indicates that the file specified contains an invalid cluster number in the file allocation table. Therefore, CHKDSK has truncated the file to zero bytes, if the first cluster is bad, or to the length of the last valid cluster. CHKDSK will also very likely encounter lost clusters that contain the file's original contents. Using the /F switch, direct CHKDSK to combine the lost clusters into a file whose contents you may be able to examine depending on the file's original type.

General Failure error reading drive *n*:

The disk in the drive specified has probably not yet been formatted or is severely damaged.

Unrecoverable error in directory
Convert directory to a file (Y/N)?

CHKDSK has encountered an error in the directory specified that prevents it from continuing its processing. CHKDSK wants to know whether or not it should convert the damaged directory to a file. In some cases you may simply want to delete the damaged directory from your disk. If so, type Y and press ENTER, otherwise, type N. If you convert the directory to a file, the files once referenced by entries in the directory will become lost clusters on your disk. Using the /F switch, direct CHKDSK to combine the lost clusters into files whose contents you may be able to examine, depending on each file's original type.

. Does not exist

The abbreviated name for the current directory does not exist. If this error occurs, you should consider making a complete backup of all of the files on your disk. This may be a sign of disk errors to come.

.. Does not exist

The abbreviated name for the parent directory does not exist. If this error occurs, back up all of the files on your disk. This may be a sign of disk errors to come.

FILENAME.EXT is cross linked on cluster *n*

DOS has erroneously assigned two files to point to the same cluster (set of sectors) on disk. Copy both of the files to a new disk and delete them. One of the files will be damaged (missing information). If the file is a text file, you will have to replace the missing data. If the file contains a program, do not execute it. Executing a damaged program can damage your disks and the information that they contain. When CHKDSK encounters cross-linked files, CHKDSK will very likely also encounter lost clusters that belong to one of the files. Using the /F switch, direct CHKDSK to combine the lost clusters into a file whose contents you may be able to combine using an editor to the correct file.

n lost allocation units found in *n* chains
Convert lost chains to files (Y/N)?

Your disk has pointers to files in the file allocation table that no longer exist. CHKDSK is prompting you to determine whether or not you want to convert the lost pointers to files in the root directory that have the form FILE*nnnn*.CHK that you can later examine (using TYPE) for lost information. If your CHKDSK command line did not contain the /F switch, you will have to reinvoke CHKDSK, specifying /F for the lost pointers to be written to disk.

Allocation error, size adjusted

The size of the file specified in a directory listing is inconsistent with the number of bytes that CHKDSK found in the file allocation table (disk road map). CHKDSK has corrected the error, assigning the file size that corresponds to the file allocation table.

All specified file(s) are contiguous

Your CHKDSK command line included a file specification that CHKDSK is to examine for disk contiguity. In this case, all of the files were contiguous; in other words, none of the files are fragmented.

Cannot CHDIR to pathname, tree past this point not processed

CHKDSK cannot continue processing your subdirectory due to disk errors. Copy as many files as you can from your disk to backup disks. This error message is associated with a damaged disk. Back up the files on your disk and use FORMAT to reformat your disk and RESTORE to place your files back on to the disk.

Cannot CHDIR to root

CHKDSK cannot select the root directory as the current directory due to a disk error. Copy as many files as you can from your disk to backup disks and use

FORMAT to reformat your disk. This error message is associated with a damaged disk.

CHDIR .. failed, trying alternate method

CHKDSK could not select the parent directory as the current directory by using the .. abbreviation. CHKDSK is trying an alternate method of selecting the current directory. If your disk contains serious errors, CHKDSK will not be able to continue processing.

FILENAME.EXT contains *n* contiguous blocks

Your CHKDSK command line included a file specification that CHKDSK is to examine for disk contiguity. In this case, CHKDSK is displaying the number of clusters in a file that are not contiguous. If many of your files are not contiguous, you may consider a BACKUP, FORMAT, and RESTORE operation.

CLS

Clears the screen display

The CLS command clears the screen display and places the cursor (and DOS prompt) in the home (upper-left) position.

Format

```
CLS
```

Notes

CLS is an internal command that requires DOS 2.0 or later. It does not affect the way DOS displays information on the screen; it merely clears the screen of all information. When CLS completes, DOS will display its prompt in the upper-left corner of your screen display.

Example

In the following example, DOS erases the current screen contents, placing the cursor and the current DOS prompt in the home position:

```
C:\> CLS   <ENTER>
```

COMMAND

Loads a secondary command processor

Invokes a secondary copy of the DOS command processor. COMMAND is used most often to invoke nested batch files in DOS versions prior to 3.3.

Format

```
COMMAND [drive:][path] [Ctty_Device][/C string]
 [/E:num_bytes] [/P][/MSG]
```

drive: The disk drive that contains the secondary command processor. If you do not specify this parameter, DOS will use the current default drive.

path   The DOS path name of the subdirectory that contains the command processor. If you do not specify a path name, DOS will use the current default directory.

Ctty_Device   A DOS 5 switch that lets you specify an alternative device for input and output operations. For more information on changing this device, refer to the CTTY command.

/C string   Directs DOS to execute the command specified by *string*. This parameter is usually used for nested batch-file invocations. If used with /P, DOS ignores /P.

/E:num_bytes   Specifies the size of the area that DOS is to allocate for the secondary command processor's environment space. This parameter must be between 160 and 32,767 bytes; the default is 160 bytes prior to DOS 5 and 256 under DOS 5.

/P   Directs DOS to leave the secondary command processor permanently in memory.

/MSG   A DOS 4 and 5 switch that directs COMMAND to load its error messages into memory, as opposed to reading the messages from disk as they are required. /MSG is most often used with floppy disk systems.

Notes

COMMAND is an external command supported by all DOS versions. It is the DOS command-line processor, responsible for displaying the DOS prompt and processing the commands you type. When DOS first starts, DOS loads a copy of COMMAND.COM into memory. After that, DOS is running, and most users won't require COMMAND.

If you are using a DOS version before 3.3, you can use COMMAND to invoke nested batch files (batch files that appear within a second batch file) as shown here:

```
CLS
COMMAND /C BATFILE
DATE
```

Beginning with DOS 3.3, DOS replaced COMMAND/C with CALL. If you don't invoke nested batch files using CALL or COMMAND/C, DOS returns control to the DOS prompt after the nested batch file completes. If the original batch file had commands that followed the nested batch file invocation, DOS will not execute the commands. If you are using DOS 3.3 or higher, use the CALL command to invoke your nested batch files.

COMMAND loads itself into memory in two parts: a resident part, which always stays in memory, and a transient part, which DOS can overwrite to provide more memory for your programs to use. If a program overwrites COMMAND.COM's transient portion in this way, DOS must reload the transient part into memory after the program completes. DOS uses the COMSPEC environment entry to determine where COMMAND.COM resides on your disk. If you move COMMAND.COM from the root, you must update COMSPEC to point to COMMAND.COM's new location. See also the EXIT command.

Examples

Assume you have on your disk the file TIMEDATE.BAT, which contains the following commands:

```
ECHO OFF
TIME
DATE
```

Using COMMAND, the batch file NESTED.BAT invokes TIMEDATE.BAT.

```
ECHO OFF
CLS
VER
COMMAND /C TIMEDATE
VOL
```

Messages

Bad or missing command interpreter

DOS could not locate the command interpreter COMMAND.COM in the root directory or directory specified in the SHELL= entry in CONFIG.SYS.

Specified COMMAND search directory bad

The subdirectory path specified as a parameter to COMMAND is invalid. Use the EXIT command to terminate the command processor and reissue COMMAND with the correct directory path.

Parameter value not in allowed range

Your COMMAND command line contains the /E switch, which lets you specify an environment size from 160 to 32,768. In this case, the value that you have specified is invalid.

Parse error
Extended error

Either message indicates you are probably running DOS from floppy disk and COMMAND cannot locate its error message file. For more descriptive messages, use the /MSG switch.

COMP

Displays the first ten differences between two files

The COMP Command displays the first ten differences between two files as hexadecimal offsets into the file.

Format

```
COMP file_spec1 file_spec2
```

or, in DOS 5

```
COMP file_spec1 file_spec2 [/D] [/A] [/L] [/N=number] [/C]
```

file_spec1   The complete DOS path name of the first file to be compared. COMP supports DOS wildcard characters.

file_spec2   The complete DOS path name of the second file to be compared. COMP supports DOS wildcard characters.

/D   Directs COMP to display the differences in decimal. This is a DOS 5 switch.

/A   Directs COMP to display the differences in ASCII. This is a DOS 5 switch.

/L   Directs COMP to display the line number in which the differences occurred instead of an offset. This is a DOS 5 switch.

/N=*number*   Directs COMP only to compare the number of lines specified. This is a DOS 5 switch.

/C   Directs COMP to consider upper- and lowercase letters as identical. This is a DOS 5 switch.

Notes

COMP is an external command supported by all DOS versions. By default, COMP compares the two files and displays the differences as hexadecimal values. If the files are identical, COMP displays the message

```
Files compare OK
```

Upon completion of the file comparison, COMP will display

```
Compare more files (Y/N)?
```

To compare additional files, type Y; otherwise, type N.
    If COMP locates more than ten differences, it will display

```
10 Mismatches - ending compare
```

Prior to DOS 5, COMP will not compare files of different sizes. If you are using DOS 5, you can include the /N switch directing COMP to compare the number of lines specified.
    If you are copying a critical file from one disk or directory to another, it is a good idea to ensure that your copy was successful with COMP.

```
C:\> COMP FILE.1  A:FILE.2   <ENTER>
Files compare ok
Compare more files (Y/N)?
```

If differences exist between the two files, you know that the file copy encountered an error. If no differences exist, you can be assured that the copy was successful.

Examples

In the following example, COMP will compare the contents of the file A.DAT to B.DAT:

```
C:\> COMP A.DAT B.DAT   <ENTER>
```

Assuming that the files contain

```
C:\> TYPE A.DAT   <ENTER>
A
AA

C:\> TYPE B.DAT   <ENTER>
B
BB
```

the command will display

```
Compare file C:A.DAT and file C:B.DAT
Compare error at OFFSET 0
File 1 = 41
File 2 = 42
Compare error at OFFSET 3
File 1 = 41
File 2 = 42
Compare error at OFFSET 4
File 1 = 41
File 2 = 42
Compare more files (Y/N)?
```

If you are using DOS 5, you can display the differences between each file in ASCII:

```
C:\> COMP A B /A   <ENTER>
 Comparing A and B...
 Compare error at OFFSET 0
 file1 = A
 file2 = B
 Compare error at OFFSET 3
 file1 = A
 file2 = B
 Compare error at OFFSET 4
 file1 = A
 file2 = B
 Compare more files (Y/N)?
```

If you omit the file name from the secondary file, DOS will match the file name on the specified drive to the primary file:

```
C:\> COMP A.DAT B:   <ENTER>
```

If you do not specify a file in the COMP command line, COMP will prompt you for it:

```
C:\> COMP   <ENTER>
 Enter the primary file name.
 A.DAT
 Enter the 2nd file name or drive id.
 B.DAT
```

Messages

Compare error at offset *nnnnnnnn*
File1=*nn*
File2=*nn*

COMP has located a difference between the two files and is displaying the offset location within the files of the difference, along with the byte values that differ. Remember, COMP displays these values in hexadecimal.

EOF mark not found

The last character in one of the files examined was not an end-of-file character, ^Z. DOS uses the CTRL-Z character as the end-of-file marker for most text files. In most cases, this message is purely informational.

Files are different sizes

The two files specified in the COMP command line differ in size. COMP will not compare files of different sizes. If you are using MS DOS 2.0 or later, use the FC command.

10 Mismatches - ending compare

COMP has identified ten differences between the two files specified and is terminating the comparison. If you are using MS DOS 2.0 or later, the FC command lets you display all of the differences between two files.

Cannot compare a file to itself

The primary and secondary file names in the COMP command line are the same. COMP will not compare one file to itself.

Enter primary file name

Your COMP command line did not specify the files that COMP is to compare. Therefore, COMP is prompting you for them. In this case, simply type in the desired file name and press ENTER.

Enter 2nd file name or drive ID

Your COMP command line did not specify the files that COMP is to compare. Therefore, COMP is prompting you for them. In this case, simply type in the desired file name or disk drive and press ENTER. If you simply type in a disk drive letter, COMP will search for a file on that disk drive that matches the primary file name.

Compare more files (Y/N)?

COMP has completed one file comparison and is prompting you to specify whether or not you want to perform another. If so, type Y and press ENTER. COMP will prompt you for the files to compare. If you instead type N, COMP will terminate and return control to DOS.

File sharing conflict

COMP could not access one of the files specified in the COMP command line due to network file sharing. Wait a few minutes for the file to be released by the program that is using it and reissue the COMP command.

COPY

Copies one or more files to a new destination

Copies one or more files to a different disk, directory, or file name.

Format

```
COPY source_file [/V] [/A] [/B] target_file [/V] [/A] [/B]
```

or

```
COPY source1+source2 [/V] [/A] [/B] [...] target_file [/V] [/A] [/B]
```

source_file   The complete DOS file specification of the file to be copied. COPY supports wildcard characters.

target_file   The name of the destination file. If a file matching the name of *target_file* exists, COPY will overwrite it. COPY supports wildcard characters.

/V   Tells COPY to use disk verification to ensure that a successful copy occurred. This switch adds processing overhead; however, it prevents a hardware error from rendering the contents of the source and target files inconsistent.

/A   Informs COPY that the preceding file was an ASCII file.

/B   Informs COPY that the preceding file was a binary file.

source1+source2   Indicates that you can use any number of source files.

Notes

COPY is an internal command supported by all DOS versions.

COPY overwrites target files that have the same name. Using the DOS ATTRIB command you can mark key files as read-only to prevent a file from being inadvertantly overwritten.

WARNING

COPY only copies the files contained in one directory at a time. To copy the files that reside in lower-level directories, use the XCOPY command.

COPY will not copy a file whose size appears in the directory list as 0 bytes. Use XCOPY instead. To combine multiple files into one file, use the plus sign (+) between the desired source files.

COPY will not allow you to copy a file to itself. If you attempt to do so, COPY will display

```
File cannot be copied onto itself
              0 file(s) copied.
```

The COPY command provides several capabilities that will likely save considerable typing and time. For example, many of you have issued a command such as

```
A> COPY FILENAME.EXT B:FILENAME.EXT   <ENTER>
```

in order to copy the contents of a file from one disk to another. Instead, if you use wildcard characters,

```
A> COPY FILENAME.EXT B:*.*   <ENTER>
```

DOS will again copy the desired file to the new disk. In this case, you have reduced the number of keystrokes DOS required you to type. Taking this process one step further, you only need to specify a disk drive ID for your destination:

```
A> COPY FILENAME.EXT B:   <ENTER>
```

By default, if you don't specify the name of the destination file, DOS will create a file with the same name as the file you are copying. The previous three commands performed identical functions. This holds true even for commands such as

```
A> COPY *.* B:   <ENTER>
```

Thus, you can greatly reduce the number of required keystrokes.

The COPY command only copies files in the current directory or specified DOS directory. If you need to copy files that reside in several subdirectories, use the XCOPY command.

Examples

The following command copies a spreadsheet file named BUDGET.DAT from the (Lotus) 123 directory to a floppy disk in drive A.

```
C:\> COPY \123\BUDGET.DAT A:    <ENTER>
```

The following command copies the contents of the CONFIG.SYS file to a file on drive A with the same name

```
C:\> COPY CONFIG.SYS A:CONFIG.SYS    <ENTER>
```

which is identical in function to the command

```
C:\> COPY CONFIG.SYS A:    <ENTER>
```

or

```
C:\> A:    <ENTER>
A:\> COPY C:\CONFIG.SYS    <ENTER>
```

In the same manner, the command

```
C:\> COPY *.* A:*.*    <ENTER>
```

copies all the files in the current directory to drive A.

If you want to copy files contained in subdirectories below the current directory, use the XCOPY command.

The following command uses the plus sign to combine the files START, MIDDLE, and END to create the file WHOLE.

```
C:\> COPY START+MIDDLE+END WHOLE    <ENTER>
```

The following command lets you append text from the keyboard to an existing file, creating a new file:

```
C:\> COPY FILENAME+CON: NEWFILE.EXT   <ENTER>
```

Messages

Cannot do binary reads from a device

You have placed the /B switch, which directs COPY to perform a binary copy, after a device name. When COPY performs a binary copy, it does not use the CTRL-Z (^Z) character to indicate an end-of-file. Since CTRL-Z is the only means of telling COPY when you have entered your required information from a device, COPY cannot perform a binary copy from a device.

Contents of destination lost before copy

The destination file name is also a file specified as a source file in the COPY operation. In this command, COPY became confused during its processing and has overwritten the file contents. If you are using the destination file as a source file in this manner, try to place the file name first in the COPY command, or at least make sure that a file name follows the file specified.

File cannot be copied onto itself

The source and destination for a file copy operation are the same. In most cases, this error occurs when you have omitted a disk drive specifier or subdirectory in the target file name.

CTTY

Modifies standard input (stdin) to point to alternate device

The CTTY command changes standard input/output from a default device to an auxiliary (alternative) device.

Format

```
CTTY DeviceName
```

DeviceName   Specifies the name of the device to which you want DOS to assign the standard input and output source. Valid device names include COM*n*, AUX, PRN, LPT*n*, NUL, and CON.

Notes

CTTY is an internal command that requires DOS 2.0 or later. Most users do not need the CTTY command. CTTY lets you connect a terminal or other device such as a modem to your computer, allowing access from the terminal as opposed to screen and keyboard. Do not execute CTTY from the DOS prompt if you do not have a device attached to the computer from which you can later issue a CTTY CON command to resume normal processing. Otherwise, you will have to turn your computer on and off to resume normal use. CTTY only works for programs that use DOS for input and output. If a program writes directly to your video hardware or uses the BIOS, CTTY will have no effect on the program.

Examples

The following command sets the standard input/output to COM1:

```
A> CTTY COM1:
```

The following batch file does not require user input; therefore, it uses CTTY NUL to disable the display of error messages and program output. Before the batch file completes, it uses CTTY CON to restore normal processing.

```
@ECHO OFF
CTTY NUL
CHKDSK > TEMP.DAT
PRINT /D:PRN TEMP.DAT
DEL TEMP.DAT
CTTY CON
```

Messages

Invalid device

Your command line either specifies an invalid device name or no device name. Only invoke CTTY when your system has a terminal device attached to a serial or parallel port.

DATE

Sets or displays the DOS system date

The DATE command sets the DOS system date that DOS uses to assign date stamps to each file you create or modify.

Format

DATE [*mm-dd-yy*]

or

DATE [*dd-mm-yy*]

or

DATE [*yy-mm-dd*]

mm The desired month (1-12).

dd The desired day (1-31).

yy The last two digits of the desired year. DATE also allows you to include the century, in the form 19*yy* or 20*yy*.

Notes

DATE is an internal command supported by all versions of DOS. The *mm-dd-yy* date format is dependent upon the COUNTRY specifier in CONFIG.SYS. If you do not specify a date, DATE will display the current date. To leave the date unchanged, press ENTER.

Prior to DOS 3.3, DATE did not modify the AT computer system clock. Users of DOS versions prior to 3.3 must use the Setup disk provided with the Guide to Operations in order to change the AT system clock. DOS 3.3 TIME (see TIME) and DATE commands actually set this clock.

The actual date is an optional command-line parameter. If you omit the date, DATE will prompt you for it. Although the DATE command does not force you to type in a date, it is a good habit to do so. DOS uses your system's current date and time to stamp files each time a file is created or modified.

```
C:\BUSINESS> DIR   <ENTER>

 Volume in drive C is DOS
 Volume Serial Number  is 1454-1231
 Directory of  C:\BUSINESS

 .           <DIR>       06-03-91   1:11p
 ..          <DIR>       06-03-91   1:11p
 BILLS   DAT     23936   06-30-91   1:47p
 IRS     MEM        10   06-30-91   1:13p
                         └───────┬───────┘
                          Date and time stamp
```

Because DOS commands such as BACKUP and RESTORE have several switches that are based upon the current date and time, you should always ensure that your system date and time is correct.

Examples

In the following example, since the date was not present on the DOS command line, DATE prompted the user for it:

```
C:\> DATE   <ENTER>
Current date is Tue 06-11-1991
Enter new date (mm-dd-yy):
```

If you simply want to display the system date without modifying it, press ENTER at the date prompt. DATE will leave the date unchanged.

In the following example, DATE will set the system date to December 8, 1991:

```
C:\> DATE 12/08/91    <ENTER>
```

This command is identical to

```
C:\> DATE 12/08/1991    <ENTER>
```

DATE fully supports a four-digit year.

Finally, this command illustrates how you can set the date from the DATE prompt:

```
C:\> DATE   <ENTER>
Current date is Tue 06-11-01-1991
Enter the new date (mm-dd-yy): 12-08-91   <ENTER>
```

Messages

Invalid date
Enter new date (mm-dd-yy):

Make sure you are entering the current system date with the month preceding the day as shown in the format given. Simply retype the command and press ENTER.

DEBUG

Invokes the DOS program debugger

Errors in programs are called bugs. DEBUG helps programmers remove bugs from their programs. Users can use DEBUG to create simple COM programs.

Format

```
DEBUG [file_spec]
```

file_spec   The complete path to the file DEBUG is to load.

Notes

DEBUG is an external command supported by all DOS versions. When you invoke it, DEBUG displays an asterisk (*) for its command prompt. DEBUG uses the following single-letter commands:

Command	Function
?	Displays a list of available DEBUG commands (DOS 5)
A	Lets you enter assembly language statements
C	Compares two memory areas

D	Displays a memory range
E	Enters data into a memory range
F	Fills a memory range with a specific value
G	Runs the command you are debugging from the current location to completion
H	Performs hexadecimal addition and subtraction
I	Displays the value in the port specified
L	Loads a file or disk sectors into memory
M	Copies a range of memory values from one location to another
N	Specifies the name of the file to be used with L and W commands
O	Writes a byte value to the port specified
P	Executes a loop, a repeated string instruction, a subroutine, or a software interrupt
Q	Quits a debugging session, returning control to DOS
R	Displays the contents of one or more registers, letting you change the register's value
S	Searches memory for the byte pattern specified
T	Executes the current instruction, displaying the register contents, the status flags, and the assembly language form of the instruction DEBUG will execute next
U	Displays the assembly language representation for a range of memory values
W	Writes the current memory contents to the file specified by the N command
XA	Allocates a region of expanded memory (DOS 4)
XD	Deallocates a region of expanded memory (DOS 4)
XM	Maps expanded memory pages (DOS 4)
XS	Displays the status of expanded memory (DOS 4)

Most users use DEBUG to create simple COM programs by entering in the program's assembly language instructions.

Example

Given the following DEBUG script file, SHOWLINE.SCR,

```
N SHOWLINE.COM
A 100
MOV AH, 2
MOV SI, 82
```

```
MOV DL, [SI]
CMP DL, D
JZ 111
INT 21
INC SI
JMP 105
MOV AH, 4C
INT 21
<ENTER>
R CX
15
W
Q
```

the following DEBUG command creates the command SHOWLINE.COM.

```
C:\> DEBUG < SHOWLINE.SCR   <ENTER>
```

Messages

Program terminated normally

The program you were tracing or executing using DEBUG's G command ended normally.

Writing *xxxx* bytes

DEBUG is writing the number of bytes you have specified in the CX register to disk.

EXE and HEX files cannot be written

The file with which you invoked DEBUG or the file you specified using DEBUG's N (name) command has an EXE or HEX extension (and format), which DEBUG cannot write.

DIR

Lists the files contained in a directory

A directory is a list of file names. DIR displays the names of each file in the directory specified.

Format

```
DIR [file_spec] [/P] [/W]
```

or, using DOS 5:

```
DIR [ file_spec ] [/P] [/W] [A: attributes ]
   [/O: sort_order ] [/S] [/B] [/L]
```

file_spec   The complete DOS file specification for the file(s) for which DIR is to display the directory listing. It can contain a disk drive identifier and path name. If you do not place a file specification in the command line, DIR will display a directory listing of the current directory. DIR fully supports DOS wildcard characters.

/P   Directs DIR to pause after each screenful of information and display the prompt

```
Press any key to continue . . .
```

/W   Directs DIR to display the files in short form (file name only), with five file names across the screen.

/A: *attributes*   A DOS 5 switch that directs DIR to display only the names of those files whose file attributes match those specified in the command line. Valid attribute values include

H	Hidden files	-H	Files that are not hidden files
S	System files	-S	Files that are not system files
D	Directories	-D	Files that are not directories
A	Files need archiving	-A	Files already archived
R	Read-only files	-R	Files that are not read-only

DIR lets you combine attributes. For example, /A:A-R directs DIR to display those files requiring archiving that are not read-only files. The colon following /A is optional.

/O: *sort_order*   A DOS 5 switch that directs DIR to display the directory listing in an order other than by name. Valid sort orders include

N	by name, A to Z	-N	by name, Z to A
E	by extension, A to Z	-E	by extension, Z to A
D	by date, oldest to newest	-D	by date, newest to oldest
S	by size, smallest to largest	-S	by size, largest to smallest
G	directories before files	-G	directories after files

The colon following /O before the attribute settings is optional.

/S   A DOS 5 switch that directs DIR to display the files in lower-level subdirectories.

/B   A DOS 5 switch that directs DIR to display names and extensions only.

/L   A DOS 5 switch that directs DIR to display names in lowercase letters.

Notes

DIR is an internal DOS command supported by all DOS versions. By default, the DIR command displays the complete name, size in bytes, and the date and time of creation (or last modification) for each file. The format of the date and time depends on the current country setting. DIR also displays the amount of free disk space in bytes. By default, DIR does not display hidden system files. If you are using DOS 5, the /A:H switch directs DIR to display the hidden file names. DIR always displays the drive letter and directory name in which the files are stored:

```
Volume in drive A is DOSDISK
Volume Serial Number is 0987-1234
Directory of  A:\

SUBDIR        <DIR>      11-01-90  12:53p
        1 File(s)    1213440 bytes free
```

If you simply invoke DIR with a file name, like this

```
C:\> DIR FILENAME   <ENTER>
```

the extension defaults to *.

Prior to DOS 5, to list all the files on disk (including files in DOS subdirectories), use the TREE command. Beginning with DOS 5, you can include the /S switch in your DIR command to display the files in lower-level directories.

To increase the usefulness of the DIR command, many users combine the DIR with the DOS I/O redirection operators:

```
DIR > PRN:              (send listing to your printer)
DIR | MORE              (display listing a page at a time)
DIR | SORT              (display a sorted directory listing)
DIR | FIND              "<DIR>"  (only display subdirectories)
```

If you are using DOS 5, you can use the environment entry DIRCMD to define the default format DIR uses to display files. For example, the following SET command assigns DIRCMD the lowercase switch, /L, and the /S switch, which directs DIR to display files in subdirectories also.

```
C:\> SET DIRCMD=/L/S   <ENTER>
```

Many DOS 5 users will assign DIRCMD in their AUTOEXEC.BAT file. If you are using DOS 4 or 5, you can view your directory list (including hidden files) using DOSSHELL.

Examples

In the following example, DIR will display a directory listing of each of the files on drive A.

```
C:\> DIR A:   <ENTER>
```

This command is functionally equivalent to

```
C:\> DIR A:*.*   <ENTER>
```

or

```
C:\> A:   <ENTER>
A> DIR   <ENTER>
```

If several files exist on drive A, many may scroll off the screen during the directory listing. If this happens, invoke DIR with the /P switch:

```
C:\> DIR A:*.* /P   <ENTER>
```

Each time DIR completes a screenful of files, it will pause, displaying the prompt

```
Press any key to continue . . .
```

When this occurs, press any key and DIR will continue.

The file specification of the DIR command can be specific:

```
C:\> DIR \DOS\CONFIG.OLD   <ENTER>
```

The following command will display the directory listing of the CONFIG.OLD file, which resides in the \DOS subdirectory on the current disk. If you are not interested in file sizes or date and time stamps, invoke DIR with the /W option:

```
C:\> DIR /W   <ENTER>
```

DIR will display a directory listing of file names only, five files across the screen:

```
Volume in drive C is DOSDISK
Volume Serial Number is 1234-4321
Directory of  C:\DOS

[.]             [..]            ANSI     EXE  APPEND   COM  ASSIGN   COM
ATTRIB   EXE  BACKUP   COM  CHKDSK   COM  COMP     COM  DISKCOMP COM
DISKCOPY COM  EDLIN    COM  FDISK    EXE  FIND     COM  FORMAT   COM
FORMATS  TBL  GRAFTABL COM  GWBASIC  EXE  HELP     EXE  JOIN     EXE
PRINT    COM  README        REPLACE  EXE  RESTORE  COM  SORT     EXE
          25 File(s)    2163104 bytes free
```

The DOS redirection operators can also be used with DIR. In this example, DOS displays a sorted directory listing:

```
C:\> DIR | SORT   <ENTER>
```

In a similar manner, this command prints the files in the current directory:

```
C:\> DIR > PRN:   <ENTER>
```

If you are using DOS 5, the following command directs DIR to display a directory listing sorted by size.

```
C:\> DIR /O:S   <ENTER>
```

Likewise, the following DOS 5 command directs DIR to display all of the files on your disk, with their names in lowercase.

```
C:\> DIR  \*.*  /S  /L  <ENTER>
```

Last, this DOS 5 command directs DIR to display only the names of subdirectories that reside in the current directory.

```
C:\> DIR /A:D  <ENTER>
```

Messages

Press any key to continue . . .

You have invoked DIR with the /P switch that suspends the directory listing display with each screenful of information. Press any key to continue the directory listing, or press CTRL-BREAK to terminate the command.

Volume label in drive *n*: has no label

DIR is simply informing you that the disk has not been assigned an optional disk volume label (11-character name). To assign a name to the disk, use the LABEL command. It is a good practice to assign a volume label to your hard disk. Starting with DOS 4, the FORMAT command will not format a hard disk until you successfully type in the disk's volume label, reducing your chance of an accidental format.

Volume label in drive *n*: is *DISKNAME*

DIR is simply displaying the disk's optional 11-character volume name.

DISKCOMP

Compares two floppy disks

The DISKCOMP command compares the contents of two floppy disks and displays differences if the disks are not identical or displays the message "Compare OK."

Format

```
DISKCOMP [primary_drive: [secondary_drive]] [/1] [/8]
```

primary_drive   The first floppy disk drive to be used for the disk comparison. If you do not specify a primary drive, DISKCOMP will use the current default.

secondary_drive   The second drive to be used for the disk comparison. If you do not specify a secondary drive, DISKCOMP will use the current default.

/1   Directs DISKCOMP to perform a single-sided disk comparison.

/8   Directs DISKCOMP to perform an eight-sector-per-track disk comparison.

Notes

DISKCOMP is an external command supported by all DOS versions. If you have a single-floppy system, the DISKCOMP command will perform a single-drive comparison, prompting you to enter the source and target disks at the correct time. If the contents of the disks are identical, DISKCOMP displays

```
Compare OK
```

Otherwise, DISKCOMP displays the side and track (in hexadecimal values) of the differences. Many users issue DISKCOMP immediately after copying the contents of one disk to another with DISKCOPY. If any undetected errors occurred during the disk copy, DISKCOMP will detect them.

If you are invoking DISKCOMP from within a DOS batch file, DISKCOMP returns the following exit status values:

Exit Status	Meaning
0	Disks compare OK
1	Disks did not compare
2	User termination via CTRL-C
3	Unrecoverable disk error
4	Invalid syntax, insufficient memory, or invalid drive

Examples

In the following example, DISKCOMP will compare the contents of the disk in drive A to those of the disk in drive B.

```
C:\> DISKCOMP A: B:   <ENTER>
```

If the disks are identical, DISKCOMP will display

```
Compare OK
```

Otherwise, DISKCOMP will display the locations of the differences:

```
Compare error on
side n, track n
```

If you need to compare single-sided disks, use DISKCOMP as follows.

```
C:\> DISKCOMP A: B: /1  <ENTER>
```

Messages

Cannot DISKCOMP to or from a Network drive

One of the disk drives that you have specified in the DISKCOMP command line references a network drive. DOS will not let you perform DISKCOMP operations to a network disk drive.

Compare another diskette (Y/N)?

DISKCOMP has completed a disk comparison operation and is prompting you as to whether or not you want to perform a second. If so, type **Y** and DISKCOMP will prompt you to enter the disks to compare. To terminate the DISKCOMP command, simply type **N** and press ENTER.

Compare error on
side *n*, track *n*

DISKCOMP has located differences between the two disks at the location specified. DISKCOMP compares two disks sector by sector, track by track, and side by side. In this case, DISKCOMP has identified a difference in the track specified.

Compare OK

The two disks are identical.

Comparing *n* tracks
n sectors per track, *n* side(s)

DISKCOMP is telling you the format of the disks that it is comparing. DISKCOMP compares two disks by comparing the disks sector by sector, track by track, side by side. This message simply tells you the number of tracks, sides, and sectors that DISKCOMP will examine on each disk.

FIRST diskette bad or incompatible

The disk in the first drive specified in the DISKCOMP command line is either damaged or incompatible with the drive that it resides in. For example, DISKCOMP will not let you examine a 1.2Mb disk in a 360Kb floppy disk drive.

SECOND diskette bad or incompatible

The disk in the second drive specified in the DISKCOMP command line is either damaged or incompatible with the disk drive that it resides in. For example, DISKCOMP will not let you examine a 1.2Mb disk in a 360Kb floppy disk drive.

Insert FIRST diskette in drive *n*:
Press any key to continue . . .

DISKCOMP is prompting you to insert one of the two disks to compare into the drive specified. If you are performing a single disk drive comparison, you will need to exchange floppy disks within the drive specified. One disk will have to be the first, while another will be the second. In this case, DISKCOMP is prompting you to enter the first disk into the drive.

Insert SECOND diskette in drive *n*:
Press any key to continue . . .

DISKCOMP is prompting you to insert one of the two disks to compare into the drive specified. If you are performing a single disk drive comparison, you will need to exchange floppy disks within the drive specified. One disk will have to be the first, while another will be the second. In this case, DISKCOMP is prompting you to enter the second disk into the drive.

Invalid drive specification
Specified disk does not exist
or is non-removable

The disk drive that you specified in your DISKCOMP command line is either invalid or a hard disk. DISKCOMP does not let you compare hard disks. If the drive specified is not a hard disk, make sure that you have placed a colon after the disk drive letter and that you are using a valid floppy disk drive letter (A, B, and so on).

Parameter not correct
Do not specify filename(s)
Command format: DISKCOMP [drive:][drive:] [/1] [/8]

Your DISKCOMP command line is invalid. Examine the DISKCOMP command format shown above and reissue the command.

Cannot DISKCOMP to or from an ASSIGNed or SUBSTed drive

One or more of the drives specified in the DISKCOMP command line is a logical drive. DISKCOMP does not support logical drives.

DISKCOPY

Copies a source floppy disk to a target floppy disk

The DISKCOPY command copies the contents of one floppy disk to another floppy disk, creating an identical copy.

Format

```
DISKCOPY [source_drive: [target_drive]] [/1] [/V]
```

source_drive   The disk drive that contains the floppy disk to copy. If you do not specify a source drive, DISKCOPY will use the current default drive.

target_drive   The disk drive that contains the disk to be copied to. If you do not specify a target drive, DISKCOPY will use the current default drive.

/1   Directs DISKCOPY to copy only the first side of the source disk to the target.

/V A DOS 4 switch that directs DOS to enable disk verification during the copy operation. Disk verification will ensure that all information written to the disk is recorded correctly. This additional verification processing will make DISKCOPY take longer to complete.

Notes

DISKCOPY is an external command supported by all DOS versions. If you have a single-floppy system, DISKCOPY will perform a single-drive copy, prompting you to enter the source and target disks at the correct time.

DISKCOPY destroys the previous contents of the target disk. If the source and target disks are not the same type of disk (a 360Kb and a 1.2Mb disk, for example), DISKCOPY will display an error message and terminate.

If the target disk has not yet been formatted, DISKCOPY will format the disk during the copy operation, displaying the message

```
Formatting while copying
```

Do not use DISKCOPY with JOINed or SUBSTed disks. (See JOIN and SUBST.)

Unless your disks are copy-protected, never use your original disks. Instead, always make a working copy of the disks that you will use on a daily basis. After you make your working copies, place your original disks in a safe location.

If you are using DISKCOPY from within a DOS batch file, DISKCOPY supports the following exit status values:

Exit Status	Meaning
0	Successful copy operation
1	A nonfatal read or write error occurred during the copy
2	User termination of copy operation via CTRL-C
3	A fatal read or write error ended the copy operation
4	Invalid disk drive, command line, or insufficient memory

If your source disk has a serial number, DISKCOPY will create and assign a new serial number for the target disk, displaying the serial number when it completes.

Examples

The following command assumes that you have two compatible floppy disk drives on your system:

```
C:\> DISKCOPY A: B:    <ENTER>
```

Once DISKCOPY begins copying a disk, it will read several tracks of data from the source and then write them to the target disk. In a single-floppy drive system, DISKCOPY repeats this process, prompting you for the source and target disks:

```
A:\> DISKCOPY   <ENTER>
Insert SOURCE Diskette in Drive A:
Press any key to continue . . .
Copying 40 tracks
9 Sectors/Track, 2 Side(s)

Insert TARGET Diskette in Drive A:
Press any key to continue . . .

Insert SOURCE Diskette in Drive A:
Press any key to continue . . .

Insert TARGET Diskette in Drive A:
Press any key to continue . . .

Copy another diskette (Y/N)?
```

If you want to perform a single-drive disk copy using your hard disk as the default drive, you must specify the same floppy disk drive twice for the source and target of the DISKCOPY operation.

```
C:\> DISKCOPY A: A:   <ENTER>
```

Messages

Cannot DISKCOPY to or from a Network drive

One of the disk drives specified in the DISKCOPY command line references a network disk drive. DOS will not let you use a network device in a DISKCOPY operation.

Copying *n* tracks
n sectors per track, *n* side(s)

DISKCOPY is simply telling you the format of the disk that it is copying. DISKCOPY copies one disk to another, sector by sector, track by track, and side by side. In this case, DISKCOPY is telling you the format of the disk it is copying.

Copy process ended

The DISKCOPY operation has failed. Normally, DISKCOPY will precede this error message with a message describing the reason for the failure.

Not ready - *n*:
Make sure a diskette is inserted into
the drive and the door is closed
Press CTRL+C to abort,
or correct this problem and press any other key to continue . . .

The disk drive latch for the drive specified is very likely still open. If so, simply close the drive latch and select the R (Retry) option.

Drive types or diskette types
not compatible

Either the two disks or disk drives specified in the DISKCOPY command are incompatible. DISKCOPY will not, for example, allow you to copy the contents of a 1.2Mb disk to a 360Kb disk.

Formatting while copying

The target disk operation was unformatted. DISKCOPY must format the disk before it can be used by DOS. In this case, DISKCOPY is simply informing you that it is formatting the disk before performing the copy operation.

Insert SOURCE diskette in drive *n*:
Press any key to continue . . .

DISKCOPY is prompting you to insert the disk that you want to copy (the source disk) into the drive specified. Once you do so, simply press any key to continue the DISKCOPY operation.

Insert target diskette in drive *n*:
Press any key to continue . . .

DISKCOPY is prompting you to insert the disk that you want DISKCOPY to copy to (the target disk), into the drive specified. Once you do so, simply press any key to continue the DISKCOPY operation.

Parameter not correct
Do not specify filename(s)
Command format: DISKCOMP [drive:][drive:] [/1] [/8]

Your DISKCOPY command line contains invalid entries. Examine the format of the DISKCOPY command shown and reissue the correct DISKCOPY command.

TARGET media has lower capacity than SOURCE
Continue anyway (Y/N)?

The source and target disks differ in capacity. If you respond with Y, DISKCOPY will attempt to format the target disk so its capacity matches the source.

SOURCE diskette bad or incompatible

The source disk (disk to copy) is damaged or incompatible with the disk drive it resides in. Make sure that you are not trying to use a 1.2Mb disk in a 360Kb disk drive and reissue the DISKCOPY command. If the command fails again, your source disk may be severely damaged.

TARGET diskette bad or incompatible

The target disk (disk DISKCOPY is to copy to) is damaged or incompatible with the disk drive it resides in. Make sure that you are not trying to copy a 1.2Mb disk to a 360Kb disk drive and reissue the DISKCOPY command. If the command fails again, your target disk may be severely damaged.

Write protect error

The target disk in the DISKCOPY command contains a write-protect tab that prevents DISKCOPY from writing to it. In most cases, this error occurs when you have forgotten to place the desired target disk in the drive specified, and DISKCOPY is attempting to overwrite a different disk. As you can see, write-protecting your disks can protect them from many errant DOS commands.

Target diskette may be unusable

DISKCOPY was unable to perform an identical disk copy of the source disk. This error normally occurs when the target disk contains damaged locations that prevent their use. To ensure that you have a complete disk copy, repeat the DISKCOPY command with a different target disk.

Unrecoverable read error on drive *n*:
side *n*, track *n*

DISKCOPY was unable to read the track of the source disk specified. Since DISKCOPY copies one disk to another sector by sector and track by track, your disk copy will be incomplete due to the missing information. In most cases, this error is associated with copy-protected software, or a damaged source disk.

Unrecoverable write error on drive *n*:
side *n*, track *n*

DISKCOPY was unable to write the track of the target disk specified. Since DISKCOPY copies one disk to another sector by sector and track by track, your disk copy will be incomplete due to the missing information. In most cases, this error is associated with a damaged target disk.

Cannot DISKCOPY to or from an ASSIGNed or SUBSTed drive

One or more of the drives specified in the DISKCOPY command line is a logical drive. DISKCOPY does not support logical drives.

DOSKEY

Recalls previously entered commands

DOSKEY is a DOS 5 command that lets you edit your previously entered commands and create macros (similar to batch files), which DOS stores in memory.

Format

```
DOSKEY [/REINSTALL] [/BUFSIZE= size] [/MACROS] [/HISTORY]
  [/INSERT |/OVERSTRIKE] [macro_name= macro_text]
```

/REINSTALL   Installs a new copy of the DOSKEY program in memory.

/BUFSIZE=*size* Specifies the size of the command and macro buffer in memory. If you are creating a large number of macros, you want to use a buffer size of 4,096 bytes. The default size is 512 bytes.

/MACROS   Directs DOSKEY to display the current list of macros. This parameter can be abbreviated as /M.

/HISTORY   Directs DOSKEY to display a list of all commands stored in the buffer (the command history). This parameter can be abbreviated as /H.

/INSERT   Lets you remain in insert mode after pressing ENTER.

/OVERSTRIKE   Disables insert mode.

macro_name= macro_text   Lets you create a macro.

Notes

DOSKEY is an external DOS command that requires DOS 5 or later. Once you enable DOSKEY, you can toggle through your previously entered commands with your arrow keys. When the desired command is displayed, you can execute the command by pressing ENTER or edit the command using the following keys.

Key Combination	Function
UP ARROW	Recalls the command issued prior to the command currently displayed
DOWN ARROW	Recalls the command issued after the command currently displayed
PGUP	Recalls the oldest command in the buffer
PGDN	Recalls the last command placed in the buffer
LEFT ARROW	Moves the cursor left one character
RIGHT ARROW	Moves the cursor right one character
CTRL-LEFT ARROW	Moves the cursor back one word
CTRL-RIGHT ARROW	Moves the cursor forward one word
HOME	Moves the cursor to the start of the line
END	Moves the cursor to the end of the line
ESC	Clears the command from display
F7	Displays all commands in memory
ALT-F7	Erases all commands stored in memory
F8	Searches memory for a command that matches the partial command line displayed
F9	Specifies a command line desired by number
F10	Displays all macros stored in memory
ALT-F10	Clears all macros

Macros are similar in concept to DOS batch files. To execute a macro, you simply type in the macro's name. A macro can contain one or more commands. DOS stores the macro in RAM. The macro you create must fit on one page. Like DOS batch files, macros support command-line parameters. Rather than using the symbols %0 to %9, macros use $1 through $9. In addition, macros support the following metacharacters.

Metacharacter	Translation
$G or $g	DOS output redirection operator
$L or $l	DOS input redirection operator
$B or $b	DOS pipe operator
$T or $t	Command separator
$$	Dollar sign character
GG or gg	Append redirection operator
$*	Entire command line minus the macro name

You cannot invoke DOSKEY macros from within a batch file. You can only invoke macros from the keyboard. DOSKEY lets you create macros with the same name as DOS internal or external commands. If you create a macro named TYPE for example, DOS will execute the macro instead of the TYPE command. To delete a macro, invoke DOSKEY with the macro name and an equal sign, without assigning a value.

Examples

The following command loads DOSKEY with a 4,096-byte buffer for commands and macros.

```
C:\> DOSKEY /BUFSIZE=4096   <ENTER>
```

The following command directs DOSKEY to display all of the commands in the command buffer.

```
C:\> DOSKEY /HISTORY   <ENTER>
```

The next command directs DOSKEY to display all of its macros.

```
C:\> DOSKEY /MACROS   <ENTER>
```

The following command creates a macro named CP that abbreviates the COPY command.

```
C:\> DOSKEY CP=COPY $1 $2   <ENTER>
```

As you can see, the macro uses the symbols $1 and $2 to access its command-line parameters. Once you create the macro, you access it using the name CP.

Last, this command creates a macro named HIST that displays the commands currently stored in the DOSKEY buffer and the current macros.

```
C:\> DOSKEY HIST=DOSKEY /HISTORY $T DOSKEY /MACROS   <ENTER>
```

The macro uses the $T metacharacter to separate the two commands.

Messages

Cannot change BUFSIZE

Your DOSKEY command included the /BUFSIZE switch after DOSKEY was installed. Once DOSKEY is installed, you cannot change the buffer size. To change the buffer size, you must restart DOS.

DOSKEY installed

The DOSKEY installation was successful.

Invalid macro definition

Your DOSKEY command line does not contain a valid macro. The format for macros is *macro_name* = *macro_text*.

DOSSHELL

Invokes the DOS 5 or DOS 4 shell

If you are using DOS 4 or 5, DOS provides a menu-driven interface to your programs and files called the DOS shell. Using the shell, you can run programs or select files and directories by clicking the program or file name with your mouse or using pull-down menus.

Format

```
DOSSHELL [/T: Resolution] [/B] [/G: Resolution]
```

/T   A DOS 5 switch that directs the shell to start in text mode.

/G   A DOS 5 switch that directs the shell to start in graphics mode.

/B   A DOS 5 switch that directs the shell to start in black and white.

Resolution   Specifies the screen resolution and must be either L, M, or H (representing low, medium, and high resolution).

Notes

DOSSHELL requires DOS 4 or later. Under DOS 4, DOSSHELL is a batch file. If you invoke DOSSHELL from your AUTOEXEC.BAT file, make sure DOSSHELL is the last command in the file or that you invoke it using the CALL command.

If you are using the DOS 5 shell and want to use your mouse, you must first install the mouse device driver. Depending on your type of mouse, installing the device driver may require a CONFIG.SYS DEVICE entry such as DEVICE=MOUSE.SYS, or it may require invoking a memory-resident command such as MOUSE.COM.

If you are using the DOS 5 shell, the shell provides a utility called the Task Swapper that lets you load several programs into memory and switch between them as your needs require. When you switch from one task to another, the Task Swapper saves the current state of the first program, and then begins running the second program specified. Only one program actually runs at any one time. When you later switch back to the first program, the Task Swapper lets you continue right where you left off. The number of programs you can load at any one time depends on the program sizes and the amount of available memory.

Example

The following command invokes the DOS 4 or 5 shell.

```
C:\> DOSSHELL   <ENTER>
```

ECHO

Displays or suppresses batch command messages

By default, each time you execute DOS batch files DOS displays the name of each command as it executes. ECHO OFF lets you disable the command name display. In addition, many batch files use ECHO to display messages to the user.

Format

```
ECHO [ON | OFF | message]
```

ON   Enables the display of batch commands as they execute.

OFF   Disables the display of batch commands as they execute.

message   The text that ECHO is to display to the user.

Notes

ECHO is an internal DOS command that requires DOS 2.0 or later. If you are using DOS 3.3 or higher, DOS lets you proceed command names in a batch file with an @ character to suppress the command name display:

```
@CLS
@DATE
@TIME
```

Rather than preceding each command name with the @ character, most batch files simply place the @ character in front of the ECHO OFF command.

```
@ECHO OFF
CLS
DATE
TIME
```

Many batch files use ECHO to display messages to the user. For example, the following batch file displays the message "Hello there!"

```
@ECHO OFF
ECHO Hello there!
```

If you aren't using DOS 5 and you want ECHO to display a blank line, you must place the ALT-255 key combination after the ECHO command.

```
@ECHO OFF
ECHO Skipping one 1
ECHO Alt-255
ECHO Done
```

To enter the ALT-255 key combination, hold down ALT. Using the numeric keypad at the right of your keyboard, type in the value **255**. When you release the ALT key, you will see the cursor move one position to the right. The ALT-255 key combination creates a special blank character. When this character appears in an ECHO command line, ECHO displays a blank line! If you are using DOS 5, you can direct ECHO to display a blank line simply by placing a period after the ECHO command:

```
@ECHO OFF
ECHO Skipping one line
ECHO.
ECHO Done
```

Depending on your DOS version, you may place the following characters immediately flush next to ECHO to generate a blank line:

```
[ ] + / \ ; ,
```

If you invoke ECHO without a message, ON, or OFF, ECHO will display its current state. If you turn ECHO OFF from the DOS prompt, DOS will not display a prompt, but will still process the commands you type.

Examples

This batch procedure displays each of its command-line parameters.

```
@ECHO OFF
:LOOP
  SHIFT
  IF '%0'=='' GOTO DONE
  ECHO %0
  GOTO LOOP
:DONE
```

The following batch file uses ECHO to display several messages on the screen:

```
@ECHO OFF
ECHO ***********************
ECHO * Batch File Example *
ECHO *                     *
ECHO * Messages displayed  *
ECHO *      by  ECHO       *
ECHO ***********************
```

Upon invocation, the batch file will display

```
**********************
* Batch File Example *
*                    *
* Messages displayed *
*      by   ECHO     *
**********************
```

The next batch file uses the IF command to test if the file AUTOEXEC.BAT resides in the root directory. If the file exists, the batch file displays the file's contents. Otherwise, the batch file displays the message "AUTOEXEC.BAT not found."

```
@ECHO OFF
IF EXIST \AUTOEXEC.BAT TYPE \AUTOEXEC.BAT
IF NOT EXIST \AUTOEXEC.BAT ECHO AUTOEXEC.BAT not found
```

The following command displays ECHO's current state.

```
C:\> ECHO   <ENTER>
ECHO is on.
```

EDIT

Invokes the DOS 5 full-screen editor

The DOS 5 EDIT command lets you create or change (edit) ASCII text files, such as CONFIG.SYS or DOS batch files.

Format

```
EDIT [file_spec] [/B] [/G] [/H] [/NOHI]
```

file_spec   The complete path name of the file to edit.

/B   Directs EDIT to display its output in black and white. Use this switch when EDIT's output is not correct on a monochrome monitor.

/G   Directs EDIT to use fast screen updating on a CGA monitor.

/H   Directs EDIT to display the maximum number of available lines for the current display.

/NOHI   Directs EDIT to use 8-color display, as opposed to 16.

Notes

EDIT is an external command that requires DOS 5 or later. If you don't specify a file name when you invoke EDIT, you can use EDIT's File menu to open an existing file or save the text you enter to a specific file.

EDIT is a full-screen editor that supports mouse operations. If you use EDIT to change an existing file, EDIT does not make a backup copy of the file's original contents. Instead, the original contents are lost.

To create the ASCII escape character using EDIT, press CTRL -P followed by ESC.

If bold characters or menu options do not appear, use the /B or /NOHI command-line options.

EDIT requires the command QBASIC.EXE to be in the command path.

Example

The following command invokes EDIT to view or modify the file CONFIG.SYS.

```
C:\> EDIT  \CONFIG.SYS  <ENTER>
```

Messages

Cannot find file QBASIC.EXE

You must make sure the file QBASIC.EXE is in the current directory, or in the command path. EDIT uses the QBASIC editor.

EDLIN

Invokes the DOS line editor

EDLIN is a line-mode editor that lets you create or change (edit) ASCII text files, such as CONFIG.SYS or DOS batch files.

Format

```
EDLIN file_spec [/B]
```

file_spec   The complete path name to the file you want to edit.

/B   A DOS 5 switch that directs EDLIN to ignore the ^Z end-of-file character.

Notes

EDLIN is an external command supported by all DOS versions. EDLIN is a line editor that lets you edit your files one line at a time.

The longest line EDLIN supports is 253 characters. You must specify a file when you invoke EDLIN. EDLIN uses a series of single-letter commands defined here:

Command	Function
?	Displays a list of EDLIN's available commands
A	Appends lines of the file from disk into memory for editing
C	Copies one or more lines from one file location to another
D	Deletes one or more lines from a file
E	Saves your changes to disk and ends the editing session
I	Enters EDLIN's insert mode to add lines to a file
L	Lists one or more lines to your screen
M	Moves one or more lines from one file location to another
P	Displays a page (23 lines) on your screen
Q	Quits the editing session without saving your changes to disk
R	Replaces one word or phrase with another
S	Searches the file for a word or phrase
T	Transfers lines from a second file into the current file
W	Writes lines of the file from memory back to disk

To create an escape character using EDLIN, press CTRL-V followed by [(a left bracket).

Example

The following example creates the batch file DATETIME.BAT.

```
C:\> EDLIN  DATETIME.BAT   <ENTER>
New file
```

```
*I <ENTER>
   1:*@ECHO OFF   <ENTER>
   2:*DATE        <ENTER>
   3:*TIME        <ENTER>
   4:*

  *E
```

Messages

New file

EDLIN did not find a file matching the file name you specified in the command line and assumes you are creating a new file.

End of input file

EDLIN is telling you it successfully read the entire file into memory. If this message does not appear, you must use EDLIN's W and A commands to move text in and out of memory.

Continue (Y/N)?

EDLIN is asking you if you want to display the next screenful of text. If you type Y, EDLIN will display the text. If you instead type N, EDLIN will redisplay its prompt.

Abort edit (Y/N)?

You have issued EDLIN's Q (quit) command. EDLIN is asking you if you want to end the editing session, discarding your changes to the file. If you type Y, EDLIN will discard the file changes and end. If you type N, EDLIN will redisplay its prompt, continuing the editing session.

O.K.?

EDLIN is asking you if you want to end a search operation or if you want EDLIN to replace the current text in a replace operation. If you type Y at the OK prompt during a search operation, EDLIN will end the search, redisplaying its prompt. If you instead type N, EDLIN will continue the search. If you type Y at the OK prompt for a replace operation, EDLIN will replace the text specified. If you instead type N, EDLIN will leave the text unchanged.

Not found

EDLIN did not find the text specified in a search or replace operation.

Line too long

The current line exceeds EDLIN's 253-character limit.

Not enough room to merge the entire file

Your system does not have enough available memory for EDLIN to merge, using the T command, all of the file specified. If necessary, use EDLIN's W command to write a portion of the file's contents to disk and try the merge operation again.

Must specify destination line number

You did not include the line number to which you want EDLIN to move or copy text. Review the M(ove) or C(opy) command format and repeat the command.

Disk full. Edits Lost

EDLIN was unable to save your file changes because of insufficient disk space on the current disk. If possible, remove unnecessary files and repeat your edits, using the E command to exit EDLIN more frequently to save your changes.

Cannot edit .BAK file—rename file

EDLIN is telling you that it will not edit the contents of a backup file. Each time you exit EDLIN using E, EDLIN copies your file's original contents to a file with the BAK extension. If you were to edit a BAK file, EDLIN would become confused, possibly overwriting the file's new contents with its previous contents. Thus, EDLIN won't let you edit files with the BAK extension.

No room in directory for file

The root directory within which you are trying to save the file is full. If possible, move files from the root into another directory, or create your file with EDLIN in another directory.

File name must be specified

EDLIN is telling you that you must include the name of the file to edit in EDLIN's command line.

EXE2BIN

Converts an EXE file into a COM file

DOS executes files with the EXE and COM extensions. COM files differ in that they require less memory and load faster than EXE files. In some cases, programmers can convert an EXE file to a COM file. EXE2BIN is a programmer's tool, as opposed to a tool for end users.

Format

EXE2BIN   *ExeFile*   [*ComFile*]

ExeFile   The complete path name to the EXE file to convert.

ComFile   The complete path name of the target COM file. If you don't specify a file name, EXE2BIN will use the same name as the source file and the BIN (for binary) extension.

Notes

EXE2BIN is an external DOS command provided with early versions of DOS and DOS 5. EXE2BIN should only be used by knowledgeable programmers. Not all EXE files can be converted to COM format. In fact, most can't. Before EXE2BIN can convert an EXE file, the following conditions must apply:

1. The EXE file must be in a valid EXE format.

2. The EXE file code and data combined must be less than 64Kb.

3. The EXE file cannot have a stack segment.

4. The program cannot include any far references.

Example

The following EXE2BIN command converts the file TEST.EXE to the COM file TEST.COM.

```
C:\> EXE2BIN TEST.EXE TEST.COM   <ENTER>
```

Messages

File cannot be converted

The EXE file violates one of the conditions for conversion specified in the Notes section.

File creation error

EXE2BIN could not create the COM file because a read-only file with the same name as the COM file exists in the same directory, or the target disk or root directory is full.

Fixups needed - base segment (hex):

The EXE file contains segment address references that the loader would typically resolve. EXE2BIN is asking you to enter (in hexidecimal) the correct segment value.

EXIT

Terminates a secondary command processor

Many applications provide an option that lets you temporarily exit the application to the DOS prompt. When you have finished issuing DOS commands, you can return to the application by typing EXIT.

Format

```
EXIT
```

Notes

EXIT is an internal command that requires DOS 2.0 or later. The DOS 4 and 5 shells and Microsoft Windows, for example, let you temporarily exit the program to the DOS prompt to issue DOS commands. When you are ready to resume your work in the program, simply type EXIT at the DOS prompt and press ENTER. DOS will return you to the program, right where you left off. The command processor is the program responsible for displaying a prompt and processing the commands you type. Under DOS, the command processor is COMMAND.COM. Just as you can invoke any program from the DOS prompt or a DOS batch file, you can invoke COMMAND.COM. When COMMAND.COM runs, DOS loads into memory a second copy of the command processor, which in turn displays a DOS prompt. When a shell program or an application, such as your word processor, lets you temporarily exit to DOS, it actually loads a second command processor. To end the secondary command processor, returning to the program, use EXIT.

Example

To terminate a secondary command processor, use the EXIT command like this:

```
C:\> EXIT   <ENTER>
```

Messages

Bad command or filename

You are using a DOS version earlier than DOS 2.0. DOS introduced the EXIT command with DOS 2.0.

EXPAND

Expands a DOS 5 compressed file

To reduce the number of distribution disks, many DOS 5 files are shipped on disk in a compressed format. During installation, these files are automatically expanded. If you ever need to restore a file from the installation disks, you must use EXPAND, to decompress the file.

Format

```
EXPAND SourceFile TargetFile
```

SourceFile   The complete path name of the file whose contents you want to expand. EXPAND supports wildcard characters.

TargetFile   The name of the expanded file. EXPAND supports wildcard characters.

Notes

EXPAND is an external command that requires DOS 5 or later. If you examine your DOS 5 distribution disks, you will see files whose last letter of their extension is an underscore (_) character, such as UNDELETE.EX_. During the DOS 5 installation, SETUP expands these files onto your hard disk as necessary. Should you ever need to copy one of these files to your disk, you will need to expand it. You cannot use a compressed file until you expand it.

Example

The following expands the file UNDELTE.EX_ on the floppy disk in drive A to your DOS directory as UNDELETE.EXE.

```
C:\> EXPAND A:UNDELETE.EX_  \DOS\UNDELETE.EXE  <ENTER>
```

Messages

Insufficient disk space on drive *n*:

The disk drive specfied does not have enough space for EXPAND to decompress the file or files specified.

Input file FILENAME.EXT already in expanded format

The file name specified does not need to be decompressed.

FASTOPEN

Increases directory search performance

Every time you invoke a program or open a file, DOS must search the disk to determine where the file is. Because the disk is a mechanical device, this search is time consuming. FASTOPEN increases the speed with which DOS locates files on disk by increasing the number of directory entries that DOS keeps in memory.

Format

```
FASTOPEN drive:[= entries] [...] [/X]
```

or, under DOS 4 or 5

```
FASTOPEN drive:=(entries, sectorlistbuffers) [...] [/X]
```

drive: The disk drive for which DOS is setting aside storage space to contain directory entries.

entries   The number of directory entries for which DOS is reserving space. This value must be in the range 10-999. The default value is 48. Each FASTOPEN entry requires about 48 bytes of memory.

sectorlistbuffers   The number of buffers FASTOPEN will use to track the actual lists of sectors that make up a recently used file. The value must be in the range 10-999. The default value is 34.

...   Indicates that FASTOPEN can reserve space for several disks in one command.

/X   A DOS 4 or 5 switch that directs FASTOPEN to create the table of directory entries in expanded memory.

Notes

FASTOPEN is an external command that requires DOS 3.3 or later. Each time a DOS application opens a file for reading or writing, DOS must locate that file on disk. DOS does this by first searching the directory specified or current directory for the file's starting location on disk. Because disks are mechanical, this directory search takes considerable time. Versions beginning with DOS 3.3 let you set aside memory to contain a table of commonly used files and their starting locations. When you later open a file, DOS first examines this table for the file's starting address. If DOS locates the file in this table, it doesn't have to read this information from disk. Thus, considerable time is saved.

FASTOPEN lets you specify the size of the table of file names DOS stores in memory. Nevertheless, this table can be a double-edged sword. If you open several files on a regular basis, FASTOPEN may save you time. If you do not use the same file or set of files repeatedly, FASTOPEN will probably increase your system overhead and give you slower performance. This is because, with every file open, DOS must search this table. If the table does not contain your file, the search is overhead.

If several disks are specified, the sum of the number of directory entries cannot exceed 999. Each directory entry that is stored requires 48 bytes. If you use a value of 999 for directory entries, DOS will spend a considerable amount of overhead simply searching its directory list. Most users, therefore, find the default value acceptable. If you are using DOS 4 or 5, tracking sector entries will improve your system performance by decreasing disk reads to the file allocation table to locate the file's sectors.

WARNING *If you are using a third-party disk defragmenter, use the program with FASTOPEN disabled or make sure you restart your system when the utility program completes. Such programs move file information from one disk location to another without FASTOPEN's knowledge. If you don't restart your system and you write to a file for whom FASTOPEN has a matching entry, FASTOPEN may write the file's contents to the wrong location on disk, damaging other files or directories.*

Example

In the following example, DOS will remember 50 directory entries for drive C:

```
C:\> FASTOPEN C:=50   <ENTER>
```

If you are using DOS 4 or later, this command also directs FASTOPEN to track 75 sector entries.

```
C:\> FASTOPEN C:=(50,75)   <ENTER>
```

Messages

Cannot use FASTOPEN for drive *n*:

The disk drive specified is either a floppy disk drive or has been ASSIGNed or SUBSTed. FASTOPEN only supports fixed disks.

FASTOPEN installed - memory resident software

FASTOPEN is simply telling you that it has successfully loaded itself in memory and is ready to assist DOS in locating your files.

FASTOPEN already installed

FASTOPEN is telling you that it has already been installed in memory. Since FASTOPEN installs memory-resident software, it can only be invoked once per user session. To change FASTOPEN parameters, you must restart DOS.

Same drive specified more than once

You have placed the same disk drive letter twice in your FASTOPEN command line. Correct the error and reissue the command.

Too many drive entries

Invoke the FASTOPEN command with fewer disk drives. Only specify your most commonly used disk drives.

Too many name entries

The total number of directory entries in the FASTOPEN command line exceeds 999. Reduce this number and reissue the command. If you specify too many entries, FASTOPEN may reduce your system's performance, since it must now spend considerable time checking each entry. Also, each FASTOPEN entry consumes 48 bytes.

FC

Displays the actual differences between two files

FC stands for File Compare. FC compares two files and displays the lines of the files that differ.

Format

```
FC [/A] [/B] [/C] [/L] [/LB n] [/N] [/T] [W] [/nnnn] file1 file2
```

/A   Directs FC to display only the first and last lines in a series of lines that differ.

/B   Directs FC to perform a binary comparison of the files.

/C   Directs FC to ignore the case of letters.

/L   Directs FC to perform an ASCII file comparison.

/LB _n_   Directs FC to use an internal buffer of _n_ lines.

/N   Directs FC to display the line numbers of lines that differ in two ASCII files.

/T   Directs FC _not_ to expand tabs into spaces.

/W   Directs FC to compress white space (spaces or tabs).

/_nnnn_   The number of lines that must again match following a difference before FC assumes them to be synchronized. The default is 2.

file1   The complete path name to the first file to compare.

file2   The complete path name to the second file to compare.

Notes

FC is an external command that requires MS-DOS 2.0 or later. FC displays differences between two files by displaying the first file name, followed by the lines that differ between the files. Next, FC displays the second file name, followed by the first line that matches in both files and the differences.

If FC is comparing binary files, it will display differences in the form

```
aaaaaaaa bb cc
```

where _aaaaaaaa_ is the offset address of the values that differ and _bb_ and _cc_ are the values that differ. If FC encounters too many errors, it will terminate, displaying the message:

```
resynch failed. Files are too different.
```

Because FC displays the differences of two files in ASCII, FC is often a much more convenient method of comparing two files than the COMP command.

If you specify wildcard characters for either *file1* or *file2*, FC will compare every file corresponding to *file1* with every file corresponding to *file2*.

Examples

The following command compares two binary files using /B switch.

```
C:\> FC TEST.EXE OLDTEST.EXE   <ENTER>
```

In this case, the output might be

```
00000002: 9A 66
00000004: 06 20
00000006: 01 03
0000000A: 00 CE
0000000E: 20 14
0000000F: 00 04
00000011: 02 08
00000012: 32 97
```

In a similar manner, assuming that the file A.DAT contains

```
1
2
3
4
5
A
A
A
6
7
8
9
10
```

and B.DAT contains

```
1
2
3
4
5
B
B
B
6
7
8
9
10
```

the command

```
C:\> FC A.DAT B.DAT    <ENTER>
```

will display

```
***** A.DAT
5
A
A
A
6
***** B.DAT
5
B
B
B
6
*****
```

If you include the /N switch

```
C:\> FC /N A.DAT B.DAT    <ENTER>
```

FC will display

```
***** A.DAT
    5:   5
    6:   A
    7:   A
    8:   A
    9:   6
***** B.DAT
    5:   5
    6:   B
    7:   B
    8:   B
    9:   6
*****
```

If the file DAYS.DAT contains

```
SUNDAY
MONDAY
TUESDAY
WEDNESDAY
THURSDAY
FRIDAY
SATURDAY
```

while WEEKDAYS.DAT contains

```
MONDAY
TUESDAY
WEDNESDAY
THURSDAY
FRIDAY
```

the command

```
C:\> FC DAYS.DAT WEEKDAYS.DAT   <ENTER>
```

will display

```
***** DAYS.DAT
SUNDAY
MONDAY
TUESDAY
***** WEEKDAYS.DAT
MONDAY
TUESDAY
*****
***** DAYS.DAT
SATURDAY
***** WEEKDAYS.DAT
*****
```

If you want FC to ignore differences between upper- and lowercase letters, you can simply add the /C switch:

```
C:\> FC /C FILE.1 FILE.2   <ENTER>
```

Messages

FC: FILENAME.EXT longer than FILENAME.EXT

The contents of each file compared identically; however, the first file specified is simply longer than the second file. FC only displays this message for binary mode comparisions.

FC: no differences encountered

Both of the files compared identically.

Out of memory

Your system has insufficient RAM for FC to create the tables that it requires to store the information from each file during the comparison. If you have installed memory-resident software or a RAM drive, you might consider removing them so that you can repeat the FC command.

Resynch failed Files are too different

The files are so different that FC could not locate a position in both files that were similar enough to resume the file comparison.

usage: fc [/a][/b][/c][/l][/lbNN][/w][/t][/n][/NNNN] file1 file2

You invoked FC without any command-line parameters and FC is displaying its optional command-line parameters.

FC: Insufficient number of filespecs

Your command line did not specify two files to compare.

FDISK

Defines disk partitions on a DOS fixed disk

DOS lets you divide your fixed disk into logical collections of cylinders, called partitions. By so doing, you can actually place several different operating systems into different partitions on one fixed disk. The FDISK command lets you add, change, display, and delete disk partitions.

Format

```
FDISK
```

Notes

FDISK is an external command that requires DOS 2.0 or later. Under DOS 3.3, the maximum partition size is 32Mb. Under DOS 4.0, the maximum partition size is 512Mb. Under DOS 5.0, the maximum partition size is 2Gb (gigabytes).

If your computer is new and DOS cannot locate your fixed disk, you will have to issue the FDISK command to define the disk to DOS. FDISK is a menu-driven program that allows you to divide your disks into multiple sections called partitions. Select the FDISK option that selects your entire disk as your DOS partition. In most cases, however, your computer retailer will have taken care of this for you.

The first sector on any fixed disk contains a master boot record, which contains information that defines which partition the computer uses for booting. FDISK is your means of interfacing with the master boot record.

You can partition a hard disk in up to four partitions. DOS can use two of these partitions. The first partition, called the primary partition, is the partition from which DOS will boot. Depending on your DOS version the size of the primary partition may be fixed. The second partition is called the extended partition. Typically, the extended partition contains all of the disk space your primary partition could not use. You must divide your extended partition into logical disk drives.

Depending on your DOS version, the size of these logical drives may be restricted to 32Mb. DOS lets you divide the extended partition in up to 23 logical drives (D through Z). Do not change your disk's current partitions without first backing up the information each partition contains.

Example

If DOS responds with

```
Invalid drive specification
```

when you try to access your hard disk, you will have to create a DOS partition and format the hard disk. FDISK lets you create DOS partitions. To invoke FDISK, place your DOS system disk in drive A and type **FDISK**.

```
A> FDISK
```

FDISK is a menu-driven program and will respond with its first menu.

```
                    MS-DOS Version 5.0
                  Fixed Disk Setup Program
             (C)Copyright Microsoft Corp. 1983-1990


                     FDISK Options

Current fixed disk drive: 1


Choose one of the following:

1: Create DOS Partition or Logical DOS Drive
2: Set active partition
3: Delete DOS Partition or Logical DOS Drive
4: Display partition information


Enter choice: [1]


Press Esc to exit FDISK
```

Messages

DOS partition created

FDISK has successfully created your DOS partition as specified. Once you exit FDISK, you must format the disk before it can be used by DOS.

Do you wish to use the entire fixed disk for DOS (Y/N).....?[Y]

FDISK is prompting you as to whether or not you want to use the entire disk as a DOS partition. Most users will want to use their entire disk as a DOS partition.

Do you wish to use the maximum size *nnn* for a DOS partition and make the DOS partition active (Y/N)...?

FDISK is prompting you as to whether or not you want to use all of the remaining disk cylinders as a DOS partition. Most users will want to do so.

Enter the number of the partition you want to make active......[*n*]

FDISK is prompting you for the number associated with the disk partition that you want to make active. Although FDISK lets you logically divide your disk into several partitions, only one partition can be active (or the partition your computer uses to start DOS). Mostly, you will keep your DOS partition as the active partition.

Fixed disk already has a DOS partition

You have selected the Create DOS Partition when a DOS partition already exists. You can only place one active DOS partition on a hard disk.

Maximum space available for partition *n* is *nnn* cylinders

You have instructed FDISK not to use the entire disk for the partition you are creating. FDISK is telling you the maximum size of the partition that you can create.

No DOS partition to delete

You have selected the FDISK menu option Delete DOS partition and the disk does not contain a DOS partition that DOS can delete.

No fixed disk present

You must inform your computer's CMOS about your hard disk type. If you are using an IBM PC AT or AT-compatible, use the SETUP program that accompanied your computer on floppy disk. If you are using a 386 or 486 system, you typically invoke SETUP by pressing a key such as DEL when you first start your computer. Refer to the documentation that accompanied your computer for more information on SETUP.

No partitions defined

You have selected the Display Partition Information option and you have not yet created partitions on the fixed disk.

No partition to make active

You have selected the Change Active Partition option and you have not yet created partitions on the fixed disk that FDISK can make active.

No space to create a DOS partition

You have selected the Create DOS Partition option and your disk does not have sufficient available free cylinders to create a DOS partition. If this error occurs, you may have to modify the size of the non-DOS partitions that you have created on the disk.

Partition *n* is already active

You have selected the Change Active Partition option and the partition that you specified was already active.

Partition *n* made active

You have selected the Change Active Partition option and specified a new boot partition. This message is purely informational.

System will now restart
Insert DOS diskette in drive A
Press any key when ready...

You have successfully created a DOS partition and FDISK is ready to restart your system so that you can format your newly created fixed disk. Place a bootable disk in drive A and press any key to continue.

Total disk space is *nnn* cylinders
Maximum available space is *nnn*
cylinders at *nn*

FDISK is telling you the current disk utilization and maximum space that you can use to create an additional disk partition.

Warning! Data in the DOS partition
will be lost. Do you wish to
continue.....? [N]

FDISK is prompting you to specify whether or not you really want to delete the current DOS partition, warning you that if you do so, all of the data that the partition contains will be lost. If you simply press ENTER, FDISK will select the default option of No.

Warning! Data in the Extended DOS
partition will be lost. Do you wish to
continue......? [N]

FDISK is prompting you to specify whether or not you really want to delete an extended DOS partition, warning you that if you do so, all of the data that the partition contains will be lost. To delete the extended DOS partition, type Y and press ENTER. If you don't want to delete the extended DOS partition, simply press ENTER and FDISK will select the default of No.

Cannot FDISK with network loaded

FDISK is telling you that you cannot execute the FDISK command on disk that is part of a local area network.

Requested partition size exceeds the maximum available space

The number of cylinders that you have directed FDISK to use for your disk partition exceeds the number of available cylinders. Repeat the option, specifying a smaller number of cylinders.

Partition selected is not bootable active partition not changed

You have selected the Change Active Partition option and specified a partition that cannot be booted. FDISK has left the active partition unchanged.

Cannot create a zero size partition

The partition size you specified was 0Mb or 0%. The minimum partition size FDISK supports is 1Mb or 1%.

Cannot create an extended DOS partition without a primary DOS partition on disk 1

FDISK is informing you that you cannot create an extended DOS partition on a disk drive until you create a primary (bootable) DOS partition on the same disk. The primary partition is the disk partition from which your computer will boot DOS.

Cannot Logical DOS drive without an Extended DOS Partition on the current drive

You tried to define a logical disk drive before creating an extended DOS partition within which the logical drive will reside. After you use FDISK to create an extended DOS partition, FDISK lets you divide the partition in up to 23 logical drives.

Cannot delete Extended DOS Partition while logical drives exist

You have attempted to remove the extended DOS partition without first individually removing the logical drives it contains. To remove the extended partition, you must first use FDISK to remove the logical drives.

All available space in the Extended DOS Partition is assigned to logical drives

There is no more disk space available to create additional logical disk drives.

All logical drives deleted in the Extended DOS Partition

FDISK has removed all the extended DOS partition's logical drives. You can now delete or change the size of the extended partition.

Extended DOS Partition already exists

You attempted to create an extended DOS partition and one is already defined. You can only create one primary and one extended DOS partition on your disk.

Extended DOS Partition created

FDISK successfully created the extended DOS partition using the size specified. You must now divide the extended partition into logical disk drives.

Extended DOS Partition deleted

FDISK has removed the extended partition. If you are using DOS 4 or DOS 5, change your primary DOS partition to use the space previously used by the extended partition.

No Logical DOS Drive(s) to delete

You have directed FDISK to delete a logical drive from the extended DOS partition, and no logical drives are defined.

Partition selected is not bootable, active partition not changed

You tried to change the active partition (the partition from which your computer boots DOS) to a partition that is not bootable. FDISK did not change the partition.

FIND

Searches file(s) or piped input for a character string

The FIND command lets you locate a sequence of characters or words within a file or within redirected output. FIND can also be used as a filter with piped input.

Format

```
FIND [/C][/N][/V][/I] "string" [file_spec] [...]
```

or

```
FIND [/C][/N][/V][/I] "string"  < file_spec
```

or

```
DOS_Command | FIND [/C][/N][/V][/I] "string"
```

/C   Directs FIND to display a count of occurrences of the string. If used with /N, the /C switch is ignored.

/N   Directs FIND to precede each line that contains the string with its line number.

/V   Directs FIND to display each line that does not contain the string.

/I   A DOS 5 switch that directs FIND to consider upper- and lowercase letters the same.

string   Specifies the string that FIND is to search for. It must be in double quotes.

file_spec   The name of the file to be searched for the string. It can be a series of file names, separated by spaces. FIND does not support DOS wildcard characters.

DOS_Command   The name of a DOS command whose output FIND is to search for the string specified.

...   Indicates that several file names can reside in the command line.

Notes

FIND is an external command that requires DOS 2.0 or later. The string FIND is searching for must be within quotation marks. If the desired string includes quotation marks as the characters themselves, you must use two sets of quotation marks—one set for the string and one for the command:

```
C:\> FIND """Look"" he said" FILENAME.EXT   <ENTER>
```

In DOS 5, you can use the TEMP environment entry to specify where DOS creates temporary files during I/O redirection operations. By directing DOS to create its temporary files on a fast RAM drive, you can improve your system performance.

Examples

In the following example, FIND is used as a filter to list each subdirectory in the current directory:

```
C:\> DIR A: | FIND "<DIR>"   <ENTER>
```

If the current directory contains the following:

```
Volume in drive A is DOSDISK
Volume Serial Number is 1234-4321
Directory of  A:\

SUBDIR          <DIR>        11-01-88   12:53p
A               <DIR>        11-01-88    1:44p
B               <DIR>        11-01-88    1:44p
C               <DIR>        11-01-88    1:44p
WSSTRIP   EXE    2816        10-03-84   10:33p
TAB       EXE   12326         5-05-85    6:25p
SUM       EXE    2834        10-24-88    2:20p
PIPE      EXE    2814        10-26-88    6:47p
PIPE2     EXE    7528        10-23-88   12:37p
          9 File(s)    1182208 bytes free
```

the previous command will display

```
SUBDIR          <DIR>        11-01-88   12:53p
A               <DIR>        11-01-88    1:44p
B               <DIR>        11-01-88    1:44p
C               <DIR>        11-01-88    1:44p
```

To list all files that are not directories, use the FIND /V option:

```
C:\> DIR A: | FIND /V "<DIR>"   <ENTER>
```

The following command displays each occurrence of the string "Mr." in the BILLING.LTR file:

```
C:\> FIND "Mr." BILLING.LTR   <ENTER>
```

In a similar manner, the following command displays each occurrence of "Mr.". However, in this example, each line is preceded by its line number:

```
C:\> FIND /N "Mr." BILLING.LTR   <ENTER>
```

The following command displays the number of directories within the current directory:

```
C:\> DIR | FIND /C "<DIR>"   <ENTER>
```

Messages

FIND: Access denied FILENAME.EXT

FIND could not access the file specified because it is locked by another program in the network or you have specified the name of a directory instead of a file.

FIND: Required parameter missing

Your FIND command line does not specify at least a search string for FIND to look for. You must specify at least FIND "*string*."

FIND: Read error in FILENAME.EXT

The file specified is very likely corrupted. Repeat the command to see if the error goes away. If you don't have a backup copy of the file, you may have to use the RECOVER command to salvage a portion of the file.

FOR

Provides repetitive execution of DOS commands

Repeats a specific command for a given set of files.

Format

Within a DOS batch file the format is

```
FOR %% variable IN (set) DO DOS_command
```

From the DOS prompt, the format is

```
FOR % variable IN (set) DO DOS_command
```

%% variable   The FOR loop control variable within a DOS batch file that FOR manipulates with each iteration. The variable name is restricted to a character; 0-9 cannot be used, since they are reserved for DOS batch parameters.

% variable   The variable name FOR manipulates if invoked from DOS' prompt.

set   A list of valid DOS file names. This list can contain DOS file names separated by commas (A, B, C), wildcard characters (*.*), or both (A, B, *.DAT).

DOS_command   The command to be executed with each iteration.

Notes

FOR is an internal command that requires DOS 2.0 or later. FOR can also be used from within DOS batch files or from the DOS prompt. Use the %% symbols before the variable name when working within batch files. Use the single % symbol from the DOS prompt. The processing that FOR performs is straightforward. Consider:

```
FOR %%V IN (AUTOEXEC.BAT, CONFIG.SYS, README.TXT) DO TYPE %%V
```

In this case, FOR will assign the variable file name AUTOEXEC.BAT during the first iteration of the command and display the file's contents:

```
TYPE AUTOEXEC.BAT
```

On the second iteration of the command, FOR assigns the file name CONFIG.SYS and displays its contents:

```
TYPE CONFIG.SYS
```

On the third iteration, FOR assigns the file name README.TXT and again displays the contents of the file:

```
TYPE README.TXT
```

When FOR prepares for the fourth iteration, it fails to find any more file names, so its processing is complete.

If you use GOTO as the command FOR executes, the first GOTO command ends FOR's execution. DOS will not return control to the FOR command for its next iteration.

Examples

In the following example, the user has issued the command from the DOS prompt. Note that the variable name is preceded by only one percent sign (%I) when FOR is invoked from the DOS command line.

```
C:\> FOR %I IN (*.FOR) DO TYPE %I   <ENTER>
```

In the following example, a DOS batch file is using FOR to compile all the C program files in the current directory with the CC command.

```
FOR %%F IN (*.C) DO CC %%F
```

Note that within a batch file, you must use double percent signs.

The following batch file uses FOR to check several possible spellings of the value in the parameter %1.

```
@ECHO OFF
FOR %%I IN (RED Red red) DO IF '%1'=='%%I' GOTO RED
REM other batch file statements here
```

Messages

FOR cannot be nested

You have placed a second FOR command as the DOS command that FOR will execute with each iteration, which is called nesting. FOR does not let you specify the FOR command as its command to execute.

FORMAT

Formats a disk for use by DOS

When you purchase floppy disks, the original disk manufacturer has no way of knowing on what computer the disks will be used—or on what operating system. Therefore, before you can use a new disk, you must format the disk for use by DOS. The FORMAT command formats a disk that is to be used with DOS.

Format

FORMAT *drive*: [/Q] [/V: *label*] [/S] [/B]

or

FORMAT *drive*: [/F:size] [/U] [/S] [/B]

or

FORMAT *drive*: [/1] [/4] [/U] [/V:*label*] [/S] [/B]

or

FORMAT *drive*: [/8] [/U] [/S] [/B]

or

FORMAT *drive*: [/T:*tracks*] [/N:*sectors*] [/S] [/B]

drive: The name of the drive that contains the disk to be formatted.

/S   Directs FORMAT to place the DOS system files on the disk, making it bootable.

/V: *label*   Directs FORMAT to include the volume label specified.

/4   Directs FORMAT to format the disk as double-sided in a quadruple-density disk drive.

/T: *tracks*　　Defines the number of tracks to a side. This switch requires DOS 3.3 or later.

/N: *sectors*　　Defines the number of sectors per track. This switch requires DOS 3.3 or later.

/1　　Directs FORMAT to format the disk as a single-sided disk.

/8　　Directs FORMAT to format the disk with 8 sectors per track; most disks use 9 or 15 sectors.

/B　　Directs FORMAT to reserve space for the system files on the target disk. Unlike the /S switch, /B does not actually place the files on disk. The /S and /V switches cannot be used in conjunction with the /B switch.

/U　　Directs DOS to perform an unconditional format, destroying all of the information previously recorded on the disk. You cannot unformat a disk unconditionally formatted. This switch requires DOS 5.

/F: *size*　　The size of the floppy disk to format, where size is one of the following:

160	160K	160Kb			
180	180K	180Kb			
320	320K	320Kb			
360	360K	360Kb			
720	720K	720Kb			
1200	1200K	1200Kb	1.2	1.2M	1.2Mb
1440	1440K	1440Kb	1.44	1.44M	1.44Mb
2880	2880K	2880Kb	2.88	2.88M	2.88Mb

/Q　　Directs FORMAT to perform a quick format of a previously formatted disk, overwriting the root directory and file allocation table. A quick format does not search the disk for bad sectors. This switch requires DOS 5.

Notes

FORMAT is an external command supported by all DOS versions. Inadvertently formatting a fixed disk can be disastrous. Before it formats a hard disk, FORMAT will first prompt you with the following to ensure that you really want to continue.

```
WARNING, ALL DATA ON NON-REMOVABLE DISK
DRIVE N: WILL BE LOST!
Proceed with Format (Y/N)?
```

To proceed with the formatting process, type **Y**; otherwise, type **N**.

Depending on your version of DOS, FORMAT may first prompt you to type in your hard disk's volume label before letting you format the hard disk. If the label you enter does not match the current hard disk label, FORMAT will not continue.

Upon completion of the formatting process, FORMAT will display the following items:

- Total disk space

- Corrupted disk space marked as defective

- Total disk space consumed by the operating system

- Total disk space available for file utilization

FORMAT reports on defective space that it finds during formatting. In addition, FORMAT places entries for each defective sector into the file allocation table (an area that DOS uses to keep track of the locations of files), which prevents DOS from using the corrupted sectors for data storage.

Do not use FORMAT in conjunction with ASSIGN, JOIN, or SUBST. FORMAT will not work with drives that are being used across a network.

If you are using DOS 5, you may be able to recover a hard disk that has been inadvertently formatted by using the UNFORMAT command.

The /Q switch directs FORMAT to perform a quick format operation of a previously formatted disk, initializing the file allocation table, and root directory. With the exception of these two areas, a quick format does not overwrite the disk's previous contents.

The /U switch directs FORMAT to perform an unconditional format, overwriting the disk's existing contents, ensuring each disk location is capable of storing information.

By default, unless you include a size switch in FORMAT's command line, FORMAT will format previously formatted disks using their existing capacity (such as 360Kb or 1.2Mb). When you begin a format operation, FORMAT will display the following message as it checks the disk to determine its previous format.

```
Checking existing disk format.
```

By default, unless you include the /U switch, the DOS 5 FORMAT command performs a safe format of disks that previously contained data, recording on the target disk the information UNFORMAT would later need to recover the disk in the event of an inadvertent disk format. When the format operation begins, FORMAT will display the following message:

```
Saving UNFORMAT information.
```

If the disk does not have sufficient space to record this information, FORMAT will display the following message:

```
Drive n error. Insufficient space for the mirror image file.
This disk cannot be unformatted.
Proceed with format (Y/N)?
```

If you are running FORMAT within a DOS batch file, FORMAT supports the following exit status codes:

Exit Status	Meaning
0	Successful format
3	Format terminated by user CTRL-C
4	Fatal error, format incomplete
5	User typed N at the prompt to continue

Examples

The following command formats the disk in drive A as a bootable DOS disk.

```
C:\> FORMAT A:/S   <ENTER>
```

Upon invocation, the command will display

```
Insert a new diskette in drive A:
and press Enter when ready...
```

Users often have to format double-density disks in their 1.2-megabyte, quad-density disk drives. The /4 switch in the FORMAT command directs FORMAT to create a 360Kb disk:

```
C:\> FORMAT A: /4   <ENTER>
```

The /B and /S switches are similar. The following command directs FORMAT to reserve space for the operating system's boot files (files that are necessary for the operating system to boot), instead of placing those files on disk. If you include the /B switch, the SYS command can later update the disk as required.

```
C:\> FORMAT A: /B   <ENTER>
```

If you are using DOS 5, the following command directs FORMAT to perform a quick format of a previously formatted floppy disk in drive A.

```
C:\> FORMAT A: /Q   <ENTER>
```

The following DOS 5 FORMAT command directs FORMAT to perform an unconditional FORMAT operation, overwriting the disk's previous contents.

```
C:\> FORMAT A: /U   <ENTER>
```

Messages

n percent of disk formatted

FORMAT is simply providing a status of the amount of the disk it has formatted. This message is purely informational.

n bytes total disk space
n bytes used for system
n bytes in bad sectors
n bytes available on disk

FORMAT is simply providing you with a summary of the disk usage for the newly formatted disk. If FORMAT continually finds damaged sectors on your disks, you might consider a new brand of disk. With the increased state of floppy disk technology today, such errors are much less common.

Attempted write-protect violation

The disk in the target drive specified in your FORMAT command line is write-protected. In most cases, this error occurs when you have forgotten to place an unused disk in the target disk drive. As you can see, write-protecting a disk protects the information stored on the disk from errant DOS commands.

Cannot format an ASSIGNed or SUBSTed drive

The target drive in your FORMAT command line is a logical drive or a drive that has been assigned to point to another drive. FORMAT does not let you format logical or assigned drives.

Cannot FORMAT a network drive

The drive specified in your FORMAT command line is a network drive. FORMAT does not let you format network drives.

Cannot find System Files

Your FORMAT command line contains the /S switch, which directs FORMAT to create a bootable target disk, and FORMAT could not locate the DOS hidden system files that it must copy to the target disk in order for the disk to be bootable. Locate the disk that you used to boot DOS and use it in the FORMAT operation.

Disk unsuitable for system disk

The disk specified contains damaged sectors in the first portion of the disk used to store the hidden system files to start DOS. Since DOS cannot place these files on the disk at this location, FORMAT cannot create a bootable disk.

Enter current Volume Label for drive *n*:

FORMAT is prompting you to enter a disk volume name that it will assign to the disk upon completion of the format operation. In this case, simply type in the 11-character disk volume name, or press ENTER for no name. Remember, assigning meaningful names to your disks will increase your disk organization.

Press any key to begin formatting *n*:

FORMAT is pausing to give you an opportunity to insert a disk in the drive specified or to cancel the format operation by pressing CTRL-C. To continue the formatting operation, press any key.

Error reading partition table

FORMAT encountered an error while attempting to read the partition table that specifies your fixed disk layout. Restart DOS and repeat the command. If this error persists, invoke the FDISK command to correct the partition table.

Error writing directory

FORMAT could not create a root directory on the disk specified. This error is normally associated with an unusable disk.

Format another (Y/N)?

FORMAT has completed the processing of one disk (either successfully or unsuccessfully) and is prompting you to determine whether or not you want to format an additional disk. If so, type Y and press ENTER; FORMAT will prompt you to insert another disk. If not, simply type N and press ENTER. FORMAT will return control to DOS.

Format complete

The format operation has successfully completed.

Insert DOS diskette for drive *n*
and press Enter when ready...

Your FORMAT command line contains the /S switch, which directs FORMAT to create a bootable DOS disk by copying the hidden system files that DOS requires to boot a disk. In this case, FORMAT is prompting you to insert a bootable DOS disk in the drive specified so that it can copy the hidden files to the target disk.

Insert new diskette for drive *n*:
and press Enter when ready...

FORMAT is prompting you to place the disk that you want to format in the drive specified. Once you do so, press ENTER, and FORMAT will continue its processing.

Invalid characters in volume label

Your FORMAT command line contains the /V switch, which directs FORMAT to assign a disk volume name to the disk upon completion of the format operation. In this case, when FORMAT prompted you to enter a disk volume name, one or more letters that you typed in were invalid for a disk label name. Remember, volume names follow the same naming conventions as DOS files. Depending on your DOS version, you may be able to use space (blank) characters within your volume name.

Bad partition table

The partition table that DOS uses to keep track of your fixed disk layout is bad. Invoke the FDISK command to correct the partition table.

Invalid media or Track 0 bad - disk unusable

The first track on the disk specified is damaged. DOS must be able to format the first track of a disk either to make the disk bootable, or to place information in that track that tells DOS that the disk is not a bootable system disk. If DOS cannot use this track, it cannot use the disk.

Non-System disk or disk error
Replace and press any key when ready

Your FORMAT command line contains the /S switch, which directs FORMAT to create a bootable disk by copying the hidden DOS system files that DOS requires at startup to the disk. In this case, the disk in the drive specified did not contain the hidden system files, or FORMAT could not read the disk. Place the disk that you used to boot DOS in the drive and press any key to continue.

Parameters not supported by drive *n*:

One or more of the switches in your FORMAT command line is invalid for the disk drive specified. Review the switches as specified in the format of the FORMAT command and reissue the command.

System transferred

Your FORMAT command line contained the /S switch, which directs FORMAT to build a bootable disk, and FORMAT has successfully copied the hidden system files to the target disk.

Volume label (11 characters, Enter for none)?

Your FORMAT command line contains the /V switch, which directs FORMAT to prompt you for a disk volume name that FORMAT will assign to the disk upon completion of the format operation. In this case, simply type in the 11-character disk volume name, or press ENTER for no name. Remember, assigning meaningful names to your disks will increase your disk organization. In addition, starting with DOS 4, FORMAT will not format your hard disk until you correctly type in the volume name. By forcing you to enter the volume name in this way, FORMAT reduces the chance of an accidental hard disk format.

Unable to write BOOT

FORMAT could not write the information to the first track of the disk that FORMAT uses to create a bootable disk or to tell DOS that the disk is not bootable. Repeat the FORMAT command to see if the error corrects itself. If not, the disk is unusable.

WARNING, ALL DATA ON NON-REMOVABLE DRIVE *n*: WILL BE LOST
Proceed with Format (Y/N)?

FORMAT is warning you that the disk specified in your FORMAT command line is a fixed disk, and continuing with the FORMAT operation will destroy all the information that the disk contains. If you want to proceed with the format operation (overwriting the information on your fixed disk), type Y and press ENTER. Otherwise, type N and press ENTER.

Must enter both /T and /N parameters

Your FORMAT command line has included either /T, which specifies the number of tracks per side on the disk, or /N, which specifies the number of sectors per track. You must specify both parameters.

Checking existing disk format

FORMAT is examining the target disk to determine its previous format capacity (such as 360Kb or 1.2Mb). Unless told to do otherwise, FORMAT formats a previously formatted disk using its previous capacity. FORMAT only provides this capability under DOS 5.

Saving UNFORMAT information

A safe format operation is storing on the target disk information UNFORMAT can use to recover the disk's contents. FORMAT only provides this capability under DOS 5.

Drive *n*: error. Insufficient space for the MIRROR image file.
There was an error creating the format recovery file.
This disk cannot be unformatted
Proceed with Format (Y/N)?

A safe format attempted to store on the target disk the information that UN-FORMAT requires to recover the disk, but could not because the disk did not have enough disk space. If you want to continue the format operation type Y. If you want to cancel the FORMAT command, returning control to the DOS prompt, type N. FORMAT only provides this capability under DOS 5.

QuickFormat another (Y/N)?

FORMAT is asking if you want to perform another quick format on a previously formatted disk. To perform a second quick format, type Y; otherwise, type N.

Existing format differs from that specified.
This disk cannot be unformatted.
Proceed with Format (Y/N)?

Your FORMAT command line specifies the desired size you want for the target disk, and upon examining the disk, FORMAT noted the disk's existing size differs from the size you have requested. As a result FORMAT cannot save the information necessary for UNFORMAT to later recover the disk. FORMAT, therefore, is asking you if you want to continue the operation. If you type Y, FORMAT will format the disk, using the capacity specified. If you type N, FORMAT will end, leaving the disk unchanged.

Invalid existing format.
This disk cannot be QuickFormatted.
Proceed with Unconditional Format (Y/N)?

FORMAT is telling you it cannot perform a quick format of the disk because the disk's format is invalid. FORMAT can only perform a quick format operation on a previously formatted DOS disk. Because FORMAT cannot perform the quick format, FORMAT is asking you if you want it to perform an unconditional format, which will overwrite the disk's existing contents. To perform the unconditional format, type Y; otherwise type N to leave the disk unchanged.

There was an error creating the format recovery file.
This disk cannot be unformatted.
Proceed with Format (Y/N)?

A safe format attempted to store on the target disk the information that UN-FORMAT requires to recover the disk, but encountered an error trying to record the information on disk. If you want to continue the format operation, type Y. If you want to cancel the FORMAT command, returning control to the DOS prompt, type N. FORMAT only provides this capability under DOS 5.

Volume label is not supported with /8 parameter.

Your FORMAT command line includes the /8 and /V switches. FORMAT does not let you use these two switches together.

GOTO

Branches to a specific location within a DOS batch file

The GOTO command tells DOS to branch to a label that is specified in a batch file. DOS label names contain any of the characters valid for DOS file names. If the label does not exist, DOS terminates execution of the batch file.

Format

```
GOTO label_name
```

label_name   The name of a label to be the target of a GOTO jump within a DOS batch file.

Notes

GOTO is an internal command that requires DOS 2.0 or later. DOS label names can be virtually any length. However, DOS only distinguishes the first eight characters of a label name. Hence, DOS will consider the label names DOS_LABEL1 and DOS_LABEL2 to be equivalent because their first eight characters are equivalent. DOS does not distinguish between uppercase and lowercase label names—it considers the labels the same.

The actual label must appear in your batch file on its own line, preceded by a colon (:). When DOS encounters a line in a batch file whose first character is a colon, DOS recognizes that the line contains a label and does not try to execute the line as a command.

If the label specified in a GOTO command does not exist, DOS will terminate the batch file when it executes the corresponding GOTO command displaying a "bad label" error message.

The most common use of GOTO is in combination with the IF command to branch to a specific location within a batch file when a specific condition is met. For more information on conditional batch file processing, see the IF command.

Examples

The following batch procedure repeatedly displays the message "Looping-press Ctrl-C to end" until you press CTRL-C or CTRL-BREAK to end the batch file.

```
@ECHO OFF
:LOOP
ECHO Looping-press Ctrl-C to end
GOTO LOOP
```

When you press CTRL-C or CTRL-BREAK, DOS will display

```
Terminate batch file (Y/N)?
```

Type Y to end the batch file, returning to the DOS prompt.

When DOS cannot find the label specified in a GOTO command, DOS terminates the processing.

```
GOTO DOSLABEL
DATE
TIME
:DOSLABL
```

This procedure will display

```
Label not found
```

In the following example, although the GOTO command branches to the DOS_LABEL2 label, DOS first finds DOS_LABEL, because DOS only examines the first eight characters of a label name.

```
GOTO DOS_LABEL2
:DOS_LABEL
ECHO LABEL1
GOTO DONE
:DOS_LABEL2
ECHO LABEL2
:DONE
```

Messages

Label not found

The label following the GOTO command was not found in the batch file. When this occurs, DOS will terminate the batch file.

GRAFTABL

Improves extended character display in graphics mode

The GRAFTABL command lets you display extended ASCII characters when the display is in medium-resolution graphics mode.

Format

```
GRAFTABL [code_page | /STATUS | ?]
```

code_page   The code page to be used for the display. Possible values are

Code Page	Country
437	United States
850	Multilingual
852	Slavic
860	Portuguese
863	French Canadian
865	Nordic

/STATUS   Directs GRAFTABL to display the code page that is currently in use. GRAFTABL lets you abbreviate /STATUS as /STA.

?   Directs GRAFTABL to display the current codepage number and available options.

Notes

GRAFTABL is an external command that requires DOS 3.0 or later. GRAFTABL is a memory-resident program. Once you install memory-resident programs, you cannot expand the size of your DOS environment. Try to issue the PATH, APPEND, and any SET commands you desire before you issue the GRAFTABL command.

Most international code-page characters use the extended ASCII values. In medium-resolution graphics mode, the extended ASCII characters may not appear in some monitors. If your code-page characters are not correct, invoke GRAFTABL.

Most users will not have to use the GRAFTABL command. If you are one of the select few to use GRAFTABL, you should probably place GRAFTABL in your AUTOEXEC.BAT file.

GRAFTABL supports the following exit status values:

Exit Status	Meaning
0	Table successfully loaded
1	Table replaced an existing table
2	File error preventing loading of a new table
3	Invalid command-line parameter
4	Incorrect DOS version

Examples

If you specify the /STA switch in the GRAFTABL command line

```
C:\> GRAFTABL /STATUS   <ENTER>
```

GRAFTABL will display the number of the current code page, as shown here.

```
Active Code Page: 437
```

The command

```
C:\> GRAFTABL 437   <ENTER>
```

directs GRAFTABL to use the code page for the United States when it displays extended characters.

Messages

DOS command line parameters supported:

You have invoked GRAFTABL with the ? parameter, directing GRAFTABL to display a list of the command-line parameters it supports.

Previous Code Page: *nnn*

GRAFTABL is displaying the code-page value it was previously using. By displaying the previous code page, GRAFTABL lets you know if your command has changed the code page in use.

GRAPHICS

Provides print-screen support for graphics mode

This command allows screen contents, which contain graphics, to be printed by print-screen operations, such as the SHIFT-PRTSC key combination.

Format

```
GRAPHICS [pro_file] [printer_type] [/B] [/R] [/PRINTBOX: id] [/LCD]
```

pro_file   The path name of a file that contains the profiles for the supported printers. By default, DOS looks for GRAPHICS.PRO. This switch requires DOS 5.

printer_type   The target printer type. Possible values are

Value	Meaning
COLOR1	Color printer with black ribbon
COLOR4	Color printer with RGB ribbon
COLOR8	Color printer with cyan, magenta, yellow, & black ribbon
DESKJET	Hewlett-Packard DeskJet
GRAPHICS	Graphics printer
GRAPHICSWIDE	Graphics printer with an 11-inch carriage

Value	Meaning (*continued*)
HPDEFAULT	Any Hewlett-Packard PCL printer
LASERJET	Hewlett-Packard LaserJet
LASERJETII	Hewlett-Packard LaserJet II
PAINTJET	Hewlett-Packard PaintJet
QUIETJET	Hewlett-Packard QuietJet
QUIETJETPLUS	Hewlett-Packard QuietJet Plus
RUGGEDWRITER	Hewlett-Packard Rugged Writer
RUGGEDWRITERWIDE	Hewlett-Packard Rugged Writer Wide
THERMAL	Thermal printer
THINKJET	Hewlett-Packard ThinkJet

/B   Directs GRAPHICS to print the background color. The default is not to print the background color. This switch is used for the COLOR4 or COLOR8 printers.

/R   Directs GRAPHICS to reverse the color of the screen image—black images on the screen will be printed as white, and white images as black.

/PRINTBOX: *id*   Selects the print box size. Valid values are std (for standard) or lcd (for liquid crystal display).

/LCD   Specifies a liquid crystal display, commonly used by portable computers.

Notes

GRAPHICS is an external command that requires DOS 2.0 or later. GRAPHICS invokes a program that remains in memory until DOS is rebooted. Therefore, the GRAPHICS command need be invoked only once during a user session. If you want to change printer profiles, the new printer profile must be the same size or smaller than the current profile. If the new profile is larger, GRAPHICS will display

```
Unable to reload with profile supplied
```

To select the profile, you must restart your system.

    If you use the GRAPHICS command to print graphics images to your printer and your printouts are too dark, use the /R switch.

    If your computer is in high-resolution graphics mode and you press SHIFT-PRTSC to print the screen contents, GRAPHICS will print the image in landscape mode.

GRAPHICS is a memory-resident program. Once you install memory-resident programs, you cannot expand the size of your DOS environment.

Examples

The following command loads the memory-resident software required to support print-screen operations that contain graphics images:

```
C:\> GRAPHICS   <ENTER>
```

The next command directs DOS to print white screen images as black, and black screen images as white.

```
C:\> GRAPHICS /R   <ENTER>
```

The following command loads support for a Hewlett-Packard LaserJet Series II printer.

```
C:\> GRAPHICS LASERJETII C:\DOS\GRAPHICS.PRO   <ENTER>
```

Messages

Printer type not in GRAPHICS profile

The printer type that you have specified in the command is invalid. Make sure that your printer type matches one of the printer types listed in the Format section.

/B invalid with a black and white printer

You command included the /B switch, which direct GRAPHICS to print the image's background color. Color values are not supported on a black-and-white printer.

Cannot find GRAPHICS profile

GRAPHICS could not locate the file GRAPHICS.PRO. Make sure you specify a complete path name to the file if the file is not in the current directory.

Printbox ID not in GRAPHICS profile

GRAPHICS could not locate the ID value you specified in the /PRINTBOX switch. Reissue the command using std or lcd as the printbox ID.

Error reading GRAPHICS profile

GRAPHICS encountered a file error while reading the file GRAPHICS.PRO. Repeat the command to see if the error persists. If so, restore the file GRAPHICS.PRO from your backups or original DOS distribution disk.

HELP

Provides DOS 5 online help

Under DOS 5, the HELP command displays general command-line syntax and a brief overview of a command's purpose.

Format

```
HELP [CommandName]
```

CommandName   The command for which you want help. If you don't specify a command name, HELP will briefly describe each command.

Notes

HELP is an external command that requires DOS 5. Under DOS 5, if you invoke a command with the /? switch, DOS will display the command's syntax and a brief description of the command. The HELP command displays the same information for a command you will view if you invoke the command using /?. Using HELP takes slightly longer than the /? switch.

Examples

The following command displays a brief description of each DOS 5 command.

```
C:\> HELP    <ENTER>
For more information on a specific command, type HELP command-name.
```

```
APPEND     Allows programs to open data files in specified directories
           as if they were in the current directory.
ASSIGN     Redirects requests for disk operations on one drive to a
           different drive.
ATTRIB     Displays or changes file attributes.
BACKUP     Backs up one or more files from one disk to another.
BREAK      Sets or clears extended Ctrl-C checking.
   :           :
   :           :
UNDELETE Recovers files which have been deleted.
UNFORMAT Restores a disk erased by the FORMAT command or restructured
           by the RECOVER command.
VER        Displays the MS-DOS version.
VERIFY     Tells MS-DOS whether to verify that your files are written
           correctly to a disk.
VOL        Displays a disk volume label and serial number.
XCOPY      Copies files (except hidden and system files) and directory
           trees.
```

The next command displays specifics on the FORMAT command.

```
C:\> HELP  FORMAT   <ENTER>
Formats a disk for use with MS-DOS.

FORMAT drive: [/V[:label]] [/Q] [/U] [/F:size ] [/B | /S]
FORMAT drive: [/V[:label]] [/Q] [/U] [/T:tracks  /N:sectors] [/B | /S]
FORMAT drive: [/V[:label]] [/Q] [/U] [/1] [/4] [/B | /S]
FORMAT drive: [/Q] [/U] [/1] [/4] [/8] [/B | /S]

  /V[:label]  The volume label.
  /Q          Performs a quick format.
  /U          Performs an unconditional format.
  /F:size     The size of the floppy disk to format (such
              as 160, 180, 320, 360, 720, 1.2, 1.44, 2.88).
  /B          Allocates space on the formatted disk for system files.
  /S          Copies system files to the formatted disk.
  /T:tracks   The number of tracks per disk side.
  /N:sectors  The number of sectors per track.
  /1          Formats a single side of a floppy disk.
  /4          Formats a 5.25-inch 360K floppy disk in a high-density drive.
  /8          Formats eight sectors per track.
```

Messages

Help not available for this command

The command you specified is not a DOS command. Invoke HELP without specifying a command to view a list of the available commands.

Help file could not be found

HELP could not find the file DOSHELP.HLP. Make sure the file is in a directory within the command path.

IF

Provides conditional processing within DOS batch files

The IF command provides conditional processing within DOS batch files, letting your batch files test if a specific file exists, two character strings are equal, or the previous command was successful.

Format

```
IF [NOT] condition DOS_COMMAND
```

NOT   Performs a Boolean NOT on the result of condition.

condition   Must be one of the following:

Condition	Meaning
ERRORLEVEL value	True if the previous program's exit status is greater than or equal to the value
EXIST *file_spec*	True if the file specified exists
string1== *string2*	True if both strings are identical

DOS_COMMAND   The name of the command that DOS is to perform if the condition is true.

Notes

IF is an internal command that requires DOS 2.0 or later. Be careful when you use IF to test the exit status value of a program.

IF evaluates to true if the exit status is greater than *or equal to* the value specified. If you combine two IF commands, you can determine the exact exit status value, as shown here.

```
IF ERRORLEVEL 1 IF NOT ERRORLEVEL 2 ECHO One
IF ERRORLEVEL 2 IF NOT ERRORLEVEL 3 ECHO Two
IF ERRORLEVEL 3 IF NOT ERRORLEVEL 4 ECHO Three
```

If you use IF to compare two strings, you should group the strings within single quotes. The IF command requires two strings to compare. If only one string is present, IF will display a "Syntax error" message. If the user does not specify a value for %1 in the following example, IF will compare the null string " to the string 'CONFIG.SYS'. If the single quotes had not been present, IF would only have one string to compare and would generate an error.

```
IF '%1'=='CONFIG.SYS' TYPE %1
```

If the user does not specify a value for %1, the IF command becomes

```
IF ''=='CONFIG.SYS' TYPE %1
```

Without the single quotes, the command would have become

```
IF == CONFIG.SYS TYPE %1
```

Because the command does not provide two strings to compare, IF will display a "Syntax error" message.

Although most users only use the IF statement from within batch files, DOS fully supports IF from the command line, as shown here:

```
C:\> IF EXIST CONFIG.SYS TYPE CONFIG.SYS    <ENTER>
```

Examples

The following batch file uses IF to determine if the CONFIG.SYS file exists in the current directory and if so, copies the file to drive A. If the file does not exist, the batch file displays the message "File not found."

```
ECHO OFF
IF EXIST CONFIG.SYS COPY CONFIG.SYS A:
IF NOT EXIST CONFIG.SYS ECHO File not found
```

If you use this expression within the following batch file, you can echo each of the batch-file parameters to the screen:

```
ECHO OFF
:LOOP
   SHIFT
   IF '%0'=='' GOTO DONE
   ECHO %0
   GOTO LOOP
:DONE
```

If you invoke the procedure with

```
C:\> ECHOTEST 1 2 3 4 5
```

it will display

```
C:\> ECHOTEST 1 2 3 4 5
C:\> ECHO OFF
1
2
3
4
5
```

The following example uses the IF command to determine whether or not the value of the batch parameter is defined:

```
ECHO OFF
IF '%1'=='' ECHO Not defined
IF NOT '%1'=='' ECHO The value is %1
```

The next batch file invokes the BACKUP command to perform a complete hard disk backup. The batch file uses BACKUP's exit status value to determine if the operation was successful.

```
@ECHO OFF
BACKUP C:\*.* A: /S
IF NOT ERRORLEVEL 1 ECHO Backup was successful
IF ERRORLEVEL 1 IF NOT ERRORLEVEL 2 ECHO No files found to backup
IF ERRORLEVEL 2 IF NOT ERRORLEVEL 3 ECHO File-sharing conflict
```

```
IF ERRORLEVEL 3 IF NOT ERRORLEVEL 4 ECHO User Ctrl-C termination
IF ERRORLEVEL 4 ECHO Fatal processing error
```

Messages

Bad command or file name

The DOS command specified in your command line after the condition does not exist as specified.

Syntax error

The format of your command is invalid, very likely yielding an invalid condition.

JOIN

Joins a DOS disk drive to a DOS path

JOIN makes two disks appear as one by joining a disk to a DOS path (the directories that DOS follows to locate a file or command).

Format

```
JOIN [drive1: [drive2:path]] [/D]
```

drive1:   The disk drive to be joined to the path provided.

drive2: path   The directory to be joined.

/D   Directs JOIN to disconnect a previously joined disk.

Notes

JOIN is an external command that requires DOS 3.1 or later. Users who have dual-drive systems often have applications that must open more files that can fit on a single floppy disk. By using the JOIN command, they can "join" the disk in drive B to a subdirectory in drive A, making the two disk drives appear as one large disk. Then their application can continue.

If you issue a JOIN command without any parameters, JOIN will display the current joins. DOS will only join a disk to an empty DOS directory.

Many shell programs perform a time-consuming complete disk and directory tree read operation each time you change disk drives. By joining a commonly used disk to your primary disk's directory tree, you can trick the shell into thinking it is only changing directories, as opposed to changing drives. As a result, the shell won't read the new disk's entire directory tree.

Do not use JOIN in conjunction with ASSIGN, BACKUP, CHKDSK, DISKCOMP, DISKCOPY, FDISK, FORMAT, LABEL, MIRROR, RECOVER, RESTORE, or SYS.

Examples

To join a disk to a directory tree, the tree must contain an empty directory to which JOIN can connect the disk. The following example connects drive A to the directory \JOINDIR on drive C.

```
C:\> JOIN A: \JOINDIR   <ENTER>
```

If the directory specified does not exist, JOINDIR will create it. In this case, references to C:\JOINDIR are identical to references to drive A. If drive A contains DOS subdirectories, simply refer to them as

```
C:\> DIR \JOINDIR\SUBDIR   <ENTER>
```

Invoking JOIN without command-line parameters displays the current joins:

```
C:\> JOIN   <ENTER>
A: => C:\JOINDIR
```

To remove a join, use the /D switch:

```
C:\> JOIN A: /D   <ENTER>
```

Messages

Directory not empty

You are attempting to join a disk to a DOS subdirectory that contains other subdirectories or files. DOS requires that your join directory be empty prior to the JOIN command.

Cannot JOIN a Network drive

The drive you are attempting to join to a subdirectory is a network drive. JOIN does not support network drives.

KEYB

Loads a foreign keyboard set

To fully support international configurations, DOS provides support for various keyboard templates. The KEYB command loads memory-resident software (a program that remains in memory until the computer is turned off or rebooted) to replace the standard keyboard layout supported by the operating system.

Format

KEYB [*keyboard_code*[,*codepage*],[*filespec*]]] [/E] [/ID:*keyboard*]

keyboard_code   The two-letter code associated with the desired keyboard.

codepage   The desired code page (see CHCP).

filespec   The name of the file containing the keyboard definitions, normally C:\DOS\KEYBOARD.SYS.

/E   Directs KEYB to assume that you are using an enhanced keyboard. This is a DOS 5 switch.

/ID: ***keyboard***   A DOS 5 switch that specifies the keyboard in use for countries that support multiple keyboard types for the same language.

Notes

KEYB is an external command that requires DOS 3.3 or later. Once a new keyboard is installed, you can toggle between it and the default keyboard by pressing CTRL-ALT-F1 for the default keyboard and CTRL-ALT-F2 for the foreign keyboard. Common keyboard layouts (and the matching code pages) include

Country	Keyboard Code	Code Page	Secondary Identification
United States	US	437 or 850	103
French Canadian	CF	863 or 860	058
Latin America	LA	850 or 437	171
Netherlands	NL	850 or 437	143
Belgium	BE	850 or 437	120
France	FR	437 or 850	120,189
Spain	SP	850 or 437	172
Italy	IT	850 or 437	141,142
Switzerland (German)	SG	850 or 437	000
Switzerland (French)	SF	850 or 437	150
United Kingdom	UK	437 or 850	166,168
Denmark	DK	850 or 865	159
Sweden	SV	850 or 437	153
Norway	NO	850 or 865	155
Germany	GR	850 or 437	129
Brazil	BR	850 or 437	
Portugal	PO	850 or 860	163
Finland	SU	850 or 437	153
Czechoslovakia (Czech)	CZ	852 or 850	
Czechoslovakia (Slovak)	SL	852 or 850	
Hungary	HU	852 or 850	
Poland	PL	852 or 850	
Yugoslavia	YU	852 or 850	

If you are using a secondary keyboard template, place the corresponding KEYB command in your AUTOEXEC.BAT file to ensure that your desired keyboard is in effect each time your system starts. If you are using DOS 4, use the CONFIG.SYS INSTALL entry to load the KEYB command. If you are using DOS 5, use LOADHIGH.

KEYB supports the following exit status values:

Exit Status	Meaning
0	Keyboard successfully loaded
1	Invalid keyboard, code page, or syntax
2	Invalid keyboard definition file
4	CON device error
5	Code page required not prepared

Examples

In the first example, DOS will use the United Kingdom keyboard template.

```
C:\> KEYB UK   <ENTER>
```

The next command selects the French keyboard template and informs DOS that the file KEYBOARD.SYS resides in the subdirectory \DOS.

```
C:\> KEYB FR,,C:\DOS\KEYBOARD.SYS   <ENTER>
```

If you are using DOS 4, the following CONFIG.SYS INSTALL entry loads the French keyboard as follows

```
INSTALL=C:\DOS\KEYB.COM FR,,C:\DOS\KEYBOARD.SYS
```

If you are using DOS 5, you can use the LOADHIGH command:

```
C:\> LOADHIGH C:\DOS\KEYB.COM FR,,C:\DOS\KEYBOARD.SYS   <ENTER>
```

Messages

Bad command or file name

The KEYB*xx* command that you are trying to execute is not on the current disk or you are using DOS 3.3, which uses the KEYB command instead.

Active code page not available from CON device

Make sure that you have placed the DISPLAY.SYS entry in CONFIG.SYS and issued the correct MODE CON CODEPAGE PREPARE command for the code page desired.

Bad or missing Keyboard Definition File

KEYB cannot locate the file KEYBOARD.SYS. Make sure that KEYBOARD.SYS is in the current directory or that you specify a complete path name to the file in the KEYB command line.

Code page requested (*nnn*) is not valid for given keyboard code

The command failed because your keyboard template and desired code page are inconsistent. Specify a code page whose character set corresponds with the keyboard template desired.

Code page specified has not been prepared

Make sure that you have specified a correct DISPLAY.SYS entry in CONFIG.SYS and that you issue the corresponding MODE CODEPAGE PREPARE command.

Current Keyboard code: *nnn* code page: *nnn*
Current CON code page: *nnn*

KEYB is simply displaying the current keyboard template and code page for the CON device.

Invalid code page specified

The three-digit code page that you have specified in the command line is invalid. Double-check your desired code page entry number and reissue the command.

Invalid keyboard code specified

The two-letter keyboard code that you have specified in the KEYB command line is invalid. Double-check your desired keyboard code and reissue the command.

KEYB has not been installed

KEYB is telling you that due to an error (whose error message should also be displayed), the KEYB command failed and a keyboard template was not installed.

One or more CON code pages invalid for given keyboard code

One of the three-digit code pages that you have specified is invalid for the keyboard code specified. Review the code-page and keyboard-code identifiers and reissue the command with the correct character set (code page).

Code page specified is inconsistent with selected code page

The code page specified in the KEYB command does not correspond to the code page currently selected for the CON device. Make sure you are specifying the correct code page in the KEYB command. If so, use the MODE CON CODEPAGE SELECT command to select the appropriate code page.

Code page specified has not been designated

The code page you specified in the KEYB command has not been prepared for use by the CON device. Use the MODE CON CODEPAGE PREPARE command specifying the desired code page.

Current keyboard does not support this code page

The code page specified is not compatible with the current keyboard template. Use the table specified in the Notes section to determine the correct code page for your desired keyboard template.

Unable to create KEYB table in resident memory

Your system has insufficient RAM to install the memory-resident portion of the KEYB command. If you have installed other memory-resident software or a RAM drive, try restarting DOS without them present in memory and reissue the KEYB command.

Read error, KEYBOARD.SYS

DOS could not read the file KEYBOARD.SYS, most likely due to a file corruption. Restart your system and repeat the command. If the error persists, restore the file KEYBOARD.SYS from your backup disks.

Unable to create KEYB table in resident memory

Your system may have insufficient memory for the code page specified. If you have installed memory-resident programs or a RAM disk, restart your system without them, repeating the KEYB command.

LABEL

Specifies a disk volume label

DOS allows you to define an 11-character name (called a volume label) for each of your disks. Disk labels help you organize your floppy disks and can prevent an inadvertent format of your hard disk.

Format

```
LABEL [target_drive:][volume_label]
```

target_drive: The disk drive that contains the disk to be labeled.

volume_label   The 11-character volume label desired. All characters that are valid in DOS file names are valid in volume labels. Depending on your DOS version, you may include blank characters within your disk label.

Notes

LABEL is an external command that requires DOS 3.0 or later. *Do not* try to use the following characters in a volume name:

```
* ? / \ | . , ; : + = [ ] ( ) & ^ < > "
```

Each time you issue the DIR command, DOS displays the volume label of the disk for which it is displaying the directory:

```
Volume in drive A is DOSLABEL
Volume Serial Number is 1234-4321
Directory of  A:\
```

Some software programs will examine the disk volume label when they direct you to insert a specific floppy disk to ensure you have inserted the correct disk.

If you do not specify a volume label in the command line, LABEL will prompt you for one:

```
Volume in drive C is DOSDISK
Volume Serial Number is 1234-4321
Volume label (11 characters, ENTER for none)?
```

If you do not want to change the disk label, press ENTER; otherwise, type in the volume name desired. If you press ENTER, LABEL will ask you if you want to delete the current volume label.

```
Delete current volume label (Y/N)?
```

To delete the label, type Y. To leave the volume label unchanged, type N.

The FORMAT command also provides you with an opportunity to assign a disk label to your disk. Get in the habit of labeling your disks with either FORMAT or LABEL.

Under DOS 4 and 5, the FORMAT command prompts you to enter the disk volume label before it will format your hard disk. By assigning a unique label to your disk, you reduce the possibility of an inadvertent disk format.

The VOL and CHKDSK commands also display the disk volume label.

Examples

The first command assigns the label DOSDISK to the floppy disk contained in drive A. Since the command line contains the desired label name, LABEL did not have to prompt the user for any information:

```
C:\> LABEL A:DOSDISK   <ENTER>
```

In the next command, the label name is not specified in the command line:

```
C:\> LABEL A:   <ENTER>
```

In such a case, LABEL will prompt

```
Volume in drive A is DOSDISK
Volume label (11 characters, Enter for none)?
```

If you are using DOS 4 or 5, the LABEL command will also display the disk's serial number:

```
Volume in drive A is DOSDISK
Volume Serial Number is 1234-5678
Volume label (11 characters, enter for none)?
```

Either type in the volume label that you desire, or press ENTER to leave the current label name unchanged. If you simply press ENTER, LABEL will ask you if you want to delete the current volume label.

Messages

Cannot label a network drive

The drive letter that you have specified in your LABEL command corresponds to a network disk drive. DOS will not allow you to assign a label to a drive in the network.

Delete current volume label (Y/N)?

You have pressed ENTER to the prompt to enter a new volume label and LABEL wants to know if you want to delete the current volume label. If so, simply type Y and press ENTER; otherwise, type N.

Invalid characters in volume label

One or more of the letters that you are using in the disk volume name are illegal. Remember, DOS label names follow the same naming conventions as your files. Depending on your DOS version, you may include spaces in your label name.

No room in root directory

LABEL could not create the volume label because the root directory of the drive specified is full. DOS creates a hidden file in which it stores your disk volume label. If DOS cannot create this file, DOS cannot assign a name to your disk.

Volume label (11 characters, ENTER for none)?

LABEL is simply prompting you to type in the name that you want to assign to the disk. Remember, DOS label names follow DOS file-naming conventions.

Volume in drive n is NAME

LABEL is simply telling you the current name for the disk in the drive specified.

Cannot LABEL a SUBSTed or ASSIGNed drive

The target drive in your LABEL command line is a logical drive or a drive that has been assigned to point to another drive. LABEL does not let you assign a volume name to logical or assigned drives.

LOADFIX

Loads a program above 64Kb in conventional memory

Loads a program that displays the "Packed file corrupt" message into conventional memory above 64Kb.

Format

```
LOADFIX ProgramName [parameters]
```

ProgramName   The path name of the program to execute.

parameters   The program's optional command-line parameters.

Notes

LOADFIX is an external command that requires DOS 5.0. Under DOS 5, you can use the DOS=HIGH,UMB CONFIG.SYS entry to load DOS into the high memory area and to maintain a link to reserved memory for use by DEVICEHIGH and LOADHIGH to load device drivers and memory-resident programs into reserved memory. Each of these techniques frees conventional memory. In some cases, DOS may execute commands in the conventional address space below 64Kb. Some programs cannot execute below 64Kb and will display the error message "Packed file corrupt" when you execute them. Using LOADFIX, you can direct DOS to load these programs above 64Kb solving the problem.

You will not need to use LOADFIX unless a program displays the "Packed file corrupt" error message.

Examples

The following command loads the program DOSSHELL.EXE above 64Kb in conventional memory.

```
C:\> LOADFIX C:\DOS\DOSSHELL.EXE   <ENTER>
```

Messages

Error: No program name given

You did not include a program name in the LOADFIX command. LOADFIX loads one program into memory above 64Kb. You must specify the name of program that displays the "Packed file corrupt" message.

Error: Missing COMSPEC

Your environment does not contain a COMSPEC entry telling LOADFIX the location of COMMAND.COM. Use SET to assign COMSPEC the correct path location of COMMAND.COM and reissue LOADFIX.

LOADHIGH

Loads a program into reserved memory

Loads a program into upper (or reserved) memory, freeing conventional memory for other use.

Format

```
LOADHIGH pathname
```

or

```
LH pathname
```

pathname   The complete path name, including the drive letter, of the program DOS is to load into reserved memory.

Notes

LOADHIGH is an internal command that requires DOS 5.0 or later. Conventional memory is your computer's memory from 0 to 640Kb. Reserved memory is the memory from 640Kb to 1Mb and is normally used for device I/O. Extended memory is the memory beyond 1Mb. Most programs run in conventional memory. LOADHIGH lets DOS load memory-resident programs in the unused portions of reserved memory. By loading programs in reserved memory, you leave more conventional memory available to your applications. If there is insufficient reserved memory available to load the program, DOS will load the program into conventional memory.

To use LOADHIGH, you must have directed DOS to save the link between reserved and conventional memory using the CONFIG.SYS DOS=UMB entry. You must also install the EMM386.EXE device driver to provide a link to reserved memory. To install a device driver into reserved memory, use the CONFIG.SYS DEVICEHIGH entry.

Example

The following command loads the memory-resident program PRINT.EXE into reserved memory.

```
C:\> LOADHIGH C:\DOS\PRINT.EXE   <ENTER>
```

MEM

Provides information on current memory usage

The MEM command is a DOS 4 command that displays your system's current memory usage. MEM is used most often by programmers.

Format

```
MEM [/DEBUG] [/PROGRAM] [/CLASSIFY]
```

/DEBUG   Directs MEM to display the location of each device driver in memory and each program's memory usage. It can be abbreviated as /D.

/PROGRAM   Directs MEM to display all of the programs that are currently in memory and a summary of their usage. It can be abbreviated as /P.

/CLASSIFY   A DOS 5 switch that directs MEM to display the status of programs in conventional memory and in the upper memory (reserved memory) area. It can be abbreviated as /C.

Notes

MEM is an external command that requires DOS 4.0 or later. MEM is primarily a programmer's tool. Most users should not require MEM.

MEM only displays information on extended memory if your system has memory above the 1Mb boundary. Likewise, MEM only displays information about expanded memory if you have an expanded memory driver installed.

Examples

By default, MEM displays

```
C:\> MEM   <ENTER>


   655360 bytes total conventional memory
   655360 bytes available to MS-DOS
   440064 largest executable program size

  1441792 bytes total contiguous extended memory
        0 bytes available contiguous extended memory
```

If you invoke MEM with the /DEBUG switch under DOS 4, MEM will display

```
C:\> MEM /DEBUG   <ENTER>

Address     Name         Size      Type
DDDDDDD     DDDDDDDD     DDDDDD    DDDDDD
000000                   000400    Interrupt Vector
000400                   000100    ROM Communication Area
000500                   000200    DOS Communication Area
000700      IBMbIO       002510    System Program
            CON                    System Device Driver
            AUX                    System Device Driver
            CLOCK$                 System Device Driver
            A: - C:                System Device Driver
            COM1                   System Device Driver
            COM2                   System Device Drive
```

```
                    COM3                         System Device Drivr
                    COM4                         System Device Driver
  002C10    IBMDOS           008E20    System Program

  00BA30    IBMbIO           00B6B0    System Data
            HIMEM            000B50      DEVICE=
            ANSI             001190      DEVICE=
            SMARTDRV         0054D0      DEVICE=
                             0015B0      FILES=
                             000100      FCBS=
                             001F40      BUFFERS=
                             0001C0      LASTDRIVE
                             000CD0      STACKS
  0170F0    CAPTURE          000080    Environment
  017180    IBMDOS           000030    — Free —
  0171C0    SHARE            0018A0    Program
  018A70    COMMAND          001640    Program
  01A0C0    COMMAND          000200    Environment
  01A2D0    CAPTURE          00BE40    Program
  026120    IBMDOS           000040    — Free —
  026170    IPX              000080    Environment
  026200    SHELLB           000E80    Program
  027090    IPX              003EE0    Program
  02AF80    NET4             000080    Environment
  02B010    NET4             009800    Program
  047860    IBMDOS           058790    — Free —

   655360 bytes total memory
   655360 bytes available
   440064 largest executable program size

  1441792 bytes total extended memory
        0 bytes available extended memory
```

Messages

Invalid switch

A switch in the MEM command line is invalid. MEM only supports the switch /PROGRAM, /DEBUG, and CLASSIFY.

MIRROR

Stores disk information used by UNDELETE and UNFORMAT

Stores critical disk information, such as the file allocation tables and root directory, used by UNFORMAT. Optionally stores information about each file you delete, assisting UNDELETE in later undeleting the files.

Format

MIRROR [*drive:*] [/ T drive [- *entries*]] [/1]

or

MIRROR [*drive:*] [/PARTN]

or

MIRROR [*drive:*] [/U]

drive: The drive letter for which you want MIRROR to record the critical disk information. If you don't specify a drive letter, MIRROR uses the current drive.

/1   Directs MIRROR to only keep the latest information about the disk. By default, MIRROR makes a backup copy of the previous information, storing the information in the file MIRROR.BAK.

/Tdrive[- *entries*]   Directs MIRROR to install a memory-resident program that records information about every file deleted from the disk specified. The entries option specifies the number of deleted files MIRROR should track, from 1 to 999. The UNDELETE program will use this information if it is available.

/U   Directs MIRROR to remove the memory-resident delete-tracking program from memory, disabling file delete tracking.

Notes

MIRROR is an external DOS command that requires DOS 5.0. The MIRROR command saves a copy of the partition table, root directory, and file allocation tables that UNFORMAT can use to recover your disk in the event of an accidental disk format operation. The more often you invoke MIRROR, the greater your chance of recovering from a format operation.

MIRROR stores its information in a file named MIRROR.FIL in your disk's root directory. The UNFORMAT command will use this information to rebuild a damaged disk.

The size of the file MIRROR.FIL depends on your disk type. If you invoke MIRROR with /Tdrive, MIRROR will create a file named PCTRACKR.DEL that MIRROR updates each time a file is deleted. The UNDELETE command will use this file, but does not require it. However using MIRROR's delete-tracking information, you greatly improve your chances of correctly undeleting a file. When delete tracking is active, UNDELETE can correctly undelete even severely fragmented files.

Depending on your disk size, the size and number of entries in the PCTRACKR.DEL file will differ.

Disk Type	Maximum Entries	Maximum Size
360Kb	25	5Kb
720Kb	50	9Kb
1.2Mb	75	14Kb
1.44Mb	75	15Kb
20Mb	101	18Kb
32Mb	202	36Kb
OVER 32Mb	303	55Kb

Use the MIRROR /PARTN command to save a copy of your disk's partition table information to a floppy disk. Store the floppy disk in a safe location.

Examples

The first command directs MIRROR to record the file allocation table and root directory for drive C and to also install delete tracking for that drive.

```
C:\> MIRROR C: /TC   <ENTER>
```

The next command directs MIRROR to save drive C's partition table information.

```
C:\> MIRROR C: /PARTN    <ENTER>
```

MIRROR will prompt you to type in the letter of the floppy disk drive containing the disk you want the partition table information written to.

Messages

Cannot install. Already present, or unknown status

You are probably attempting to install MIRROR for a second time, this time with delete tracking active. MIRROR installs memory-resident software and can only be invoked one time. To reinstall MIRROR with a different configuration, you must restart your system.

WARNING! Unrecognized DOS INT 25h/26h handler. Some other TSR programs may behave erratically while Delete-tracking is resident! Try installing MIRROR program before your other resident programs.

MIRROR is warning you that it does not recognize the software that DOS uses to read and write to disk. If you have installed another memory-resident program that intercepts disk operations, the program may not be compatible with MIRROR. Because the two programs are both intercepting the information DOS is reading from or writing to disk, a disk error may occur that renders your disk unusable. If this error occurs, determine which program is conflicting with MIRROR, and invoke the MIRROR program first.

Also, make sure you have current disk backups while you test the compatibility of the two programs.

Error reading system area

MIRROR experienced a disk read error while trying to read your disk's file allocation table or root directory. Disk read errors are a sign of serious disk problems. If this error message occurs, perform a system backup immediately.

Insufficient space for MIRROR image file

Your disk does not have enough available space for MIRROR to store copies of the root directory and file allocation table. If possible, delete unnecessary files or move files to a new disk and invoke MIRROR again.

Insufficient memory to read all system info

Your system does not have enough available memory for MIRROR to continue. If this error message occurs, you will have to remove memory-resident programs, possible modify your CONFIG.SYS entries, and reboot DOS before MIRROR can successfully run.

**There are no entries available in the root directory
of the drive. Delete one or more files from the root directory**

MIRROR cannot create the file MIRROR.FIL in the root directory because the
root directory is full. Most hard disk root directories will store up to 512 files. If
your root directory is full, it probably contains files that should be stored in a
different directory. This error is a sign that it is past time to clean up your root
directory.

MKDIR

Creates a DOS directory

DOS subdirectories let you organize your files by grouping related files into a
list called a directory. A directory is much like a drawer of a filing cabinet. The
MKDIR command creates directories on your disk.

Format

MKDIR [*drive:*]*path*

or

MD [*drive:*]*path*

drive: The drive on which to create the directory. If a drive is not specified, MKDIR
will use the current drive.

path   The name of the DOS directory that MKDIR is to create.

Notes

MKDIR is an internal command that requires DOS 2.0 or later. Because of its
frequency of use, DOS lets you abbreviate the MKDIR command as MD.

Every DOS disk has a root directory (\) from which all other subdirectories grow.
If you do not use DOS subdirectories, your disks are restricted to a limited number
of files, as shown here:

Disk Space	Maximum Subdirectories in Root Directory
160Kb	64
180Kb	64
320Kb	112
360Kb	112
720Kb	112
1.2Mb	224
1.44Mb	224
Fixed disk	Typically 512

MKDIR enables you to create subdirectories. Each time you create a DOS directory, MKDIR has two choices. First, if the directory name starts with a slash (as in \SUBDIR), MKDIR will start with the root directory to create the directory. If, however, the name does not start with a slash (as in SUBDIR), MKDIR will create the directory within the current directory.

Use the following "rules of thumb" when you create your DOS directories:

- DOS directory names conform to the same format as DOS file names (an eight-character file name followed by an optional three-character extension). The following are examples of valid DOS directory names: FILENAME.EXT, HARDWARE.SAL, and SOFTWARE.INV.

- The maximum path name (the representation of all directories and subdirectories) that DOS can process is 63 characters:

```
C:\> MD \COMMANDS\UTILITY\DATAFILE\INPUT\LOWLEVEL\PASCAL
   \SOURCE\ROUTINE
```

- If you do not specify a complete DOS path name when you create a directory, DOS assumes that you are creating the directory in the current directory.

- To manipulate directories contained on other disks, precede the directory name with a drive letter (such as B:\CARS).

- Do not create directory names that are identical to the names of files contained in the same directory.

- Root directories on each disk are restricted to a specific number of files because of the disk layout. Directories, however, can contain an unlimited number of files.

- Divide your disk logically into directories.

When you examine DOS path names, ask yourself the following question: "Does the path name start with a back slash (\)?" If it does, the directory path is specified, starting at the root or upper-level directory.

```
A> MKDIR \DOS\SOURCE\UTIL
```

If not, the path name starts from the current directory.

```
A> MKDIR TEMPFILE\FILENAME
```

Examples

In the following example, MKDIR creates a directory called IBM in the root:

```
C:\> MKDIR \IBM    <ENTER>
```

In a similar manner, the command

```
C:\> MKDIR \IBM\NOTES    <ENTER>
```

creates a subdirectory called NOTES in the IBM directory. This command is equivalent to the commands

```
C:\> CHDIR \IBM    <ENTER>
C:\> MKDIR NOTES    <ENTER>
```

Note that the second command does not have a slash in front of the directory name NOTES. If it did, MKDIR would create the directory in the root instead of in the \IBM directory.

Assuming that the current directory is still the root, the command

```
C:\> MKDIR MISC    <ENTER>
```

also creates a directory off the root. In this case, the directory name does not contain a slash, so MKDIR creates the directory in the current directory (which, in this case, is still the root).

Had the current directory been other than the root, the correct command would have been

```
C:\> MKDIR \MISC    <ENTER>
```

Messages

Unable to create directory

One of the directories in your directory path may be invalid, a file with the same name as the directory already exists on disk, or the root directory of the target disk drive is full.

Directory already exists

A directory with the same name you are trying to create already exists.

MODE

Specify device characteristics

Many hardware devices require unique data communication setups or let you specify different characteristics. The MODE command lets you set data communications parameters for a serial port, change your video display, select international code pages, configure your printer, and even increase your keyboard response.

Format

For video display

MODE *n*

or

MODE [*n*],*m*,[*t*]

or, using DOS 5

MODE CON[:] [COLS= *columns*][LINES=*lines*]

For COM ports

DE COM#[:] *baud*[, *parity*[, *data*[, *stop*[,P]]]]

or, using DOS 5

```
MODE COM#[:]  BAUD=baud  [PARITY=parity][DATA=data]
  [STOP=stop]  [RETRY=R]
```

For parallel printers

```
MODE LPT#[:]  [cpl][,vli][,P]
```

or, using DOS 5

```
MODE LPT#:  [COLS=cpl][LINES=vli][RETRY=r]
```

For printer redirection

```
MODE LPT n[:]=COM n[:]
```

For code-page operations

```
MODE device CODEPAGE operation
```

For keyboard operations using DOS 4 or 5

```
MODE CON[:]  [RATE= rate]  [DELAY= delay]
```

baud   The device baud rate can be 110, 150, 300, 600, 1,200, 2,400, 4,800, 9,600, or 19,200. MODE only requires you to specify the first two digits of the baud rate.

n   The screen-display attribute. It must be one of the following values:

Value	Setting
40	40-column display
80	80-column display
BW40	Black-and-white 40-column display
BW80	Black-and-white 80-column display
CO40	Color 40-column display
CO80	Color 80-column display
MONO	Monochrome display

m   The direction to shift the screen display, either one character to the left or right.

t   Requests MODE to display a test pattern to aid in character alignment.

columns   The number of characters per line, either 40 or 80.

lines   The number of lines on the screen: 25, 43, or 50.

parity   The device parity: E for even parity, N for no parity, O for odd parity, M for mark parity, and S for space. The default is even parity.

data   The number of data bits, 5, 7, or 8. The default is 7 data bits.

stop   The number of stop bits: 1, 1.5, or 2. For 110 baud, the default is 2; otherwise, it is 1.

cpl   Characters per line (80 or 132).

vli   Vertical lines per inch (6 or 8).

r   The retry action on the following timeout errors:

Value	Action
E	Returns a busy status error (the default)
B	Returns a busy status
R	Returns a ready status
N	Performs no action
P	Continues retries on timeout errors

P   Specifies continuous retries on timeout errors.

LPT*n*   The parallel printer number, such as LPT1.

COM*n*   The serial port number, such as COM1.

device   The device to manipulate a code page for (CON, LPT *n*).

operation   The code-page operation desired:

```
prepare=[[codepage] [filename]]
```

or

```
select= codepage
```

or

```
refresh /STATUS
```

rate   The keyboard typematic rate in clock ticks. Values range from 1 to 32.

delay   The amount of time you must hold down a key before DOS begins to repeat the character. Values are 1, 2, 3, and 4, which correspond to 0.25, 0.50, 0.75, and 1.0 seconds.

Notes

MODE is an external DOS command supported by all DOS versions. MODE is one of the most difficult DOS commands, mainly because it is used for complex concepts (such as serial data communication or printer redirection). Unless you are using a serial laser printer or modem, you probably will never have to issue the MODE command to configure a serial port. If your printer attaches to a serial port, the documentation that accompanied your printer should specify the MODE command that you need. Place this command into your AUTOEXEC.BAT file to automatically configure your printer port each time your system starts.

By default, DOS uses the parallel printer port for printed data. If your printer is connected to a serial device, you can redirect the parallel output to the serial device with MODE.

If you are using DOS 3.3 or higher, the MODE command allows you to prepare and select code pages for your screen display and printer. The PREPARE operation directs DOS to get a code page ready for use for the device specified. The SELECT operation chooses a specific code page to be used by the device. In some cases, you may have downloaded a code page to your printer device and then turned the printer off. To restore the code page, you use the REFRESH operation. Last, the /STATUS switch lists the code pages that are currently in use or are prepared for the device specified.

MODE supports the following abbreviations:

CP	CODEPAGE
/STA	/STATUS
PREP	PREPARE
SEL	SELECT
REF	REFRESH

Beginning with DOS 4, the MODE command lets you set your keyboard's typematic rate, which controls how long you must hold down a key before the key repeats. Use the following repeat rate settings.

Repeat Rate	Characters per Second	Repeat Rate	Characters per Second
1	2.0	17	8.0
2	2.1	18	8.6
3	2.3	19	9.2
4	2.5	20	10.0
5	2.7	21	10.9
6	3.0	22	12.0
7	3.3	23	13.3
8	3.7	24	15.0
9	4.0	25	16.0
10	4.3	26	17.1
11	4.6	27	18.5
12	5.0	28	20.0
13	5.5	29	21.8
14	6.0	30	24.0
15	6.7	31	26.7
16	7.5	32	30.0

Examples

The first command sets the screen display to 40 columns per line.

```
C:\> MODE 40   <ENTER>
```

If you are using DOS 5, an equivalent command is

```
C:\> MODE CON: COLS=40   <ENTER>
```

The command

```
C:\> MODE 80   <ENTER>
```

resets the screen to 80-column mode. Next, many users have serial printers connected to their systems. To route the printer data to the serial printer, you must use MODE. This command routes the parallel data from LPT1 to the serial port COM1.

```
C:\> MODE LPT1:=COM1:   <ENTER>
```

The next command specifies data communication parameters for COM1.

```
C:\> MODE COM1 96,N,8,1   <ENTER>
```

If you are using DOS 3.3 or higher and an EGA or VGA monitor, the following command prepares the display for the Multilingual and Portuguese code pages.

```
C:\> MODE CON CODEPAGE PREPARE=(850,860) \DOS\EGA.CPI   <ENTER>
```

Note that you must specify the code-page information file (CPI) in the command line. Once you prepare a code page for a device, you select the code page via the SELECT option:

```
C:\> MODE CON CODEPAGE SELECT=860   <ENTER>
```

The following command prepares and IBM 4201 ProPrinter to use the Multilingual and Portuguese code pages.

```
C:\> MODE LPT1 CODEPAGE PREPARE=(850,860) \DOS\4201.CPI   <ENTER>
```

If you are using DOS 4 or higher, you must use two sets of parentheses in the previous command:

```
C:\> MODE LPT1 CODEPAGE PREPARE=((850,860) \DOS\4201.CPI)   <ENTER>
```

Using DOS 4 or higher, the following MODE command sets your keyboard's typematic rate to its fastest response time.

```
C:\> MODE CON: RATE=32 DELAY=1   <ENTER>
```

Messages

Infinite retry on parallel printer time-out

You have specified the P parameter in the MODE command line to enable infinite retries when your printer has a timeout condition. When continuous retry is enabled, your computer will continually attempt to access your printer device until the user presses CTRL-BREAK to return control back to DOS.

Resident portion of MODE loaded

MODE is informing you that it has loaded memory-resident software to perform the task specified. MODE loads memory-resident software when you redirect a parallel port's output to a serial port or when you direct MODE to retry operations on device timeout errors.

No retry on parallel printer time-out

Your MODE LPT *n* command line did not specify the P parameter, which directs DOS to perform continuous retries to access the printer device. This is the default setting. Most users will not have a need to enable continuous retries on printer operations.

ANSI.SYS must be installed to perform requested function

MODE is telling you it cannot select 43 or 50 lines per screen for EGA and VGA monitors until you install the ANSI.SYS device driver using CONFIG.SYS.

LPT *n*: set for 80

MODE is simply telling you that it has set your printer to 80 characters per line. Depending upon your printer type, MODE may not actually be able to set your printer as specified. Regardless, MODE will still display the message shown above.

LPT *n*: set for 132

MODE is simply telling you that it has set your printer to 132 characters per line. Depending upon your printer type, MODE may not actually be able to set your printer as specified. Regardless, MODE will still display the message shown above.

Printer lines per inch set

Has set the number of lines of text per inch on your printer to either 6 or 8 lines per inch as specified in the MODE command line. Depending upon your printer type, MODE may not be able to set your printer as specified in the MODE command line. Regardless, MODE will display the message shown above.

COM *n*: *baud, parity, data bits, stop bits, time out*

MODE is displaying the current data communication parameters for the communication port specified. Use this message to determine your COM port settings.

LPT *n*: rerouted to COM *n*:

Your MODE command line has redirected output that DOS normally routes to the parallel port LPT *n* to the serial communications port specified. If you are using a serial printer, you will probably want to redirect output to your serial port in this manner.

LPT *n*: not rerouted

Your MODE command line has set DOS printer output back to the parallel port specified following a previous MODE command that redirected printer output from a parallel device to a serial device.

Active code page for device *nnn* is *nnn*

Your MODE command line specified the CODEPAGE /STATUS option, which directs MODE to display the current code page for the device specified. This message is purely informational.

Requested Screen Shift out of range

You cannot shift the screen any further in the specified direction.

Code page not prepared

Your MODE command either includes the CODEPAGE /STATUS option, which directs MODE to display the current code page, or CODEPAGE SELECT, which directs MODE to select a code page for the specified device. If your command line contains /STATUS, this message is purely informational. If instead, you issued a CODEPAGE SELECT command, you must first issue the CODEPAGE PREPARE option with the MODE command.

Code pages cannot be prepared

Your MODE command contains a CODEPAGE PREPARE option that MODE cannot complete. Make sure that you have installed the DISPLAY.SYS and PRINTER.SYS device drivers in your CONFIG.SYS file.

Codepage operation not supported on this device

Either the device name that you have specified in the MODE command is invalid, or you have not installed the DISPLAY.SYS or PRINTER.SYS device driver in CONFIG.SYS.

Device error during operation

The MODE command could not successfully complete due to a variety of possible errors. Make sure that you have installed the DISPLAY.SYS or PRINTER.SYS device driver in CONFIG.SYS, that the device is turned on, and that you are using a valid code-page information file.

Device or codepage missing from font file

Your MODE command line contains a CODEPAGE PREPARE option that MODE cannot complete. Make sure that your command line specifies a valid code-page number and that the device name is correct.

Failure to access codepage font file

Your CODEPAGE PREPARE command failed because MODE could not locate the code-page information file specified. Make sure that the code-page information file specified is in the current directory or contains a complete subdirectory path.

Font file contents invalid

Your CODEPAGE PREPARE command failed because MODE could not read the contents of the code-page information file. Reissue the command with the original DOS code-page information file.

Failure to access device

MODE could not access the device specified in your MODE command line. Make sure that you have correctly specified the device name and that you have correctly installed any required device drivers in CONFIG.SYS.

Previously prepared codepage replaced

Your MODE command has prepared a new code page for the device specified, overwriting the previously prepared code pages. This message is informational.

Device *nnnn* not prepared

Your MODE CODEPAGE PREPARE failed. Make sure that you have correctly specified the device name and installed the device drivers DISPLAY.SYS and PRINTER.SYS in CONFIG.SYS.

**RATE and DELAY must be specifed together
RATE=X DELAY=X**

Your MODE command specified only one of the two parameters required, the keyboard typematic rate. Repeat the command specifying both the repeat rate and the delay interval.

Unable to perform refresh operation

MODE was unable to download the current code page to the device specified. Use MODE to prepare and select the code page for the device.

MORE

Displays a command's output a screenful at a time

MORE lets you view a file or a program's output a screenful at a time, pressing any key when you are ready to view the next screenful of information.

Format

```
DOS_command | MORE
```

or

```
MORE < DOS_file
```

DOS_command   The name of a DOS command whose output becomes the MORE command's input.

DOS_file   The name of an existing ASCII file.

Notes

MORE is an external command that requires DOS 2.0 or later. MORE reads data from the standard input device, displaying the information on the standard output device, a screenful at a time, until an end-of-file marker is encountered. Each time a screenful of data is displayed on the screen, MORE displays the message

```
– More –
```

Press any key to continue the output or press CTRL-C to terminate the command. If you invoke MORE without specifying a redirected input file, MORE will read lines of input from the keyboard until you enter the ^Z end-of-file character (by pressing F6 or CTRL-Z).

If you are using DOS 5, you can use the TEMP environment entry to specify where DOS creates temporary files during I/O redirection operations. By directing DOS to create its temporary files on a fast RAM drive, you can improve your system performance.

Examples

The following command displays the files in your directory a screenful at a time.

```
C:\> DIR | MORE    <ENTER>
```

By including the SORT command, you can enhance the previous command to display a sorted directory listing one screenful at a time.

```
C:\> DIR | SORT | MORE    <ENTER>
```

To display the contents of a file named DATA.DAT one screenful at a time, use MORE as shown here:

```
C:\> MORE < DATA.DAT    <ENTER>
```

NLSFUNC

Provides device support for international code pages

NLSFUNC stands for National Language Support Function. It is used by international DOS users who must change character sets.

Format

```
NLSFUNC [CountryFile]
```

CountryFile   The complete DOS file specification for the file that contains the country information. This file is usually C:\DOS\COUNTRY.SYS.

Notes

NLSFUNC is an external command that requires DOS 3.3 or later. The only users who will have to issue NLSFUNC are those concerned with code-page support for international character sets. If you are modifying code pages, you must issue the NLSFUNC command before you can invoke CHCP.

If your NLSFUNC command line does not specify the country file, NLSFUNC uses the file specified in your CONFIG.SYS COUNTRY entry as the default. If NLSFUNC cannot locate the default file, NLSFUNC does not display an error message. Instead, CHCP will display an error message the first time you try to change code pages.

If you are using DOS 4 or later, you can use the CONFIG.SYS INSTALL entry to load NLSFUNC during system startup. If you are using DOS 5, invoke NLSFUNC using LOADHIGH.

Examples

The following command informs DOS that the country information file COUN-TRY.SYS is in the DOS directory on drive C:

```
C:\> NLSFUNC C:\DOS\COUNTRY.SYS   <ENTER>
```

If you are using DOS 4, invoke NLSFUNC from within your CONFIG.SYS file using the INSTALL entry, as shown here.

```
INSTALL=C:\DOS\NLSFUNC.EXE C:\DOS\COUNTRY.SYS
```

Likewise, if you are using DOS 5, invoke NLSFUNC using LOADHIGH.

```
C:\> LOADHIGH C:\DOS\NLSFUNC.EXE C:\DOS\COUNTRY.SYS   <ENTER>
```

Messages

File not found

NLSFUNC could not find the file COUNTRY.SYS. If COUNTRY.SYS is not in the current directory, make sure that you specify the location of this file in the NLSFUNC command line.

NLSFUNC already installed

You have already invoked NLSFUNC. NLSFUNC installs memory-resident software, which only needs to be invoked once per user session at the computer.

Resident portion of NLSFUNC loaded

NLSFUNC is simply telling you its memory-resident software has been loaded in memory. This message is purely informational.

PATH

Defines a command-file search path

The PATH command defines the search path (the list of directories that DOS will follow) to locate an external command when the complete path is not given or the file is not found in the given path. By defining a command-file search path, you can easily execute your commonly used commands, regardless of your current directory.

Format

PATH [*drive:*] [*path*] [; [*drive:*] [*path*]...]

drive: The disk drive that DOS is to include in the command-file search path.

path   A DOS directory to be included in the command-file search path.

...   Indicates that a disk drive and subdirectory may be specified several times.

Notes

PATH is an internal command that requires DOS 2.0 or later. Each time you type in a command name from the DOS prompt, DOS first checks to see if the command is an internal command that resides in your computer's fast electronic memory. If so, DOS executes the command. If DOS fails to locate a command internally, DOS then searches the current directory or the directory specified in the command line. If DOS cannot find a matching EXE, COM, or BAT file, DOS checks to see if you have defined a command-file search path. If so, DOS searches each of the directories specified in the command path for the command. The PATH command lets you define disk drives and subdirectories to be included in this search path.

To reduce overhead with each command reference, place the directories that are most likely to contain command files first in your PATH command. Each time DOS fails to locate a command in the current directory, DOS searches the first entry in your PATH path. If DOS still doesn't locate your file in that directory, it searches the second, third, and so on. If your commonly used commands are in the directories specified at the end of the PATH command, DOS has to perform needless directory searches. These additional searches increase your system overhead.

The maximum length of the command path is 122 characters. If you need to create a path longer than this, use the SUBST command to abbreviate directory path names. DOS stores the current path in the environment. Using the SET command, you can display (and set) the current path.

Examples

In the following example, if DOS cannot find the command, it will search the drive C directories DOS, BATCH, and UTIL.

```
C:\> PATH C:\DOS;C:\BATCH;C:\UTIL   <ENTER>
```

If you don't include a drive letter before each path name, DOS will search the current disk for the path.

If you invoke PATH without a command line, PATH will display the current command path.

```
C:\> PATH   <ENTER>
PATH=C:\DOS;C:\BATCH;C:\UTIL
```

To remove the command path, invoke PATH with a semicolon:

```
C:\> PATH ;   <ENTER>
```

Messages

No Path

There is currently no command-file search path defined. Therefore, DOS will only search for your batch or executable files in the current subdirectory or subdirectory specified.

Out of environment space

You have very likely installed a memory-resident program (GRAPHICS, PRINT, or a third-party product), which prevents DOS from expanding the environment to store your new entry. If necessary, restart DOS and issue your PATH command prior to invoking the memory-resident program. Remember, by using SHELL= in CONFIG.SYS, you can specify the desired size of your DOS environment.

PAUSE

Displays an optional message pausing batch-file execution

The PAUSE command temporarily suspends a batch file's processing until you press a key to continue.

Format

```
PAUSE [message]
```

message   An optional message of up to 121 characters that PAUSE is to display when it suspends batch processing.

Notes

PAUSE is an internal command supported by all DOS versions. When DOS encounters a PAUSE command within a batch file DOS will temporarily suspend the batch file and display the following:

```
[optional message text]
Press any key to continue . . .
```

The optional message is normally an instructional message the batch file displays to the user, such as to turn on the printer. To continue batch processing, press any key; otherwise, press CTRL -BREAK to cancel the batch file. If you press CTRL -BREAK, DOS will display the following:

```
Terminate batch job (Y/N)?
```

If you type **Y**, the batch file will end and DOS will redisplay its prompt. If you instead type **N**, DOS will terminate the current command, continuing the batch file's execution with its next command.

Depending on your DOS version, PAUSE may display the following message:

```
Strike a key when ready...
```

The ECHO OFF command (see ECHO) suppresses the display of messages from PAUSE.

If your batch file runs a long program and then invokes PAUSE to inform the user the program has completed, you might consider including the CTRL-G (^G) character in PAUSE's optional message sounding the computer's bell to get the user's attention.

Examples

When DOS encounters the PAUSE command in a batch procedure, as shown here,

```
PAUSE Insert a blank disk in drive B
```

it will pause and display

```
C:\> PAUSE Insert a blank disk in drive B
Press any key to continue . . .
```

In a similar manner, the following PAUSE command will not display an instructional message, but will still suspend processing.

```
C:\> PAUSE
Press any key to continue . . .
```

Messages

Press any key to continue...

Without the message you have specified in the PAUSE command line, the current ECHO status is OFF. When ECHO is OFF, DOS suppresses the display of messages by PAUSE.

PRINT

Prints a DOS file via the print queue

The PRINT command lets you print one or more ASCII files from the DOS prompt while continuing to issue other DOS commands.

Format

```
PRINT [/D:device_name] [/C] [/T] [/P] [/B:buffer_size]
 [/M:max_ticks] [/Q:queue_size] [/S:time_slice] [/U:busy_ticks]
 file_spec [...]
```

/D: *device_name*   The name of the device that DOS is to use for the printer. The default device is PRN.

/C   Directs PRINT to cancel the print job of the file whose name precedes the /C and all those that follow.

/T   Directs PRINT to cancel all the print jobs in the printer queue.

/P   Directs PRINT to add to the print queue the file that precedes the /P and all the files that follow.

/B: *buffer_size*   The amount of memory (in bytes) that is set aside for PRINT. The default size is 512. By increasing this size in multiples of 512 (1,024, 2,048, 4,096), you will improve PRINT's performance by decreasing the number of required disk I/O operations. Increasing this value, however, does consume memory.

/M: *max_ticks*   The maximum number of CPU clock ticks that PRINT can consume before it must return control to DOS. This value can be in the range from 1 to 255; the default value is 2. This switch is only valid the first time that you invoke PRINT. Increasing this value will improve PRINT's performance, since it has more control of the CPU. However, if you make this value too large, the rest of your applications will become sluggish when PRINT is working.

/Q: *queue_size*   The number of entries that the PRINT queue can store. This value must be in the range from 1 to 32; the default value is 10. This switch is only valid the first time you invoke PRINT.

/S: *time_slice*   The PRINT time slice. This value must be in the range from 1 to 255; the default value is 8. This switch is only valid the first time you invoke PRINT.

/U: *busy_ticks*   The number of CPU clock ticks that PRINT will wait before the printer becomes available for the next series of characters. (CPU clock ticks occur 18.2 times per second on the IBM PC.) This value must be in the range from 1 to 255; the default value is 1. This switch is only valid the first time you invoke PRINT.

file_spec   The complete DOS path name of the file to be added to or removed from the print queue. PRINT supports DOS wildcard characters.

...   Indicates that several file names can be placed on the PRINT command line.

Notes

PRINT is an external command that requires DOS 2.0 or later. The PRINT command sends files to the printer in a background mode, which means that you can continue your processing in the foreground while the printing takes place. PRINT places files in a print queue (or waiting line). PRINT selects files from the queue for printing in the order of their entry in the queue.

If you want to print files using the DOS 4 or 5 shell, you must first install PRINT's memory-resident software. If you plan to print from within the shell, place a PRINT command in your AUTOEXEC.BAT.

Examples

The following command installs a print queue with storage for 32 files:

```
C:\> PRINT /Q:32   <ENTER>
```

Remember that many switches are only valid the first time you issue a PRINT command.

The following command prints a copy of your AUTOEXEC.BAT file.

```
C:\> PRINT \AUTOEXEC.BAT   <ENTER>
```

PRINT lets you specify the names of two or more files you want to print. The following command, for example, prints the files AUTOEXEC.BAT and CONFIG.SYS.

```
C:\> PRINT \AUTOEXEC.BAT   \CONFIG.SYS   <ENTER>
```

PRINT fully supports DOS wildcard characters. The next command prints all the files in the current directory with the DAT extension.

```
C:\> PRINT *.DAT   <ENTER>
```

The following command terminates the current print job and removes remaining jobs from the print queue.

```
C:\> PRINT /T   <ENTER>
```

The next command removes the AUTOEXEC.BAT file from the print queue:

```
C:\> PRINT AUTOEXEC.BAT /C   <ENTER>
```

Messages

FILENAME.EXT File not found in print queue

PRINT could not find the file specified in a command that contains a /C switch (which directs PRINT to remove the file from the print queue). Redisplay the files in the print queue and then reissue the command.

FILENAME.EXT is currently being printed

PRINT is simply telling you the name of the file that it is currently printing.

FILENAME.EXT is in queue

PRINT is telling you that the file specified is in the print queue, waiting to be printed.

FILENAME.EXT Pathname too long

The complete path name specified exceeds 63 characters. DOS will not process paths longer than 63 characters in length.

Access denied

The file specified is currently locked by another application. Wait a few minutes and repeat the PRINT command.

All files canceled by operator

You have canceled the printing of all of the files in the print queue via the /T command-line switch.

Errors on list device indicate that it may be offline. Please check it.

Your printer may either be turned off or have been placed offline. Turn your printer on or place it online and printing will continue.

File FILENAME.EXT canceled by operator

The file specified was removed via a /C switch in the PRINT command line and will not be printed.

List output is not assigned to a device

The device name specified at PRINT's prompt for a target device is invalid. Reissue the command specifying a device name such as PRN, LPT1, COM1, and so on.

Name of list device [PRN:]

PRINT is simply prompting you to enter the name of the target device that you want printed output to be written to. By default, PRINT uses the device PRN. If you simply press ENTER, PRINT will select this device. If your printer is attached to a different port, such as COM1, type in that device name.

Printer out of paper error

Your printer is out of paper. Take the printer offline, add additional paper, and place the printer back online. PRINT will continue printing your output.

PRINT queue is empty

You have no files in your print queue, either printing or waiting to be printed.

PRINT queue is full

Your printer queue is full and cannot hold an additional file until it has printed another file. Remember, the /Q switch allows you to specify a queue size up to

32 entries. You can only specify /Q the first time that you invoke the PRINT command.

Resident part of PRINT installed

PRINT has installed the memory-resident software that DOS requires to handle your files and control of the printer. This message is purely informational.

PROMPT

Defines the DOS system prompt that appears on the display

The PROMPT command defines how the DOS prompt appears on your screen display.

Format

```
PROMPT [prompt_string]
```

prompt_string   The character string that defines the DOS prompt. It can contain characters or the following metacharacters:

Character	Meaning
$b	| character
$d	Date
$e	ESC character
$h	Backspace cursor one position
$g	> character
$l	< character
$n	Current drive
$p	Current drive and directory
$q	= character
$t	Current time
$v	DOS version
$_	Carriage return/line feed
$$	$ character

Notes

PROMPT is an internal command that requires DOS 2.0 or later. If no string is specified, PROMPT resets the system prompt to the current default drive letter followed by a greater-than sign.

Some users will define "cute" system prompts, such as

```
WHAT'S NEW?
```

The DOS prompt, however, can be very useful. You should set your prompt to pg, which displays the current drive and directory as shown here.

```
A>  PROMPT $p$g   <ENTER>

A:\>
```

Note how the prompt changes with the directories.

```
A:\> C:            <ENTER>

C:\> CD DOS        <ENTER>

C:\DOS> CD \123    <ENTER>

C:\123>
```

The PROMPT command creates an entry in the DOS environment. Each time it completes a command, DOS searches the environment for an entry in the form PROMPT=. If DOS finds the entry, it uses the value to set the system prompt. If the entry does not exist, DOS uses the default prompt of the current drive letter, followed by a greater-than sign.

If you are using DOS 3.3 or higher, your batch files can use the named parameter %PROMPT% to determine and save the current system prompt.

The ANSI.SYS device driver lets you enhance your screen and keyboard capabilities using various escape sequences. Using the $e metacharacter, you can generate the ASCII escape character that starts an escape sequence.

If you use the current system date or time within your prompt, DOS does not continuously update the date or time displayed in the prompt. Instead, DOS displays the current date or time each time you press ENTER *to redisplay a new prompt.*

NOTE

Examples

The following command simply sets the DOS prompt to the current drive and directory, followed by a greater-than sign.

```
C> PROMPT $p$g    <ENTER>

C:\DOS>
```

As your current directory or drive changes, so, too, will your prompt.

The following command sets the system prompt to the current system time:

```
C> PROMPT $t    <ENTER>

15:20:18.81    <ENTER>
15:20:43.78    <ENTER>
15:20:87.12    <ENTER>
```

To display only the hours and minutes, you can change the prompt to use the $h backspace character to erase the seconds and hundredths of seconds, displaying *hh: mm:*.

```
C> PROMPT $t$h$h$h$h$h    <ENTER>
```

The DOS prompt can be used to keep track of the current directory. In this case, the command

```
C> PROMPT [$p]    <ENTER>
```

directs DOS to display the current directory name within left and right brackets as shown here:

```
[C:\SUBDIR]
```

Messages

Out of environment space

The environment is full. Until you install memory-resident software such as PRINT, GRAPHICS, or a third-party product, DOS allows your environment to grow to up to 32Kb as your processing needs require. If, however, you install memory-resident software, your environment size becomes fixed. Therefore, try to invoke all of your

SET commands prior to loading memory-resident software. Also, remember that the SHELL= entry in CONFIG.SYS allows you to specify the environment size.

QBASIC

Runs Microsoft's QBasic interpreter

QBasic is an editor and interpreter that lets you create and run programs in the BASIC programming language.

Format

```
QBASIC [/B] [/EDITOR] [/G] [/H] [/MBF]  [/NOHI] [/RUN]  [ProgramName]
```

/B   Directs QBasic to display its output in black and white.

/EDITOR   Directs QBasic to invoke the DOS editor.

/G   Directs QBasic to perform fast screen output on a CGA.

/H   Directs QBasic to display its output using the maximum number of lines your screen display supports.

/MBF   Converts QBasic's built-in functions so that MKS$ becomes MKSMBF$, MKD$ becomes MKDMBF$, CVS becomes CVSMBF, and CVD becomes CVDMBF.

/NOHI   Disables QBasic's high-intensity video.

/RUN   Directs QBasic to run the program before displaying the program instructions with the QBasic environment.

Notes

For more information on QBasic, refer to the Osborne/McGraw-Hill book, *QBasic Made Easy*, 1991.

Example

The following command runs the program GORILLA.BAS, provided with DOS 5 as a QBasic demonstration.

```
C:\> QBASIC /RUN GORILLA.BAS   <ENTER>
```

RECOVER

Recovers a damaged disk or file

If a DOS disk or file becomes damaged and loses sectors (the areas on the disk that contain information), you can use the RECOVER command to retrieve portions of the disk or file up to the point of the corruption.

Format

RECOVER *file_spec*

or

RECOVER *drive:*

drive: The drive identifier of the disk to be recovered.

file_spec   The complete path name of the damaged file to be recovered.

Notes

RECOVER is an external DOS command that requires DOS 2.0 or later. Use CHKDSK to examine your disk before you invoke RECOVER.

RECOVER sometimes allows you to recover a portion of a file if your file develops a bad sector. At best, however, RECOVER can only save a portion of your file. Do not rely upon this command. Instead, perform file and disk backups on a regular basis.

If the file is a text file, you can edit the file later and restore the missing contents. If, however, the file is an executable file, you should not execute it—remember, the file is missing sectors. Maintain a good backup of your files so that you do not have to rely on RECOVER.

If you use RECOVER to recover a complete disk, it will create files in the root directory with names in the form FILE*nnnn*.REC, where *nnnn* is a four-digit number beginning with 0001 (FILE0001.REC). Using an editor or DEBUG, you can examine the contents of the file to determine the its correct name.

RECOVER does not work with disk drives connected to a network. Do not use RECOVER in combination with the ASSIGN, JOIN, or SUBST commands.

RECOVER does not undelete files. RECOVER salvages portions of a damaged file or disk. Do not use RECOVER on a disk or file that is not damaged.

Examples

The following command attempts to recover the contents of the disk in drive A.

```
C:\> RECOVER A:   <ENTER>
```

In this case, RECOVER will create several files with names that are in the format FILE *nnnn*.REC.

The command

```
C:\> RECOVER FILENAME.EXT   <ENTER>
```

will simply recover the contents of the FILENAME.EXT file up to the damaged sector.

Messages

Cannot RECOVER a Network drive

The disk drive that you are specifying in the RECOVER command line is a network device. DOS does not allow you to use RECOVER on a network disk.

Warning - directory full *n* file(s) recovered

The root directory of your disk drive is full. Copy the files FILE*nnnn*.REC to a new disk, delete the current files, and repeat the RECOVER command to continue recovering files on the disk drive.

REM

Documents a DOS batch file

The REM command lets you place comments or remarks within your DOS batch files to explain the batch file's processing.

Format

```
REM [message]
```

message   A character string of up to 121 characters.

Notes

REM is an internal DOS command support by all DOS versions. DOS does not execute lines containing the REM command; instead, DOS simply ignores the line and continues the batch file's execution with the next line.

If you are using empty REM statements to space your batch file's commands, you can replace the statements with blank lines.

Place the ECHO OFF command at the start of your batch files to prevent DOS from displaying each REMark on the screen as the batch file executes.

Do not place the I/O redirection operators (>, >>, <, |) in a remark. DOS will try to use them.

At a minimum, your batch file should use REM to explain the batch file's purpose, the author, and when it was written.

```
@ECHO OFF
REM Name: DISPLAY.BAT
REM Purpose: Display the contents of each file specified.

REM Written by: Kris Jamsa
REM Date Written: 6/30/91

:LOOP
  IF '%1'=='' GOTO DONE
  FOR %%I IN (%1) DO TYPE %%I
  SHIFT
  GOTO LOOP
:DONE
```

Note that if you are using DOS 4 or later, you can also place REM statements within your CONFIG.SYS file to explain the file's entries.

Example

The following batch file uses REM to add several meaningful comments, which explain the batch file's processing, to the batch file presented in the Notes section.

```
@ECHO OFF
REM Name: DISPLAY.BAT
REM Purpose: Display the contents of each file specified.

REM Written by: Kris Jamsa
REM Date Written: 2/30/91

REM The format to invoke DISPLAY.BAT is as follows:
REM    C:\ DISPLAY FILENAME.EXT [optional additional file names]
REM Loop through all of the file names specified in the command line

:LOOP
  REM When %1 is null, the batch file is done
  IF '%1'=='' GOTO DONE

  REM By using the FOR command, the batch file supports wildcards
  FOR %%I IN (%1) DO TYPE %%I

  REM Assign the next file name to %1
  SHIFT
  GOTO LOOP
:DONE
```

Messages

Because DOS does not execute REM commands, there are no possible error messages.

RENAME

Rename the file(s) specified

The RENAME command renames one or more files on your disk.

Format

REN *CurrentName NewName*

or

```
RENAME CurrentName NewName
```

CurrentName   The complete DOS path name of the file to be renamed. It can contain a drive and DOS subdirectory path. RENAME supports DOS wildcard characters for this parameter.

NewName   The target file name for the rename operation. It cannot have a drive or DOS subdirectory path. RENAME supports DOS wildcard characters for this parameter.

Notes

RENAME is an internal DOS command supported by all DOS versions. Because of its frequency of use, DOS lets you abbreviate RENAME as REN. The REN command does not rename DOS subdirectories.

You must specify a target file after indicating the file you want to rename. The target file must be in the same directory on the same disk drive as the source file. This is because RENAME does not copy the contents of a file, but simply renames the file in its directory entry.

To move a file from one drive or directory to another, you must instead first copy the file to the desired drive or directory, and then delete the file using DEL.

RENAME can change the name of a read-only file.

Examples

The following command renames the file CONFIG.BAK as CONFIG.SAV.

```
C:\> REN CONFIG.BAK CONFIG.SAV   <ENTER>
```

The following command gives all of the files in the current directory with the extension BAK a new extension of SAV:

```
C:\> REN *.BAK *.SAV   <ENTER>
```

If you specify a disk drive identifier or directory for the target file, REN will display

```
C:\> REN AUTOEXEC.OLD A:AUTOEXEC.OLD   <ENTER>
Invalid parameter
```

Remember, REN cannot move a file from one directory or disk to another.

The following command renames the file OLDNAME.EXT on drive A to NEWNAME.EXT. The file remains on drive A.

```
C:\> REN A:OLDNAME.EXT NEWNAME.EXT   <ENTER>
```

Note the target file name does not include the drive letter. RENAME knows the target file is on drive A, because the source file is on drive A, and RENAME cannot move a file from one disk to another.

Messages

Invalid parameter

Your RENAME command very likely contains a disk drive letter or directory path before the target name. RENAME cannot move a file from one disk or directory to another, and therefore does not let you specify a drive letter or directory before the target file name.

Duplicate file name or File not found

RENAME could either not find the file you want to rename, or a file already exists in the target directory with the new name you desire. RENAME will not let you overwrite an existing file.

REPLACE

Selectively replaces or updates a file

The REPLACE command allows selective file replacements and updates when new versions of software become available.

Format

```
REPLACE source_file_spec [target_file_spec] [/A] [/P]
  [/R] [/S] [/U] [/W]
```

source_file_spec   The complete DOS file specification for the files that RE-PLACE is to use in the file replacement. REPLACE supports DOS wildcard characters.

target_file_spec   The drive and directory path of the destination files being added or replaced.

/A   Directs REPLACE to add files to the target directory instead of replacing them. With this switch, REPLACE only places those files onto the target that are not currently present.

/P   Directs REPLACE to prompt you with the screen message "Replace *DRIVE:FILENAME.EXT* (Y/N)?" before adding or replacing files.

/R   Directs REPLACE to also replace the files on the target location that are currently marked as read-only. Without this switch, REPLACE stops replacement operations with the first file marked read-only.

/S   Directs REPLACE to search the subdirectories on the target location for other occurrences of the file to be replaced. This switch cannot be used with /A.

/U   Directs REPLACE to replace only those files in the target directory that are older than the files in the source. This is a DOS 5 switch.

/W   Directs REPLACE to prompt "Press any key to continue..." before starting the file-replacement operations.

Notes

REPLACE is an external command that requires DOS 3.2 or later. The REPLACE command exists primarily to aid program developers when they have updates to programs that users may have distributed across several directories. Most end users will never have to issue the REPLACE command.

If you use REPLACE to update your fixed disk with a new version of DOS, keep in mind that REPLACE cannot update the hidden system files IO.SYS and MSDOS.SYS, which are required for your system to boot.

If you are using REPLACE within a DOS batch file, REPLACE supports the following exit status values:

Exit Status	Meaning
0	All files successfully replaced
2	The source files were not found
3	The source or destination path was not found
5	File access violation
8	Insufficient memory
11	Invalid command-line syntax
15	Invalid drive specified
22	Incorrect DOS version

Examples

The following command will replace any files in the current directory that have the DAT extension using files in drive A:

```
C:\> REPLACE A:*.DAT C:    <ENTER>
```

The next command will replace all of the files on drive C that have the extension DAT with the corresponding file from drive A:

```
C:\> REPLACE A:*.DAT C:\ /S    <ENTER>
```

Messages

n File(s) added

Your REPLACE command line contains the /A switch, which directs REPLACE to add files to the target disk, and REPLACE is simply telling you the number of files that REPLACE has added to the disk.

n file(s) replaced

REPLACE is simply telling you the number of files that it has replaced on the target disk.

Access denied -'*pathname*'

REPLACE could not replace the file specified because it has been marked read-only. If you want REPLACE to replace a read-only file, use the /R switch.

Add pathname? (Y/N)

You have invoked REPLACE with the /A and /P switches to selectively add files to the target disk. In this case, to add the file to the disk, type Y and press ENTER. If you type N and press ENTER, REPLACE will not modify the file.

Adding pathname

Your REPLACE command line contains the /A switch, which directs REPLACE to add files found on the source disk to the files that reside on the target. In this case, REPLACE is simply telling you that it is adding the file specified to the target disk.

File cannot be copied onto itself *'path'*

A source file for your REPLACE command is identical to the target. Change the target file name and reissue the command or add a disk drive or directory specifier as required.

No files added

Your REPLACE command line contains the /A switch, which directs REPLACE to only add those files from the source disk that don't currently reside on the target disk. In this case, REPLACE found no files to add to the disk.

No files found *'path'*

No files existed in the source path specified. Make sure that the directory specified is valid and contains files, repeating the command as necessary.

No files found

REPLACE did not find any files on the target disk that needed to be replaced by files on the source.

Parameters not compatible

Two or more of the switches specified in the REPLACE command line are incompatible. Review the format of the REPLACE command and reissue the REPLACE command.

Path too long

A subdirectory path name in your REPLACE command line exceeds 63 characters. DOS does not support subdirectory path names of this length.

Press any key to continue . . .

Your REPLACE command contains the /A switch, which directs REPLACE to add files from the source disk to the target and also /W, which directs REPLACE to pause and allow you to insert the desired floppy disks into the correct disk drives.

Replace FILENAME.EXT? (Y/N)

Your REPLACE command line contains the /P switch, which allows you to perform selective file replacements. To replace the file specified, type Y and press ENTER. If you type N, REPLACE will not update the file specified.

Source path required

Your REPLACE command line does not specify the location of the files to use in the replacement operation. You must specify the files you want REPLACE to use in the command line.

RESTORE

Restores files saved by BACKUP

The BACKUP command places files onto a disk in a manner only accessible by the RESTORE command. To copy a file from the backup disk, you must use RESTORE.

Format

```
RESTORE source_drive: target_drive:file_spec [/P] [/S]
        [/B:mm-dd-yy] [/A:mm-dd-yy] [/E:hh:mm:ss] [L:hh:mm:ss]
        [/M] [/N] [/D]
```

***source_drive*:**   The drive containing the file to be restored.

target_drive*: *file_spec   The files you want to restore from the backup disk. RESTORE supports DOS wildcard characters.

/P   Directs RESTORE to prompt the user before restoring those files that have been modified or set to read-only since the backup.

/S   Directs RESTORE to restore files contained in subdirectories.

/B: *mm-dd-yy*   Directs RESTORE to restore only those files modified on or before the date specified.

/A: *mm-dd-yy*   Directs RESTORE to restore only those files modified after the specified date.

/E: *hh:* *mm:ss*   Directs RESTORE to restore only those files modified at or before the time specified. This switch requires DOS 3.3 or higher.

/L:*hh:mm:ss*   Directs RESTORE to restore only those files modified at or after the time specified. This switch requires DOS 3.3 or higher.

/M   Directs RESTORE to restore only those files modified since the last backup.

/N   Directs RESTORE to restore only those files no longer existing on the target disk.

/D   Directs RESTORE to display a list of files on the backup disk that match the file specification given. RESTORE will not actually restore any of the files; instead, it will simply list them. This switch requires DOS 5.

Notes

RESTORE is an external command that requires DOS 2.0 or later. The RESTORE command will not restore the DOS hidden system files that DOS uses to boot your system.

If you do not perform regular system backups, the RESTORE command is essentially worthless to you. Get in the habit of backing up your disks on a regular basis. Next, place those backups into a safe location.

DOS 3.3 allows you to keep a log of the files contained on your backup disks. Use this log to help you locate specific files on your disks for restoration.

Last, remember to label your backup disks in a meaningful manner. If you later need to restore your files, you will be organized enough to do so.

IF you are using RESTORE within a DOS batch file, RESTORE supports the following exit status values:

Exit Status	Meaning
0	Successful file restore
1	No matching files found to restore
3	User termination via CTRL-C
4	Fatal processing error, restore incomplete

Examples

The following command restores all files from the backup disk in drive A, including those in subdirectories:

```
C:\> RESTORE A: C:*.* /S  <ENTER>
```

If the backup operation required you to use several floppy disks, RESTORE will prompt you to place subsequent disks in the specified drive each time it needs a new backup disk.

This command restores all the files from the backup disk that contain the extension DAT:

```
C:\> RESTORE A: C:*.DAT /P  <ENTER>
```

RESTORE will prompt you with

```
Warning! File FILENAME.EXT
was changed after it was backed up.
Replace the file (Y/N)?
```

before it restores files that have been modified since the backup.

Under DOS 5, the following command directs RESTORE to list all the files on the backup disk that match the specification *.LTR.

```
C:\> RESTORE A: C:\*.LTR /D  <ENTER>
```

Messages

*** Files were backed up on *mm-dd-yy*

RESTORE is simply telling you the date that the files on the backup disk were backed up. If this date does not correspond to your last known BACKUP operation, you may not be using your latest backup disks.

*** Not able to restore file ***

The file specified may be currently in use by another program in the network. It is a good practice to only perform BACKUP and RESTORE operations when your network is disabled.

*** Restoring files from drive *n* ***
Diskette *nnn*

RESTORE is simply telling you the disk drive letter and the backup disk number that it is currently using to restore files.

Insert backup diskette *n* in drive *n*
Strike any key to continue . . .

RESTORE is simply telling you that it is ready for the next backup disk. Once you have inserted the disk in the drive specified, simply press a key, and RESTORE will continue its processing.

Source and target drives are the same

The disk drives that you have specified in your RESTORE command line are the same. RESTORE does not support this type of processing. Reissue the command with a different source and target disk drive.

Source does not contain backup files

The disk in the source drive specified in the RESTORE command line does not contain backup files. Repeat the command inserting a disk in the drive that contains files placed on the disk by the BACKUP command.

The last file was not restored

RESTORE did not restore the last file specified on the screen display either because the target disk is full or the backup file is bad. If your disk is full, you may need to remove other unnecessary files from your disk before you can restore the files.

WARNING! Diskette is out of sequence
Replace diskette or continue if ok
Press any key to continue . . .

You have inserted a backup disk in the wrong order. If you want RESTORE to continue with this disk, simply press ENTER. If you want to insert a different disk, do so and press ENTER.

**WARNING! File FILENAME.EXT
is a read-only file
Replace the file (Y/N)?**

Your RESTORE command line contains a /P switch, which allows you to selectively restore files marked as read-only. If you want to restore the file specified, simply type Y and press ENTER. If you don't want RESTORE to restore the file, simply type N and press ENTER.

**WARNING! File FILENAME.EXT
was changed after it was backed up
Replace the file (Y/N)?**

Your RESTORE command line contains a /P switch, which allows you to selectively restore files that have changed since the backup operation was performed. If you want to restore the file specified, simply type Y and press ENTER. If you don't want RESTORE to restore the file, simply type N and press ENTER.

WARNING! No files were found to restore

RESTORE did not find any matching files to restore from the back up disk. Make sure that you have correctly specified the files desired including the original subdirectories.

RMDIR

Removes the directory specified

The RMDIR command lets you remove an empty directory from your disk when the directory is no longer needed.

Format

```
RMDIR [drive:]path
```

or

```
RD [drive:]path
```

drive: The drive from which the subdirectory will be removed. If this parameter is not specified, RMDIR will use the current drive.

path   The name of the DOS subdirectory to remove.

Notes

RMDIR is an internal command that requires DOS 2.0 or later. Due to its frequency of use, DOS lets you abbreviate RMDIR as RD. Use the RMDIR command to remove a specified directory. This command will only remove empty subdirectories that do not contain files. Beware of hidden or system files in the directory that don't appear in the directory listing. If you attempt to remove a directory that appears empty but contains hidden or system files, RMDIR will display the following error message:

```
Invalid path, not directory,
or directory not empty
```

Under DOS 5, you can use the ATTRIB command to display the names of hidden or system files that may reside in the current directory.
RMDIR will not remove the current directory.

Examples

The following command attempts to remove the IBM subdirectory from the root directory of the current drive. If the directory contains files, RMDIR cannot remove the directory.

```
C:\> RMDIR \IBM   <ENTER>
```

Similarly, the command

```
C:\> RMDIR \MISC\IBM\SALES   <ENTER>
```

removes the subdirectory \SALES from the directory \MISC\IBM on the current drive.

Messages

Invalid path, not directory, or directory not empty

The directory name (or path name) that you are specifying is invalid, the name specified is not a DOS subdirectory, or the directory still contains files or sub-directories. DOS will not allow you to remove a subdirectory that contains files. If no files appear in a listing of the directory, the directory may contain hidden files.

SELECT

Selects an international format for a new disk

SELECT lets international DOS users choose their country-specific character sets and keyboard templates when they format a new system disk.

Format

```
SELECT [[A: | B:] drive:[path]] country keyboard
```

A: | B: The source drive of the keyboard files.

*drive***:** The target drive to which international files are copied.

path The target path for the file copy.

country The three-digit code that specifies the country to be used.

keyboard The two-character identifier that specifies the keyboard layout to be used (see KEYB).

Notes

DOS 5 does not support SELECT. Also, DOS 4 uses SELECT to install DOS on a hard disk. The discussion below relates to versions prior to DOS 4.

The SELECT command uses the DISKCOPY command (see DISKCOPY) to make a copy of the DOS disk (DOS 3.2 uses XCOPY). The command also creates the CONFIG.SYS (see CONFIG) and AUTOEXEC.BAT (see AUTOEXEC) files that are required for international support on the target disk.

The following country codes are supported:

Code	Country	Code	Country
001	United States	002	French-Canadian
003	Latin America	031	Netherlands
032	Belgium	033	France
034	Spain	039	Italy
041	Switzerland	044	United Kingdom
045	Denmark	046	Sweden
047	Norway	049	Germany
061	English	351	Portugal
358	Finland	785	Arabic countries
972	Israel		

SELECT also uses the following keyboard identifiers:

Identifier	Country	Identifier	Country
US	United States	FR	France
GR	Germany	IT	Italy
SP	Spain	UK	United Kingdom
PO	Portugal	SG	Swiss German
DK	Denmark	BE	Belgium
NL	Netherlands	NO	Norway
LA	Latin America	SV	Sweden
SU	Finland		

Upon completion, SELECT will place the line

```
COUNTRY=xxx
```

in the CONFIG.SYS file and

```
KEYB xx
```

in the AUTOEXEC.BAT file on the target disk.

SELECT supports single- or dual-floppy drive systems. If you have a bootable system disk to which you want to assign a specific country code, you will not need to use the SELECT command. Instead, place the COUNTRY= entry for the correct country in CONFIG.SYS and the KEYB command for your desired keyboard in AUTOEXEC.BAT.

Examples

The following command directs SELECT to create a disk that fully supports German language characteristics.

```
C:\> SELECT A: 049 GR   <ENTER>
```

Messages

Cannot execute FILENAME.EXT

SELECT cannot execute FORMAT, DISKCOPY, or XCOPY, which SELECT uses to create your bootable international disk. If this error occurs, make sure that the file containing the command specified is available in the current directory or command path.

Insert DOS diskette in drive A. Strike any key when ready

SELECT is prompting you to insert the DOS disk that you used to boot DOS in drive A. SELECT uses this disk to create a bootable international disk.

Insert KEYB *xx*.COM diskette in drive *n*: Strike any key when ready

SELECT is prompting you to insert the disk containing the KEYB *xx*.COM file specified into the drive given. SELECT will then copy this file to the international disk that you are building. Once you place this disk in the drive specified, simply press any key to continue.

Insert target diskette in drive *n*: Strike any key when ready

SELECT is prompting you to place the disk that will contain your international configuration into the disk drive specified so that it completes its processing. Once you have placed the disk into the drive specified, simply press any key to continue.

Invalid country code

The international country code (three-digit number) that you have specified in the SELECT command line is invalid. Review the list of valid country codes and reissue the SELECT command.

Is KEYB xx.COM on another diskette (Y/N)?

SELECT could not find the KEYB xx.COM file specified on the current disk. Thus, SELECT is prompting you to determine whether or not the file is on a different disk. If you type **Y**, SELECT will prompt you to insert the disk containing the KEYB xx.COM file. If you instead type **N**, SELECT will terminate its processing.

Invalid keyboard code

The two-letter keyboard code that you have specified in the SELECT command line is invalid. Review the list of valid keyboard codes and reissue the correct SELECT command.

Keyboard routine not found

SELECT could not find the KEYB xx.COM file on the disk that you just inserted following the SELECT prompt to insert the disk containing the KEYB xx.COM file. SELECT will terminate its processing.

SELECT is used to install DOS the first time. SELECT erases everything on the specified target and then installs DOS. Do you want to continue (Y/N)?

SELECT is warning you that if you proceed with the command, it will erase all of the files on the target disk, creating a bootable disk with the international support specified. If you want to continue this command, type **Y** and press ENTER, otherwise, type **N** to terminate the command.

Unable to copy keyboard routine

SELECT was unable to copy the KEYB xx.COM to the target disk. In most cases, this error occurs when the target disk is damaged.

Code page switching not supported for this country

The country code specified does not support code-page switching. In most cases, users will not require support for code-page switching.

Read error, KEYBOARD.SYS

SELECT could not read the file KEYBOARD.SYS. In most cases, this error message indicates that the file KEYBOARD.SYS has become damaged. Retry the SELECT command with the original KEYBOARD.SYS file.

Invalid signature in KEYBOARD.SYS file

The KEYBOARD.SYS file may have become damaged. Retry the SELECT command with the original KEYBOARD.SYS file.

Invalid signature in COUNTRY.SYS file

The COUNTRY.SYS file may have become damaged. Retry the SELECT command with the original copy of COUNTRY.SYS.

SET

Places or displays DOS environment entries

When DOS boots, it reserves an area of memory called the environment, which provides a storage location for system specifics. DOS commands such as PROMPT and PATH place entries in the environment. The SET command sets or displays entries in the DOS environment.

Format

```
SET [name=[value]]
```

name   The name of the DOS environment entry to which you are assigning a value.

value   A character string that defines the assigned value.

Notes

SET is an internal DOS command that requires DOS 2.0 or later.

The DOS environment always contains the COMSPEC= and PATH= entries. COMSPEC= tells DOS where to locate the command-line processor COMMAND.COM. PATH= defines the current command search path. Other commands that set environment entries include PROMPT, PATH, and APPEND. If you are using DOS 5, the DIRCMD entry defines the format DIR uses to display directory listings (see DIR). If you are using DOS 5, the TEMP environment entry tells DOS where to create its temporary files needed for I/O redirection with the DOS pipe. By directing DOS to create these files on a fast RAM drive, you can improve your system performance.

The SET command converts all entry names to uppercase. SET with no parameters displays the current environment.

Most of you have probably used the DOS batch parameters %0 to %9. Beginning with DOS 3.3 you can use named parameters, which are environment entries whose names are surrounded by percent signs (%NAME%). Consider the following batch file:

```
CLS
TYPE %FILE%
```

When DOS encounters the %FILE% in the batch file, it will search your environment entries for an entry matching FILE=. Assuming that your environment contains

```
COMSPEC=C:\DOS\COMMAND.COM
PATH=C:\DOS;C:\UTIL
PROMPT=$p$g
FILE=TEST.BAT
```

DOS would display the contents of the file TEST.BAT.

Examples

With no command-line parameters, SET displays the current environment entries:

```
C> SET   <ENTER>
COMSPEC=C:\DOS\COMMAND.COM
PATH=C:\DOS
```

In the following example, SET will create a new environment entry called FILE and assign it the value TEST.DAT:

```
C> SET FILE=TEST.DAT   <ENTER>
```

You can verify this by again issuing the SET command:

```
C> SET   <ENTER>
COMSPEC=C:\DOS\COMMAND.COM
PATH=C:\DOS
FILE=TEST.DAT
```

To remove the value for an entry, use SET as shown here:

```
C> SET FILE=   <ENTER>
```

Invoking SET now displays

```
C> SET   <ENTER>
COMSPEC=C:\DOS\COMMAND.COM
PATH=C:\DOS
```

Under DOS 5, the following command directs DOS to create its temporary files used for I/O redirection via the DOS pipe on the fast RAM drive D.

```
C:\> SET TEMP=D:   <ENTER>
```

Messages

Out of environment space

The environment is full. Until you install memory-resident software such as PRINT, GRAPHICS, or a third-party product, DOS allows your environment to grow to up 32Kb as your processing needs require. If, however, you install memory-resident software, your environment size becomes fixed. Try to invoke all of your SET commands prior to loading memory-resident software. Also, remember that the SHELL= entry in CONFIG.SYS allows you to specify the environment size.

SETVER

Reports a DOS version number to a program

Many older applications, and in some cases older DOS commands, will not run under DOS 5. The SETVER command instructs DOS to report a specific version when a specific program executes.

Format

```
SETVER [program_name] [version]
```

or

```
SETVER program_name /DELETE
```

program_name　The complete path name of the program to which you want SETVER to report a different DOS version number.

version　The DOS version number you want SETVER to report. The version number must be in the range 2.11 to 9.99.

/DELETE　Directs SETVER to remove the version number assignment from the program.

Notes

SETVER is an external program that requires DOS 5. Before you can use SETVER, you must install it as a device driver using the CONFIG.SYS DEVICE entry

```
DEVICE=C:\DOS\SETVER.EXE
```

SETVER manages a list of programs to which you want DOS to report it is running a specific version. Each time you change this list, you must restart your system for the change to take effect. SETVER stores the version list within the file SETVER.EXE.

If you do not type in a program name, SETVER will display the current version number assignments.

If you are using SETVER within a DOS batch file, SETVER supports the following exit status values:

Exit Status	Meaning
0	Successful version assignment
1	Invalid command-line switch
2	Invalid file name specified
3	Insufficient memory
4	Invalid version number format
5	Program name not found in list
6	Could not find SETVER.EXE
7	Invalid drive specified
8	Too many command-line parameters
9	Command-line parameters missing
10	Error reading SETVER.EXE
11	Corrupt version list in SETVER.EXE
12	The specified SETVER.EXE does not support version list
13	Insufficient space in list for a new entry
14	Error writing SETVER.EXE

Examples

The following command lists the current version number assignments:

```
C:\> SETVER     <ENTER>
WIN200.BIN      3.40
WIN100.BIN      3.40
WINWORD.EXE     4.10
EXCEL.EXE       4.10
HITACHI.SYS     4.00
MSCDEX.EXE      4.00
REDIR4.EXE      4.00
NET.EXE         4.00
NET.COM         3.30
NETWKSTA.EXE    4.00
DXMA0MOD.SYS    3.30
BAN.EXE         4.00
BAN.COM         4.00
MSREDIR.EXE     4.00
METRO.EXE       3.31
IBMCACHE.SYS    3.40
REDIR40.EXE     4.00
DD.EXE          4.01
DD.BIN          4.01
LL3.EXE         4.01
REDIR.EXE       4.00
SYQ55.SYS       4.00
SSTDRIVE.SYS    4.00
ZDRV.SYS        4.01
ZFMT.SYS        4.01
TOPSRDR.EXE     4.00
```

This command assigns DOS version number 3.2 to EXE2BIN.EXE.

```
C:\> SETVER EXE2BIN.EXE 3.2    <ENTER>
WARNING - The application you are adding to the MS-DOS version
table may not have been verified by Microsoft on this version of
MS-DOS. Please contact your software vendor for information on
whether this application will operate properly under this version
of MS-DOS. If you execute this application by instructing MS-DOS
to report a different MS-DOS version number, you may lose or
corrupt data, or cause system instabilities. In that
```

```
circumstance, Microsoft is not responsible for any loss or
damage.

Version table successfully updated
The version change will take effect the next time you restart
your system
```

To remove a command from the set version list, include the /DELETE switch:

```
C:\> SETVER TEST.EXE /DELETE    <ENTER>
```

Messages

Version table successfully updated
The version change will take effect the next time you restart your system

SETVER is informing you that the command was successful and is reminding you that you must restart your system for the change to take effect.

ERROR: Invalid version number, format must be 2.11-9.99

The version number you specified in your command line is not in the valid range of DOS version numbers from 2.11 to 9.99.

ERROR: Missing parameter

Your SETVER command line does not contain both a file name and a version number to assign to the file. You must specify both.

There is no more space in version table new entries

SETVER is telling you that the version table is full. If you want to add this entry to the table, you will have to delete an existing table entry. Invoke SETVER without any parameters to view the existing entries.

SHARE

Installs DOS file-sharing support

SHARE lets users in a network access the same file at the same time.

Format

```
SHARE [/F: file_space] [/L: locks]
```

/F: *file_space*   Allocates memory (in bytes) for the area in which DOS will store file-sharing information. Each open file requires 11 bytes plus the length of the file name (up to 63 characters). The default file space is 2,048 bytes.

/L: *locks*   Allocates memory for the number of file locks desired. The default is 20.

Notes

SHARE is an external command that requires DOS 3.0 or later. If your computer is part of a local area network, ask your network supervisor for the proper SHARE values.

SHARE invokes memory-resident software that performs the file and record locking. You can only invoke SHARE once per user session. When it has been invoked, the only way to remove file sharing is to reboot. The SHARE command places considerable overhead (slows down the speed of operation) on all your file operations; so, you should only install it when file sharing is in effect.

DOS versions greater than 3.0 support file and record locking. When file sharing is active, each time a program opens a file, DOS checks to see if the file is locked by another program, preventing the file-open operation. If the file is locked, DOS will not let the program open the file. In addition, each time a program reads or writes to a file, DOS checks for locking to make sure the section of the file the program wants to use is not locked.

If you are using DOS 4 and disk partitions larger than 32Mb, you should invoke SHARE to prevent an older program that uses file control blocks (FCBs) from damaging your disk. Prior to DOS 2, DOS used file control blocks for file input and output operations. File control blocks only know about disk partitions 32Mb and smaller. If you run an older program that uses file control blocks to write to disk, and your disk partition is larger than 32Mb, the program may actually write its output anywhere on your disk, possibly corrupting files, directories, or even preventing DOS from accessing your files at all. To correct the file control block problem with large partitions under DOS 4, you should invoke SHARE. If you are using DOS 5, you don't need to invoke SHARE in this way.

If you are using DOS 4, you can use the CONFIG.SYS INSTALL entry to invoke SHARE each time your system starts.

Examples

The following command invokes file sharing with default values of 2,048 bytes of space and 20 locks.

```
C:\> SHARE   <ENTER>
```

The next command installs file-sharing support with 40 locks:

```
C:\> SHARE /L:40   <ENTER>
```

If you are using DOS 4 with large disk partitions, place the following INSTALL entry in your CONFIG.SYS file.

```
INSTALL=C:\DOS\SHARE.EXE
```

Messages

Not enough memory

Your computer does not have enough memory to invoke the SHARE memory-resident software. If possible, remove other memory-resident software and RAM drives.

SHIFT

Shifts each batch parameter left one position

Your DOS batch files can easily access the first nine batch file command-line parameters using the symbols %1 through %9. If you invoke your batch file with more than nine parameters, you can use the SHIFT command to access them.

Format

```
SHIFT
```

Notes

SHIFT is an internal command that requires DOS 2.0 or later. This command shifts each batch parameter one position to the left. If more than ten parameters are passed to a DOS batch procedure, you can use the SHIFT command to access each parameter past %9.

If no parameter exists to the right of a parameter, SHIFT will assign the parameter a NULL string. Once you shift the value out of %0, you cannot get the value back.

Example

The following batch file displays all the batch parameters specified on the command line:

```
@ECHO OFF
:LOOP
  SHIFT
  IF '%0'== '' GOTO DONE
  ECHO %0
  GOTO LOOP
:DONE
```

If the previous file were named TEST.BAT, invoking the batch file as

```
C:\> TEST 1 2 3 4   <ENTER>
```

would display

```
C:\> TEST 1 2 3 4   <ENTER>
1
2
3
4
```

SORT

Sorts in a given order

The SORT command lets you view a file's contents or a program's output in sorted order.

Format

```
DOS_COMMAND | SORT [/R] [/+ n]
```

or

SORT [/R] [/+ *n*] < *file*

/R   Directs SORT to sort the data in reverse order.

/+n   Allows you to specify the column on which to sort the data.

file   The name of an existing DOS file.

DOS_COMMAND   The name of a command whose output SORT is to sort.

Notes

SORT is an external command that requires DOS 2.0 or later. The SORT command reads data from the standard input device, sorting the information and displaying it on the standard output device until an end-of-file marker is encountered. SORT is usually used with the < and | redirection operators.

SORT can sort files (or redirected program output) as large as 64Kb. If you invoke SORT without specifying a redirected input file, SORT will read lines of input from the keyboard until you enter the ^Z end-of-file character (by pressing F6 or CTRL-Z) or press CTRL-C to end the command.

If you are using DOS 5, you can use the TEMP environment entry to specify where DOS creates temporary files during I/O redirection operations. By directing DOS to create its temporary files on a fast RAM drive, you can improve your system performance.

Examples

The following command displays a sorted directory listing.

```
C:\> DIR | SORT   <ENTER>
```

The following command directs SORT to sort the information contained in the DATA.DAT file.

```
C:\> SORT < DATA.DAT   <ENTER>
```

In a similar manner, the command

```
C:\> SORT /R < DATA.DAT   <ENTER>
```

directs SORT to sort the same file, this time in reverse order.

If your data file contains

```
Bill Smith    334-1343
Mary Jackson  323-3321
Kris Anderson 333-4322
Kal  Davis    512-3321
Jane Frank    340-2211
Alex Dawson   653-6664
Ed   Miller   332-2231
```

the command

```
C:\> SORT /+6 < FILENAME.EXT   <ENTER>
```

directs SORT to sort the file based on the data starting in column 6. In this case, SORT will display

```
Kris Anderson 333-4322
Kal  Davis    512-3321
Alex Dawson   653-6664
Jane Frank    340-2211
Mary Jackson  323-3321
Ed   Miller   332-2231
Bill Smith    334-1343
```

The following command displays a directory listing sorted by file extension.

```
C:\> DIR | SORT /+10   <ENTER>
```

SUBST

Substitutes a drive name for a DOS path name

Because DOS path names can become large, DOS allows you to use the SUBST command to substitute a drive identifier for a path name.

Format

```
SUBST [ drive:] [path_name] [/D]
```

drive: The drive identifier that will be used to reference the path.

path_name   The DOS path name to be abbreviated.

/D   Directs SUBST to remove a previous disk substitution.

Notes

SUBST is an external command that requires DOS 3.1 or later. Some older software programs do not support DOS subdirectories. If you are using such a program, you can trick the program into using a subdirectory by substituting the desired directory name with a disk drive letter. Likewise, if your command path is pushing its 122-character limit, you can use SUBST to abbreviate one or more of the path entries.

By default, the last logical disk drive that DOS will reference is drive E.

```
C:\> SUBST E: \ DIRNAME   <ENTER>
```

If you need to specify a disk drive greater than E, use the LASTDRIVE= entry in CONFIG.SYS to define the drive letter of the last drive you will need. For instance, the following entry directs DOS to support the drive letters A through K:

```
LASTDRIVE=K
```

Do **not** use the following commands with a substituted disk:

ASSIGN	FDISK	RESTORE
BACKUP	FORMAT	SYS
CHKDSK	LABEL	UNDELETE
DISKCOMP	MIRROR	UNFORMAT
DISKCOPY	RECOVER	

Examples

In the following example, DOS lets you abbreviate the subdirectory \DOS\HELP-FILE\COMMANDS to the drive letter E:

```
C:\> SUBST E: \DOS\HELPFILE\COMMANDS   <ENTER>
```

A command like

```
C:\> DIR E:   <ENTER>
```

will then display the contents of the \DOS\HELPFILE\COMMANDS directory. If that subdirectory contains other subdirectories, you can still use the drive letter

```
C:\> DIR E:SUBDIR   <ENTER>
```

Invoking SUBST without command-line parameters displays current substitutions:

```
C:\> SUBST   <ENTER>
E: => C:\DOS\HELPFILE\COMMANDS
```

Messages

Cannot SUBST a Network drive

The SUBST command failed because the disk drive specified in the command line refers to a network disk. DOS does not allow you to substitute a network disk drive. Depending on your network software, this error message may appear as "Path not found."

SYS

Creates a bootable disk

To start your system, DOS requires that two hidden files reside in the disk's root directory. The SYS commands lets you copy these hidden files from a bootable disk to a newly formatted disk.

Format

```
SYS target_drive:
```

or, under DOS 4 and 5

```
SYS SystemPath target_drive:
```

target_drive: The target disk drive for the hidden operating system files.

SystemPath   The complete path name to the disk and directory containing the system files you want transferred. If you don't specify a path, SYS uses the root directory of the current drive.

Notes

SYS is an external command supported by all DOS versions. SYS enables you to transfer to the target disk the hidden operating system files that perform the initial system startup. Prior to DOS 5, the SYS command does not copy the COMMAND.COM file to the target disk. To do so, you must use COPY.

Prior to DOS 4, SYS will only transfer files to an empty target disk or to a disk that was formatted previously with the /S or /B switch. The hidden system files IO.SYS and MSDOS.SYS must be the first two files in the root directory. If the root directory already contains files, you may not be able to transfer the hidden files to the disk. In such cases, SYS will display a message indicating that there is no room for the system files:

```
No room for system on destination disk
```

If SYS successfully transfers the system files to the disk, SYS will display the following message:

```
System transferred
```

Beginning with DOS 4, SYS will rearrange the files in the target disk's root directory, if necessary, to place the files IO.SYS and MSDOS.SYS in the first two directory entries, as required.

SYS does not work with JOIN or SUBST.

Examples

In this example, SYS will transfer the hidden operating system files to the disk in drive A:

```
C:\> SYS A:   <ENTER>
```

If you are using DOS 4 or 5, the following SYS command specifies the path to the system files.

```
A:\> SYS C:\ A:   <ENTER>
```

Messages

System transferred

SYS successfully copied the hidden system files to the target drive.

Cannot SYS a Network drive

The command failed because DOS will not allow you to copy system files to a network device.

Incompatible system size

SYS could not copy the hidden system files as contiguous files on the target disk. The disk may not be bootable.

Insert destination disk in drive *n* and press any key when ready

SYS is prompting you to insert the disk that you want SYS to transfer the system files to into the disk drive specified.

Insert system disk in drive *n* and press any key when ready

SYS is prompting you to insert a DOS disk in the disk drive specified so that it can copy the hidden system files from the disk to the target disk specified in your SYS command line.

No room for system on destination disk

SYS could not place the hidden system files on the target drive specified. The hidden DOS files must be the first files that DOS places on a disk. If SYS displays this message, you will very likely have to use FORMAT /S to create a bootable system disk. If you are using a fixed disk, make sure that you completely back up all of the files on your disk before doing so. Once the FORMAT /S command completes, you can restore the original files back to the disk drive, adding the required DOS command files.

No system on default drive
Insert system disk in drive *n*
and press any key to continue...

SYS could not find the hidden files on the disk in the current drive. Place a bootable DOS disk in the drive specified and press ENTER.

Cannot specify default drive

You must specify a disk drive letter other than the default disk. If necessary, change the default and reissue the SYS command.

TIME

Sets or displays the DOS system time

Sets the current system time DOS assigns to each file each time you create or modify a file.

Format

TIME [*HH*:*MM*[:*SS*[.*hh*]]]

HH:MM   The desired hours (0-23) and minutes (0-59).

SS   The desired seconds (0-59).

hh   The desired hundredths of a second (0-99).

Notes

TIME is an internal command supported by all DOS versions. The *HH:MM:SS.hh* time format is dependent upon the COUNTRY specifier in CONFIG.SYS. If you do not specify a time in the command line, TIME will display the current time and prompt you to enter a new time. To leave the time unchanged, press ENTER.

Prior to DOS 3.3, the TIME command did not modify the AT computer system clock. To change the AT system clock, users of DOS versions prior to 3.3 must use the Setup disk provided with their DOS' *Guide to Operations*. Beginning with DOS 3.3, the TIME and DATE commands (see DATE) actually set this clock.

The actual time is an optional command-line parameter. If you omit the time, TIME will prompt you for it. Although the TIME command does not force you to type in a time, it is a good habit to do so. DOS uses your system's current date and time to stamp files when a file is created or modified.

```
C:\BUSINESS> DIR   <ENTER>

 Volume in drive C is DOS
 Volume Serial Number is 1234-4321
 Directory of C:\BUSINESS

 .            <DIR>        06-03-91    1:11p
 ..           <DIR>        06-03-91    1:11p
 BILLS    DAT     23936    06-30-91    1:47p
 IRS      MEM        10    06-30-91    1:13p
```
                                Date and time stamp

Because DOS commands, such as BACKUP and RESTORE, have several switches that are based upon the current date and time, you should always ensure that your system time and date is correct.

If you are using DOS 4 or 5, you can enter a time based on a 12-hour clock and include AM or PM following the time, as appropriate. In this case, the following TIME commands are identical.

```
C:\> TIME 14:30    <ENTER>
C:\> TIME 2:30P    <ENTER>
C:\> TIME 2:30PM   <ENTER>
```

If you are using an earlier version of DOS, you must enter the time using a 24-hour format.

Examples

If you do not specify a time on the command line, TIME will prompt you for one:

```
C:\> TIME  <ENTER>
Current time is  4:08:41.15p
Enter new time:
```

To leave the time unchanged, simply press ENTER. Otherwise, type in the time desired.

The following command sets the clock to 12:00 noon.

```
C:\> TIME 12:00   <ENTER>
```

The next command sets the clock to midnight.

```
C:\> TIME 00:00:00.000   <ENTER>
```

If the time that you specify is invalid, as in

```
C:\> TIME 15:65:00   <ENTER>
```

TIME will display an error message and reprompt you for the time:

```
Invalid time
Enter new time:
```

Messages

Invalid time
Enter new time:

The time that you have typed in is invalid. Simply enter a new time in the format *hh:mm:ss.nnn* and press ENTER. TIME only requires you to enter the hours and minutes.

TREE

Displays directory structure

DOS refers to the directories on your disk as the directory tree. The TREE command displays all of the directories on your disk and, optionally, the files each directory contains.

Format

```
TREE [drive:] [path] [/F] [/A]
```

drive: The drive letter of the disk whose directory TREE is to display. If you don't specify a drive, TREE uses the current drive.

path   The directory at which you want TREE to begin its display. If you don't specify a directory name, TREE uses the current default.

/F   Directs TREE to display the name of each file in a directory as well.

/A   Directs TREE to display the directory tree using standard text characters instead of graphics characters. This switch requires DOS 4 or higher.

Notes

TREE is an external command that requires DOS 2.0 or later. As you begin to create more directories on your disk to organize your files, you can use TREE to view a graphic representation of your directory structure. If you include the /F switch, you can direct TREE to display the names of the files in each directory, helping you determine which directories are good candidates for additional subdirectories to improve their organization.

Beginning with DOS 4, the TREE command uses graphics characters to display your directory structure.

You can use the I/O redirection operators to print your directory tree as follows.

```
C:\> TREE > PRN   <ENTER>
```

Examples

The following command displays the directory structure below the current directory.

```
C:\SUBDIR> TREE   <ENTER>
```

To display the directory tree structure for the entire disk, you must specify the root directory in TREE's command line or make sure the root is the current directory.

```
C:\SUBDIR> TREE \   <ENTER>
```

To display the files in each directory, use the /F switch:

```
C:\> TREE  C:\ /F   <ENTER>
```

Messages

No sub-directories exist

TREE is telling you that it did not find any DOS subdirectories on the disk specified. This message is purely informational.

TYPE

Displays a text file's contents

The TYPE command displays the contents of an ASCII text file on your screen.

Format

```
TYPE file_spec
```

file_spec   The complete DOS file specification for the file to be displayed. It can contain a drive letter and DOS path name.

Notes

TYPE is an internal command supported by all DOS versions. The TYPE command is restricted to ASCII files. Do not use TYPE with files containing a COM or EXE extension—these files contain characters that will cause your screen to beep and display uncommon characters.

If the file specified in the TYPE command line does not exist, TYPE will display

```
File not found - FILENAME.EXT
```

When you use the TYPE command, don't forget that you can control your output by using the MORE command

```
A> TYPE FILENAME.EXT | MORE
```

and, also, by pressing CTRL-S. When DOS encounters the CTRL-S, it will suspend scrolling of the current output. To resume scrolling, press any key.

Many word processors place embedded characters within a document that possibly direct the word processor to enable boldface type, italics, or to align margins. Although such characters are meaningful to your word processor, they are not meaningful to TYPE, which may display strange, unrecognizable characters. If you create a non-ASCII file using your word processor, you must use your word processor to view the file's contents.

TYPE only displays a file's contents. To change a file, you must use one of the DOS editors EDIT or EDLIN or use a word processor.

Examples

The following command directs TYPE to display the contents of the CONFIG.SYS file.

```
C:\> TYPE \CONFIG.SYS   <ENTER>
```

In a similar manner, the command

```
C:\> TYPE \AUTOEXEC.BAT   <ENTER>
```

directs TYPE to display the contents of the file AUTOEXEC.BAT that resides in the root directory.

UNDELETE

Recovers a previously deleted file

When you delete a file, the file actually remains on your disk until DOS overwrites the file's contents with another file. The UNDELETE command lets you recover recently deleted files. If you don't immediately recover a deleted file, the file may be overwritten by your next command, making the file's undeletion impossible.

Format

```
UNDELETE [path_name] [/LIST | /ALL] [/DT | /DOS]
```

path_name   The subdirectory path of the file or files you want to undelete. If you don't specify a path name, UNDELETE uses the current directory.

/LIST   Directs UNDELETE to list all of the files available for recovery.

/DT   Recovers only those files listed in the delete tracking (DT) file created by MIRROR.

/DOS   Recovers only those files listed by DOS as deleted. DOS will prompt you to enter the first letter of each file name.

/ALL   Recovers all of the files listed by DOS as deleted without prompting you to enter the first letter of the file. Instead, UNDELETE will assign the character # to the first letter of each file. If a file exists with the same name, UNDELETE will attempt to use, instead, the %&-0123456789A to Z characters, in that order.

Notes

UNDELETE is an external command which requires DOS version 5.

If you are recovering files using /DOS, the recovered files may contain errors due to file fragmentation. If you inadvertently delete a file, do not copy any files to the disk until you successfully recover the deleted file.

Examples

When DOS deletes a file, it replaces the first character in the file's name with a special symbol. To recover a file, UNDELETE may ask you to type in the file's original first character. For example, the following command directs UNDELETE to undelete the file DOSKEY.COM.

```
C:\TESTDIR> UNDELETE  DOSKEY.COM   <ENTER>


Directory: C:\TESTDIR
File Specifications: DOSKEY.COM

   Deletion-Tracking file not found.

   MS-DOS Directory contains    1 deleted files.
   Of those,   1 files may be recovered.

 Using the MS-DOS Directory.

    ?OSKEY   COM     5693 12-13-90  4:09a  ...A  Undelete (Y/N)?
```

Typing **Y** directs UNDELETE to undelete this file. UNDELETE will prompt you for the first letter of the file name. Type **D**, and UNDELETE will recover the file:

```
Please type the first character for ?OSKEY   .COM: D

File successfully undeleted.
```

The following UNDELETE command displays the names of all files available for recovery in the current directory.

```
C:\> UNDELETE /LIST /ALL   <ENTER>
```

If you have enabled file delete tracking with MIRROR, UNDELETE will use the information MIRROR has saved.

The following command undeletes all of the recoverable files in the current directory based on delete-tracking information.

```
C:\> UNDELETE *.* /DT   <ENTER>
```

Similarly, the following command undeletes all of the recoverable files in the current directory using only DOS file information.

```
C:\> UNDELETE *.* /DOS   <ENTER>
```

Messages

Cannot operate on the specified drive

You are probably trying to access a network drive. Like most disk utilities, UNDELETE does not support network drives.

Cannot operate on a SUBST drive

The disk drive specified in the command line is a logical drive created by the SUBST command. UNDELETE only supports physical disk drives.

Cannot specify both /DT and /DOS

Your UNDELETE command line is attempting to access files marked as deleted by the delete-tracking file and DOS. To recover all files, use the /ALL switch.

Deletion tracking file not found

Your UNDELETE command line contained the /DT switch, and UNDELETE does not have delete-tracking information available. You must use the /DOS switch and attempt to restore the files as recorded by DOS.

Only some of the clusters for this file are available.
Do you want to recover this file with only the available
clusters? (Y/N)

UNDELETE is telling you that part of the file specified has been overwritten on disk. UNDELETE can, however, restore part of the file. If you want UNDELETE to restore as much of the file as it can, type Y. If you want UNDELETE to ignore the file, type N.

The file cannot be recovered

The file specified has been overwritten on disk and cannot be recovered. You must locate your backup copy of the file.

Please type the first character for FILENAME.EXT

UNDELETE is attempting to recover the file specified and needs you to type in the original first character of the file name.

All of the clusters for the file are available. Undelete (Y/N)?

UNDELETE is informing you that the file is fully recoverable. If you want to recover the file, type Y. If you don't want to recover the file, type N.

UNFORMAT

Restores an erased or formatted disk

UNFORMAT is a DOS 5 command that works in conjunction with the MIRROR command to rebuild an accidentally formatted disk or a disk damaged by an inadvertent RECOVER.

Format

```
UNFORMAT drive: [/J]
```

or

```
UNFORMAT drive: [/L] [/TEST] [/U] [/P]
```

or

```
UNFORMAT drive: [/L] [/PARTN]
```

drive: The drive letter of the disk to rebuild.

/J   Directs UNFORMAT to verify the current root directory and file allocation table to match the last file created by MIRROR. This qualifier does not rebuild the disk.

/L   Directs UNFORMAT to list each file and subdirectory it finds.

/TEST   Directs UNFORMAT to display how it will rebuild the disk, without actually rebuilding the disk.

/PARTN   Directs rebuild to restore a corrupted partition table using the file that MIRROR previously recorded to a floppy disk.

/U   Directs UNFORMAT to unformat the disk without using the MIRROR's disk information file.

/P   Directs UNFORMAT to send its messages to the printer and the screen, generating a log file.

Notes

UNFORMAT is an external command that requires DOS 5. UNFORMAT cannot restore a disk formatted with the /U option.

UNFORMAT will always attempt to use the information previously stored by the MIRROR command. If the MIRROR file is not available or is very old, you can direct UNFORMAT with the /U switch to try to recover the disk using only the current file allocation table and root directory. This method, however, is much less reliable. The more often you invoke MIRROR, the greater your chance of successfully unformatting your disk. Using the /J switch, you can direct UNFORMAT to compare the current disk contents to the information recorded in MIRROR's file. If differences exist, invoke MIRROR to update the file. When you use the /J switch,

UNFORMAT does not unformat the disk. If a file is fragmented (stored in locations dispersed across your disk), UNFORMAT may not be able to fully recover the file's contents. As a result, UNFORMAT will ask if it should truncate the file, giving you as much of the file as it can, or if it should delete the file.

If the file is an ASCII file whose contents you can edit, direct UNFORMAT to truncate the file. If the file contains a program or command, direct UNFORMAT to delete it, because you would not want to execute a partial program. The UNFORMAT /PARTN switch lets you recover a damaged partition table using information previously saved by MIRROR.

Examples

The following UNFORMAT command uses the /J switch to verify that the information in the file saved by MIRROR matches the current disk contents.

```
C:\> UNFORMAT C: /J   <ENTER>
```

If the file matches your disk, UNFORMAT will display the following.

```
The system area of drive C has been verified
to agree with the MIRROR image file.
```

If differences exist, UNFORMAT will display

```
The system area does NOT agree with the MIRROR image file.
```

If differences exist between MIRROR's file and your disk, invoke MIRROR to bring the file up to date.

The following command uses UNFORMAT to restore a corrupted partition table for drive C.

```
A> UNFORMAT C: /PARTN   <ENTER>
```

In this case, UNFORMAT will prompt you to place the floppy disk containing the correct partition table information saved by MIRROR into a floppy drive.

The following UNFORMAT command uses the /TEST qualifier to determine if UNFORMAT can rebuild a formatted floppy disk in drive A.

```
C:\> UNFORMAT A: /TEST   <ENTER>
```

Messages

Cannot process network drive

The drive specified in the UNFORMAT command line is a network drive. Like most disk utilities, UNFORMAT does not support network drives.

Are you sure you want to do this?
If so type Y; anything else cancels.

UNFORMAT is giving you the opportunity to cancel the current operation. UNFORMAT normally displays this message before it performs an operation that will actually update your disk. To continue the operation, type Y and press ENTER. To cancel the operation, type anything but Y.

CAUTION!! This attempts to recover all the files lost after
a format assuming you've not been using the MIRROR command. This
method cannot guarantee complete recovery of your files.

Your UNFORMAT command line probably contains the /L qualifier that disables UNFORMAT's use of the file MIRROR.FIL created by the MIRROR command. If you don't use the MIRROR file to rebuild your disk, you have a greater chance of losing files.

The LAST time the MIRROR or FORMAT command was used was at
19:32 on 06-12-91
The PRIOR time the MIRROR or FORMAT command was used was
at 11:59 on 06-12-91

If you wish to use the LAST file as indicated above, press L. If you wish
to use the prior file as indicated above, press P. Press ESC to cancel
UNFORMAT.

UNFORMAT is asking you which of MIRROR's disk information files you want to use. Each time you invoke MIRROR to save your disk's status, MIRROR renames its previous status file as MIRROR.BAK. Should you later need to UNFORMAT your disk, UNFORMAT lets you select the current or previous file. Type **L** to use the latest file or **P** to use the previous file.

FILENAME.EXT *nnn* 12-25-90 8:30p.m. ONLY *nnn* bytes are recoverable Truncate or Delete this file?

The file specified is truncated, and UNFORMAT can only recover a portion of it. UNFORMAT is asking you if you want it to recover as much of the file as it can or if you want it to delete the file. If the file is an ASCII file whose contents you can edit, type **T** directing UNFORMAT to truncate the file. If the file is an executable program, type **D**, directing UNFORMAT to delete the partial file.

VER

Displays the DOS version number

The VER command displays the current DOS version number.

Format

```
VER
```

Notes

VER is an internal command that requires DOS 2.0 or later. DOS version numbers are comprised of a major and minor version number. For example, DOS 5.0 has a major version number of 5 and a minor version number of 0.

Example

The following command directs VER to display the current version number:

```
C:\> VER   <ENTER>
```

For DOS 3.3, the output is

```
IBM Personal Computer DOS Version  3.30
```

For DOS 5, the output is

```
MS-DOS Version 5.00
```

VERIFY

Enables or disables disk verification

Periodically, a disk drive may not correctly record the information on disk as DOS intended. Although that is rare, such occurrences can leave incorrect data on your disk. If you enable disk I/O verification by issuing the VERIFY command, DOS will double-check the data it writes to disk by comparing it with the original data.

If a discrepancy exists, DOS will detect it. However, because DOS must compare each sector that it writes to disk, disk verification causes significant system overhead (that is, slows down the speed of operation).

Format

```
VERIFY [ON | OFF]
```

ON   Enables DOS disk verification.

OFF   Disables DOS disk verification.

Notes

VERIFY is an internal DOS command that requires DOS 2.0 or later. If you invoke VERIFY without a command-line parameter, it will display its current state, ON or OFF.

The VERIFY command ensures that DOS is successfully recording all the information it is writing to disk. VERIFY does this by comparing each disk sector, immediately after it is written, to the actual information that should have been recorded. If a difference exists, DOS knows that it has recorded data incorrectly.

Although this seems to be a good idea, such disk errors are very rare. VERIFY is increasing the overhead on your system by writing and comparing multiple sectors. Most users should use the default value of

```
A> VERIFY OFF
```

Remember, beginning with DOS 3.3, you can use the /V switch with the COPY and XCOPY commands to enable disk verification for the duration of the copy operation.

```
A> COPY FILENAME.EXT B: /V
```

DOS will verify the contents of the file as it is recorded to disk.

Examples

The following command enables disk I/O verification:

```
C:\> VERIFY ON    <ENTER>
```

Invoking VERIFY without command-line parameters causes VERIFY to display its current state:

```
C:\> VERIFY    <ENTER>
VERIFY is on
```

Messages

Must specify ON or OFF

You have invoked the VERIFY command specifying a command-line parameter other than ON or OFF. Reissue the command with no command-line parameters (to display the current verify setting), or with either ON (enable disk verification) or OFF (disable disk verification).

VOL

Displays a disk volume label

The VOL command displays a disk volume label (or name) for the drive specified. A DOS volume label is an 11-character name assigned to a disk.

Format

```
VOL [drive:]
```

drive: The disk drive that contains the disk for which VOL is to display the disk volume label. If you do not specify this parameter, VOL will use the current drive.

Notes

VOL is an internal command that requires DOS 2.0 or later. Disk labels can consist of the same characters as DOS file names, although some DOS versions support spaces (blank characters). To assign a volume label, use the LABEL command or the FORMAT command (for unused disks).

If you are using DOS 4 or later, the VOL command also displays the disk's optional serial number.

Example

In the following example, VOL displays the disk volume label of the disk contained in the current drive:

```
C:\> VOL   <ENTER>

Volume in drive C is DOSDISK
```

If you are using DOS 4 or later, VOL will also display the disk serial number:

```
C:\> VOL   <ENTER>

 Volume in drive C is DOS
 Volume Serial Number is 4E13-1342
```

Messages

Volume in drive *n* has no label

VOL is simply telling you that DOS has never assigned a label to the disk in the drive specified. To assign a label to a disk, use the LABEL command.

XCOPY

Copies source files and subdirectories to a target disk

The XCOPY command copies one or more files providing extended capabilities not available with the COPY command.

Format

```
XCOPY source_file_spec [target_file_spec] [/A | /M] [/D:mm-dd-yy]
    [/E] [/P] [/V] [/S] [/W]
```

source_file_spec   The complete DOS file specification for the source files to be copied by XCOPY. XCOPY supports DOS wildcards.

target_file_spec   The destination name for the files copied by XCOPY. XCOPY supports DOS wildcards.

/A   Directs XCOPY to copy only files that have the archive bit set.

/D:*mm-dd-yy*   Directs XCOPY to copy only those files created since the specified date.

/E   Directs XCOPY to place subdirectories on the target disk if the subdirectory is currently empty.

/M   Functions like the /A switch; however, /M directs XCOPY to clear each file's archive bit as it copies the file.

/P   Directs XCOPY to prompt "FILENAME.EXT (Y/N)?" before copying each file.

/V   Directs XCOPY to compare the contents of the target file and the source file to verify that the file copy was successful.

/S Directs XCOPY to copy the contents of lower-level subdirectories to the target location.

/W Directs XCOPY to prompt "Press any key to begin copying file(s)" before beginning.

Notes

XCOPY is an external command that requires DOS 3.2 or later. XCOPY copies source files and subdirectories to a target destination, and provides many more capabilities than COPY.

XCOPY lets you copy the files in a directory and within lower-level directories and lets you perform selective file copies based on a file's archive attribute or date and time stamp. In fact, many users invoke XCOPY to perform simple backup operations.

If you are using XCOPY within a DOS batch file, XCOPY provides the following exit status values.

Exit Status	Meaning
0	Files successfully copied
1	No files found to copy
2	User termination via CTRL-C
4	Insufficient memory, invalid disk or invalid syntax
5	Fatal disk write error prevented copy

Examples

The following XCOPY command copies the files in the current directory of drive C to the disk in drive A. Using the /S switch, the command creates an identical copy of the directory on the floppy drive, including all of the files in subdirectories below the directory.

```
C:\SOMEDIR> XCOPY *.*  A:\ /S  <ENTER>
```

This command modifies the previous command, using the /A switch to only copy those file's whose archive bit is set.

```
C:\SOMEDIR> XCOPY *.*  A:\ /S /A  <ENTER>
```

If you use /M instead of /A, XCOPY will clear the archive bit of each file it successfully copies.

The following command copies all of the files in the current directory that have been created or modified since June 30, 1991, to the disk in drive A.

```
C:\> XCOPY *.* /D:6/30/91 A:    <ENTER>
```

To use XCOPY to copy the entire directory contents on a hard disk to floppy disks, first set the attribute of each file in the hard disk directory to indicate each requires a backup, as shown here:

```
C:\> ATTRIB +A *.* /S   <ENTER>
```

Next, issue the command

```
C:\> XCOPY *.* A:\ /M /E /S   <ENTER>
```

XCOPY will begin transferring files to the floppy disk, maintaining the existing disk structure. When the target disk becomes full, simply insert a new floppy disk in drive A and again invoke the command:

```
C:\> XCOPY *.* A:\ /M /E /S   <ENTER>
```

Because XCOPY clears the archive bit for each file it has successfully copied, XCOPY will continue where it left off.

Messages

drive:path\filename.ext (Y/N)?

You have invoked the XCOPY command with the /P switch, which lets you perform selective file copy operations. If you don't want to copy this file, simply respond with **N**; to copy the file, type **Y** and press ENTER.

Access denied

Either the source file specified in your XCOPY command is locked by another application, or the target file name has been marked as read-only.

Cannot perform cyclic copy

Your XCOPY command line contains the /S switch, and your source and target specifications are such that a subdirectory specified in the target is also a subdirectory in the target. XCOPY will read from the subdirectory, writing files back to the directory.

**Does *FILENAME* specify a file name
or directory name on the target
(F=file, D=directory)?**

XCOPY could not determine if the target of the file copy operation is supposed to be a file name or directory. If you want XCOPY to write all of the information to a file, simply type **F** and press ENTER. If you want XCOPY to create a subdirectory, type **D** and press ENTER.

Exit Status Values

This appendix lists the exit status values DOS commands provide for use with IF ERRORLEVEL in your batch files.

BACKUP

Status Value	Meaning
0	Successful backup operation
1	No files found to back up
2	File-sharing conflicts prevented a complete backup
3	Backup operation ended by user CTRL-C
4	Backup operation ended due to fatal error

DISKCOMP

Status Value	Meaning
0	Disks are the same
1	Disks are not the same
2	Comparison ended by user CTRL-C
3	Comparison ended due to fatal disk error
4	Initialization error prevented comparison

DISKCOPY

Status Value	Meaning
0	Successful disk copy operation
1	Non-fatal disk read/write error
2	Disk copy operation ended by user CTRL-C
3	Disk copy ended due to fatal processing error
4	Initialization error prevented copy operation

FORMAT

Status Value	Meaning
0	Successful format operation
3	Format process ended by user CTRL-C
4	Format process ended due to fatal processing error
5	Format processes ended by user at the prompt "Proceed with Format (Y/N)?"

GRAFTABL

Status Value	Meaning
0	Character set successfully loaded
1	Previously loaded character set replaced
2	File access error prevented character set loading
3	Invalid command-line parameter prevented character set loading
4	Incorrect DOS version

KEYB

Status Value	Meaning
0	Keyboard template successfully loaded
1	Invalid keyboard code, code page, or command syntax prevented template loading
2	Keyboard definition file was not found

4   Error accessing CON device prevented template loading
5   Requested code page was not previously prepared

REPLACE

Status Value	Meaning
0	Successful file replacement
2	Source files not found
3	Source or destination directory path not found
5	Access to destination file denied
8	Insufficient RAM to execute REPLACE
11	Invalid command-line syntax
15	Invalid disk drive specified
22	Incorrect DOS version (not provided by MS-DOS)

RESTORE

Status Value	Meaning
0	Successful file restoration
1	No files found to restore
2	File sharing conflict prevented complete restoration (not provided by MS-DOS)
3	Restore operation ended by user CTRL-C
4	Restore operation ended by fatal error

SETVER

Status Value	Meaning
0	Successful version assignment
1	Invalid command switch
2	Invalid file name specified
3	Insufficient RAM for SETVER to execute
4	Invalid version number specified
5	Entry specified not found in version table
6	System files not found

7	Invalid drive letter specified
8	Too many command-line parameters specified
9	One or more command-line parameters missing
10	Error reading system files
11	System file version table is corrupt
12	System files specified don't support a version table
13	Insufficient version table space for new entry
14	Error writing to system files

XCOPY

Status Value	Meaning
0	Successful file copy operation
1	No files found to copy
2	File copy operation terminated by user CTRL-C
4	Initialization error prevented file copy operation
5	Disk write error during copy operation

ASCII and Extended ASCII Character Sets

Dec	Hex	ASCII Symbol	Control Code	Ctrl Key	Dec	Hex	ASCII Symbol	Control Code	Ctrl Key
0	00		NUL	^@	16	10	▶	DLE	^P
1	01	☺	SOH	^A	17	11	◀	DC1	^Q
2	02	☻	STX	^B	18	12	↕	DC2	^R
3	03	♥	ETX	^C	19	13	‼	DC3	^S
4	04	♦	EOT	^D	20	14	¶	DC4	^T
5	05	♣	ENQ	^E	21	15	§	NAK	^U
6	06	♠	ACK	^F	22	16	▬	SYN	^V
7	07	•	BEL	^G	23	17	↨	ETB	^W
8	08	◘	BS	^H	24	18	↑	CAN	^X
9	09	○	HT	^I	25	19	↓	EM	^Y
10	0A	◙	LF	^J	26	1A	→	SUB	^Z
11	0B	♂	VT	^K	27	1B	←	ESC	^[
12	0C	♀	FF	^L	28	1C	∟	FS	^\
13	0D	♪	CR	^M	29	1D	↔	GS	^]
14	0E	♫	SO	^N	30	1E	▲	RS	^^
15	0F	☼	SI	^O	31	1F	▼	US	^_

Dec	Hex	ASCII Symbol	Dec	Hex	ASCII Symbol
32	20		72	48	H
33	21	!	73	49	I
34	22	"	74	4A	J
35	23	#	75	4B	K
36	24	$	76	4C	L
37	25	%	77	4D	M
38	26	&	78	4E	N
39	27	'	79	4F	O
40	28	(	80	50	P
41	29	)	81	51	Q
42	2A	*	82	52	R
43	2B	+	83	53	S
44	2C	,	84	54	T
45	2D	-	85	55	U
46	2E	.	86	56	V
47	2F	/	87	57	W
48	30	0	88	58	X
49	31	1	89	59	Y
50	32	2	90	5A	Z
51	33	3	91	5B	[
52	34	4	92	5C	\
53	35	5	93	5D	]
54	36	6	94	5E	^
55	37	7	95	5F	_
56	38	8	96	60	`
57	39	9	97	61	a
58	3A	:	98	62	b
59	3B	;	99	63	c
60	3C	<	100	64	d
61	3D	=	101	65	e
62	3E	>	102	66	f
63	3F	?	103	67	g
64	40	@	104	68	h
65	41	A	105	69	i
66	42	B	106	6A	j
67	43	C	107	6B	k
68	44	D	108	6C	l
69	45	E	109	6D	m
70	46	F	110	6E	n
71	47	G	111	6F	o

Dec	Hex	ASCII Symbol	Dec	Hex	ASCII Symbol
112	70	p	152	98	ÿ
113	71	q	153	99	Ö
114	72	r	154	9A	Ü
115	73	s	155	9B	¢
116	74	t	156	9C	£
117	75	u	157	9D	¥
118	76	v	158	9E	Pt
119	77	w	159	9F	ƒ
120	78	x	160	A0	á
121	79	y	161	A1	í
122	7A	z	162	A2	ó
123	7B	{	163	A3	ú
124	7C	|	164	A4	ñ
125	7D	}	165	A5	Ñ
126	7E	˜	166	A6	ª
127	7F	⌂	167	A7	º
128	80	Ç	168	A8	¿
129	81	ü	169	A9	⌐
130	82	é	170	AA	¬
131	83	â	171	AB	½
132	84	ä	172	AC	¼
133	85	à	173	AD	¡
134	86	å	174	AE	<<
135	87	ç	175	AF	>>
136	88	ê	176	B0	▓
137	89	ë	177	B1	▓
138	8A	è	178	B2	▓
139	8B	ï	179	B3	│
140	8C	î	180	B4	┤
141	8D	ì	181	B5	╡
142	8E	Ä	182	B6	╢
143	8F	Å	183	B7	╖
144	90	É	184	B8	╕
145	91	æ	185	B9	╣
146	92	Æ	186	BA	║
147	93	ô	187	BB	╗
148	94	ö	188	BC	╝
149	95	ò	189	BD	╜
150	96	û	190	BE	╛
151	97	ù	191	BF	┐

Dec	Hex	ASCII Symbol	Dec	Hex	ASCII Symbol
192	C0	└	224	E0	α
193	C1	┴	225	E1	β
194	C2	┬	226	E2	Γ
195	C3	├	227	E3	π
196	C4	─	228	E4	Σ
197	C5	┼	229	E5	σ
198	C6	╞	230	E6	μ
199	C7	╟	231	E7	τ
200	C8	╚	232	E8	φ
201	C9	╔	233	E9	θ
202	CA	╩	234	EA	Ω
203	CB	╦	235	EB	δ
204	CC	╠	236	EC	∞
205	CD	═	237	ED	∅
206	CE	╬	238	EE	∈
207	CF	╧	239	EF	∩
208	D0	╨	240	F0	≡
209	D1	╤	241	F1	±
210	D2	╥	242	F2	≥
211	D3	╙	243	F3	≤
212	D4	╘	244	F4	⌠
213	D5	╒	245	F5	⌡
214	D6	╓	246	F6	÷
215	D7	╫	247	F7	≈
216	D8	╪	248	F8	°
217	D9	┘	249	F9	•
218	DA	┌	250	FA	·
219	DB	█	251	FB	√
220	DC	▄	252	FC	η
221	DD	▌	253	FD	2
222	DE	▐	254	FE	■
223	DF	▀	255	FF	

DOS 4 and DOS 5
Shell Menu Maps

Just as the TREE command can render the sometimes complex directory structure of your disk clearer by using a graphical representation, so this section will use graphical maps to help you more clearly understand the command structure of the DOS 4 and DOS 5 shell menu options.

Figure C-1 shows the command structure of the DOS 4 shell.

Figure C-2 shows the command structure of the DOS 5 shell.

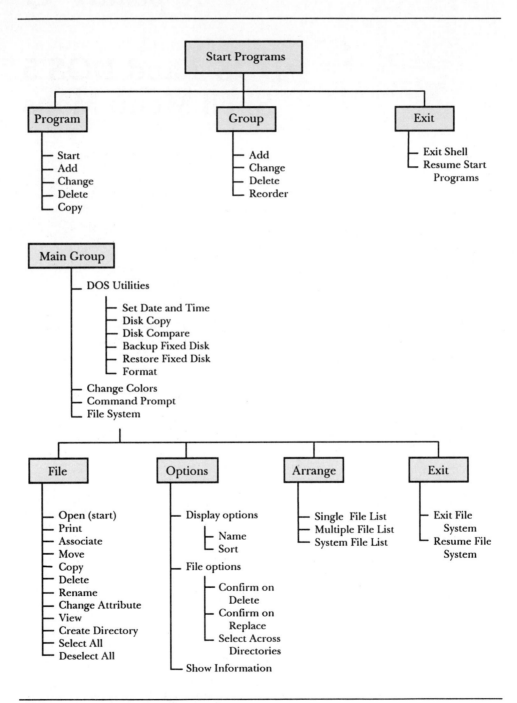

Figure C-1. *DOS 4 Shell menu map*

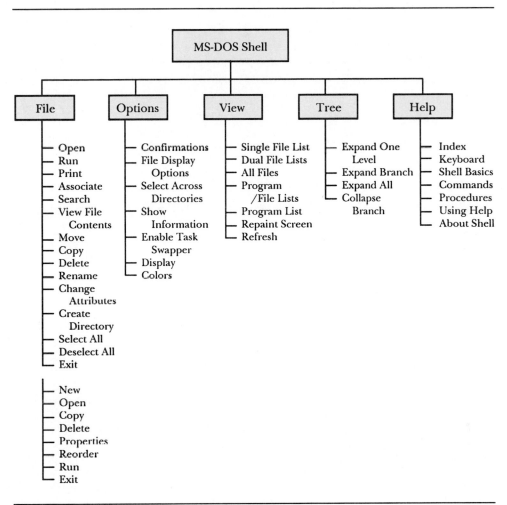

Figure C-2.   DOS 5 Shell menu map

International
Keyboard Templates
and Code Pages

Keyboard Layouts

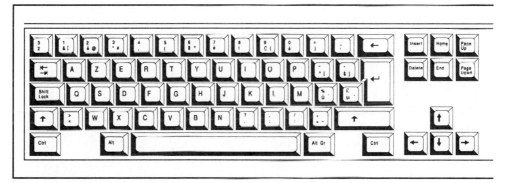

Belgium

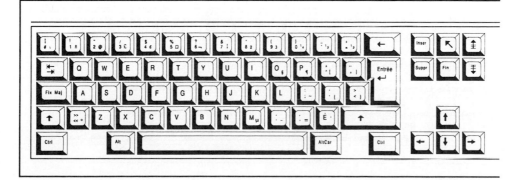

Canada

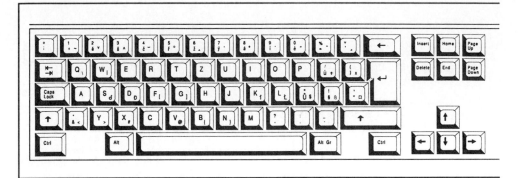

Czechoslovakia (Czech)

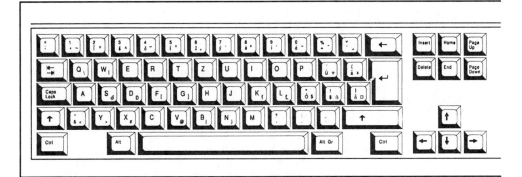

Czechoslovakia (Slovak)

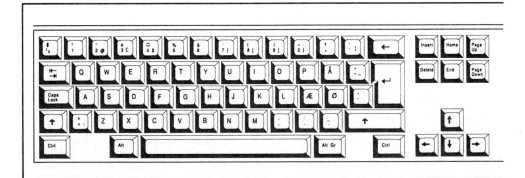

Denmark

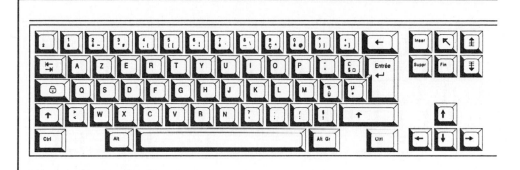

France

Germany

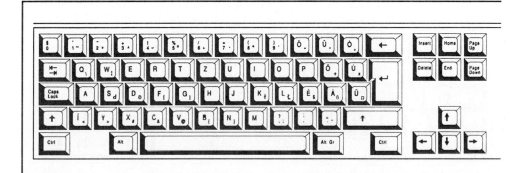

Hungary

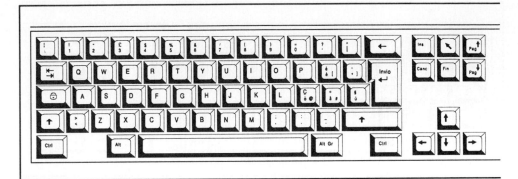

Italy

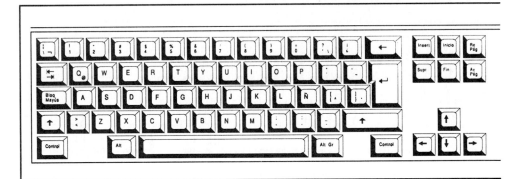

Latin America

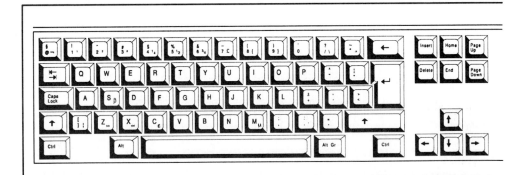

Netherlands

Norway

Poland

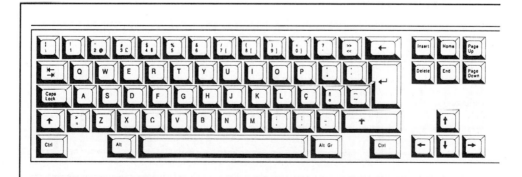

Portugal

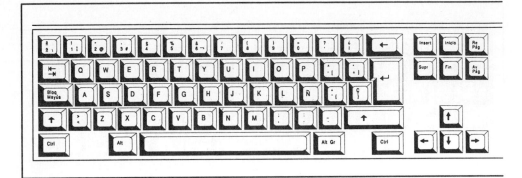

Spain

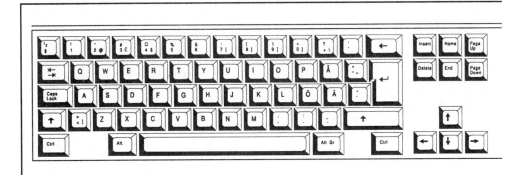

Sweden/Finland

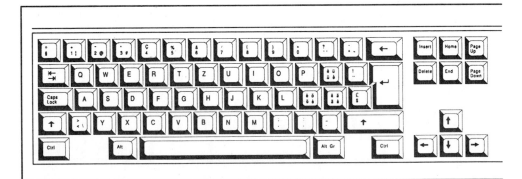

Switzerland

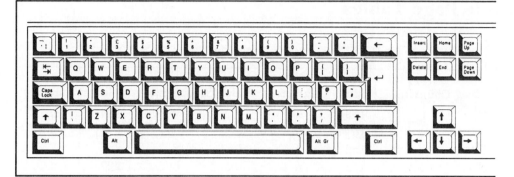

United Kingdom

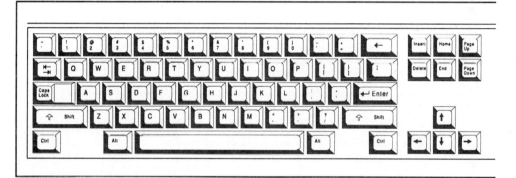

United States

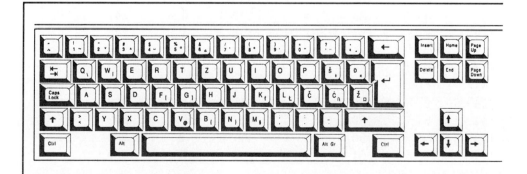

Yugoslavia

Code Page Tables

Value	Character	Value	Character	Value	Character	Value	Character
128	Ç	160	á	192	∟	224	α
129	ü	161	í	193	⊥	225	β
130	é	162	ó	194	⊤	226	Γ
131	â	163	ú	195	├	227	π
132	ä	164	ñ	196	─	228	Σ
133	à	165	Ñ	197	┼	229	σ
134	å	166	ª	198	╟	230	μ
135	ç	167	º	199	╟	231	τ
136	ê	168	¿	200	╚	232	φ
137	ë	169	⌐	201	╔	233	θ
138	è	170	¬	202	╩	234	Ω
139	ï	171	½	203	╦	235	δ
140	î	172	¼	204	╠	236	∞
141	ì	173	¡	205	═	237	ø
142	Ä	174	<<	206	╬	238	∈
143	Å	175	>>	207	╧	239	∩
144	É	176	▓	208	╨	240	≡
145	æ	177	▓	209	╤	241	±
146	Æ	178	▓	210	╥	242	≥
147	ô	179	│	211	╙	243	≤
148	ö	180	┤	212	╘	244	⌠
149	ò	181	╡	213	╒	245	⌡
150	û	182	╢	214	╓	246	÷
151	ù	183	╖	215	╫	247	≈
152	Ÿ	184	╕	216	╪	248	°
153	Ö	185	╣	217	┘	249	•
154	Ü	186	║	218	┌	250	·
155	¢	187	╗	219	█	251	√
156	£	188	╝	220	▄	252	η
157	¥	189	╜	221	▌	253	2
158	Pt	190	╛	222	▐	254	■
159	ƒ	191	┐	223	▀	255	

Table D-1.   *Code Page 437, United States*

Code Page Tables (*continued*)

Value	Character	Value	Character	Value	Character	Value	Character
128	Ç	160	á	192	∟	224	Ó
129	ü	161	í	193	┴	225	ß
130	é	162	ó	194	┬	226	Ô
131	â	163	ú	195	├	227	Ò
132	ä	164	ñ	196	─	228	õ
133	à	165	Ñ	197	┼	229	Õ
134	å	166	ª	198	ã	230	µ
135	ç	167	º	199	Ã	231	Þ
136	ê	168	¿	200	╚	232	þ
137	ë	169	®	201	╔	233	Ú
138	è	170	¬	202	╩	234	Û
139	ï	171	½	203	╦	235	Ù
140	î	172	¼	204	╠	236	ý
141	ì	173	¡	205	═	237	Ý
142	Ä	174	<<	206	╬	238	¯
143	Å	175	>>	207	¤	239	´
144	É	176	▒	208	ð	240	
145	æ	177	▓	209	Đ	241	±
146	Æ	178	█	210	Ê	242	‗
147	ô	179	│	211	Ë	243	¾
148	ö	180	┤	212	È	244	¶
149	ò	181	Á	213	ı	245	§
150	û	182	Â	214	Í	246	÷
151	ù	183	À	215	Î	247	¸
152	ÿ	184	©	216	Ï	248	°
153	Ö	185	╣	217	┘	249	¨
154	Ü	186	║	218	┌	250	·
155	ø	187	╗	219	█	251	¹
156	£	188	╝	220	▄	252	³
157	Ø	189	¢	221	¦	253	²
158	×	190	¥	222	Ì	254	■
159	ƒ	191	┐	223	▀	255	

Table D-2.   *Code Page 850, Multilingual*

Code Page Tables (*continued*)

Value	Character	Value	Character	Value	Character	Value	Character
128	Ç	160	á	192	└	224	Ó
129	ü	161	í	193	┴	225	ß
130	é	162	ó	194	┬	226	Ô
131	â	163	ú	195	├	227	Ń
132	ä	164	A	196	─	228	ń
133	ů	165	ą	197	┼	229	ň
134	ć	166	Ž	198	Ă	230	Š
135	ç	167	ž	199	ă	231	š
136	ł	168	Ę	200	╚	232	Ŕ
137	ë	169	ę	201	╔	233	Ú
138	Ö	170		202	╩	234	ŕ
139	ö	171	ź	203	╦	235	Ü
140	î	172	Č	204	╠	236	ý
141	Ź	173	Ş	205	═	237	Ý
142	Ä	174	»	206	╬	238	ţ
143	Ć	175	«	207	¤	239	´
144	É	176	░	208	đ	240	–
145	Ĺ	177	▒	209	Đ	241	″
146	ĺ	178	▓	210	Ď	242	˛
147	ô	179	│	211	Ë	243	˜
148	ö	180	┤	212	ď	244	˘
149	Ľ	181	Á	213	Ň	245	§
150	ľ	182	Â	214	Í	246	÷
151	Ś	183	Ě	215	Î	247	˛
152	ś	184	Ş	216	ě	248	°
153	Ö	185	╣	217	┘	249	¨
154	Ü	186	║	218	┌	250	·
155	Ť	187	╗	219	█	251	ű
156	ť	188	╝	220	▄	252	Ř
157	Ł	189	Ż	221	Ţ	253	ř
158	×	190	ż	222	Ů	254	■
159	č	191	┐	223	▀	255	

Table D-3.   Code Page 852, Slavic (Latin II)

Code Page Tables (*continued*)

Value	Character	Value	Character	Value	Character	Value	Character
128	Ç	160	á	192	└	224	α
129	ü	161	í	193	┴	225	β
130	é	162	ó	194	┬	226	Γ
131	â	163	ú	195	├	227	π
132	ã	164	ñ	196	─	228	Σ
133	à	165	Ñ	197	┼	229	σ
134	Á	166	ª	198	╞	230	μ
135	ç	167	º	199	╟	231	τ
136	ê	168	¿	200	╚	232	Φ
137	Ê	169	Ò	201	╔	233	θ
138	è	170	¬	202	╩	234	Ω
139	ì	171	½	203	╦	235	δ
140	Ô	172	¼	204	╠	236	∞
141	ì	173	¡	205	═	237	ø
142	Ã	174	<<	206	╬	238	∈
143	Â	175	>>	207	╧	239	∩
144	É	176	▒	208	╨	240	≡
145	À	177	▓	209	╤	241	±
146	È	178	█	210	╥	242	≥
147	ô	179	│	211	╙	243	≤
148	õ	180	┤	212	╘	244	⌠
149	ò	181	╡	213	╒	245	⌡
150	Ú	182	╢	214	╓	246	÷
151	ù	183	╖	215	╫	247	≈
152	Ì	184	╕	216	╪	248	°
153	Õ	185	╣	217	┘	249	•
154	Ü	186	║	218	┌	250	·
155	¢	187	╗	219	█	251	√
156	£	188	╝	220	▄	252	η
157	Ù	189	╜	221	▌	253	²
158	Pt	190	╛	222	▐	254	■
159	Ó	191	┐	223	▀	255	

Table D-4.   Code Page 860, Portuguese

Code Page Tables (*continued*)

Value	Character	Value	Character	Value	Character	Value	Character
128	Ç	160	ı	192	∟	224	α
129	ü	161	´	193	⊥	225	β
130	é	162	ó	194	┬	226	Γ
131	â	163	ú	195	├	227	π
132	Â	164	¨	196	─	228	Σ
133	à	165	˷	197	┼	229	σ
134	¶	166	³	198	╞	230	μ
135	ç	167	¯	199	╟	231	τ
136	ê	168	Î	200	╚	232	Φ
137	ë	169	⌐	201	╔	233	θ
138	è	170	¬	202	╩	234	Ω
139	ï	171	½	203	╦	235	δ
140	î	172	¼	204	╠	236	∞
141	═	173	¾	205	═	237	ø
142	À	174	<<	206	╬	238	∈
143	§	175	>>	207	╧	239	∩
144	É	176	▓	208	╨	240	≡
145	È	177	▒	209	╤	241	±
146	Ê	178	▓	210	╥	242	≥
147	ô	179	│	211	╙	243	≤
148	Ë	180	┤	212	╘	244	⌠
149	Ï	181	╡	213	╒	245	⌡
150	û	182	╢	214	╓	246	÷
151	ú	183	╖	215	╫	247	≈
152	¤	184	╕	216	╪	248	°
153	Ô	185	╣	217	┘	249	•
154	Ü	186	║	218	┌	250	·
155	¢	187	╗	219	█	251	√
156	£	188	╝	220	▄	252	η
157	Ù	189	╜	221	▌	253	²
158	Û	190	╛	222	▐	254	■
159	ƒ	191	┐	223	▀	255	

Table D-5.   *Code Page 863, French Canadian*

Code Page Tables (*continued*)

Value	Character	Value	Character	Value	Character	Value	Character
128	Ç	160	á	192	└	224	α
129	ü	161	í	193	┴	225	β
130	é	162	ó	194	┬	226	Γ
131	â	163	ú	195	├	227	π
132	ä	164	ñ	196	─	228	Σ
133	à	165	Ñ	197	┼	229	σ
134	å	166	ª	198	╞	230	μ
135	ç	167	º	199	╟	231	τ
136	ê	168	¿	200	╚	232	Φ
137	ë	169	⌐	201	╔	233	θ
138	è	170	¬	202	╩	234	Ω
139	ï	171	½	203	╦	235	δ
140	î	172	¼	204	╠	236	∞
141	ì	173	¡	205	═	237	ø
142	Ä	174	<<	206	╬	238	∈
143	Å	175	¤	207	╧	239	∩
144	É	176	▒	208	╨	240	≡
145	æ	177	▓	209	╤	241	±
146	Æ	178	█	210	╥	242	≥
147	ô	179	│	211	╙	243	≤
148	ö	180	┤	212	╘	244	⌠
149	ò	181	╡	213	╒	245	⌡
150	û	182	╢	214	╓	246	÷
151	ú	183	╖	215	╫	247	≈
152	ÿ	184	╕	216	╪	248	°
153	Ö	185	╣	217	┘	249	•
154	Ü	186	║	218	┌	250	·
155	ø	187	╗	219	█	251	√
156	£	188	╝	220	▄	252	η²
157	Ø	189	╜	221	▌	253	
158	Pt	190	╛	222	▐	254	■
159	ƒ	191	┐	223	▀	255	

Table D-6.   Code Page 865, Norwegian

Installing DOS
Version 4

Depending upon whether or not your hard disk currently contains files, the steps you must follow to install DOS 4 on your disk will differ.

Installing DOS 4 on a New Disk

If you are installing DOS 4 on a new disk, you may need to perform the following steps before starting the DOS 4 installation.

1. Use your computer's Setup program to update your computer's CMOS settings about your hard disk.

2. Partition the hard disk using FDISK, as discussed in Chapter 45.

3. Format your hard disk using the DOS 4 FORMAT command.

If you need to partition your hard disk, place the DOS 4 disk labeled "Install" in drive A and turn on your computer. Your screen will display the following message.

```
Insert SELECT diskette in drive A:

Press Enter to continue installing DOS,
or press Esc to exit.
```

Press ESC to exit the installation to the A> prompt. Invoke FDISK and partition your disk, as discussed in Chapter 45.

```
A> FDISK   <ENTER>
```

When you finish partitioning your disk, your system will restart. Press ESC to exit to the A> prompt as before. Invoke the FORMAT command to prepare your hard disk for use as follows.

```
A> FORMAT   C:  /S   <ENTER>
```

When the FORMAT completes, you are ready to perform the DOS 4 installation. Continue your reading at the section titled "Performing the Installation."

Installing DOS 4 on a System Currently in Use

If your disk contains a previous version of DOS, you need to first back up the files on your disk to floppy disks before continuing. You may want to review Chapter 22 for specifics on the BACKUP command. Use the following command to back up your entire hard disk to floppy disks in drive A.

```
C:\> BACKUP   C:\*.*   A:   <ENTER>
```

If your backup operation successfully completes, you are ready to continue. If BACKUP is not successful, do not continue the DOS 4 installation until you completely back up your hard disk.

Changing Your Existing Partitions

DOS 4 increases the maximum disk partition size from 32Mb to 512Mb. Depending on your disk size, you may want to change your disk's current partitions. If you plan to change your partition size, first back up every partition on your disk. Next, place the DOS 4 disk labeled "Install" in drive A and restart your computer. When Install displays the following message

```
Insert SELECT diskette in drive A:

Press Enter to continue installing DOS,
or press Esc to exit.
```

press ESC to exit to the A> prompt and invoke FDISK, selecting your desired partition sizes, as discussed in Chapter 45.

```
A> FDISK   <ENTER>
```

When FDISK completes, your system will restart. Press ESC to exit to the A> prompt and issue the following FORMAT command.

```
A> FORMAT  C:/S  <ENTER>
```

When FORMAT completes, you are ready to continue the installation.

Performing the Installation

Place the DOS 4 disk labeled "Install" in drive A and restart your computer. After your computer restarts, your screen will display the following message.

```
Insert SELECT diskette in drive A:

Press Enter to continue installing DOS,
or press Esc to exit.
```

Place the disk labeled "Select" into drive A and press ENTER to continue the installation. Your screen will display the following message.

```
                      Continuing Installation


Insert INSTALL diskette in drive A
```

Place the Install disk back in drive A and press ENTER. Your screen will display the following message, informing you that the installation requires one 5 1/4- or one 3 1/2-inch disk to hold temporary installation files.

```
                              Welcome

Welcome to DOS 4.0 and the SELECT program. SELECT will install
DOS 4.0 on your fixed disk or diskette.
If you install DOS 4.0 on a diskette, the number of
blank diskettes you need depends on the type and
capacity of your diskette drive:

   Drive Type (Capacity)       Number of Diskettes

   5.25-Inch Drive (360KB)     five  5.25 (360KB)
   5.25-Inch Drive (1.2MB)     five  5.25 (360KB)
   3.5-Inch Drive (720KB)      three 3.5  (720KB)
   3.5-Inch Drive (1.44MB)     three 3.5  (720KB)

If you install DOS 4.0 onto a fixed disk, you need
one blank diskette:

   5.25-Inch Drive             one   5.25 (360KB)
   3.5-Inch Drive              one   3.5  (1 or 2MB)

   Press Enter (<-) to continue or Esc to Cancel
```

Press ENTER to continue the installation. Your screen will display the following message describing the different keys you can use throughout the installation.

```
                           Introduction

As you view the SELECT displays, you will be asked to make a
choice or type an entry. If you are uncertain about what to
choose or type you can accept the predefined choice or press the
F1 help key for more information about an item.

You will be using these keys in the SELECT program:

   Enter                   To proceed to the next step.
```

```
    Esc                         To cancel the current display.
    Tab                         To move to the next entry field.
    PgUp/PgDn                   To scroll information one page at a
                                    time.
    Up/Down Arrow               To move the highlight bar to the next
                                    item.
    F1                          To view the help information.
    F3                          To exit SELECT.
    F9                          To view key assignments while viewing
                                    help.
    Left/Right Arrow            To scroll data fields horizontally
                                    to the left or right.

You can press Enter, Esc, and F1 keys when they appear on the
display.
```

When you press ENTER, your screen will display the following prompt for you to select a specific configuration.

```
                    Specify Function and Workspace

  SELECT sets up your computer to run DOS and your programs
  most efficiently based on the option you choose.

  Note: You can review the results of your choice later
  in this program.

  Choose an option:

      1. Minimum DOS function; maximum program workspace

      2. Balance DOS function with program workspace

      3. Maximum DOS function; minimum program workspace
```

If your computer has 256Kb or less, select option 1. If your computer has 256Kb to 512Kb, select option 2; if your computer has at least 512Kb, select option 3.

Your screen will now display the following message prompting you to select the U.S. keyboard and country or to select an international configuration.

```
                    Select Country and Keyboard

Predefined country............: United States          (001)
Predefined keyboard...........: None

Choose an option:

    1. Accept predefined country and keyboard

    2. Specify a different country and keyboard
```

After you make your selection, your screen will display the following message, asking whether you want to install DOS 4 on your hard disk C or on floppy.

```
                    Select Installation Drive

Choose the drive to install DOS on:

    1. C

    2. A
```

Select drive C and press ENTER. Your screen will display a message asking you to specify the directory on your hard disk within which you want DOS files to reside:

```
                     Specify DOS Location

You can accept the DOS directory name shown or type a new
directory name.

DOS Directory . . . .C:\[DOS                      ]

To select option 1 below, press Enter. To change your
option, press the tab key, highlight your choice and then
press Enter.

    1. Update all DOS files on fixed disk

    2. Copy non-system files to directory specified
```

Select the directory name C:\DOS and press ENTER. Your screen will display a message prompting you for the number of printers attached to your computer.

```
                          Number of Printers


How many printers do you have? . . . . [0]  (0-7)
```

Type in the correct number and press ENTER. Your screen will display a list of printer names. If your printer is listed, use your arrow keys to highlight it and press ENTER.

If your printer is not listed, highlight either the option Other Parallel Printer or Other Serial Printer depending on your printer type and then press ENTER. If you don't know if you are using a serial or parallel printer, turn to Chapter 13, "Printing."

If you select a parallel printer, your screen will display the message asking you to select a printer port. Most users will select the parallel port LPT1. If you select a serial printer, your screen will ask you to identify the serial port to which your printer is attached. In most cases, you will use COM1.

Your screen will display the following message, asking you if you want to accept the system configuration you just specified or if you want to review, and possibly change, one or more items.

```
                          Installation Options

SELECT defined a configuration based on the options

you chose for DOS functions and program workspace.


Choose an option:

    1. Accept configuration and continue with installation

    2. Review, change, or add installation choices
```

If you are satisfied with the configuration, select option 1 and press ENTER to continue. If you made a mistake earlier in the installation, select option 2 and correct the entry.

Next, your screen will display the following message informing you that you will soon need your unused floppy disk.

```
                    Continuing Installation

Before proceeding, SELECT needs to make a copy of
the INSTALL diskette.

During installation to a fixed disk, SELECT records
information to a diskette for later use in the
installation process. Have your blank diskette,
labeled "SELECT COPY", ready for this purpose.

For now, leave the INSTALL diskette in drive A and
press ENTER to continue.
```

Attach the gummed label "Select Copy" to the disk and keep it nearby. Press ENTER to continue. The installation will begin copying files, eventually displaying the following message for you to insert your unused Select Copy disk in drive A.

```
                    Continuing Installation


Remove the INSTALL diskette from drive A

Insert the SELECT COPY diskette in drive A
```

Place your Select Copy diskette in drive A, and press ENTER. The installation will copy files to your Select Copy disk. Eventually, the installation will prompt you to place specific disks in drive A. Insert the disk specified and press ENTER. After the files on each disk are copied to your hard disk, the installation will display the following screen.

```
                    Installation Complete

Installation of IBM DOS 4.0 is complete.


REFER TO THE "GETTING STARTED WITH DOS 4.0" BOOK
FOR INFORMATION ON USING THE DOS SHELL.


Remove all diskettes. Press Ctrl+Alt+Del to start DOS.
```

Remove the floppy disk currently in drive A and press the CTRL-ALT-DEL key combination to start DOS 4 from your hard disk.

Restoring Your Disk's Previous Files

If your disk contained files before the DOS 4 installation that you backed up to floppy disk, you can now restore those files to your hard disk.

To begin, use the following ATTRIB command to set your DOS 4 files to read-only, protecting the files from being overwritten by RESTORE.

```
C:\> ATTRIB  +R  C:\*.* /S <ENTER>
```

When the ATTRIB command completes, issue the following RESTORE command to restore your hard disk's previous files.

```
C:\> RESTORE  A:  C:\*.*  /3 /P  <ENTER>
```

The /P switch directs RESTORE to display the following prompt each time one of your older DOS files conflicts with a new DOS 4 file.

```
Warning!  File FILENAME.EXT
is a read-only file
Replace this file  (Y/N)?
```

Because you don't want your older DOS files to overwrite a new DOS file, type N. RESTORE will repeat this message for several files. Respond with N each time.

When the RESTORE command completes, issue the following command to remove the read-only attribute from your DOS files.

```
C:\> ATTRIB -R C:\DOS\*.*  <ENTER>

Your system upgrade is complete.
```

Upgrading to DOS 5

If you purchase DOS 5 with a new computer, the company that sells you the computer should install DOS on your hard disk for you. Therefore, this appendix examines the steps you must perform to upgrade from a previous DOS version to DOS 5. If your computer retailer did not install DOS 5 for you, follow the upgrade procedures provided with the documentation that accompanied your computer. Should the documentation direct you to use FDISK, turn to Chapter 45 of this book for more information. Likewise, for specifics on formatting your disk, turn to Chapter 7 or to FORMAT in the Command Reference section of this book.

Upgrading to Version 5.0

To upgrade to DOS 5.0, you must currently be using DOS version 2.11 or later, have a minimum of 512Kb of memory and at least 2.8Mb of available space on your hard disk. Use the DIR command to determine the number of free bytes your disk contains.

```
C:\> DIR   <ENTER>
```

Although the upgrade does not require you to do so, I strongly recommend you back up your entire hard disk to floppy disks before performing the upgrade or that you select the upgrade option that backs up your disk for you. To determine how many floppy disks the backup operation will require, invoke CHKDSK to determine the amount of disk space currently in use.

```
C:\> CHKDSK   <ENTER>
```

Subtract the number of bytes available from the total disk size to determine the number of bytes in use. Next, divide the number of bytes in use by the floppy disk size you intend to use to back up your disk. Table F-1 lists commonly used floppy disk sizes.

The DOS 5 upgrade provides you with an opportunity to back up your hard disk during the upgrade. If, instead, you want to back up your entire disk now, issue the following BACKUP command.

```
C:\> BACKUP  C:\*.*  A: /S  <ENTER>
```

For more information on BACKUP, turn to Chapter 22.

In addition, the upgrade creates two floppy disks to which you will attach the labels "UNINSTALL #1" and "UNINSTALL #2." Should the upgrade fail for any reason, you can use these disks to remove the DOS 5 files, restoring your previous DOS version to its original condition.

To begin the upgrade, place Disk 1 of your DOS version 5 disks in drive A and invoke SETUP.

```
C:\> A:SETUP   <ENTER>
```

SETUP displays the message shown in Figure F-1 on your screen telling you the upgrade creates the UNINSTALL disks, and that, rather than deleting the files in your existing DOS disk, SETUP renames the directory OLD_DOS.1. After you are sure the upgrade was successful and you can use your computer as required, you can remove the directory containing your previous DOS version files from your disk.

Disk	Data Capacity
360 Kb	362,496 bytes
720 Kb	730,112 bytes
1.2 Mb	1,213,952 bytes
1.44 Mb	1,457,664 bytes

Table F-1.   *Storage Capacity of Commonly Used Disks*

```
Microsoft(R) MS-DOS(R) Version 5.00

        Welcome to Setup

        Setup upgrades your original DOS files to MS-DOS version 5.0.
        During Setup you need to provide a floppy disk (or disks).
        Setup will use the disk(s) to store your original DOS files.
        Label the disk(s) as follows.

            UNINSTALL #1
            UNINSTALL #2 (if needed)

        The disk(s), which can be unformatted or newly formatted,
        must be used in drive A:.

        Setup copies some files to the Uninstall disk(s), and
        others to a directory on your hard disk called OLD_DOS.x.
        Using these files, you can restore the original DOS on your
        hard disk if you need to.



 ENTER=Continue  F1=Help  F3=Exit  F5=Remove Color
```

Figure F-1.   Setup's initial explanatory screen

To continue the upgrade, press ENTER.

Next, Setup will display the following screen, asking you if your computer is connected to a local area network.

```
    If you use a network, you will probably
    need to complete a few additional steps
    before installing MS-DOS version 5.0.

    If you use a network, press Y.
    If you do not use a network, press N.
```

If your computer is connected to local area network, type Y. Setup will display a screen directing you to review steps about upgrading your network software in Microsoft's *MS-DOS Getting Started* manual. If your computer is not connected to a network, type N to continue the upgrade. Setup will now display the screen shown in Figure F-2, providing you with an opportunity to back up your hard disk before performing the upgrade. If you did not previously back up your hard disk, do so now. If your hard disk backups are current, select the Do not back up hard disk(s) option to continue the upgrade.

Setup will now display a screen similar to Figure F-3, containing what it believes to be your current system configuration.

```
Before upgrading to MS-DOS version 5.0, Setup can back up
your hard disk(s).

Use the UP ARROW or DOWN ARROW key to select the option
you want and press ENTER.

┌─────────────────────────────────────────────────────────┐
│ Do not back up hard disk(s).                             │
│ Back up hard disk(s).                                    │
└─────────────────────────────────────────────────────────┘
```

Figure F-2.   Setup's prompt for a backup operation

If the items Setup displays are correct, press ENTER to continue. If an item is not correct, use your arrow keys to highlight the entry and press ENTER. Setup will display a list of options from which you can select the correct setting.

When the settings are correct, Setup will display the following screen, informing you that it is going to begin the upgrade.

```
Setup is ready to upgrade to MS-DOS version 5.0. If you
continue, you may not be able to interrupt Setup until it
has completed installing MS-DOS on your system.

To upgrade to MS-DOS version 5.0 now, press Y.

To exit Setup without upgrading, press F3.

To review your configuration selections, press any other key.
```

To perform the upgrade, type Y. To exit Setup without performing the upgrade, press F3.

```
Setup has determined that your system includes the
following hardware and software components.

┌─────────────────────────────────────────────────────────┐
│ DOS Type       :MS-DOS                                   │
│ DOS Path       :C:\DOS                                   │
│ MS-DOS Shell   :Do not run MS-DOS Shell on startup.      │
│ Display Type   :VGA                                      │
│ Continue Setup: The information above is correct.        │
└─────────────────────────────────────────────────────────┘

If all the items in the list are correct, press ENTER.
If you want to change an item in the list, use the UP
ARROW or DOWN ARROW key to select it.  Then press ENTER
to see alternatives for that item.
```

Figure F-3.   Setup's system configuration screen

Setup will create two disks, UNINSTALL #1 and UNINSTALL #2, you can use to remove DOS 5 from your hard disk and restore your previous DOS version. Setup will display the following screen prompting you to place the UNINSTALL #1 disk in drive A.

```
        Label a floppy disk
            UNINSTALL #1
     and insert it into drive
                A:

     When ready, press ENTER.

     WARNING:  All existing files
     on this disk will be deleted.
```

If the floppy disk you insert is not formatted, Setup will display a prompt for you to select a high- or low-density format. Select the format that corresponds to your disk. Setup will repeat this process, prompting you to place the disk UNINSTALL #2 in drive A.

Setup may now prompt you to insert the next DOS 5 disk into drive A. Place the UNINSTALL disks in a safe location. As Setup progresses, it will ask you to insert additional disks. Insert each disk as required and press ENTER. As Setup copies DOS 5 files to your hard disk, Setup will display a bar line, letting you view the percentage of the upgrade that is complete.

```
80% complete
```

When it completes the upgrade, Setup displays the following screen, telling you to remove the last floppy disk from drive A and to press any key to reboot your system in DOS 5.

```
Setup is now complete. Please remove any floppy
disks from your drives and then press ENTER to
start MS-DOS version 5.0.

NOTE:
     Your original AUTOEXEC.BAT and CONFIG.SYS
     (if any) were saved as AUTOEXEC.DAT and
     CONFIG.DAT on the Uninstall disk.
```

Remove the last floppy disk from drive A and press any key to restart your system.

When you are sure your system is working and your key programs are compatible with DOS 5, you can use the DELOLDOS command to remove your previous DOS version command files from the OLD_DOS.1 directory.

```
C:\> DELOLDOS    <ENTER>
```

DELOLDOS will display a prompt asking you to confirm the file deletion. Type Y to delete the files. When DELOLDOS completes, press any key to return to DOS. Not only does DELOLDOS delete your old DOS version files, it also deletes itself, since you won't need it again. Your system is now fully upgraded to DOS 5.

Using the UNINSTALL Disks

The DOS 5 upgrade creates the UNINSTALL disks to help you recover from an upgrade error that prevents Setup from successfully upgrading your computer to DOS 5. If you need to use the UNINSTALL disks, place the disk UNINSTALL #1 in drive A and use CTRL-ALT-DEL to restart your system. Follow the instructions that appear on your screen to restore your previous DOS version.

You can use the UNINSTALL disks to restore your previous DOS version at any time until you perform one of the following operations:

1. Delete the previous DOS command files from your hard disk using the DELOLDOS command.

2. Change the hard disk partition.

3. Delete or move the hidden system files IO.SYS or MSDOS.SYS.

NOTE   *Should you ever need to boot DOS 5 from floppy and you don't have a DOS 5 system disk, boot your computer using the UNINSTALL disk #1. Press F3 at UNINSTALL's first screen and type Y to exit to a DOS 5 prompt.*

Common Error
Messages

The Command Reference section of this book provides a detailed description of the error messages you may encounter while working with a specific command. This appendix discusses error messages common to many commands.

Abort, Retry, Fail?

DOS has encountered an error it cannot resolve without user intervention, such as an open floppy disk drive latch or an offline printer. To end the command generating this error message, type A for Abort. If you can correct the cause of the error, for example, closing the floppy disk drive latch, do so and type R to retry the command. The Fail option, the least often used, directs DOS to fail the operation that caused the error and continue the program's execution. If you are copying files from a disk and DOS encounters a disk read error, you may be able to use Fail to fail the reading of the bad sector and continue the file copy with the next file.

Access denied

The command attempted to delete or change a read-only file or specified a file name as the desired directory in a CHDIR command. DOS does not let you change read-only files. If you really want to change or delete the file's contents, use ATTRIB to remove the file's read-only setting.

Bad command or file name

DOS could not locate the command specified as an internal or external command or DOS batch file. Double-check the command's spelling. Make sure the directory containing the command is in the command path (see PATH) or that you are specifying a complete directory path name to the command.

Bad or missing Command interpreter

DOS could not find the file COMMAND.COM during system startup. By default, DOS looks in the root directory of the boot disk for the command interpreter file COMMAND.COM. If your CONFIG.SYS file contains a SHELL entry, you can direct DOS to look in a location other than the root. If this error occurs, boot DOS from a floppy disk and either move COMMAND.COM to the root directory or place a SHELL entry in CONFIG.SYS that contains a complete path to COMMAND.COM.

Batch file missing

DOS cannot continue the execution of the current batch file because it cannot find the batch file in the current directory or command path. This error message may occur if a batch file deletes itself as part of its processing.

Cannot load COMMAND, system halted

The previous command overwrote the transient portion of COMMAND.COM in memory. When this occurs, DOS uses the COMSPEC environment entry to locate the file COMMAND.COM to reload the transient portion. In this case, DOS was unable to find or load COMMAND.COM. Use CTRL-ALT-DEL to restart your system.

Cannot read file allocation table

See "File allocation table bad."

Current drive is no longer valid

The current drive is either a floppy drive with no disk in it or a network drive that is no longer accessible. You must either change the current drive or, in the case of a floppy drive, insert a disk.

Data error reading drive n:
Disk error reading drive n:

Either of these error messages means DOS cannot read the data stored on the disk drive specified. DOS will follow this message with the "Abort, Retry, Fail" prompt. Use the Fail option to read as much of the data from the disk as you can. If you cannot read any information, you might try using the RECOVER command. Then, use FORMAT to reformat the disk.

Disk error writing drive n:

DOS cannot write information to the disk drive specified. DOS will follow this message with the "Abort, Retry, Fail" prompt. Abort the operation trying to write information to the disk. Use CHKDSK to examine the disk. If possible, salvage as much data from the disk as you can using COPY and RECOVER. Then, use FORMAT to reformat the disk.

Divide overflow

The command performed an invalid division operation, normally a divide by zero. Restart your system using CTRL-ALT-DEL and determine if the error persists. If so, contact the manufacturer of the software program for assistance.

Error writing directory

DOS cannot write to the directory specified. Restart your system and use CHKDSK to examine your disk. Copy as much information from the disk as you can, then use FORMAT to reformat the disk.

Error writing file allocation table

DOS cannot write to the file allocation table specified. DOS uses the file allocation table to track the location of every file on your disk. To keep a file allocation table error from preventing DOS accessing your files, DOS stores two copies of the file allocation table on most disks. Use BACKUP or COPY to copy information from the disk, then use FORMAT to reformat the disk.

File allocation table bad
File allocation table bad drive *n*:
Cannot read file allocation table

Any of these three error messages means the file allocation table for the disk specified may be damaged. Use CHKDSK to examine the disk. DOS uses the file allocation table to track the location of every file on your disk. To keep a file allocation table error from preventing DOS accessing your files, DOS stores two copies of the file allocation table on most disks. If one of the file allocation tables becomes damaged, DOS uses the second. Use COPY or BACKUP to copy as many files from your disk as you can. Use FORMAT to reformat the disk.

File creation error

The command attempted to create a file whose name is already in use as a directory name within the same directory, or the command attempted to create a file in the root directory and the root is full.

File not found

The command could not locate the file you specified in the command line. Double-check your spelling of the file name. Make sure you are specifying a correct path to the file. Use the DIR command to ensure that the file is in the directory you are referencing.

General failure error reading (or writing) drive *n*:

DOS cannot access the disk drive specified. This message is followed by an "Abort, Retry, or Fail" prompt. Select the Abort option. In most cases, this error occurs when the disk in the drive specified has not been formatted.

Incorrect DOS Version

The command or program you are trying to execute requires a different DOS version than you are using. Locate either the correct DOS version or the program version that runs under your version of DOS. If you are using DOS 5, you may be able to execute the program using SETVER.

Incorrect number of parameters
Invalid number of parameters
Too many parameters

Any of these three error messages means that the command line you entered has too many or too few parameters. Examine the command's format in the Command Reference section of this book and issue the command with the correct parameter count.

Insert disk with batch file and press any key when ready

The floppy disk from which you originally started the batch file is no longer in the current drive. To continue the batch file's execution, place the disk containing the batch file back into the drive and press any key.

Insert disk with \COMMAND.COM in drive *n*:
and strike any key when ready

The previous command overwrote the transient portion of COMMAND.COM in memory. When this occurs, DOS uses the COMSPEC environment entry to locate the file COMMAND.COM to reload the transient portion. In this case, DOS is prompting you to insert a floppy disk into the drive specified that contains COMMAND.COM, so DOS can reload the transient portion.

Insufficient disk space

The disk specified is full, preventing the previous command from successfully finishing. If possible, free up space on the disk by removing unneeded files or copying one or more files to a different disk. If you are trying to copy files from one disk to another, see the XCOPY command in the Command Reference section of this book.

Insufficient memory
Not enough memory

Either of these error messages means that your computer does not have enough available memory for the command to execute. If you have loaded memory-resident programs or a RAM drive, you may need to restart DOS without them to successfully execute this command. If you are using DOS version 5, refer to the CONFIG.SYS DEVICEHIGH entry and the LOADHIGH command for ways to free up conventional memory.

Intermediate file error during pipe

The DOS pipe creates temporary files to which it redirects a program's output. If the disk is write-protected or its root directory is full, DOS cannot create the needed files. If you are using DOS 5, you can use the TEMP environment entry to specify where you want DOS to create the pipe's temporary files.

Internal stack overflow, system halted

A series of successive hardware interrupts used up all of the DOS interrupt stack space. Use the CONFIG.SYS STACKS entry to allocate more stack space and restart your system.

Invalid Argument
Invalid Parameter

Either of these error messages means that one or more parameters you specified in the command is invalid. Refer to the command in this book's Command Reference, noting the valid parameters, and reissue the command. If you are using DOS 5, invoke the command with the /? switch to display a list of valid parameters.

Invalid COMMAND.COM in drive *n*:

The previous command overwrote the transient portion of COMMAND.COM in memory. When this occurs, DOS uses the COMSPEC environment entry to locate the file COMMAND.COM to reload the transient portion. In this case, when DOS reads COMMAND.COM from the disk specified, the version of COMMAND.COM on disk did not match the version DOS is currently running. Insert a disk containing the correct version of COMMAND.COM and press any key to continue.

Invalid drive in search path

A disk drive in either the command-file search path defined by PATH or the data-file search path defined by APPEND does not exist. Invoke either PATH or APPEND with no arguments to view their current settings and remove or correct the invalid disk reference.

Invalid drive or file name

A drive letter or file name specified in the command line is invalid. Make sure you are specifying a valid disk drive letter, followed by a colon, or that you are providing a correct path name to the file specified.

Invalid drive specification

The disk drive specified in your command line is invalid. Make sure you are using a valid disk drive letter followed by a colon. If you are trying to access your hard disk for the first time, the disk may not yet have been partitioned by FDISK.

Invalid number of parameters

See "Incorrect number of parameters."

Invalid Parameter

See "Invalid Argument."

Invalid parameter combination
Parameters not compatible

Either of these error messages means that your command line contains two or more conflicting switches. Refer to the command in this book's Command Reference, noting the valid parameters, and reissue the command. If you are using DOS 5, invoke the command with the /? switch to display a list of valid parameters.

Invalid path
Path not found

Either of these error messages means that the directory path you have specified in your command does not exist. Double-check your spelling and make sure you are providing a correct path name relative to your current directory. Reissue the command with a correct path name.

Invalid switch

One or more of the switches you have specified in the command line is not supported by this command. Refer to the command in this book's Command Reference, noting the valid switches, and reissue the command. If you are using DOS 5, invoke the command with the /? switch to display a list of valid parameters.

Invalid syntax

The command line entered violates the command's format. If you are using the FOR command, make sure you include the keyword DO. If you are using an IF command within a batch file to compare one string to a batch parameter, enclose both strings within single quotes to ensure the IF command has two strings to compare if the user does not provide a corresponding batch line parameter.

No such file or directory

A file or directory specified in the command line does not exist. Double-check your spelling of the file or directory name. Make sure you are specifying a correct path name. Use DIR to ensure that the file or directory is in the directory you are referencing.

Not enough memory

See "Insufficient memory."

Not ready error reading (or writing) drive *n*:

The command attempted to read information from or write information to the disk in the drive specified, and the drive was not ready. This error occurs when you don't have a floppy disk in the drive specified or you have not closed the disk drive latch. This message is followed by the "Abort, Retry, or Fail" message. If you want to end the command trying to access the disk, select Abort. If you have inserted the disk or closed the disk drive latch, select Retry.

Parameter value not allowed
Parameter value not in allowed range

Either of these error messages means that the value you have specified for one of the parameters in the command line is invalid. Refer to the command in the Command Reference section of this book to determine the valid range of values.

Parameters not compatible

See "Invalid parameter combination."

Path not found

See "Invalid path."

Path too long

The path specified exceeds the DOS maximum of 64 characters.

Program too big to fit in memory

You do not have enough available memory to run the program specified. If you have loaded memory-resident programs or created a RAM drive in your computer's conventional memory, start your system without loading them into memory.

Out of environment space

The command could not place an entry in the DOS environment because the environment is full and DOS cannot increase its size due to memory-resident programs. Use the CONFIG.SYS SHELL entry to increase the amount of space DOS reserves for the environment and restart your system.

Sector not found reading (or writing) drive n:

DOS could not find the sector corresponding to a disk read or write operation on the drive specified. Use CHKDSK to examine the disk. Restart your computer and retry the program. If the error persists, perform a backup, format, and restore operation.

Seek error reading (or writing) drive n:

A seek operation moves the disk drive heads to a specific track. A seek error occurs when the drive is unable to seek to the track specified. Use CHKDSK to examine the disk. Restart your computer and retry the program. If the error persists, perform a backup, format, and restore operation.

Specified COMMAND search directory bad

The CONFIG.SYS SHELL entry lets you specify the location of the DOS command interpreter COMMAND.COM. In this case, the location specified does not exist or does not contain COMMAND.COM. If necessary, restart your system using a bootable floppy disk in drive A, and correct the CONFIG.SYS SHELL entry.

Terminate batch job (Y/N)?

You have pressed either CTRL-BREAK or CTRL-C during the execution of a DOS batch file. If you type **Y**, DOS will end the batch file's execution, returning control to the DOS prompt. If you instead type **N**, DOS will end only the current command's execution, continuing the batch file with the next command.

Too many open files

The command could not execute because DOS did not have enough file handles available. Use the CONFIG.SYS FILES entry to increase the number of available file handles and restart your system. At a minimum, your system should provide 20 file handles.

Too many parameters

See "Incorrect number of parameters."

Write protect error writing drive *n*:

The command attempted to write information to or delete files from a write-protected disk. If you want to change the disk's contents, you must first remove the write-protect tab from a 5 1/4-inch floppy disk or move the write-protect bar on a 3 1/2-inch microfloppy disk. If you don't want to change the disk's contents, make sure you are specifying the command's source and target disks in the correct order.

Index

symbol
    assigned by UNDELETE as first
        character of retrieved files, 487
    in EDLIN, 647
$*, to access entire macro line, 474-475
$E, to generate an Esc character, 615
$T, to separate multiple commands in
    DOSKEY macro, 474
% symbol, 921
%% symbols, 921
*, wildcard character, 147-155, 158
    to match groups of files with similar
        names, 147, 233-234, 237, 482-483
    to reference all files (ignore base name
        and extension), 145-146, 150-151
+, wildcard character
    to add file names to command lines, 144
    to append file contents to another file,
        144-145
101-key keyboard, 616-619
-, prompt in DEBUG, 508
. (period), in EDLIN, 647
?
    in EDLIN (DOS 5), 648
    as first character in file name for
        UNDELETE, 481
    wildcard character to substitute for
        individual character, 155-158
@, to supress display of current command
    name, 249, 255
@ character, supressing command name
    display with, 892
/? switch, 772, 774
\ backslash character
    before directory name with DIR, 66
    root directory symbol, 163, 175

A
A20 handler, 590
A20 handler values, 591
/A20CONTROL switch, 590
Abort, Retry, Fail? prompt, 102-105, 118,
    208
Access time, 805
Active partition, 913
Active Task List, adding programs to in
    DOS 5 shell, 752
Add Group dialog box in DOS 4 shell, 719
Add Program dialog box in DOS 4 shell, 716
Add Program dialog box in DOS 5 shell, 759
Allocation units for disk space, 124-127, 597.
    See also Clusters of sectors
        CHKDSK display of information about,
            436-437
        converted to files, 443
        lost, 443
        required, calculating, 444
        size of, 448-449, 555
ALT-255 key combination, 892
ALT-F7 function key to discard the current
    command buffer contents, 468, 471
ANSI.COM, creating to execute escape
    sequences, 620-621
ANSI.SYS device driver, 609-626, 972
        assigning text attributes with, 626
        background color values, 614
        cursor positioning with, 623-624, 625
        foreground color values, 614
        installing, 609-610
        redefining keys with, 616-619
        selecting a video mode with, 624-625
ANSI.SYS video mode escape sequences, 625

APPEND command, 54, 827-830
/E switch, 827-828
/PATH:on|off switch, 828
/X:on|off switch, 827-828
/X switch, 827, 828
to define a data-file search path,
203-204, 559
Append redirection operator (>), 301-302,
332-333, 339
in macros with GG, 476
Applications, exiting temporarily, 900-901
ASCII character set, 1049-1052
ASCII characters
displaying extended, 935-937
extended, 262-263
method for entering, 181
ASCII characters, extended, displaying with
GRAFTABL, 774-775
ASCII escape character, 610
creating, 895
ASCII file, copying, 864
ASCII files
displaying contents of, 132
printing, 231, 237
printing via the print queue, 157-161
viewing, 1028-1029
viewing in DOS 5 shell, 735
ASCII text files, editing, 895
Assembly language for DEBUG, 508-511,
520-522
ASSIGN command, 54, 830-832
/STATUS switch, 830, 831, 832
/STATUS switch to display current
disk assignments, 452-453, 459
commands not to use with, 453
redirecting DOS from floppy to hard
disk with, 451-453, 457-459, 461-463
removing drive assignment by using no
command parameters with, 459
Associate File dialog box, in DOS 5 shell, 733
Asterisk wildcard. *See* * wildcard character
AT system clock, changing, 1024
ATTRIB command, 54, 832-835, 1004
+-A switch, 832
+-H switch, 832-833
+-R switch, 832
+-S switch, 832
/S switch, 833
/S switch to set or display attributes of
subdirectory files, 386, 404

ATTRIB command, *continued*
to display attributes of files in current
directory, 404, 409
manipulating file attributes with,
385-389
to set or clear file's archive-required
attribute, 214-215, 372, 385-387, 402
to set or clear file's hidden attribute,
386
to set or clear file's read-only attribute,
385-386, 388, 402
to set or clear file's system attribute,
386, 409
Attribute byte, 372
of a file, 832
Attribute values, for displaying files, 874
Attributes, displaying files according to, 874
AUTOEXEC.BAT, 303-313, 432-433
adding lines to, quick method for, 145
to automatically execute commands
when system starts, 192, 310, 411
backup copy of, 309-310, 344-345
caution required to change, 309
conditional installation of
memory-resident software by, 514
CONFIG.SYS and, 308-309
DIRCMD environment entry in, 307,
310
disabling, 312-313
displaying contents of, 121-132
DOS search for, 41, 303, 310
DOSKEY command for macros in, 473
DOSSHELL command in, 304, 307-308
FASTOPEN command in, 198,
304-306, 310
Hands On for, 310
LOADHIGH command in, 559
MIRROR command in, 499
MODE command in, 222
PATH command in, 192-194, 199, 304
PRINT command in, 243-244, 306,
309
printing contents of, 225-226, 233, 237
PROMPT command in, 304-305
restarting DOS after changing, 89-90
in root directory, 164
sample, 308
SET DIRCMD command in, 304, 321
SET TEMP command in, 304, 307
SHARE command in, 304, 307-308

AUTOEXEC.BAT, *continued*
shielded from changes other software makes, 312
sorted output from, 359
TEMP environment entry in, 306-307, 310
testing for presence of, 268-269, 278-279
VERIFY command in, 550
AUX serial port, 220

B

Background color values, ANSI.SYS, 614
Backslash character, 846
BACKSPACE key to erase previous character, 45, 85, 617
Backup, 365-384, 479-480, 501, 547, 563
complete, 367-370, 377-378
to copy key file or directory, 373
daily, 370-373
Hands On, for, 377-379
hard disk, 368-370
incremental, 370, 376-377
log of each, 375-376, 383
process, 366-368
third-party programs to perform, 376
BACKUP command, 36, 54, 365-384, 833, 835-841, 999
/A switch, 836
/A switch to append files to previous incremental backup disks, 372
/D: switch, 836
/D switch to copy files created or changed after specified date, 380
/F switch, 836
/L: switch, 836
/L switch to use BACKUP.LOG file, 375-376, 380, 383
/M switch, 834, 836
/M switch to copy files whose archive attribute is set, 372
/S switch, 836
/S switch to copy subdirectory files, 369
/T switch, 836
/T switch to copy files created or changed after specified time, 380
exit status values, 382
prompts, 369-370
used in batch files, 382-383
used with large files, 381-382
Backup disks, log of files, 1000

Backup Fixed Disk option, DOS 4 shell, 700
Backup Fixed Disk option in DOS 5 shell, 746
BACKUP log file, 837
BADLABEL.BAT file, 295
BAK extension, with EDLIN files, 642-643
BAK file, in EDLIN, 898
BAS (BASIC) file extension, 64
BASIC programming language
creating and running programs, 989-990
invoking, 775
BAT (batch file) file extension, 64
Batch command messages, displaying or suppressing, 891-894
Batch file
branching to a specific location within, 933-935
invoking from within a second batch file, 842
suspending the processing of, 980-981
Batch files, 245-302
backups performed using, 382-383
branching within, 285-288, 296
built "on the fly," 345-348
conditional entries within, 942-945
decision-making, 265-284
defined, 245, 255
differences between macros and, 472-473
disabling command-name display in, 248-249
documenting, 991-993
ending, 249-250
grouping commands with, 245-263
Hands On for, 254, 257-258
labels in, 286-287, 296
locating commonly used, 251
menu-driven, 300-301
naming, 59, 248
nested, 293-295, 297
passing information to, 273-276, 278
pipe restrictions for, 361-362
procedure for creating simple, 245-251
remarks to document, 252
space consumed by, 606-607
temporary suspension of, 253-254, 256
as text files, 132
Batch parameters, 273-276, 278, 348, 1010
accessing more than nine, 290-293, 296-297
shifting, 1016-1017
BATCH subdirectory, 254

BATCOPY.BAT file, 253-254
Baud rates, 782, 794
Bell, sounding the computer's, 981
Binary file, copying, 864
Blank lines, ECHO command to insert, 260-262
Blocks, contiguous, 856
BLUEBACK.BAT file, 611
Board, installing new, 26-28
BOOK= environment entry, 316-317
Boot record, 40, 122-123, 125, 448-449, 601-602
    master, 39-40, 504
Bootable disk, creating, 1021-1024
BOX.BAT file, 262
Boxes, extended ASCII characters to make, 262-263
BREAK= configuration entry, 413, 431, 558
BREAK command, 53, 770, 785, 841-842
    to perform extended CTRL-BREAK checking, 424
Buffer size, changing, 890
BUFFERS= configuration entry, 412-413, 415, 420-422, 556-557
Bytes defined, 12, 18

C

CALL command, 53, 842-843, 858
    to invoke a batch file from within another, 294-295, 308
CD command, 845-849
Central processing unit (CPU), 2
    types, 28
Change Attributes dialog box in DOS 5 shell, 739
Change line signal, 428
Character set, 675
Character sets, ASCII, 1049-1052
Character string
    defined, 273
    IF command to compare, 273, 275-276
    testing for identity with another string, 277
CHARCNT utility command, 353
Chassis, computer, 2-5
    components, 23-29. *See also individual components*
    cover, removing, 23
    screws, 23
CHCP command, 53, 685, 688-689, 691, 843-845

CHDIR command, 845-849
CHDIR command (CD), 53, 165-168, 174-175, 194-195, 247-248
    to access application program directory, 189-190, 265, 559, 563
CHECK1ST.BAT file, 269-270
CHECKFOR.BAT file, 268-269
CHKDCOPY.BAT file, 272
CHKDSK command, 54, 435-450, 540, 555, 559-560, 565, 576, 598, 603-604, 613, 837, 849-856
    /F switch, 849, 852, 853, 855
    /F switch to handle errors, 442-444, 450
    /V switch, 849, 852
    /V switch to display file names for verification, 446-447
    detecting fragmented files, 799, 803
    to determine space hard disk is using, 366, 368, 377, 555
    disk label displayed by, 540-541
    to examine files for fragmentation, 559-560
    Hands On for, 446-447
    hard disk's restored structure reviewed with, 495
    invoking, 435-436, 446
    memory displayed by, 565, 576
Clicking, the mouse, 714
Clock, system, changing, 1024
CLR (color information) file extension, 64
CLS command, 856-857
CLS command (clear screen), 44-45, 51, 53, 55-56
Clusters of sectors, 125-127, 179-181, 441, 597, 631, 795
    allocating, 555
    available after file deletion, 484-485, 561-563
    available on common disk types, 598
    knowing the disk's, 554-555
    lost, 443-445, 447, 604
CMOS chip, 811
Code page, 691
    displaying or changing the current, 843-845
Code pages
    changing with CHCP, 685-686
    preparing and selecting, 675-676, 969
    preparing for use, 682-685
    refreshing, 685
    supported by DOS, 677

CODEPAGE, /STATUS switch, 684-685

Code-page combinations, 679

Codepage operations, 967

CODEPAGE PREPARE command, 973, 974

CODEPAGE REFRESH command, 685

CODEPAGE SELECT command, 973

Code-page switching, 691

Cold boot of DOS, 90

COLOR.BAT file, 275

Color Scheme dialog box in DOS 5 shell, 755

COLORS.BAT file, 299

COM1:, COM2:, COM3:, or COM4: serial port, 219-222, 225, 227-228, 242, 344

COM (command) file extension, 58-59, 64

COM file, converting an EXE file into, 899-900

COM port settings, determining, 972

COM ports, setting characteristics, 966-967

Command buffer

    cursor movement keys for viewing, 466

    default of 512 bytes of memory allocated to DOSKEY, 466

    discarding contents of, 468, 471

    editing previous commands in, 468-469, 471

    erasing command from, 467-468

    filled, 466

    insert mode for, 469

    previous, 465-468

    setting size of, 469-471

COMMAND.COM file, 789, 858

    command history passed from DOSKEY command to, 477

    contents, 324

    customizing, 428-430

    duplication of, 326

    invoking, 40-41, 901

    loading, 324-325

    required for DOS to start, 121-122

    in root directory, 164

    SHELL= entry to specify location of, 312-313, 326, 428

COMMAND command, 54, 857-859

    /C switch, 857

    /C switch to nest batch files, 294-295, 308

    /E: switch, 857

    /MSG switch, 857

    /P switch, 857

Command history, 467

Command interpreter, locating the, 859

Command line

    defined, 50

    parameters, 50

Command path, maximum length of, 979

Command processor, loading a secondary, 857-859

Command reference, 827-1043

Command-file search path, defining, 978-980

Command-line switches in DOS 4 shell, 713

Command-name display for batch files, disabling, 248-249

Commands

    DOS 5, online help for, 772-774

    EDLIN, 896

    repetitive execution of, 920-922

Commands (EDLIN), 639

Communication protocol, 781

COMP command, 54, 392-397, 403, 859-864

    /A switch, 860

    /A switch to display values in ASCII, 393, 395, 406

    /C switch, 860

    /C switch to ignore case differences, 396, 406

    /D switch, 860

    /D switch to display differences in decimal values, 393-395

    /L switch, 860

    /L switch to display line number of each difference, 395-396

    /N:n switch to compare specified number of lines, 397

    /N= switch, 860

Compressed format, expanding, 901-902

Computer, turning on, 32-33

Computer program defined, 16, 18

Computer's bell, sounding the, 981

COMSPEC= entry, 1009

COMSPEC= environment entry, 316, 324-326, 429, 433

CON (keyboard) device, 86, 778

Conditional processing, within DOS batch files, 942-945

CONFIG.SYS BREAK entry, 771

CONFIG.SYS COUNTRY entry, 678, 687

CONFIG.SYS DEVICEHIGH entry, 580, 585-586, 957

CONFIG.SYS DOS=UMB entry, 957

CONFIG.SYS DOS entry, 585

CONFIG.SYS file, 411-433
    AUTOEXEC.BAT file and, 308-309
    backup copy of, 344-345
    comments in, 413, 418-419, 421
    displaying the contents of, 141-142, 412
    entries, 411-419, 431. *See also individual*
        configuration entries
    Hands On for, 419-420
    minimum contents of, 419-420
    printing contents of, 233
    restarting DOS after changing, 89-90
    in root directory, 164, 432
    SYSINIT program search for, 40
    testing for presence of, 268-269,
        411-412
CONFIG.SYS INSTALL entry, 948, 949
CONFIG.SYS placing REM statements in, 992
Confirmation dialog boxes, enabling and
    disabling in DOS 5 shell, 740-741
Confirmation options, changing in DOS 4
    shell, 709
Contiguous blocks, 856
Contiguous files, 796, 806, 855
Controller overhead, 805
Conventional memory, 566-567, 584, 594, 956
Conventional Memory KB Required option in
    DOS 5 shell, 761
Coprocessors, 28
COPY command, 53, 83, 864-867, 1038
    /A switch, 864
    /B switch, 864
    /V switch, 864
    /V switch to verify disk write, 545, 557
    to copy files from floppy to hard disk,
        209
    to copy files from hard disk to floppy,
        208, 213
    to copy files to printer, 220-221,
        225-226, 231-232
    to copy groups of files, 151-153, 208
    to create files, 92
    to duplicate file's contents, 131,
        133-137, 139-141
COPYMSG.BAT file, 344-345
COUNTRY=, 844
COUNTRY= configuration entry, 413, 418
COUNTRY= entry, 1006
Country codes, supported in SELECT, 1006
COUNTRY specifier, 869
COUNTRY.SYS, 686, 976-977
Country-code values, 679

CPI (code-page information file) file
    extension, 64, 690
CPU clock ticks, 982
/CPUCLOCK switch, 591
CRC (cyclic redundancy check), 635
Create Directory dialog box in DOS 5 shell,
    739
Cross-linked files, 604, 855
CTRL-ALT-DEL (restart DOS), 89-91, 93, 332,
    334
CTRL-ALT-F1, for default keyboard, 947
CTRL-ALT-F2, for foreign keyboard, 947
CTRL-BREAK, 841-842
CTRL-BREAK checking, enabling extended,
    770-771, 785
CTRL-BREAK (end command execution), 89
    checking, 423-424, 431, 558
CTRL-C (cancel command execution), 88-89,
    91-92, 332, 334, 423, 444, 449
    to cancel printing, 234
    to terminate batch file, 249-250, 255-256
CTRL-G (bell), 262-263
CTRL-LEFT ARROW (move cursor one word to
    left), 469
CTRL-PRTSC (printer echo), 224-226
CTRL-RIGHT ARROW (move cursor one word to
    right), 469
CTRL-S (suspend scrolling), 97-98, 201
CTRL-Z character, 863
CTRL-Z (end-of-file), 86-87, 92
CTTY command, 53, 789, 867-868
Cursor positioning, with ANSI.SYS, 623-624,
    625
Cursor-movement key combinations, in EDIT,
    666
CUSTOM.BAT file, 312
Cut and paste, 674
Cut-and-paste operations, performing in
    EDIT, 673
Cyclic redundancy check (CRC), 635

D ───────────────────────

DAILY.BAT file, 382-383
DAT (data) file extension, 64
Data transfer time, 805
Data-file search path, defining, 827
Date, displaying current in the prompt, 988
DATE command, 49-51, 53, 55, 57, 869-871
    batch file with, 246-247
    canceling, 92

Date stamp for files, 65-66, 72
    suppressing DIR display of, 79
Date, system
    displaying or setting, 49-50, 55, 57
    DOS use of, 66
    entering, 33, 246-247
DATETIME.BAT file, 246-248, 473-474
DEBUG command, 507-536, 871-873
    assembly language used for instructions
      to, 508, 520-522
    creating commands with, 272, 283,
      507-513
    quitting, 510
    script files, 511-513
DEBUG commands, 507-536
    ?, 519-521
    A, 520-522
    C, 520, 522-523
    D, 520, 523
    E, 520, 524
    F, 520, 524-525
    G, 520, 525-526
    H, 520, 526
    I, 520, 526-527
    L, 520, 527
    M, 520, 527-528
    N, 520, 528, 534
    O, 520, 528-529
    P, 520, 529
    Q, 510, 520, 529-530
    R, 509-510, 520, 530-531
    S, 520, 531-532
    T, 520, 532-533
    U, 520, 533
    W, 510, 520, 533-534
    XA, 520, 534-535
    XD, 520, 535
    XM, 520, 535
    XS, 520, 535-536
DEBUG-created commands
    BEEP.COM, 510-511
    HELLO.COM, 508-512
    HOUR.COM, 272-273, 512
    SCANCODE.COM, 300, 514-516
    SHOWLINE.COM, 516-518
    Y OR N.COM, 513-514
Default directory, changing or displaying the,
    845-849
Defragment utilities, third-party, 801

DEL command, 53, 93, 146
    /P switch to display each file name and
      prompt for deletion, 143-144
    to delete files, 131, 140-141
    to delete groups of or all files, 154-155,
      159
    DIR used to prevent accidental
      deletions with, 154-155
DEL key to delete character from command
    buffer, 85, 469, 617
Delete Item dialog box in DOS 5 shell, 759
Delete tracking, 961
Deleted files, recovering, 1029-1032
DELETEIT.BAT file, 346-347
DEVICE= configuration entry, 412-413, 419,
    421
Device, PRN, 985
Device characteristics, specifying, 966-975
Device code pages
    preparing, 682-684
    selecting, 684
Device code pages, displaying information
    about, 684-685
Device drivers
    software, 419, 421
    in various versions of DOS, 420
Device drivers. *See also individual drivers*
Device name(s)
    informing parallel or serial board of,
      227-228
    of standard devices, 343-344, 417
DEVICEHIGH= configuration entry, 413,
    430, 585-586
DEVICEHIGH entry, 580
Devices
    assigned default, 343
    block, 427
    character, 427
    displaying current status of, 783-784
Dialog box, 663, 674, 714
    DOS 4 shell, 698
    File Open, 667
Dialog box switches in DOS 4 shell, 723
Dialog boxes, designing in DOS 5 shell,
    763-764
Differences between two files, displaying,
    859-864
DIP (Dual Inline Package) switch, 228
DIR1LINE.BAT file, 298

DIR command, 53, 62-80, 79, 298, 319, 321,
   537, 613, 873-878
      /A: switch, 874
      /A switch to list files by attribute,
         77-78, 319
      /B switch, 875
      /B switch to display only base file
         names and
      /L switch, 875
      /L switch to display file names using
         lowercase letters, 78, 319, 321, 357
      /O: switch, 874-875
      /O switch to specify sort order, 76-77,
         319
      /P switch, 874
      /P switch to pause display, 67-68, 72,
         334, 355
      /S switch, 875
      /S switch to display file names in
         subdirectories, 78, 319
      /W switch, 874
      /W switch to display file names five
         across, 70-73, 257
      disk label displayed by, 540, 547
      for drive other than the default,
         100-101, 103-104
      file attribute options for, 77
      Hands On for, 71-73
      invoking, 62
      output sent to printer for, 329-330
DIRCMD= environment entry, 307, 310, 318,
   320
DIRCMD entry, 1009
DIRCMD environment entry, 876
Direct memory access (DMA), 593-594
Directories
      deleting in DOS 5 shell, 737
      expanding the next level of in DOS 5
         shell, 729
Directory
      163-183, 185-205. *See also* Root directory
      allocating clusters for, 555
      for application listed in PATH
         command, 304
      backing up specific, 373
      changing, 165-168, 175
      changing or displaying the current,
         845-849
      creating, 168-173, 175-176, 963-966
      creating in DOS 4 shell, 707
      creating in DOS 5 shell, 739-740

Directory, *continued*
      current, 164-165, 196
      defined, 61-62, 72
      deleting unnecessary files from, 555
      disk drive as, 456-459
      disk space used for, 438
      displaying current in the prompt,
         987-988
      displaying files in, 62-63, 66-70
      displaying screenfuls of files in, 356, 387
      displaying selected groups of files in,
         157
      entry available after file deletion,
         484-485, 561-563
      file control block, 551-552
      Hands On for, 174, 176-177, 200-202
      limiting the number of files per,
         554-555
      parent, 196-197, 200, 202
      printing a listing of, 329-330, 340
      protecting a private, 181-182
      removing empty, 173-174, 176
      restoring specific, 375-376
      running older programs that do not
         support, 458
      saving and restoring, 301-302
      searching, 553-554
      sorting file names and information in,
         74-79, 319, 340, 356-360
      system performance considerations for,
         553-555
      tree, 170-171, 185-189, 199, 226
      wide format for listing, 70-71
Directory branches, collapsing in DOS 5 shell,
   729
Directory entries, 600-601
      increasing the number of, 903
Directory names, 964
      abbreviating, 194-197, 199-200, 455, 458
      meaningful, 172-173
      substituting unused drive letter for,
         205, 453-455
Directory structure, displaying, 1026-1028
Directory structures, checking, 849-856
Directory tree
      arranging in DOS 4 shell, 709, 710
      expanding in DOS 5 shell, 729
      joining a disk to, 946
Directory trees, displaying two in DOS 5 shell,
   742, 743
Directory trees in DOS 5 shell, 729

Disk, creating a bootable, 1021-1024
Disk access time, 26
Disk buffers, 412-417
    flushing, 416-417
Disk cache, creating, 575-576
Disk clusters, 795
Disk Compare menu option, DOS 4 shell, 699
Disk controller
    connections of, 24-25
    defined, 26
    function of, 26, 107
    improving timing coordination
        between computer and, 556-557
    types (ESDI and IDE), 26
    upgraded when new drive is installed,
        107
Disk Copy utility, DOS 4 shell, 699
Disk crash, 636
Disk defragmenter, third-party, with
    FASTOPEN, 904
Disk drive
    as a directory, 456-459
    changing the default, 99-100, 104
    identity swapping, 451-453
    joining to a DOS path, 945-947
    logical, 451, 453-455, 459-460
    specifying last, 413, 424
    system performance considerations of,
        556-557
Disk drive, floppy, 7, 18
    A> as first, 33
    activation light, 7, 14, 18, 33
    disk ejection button of, 7, 14
    disk insertion in, 13-15
    external, 108
    Hands On for, 19
    latch, 7, 14-15
    logical drive as second (B>), 462-463
    names, 14, 16, 20, 22, 99
    spindle for 3 1/2-inch, 10
    starting DOS from, 32
    updating, 106-108
Disk drive icons, in DOS 5 shell, 727
Disk drive references, routing, 830
Disk formatting, performing in DOS 4 shell,
    700-701
Disk fragmentation, 127, 179-180
    detecting and correcting, 795-806
    RESTORE command for backup files
        to correct, 374

Disk head crashes, 636
    avoiding, 628
Disk head parking, 627-630, 635
Disk head seek, 806
Disk interleaving, 556
Disk parking, 627-630, 636
Disk partition, creating one large, 811-813
Disk partitions
    creating primary and extended, 813-817
    defining, 911-917
Disk sector, interleaving, 630-632
Disk space
    displaying free, 875
    reporting on status of, 850
    total, 438
Disk space, available
    CHKDSK display of, 439
    copying files that require more than,
        214-215
    determining, 66, 113-114, 366
    suppressing DIR display of, 79
Disk storage, 6-8, 11
Disk transfer time, 26
Disk Utilities group, selecting in DOS 5 shell,
    745
Disk verification, 545, 549-550, 1037-1038
Disk volume label, 878
    displaying, 1039-1040
    specifying, 952-955
Disk-caching software, 557
DISKCOMP command, 54, 878-882
    /8 switch, 879
    /1 switch, 879
    to compare contents of two like floppy
        disks, 537, 542-543, 548
DISKCOPY, detecting errors after
    completing, 879
DISKCOPY command, 54, 209-213, 837,
    882-887
    /1 switch, 882
    /V switch, 883
    exit status values for, 270-271
    using one drive for, 211-213
    using two drives for, 209-211
Disks
    backing up in DOS 5 shell, 746
    copying in DOS 5 shell, 745-746
    formatting, 923-933
    formatting in DOS 5 shell, 747
Display connector, plugging in, 4

DISPLAY.SYS device driver, 677, 687

DMA (direct memory access), 593-594

DOS 1.0, 822

DOS 1.1, 823

DOS 2.0, 823-824

DOS 3.0, 824-825

DOS 4, installing, 1071-1079

DOS 4.0, 825

DOS 4 shell, 693-714

    Add Group dialog box, 719

    Add Program dialog box, 716

    adding programs to the main group, 715-718

    arranging the directory tree, 709, 710

    associating file types with a program, 704-705

    Backup Fixed Disk option, 700

    changing a group program entry, 717

    changing confirmation options, 709

    changing files, 706-707

    command structure, 1054

    command-line switches, 713

    comparing disks, 699

    copying a program entry from one group to another, 720

    copying disks, 699

    copying files, 705

    creating a directory, 707

    customizing screen colors, 696

    deleting files, 706

    dialog box, 698

    dialog box switches, 723

    editing a group, 720

    exiting, 695

    file icons, 703

    file system, 702-709

    Format option, 700-701

    group, 695

    groups, 718-721

    main menu, 694

    menu maps, 1054

    moving files, 705

    online help, 701

    opening files, 703-704

    printing files, 704

    rearranging entries within a group, 721

    removing a group, 720

    removing a program name from a group, 718

    renaming files, 706

    Restore Fixed Disk option, 700

DOS 4 shell, *continued*

    setting system date and time, 698-699

    SHELLC command, 714

    starting, 693-695

    utilities, 696-701

    utilities option, 696

    viewing file contents, 707, 708

DOS 4 workspace, setting up, 1075

DOS 5

    editor, EDIT, 659-674

    installation disk files, restoring, 901-902

    memory management, 579-587

    online help for commands, 772-774

    upgrading to, 1081-1086

DOS 5.0, 825-826

    booting, 1086

    booting without a system disk, 1086

    new commands, 826

DOS 5 shell, 725-753, 755-765

    Add Program dialog box, 759

    adding programs to the Active Task List, 752

    Associate File dialog box, 733

    associating programs with a file type, 732-733

    backing up disks, 746

    Backup Fixed Disk option, 746

    Change Attributes dialog box, 739

    changing attributes of files, 738-739

    changing program group entries, 761

    changing the display, 742-744

    changing the display of, 740

    changing the order of group items, 758

    collapsing a directory's branches, 729

    Color Scheme dialog box, 755

    command structure, 1055

    Conventional Memory KB Required option, 761

    copying disks, 745-746

    copying files, 736

    copying program entries, 761

    Create Directory dialog box, 739-740

    creating a directory, 739-740

    Delete Item dialog box, 759

    deleting directories, 737

    deleting files, 737

    designing dialog boxes in, 763-764

    directory trees, 729

    disk drive icons, 727

    displaying all files, 742, 744

    displaying file specifics, 741

DOS 5 shell, *continued*
    displaying in graphics mode, 728-729
    displaying two directories and file lists,
        742, 743
    editing program groups, 758
    Enable Task Swapper option, 751-753
    enabling and disabling confirmation
        dialog boxes, 740-741
    exiting, 730
    expanding a directory tree, 729
    expanding the next level of directories,
        729
    file icons, 728
    file menu, 727
    files, working with, 730-742
    formatting disks, 747
    help menu options, 749
    Help Text option, 760-761
    key combinations, reserved, 760
    menu maps, 1055
    moving files, 734-735
    moving or copying files with the
        mouse, 736-737
    New Program Object dialog box, 757
    online help, 748, 749
    Password option, 757-758
    printing files, 732
    program entries, 759-761
    program groups, 756-759
    program icons, 745
    removing program groups, 758
    renaming files, 738
    reserved key combinations, 760
    reserving keys for program use, 761
    restoring fixed disk, 746-747
    running programs, 731-732
    running programs from the program
        list, 745-747
    searching for specific files, 733-734
    selecting Disk Utilities group, 745
    selecting files, 730-731
    setting screen colors in, 755-756
    shell confirmation options, 741
    shell interface, 726
    starting, 725-728
    Undelete command, 747
    undeleting files, 747
    viewing ASCII files, 735
    viewing file contents, 734
    XMS Memory KB Required option, 761

DOS
    boot record, 39-40
    case insensitivity of, 46, 65
DOS= configuration entry, 413, 430, 585
DOS
    disks, distribution, 32
    history of, 821-826
    located and loaded by computer during
        power up, 38-39, 51
    memory management, 565-595
    on-line help in version, 5, 54-55
    purpose of, 17-18
    reinstalled from floppy disk, 36
    starting, 31-41
    troubleshooting the startup of, 34, 36
    version number, displaying, 44-45,
        55-56
    versions of, 17
DOS=HIGH, UMB CONFIG.SYS entry, 955
DOS ATTRIB command, 865
DOS batch file
    branching to a specific location within,
        933-935
    documenting, 991-993
DOS boot record, 601-602
DOS commands
    43-59. *See also individual commands*
    correcting mistyped, 45-46
    crisis prevention, 479-506
    for a different directory, issuing,
        100-191
    for disks, 537-552
    entering and executing, 43-44
    Hands On for, 55
    internal versus external, 51-54, 69
    listing, 165-166
    pretender, 451-463
    redirecting output of, 331
    repeated character by character with F1
        function key, 85
    repeated for a set of files, 288-290, 296
    repeated in entirety with F3 function
        key, 83-85
    repetitive execution of, 920-922
    simplifying execution of external,
        189-194
DOS directory, creating, 963-966
DOS directory names, 964
DOS disk drive, joining to a DOS path,
    945-947

DOS editor, invoking from QBasic, 989
DOS environment
　　315-327. *See also individual environment
　　　　entries*
　　adding entry to, 316-317
　　displaying current, 280-281, 315
　　increasing size of, 323-326, 429-430
　　removing entry from, 317-318
　　setting or displaying entries in,
　　　　1009-1011
　　space, 317
　　specifying the desired size of, 980
　　ways DOS uses, 318-320
DOS file names, 964
DOS files, printing via the print queue,
　　982-986
DOS file-sharing support, installing, 1014-1016
DOS partition, 38-40
DOS partitions, 911-917
DOS path, joining a disk drive to, 945-947
DOS path name, substituting a drive name
　　for, 1019-1021
DOS prompt, 33, 43
　　current directory shown in, 164-165
　　customizing, 165, 326-327
　　defining, 986-989
　　exiting to, 900-901
DOS shell
　　display of version, 4, 5, 34-35
　　invoking, 307, 890-891
DOS subdirectories, 847
DOS system commands, 767-794
DOS version number
　　displaying, 1036-1037
　　reporting, 1011-1014
DOSHELP.BAT file, 288
DOSKEY command, 54, 465-478, 887-890.
　　See also Command buffer
　　/BUFSIZE= switch, 887
　　/BUFSIZE switch to specify buffer size
　　　　in bytes, 469-470, 476
　　/H switch, 888
　　/HISTORY (/H) switch to display
　　　　command history, 467, 469, 471, 473
　　/HISTORY switch, 888
　　/INSERT switch, 888
　　/INSERT switch to automatically begin
　　　　in insert mode, 470
　　/MACROS switch, 887
　　/MACROS switch to display defined
　　　　macros, 470, 476

DOSKEY command, *continued*
　　/OVERSTRIKE switch, 888
　　/REINSTALL switch, 887
　　/REINSTALL switch to reload
　　　　DOSKEY using new switch values,
　　　　470
　　arrow keys used by, 88, 466, 469
　　default of 512 bytes of memory in
　　　　command buffer for, 466
　　Hands On for, 470-471
　　I/O redirection with, 475-477
　　to recall recently entered commands,
　　　　94, 465-471
DOSKEY macros, 607
DOSSHELL command, 54, 890-891
　　/B switch, 891
　　/G switch, 891
　　/T switch, 891
　　in AUTOEXEC.BAT file, 304, 307
DOSSHELL.INI file, 765
Double-clicking, the mouse, 714
DOWN ARROW key, 617
　　in command buffer, 466
DOWP.BAT file, 247-248, 252
Drive, displaying current in the prompt,
　　987-988
DRIVER.SYS device driver to use external
　　floppy drive, 108
DRIVPARM= configuration entry, 413,
　　427-428, 432
Dual File Lists option, in DOS 5 shell, 742, 743

E

ECHO command, 53, 611, 891-894
　　to display blank lines, 260-262
ECHO OFF or ECHO ON in batch files, 249,
　　251-256, 345-348
EDE2BIN command, 899-900
EDIT command, 54, 613, 894-895
　　/B switch, 894
　　/G switch, 894
　　/H switch, 895
　　/NOHI switch, 895
EDIT, DOS 5 editor, 659-674
　　Clear option, 673
　　Copy option, 673
　　customizing the screen display,
　　　　668-669
　　Cut option, 673
　　editing existing files in, 662
　　exiting without saving changes, 662-663

EDIT, DOS 5 editor, *continued*
    File menu, 660-661
    Help option, 664-665
    insert mode, 662
    moving around in files, 665-666
    moving documents in, 665-666
    overstrike mode, 662
    Paste option, 673
    Print option, 663
    saving files, 667-668
    Search menu, 671-673
    selecting files for editing, 666-667
    starting, 659-662
Editor, 657
EDLIN command, 54, 611-613, 895-899
    /B switch, 896
    appending lines in, 651-652
    C command, 649-650
    combining files in, 57
    commands, summarizing, 648
    creating text files with, 637-657
    D command, 650
    deleting lines with, 650-651
    displaying pages with, 653
    E command, 651
    insert mode, entering, 644, 651
    inserting new text, 644-645
    L command, 652
    line number, 648-649
    M command, 653
    moving around in files with, 643-644
    P command, 653-654
    Q command, 654
    R command, 654-655
    replacing words or phrases in, 655
    S command, 656
    searching for a word or phrase, 656
    single-letter commands, 639
    T command, 656-657
    W command, 649, 657
EDLIN commands, E, 612
EMM386.EXE device driver, installing, 957
EMM386.EXE driver, 591-594
EMM driver, 567
EMS software, 567
Enable Task Swapper option in DOS 5 shell,
    751-753
END moves the cursor to the end of the
    command, 469
End-of-file marker, 863

ENTER key scan code value, 617
Entries, directory, 600-601
Entries within a group, rearranging in DOS 4
    shell, 721
Environment, setting or displaying entries in,
    1009-1011
Environment space, out of, 980
ERASE command, 53
Erased disk, restoring, 1032-1036
Error messages, common, 1087-1096
Error messages. *See also Command Reference
    entries under individual commands*
Error messages by category
    command, 52-53, 192, 476
    disk or drive, 36, 40, 108, 152-153,
        214-215, 334, 391, 442-445, 542-543
    environment, 324
    file, 124, 132, 134, 138-139, 156,
        361-362, 388-389
    label, 286, 295
    parameter, 437
    stack, 425-426
Error messages loaded into memory, 430
Errors, detecting after disk copy, 879
Esc, 610
ESC key (cancel a command), 96-98, 468
Escape character
    ASCII, 610
    creating in EDLIN, 896
Escape character (ASCII), creating, 895
Escape sequences, 610, 626
    creating with a word processor, 613
    creating with EDIT, 613
    creating with EDLIN, 611-613
ESDI (Enhanced Small Device Interface), 26
EXE2BIN command, 54
EXE (executable) file extension, 58-59, 64
    TYPE command not able to display
        contents of file with, 132
EXE file, converting into a COM file, 899-900
EXIT command, 53, 785-786, 900-901
    using to resume a program, 771-772
Exit-status values, 1045-1048
EXPAND command, 54, 901-902
    to decompress DOS 5 program file, 409
Expanded memory, 567-571, 584, 594
Expansion slots, 24, 26
    cover, removing, 27
    installing new computer boards in,
        26-28

Extended ASCII character set, 1049-1052
Extended ASCII characters
    displaying, 935-937
    displaying with GRAFTABL, 774-775
Extended CTRL-BREAK checking, 841-842
    enabling, 770-771, 785
Extended memory, 571-573, 584, 594, 957
    specifying for a program in DOS 5
        shell, 761
Extended partition, 808, 820, 911, 916
Extension(s), file. *See also individual types*
    DOS, 63-64
    file operations using wildcards on all
        files with the same, 154, 157-159
    period preceding, 65
    sorting directory listing by, 319
    three-character maximum for, 63
    user, 63-64

F ———————————————————————————

F1 function key to repeat previous DOS
    command character by character, 85,
    90-91, 95
F2 function key to repeat previous DOS
    command line up to specified character,
    95, 98
F3 function key to repeat entire previous DOS
    command line, 83-85, 90-95
F4 function key to copy characters that
    include and follow specified character, 95,
    98
F5 function key to edit command line, 96, 98
F6 function key to generate end-of-file
    character, 86-87, 91
F7 function key to display all command names
    in the buffer, 467-468, 471
F8 function key to display the first matching
    command name, 468, 471
F9 function key to prompt for a buffer
    command's number, 468
F10 TREE.BAT file, 616
FASTOPEN command, 54, 197-198, 200, 202,
    554, 903-905
    /X switch, 903
    in AUTOEXEC.BAT file, 303-306, 559
FC command, 54, 397-399, 403, 905-911
    /A switch, 906
    /A switch to display only first and last
        lines that differ, 399
    /B switch, 906

FC command, *continued*
    /B switch to perform byte-by-byte
        comparison, 399
    /C switch, 906
    /C switch to ignore case differences,
        399
    /L switch, 906
    /L switch to perform ASCII line-by-line
        comparisons, 399, 407
    /LB switch, 906
    /LB switch to set number of lines
        checked before cancellation, 399
    /N switch, 906
    /N switch to display line numbers for
        differences, 398-399
    /*nnn* switch to set number of lines to
        match, 399
    /T switch, 906
    /T switch to not change tabs to spaces,
        399
    /W switch, 906
    /W switch to compress white space, 399
FCBS= configuration entry, 413, 425, 431
FCBs (file control blocks), 1015
FDISK command, 39, 54, 504, 810-811,
    911-917
    changing partitions with, 818-819
File, read-only, 833
File allocation table, 852, 853, 855
    checking, 849-856
File allocation table (FAT), 444, 597-600, 607
    initializing hard disk's, 498
    reserving space for, 122-123
    storing current, 500, 602
    two copies stored on disk of, 122, 127
File attributes, 77
    combining, 389
    displaying, 386-387, 402
    Hands On for, 404-407
    manipulating, 385-389
    removing, 389
    setting, 387-389, 402
File Compare command, 905-911
File control blocks (FCBs), 425, 431, 544, 1015
    effects on hard disk of, 548, 551
    lack of directory path information in,
        552
File fragmentation, 489-490, 497, 556, 559-560
    correcting, 799-801
    detecting, 799

File handle
    assignments, 343-344
    created for DOS, 551-552, 2.0
File icons
    DOS 4 shell, 703
    DOS 5 shell, 728
File lists, displaying two in DOS 5 shell, 742, 743
File locks, allocating memory for, 1015
File names, 964
    base name part of, 63-65, 72
    changed for copies during file copy operations, 134
    concatenated in the command line, 161-162
    creating meaningful, 64
    displayed in directory in lower case, 78, 319, 321
    duplicated for copies during file copy operations, 135-136
    listing, 62-63, 66-69
    listing specific, 69-70
    parts of, 63
    quick location of, 197-198, 200
    sorting, 74-79
    valid characters for, 65
File names. *See also* Extension(s), file
File Open dialog box, 667
File system, DOS 4 shell, 702-709
File system window, DOS 4 shell, 702
File types, associating with a program in DOS 4 shell, 704-705
File undeletion, effect of fragmentation on, 802
Files, 61-80
    in a directory, listing, 873-878
    accessed in different directory or disk, 101, 104
    adding, 996
    adding or replacing application, 399-401, 403
    adding to the print queue, 982
    appended to other files, 332-333
    backing up, 835
    backup copies to protect, 365-384
    BACKUP, restoring, 175-179
    changing attributes in DOS 4 shell, 706-707
    changing attributes of in DOS 5 shell, 738-739

Files, *continued*
    changing the display of in DOS 5 shell, 740
    comparing, 392-399, 403
FILES= configuration entry to set number of file handles, 344, 412-413, 417, 420-422
Files
    contiguous, 796, 855
    copying, 86-87, 133-137, 140, 207-215, 220-221
    copying ASCII, 864
    copying binary, 864
    copying critical, 860-861
    copying in DOS 4 shell, 705
    copying in DOS 5 shell, 736
    cross-linked, 444-445, 449-450, 604, 855
    deleting, 138-139, 140, 146, 157
    delcting in DOS 4 shell, 706
    deleting in DOS 5 shell, 737
    destination or target, 134-135
    determining latest version of, 65-66
    disk space used by, 439
    displaying all in DOS 5 shell, 742, 744
    displaying count of current directory's, 66
    displaying differences between two, 859-864, 905-911
    displaying in lower-level subdirectories, 875
    displaying names of hidden or system, 1004
    displaying the specifics of in DOS 5 shell, 741
    editing existing with EDLIN, 641-642
    expanding compressed, 409
    fragmented, 597-598, 795-806, 850, 851
    fragmented, reasons for, 797-799
    hidden. *See* Hidden files
    manipulating, 385-410
    moving in DOS 4 shell, 705
    moving in DOS 5 shell, 734-735
    moving or copying with the mouse in DOS 5 shell, 736-737
    opening in DOS 4 shell, 703-704
    operations on, fundamental, 131-146
    overwritten after accidental deletion, 483-484, 490
    overwritten during copy operation, 136-137

Files, *continued*

overwritten during redirection of output, 331

overwritten during restoration with backup files, 375

printing in DOS 4 shell, 704

printing in DOS 5 shell, 732

printing in EDIT, 663

printing list of, 404

printing via the print queue, 982-986

read-only, 77, 319, 385-386, 389, 401, 405

read-only, replacing, 996

recovering deleted, 1029-1032

redirecting input to, 335-337

redirecting output to, 331

renaming, 134, 137-138, 140-141, 993-995

renaming in DOS 4 shell, 706

renaming in DOS 5 shell, 738

replacing older, 996

replacing selectively, 995-999

restoring fixed disk, in DOS 5 shell, 746-747

restoring for DOS, 4, 1079

restoring read-only, 999, 1003

restoring specific, 375-376

retrieving damaged, 990-991

saving the name and location of frequently used, 197-198, 200, 305-306, 554

searching a directory for, 996

searching for a string, 917-920

searching for specific in DOS 5 shell, 733-734

selecting in DOS 5 shell, 730-731

sharing, 543-544, 548

sorting, 1018

source, 134-135

system performance considerations for, 556

testing for existence of, 266-269, 277-279

transferring system, 789-791

undeleting accidentally erased, 479-487

undeleting in DOS 5 shell, 747

updating, 995-999

viewing, 1028-1029

viewing contents in DOS 4 shell, 707, 708

viewing contents in DOS 5 shell, 734

Files, *continued*

working with in DOS 5 shell, 730-742

File-sharing information, storing, 1015

File-sharing support, installing, 1014-1016

Filter

defined, 352

example, 357, 360

with piped input, 917

FIND command, 54, 917-920

/C switch, 918

/C switch to display count of lines containing search string, 338, 341

/I switch, 918

/I switch to make upper- and lowercase equivalent, 338

/N switch, 918

/N switch to use line numbers for matching lines, 338

/V switch, 918

/V switch to display lines that do not contain string, 338

/V switch to remove lines from sorted output, 75

piping DIR output to, 352, 357, 362

to search redirected input, 337-338, 342

FIRST utility command, 353

Flippies, 823

Floppy disk, 8-13

bad sectors on, 114-115, 119, 437, 439

bending or creasing damaging to, 12

bootable system, 121-122

care instructions for, 11-12

components of, 8

copying entire contents of, 209-213

copying files from hard disk to, 207-208, 213

copying files to hard disk from, 208-209

defined, 2

duplicating key, 11

envelope for, 8, 11

formatting, 111-129, 367

function of, 3

hard disks versus, 6-7

hub, 9-10

index hole, 9

inserting, 13-14

jacket, 9

label, proper technique for writing on, 12

magnetic flux damaging to, 11

Floppy disk, *continued*
    prepared for use with FORMAT
      command, 115-119
    read/write opening, 9-10
    sectors, 112-115, 209-210, 440, 546-547
    serial number for, 437-438, 539
    shutter, 10
    sizes and storage capacities of, 7, 12-13, 367
    of smaller capacity than drive's, formatting, 117
    smoke particles damaging to, 11
    source and target, 209-213
    temperature extremes damaging to, 12
    touching, 11
    tracks, 112-114, 209-210, 440
    with UNFORMAT.COM, recovery of hard disk using, 492-493
    volume label for, 116, 119, 437-438, 537-541, 548
    write-protect notch and tab, 9-10, 14, 209-210
Floppy disk drives. *See also* Disk drive
Floppy disks
    common sizes of, 1082
    comparing the contents of two, 878-882
    copying, 882-887
    storage capacity of commonly used, 1082
    unformatting, 924
    write-protecting, 927
FOR command, 53, 289-290, 296, 920-922
    to provide wildcard support, 162
FOR loop control variable, 921
Foreground color values, ANSI.SYS, 614
Foreign keyboard set, loading, 947-951
Form factor values, 428-429
Format, international, selecting, 1005-1009
FORMAT command, 54, 111-128, 133, 602-603, 853, 878, 923-933, 953, 1039
    /4 switch, 924
    /8 switch, 924
    /4 switch to format 360Kb disk in 1.2Mb drive, 117, 119
    /B switch, 924, 926
    /F switch, 924
    /F switch to format 720Kb disk in 1.44Mb drive, 117, 119, 368
    /L: switch, 924
    /N switch, 924
    /1 switch, 924

FORMAT command, *continued*
    /Q switch, 924, 925
    /S switch, 789, 924, 926, 929, 930
    /S switch to format disk as bootable system disk, 121, 367, 492
    /T: switch, 924
    /U switch, 924, 925, 927
    /V switch, 924, 929, 930
    disk-size switches to format disk with less storage capacity than drive's, 117
    FAT space on disk reserved by, 122-123
    Hands On for, 118-119
    messages displayed by, 115-116
    on hard disk, reasons to use, 117-118
    previous disk contents, 127, 498-499
    recovering hard disk contents after accidental, 488, 492-498
    root directory space on disk reserved by, 123-124
    volume serial number assigned by, 437-438
Formatted disk, restoring, 1032-1036
Formatting
    high-level, 636
    low-level, 632-633, 636
Fragmentation, eliminating, 803
Fragmented files, 597-598, 795-806, 806, 850, 851
    reasons for, 797-799
Full-screen editor, invoking, 894-895
Function keys, assigning commands to, 616

G

GOTO command, 53, 933-935
    to branch to another location within a batch file, 285-288, 296
    with FOR, 922
GRAFTABL, displaying extended ASCII characters with, 774-775
GRAFTABL command, 54, 774-775, 786, 935-937
    /STATUS switch, 935
Graphics, printing the screen's contents with, 222-223
GRAPHICS command, 54, 222-223, 225, 937-940
    /B switch, 938
    /B switch to print color background images, 222
    /LCD switch, 938

GRAPHICS command, *continued*
/LCD switch to use LCD screen aspect ratio, 222
/PRINTBOX option to select size of print box, 223
/PRINTBOX switch, 938
/R switch, 938
/R switch to reverse white-on-black images, 222
specifying path to printer profile file, 222
specifying printer type, 222
GRAPHICS.PRO file, 222
GREENFOR.BAT file, 614
GREET.BAT file, 272
GREETING.BAT file, 251, 513
Group, 695
editing in DOS 4 shell, 720
removing in DOS 4 shell, 720
Group program entry, changing in DOS 4 shell, 717-718
Groups, working with in DOS 4 shell, 718-721

H ─────────────────────

Hard copy defined, 217
Hard disk
access time, 24
backup, 368-370, 377
components, 7
contents recovery after accidental FORMAT command, 488, 492-498
defined, 2
drive letter, C as, 33
formatting, 38, 117-118
large-capacity, 543-544
partitions, 38-39, 307-308, 504-505, 544
recovering file from damaged sectors on, 546-547
running older programs on, 451-452
speed and storage capacity of, 6
transfer time, 26
Hard disk partitions, 807-809
Hardware
components, 1-2
setup, 2-6
Hardware interrupt support, 425-426, 431-432
Head crashes, avoiding, 628
Heads, read/write, 627-630
HELLO.BAT file, 257
Help, DOS version 5 on-line, 54-55

HELP command, 786, 940-942
/? switch, 940
Help Text option, DOS 5 shell, 760-761
Hewlett-Packard LaserJet II printer
communications settings for, 220
GRAPHICS command settings for, 223
Hewlett-Packard printer types, 223
Hidden bit, of a file, 833
Hidden files
CHKDSK report of space used by, 438
displaying a directory's, 77, 319, 408-409
displaying the names of, 1004
MIRROR command limitation of, 490
for MS-DOS and PC-DOS, 39, 408
omitting listing display of, 319
purpose of, 408
reporting on the number of, 850
High-memory area
loading DOS 5 into, 579
loading DOS into, 955
High-level formatting, 636
HIMEM.SYS device driver, 589-591
/A20CONTROL switch, 590
/CPUCLOCK switch, 591
/HMAMIN switch, 590
/INT15 switch, 590
/MACHINE switch, 590
/NUMHANDLES switch, 590
/SHADOWRAM switch, 590-591
installing, 572
HLP (help), file extension, 64
/HMAMIN switch, 590
HOME
to move the cursor to the start of the command, 469
scan code value of, 617

I ─────────────────────

I/O redirection operators, 875, 992
IBM printer types, 223
IBMBIO.COM file, 39
IBMDOS.COM file, 39
IDE (Integrated Drive Electronics), 26
IF command, 53, 266, 942-945
case sensitivity of, 273
to compare two character strings, 273
pipe restrictions with, 361-362
IF ERRORLEVEL batch file command, 266, 269-273, 277, 513

IF EXIST command, 266-269, 277
    NOT operator for, 267-269
IF STR command, 266
IFEXIST utility command, 353
IFSTR utility command, 353
IMPTROOT.BAT file, 267-268
INFINITE.BAT file, 295, 297
Infinite loop, 298
INI (windows initialization) file extension, 64
Input redirection operator (), 334-339
    combined with output redirection
        operator, 339-340
    combined with pipe operator, 353-354
    to create DEBUG commands with
        script file, 511
    in macros with $L, 476
    sorting with, 340-341
INS key
    to insert letter in command line, 96
    scan code value of, 617
    as toggle, 84, 469
Insert mode (EDLIN)
    entering, 644
    selecting, 638
Insert mode of DOS, 84
INSTALL= configuration entry, 308, 413, 426,
    432, 559
Installation disk files (DOS5), restoring,
    901-902
/INT15 switch, 590
Interactive processing, 245
Interleave, specifying, 631-632
INTERNAL.COM file, 52
International code pages, providing support
    for, 976-978
International configuration, setting an,
    676-678
International format, selecting, 1005-1009
International keyboard templates, 681
International symbol sets, specifying, 418
International users, support for, 675-691
Invalid cluster, 854
IO.SYS file, 39-40, 121, 789-791, 1022

J

JOIN command, 54, 456-463, 945-947
    /D switch, 945-946
    /D switch to remove drive from
        directory tree, 457, 461
    commands not to use with, 453

Jumper settings, device names selected with,
    228

K

Key combination defined, 88
Key combinations, reserved in the DOS 5
    shell, 760
Key device drivers, loading, 677-678
KEYB command, 54, 687-688, 947-951, 1006
    /E switch, 947
    /ID: switch, 947
Keyboard, 81-98
    101-key, 616-619
    copying files from, 86-87
    cursor-control keys on, 87-88
    enhanced versus conventional, 427
    four major sections of, 81-88
    function keys on, 82-87. *See also*
        individual function keys
    Hands On for, 90, 92-93
    IBM PC, 82
    numeric keypad on, 87
    PC AT, 82
    plugging in, 304
    PS/2, 82
    redirecting input from, 335-337
    scan code values, 514-515, 617
    selecting in DOS, 4, 1076
    setting response rate with MODE,
        777-778, 779
    as standard input device, 342-343, 417
    typematic rate, setting, 969-970, 971
    typewriter keys on, 82
    uses of, 1, 3
Keyboard codes, 948
Keyboard identifiers, in SELECT, 1006
Keyboard layouts, common, 947-948
Keyboard operations, setting, 967
Keyboard scancode values, 617-619
KEYBOARD.SYS file, 949
Keyboard template, selecting, 680-682
Keyboard templates
    international, 681
    supporting, 122-126
KEYB*xx* command, 54
Keys
    redefining with ANSI.SYS, 616-619
    reserving for program use with DOS 5
        shell, 761
Kilobytes (k-bytes or Kb) defined, 12, 18

L

LABEL command, 54, 878, 952-955, 1039
    replacing disk volume label using,
      539-540
LAST utility command, 353
LASTDRIVE= configuration entry, 413, 424,
    431, 455
LASTDRIVE= entry, 1020
LEFT ARROW moves the cursor one
    character position to the left, 469
LIM EMS version 3.2, 567
LIM EMS version 4.0, 571
Line editor, 657
    DOS, 895
Line number, in EDLIN, 648-649
LINECNT utility command, 353
Liquid crystal display, specifying, 938
LISTPAR.BAT file, 279
LISTTREE.BAT, 302
LOADFIX command, 54, 582, 586, 955-956
LOADHIGH command, 54, 554, 580-582,
    581, 582, 585-587, 586, 589, 948, 949,
    956-957
      in AUTOEXEC.BAT file, 559
      installing KEYB, 681
Log, of files on backup disks, 1000
Log file, BACKUP, 837
Logical drives, 815, 816, 819, 820, 911
Lost chains, converting to files, 855
Lost clusters, 604, 853, 854
Lowercase letters, displaying file names in, 875
Low-level formatting, 632-633, 636
LPT1;, LPT2:, or LPT3: parallel port,
    219-220, 225, 227-228, 344
LTR (letter) file extension, 64

M

/MACHINE switch, 590
Macros, 465-478
    command-line parameters in, 474-475
    for commands users should not access,
      473
    created from DOSKEY's
      previous-command buffer, 470,
      472-474
    difference between batch files and,
      472-473
    display defined, 470
    DOSKEY, 607, 888-889
    executing, 472-473, 477
    I/O redirection operators in, 475-477

Macros, *continued*
    nesting or linking not allowed for,
      475-477
    restrictions for, 476-477
    separating multiple commands in, 474
Main group, adding programs to in DOS 4
    shell, 715-718
Mark parity, 783
Marker, dragging, 666
Master boot record, 39-40, 504, 819, 911
Maximum path name, 964
MD command, 963-966
Megabytes (Mb) defined, 12-13, 18
MEM command, 54, 576-578, 583, 585, 587,
    957-959
    /C switch, 957
    /CLASSIFY switch, 581-582, 957
    /D switch, 957
    /DEBUG switch, 578, 585, 957-958
    /PROGRAM switch, 577-578, 585, 957
MEM (memo) file extension, 64
Memory
    contained in computer, CHKDSK
      report of, 439-440
    conventional, 566-567, 584, 594
    expanded, 520, 534-536, 557, 567-571,
      584, 594
    extended, 557, 571-573, 584, 594
    for PRINT, 982
    range, DEBUG commands for, 520,
      522-525
    reporting on the amount of, 850
    reserved, 579, 595
Memory management, 565-595
Memory management (DOS 5), 430, 579-587
Memory map, 323-324
Memory types, 565-573
Memory usage
    displaying current, 957-959
    viewing, 576-579
Memory-resident programs, loading into
    reserved memory, 957
Memory-resident software
    commands that install, 240
    DOSKEY, 466, 477
    INSTALL= configuration entry for,
      426, 432
    MIRROR, 488-490, 500
    selective installation of, 514
    SHARE, 543, 548
MEN (menu option) file extension, 64

MENU.BAT file, 300, 514
Metacharacter translations, PROMPT, 768
Metacharacters
  defining the DOS prompt, 767, 793, 986
  in DOSKEY macros, 889
Microsoft Windows, 34
  interface display, 34-35
MIRROR command, 54, 488-490, 500,
  960-963, 1033
    /1 switch, 960
    /PARTN switch to save master boot
      record to floppy disk, 504-505
    /T switch, 960
    /T switch to install file-deletion
      tracking, 489, 499-500, 502
    /U switch, 960
    /U switch to change setting, 490
    in AUTOEXEC.BAT to save disk's
      systems information, 499
    two copies of disk information
      maintained by, 493
    updating image file of, 494-495
MIRROR.FIL file, 961
MIRROR/PARTN command, 961
MKDIR command, 846, 963-966
MKDIR command (MD), 63, 168-176, 194,
  563, 601
MODE code-page commands, 688
MODE CODEPAGE SELECT command, 684,
  688
MODE command, 54, 558, 775-784, 845,
  966-975
    /STATUS switch, 783, 969
    added to AUTOEXEC.BAT file, 222
    to assign serial port settings, 220, 226
    P retry option, 776-777
    preparing device code pages, 682-684
    video display settings supported by, 779
MODE CON CODEPAGE SELECT
  command, 951
Monitor
  intensity level, problem with, 36
  plugging in, 5
  uses of, 1, 3
MONTHLY.BAT file, 382-383
MORE command, 54, 335, 342, 356, 975-976
  controlling output with, 1028
  with pipe operator to display files a
    screenful at a time, 387, 404
MOS (mouse driver) file extension, 64

Motherboard, 80386, 29
  contents of, 27-28
  defined, 23-24
Mouse
  defined, 2
  function of, 3
MS-DOS
  hidden files, 39
  PC-DOS versus, 17
MSDOS.SYS file, 39-40, 121, 789-791, 1022
Multitasking, 753

N

Named parameter %PROMPT%, 987
Named parameters, 162, 281, 322-323, 1010
National Language Support Function
  (NLSFUNC), 976
NESTED.BAT file, 293-294
Network, shared files on, 543-544
New Program Object dialog box in DOS 5
  shell, 757
NLSFUNC (National Language Support
  Function) command, 54, 685-686, 688-689,
  844, 845, 976-978
NOEMS parameter, 580
NOEND.BAT file, 294
NOMSG.BAT file, 345
Non-ASCII files, viewing, 1028-1029
NOUMB entry, 580
NUL (nonexistent) device, 344-345
/NUMHANDLES switch, 590
NUMLOCK key, 87

O

Online help, in DOS 4 shell, 701
Online help key combinations, in EDIT, 665
Operating system. *See* DOS (disk operating
  system), MS-DOS, and PC-DOS
Output
  displaying a screenful at a time, 975-976
  displaying with QBasic, 989
  searching redirected, 917
Output redirection operator (>), 329-332, 339
  combined with input redirection
    operator, 339-340
  combined with pipe operator, 353-354
  to discard output, 344-345
  Hands On for, 340
  in macros using $G, 475-476
  to print file listing, 404

Overstrike mode of DOS, 84

P

P retry option, in MODE, 776-777
"Packed file corrupt" error message, 582, 955
Page buffers, 567-570
Page frame, 592
Page-frame-use address values, 593
Pages, 567-570
Parallel communication, 794
Parallel devices, 781, 782
Parallel ports, 781
Parallel printer, time-out, 971, 972
Parallel printers, 781
    configuring, 967
Parameters
    batch, 1010
    named, 1010
    replaceable, 763, 764, 765
Parity bits, 782
PARKC.COM utility, creating, 630
Parking, disk head, 627-630
Partition table, restoring a corrupted, 1033
Partitions, 820, 911-917
    changing existing in DOS 4, 1072-1073
    changing with FDISK, 818-819
    hard disk, 807-809
    maximum sizes of, 808
Password option in DOS 5 shell, 757-758
PATH= entry, 1009
Path
    joining a disk drive to, 945-947
    maximum length, 979
PATH command, 53, 190-194, 199-201,
    303-304, 978-980
    avoiding 122-character limit of, 455
    current command path displayed by,
      559
    environment entries created by, 326-327
    to locate frequently used batch files, 251
    system performance considerations of,
      555
Path name
    maximum, 964
    substituting a drive name for, 1019-1021
PAUSE command, 53, 256, 980-981
    to temporarily suspend batch file,
      253-254
PAUSE/BREAK key scan code value, 617

PC-DOS, 17
    hidden files, 39
PCTRACKR.DEL file, 961
PGUP and PGDN keys
    in command buffer, 466
    scan code values for, 617
Pipe operator (|), 306, 318, 349-363
    batch file use of, 361-362
    commands operable with, 352-353
    filter side of, 352
    Hands On for, 355-358
    I/O redirection operators combined
      with, 353-354
    input side of, 352
    location on keyboard of, 349-350
    in macros with $B, 476
    and MORE command to display files a
      screenful at a time, 387, 404
    pitfalls of using, 354-355
    purpose of, 350-352
Plus and minus offsets, in EDLIN, 647
Port
    defined, 3-4
    parallel (PRN), 218-220. *See also* PRN
    serial, 218-222, 225-228, 242, 344
    video, 4
Power strip, surge suppressor versus, 5
Power supply, 24-25
    problem, symptoms of, 36
Power-on self-test, 33, 36
PREPARE operation (MODE), 969
Previous-command buffer. *See* Command
  buffer
Primary partition, 808, 820, 911, 916
Print box size, selecting, 938
Print buffer, 241-242
PRINT command, 54, 231-244, 304, 982-986
    /B: switch, 982
    /B switch to set buffer size, 241-242,
      306
    /C switch, 982
    /C switch to remove specific file from
      print queue, 234-236, 238, 244
    /D: switch, 982
    /D switch to specify list-device name,
      242, 306
    /M: switch, 982
    /M switch to specify time PRINT uses
      CPU each run-time, 243, 306

PRINT command, *continued*
/P switch, 982
/P switch to add file to queue, 244
/Q: switch, 982, 985-986
/Q switch to queue files being printed, 233, 241
/S: switch, 982
/S switch to specify clock ticks for another program to run, 243
/T switch, 982
/T switch to remove all files from print queue, 234-235, 238
/U: switch, 983
/U switch to specify wait time for more characters, 243, 306
background printing with, 232, 237, 242
Hands On for, 236-238
list device for, 232
memory allocated to, 244
memory-resident software of, 240-244
Print job, canceling, 982
Print queue, 233-236
adding files to, 982
installing a high-performance, 306
number of entries stored in, 982
PRINT time slice, 982
Printer
application program setup for, 224
copying files to, 220-221, 225-226, 231-232
Hands On for, 224-226
laser, 218
On Line button on, 217-218
preparing to print with, 217
profile file, 222
purpose of, 2-3
redirecting output to, 329-331
sending information to both screen and, 224-225, 257-258
tractor-feed, 218
type, 218-219, 222-223, 225
Printer cable, connection to port of, 4-5
Printer output, customizing, 776-777
Printer redirection, 967
PRINTER.SYS device driver, 677, 687
printer types supported by, 678
Printer timeout errors, retry options for, 777
Printer type, for graphics printing, 937-938
Printers
installing in DOS 4, 1077
parallel, 781

Printers, *continued*
parallel, configuring, 967
Printing, 217-229
canceling, 234-236
copying file to printer for, 220-221
directory listing, 329-330, 340
multiple files, 233-234
the screen's contents, 221-223
Print-screen support, for graphics mode, 937-940
PRN
parallel port, 219-221
as PRINT command's default device, 232
PRN device, 985
PRO (printer profile) file extension, 64
Processor sizes, 28
Program
loading above 64KB, 955-956
loading into upper (reserved) memory, 956-957
Program debugger, invoking, 871-873
Program entries, copying, 761
Program entries in DOS 5 shell, 759-761
Program entry, copying from one group to another in DOS 4 shell, 720
Program group, 724
Program group entries, changing in DOS 5 shell, 761
Program group items, changing the order of, 758
Program groups
in DOS 5 shell, 756-759
editing in DOS 5 shell, 758
removing in DOS 5 shell, 758
Program icons in DOS 5 shell, 745
Program list, running programs from in DOS 5 shell, 745-747
Program name, removing from a group in DOS 4 shell, 718
Programs
associating with a file type in DOS 5 shell, 732-733
cycling through active in DOS 5 shell, 752
running in DOS 5 shell, 731-732
PROMPT command, 53, 303-304, 615, 767, 768, 785, 847, 986-989
controlling screen colors with, 615
to customize DOS system prompt, 164-165, 767-770

PROMPT command, *continued*
    environment entries created by, 326-327
    Metacharacter translations, 768
Protected mode, 573
PRTSC key scan code value, 617

Q

QBASIC command, 775, 989-990
    /B switch, 989
    /EDITOR switch, 989
    /G switch, 989
    /H switch, 989
    /MBF switch, 989
    /NOHI switch, 989
    /RUN switch, 989
QBASIC.EXE command, 895
QBasic interpreter, running, 989-990
Quick format, 924

R

RAM, macros executed in, 472-473, 477
RAM disk drive to store temporary files,
    306-307, 318-319, 361, 556
RAM drive, creating, 573-575, 584-585
RAMDRIVE.SYS device driver, 306, 574,
    584-585, 588
    /A switch, 574, 588
    /E switch, 574, 588
RD command, 1003-1005
Read/write heads, 627-630, 796
Read-ahead, 416
Read-only file, 833
Read-only files, replacing, 996
Real mode, 573
RECOVER command, 36, 54, 537, 546-547,
    549, 990-991
REDBACK.BAT file, 614
Redirected output, searching, 917
Redirected program output, sorting, 1018
Redirection operators 329-348. *See also*
    individual operators
        I/O, 875, 992
REFRESH operation (MODE), 969
Registers, displaying contents of, 520, 530-531
REM command, 53, 252, 256, 258, 413,
    418-419, 421, 991-993
Remarks in batch files, 252, 256, 258
RENAME (REN) command, 53, 159, 993-995
    to assign original file names to
        undeleted files, 487

RENAME (REN) command, *continued*
    to change a file's name, 131, 137-138,
        140-141
    to rename groups of files, 153-154
REPLACE command, 54, 399-401, 403,
    995-999
    /A switch, 401, 996
    /P switch, 401, 996
    /R switch, 401, 996
    /S switch, 400-401, 996
    /U switch, 401, 996
    /W switch, 401, 996
Replaceable parameters, 763, 764, 765
Reserved keys in the DOS 5 shell, 760
Reserved memory, 579, 595, 956-957
    loading a program into, 956-957
RESTORE command, 54, 374-384, 563, 853,
    999-1003
    /A: switch, 1000
    /A switch to restore files created on or
        after a specified date, 380
    /B: switch, 999
    /B switch to restore files created on or
        before a specified date, 380
    /D switch, 1000
    /D switch to display list of matching
        files without restoring, them, 381
    /E: switch, 1000
    /E switch to restore files created earlier
        than specified time, 380
    /L: switch, 1000
    /L switch to restore files created later
        than specified time, 380
    /M switch, 1000
    /M switch to restore only files changed
        since last backup, 381
    /N switch, 1000
    /N switch to restore only files no
        longer on hard disk, 381
    /P switch, 999
    /P switch to prompt before overwriting
        a read-only file, 381
    /S switch, 999
    /S switch to restore subdirectory files,
        374
    exit status values, 384
    used in batch files, 382-383
    used with large files, 381-382
Restore Fixed Disk option, DOS 4 shell, 700
Restoring backup files, 374-376
Retry options for printer timeout errors, 777

RIGHT ARROW key
    to move the cursor one character
        position to the right, 469
    scan code value, 617
RMDIR command, 1003-1005
RMDIR (RD) command, 53, 173-174, 176-177,
    563
Root directory, 163-164, 175, 602, 603, 846
    AUTOEXEC.BAT in, 164
    creating subdirectories in, 963-964
    displaying files in, 77, 164
    examined after rebuilding hard disk
        contents, 495
    as initial current directory, 182
    initializing hard disk's, 498
    maximum subdirectories in, 963-964
    number of sectors reserved for, 602
    reserved space for, 123-125
    saving current state of, 500
    sectors, 124-125
    temporary files created in, 318
Rotational delay, 805, 806
RPT (report) file extension, 64

S

SAVEDIR.BAT file, 301-302
SAVEIT.BAT file, 302
Scancode values, keyboard, 617-619
SCR (script file) file extension, 511
Screen
    clearing, 44, 55-56
    printing contents of, 221-223, 225
    sending information to both printer
        and, 224, 257-258
    as standard output device, 342-343, 417
Screen. *See also* Monitor
Screen colors
    controlling with ANSI.SYS, 613-615
    controlling with PROMPT, 615
    customizing, in DOS 4 shell, 696
    setting in DOS 5 shell, 755-756
Screen display
    clearing, 856-857
    customizing, in EDIT, 668-669
Screen editor, 657, 674
Screen size, setting in DOS 5, 626
Screenful at a time, displaying output,
    975-976
Scroll bars, 665, 674, 714, 728
SCSI (Small Computer System Interface), 26
Search menus, in EDIT, 671-673

Search path
    command-file, 978-980
    defining, 978-980
    defining a data-file, 827
Sector entries, tracking, 904
Sector interleaving, 636
Sectors on disk, 39
    bad, 114-115, 119, 437, 439
    disk interleaving to change order of, 556
    read-ahead, 416
Seek time, 805, 806
SELECT command, 54, 1005-1009
SELECT operation (MODE), 969
SELERASE.BAT file, 345-346
Serial communication, 794
Serial devices, 781, 782
Serial number, of a disk, 953
Serial port, configuring, 969
Serial ports, 781
    configuring, 780-783
SET command, 53, 302, 315-318, 321, 876,
    1009-1011
    to add an environment entry, 316-317,
        320
    to assign a value to a name, 282
    to assign a value to an environment
        entry, 304
    to display the current DOS
        environment, 281, 315-316, 320, 769
    to remove an environment entry,
        317-318, 320
SET PROMPT=, 769
SETUP program, 409, 807
SETVER command, 54, 791-793, 1011-1014
    /DELETE switch, 1012, 1014
    /QUIET switch, 793
/SHADOWRAM switch, 590-591
SHARE, /F: switch, 1015
SHARE command, 54, 304, 307-308, 537, 543,
    548, 1014-1016
    /F switch to specify bytes for memory
        table, 544
    /L switch to specify number of locks,
        544
    file control blocks needed for, 425, 431
SHELL= configuration entry, 312-313, 324,
    326, 413, 429
    /P switch required to execute
        AUTOEXEC.BAT file, 313, 428
    to increase environment size, 430
    to specify command processor, 432-433

Shell confirmation options, DOS 5 shell, 741

Shell, DOS, invoking, 890-891

SHELLC command, in DOS 4 shell, 714

SHIFT command, 53, 290-293, 296-297, 1016-1017

  to access more than nine batch parameters, 290-293

  to access multiple files, 162

SHIFTALL.BAT file, 292

SHIFTONE.BAT file, 291

SHIFT-PRTSC to print the screen's contents, 221-223, 225

SHIFTTWO.BAT file, 291

SHOWALL.BAT file, 273-274

SHOWBAT.BAT file, 289

SHOWENV.BAT file, 281-282

Shugart Technology (ST) controller, 26

Single-drive disk copy, performing, 884

SKIPDIR.BAT file, 296

SMARTDRV.SYS device driver, 575-576, 585, 587

  /A switch, 576, 587

Software defined, 15-16, 18

SORT command, 54, 335-337, 350-352, 976, 1017-1019

  /+*n* column switch to sort files or file names by size, 76, 336-337

  /+*n* switch, 1018

  /R switch, 1018

  /R switch to sort files in descending order, 75, 336-337, 341, 351

  to sort file entries in ascending order, 74

  to sort file entries in reverse order, 356-357

Sort orders, for displaying files, 874-875

SORTIT.BAT file, 362

Space parity, 783

Speaker, PC, 24

Stack defined, 425

STACKS= configuration entry, 413, 426, 431-432

Standard input device, keyboard as, 342-343

Standard input/output, changing to an alternate device, 867-868

Standard output device, screen as, 342-343

Start bits, 783

Stop bits, 783

Subdirectories

  creating, 964

  DOS, 847

SUBST command, 54, 830, 831, 979, 1019-1021

  /D switch, 1020

  /D switch to remove substitution, 460

  commands not to use with, 453

  to substitute unused drive letter for directory name, 205, 453-455, 458-463

Surge suppressor, 5-6

SWITCHES= configuration entry, 413

Symbol set, selecting, 678-680

SYS command, 54, 1021-1024

SYS (system) file extension, 64, 419

SYSINIT program, 344

System, hung, 332

System bit, of a file, 833

System clock

  changing, 1024

  pre-DOS 3.3 method of setting, 50

System commands, DOS, 767-794

System configuration entries, 308, 312-313

System date, setting, 869-871

System date and time, setting in DOS 4 shell, 698-699

System files

  displaying the names of, 1004

  transferring, 789

System performance, improving, 197-198, 200, 414, 553-563

  from directories, 553-555

  from disks, 556-557

  from files, 556

  from the system, 557-558

System prompt. *See* DOS prompt

System prompt, customizing, 767-770

T ─────────────────────────

TAB key, 617

Task Swapper, 751, 753, 891

TEE utility command, 353

TEMP= environment entry, 304, 306, 310, 318, 361, 556

TEMP environment entry, 575, 919, 1009

Temporary files
    created during pipe operations,
      360-361, 556
    created in root directory, 318
    RAM drive to store, 306-307, 318-319,
      361
Terminal device, changing, 789
Terminate-and-Stay-Resident (TSR)
    commands, 240
TESTAUTO.BAT file, 278
TESTFILE.BAT file, 279
Text attributes, assigning with ANSI.SYS, 626
Text files
    creating with EDLIN, 637-657
    displaying contents of, 132
    printing, 231, 237
Text files, ASCII, editing, 895
Text-scrolling key combinations, in EDIT,
    666
Ticks, CPU clock, 982
Time, displaying current in the prompt, 988
TIME command, 46-48, 51, 53, 55-56,
    1024-1026
    batch file with, 246-247
Time slice, PRINT, 982
Time stamp for files, 65-66, 72
    suppressing DIR display of, 79
Time, system
    correcting invalid, 48
    displaying current, 46, 56
    DOS use of, 66
    entering, 33, 246-247
    military (24-hour) and standard, 47-48
    setting, 47-48, 55-56
    specifying precise, 48
TopView, conflict with APPEND, 829
TREE command, 54, 185-190, 199, 201, 616,
    875, 1026-1028
    /A switch, 1027
    /F switch, 1027
    /F switch to display all files in
      directory, 188, 201
    printer echoing with, 257-258
    printing directory structure with, 226,
      356
TREEPRT.BAT file, 257-258
TXT (text) file extension, 64
TYPE3.BAT file, 289

TYPE command, 53, 140, 610, 613, 851,
    1028-1029
    to display file contents, 92-93, 131-133
    wildcards used with, 161-162, 288-290
TYPEALL.BAT file, 290, 292
Typematic delay, 794
Typematic rate, setting, 777-778, 779,
    969-970, 971

U

UMB (upper memory block) entry, 580
Unconditional format, performing, 924
UNDELETE command, 54, 479-491, 500,
    1029-1032
    /ALL switch, 1030
    /ALL switch to undelete each matching
      file without prompting, 486, 502
    /DOS switch, 1030
    /DOS switch to undelete files known
      about by DOS, 491
    /DT switch, 1029
    /DT switch to undelete files for which
      file tracking is active, 491
    /LIST switch, 1029
    /LIST switch to display file names,
      484-485, 491, 501
    to determine the number of unused
      directory entries, 562
    effect of fragmented files, 802-803
    file location by, 488-489, 491
    to retrieve accidentally deleted files, 139
    steps in using, 481
    storing information used by, 960-963
Undelete command in DOS 5 shell, 747
Underscore character, in file extensions, 902
Unformat a disk, 924
UNFORMAT command, 54, 492-502, 925,
    1032-1036
    /J switch, 493-494, 1033
    /L switch, 1033
    /P switch, 498, 1033
    /PARTN switch, 505-506, 1033
    /TEST switch, 496-498, 1033
    /U switch, 498, 1033
    MIRROR command support of, 488, 492
    to recover contents of accidentally
      formatted hard disk, 118-119,
      127-128, 492-501

UNFORMAT command, *continued*
    storing information used by, 960-963
UNINSTALL disks, 1082, 1086
UP ARROW key
    in command buffer, 466
    scan code value, 617
Upper-memory, loading a program into,
    956-957
Upper-memory block (UMB), 580
Utilities, DOS 4 shell, 696-701

V

VER command, 1036-1037
VER command (version number), 44, 51, 53,
    55-56
VERIFY command, 53, 1037-1038
    to toggle disk verification, 545, 549-550
Version number, DOS, reporting, 791-793,
    1011-1014
Version number (DOS), displaying, 1036-1037
Version number of DOS, displaying, 44, 51,
    53, 55-56
Version table, 1014
Video display
    customizing with MODE, 778-780
    setting, 966
Video display settings, supported by MODE,
    779
Video mode, selecting with ANSI.SYS, 624-625
Video mode escape sequences, ANSI.SYS, 625
VOL command, 53, 537, 548, 1039-1040
    disk volume label displayed with, 541
Volume label
    for a disk, 878, 952-955
    displaying, 1039-1040

W

Warm boot of DOS, 90
Weitek math coprocessor, W parameter for,
    592
WHITEBLU.BAT file, 615
WIDEDIR.BAT file, 257

WILD.BAT to add wildcard support to DOS
    commands, 161
Wildcard characters 143-146. *See also*
    individual wildcard symbols
    batch files for commands not
        supporting, 288-289, 296
    copying files with, 208-209
    decompressing multiple files with, 409
    Hands On for, 157-159
    printing with, 233-234, 237
    undeleting groups of files with, 482-483
WORDCNT utility command, 353
Workspace in DOS 4, setting up, 1075
Write-protect tab, 886
Write-protect violation, 927
WRONGIF.BAT file, 271

X

XCOPY command, 54, 402-403, 557, 833,
    835, 1038, 1040-1043
    /A switch, 392, 1040
    /D: switch, 1040
    /D:MM-DD-YY switch to copy files
        created or changed after specified
        date, 392
    /E switch, 392, 1040
    /M switch, 390-392, 405, 1040
    /P switch, 392, 1040
    /S switch, 391-392, 1041
    /V switch, 392, 545, 557, 1040
    /W switch, 392, 1041
    archive-required attribute cleared by,
        215, 390-391
    extended copy capabilities of, 389-390
    to set or clear file's archive-required
        attribute, 390
XMS Memory KB Required option in
    DOS 5 shell, 761

Y

Y_OR_N.COM file, 283-284, 513-514

Osborne McGraw-Hill

Computer Books

(800) 227-0900

Bookmarker Design — Lance Ravella

Tear off for Bookmark

▼

You're important to us...

We'd like to know what you're interested in, what kinds of books you're looking for, and what you thought about this book in particular.

Please fill out the attached card and mail it in. We'll do our best to keep you informed about Osborne's newest books and special offers.

▶ **YES, Send Me a FREE Color Catalog of all Osborne computer books**
To Receive Catalog, Fill in Last 4 Digits of ISBN Number from Back of Book (see below bar code) 0-07-881 _ _ _ — _

Name: _____ Title: _____

Company: _____

Address: _____

City: _____ State: _____ Zip: _____

I'M PARTICULARLY INTERESTED IN THE FOLLOWING *(Check all that apply)*

I use this software
- ☐ WordPerfect
- ☐ Microsoft Word
- ☐ WordStar
- ☐ Lotus 1-2-3
- ☐ Quattro
- ☐ Others _____

I program in
- ☐ C or C++
- ☐ Pascal
- ☐ BASIC
- ☐ Others _____

I chose this book because
- ☐ Recognized author's name
- ☐ Osborne/McGraw-Hill's reputation
- ☐ Read book review
- ☐ Read Osborne catalog
- ☐ Saw advertisement in store
- ☐ Found/recommended in library
- ☐ Required textbook
- ☐ Price
- ☐ Other _____

I use this operating system
- ☐ DOS
- ☐ Windows
- ☐ UNIX
- ☐ Macintosh
- ☐ Others _____

I rate this book:
- ☐ Excellent ☐ Good ☐ Poor

Comments _____

Topics I would like to see covered in future books by Osborne/McGraw-Hill include:
_____

IMPORTANT REMINDER
To get your FREE catalog, write in the last 4 digits of the ISBN number printed on the back cover (see below bar code) 0-07-881 _ _ _ — _

Osborne McGraw-Hill

Computer
Books

(800) 227-0900